Paul and the Stoics

Paul and the Stoics

TROELS ENGBERG-PEDERSEN

Westminster John Knox Press
Louisville, Kentucky

Published in Great Britain by T&T Clark Ltd
59 George Street, Edinburgh EH2 2LQ, Scotland

www.tandtclark.co.uk

This edition published under license from T&T Clark Ltd by
Westminster John Knox Press
100 Witherspoon Street, Louisville
Kentucky 40202–1396

First published 2000

Library of Congress Cataloging-in-Publication Data
is on file at the Library of Congress, Washington, D.C.

ISBN 0–664–22234–X

Typeset by Waverley Typesetters, Galashiels
Printed and bound in Great Britain by Bell & Bain Ltd, Glasgow

To
ABRAHAM J. MALHERBE
WAYNE A. MEEKS
mentors and friends

Contents

Preface

This is a book about Paul far more than the Stoics. It is part of the current fascinating and laborious retrieval of Paul from the dominant Protestant tradition of reading him, a retrieval that began almost exactly a hundred years ago in works by Paul Wernle, William Wrede and Albert Schweitzer and took off again, after the period of Dialectical Theology or Neo-Orthodoxy, in Pauline classics of the last quarter of the 20th century by Krister Stendahl, E. P. Sanders, Gerd Theissen and others. The book is an attempt to solve, from within the new perspective on Paul, issues in the understanding of his thought that have partly remained on the agenda from the traditional reading and partly arisen from the new perspective itself. In order to achieve this, the book aims to situate Paul's thought firmly within the ancient ethical tradition as this was inaugurated by Plato's Socrates, developed by Aristotle and given classic shape in Stoicism. There is no claim that the resulting interpretation is the only valid one. The days are fortunately gone when anybody could make a claim for interpretive hegemony. Instead, the position is that there is a reading here which helps to solve a number of issues and that should be seen as complementing other recent interpretations of Paul—not least those stressing his Jewish profile—rather than as a substitute for them.

The book has had a long gestation. I had published a book on Aristotle's ethical theory in 1983. In 1984 I then became attached as a non-teaching research scholar to the Department of Biblical Exegesis, Copenhagen University, while working on a similar book on Stoic ethics which was eventually published in 1990. Concomitantly I began serious work on Paul. This was furthered by a research professorship from 1986 to 1991, awarded by the Danish Research Council for the Humanities—but hampered by my (otherwise very stimulating) involvement as co-director of an interdisciplinary research project on the Hellenistic period, running from 1989 to 1995 and also funded by the Humanities Council. With the end of that project, I was finally able to spend all my research time on Paul while also, since 1989, teaching New Testament as a full-time lecturer at the Department of Biblical Exegesis. The present book is the result—the third in a kind of trilogy: Aristotle, the Stoics, Paul.

While working on this project I have incurred numerous debts that I would like to acknowledge here. The Danish Research Council for the Humanities deserves thanks for financial support over the years. My co-directors in the Hellenism project, Per Bilde, Lise Hannestad and Jan Zahle, are warmly thanked for a period of intensive co-operation that had almost nothing to do with Paul and little with ancient philosophy, but nevertheless taught me very much about the overall historical situation of these bodies of thought.

Since 1984 the Department of Biblical Exegesis has been my daily scholarly base. As I am writing, it is uncertain whether at the end of the year 2000 I shall be leaving the Department in order to take up another position at Copenhagen University. This makes me all the more conscious of the stimulating scholarly milieu in the New Testament section that it has been my good fortune to take part in. I thank my colleagues, Lone Fatum, Geert Hallbäck, Niels Hyldahl, Mogens Müller and Henrik Tronier, warmly for this. Thanks are also due, for his continuous active support over the years, to the present Dean of the Faculty of Theology, John Strange.

I have been lucky to become gradually part of an international network of New Testament and Pauline scholars working on similar kinds of projects, mainly in the Nordic countries, the United Kingdom and the United States. My colleagues at Oslo University, David Hellholm, Halvor Moxnes and Turid Karlsen Seim, have been a constant source of stimulus. Two New Testament scholars in Glasgow, John Barclay and John Riches, and one in Sheffield, Loveday Alexander, have taught me a lot. And in the United States I have learned greatly from yearly participation (since 1987) in the Annual Meeting of the Society of Biblical Literature. The work done in the Society's renowned Pauline Theology Group convinced me of the validity of trying to combine the new perspective on Paul with a more traditional concern about his 'ideas' or 'theology'. I would like to thank the two directors of the group, Jouette Bassler and Calvin Roetzel, and a number of other participants in its work for stimulating input over the years: Paul Achtemeier, James Dunn, Victor Furnish, Richard Hays, Robert Jewett, Leander Keck, Paul Meyer, Paul Sampley, Tom Wright and others.

More recently, I have learned a great deal from participation in another group under the Society: the Hellenistic Moral Theology and the New Testament Group. I am grateful to its two consecutive directors, John Fitzgerald and L. Michael White, for involving me in work that is so close to my own basic interests. Another member of the group's steering committee, Stanley Stowers, deserves a special word of thanks too.

That leads me back to where it all, in a sense, began. In the fall of 1988 together with my family I visited Yale University at a high point in that distinguished university's New Testament career. Abraham Malherbe and Wayne Meeks were there and so were Leander Keck, Susan Garrett, Richard Hays, and a large group of highly gifted and interesting Ph.D. students. Others had just left but became known to me nevertheless: Dale Martin, Alan Segal, Stanley Stowers and more. What I basically learned at Yale was the fundamental importance of social history, in particular the intricate and ultimately perhaps unfathomable 'correlation' of symbols, ideas and patterns of belief on the one hand and social facts on the other. That added a wholly new dimension to my thinking on Paul, which had previously been more one-sidedly 'philosophical'. Readers of the present book may feel that it remains too exclusively concerned with 'ideas'. But the whole picture is there, I contend. And I would not have the book read as saying anything else.

I thank all my Yale friends for everything that they have given me over the years. Two stand out, however: Abe Malherbe and Wayne Meeks. As a small token of my deep appreciation and gratitude, I dedicate the book to them.

Copenhagen University   TROELS ENGBERG-PEDERSEN

An Essay in Interpretation

This book is the result of a long-standing effort to reach a comprehensive and coherent understanding, not only of the relationship between Paul and Stoicism, but also, and indeed mainly, of Paul. It springs from a sense that there is a need now in Pauline scholarship to reopen vigorously the old question of the coherence of Paul's ideas in the letters, *but* to do it from a different perspective than the traditional, theological one within which it has hitherto been seen. And its central thesis is that the major obstacles to finding coherence in Paul's ideas that scholars have stumbled against throughout much of the 20th century can be sufficiently removed once one reads Paul—the whole of Paul, not just this or that fairly restricted motif—in the light of Stoicism and the ancient ethical tradition generally.

This agenda owes a vital impetus to the change in Pauline studies that has been taking place over the last 25 years, as exemplified in the work of such widely different scholars as Abraham J. Malherbe, Wayne A. Meeks, Heikki Räisänen, E. P. Sanders, Krister Stendahl and Gerd Theissen.[1] What binds together their work and distinguishes it both from the traditional theological reading to which they were reacting and also from other contemporary work of the same theological kind is a determination to stay squarely historical-critical in the analysis of Paul and either to circumvent (Malherbe, Meeks, Theissen) or directly to question (Räisänen, Sanders, Stendahl) a more distinctly theological reading. For present purposes the latter may be defined here as that of Dialectical Theology or Neo-Orthodoxy as exemplified by scholars such as Rudolf Bultmann and Ernst Käsemann (notwithstanding the clear differences between the two) and its heirs among contemporary students of Paul. The reaction to that kind of reading among scholars like those mentioned first has been enormously fruitful and healthy. It has reinstalled the best of historical criticism of Paul from scholars who worked before Neo-Orthodoxy, such as William Wrede and Albert Schweitzer, or alongside Neo-Orthodoxy, e.g. Martin Dibelius, or even as one *side* of Neo-Orthodoxy, such as one finds in the work of Bultmann himself. For want of a better word, I shall call this historical-critical approach 'naturalistic', as distinct from the overtly 'theological' perspective that formed the core of Neo-Orthodoxy. The present work explicitly adopts the naturalistic approach. It is the aim of this introductory chapter to develop how it does it, how a 'naturalistic' approach will therefore be understood here and how it differs from one based on a 'theological' perspective. At the end of the chapter we shall also consider whether what we shall offer here may or may not in the end be dignified with the term 'theology'.

I emphasize that the approach adopted in this book is 'naturalistic' *and not* 'theological'. After more than one hundred and fifty years of historical criticism that might seem obvious in a piece of scholarship on Paul. In fact it is not. As we shall see, far too much scholarship that has a mainstream historical profile is *also* 'theological', though most often only implicitly and unavowedly. The historical-*critical* edge has been lost. By contrast, the present work cannot at all get off the ground unless one takes the historical-critical, 'naturalistic' perspective wholly seriously. One must bracket completely, at least initially, any 'theological' interest one may have in aligning oneself with Paul's own perspective, which is definitely a 'theological' one that begins, logically, 'from above' in ideas about God and his acts. One must part company with Paul and give up reading him merely from within. Instead, one must read the whole of Paul—including his 'theological' ideas—coolly from the outside. That is just what the representatives of historical criticism mentioned above—both old and new—have done.[2] (Later in this chapter we shall clarify the distinction between reading 'from within' and 'from the outside'.)

In point of fact, however, the agenda for the book also owes something to the traditional theological reading itself, namely its concern with Paul's ideas and the question of their coherence. By focusing on this, it aims to take issue with the work of Malherbe, Meeks (and Theissen) and Sanders and Räisänen (and Stendahl) by enlarging it in a direction they have not wanted to go. (i) Where Malherbe has convincingly shown that Paul made easy use of a whole range of particular moral philosophical sets of ideas (*topoi*) of Cynic and Stoic descent, he has not attempted to show the same for the *whole* of Paul's thought at the level of its possible, comprehensive coherence.[3] It is this task that is undertaken here. (ii) Where Meeks has strongly elaborated the rich and concrete social historical dimension underlying the Pauline letters based on an entirely healthy distrust of 'ideas', that distrust has also prevented him from trying to develop the coherence of Paul's many ideas as ideas—in order to 'correlate' them in their entirety with their *Sitz im Leben* and with Paul's community formative aim.[4] Meeks rightly employs the notion of a 'grammar' to describe what (to continue the Wittgensteinian picture) we may call the Pauline 'form of life'. And he rightly insists that both the grammar and the form of life contain far more than just the ideas. Still, it does contain a wide variety of ideas of very different types. It is the logical coherence of these ideas—as *part* of the grammar and form of life—that will constitute our theme. (iii) Where Sanders and Räisänen have successfully demolished traditional theological readings of Paul's ideas on the Jewish law and Judaism, they have not succeeded in developing a coherent and comprehensive alternative account of Paul's ideas on Christ, the law, gentiles and Judaism, indeed, they have explicitly rejected that such an account can be found. As against this, I claim that there is a need to reopen the search for such an account on a different basis than the one Sanders and Räisänen were reacting against.[5] Thus in all three cases this book presupposes the basic, very important insights reached by this group of scholars in their wholly justified reaction to the earlier, theological reading. But it also attempts to reinstall from that reading a search for a fairly strong degree of coherence in Paul's ideas—though not of the traditional, theological kind, but precisely as seen from the basic, historical-critical perspective that lies behind the new insights. It is the combination of these two sides that constitutes the (first half of) the basic methodological profile of the book.

The quest for coherence in ideas is probably in some way endemic to the act of reading itself. But its claim to being *the* appropriate reading strategy has of course been fundamentally questioned by various modern approaches, most famously that of deconstruction. Also, the kind of questioning of the old truths that one finds, for instance, in Räisänen was built on a healthy scepticism about the degree of coherence to be found in Paul. Why, then, is there a 'need' to reopen the old quest for the coherence in Paul's thought? The quick answer is that seen in the abstract there is absolutely no such 'need'. Instead, there is a fact, the fact that, as I shall claim, we do find a fairly strong degree of coherence of Paul's thought once we open ourselves up again to such a *possibility—and* begin to read it, not theologically but naturalistically as one more participant in a discourse shared with Stoicism and the ancient ethical tradition more generally. I had been working on Aristotle's ethics.[6] I then turned to Stoic ethics and began to study Paul concomitantly with that.[7] When I had finished with the Stoics, I concentrated all my efforts on Paul. I was struck by the degree to which my initial intuitive sense was confirmed: that very much of what appeared problematic and incoherent in Paul's letters falls into place and makes coherent sense once it is seen in the light of certain central ideas in Stoic ethics and, more generally, the ancient ethical tradition—which in the present context will in the main be represented by Aristotle and the Stoics.[8]

The present book sets forth the result of this work. It has been written very specifically for Pauline scholars and students and for other theologians with a professional wish to understand Paul. It argues that we may reach solutions that fit in with the three modern types of reading to problems in Paul's thought that have been in focus within the traditional, theological type of reading by drawing on a nucleus of ideas that were very sharply articulated in Stoicism and the ancient ethical tradition. There is no suggestion that the perspective to be developed here is the only one that may be adopted for a 'good' interpretation of Paul. Of course not. For instance, one might well be relatively unconcerned about the 'coherence of ideas' in Paul and concentrate on other matters. One thing that has finally become clear over the last few decades of New Testament scholarship is that there is a whole range of perspectives that may yield 'good' interpretations of Paul, and that we do not need to choose between them. The claim is only that *if* one is concerned about a certain range of interpretive problems of literary structure and coherence of thought that have engaged students of Paul's letters through much of the 20th century, then there is a perspective here that contributes to solving those problems and to that extent provides a reading that is 'good'.

Later in this chapter we shall consider in slightly more detail the relationship of the present approach to the three major trends in recent Pauline scholarship already referred to. We shall also situate it more broadly within a pattern of major readings of Paul since the rise of historical criticism. In that connection we shall introduce one more element in the profile of this approach (in addition to its concern with ideas) that connects it with a more traditional, theological reading of Paul and removes it quite dramatically from being *just* a historical-critical one. Right now, however, we should make a brief sketch of the main problems with which we shall be concerned, the general topics under which they fall and the overall profile of the proposed solutions.

The subject-matter of the present reading

The problems constitute a very mixed bag of literary and exegetical ones, traditionally theological ones, historical ones and interpretive or hermeneutical ones, all of which will immediately strike the scholar as being exceedingly well known. How do the Pauline letters hang together structurally? What is their genre? Are they letters of parenesis? What is parenesis? What is the relationship between Paul's indicative statements and his imperatives? Indeed, between 'theology' and 'ethics'? What is the meaning and role of Paul's teaching on righteousness? Did he have a theory of sinlessness in Christ? If so, what is the point of his imperatives? How did he see the Jewish law in relation to Christ faith? And how the relationship between Jews and gentiles in Christ? Also, is the teaching on righteousness only a side issue? How does it relate to the comprehensive idea of 'participation', of 'being in Christ'? Indeed, how does Paul's 'mystical', strongly reifying and 'substantive' language of bodily participation in Christ cohere with the distinctly cognitive language of his talk about righteousness, 'ethics' and parenesis?

All these problems come together in a single question: Does it all hang (sufficiently) together or must we be content with only a highly suggestive string of 'disparate limbs' of literary exposition and of thought?

Theological tradition has implicitly answered this question very strongly on the side of coherence on matters of thought and content. By contrast, 20th-century scholarship (e.g. since William Wrede) has—in a sinuous process that has rightly rejected the traditional solutions where they turned up again between 1920 and 1970 in Neo-Orthodoxy—moved towards a far greater openness to incoherence on such central issues of content as righteousness, the law, Jews and gentiles and also the relationship between Paul's use of 'substantive' and cognitive language.[9] As against this, scholarship has, through the development of a number of literary approaches, moved towards finding more coherence at the literary level of the letters.[10]

The basic question addressed in the book is therefore this: Is it possible to find a greater degree of coherence at the level of the content of Paul's exceedingly rich and complex thought than one sees in the best critical modern scholarship as exemplified by the scholars mentioned earlier? Is it even possible to connect such a degree of coherence with the recent insights into greater coherence at the literary level?

We may group the various problems listed above under some general topics. It is the discussion of these topics as they are evidenced in the letters and the clarification of their interrelationship through the light thrown on them by Stoicism that constitutes the overall profile of the book.

One topic concerns the definition and relationship between what appear to be different categorial types of ideas in Paul: 'theological' *cum*

'cosmological', 'anthropological', 'ethical'. Here I owe a large debt to a
seminal essay by the American cultural anthropologist Clifford Geertz
(1957). Writing at a time (the 1950s) when analytic philosophy was
keenly interested in preventing people from committing the so-called
'naturalistic fallacy' (that of concluding from 'is' to 'ought'), Geertz
insisted that no matter what the philosophers were saying, in the religions
of actual experience that supposed fallacy is committed all the time. In
particular, there is a constant interchange between a people's (religious)
'world view' (their 'is') and its 'ethos' (their 'ought'). Geertz' case is wholly
persuasive. In Paul, as we shall see, the different categorial types cannot
in the end be kept distinct. For instance, 'theology' and 'ethics' were not
seen in antiquity as being sharply distinguished in the way they have
become in modernity as a result of a growing secularization. And that
holds both for the ancient ethical tradition in general and even more for
Paul. Still, the various categories can be separated notionally; and for
analytical purposes they need to be. In order to remind us of the point
about inseparability, however, I shall go on to place the categorial terms
in scare-quotes.

Thus in Paul there are ideas about God and Christ and how the world
is put together in time and space. These we may call broadly 'theological'
or 'religious' and 'cosmological'. There are also ideas about how human
beings relate to God, Christ and the world cosmologically understood;
and ideas about how they relate to other human beings in and outside
the group of Christ-believers. These ideas we may call broadly 'anthropological' and the latter group more especially 'ethical'. One central topic
that will concern us is exactly how these various types of ideas hang
together logically. Is it possible to construct some kind of overarching
theory that will explain what Paul says about one type by referring to
something he says of another and vice versa? Can we see an underlying
logic that holds together what he says right across the board? In a way,
that is what readers of Paul have traditionally been after when they were
looking for his 'theology'. We shall be after the same kind of thing, but
now as seen from the 'naturalistic' perspective that distinctly does not
start 'from above' nor operate merely from the inside. Instead, we shall
look at the whole material from the outside through historical-critical
lenses without giving any special pride of place to either the 'theological'
cum 'cosmological' ideas or the 'anthropological' and 'ethical' ones.

Some of these formulations may have reminded readers of Rudolf
Bultmann. Did he not claim, famously, that 'every sentence [in Paul]
about God is at the same time a sentence about man and vice versa'
and so 'the Pauline theology is as the same time anthropology'?[11] I am

not at all averse to seeing that connection. On the contrary, Bultmann was right—when suitably interpreted (in a 'naturalistic' direction that Bultmann himself hardly intended to go). That idea of his is another one that needs to be resuscitated and combined, in a Geertzian manner, with the historical-critical perspective from the outside.

A second general topic has a Bultmannesque flavour too and will come in repeatedly in the articulation and solution of the problems listed: that of self-understanding. The many ideas that Paul introduces are not just free-floating ones that one may or may not have, as it were haphazardly and with little or no connection to the person one is. Rather, they are located by Paul in a quite specific place. They either actually go into (in Paul's own case) or else should go into (in the case of his addressees) people's self-understanding, their most basic understanding of who they themselves are as shown by the relationship they stand in with God, Christ, the world and the others. The general topic of people's self-understanding is another (old-fashioned) one that I claim should be re-installed in our interpretation of Paul.

That clearly recalls Bultmann. But again, this Bultmannesque motif should not be understood in Bultmann's own way. Self-understanding is in formal terms necessarily something that is tied to an individual, to an I or a self.[12] But the way this was construed in the ancient ethical tradition and in Paul has very little to do with modern 'individualism' as reflected in Bultmann's own existentialism. First, Paul's construction of the self and the initial I-perspective is not at all 'individualistic' in any modern sense. And secondly, as we shall see, the basic thrust of Paul's writing is towards some form of communitarianism. The overarching theory to be found in Paul about how the self should see its relationship with God, Christ, the world and the others is about a move *from* an I-perspective to a totally shared one.

But neither is Paul in fact merely concerned with self-*understanding*. On the contrary, the whole point of his thought as we have it in his letters lies elsewhere: in practice. It is social practice that is his primary target. In this connection we shall be much concerned with the logical place of parenesis (exhortation) within the letters and indeed with the inner logic of parenesis itself as seen in relation to the other type of speech-act that Paul employs in the supposedly non-parenetic parts of his letters, description. That is another general topic that will come in repeatedly in the articulation and solution of the problems listed: the understanding of Pauline parenesis. For instance, this pertains directly to the traditional problem of the indicative and the imperative in Paul. I shall argue that there is no genuine 'problem' here at all if one puts the proper interpretation on the logic of parenesis. Indicative and imperative are logically connected in the way that the indicative spells out the content itself of the new state in which Christ-believers already find themselves, a content that the parenesis then urges them to actualize or show in practice. Thus the parenesis logically presupposes the indicative and the latter is logically directed towards the former.

This general topic of thought is also directly relevant to another problem among those listed: that of the literary structure of the letters. In particular, how should one understand Paul's 'turn to parenesis' towards the end of some of them? Does it constitute a change of subject? And if so, are those sections only of secondary importance compared with the earlier 'theological' sections? These two questions should receive negative answers. Paul's specific sections of parenesis do not change the subject and they are of primary importance in the letters.

Thus the basic topics that will concern us all through are these: the relationship between the various categorial types of ideas; the role of self-understanding; that of practice; the understanding of parenesis; and the literary structure of the letters.

Finally, there is a range of topics that have the form of corollaries to those listed. In calling them corollaries, I am indicating that they are only somewhat incidental to those that will be our primary concern. That does not, however, make them any the less interesting. On the contrary, they address a number of issues that have traditionally been of the greatest directly theological concern in the reading of Paul. One such corollary is about Paul's understanding of the role of the Jewish law in relation to Christ. As we shall see, Paul did not find anything wrong with the law. The only 'problem' with it was that it was insufficient. It could not make people do what it aimed to make them do: keep it. That, by contrast, is precisely what the Christ faith both could and did. In fact, the Christ faith in principle generates actual, realized sinlessness—another traditional theological topic. And that, furthermore, is part of the meaning of the claim that it makes people righteous—yet another one. Since sinlessness is also to be explained by reference to the spirit, any supposed contrast between talk of righteousness and talk of the spirit is void—and that of course pertains to one more traditional theological issue.

Further: the point about sinlessness also means that there is no need, or indeed room, for ideas about the relationship between present and future righteousness like the one captured in the phrase 'already, but also not yet'. There *is* plenty of room for the idea of moral and spiritual progression from the state of basic conversion to something more total. That idea evidently presupposes that a person may not have fully reached the end yet. But as we shall see, that does not constitute a problem for the claim that the basic conversion in principle means sinlessness. An idea like 'both righteous and a sinner' has no foothold in Paul.

I emphasize that these various points are only corollaries of the reading to be developed. I did not start out from trying to address them head on, but rather from the kind of reading that, initially, attempts to make coherent sense of the text from a genuinely historical-critical perspective. Nor shall I give them any independent, full treatment here. Instead, they will come in from time to time precisely in the form of corollaries. Still, they are there, which is another sign that the present overall reading based on a single specific perspective is also a quite comprehensive one. That, among other things, is what will also make it a 'good' one.

Closer comparison with the three recent types of reading

Let us consider in a little more detail the relationship of the present approach to those of Malherbe, Meeks and Sanders, Räisänen and Stendahl. In the next section we shall range more broadly over the last hundred years of Pauline exegesis in order to see where the present approach is in line with that and where it differs.

(i) We may begin from the perspective adopted by Malherbe. His approach has two sides to it. On the one hand, as we noted, he has picked up a number of specific motifs (*topoi*) in the moral philosophers of the ancient ethical tradition and shown in detailed exegesis of particular texts that Paul uses them too. Malherbe therefore insists that Paul should not be seen 'against' something which has traditionally been called his Greco-Roman 'background'. Instead, we should understand him as being 'part of' a shared 'context': a shared Greco-Roman discourse in which he participated as a Hellenistic Jew.[13] However (and this is the other side), Malherbe is also keen on showing that Paul had an agenda of his own and that his use of the moral-philosophical *topoi* should be seen as part of *that*. For Malherbe the overall shape of Paul's thought remains different at crucial points from that of the moral philosophers. And Paul might precisely use the shared discourse to bring out that difference.[14]

We should be in complete agreement with the first side of this approach. The point about 'context' is especially well taken. One might formulate it like this. We should *start out* from expecting *similarities* between Paul and the moral philosophers in his use of the various *topoi* of contemporary 'popular moral philosophy'. Only later may we then claim, as it were forced by the material itself, to have hit upon dissimilarities.[15]

However, this formulation also points to two differences between the present approach and that of Malherbe, two differences where we shall move further in the direction in which Malherbe has rightly pointed. First, we shall see that there is a basic similarity between Paul and the Stoics not just with regard to a number of particular, relatively minor *topoi*, but to a whole cluster of motifs that together constitute a major pattern of thought. That is the pattern that goes into Paul's idea of 'conversion' or 'call' understood as a change in self-understanding: a move away *from* an identification of the self with itself as a bodily, individual being, *via* an identification with something outside the self, and *to* a perspective shared with and also directed towards others, a perspective that will then also issue immediately in practice. Though in a sense only a matter of quantity, this difference has rather wide ramifications. For instance, one might claim that this supposed major similarity between Paul and the Stoics might also be used to *explain* the many more restricted similarities that Malherbe has investigated: they are not just haphazardly there; instead, they form part of a major area of overlap.[16]

The second difference is that in the light of the first one, we shall be more reluctant than Malherbe is to claim that Paul's thought remains different from that of the moral philosophers at crucial points. Of course, Paul is speaking of Christ, and no ancient moral philosopher did that. Also, we cannot rule out beforehand that Paul does differ from the Stoics in important respects—on the contrary, that is to be expected and may indeed even be welcomed. But we must be extremely careful not to jump to any conclusions here, and the danger of doing so is enormous in view of what has become over the last two thousand years an inveterate tradition of contrasting the two great 'traditions' in European culture, the Jewish and the Greek.

The research done by Malherbe and his successors continues a line of scholarship that reached its first peak almost a hundred years ago. It issued in such work as Bultmann's early analysis of Paul's relationship with the Greco-Roman diatribe and Lietzmann's and Dibelius' emphasis on the importance of Greco-Roman material for the analysis of early Christian parenesis.[17] It is interesting to note, however, that Malherbe differs rather strongly from his predecessors, at least initially, in his stress on 'shared context' and his corresponding denial of the relevance of thinking in terms of the two contrasting 'traditions' when one is analysing the details of Paul's argument. Bultmann and Dibelius would not have gone so far as that. For them the two 'traditions' remained present as two lenses or parameters against which Paul should constantly be seen.

Still, I am suggesting that even Malherbe has not taken the whole step away from the traditional picture of the two 'traditions'. In Paul's case, the area of overlap is an even more extensive one.

In brief, the present work argues for similarity of ideas between Paul and the Stoics right across the board and fundamentally questions the widespread view that in the end there remains a basic, intrinsic difference between the perspectives of Paul the (Hellenistic) Jew and the ethical tradition of the Greeks.[18]

With this identification of the profile of the present work we have also identified the difference between this work and almost all other attempts to sort out similarities and differences between Paul and the Stoics. As already noted, this project of comparison is an old one. It goes back not only to the work done a hundred years ago, but right back to the apocryphal exchange of letters between Paul and Seneca.[19] It has not been entirely off the agenda at any point during the 20th century.[20] And it continues in the present day.[21] Is there more to be gained here? Not, one would think, when the project is executed as an exercise in the stocktaking of Paul's religious-historical 'background'. Instead, it should be undertaken (as it is, for instance, by Malherbe himself) as contributing to the exegetical elucidation of what Paul is actually saying. But it becomes even more potentially fruitful when it no longer restricts itself to individual passages and more or less minor *topoi*, but sees the possibility of doing what the present work attempts: to show that there is similarity right across the board; that the Christ-believing Paul is just as much a part of the ancient ethical tradition as we have recently learned to see him as part of (non-Christ-believing) Hellenistic Judaism;[22] that as regards Paul, the traditional dichotomies between Jerusalem and Athens, religion and philosophy, Christianity and humanism are without application; and more of the same kind. It is within this wider perspective that the present work should also be seen.[23]

(ii) The second scholarly perspective to be discussed here is the one that was inaugurated in the 1970s by Theissen in Germany and by Meeks in the USA. As exemplified in the latter's book *The First Urban Christians* (1983), this approach starts out from doing a kind of social history of the Pauline groups that is informed by sociological theory. It then moves on to analyse the central practices (ritual and other) that held the Pauline groups together by drawing on a number of theoretical motifs derived from cultural anthropology. And it ends by correlating the whole thought world of the Pauline Christians with their social world. Superficially, this approach might seem widely different from the one I am pursuing.

Methodologically, at least, Meeks' approach distrusts 'ideas' and aims to go behind those ideas that, as everybody of course agrees, are clearly present in the Pauline texts. Indeed, Meeks' approach welcomes, at least in principle, a kind of ideology critique that precisely aims to pull the carpet away from under the 'ideas' by confronting them with the actual practices. As against this, in the present book we shall be working wholly with ideas and not at all aim to go behind them in the direction of ideology critique. Nor shall we discuss social history or the many symbolic and metaphorical ideas of a non-discursive kind that Meeks correlates with the social world of the Pauline Christians. Could anything be more different, then?

Indeed, yes. For one thing, I personally share the interest in social practice and the impulse towards ideology critique. I also agree that when it comes to analysing Paul's thought world, such entities as symbols, metaphors and the like may be just as important as fully worked out, discursive and (quasi-)philosophical ideas. Still, Paul's explicit ideas should at least be allowed a place when one considers correlations between his thought world and his addressees' social world. And the ideas are of course presupposed when one moves on to something like an ideology critique of them. So they should be made clear. In fact, the connection between the present approach and the one represented by Meeks is even closer if, as suggested above, Paul's ideas are all directed towards practice and indeed towards social practice. As we shall see, the nucleus of ideas to be discussed constitutes the very idea of a form of life that is essentially communitarian. Moreover, Paul's aim with presenting these ideas to his addressees is a community-formative one. But community formation is also the ultimate theme of Meeks' analysis.

We should take it, therefore, that the present analysis complements Meeks' approach in a manner that is not just of minor importance. The two relevant questions are these: How much of what was actually taking place socially in Paul's community-formative practice was understood and grasped by Paul himself? And to what extent did he not only understand a sizeable part of this but also present it to his addressees themselves in order to *further* the community-formative process? If the answers to these questions are 'much' and 'to a large extent', then the particular dimension with which I am concerned, of Paul's discursive ideas concerning community formation, must be given due weight as *part* of an analysis that is focused on showing how the Christ faith functioned in concrete practice.

Another way of showing the connection between the present approach and one like Meeks' is as follows. Meeks aims to show how the Pauline thought world functioned by starting 'from below', from the social situation and the social practices. The same is true of the present approach, even when it focuses on ideas. We too shall start 'from below', in the notion of an individual self-understanding that itself reflects a certain social reality, and proceed from there to showing how that self-understanding may gradually develop into an articulation of a whole form of life that includes both an overarching world-view and also directions for a *different* kind of social, inter-human life. It seems obvious that such an approach constitutes a close complement to Meeks'. If it succeeds, it will teach us how the participants in the new social experiment whose external features Meeks has analysed themselves saw their world.

There are many different versions, of course, of the kind of approach instantiated here by Meeks, with a basis in modern sociology and cultural anthropology. We may mention two—connected with the names of Bruce J. Malina and Dale B. Martin—that differ from each other but are also in close affinity on a point of great importance to the present approach, a point, however, which we should only accept with some caution.[24] The point of similarity is to be found in the emphasis these scholars put on a supposed difference of Paul's whole thought world from modern, 'western' (that is, North-American?) individualism. There is a difference, however, in the way the point is made. Drawing on modern cultural anthropology, Malina and his colleagues have referred to social symbolical structures underlying Paul's text which they consider to be less relevant to north-western industrialized societies, but characteristic of the Mediterranean world both in antiquity and to some extent also now: honour and shame, purity and impurity, 'self' and community and the like. Martin draws on some of the same insights but is more keen on locating them historically in the specific historical context of these texts. But he too emphasizes the extent to which Paul's thought world differs from the modern one on such points as the understanding of the body, the 'self' and more. The ancients just had different views from ours on a number of salient features in their world-view. Both Martin and Malina therefore regularly emphasize the dangers of anachronism in the reading of Paul.

The specific point where caution is called for concerns Paul's talk of the 'self'. It is quite appropriate to warn against an 'individualistic' reading of Paul. But it is false not to allow that Paul is in fact doing philosophy about the self (the 'I') and its relation to God, Christ, the world and the others to exactly the same extent as a similar philosophy (of self and others) was being done in antiquity by the philosophers who make up the ancient ethical tradition. That kind of philosophy, in the precise form that we shall consider later, is actually there, both in the philosophers and in Paul. The fact that it is also, to a large extent, directly accessible to us, should not lead us to write it off out of a (in this case) misplaced fear of anachronism. Rather, we should allow this dimension to be *in* the picture—while also stressing those other features in Paul's world-view to which Malina and Martin have rightly drawn our attention, features that distinguish that world-view from our own. I must admit, however, that whereas I can easily see how my own emphasis on Paul's 'philosophy' may be incorporated into the comprehensive picture drawn by Meeks, I have more difficulty in seeing how the same thing can be done in relation to the approaches adopted by Malina and Martin—just because they explicitly reject anything that smacks of 'individualism'. But that will be a problem for us as interpreters, not for Paul himself, in whose thought world we do find elements of the various features highlighted by Malina, Martin—and myself.

(iii) The third perspective with which this book is in basic agreement is the 'new' perspective on Paul connected with the names of Sanders and Räisänen and on one crucial point prepared for by Stendahl.[25] As already noted, this perspective is presupposed here with regard to its fundamental insight that all of Paul's reflections on the relationship between the Christ faith and the Jewish law and Judaism in general spring from a highly positive attitude towards everything distinctively Jewish, an attitude that Paul had both before and after he was called to the Christ faith. His reflections in this area are to be understood as retrospective attempts of a 'good' Jew to fit everything in Judaism that was not intrinsically connected with the Christ faith into a coherent picture of God's handling of Jews and gentiles in relation to that one, new crucial event, the arrival of Christ.

Paul was in no way 'against' the Jewish law. He had never agonized over it (Stendahl's basic point), nor did he find it misplaced because of its supposedly inordinate 'quantity'—that it could never be fulfilled —or because of its 'quality'—that the whole direction of the law was in any case wrong since it only ministered to a human sense of self-sufficiency. Indeed, both in Galatians (3:22) and Romans (7:12) Paul heaps praise on the law. His 'problem' was rather how to fit in the law now that something else had been offered as playing the crucial role for salvation, something, moreover, that would give access to God's salvation even to gentiles, who by definition lived outside the Jewish law. It was the latter fact that set the task for Paul's thinking about his Jewish heritage.

We should even emphasize a point here that has gradually become ever clearer within this approach: that Paul did not in any way see his own form of Christ faith as constituting a break with Judaism. On the contrary, in the best sectarian manner he conceived of it as the true apogee of Judaism. In accordance with this, Paul's own missionary task was to bring the gentiles 'to Zion', even though the manner in which this might happen would probably be rather different from the way it had traditionally been expected.[26]

However, in spite of the basic sanity of the viewpoint displayed in Sanders' and Räisänen's handling of Paul's treatment of the law, we have already noted an important point where we must disagree. On their view, even though Paul attempted, more or less valiantly, to fit the Jewish law into his new conception, he was not very successful. Instead, he struggled on from letter to letter. There is little consistency and the inconsistencies are to be explained by Paul's psychological needs both to maintain the holiness of the law and also to insist that it had now been pushed aside by Christ. Some of this is quite right. In particular, it is obviously the case that Paul did not sit down to work out at philosophical leisure a complete 'system' that would fit the Jewish law seamlessly into his new conception of the world. Instead, he wrote letters that were basically occasional pieces. That even holds of Romans, which might otherwise well be said to constitute Paul's most sustained attempt to get to grips with the law and Judaism more generally. Still, it is wrong to resort to psychological explanation or to such expediencies as claiming the substance of a chapter like Romans 2 to be merely taken over from some external tradition without being properly integrated into Paul's own thought.[27]

The basic problem here is that of not allowing for what one might call Paul's philosophical impulse. It is true that Paul wrote occasional pieces. It is also true that he was not a philosopher. Indeed, he would never have accepted that kind of designation for a whole number of reasons, first among which was his sense of his practical, missionary task—and also that of being in some sort of basic opposition to the whole world (with its rulers and authorities) to which belonged the philosophers with their concern for 'wisdom' (cf. 1 Cor 1–2). But it is false to deny him a 'thinker's' impulse towards developing a coherent picture of the world in which he now found himself.[28] And once one does allow for that, one will discover far more by way of systematic thought in Paul than either Sanders or Räisänen has been prepared to see. To the extent that this systematic thought constitutes a concerted effort on Paul's part to spell out the meaning of the Christ event (as it were, *after* the event), we may even dignify it with the term 'theology' or 'theologizing'.[29] There is much more of that in Paul than Sanders and Räisänen would have us believe. It is a basic aim of the present book to show this and to connect the comprehensive pattern of Paul's thought that we shall discover through applying a Stoic lens to it with the literary structure of the letters.

Readings of Paul since the rise of historical criticism

This leads us to the final point of comparison with the present approach: that of a traditional theological perspective. That is not, however, a single, well-defined entity. We need to go back and sketch, in broad, somewhat systematized outline, the main positions in the scholarly exploration of Paul since the rise of historical criticism. The guiding question will be how they have handled what I shall call the 'original' Christian way of reading Paul: that of in principle accepting everything in Paul and transferring it lock, stock and barrel into one's own understanding of the world. To see how reflective positions over the last hundred and fifty years have handled this, we need a few hermeneutical tools.

The first is the notion of reading 'from within'. I shall understand it here as being defined by the second and third of the following three fundamental, phenomenological facts about reading: that until some obstacle arises, a reader will immediately read 'eye to eye' with the author, (a) expecting to be able to *understand* the author, that is, to 'speak the same language as' him or her, (b) aiming in addition to understand the *author's* point of view as *distinct* from the reader's own, and (c) immediately expecting the author to express a *truth*—or at least what I shall call a 'real option' (on which see more in a moment). In short, until some obstacle arises, the reader expects to *learn*. In relation to this, what the original Christian way of reading Paul has done is just to read him from within, either from a lack of sense of any obstacles or from neglecting them even if they were somehow felt to be there. By contrast, the essence of historical criticism and the later approaches that build on that is to acknowledge, and indeed insist on, such obstacles and to reflect on whether and to what extent they can be circumvented. Is reading Paul from within at all possible? And if it is, to what extent?

To see how the reflective positions from historical criticism onwards have handled this issue, we may focus on the third element in reading from within, and more especially on the notion of a real option. I take this over from the British philosopher Bernard Williams. Williams has for his own purposes distinguished between ethical outlooks of a large-scale kind (whole bodies of beliefs and attitudes) which constitute a 'real option' for us and others which do not. 'Many outlooks that human beings have had are not real options for us now. The life of a Bronze Age chief or a medieval samurai are not real options for us: there is no way of living them.' By contrast, 'an outlook is a real option for a group either if it already is their outlook or if they could go over to it; and they could go over to it if they could live inside it in their actual historical circumstances and retain their hold on reality, not engage in extensive self-deception, and so on.'[30]

There are obvious problems with Williams' idea and Williams has been duly criticized for it. For instance, who are the 'we' (in 'us now')? Also, one should always be suspicious when a philosopher states that we 'cannot' do this or the other thing. Still, in the way I shall apply Williams' notion to Paul, I believe everybody will agree that it has bite. Here a further remark of Williams holds true, which he makes after having singled out a peculiar level of reflectiveness and self-consciousness as the mark of the modern world in contrast with more traditional societies: 'There is no route back from reflectiveness. I do not mean that nothing can lead to its reduction; both personally and socially, many things can. But there is no *route* back, no way in which we can consciously take ourselves back from it.'[31]

The relevance to Paul is as follows. To put it bluntly, by far most of Paul's basic world-view, in other words, the basic apocalyptic and cosmological outlook that was his, does not constitute a real option for us now—in the way in which it was understood by Paul. This is the basic fact to which the last hundred and fifty years of reflective, scholarly reading of Paul has constituted so many responses. But note: in the way in which it was understood by Paul. For an underlying idea behind the various reading strategies that have been adopted has precisely been to find ways of making what Paul says come out as a real option for us by understanding it in ways that are different from the one in which it was understood by Paul himself—though hopefully in ways that are also sufficiently closely *connected* with that.

The first, and quite radical, such strategy was that of historical criticism. For by far most of the two millennia since his own time, Paul had been read more or less innocently from within in the original way of reading him. Gradually during the 19th century, however, readers of Paul came to realize that they were no longer able to do that. Central parts of what Paul is saying were no longer felt to present a real option when read at eye level with Paul himself, in the way in which it was understood by him. How then might readers reach truth, now that the direct road to truth had been blocked? The solution was to move outside the orbit of reading the text from within, at least as regards its second and third elements. Instead, one began to read it self-consciously from the outside. The realization of a 'historical gap' between now and then was felt to make such a step necessary. This is the crucial step that was taken in the kind of markedly historical criticism that rose to unprecedented heights exactly a hundred years ago. One might paraphrase the use of the term 'historical' here as meaning '*not* as something to be accepted immediately in a reading from within, but as something that is different from us'.

This change did not, however, extinguish altogether the original impulse to reading. In spite of taking the distancing, historicizing step, scholars went on, individually, to read Paul as if one or the other element in his thought did not fall under the distancing perspective. Also, it would not be false to say that the original impulse to reading was completely alive even within the distancing perspective itself. Only now it had been turned to a quite new object. Where the pursuit was originally directed towards the truths that Paul had been trying to formulate, its object had now become truth *about* those 'truths'. That object might only be reached by reading from the outside. An excellent example of this attitude may be found in such classics as the books on Paul by William Wrede (1907) and Albert Schweitzer (1930).

However, that change only served to reinforce the sense that the original impulse to reading Paul was left in a somewhat precarious position. Were there no *direct* truths to be gleaned from Paul or at least some real options for us to consider? It is not surprising, therefore, that readers of Paul soon became dissatisfied with a merely historical-critical reading of him. But what could be done about it? If the facts remained the same, if the main features of Paul's 'theology' and 'cosmology' were no more of a real option now than before, how could one salvage a reading of it from within? What possibility remained?

Rudolf Bultmann's approach constituted the logical answer. Bultmann did not give up the historical perspective, which had come to stay. But he sought ways of supplementing it that would reopen the possibility of reading Paul from within. Since the problem resided in reading Paul's 'theology' *cum* 'cosmology' from within in the way it was understood by Paul himself, Bultmann's solution was to read the 'theology' *cum* 'cosmology' from within but *not* (quite) in the way it was understood by Paul himself. Instead, what Bultmann offered was an *interpretation* of Paul's apocalyptic talk which took away all that was offensive in it by substituting for it a new understanding of the 'theology' *cum* 'cosmology' (the existentialist one) which *was* a real option (in Bultmann's time).[32]

The daring and clarity of Bultmann's attempt are impressive. But once again it is unsurprising that readers of Paul would soon become dissatisfied with it. As soon as Bultmann's existentialist frame fell out of favour, no stimulus was left to accept the reinterpretation of Paul that had been required in order to make him fit. Then it quickly became clear that Bultmann's 'interpretation' was in fact a *re*interpretation. It was not an interpretation that could be historically anchored in Paul himself, as Bultmann himself had, at least partially, claimed for it.[33] When the *modern* stimulus to seeing Paul in that particular way was removed, the basic props in Bultmann's reading also fell away. And then those historical facts about Paul that the earlier historical criticism had brought into the open reasserted themselves. The result was the 'rediscovery', e.g. by Ernst Käsemann, of Paul's apocalyptic frame of reference.[34]

With Käsemann, however, a deplorable development began, which still governs much, though fortunately not all, of Pauline criticism. In spite of the fact that scholars have generally accepted the historical-critical paradigm, they often do not realize that as long as what they are elucidating is the genuinely historical meaning of Paul's 'theology' *cum* 'cosmology', that is, its meaning in the way it was understood by Paul himself, they cannot also behave as if they were reading Paul from within and so present their reading to its readers as a real option for them. For if scholars are truly historical in their readings, then the picture that will come out of their efforts does *not* constitute a real option for us.

This unresolved dilemma is far too pervasive in present-day Pauline scholarship for comfort. Scholars sense the need to be historical and to honour the time gap between Paul and us. But they also wish to read Paul from within, believing that the content of Paul's thought *must* constitute a real option for us. Personally, I do not wish to deny that to some extent it does. Indeed, writing as a scholar who is also a Christian, I distinctly believe it does. But precisely only to some extent. (We shall see in a moment exactly how.) For one thing is certain. One cannot just provide a historical interpretation of Paul's 'theology' *cum* 'cosmology' and then go immediately on to offer it in the form in which it was understood by Paul himself as a real option for us. One must do something more. There are two possibilities. Either one will put the emphasis on 'a real option for us'. Then one may do what Bultmann did—in actual fact, though he would have denied it: offer a reinterpretation of the 'theology' *cum* 'cosmology' that constitutes an independent 'reading' of Paul which is not primarily concerned to be historically responsible. That is a perfectly legitimate task as long as the reading is not clothed *as a historical* one. Or else one will put the emphasis on 'historical interpretation'. Then one must give up insisting on the possibility of reading Paul's 'theology' *cum* 'cosmology' from within and accepting instead that any truths one may succeed in formulating in relation to Paul's text are truths from the outside, truths *about* Paul's talk of God, not the truths *of* it. That is what the original historical criticism did. And that too is what is in fact done in those many relatively new approaches to Paul—broadly of an either social historical or literary brand—which have come to the fore during the last quarter of the 20th century, even though they do not, unfortunately, always acknowledge to themselves that that *is* what they are doing. Let us consider briefly how these approaches, some of which we have already touched on, relate to the fundamental problem: that Paul's 'theology' *cum* 'cosmology' is no longer a real option for us in the way in which it was understood by Paul himself.

What characterizes these approaches in comparison with the original historical criticism are two things: (*a*) They bring to the Pauline text a fully worked out methodological perspective that has been developed outside the text, and then attempt to elucidate the text in terms of that perspective. (*b*) And what they attempt to elucidate is the whole of Paul, either the whole of his form of life or the whole of the specific text (a whole letter) that they study. As already hinted, we may divide these approaches into two broad groups. On the one side there are approaches of a sociological or cultural anthropological bent. They study the Pauline form of life, as opposed to the literary, more or less autonomous surface of the text, using the text as a window on to a real, lived type of existence. On the other side there are approaches whose central focus is on the text itself. They include the various modern literary approaches that are historically derived from Russian formalism of the 1920s: New Criticism, narrative criticism, structuralism, rhetorical criticism and the like. How do the approaches in these two groups handle the fundamental problem?

One might think that the literary approaches constitute an attempt to overcome the modern, historical alienation from Paul's own perspective. Do they not read the text as it stands? Both yes and no. In some cases where the specifically literary self-consciousness is low in practitioners of this approach, what we get is not very different from the usual, mainstream type of approach to Paul. Such practitioners too will feel that by providing a 'literary' reading they are both able to get around subscribing lock, stock and barrel to Paul's 'theology' *cum* 'cosmology' in his own terms and also to stay very *close* to his own perspective. As before, however, that is a fallacy. Properly understood, what a literary, text-oriented approach has to offer is just as far removed from being a historically oriented reading from within as any approach in the other modern group. Both reflect the level of reflectiveness and self-consciousness that Bernard Williams identified as the peculiar mark of the modern world. Whether they like it or not, both read from the outside in relation to Paul's own viewpoint. To the extent that they believe otherwise, they are under an illusion. They do *not* provide *direct* access for us to Paul's own world.

They do, however, give us something more than a merely historical picture to relate to. That is due to two features of the modern approaches that might seem to stand in some tension but in fact do not, their methodological selectivity and their aim at material comprehensiveness. As noted, the modern approaches generally attempt to elucidate *as much* of Paul and his text as possible when seen from within the methodological perspective that is applied. They do this by attempting to bring out *connections* between the 'theology' *cum* 'cosmology' and the rest. Thus, for instance, among non-just-literary approaches a reading of Paul that is informed by modern sociology of knowledge will begin in the way we noted in connection with Meeks: from the level of the social world and social practices *under*lying the text. But from there it will move into Paul's text aiming to bring out connections between all its levels, both intrinsically between textual levels ('theology', 'cosmology', 'anthropology', 'ethics' and the like) and extrinsically between text and reconstructed social world. As we saw, such connections may have the form of *correlations*, which leaves the exact character of the connectedness somewhat open. Or they may focus on the idea of the social *function* of the 'theology' *cum* 'cosmology' in relation to the rest. A reading informed by modern sociology of knowledge may also bring in branches from the other, literary group of approaches, e.g. rhetorical criticism, with the aim of showing how Paul's own letter-writing practice fits into the rest. All through, the aim is to build up as comprehensive a picture as is possible of the form of life to which Paul's letters bear witness. The same aim will be found in various approaches of a cultural anthropological kind, only here focus will from the start be more on the symbolic content of terms and practices than on their strictly socio-political basis.

The literary approaches too aim at comprehensiveness. Once more the aim is to integrate talk that belongs at different levels of Paul's text, though here with less emphasis, if any at all, on aspects of *extra*-textual practice underlying the text itself. By thus providing a reading of the text as a whole, its structure, the literary connections across the whole tapestry and the like, literary approaches offer an interpretation of Paul's 'theology' *cum* 'cosmology' as part of the overall web of meaning. It has now been *integrated* into a more comprehensive meaning. And thus, as in the case of the other, non-just-literary type of approach, there now is something comprehensive and thought-provoking to relate to for the person who is interested in 'Paul's theology', but cannot see it directly as a real option in the way it was understood by Paul himself. Via the route over the modern selective viewpoint combined with the attempt at maximal material comprehensiveness, the modern approaches manage to provide readings that still do not make Paul's own form of life a real option for us, but does present it to the modern reader in a clothing that makes it possible to draw *analogies* between that form of life (as re-described) and ways of living that are in fact real options for us.

The quest for comprehensiveness governed by a methodologically based, selective viewpoint is wholly understandable and to a large extent justified. It aims to find a comprehensive form of truth in the Pauline material, even though only a truth *about* Paul, by way of substitution for the kind of truth with which Paul was himself grappling. The truth that these approaches have to offer definitely remains a truth from the outside in relation to Paul's own viewpoint. Still, in the way they are pledged to reading as much of Paul as possible, *including* his 'theological' *cum* 'cosmological' talk, and to doing it from a modern perspective, they do offer something to satisfy the interest in 'Paul's theology' that almost all his readers will have. There are obviously a number of external reasons why Pauline scholars have become attracted to the various modern approaches. But there can be no doubt that a major reason for their attractiveness is the fact that by their double character of methodological selectivity and material comprehensiveness they offer, in a reflected way, a full substitute for what we would like to have, but cannot get: the sense of reading 'Paul's theology' directly from within as a real option for us.

The formal shape of the present approach

Against this background we are finally able to define the hermeneutical profile of the present approach in its entirety. It has three stages that are logically distinct, but cannot always be kept separate in practice.

The first stage accepts the historical-critical challenge to the full and insists that the task is through and through historical and hence completely detached from the one of looking for real options for us in the Pauline material. Here we need to keep constantly alive to ourselves all those elements in Paul's comprehensive 'world-view' that do not constitute a real option for us, but to which we do have some imaginative access (albeit hardly to the degree one would have were one to live that form of life). This stage, therefore, insists on the historical distance between Paul and ourselves, which once and for all prevents us from seeing Paul's own form of life as a real option for us.

At the next stage, however, the present approach also accepts the basic structure of the modern approaches with their methodological selectivity and material comprehensiveness. As already noted, we shall only be directly concerned here with Paul's discursive ideas, which leaves out much material in the letters. On the other hand, the present approach shares with the literary ones the concern to cover as much material in the text as possible in order to bring out a comprehensive logical pattern that informs Paul's use of the many different ideas. With the sociologically and anthropologically oriented approaches the present one also shares the concern to see such a pattern as articulating a whole form of life, either one that was actually practised among the Pauline Christ-believers or one that constituted a sort of ideal or intended point of convergence for the actual life practices of Paul's addressees. Such a reading will stay wholly on the outside in relation to Paul's own viewpoint reflecting as it does the reflectiveness and self-consciousness of the modern world. It will also maintain the acknowledgement of the historical distance that forms the core of historical criticism. In addition, by elucidating the Pauline material in terms of well-defined *modern* categories, the present reading will also share with the modern approaches the feature of presenting a picture that makes it possible to draw analogies between Paul's own form of life (as redescribed) and ways of living that in fact constitute real options to us. Here the modern approaches with their emphasis on starting out from *modern* concepts and with their methodological selectivity provide readings of the Pauline material that make it *intelligible* (but no more than that) in ways that allow the modern reader to draw *analogies* (but again no more than that) to forms of life that do constitute real options for us. We can, if we want to, *compare* Paul's own form of life as redescribed from a modern perspective with modern forms of life to which we have direct access.

In both respects—the historically distancing one and the methodological, *partially* integrating one—the results of such a reading will be, in a broad sense, of 'theological interest'. Even if we are not able to take over Paul's own way of understanding the world, it remains of interest to our own independent, theological reflection to see exactly how Paul himself did understand it and under what redescriptions we may understand his world in such a way that we may draw analogies from it to our own.

In addition to the two stages identified, there is a third, quite complicated one. Here we shall take a step that will be regarded with scepticism by those reflective modern scholars with whom we have hitherto been in company. Unreflective scholars, by contrast, might greet it with alacrity. That only makes it all the more important to explain how it should be understood. What we shall do at this stage is move in the direction of articulating a set of (almost) genuinely Pauline ways of understanding that have a claim to constituting a real option for us even when we look at them in the cool light of historical criticism. As before, that cannot be done for the whole of Paul's 'theology' *cum* 'cosmology'. No trick can remove the basic stumbling-block here that gave rise to historical criticism. But it can be done, in a historically responsible way, for those sides of Paul's thought that we termed 'anthropological' and 'ethical' *even though* the result of the strictly historical analysis will be that they hang tightly together with the 'theological' *cum* 'cosmological' side of his thought. Let me explain how. And let me also explain why it is important—even exegetically important—to open up for this kind of application of the notion of a real option to Paul.

First, however, we should make explicit that a real option is just that—an option. There is no idea here that what one may get out of Paul by analysing him in the way to be suggested necessarily constitutes an ('anthropological' or 'ethical') *truth*. It is just an option. The aim is merely to articulate, in as differentiated and comprehensive a manner as possible, a form of life that is precisely *possible*—as it were for our consideration. Whether and in what manner both the writer and the reader will end up subscribing to this particular option after having compared it with a range of other available options is entirely up to each of us. This point is of great importance since it helps to define the level at which we shall be operating. Basically, as I said, the level is the disinterested one of historical criticism enlarged with the *cognitively* 'interested' position of the modern approaches. But even where we shall be moving towards bringing in more of ourselves, the level will remain one of an *articulation* of a *possible* form of life, certainly not of recommendation of a preferred one—though now an articulation that is 'interested' in a more than merely cognitive way: *existentially* so.

How may one consider the 'anthropological' and 'ethical' sides of Paul's thought as a real option for us if they also hang tightly together in actual historical fact with the 'theological' *cum* 'cosmological' side which does not constitute such an option? The first answer is that there is in fact no problem here. What constitutes a real option for us evidently depends on ourselves. Seen in that light we are free to cut into the existentially disinterested picture drawn by historical criticism and the modern approaches and state that certain parts of that picture constitute a real option for us even though they hang intimately together, within that picture itself, with other parts that we cannot accept as real options. The requirement that we engage in this operation in a historically responsible manner is fulfilled when we acknowledge and emphasize that what we present as a real option is not *exactly what it is* in Paul since we have cut off connections with other parts of his thought that we are not prepared to take over.

The second answer is that in this operation we are in fact much helped by Paul himself when he develops the 'anthropological' and 'ethical' sides of his thought in such a way that they acquire a weight of their own, certainly not in complete independence from the other sides, but of sufficient comprehensiveness and sophistication for it to be possible for us to *consider* them on their own. That *is* of help. For if what we might consider worth cutting off as a real option for us was itself only of minor significance and proportions and if it was *just* and *totally* dependent on the rest of Paul's thought, then while we might well proceed to our cutting operation, there would not be much point to it. Instead, we would do better to leave Paul completely behind in our own existential search. As it is, the part of Paul's thought that we may consider a real option for us is of large proportions and of major significance within that thought itself even when looked at coolly in the historically distancing perspective. The road is clear, therefore, for us to *address* it (also) as a real option.[35]

The specific way in which Paul himself helps us here is the following. As already noted, he does not just present his 'theological' *cum* 'cosmological', 'anthropological' and 'ethical' ideas as it were from the outside, as either merely lying alongside one another or else in a manner that shows, but still from the outside, their intrinsic connectedness. Instead, he locates them all in a single place: in the human self-understanding, Paul's own and that of his addressees. What Paul does throughout his letters is to articulate a comprehensive form of life—which in itself includes all his 'theological' *cum* 'cosmological', 'anthropological' and 'ethical' ideas—*from the inside out*: as lived and experienced by Paul himself and his addressees. Everything is, as it were, seen *from* a human perspective, the one Paul aims to share with his addressees. This fact allows us to cut into a very sizeable part of Paul's thought without being too bothered that there are other, and even closely connected, parts that are left out. Paul's 'theological' *cum* 'cosmological' ideas will be left out as considered on their own. But they *will* be included in the form in which they actually show up in the letters: as entering into the comprehensive self-understanding that Paul is aiming to articulate.

How can one distinguish in that way? If Paul's 'theology' *cum* 'cosmology' does not itself constitute a real option for us, then neither will those ideas do so when seen as part of Paul's and his addressees' own perspective, as it were from the inside out. That is quite correct. However, what constitutes a real option for us is not in the end those ideas themselves, even as part of the perspective from the inside out, but their function: the role they play in *informing* and *reflecting* the *other* ideas (the 'anthropological' and 'ethical' ones) that enter into that perspective. What we *can* see as a real option is a perspective on a form of life in which *certain* ideas 'from above' *like* Paul's 'theological' *cum* 'cosmological' ones do enter into some kind of symbiosis with those other ideas that more immediately constitute a real option for us.[36]

Put briefly, then, the reading of Paul to be given here is of the same kind as the one enlightened modern scholars and philosophers give of, say, Plato, Aristotle or the Stoics. These ancient philosophers had their 'theologies' too, which played a larger or smaller role also in their 'ethics'. In Stoicism, for instance, the role of their 'theology' was far from negligible. To most moderns these 'theologies' do not constitute a real option for a number of reasons, one of which is that they too were intimately connected with 'cosmologies' that are no longer acceptable to us. But that does not prevent modern scholars and philosophers from reading the 'ethics' of the ancients as real options for us, not necessarily as stating certified and convincing truths, but precisely as options. And the way this is in fact done is precisely the one that has been developed here.

Why, then, is it important—even exegetically—to engage in this particular kind of reading? Why is it important to address Paul's articulation of his own and his addressees' perspective on the Christ-believing form of life from a sense that over sizeable areas it constitutes a real option for us? Why not just stay historical-critical and existentially disinterested? Before answering this question, we may at least claim that simply stating that that is what we shall be doing has an advantage over most traditional analyses of Paul. We have complained that scholars often engage in historical-critical analysis of Paul—or some modern successor to it—*as if* their results were also immediately available to us as real options. That is a mistake. Scholars ought see this and to make clear to themselves and their readers exactly where and how their own existential interest is involved in their professional scholarly work. We have at least done that here.

But back to the question: Is such clarity of any intrinsic value to the scholarly work itself? It is, in at least two ways. First, it will constitute an

important check on that work, preventing one's *more* than scholarly
interest from unduly distorting it. That, one might say, is the negative
importance of the scholar's clarity about his or her own interests in
reading. But second, such clarity also has positive import. For it allows
the scholar to engage in a more fruitful analysis than would otherwise be
possible of those areas in Paul that are taken to constitute a real option.
The idea is this. If we may see sizeable parts of Paul's 'anthropology' and
'ethics' as a real option for us, then we may also be allowed to speculate
more freely about how to fill in gaps in Paul's thought in this area based
on our own understanding of the area. Such a reading may be called a
'phenomenological' one. By calling it so I do not intend to suggest
that we shall be moving in an area of self-identical eternal truths that
may be read off the phenomena themselves in any historical period and
any culture. For we shall remain in a variable area of options and no
options. Thus while the phenomenological approach will allow us to fill
in gaps in our reading of Paul based on our own understanding of the
phenomena, it will do so, and may generally be applied, only *tentatively*:
in an *attempt* to give sense to what Paul is saying. For we shall of course
be constrained all through by our basic aim of providing a reading that
is *historically* valid. Still, in order to be able to engage at all in this
tentative kind of phenomenological reading, we must take it beforehand
(tentatively!) that Paul's thought in this area does constitute a real option
for us.

   To see the last point let us consider an example. One feature of Paul's
'theology' *cum* 'cosmology' is an idea of a kind of physical participation
in Christ on the part of Christ-believers: they are 'one with' Christ in a
manner that was probably understood by Paul in a very reified way.
(Fortunately, however, he also understood it in other ways that are more
accessible to us.) Now scholars often speak of Paul's idea here as if it
made immediate sense and indeed was more or less readily acceptable to
us. But it is not. On the contrary, it looks as if it is very far from constituting a real option for us. That also means, however, that it is very difficult
to develop, even as part of doing one's existentially neutral, historical
work, what it at all meant to Paul. Since it appears so strange to us, one
really cannot feel sure that one has got it sufficiently right for it to be
possible to develop it further and combine it with other similar ideas.
A shared level of discourse is lacking. But that is just another way of
saying that one cannot recur to a shared field of 'phenomena' to fill it
in. By contrast, with the 'anthropological' and 'ethical' ideas with
which we shall be centrally concerned, there is far more of an initial
likelihood that we do share Paul's level of discourse. And so the road is

open to a 'phenomenological' reading that presupposes that, at least tentatively.

To summarize, the approach adopted here has three logical parts: (i) In its existentially neutral, historical-critical aspect it is dedicated to making as much historical sense as possible of Paul's thought world taken in its entirety. As noted earlier, the present approach presupposes the insights of Malherbe and others (on Paul's relationship with Hellenism), of Meeks, Theissen and others (on the importance of social reality) and of Stendahl, Sanders, Räisänen and others (on Paul's relationship with Judaism). (ii) By almost exclusively focusing on ideas, it differs from an approach like Meeks'. But otherwise it should be understood as being informed by an underlying concern just like Meeks' to provide a methodologically based, comprehensive picture of the intrinsic connections between the various levels of Paul's thought world and between those taken together and his social world. Only, by focusing specifically on his ideas the present investigation does no more than provide a complement in this particular respect to Meeks' more comprehensive project. (iii) In its existentially interested aspect it cuts out a sizeable portion of Paul's thought world—the 'anthropological' and 'ethical' one—and attempts to elucidate that both as part of the more comprehensive perspective on the Christ-believing form of life that Paul aims to present to his addressees—but also as constituting a real option for us (though no more than that). Here it differs distinctly from a traditional theological reading, which aims, in whatever way and to different degrees, to see also the upper parts of Paul's thought (the 'theology' *cum* 'cosmology') as a real option, and indeed as stating the truth. In relation to that, the present reading remains at a lower level.

A final question: The proposed reading will be a piece of historical-critical scholarship. It will also be a philosophical and phenomenological reading in the way we have just seen. Will it also be a theological one?

A theological reading?

Before turning to this question, it is worth comparing the present approach with that of Rudolf Bultmann. As already noted, there are clear similarities, but also marked differences. The similarities include Bultmann's well-known focus on Paul's 'anthropology' and self-understanding and his use of philosophy (in Bultmann's case, of Heideggerian descent) to elucidate the 'anthropology'. The similarities also include Bultmann's insistence that the 'anthropology' cannot be separated from the 'theology' and Bultmann's clear recognition of the problem this raises since

Paul's 'theology' *cum* 'cosmology' is so thoroughly marked by its 'mythic' features.

But there are also large differences. One is that whereas Bultmann employed a philosophical key of modern descent to elucidate Paul, the present approach makes use of a set of philosophical ideas that were contemporary with Paul. Correspondingly, I claim (hopefully with more success than Bultmann) to be giving an interpretation of Paul that is through and through historically valid. Another difference is that whereas Bultmann saw Paul as being himself engaged in a sort of existentialist re-interpretation of the 'mythic' features of his 'theology' *cum* 'cosmology', I strongly deny anything like this, taking it instead that Paul subscribed completely to the entirely realistic apocalyptic world-view that is a constituent part of his 'theology'. This connects with a third difference, which is that whereas Bultmann felt able to present his reading of Paul as in its entirety stating *the* truth about human life, the present approach argues neither for 'the' truth (but only for a real option), nor for the direct relevance of *all* sides of Paul's thought. That is precisely what raises the question whether this reading may after all qualify as a theological one.

There are other, less general but equally important, differences between Bultmann's reading and the present one. For example, I have already distinctly rejected Bultmann's very individualistic reading of the kind of self-understanding he found in Paul. I have also rejected most of the features of Bultmann's reading that were taken over more or less wholesale from traditional Protestantism: the construal of Paul's relationship with the Jewish law and Judaism more generally; the characteristic construal of the relationship between the indicative and the imperative in Paul with its 'forensic' understanding of the indicative (God's act 'from above' of declaring Christ-believers righteous) and its authoritarian understanding of the imperative (God's command 'from above' to Christ-believers who remain sinners); and more. In spite of all this, the level of sophistication in Bultmann's grasp of the basic hermeneutical issues in a philosophically responsible reading of Paul remains far greater than what one finds in most later treatments of him. To that extent, at least, it constitutes a model.

The final question, then: to what extent will the present approach provide a reading that may qualify as a genuinely theological one? Let us understand the question in the following way: will it provide an interpretation of Paul's talk about God, Christ and more which presents that talk as at least a real option, if not the actual truth about human beings and the world? The most straightforward answer is to say that on such a stringent understanding of what makes a reading of Paul a theological one, the one to be proposed here will not be that. For we have explicitly renounced any attempt to provide some interpretation here of the 'cosmological' ideas in which Paul's whole understanding of the Christ story is couched that will turn them into real options for us. Instead, as regards real options and truth we shall focus exclusively on his 'anthropological' and 'ethical' ideas.

There is a special perspective, however, that would turn even such a reading into a theological one in some sense of the term. It formulates a line of thought which one might see as a more or less radical extension of Bultmann's original claim about the relationship between 'theology' and 'anthropology' in Paul—and of Clifford Geertz' corresponding claim about the interrelationship between 'world-view' and 'ethos'. On this view, everything Paul says about the 'anthropological' and 'ethical' sides of the Christ-believing form of life would be understood as a sort of *'interpretation'* of the specifically 'theological' *cum* 'cosmological' sides of that life, a statement of their *meaning*. Conversely, one might see the 'theological' *cum* 'cosmological' ideas as metaphysical 'constructions' whose function it is to give ontological substance to the 'anthropological' and 'ethical' ideas. It goes without saying that such an understanding of what is going on in Paul's letters has removed itself drastically from Paul's own straightforward and wholly realistic perspective. It is also a very real question what the content is of calling such a reading a 'theological' one. Still, it is an idea to be explored rather than just rejected.

If we remain on firmer ground, however, we shall probably do better to admit that under the stringent construal of what makes a reading a theological one, the present one will not be that. But neither will it, of course, be any *less* theological than any other attempt to get at historical-critical truth *about* Paul.

The plan of the book

I begin (chapter 2) from presenting in broadest outline a thought model of Stoic descent that I take to underlie substantial stretches of Paul's thought and practice. I then (chapter 3) turn directly to Stoicism in order to show in more detail how various specific features of the model are derived from that philosophy. In chapter 4 I turn to Paul aiming to show how the model in its specifically Stoic form may be seen to illuminate a whole number of widely different motifs in the Pauline material and to solve, or at least dramatically lessen the tension in, the problems listed earlier in this chapter. Since I wanted to discuss whole letters and could not treat all the letters in sufficient depth in a single book, I decided to focus on three of them: Philippians, Galatians and Romans. The choice is somewhat arbitrary. Philippians and Galatians suggested themselves because they are (*a*) of sufficient size, complexity and importance (compared with 1 Thessalonians and Philemon), (*b*) not *too* complex (compared with 1 and 2 Corinthians) and (*c*) rather different in character. Romans has the same degree of complexity as 1 and 2 Corinthians, albeit of a different kind, but Romans was included for obvious strategic reasons. If I could not show the fruitfulness of my reading of Paul for Romans, it would be too easy for scholars to dismiss it. Philippians is discussed in chapters 4–5, Galatians in chapters 6–7 and Romans in chapters 8–10. Chapter 11 summarizes our results.

2

The Model

This chapter presents the model I claim underlies much of Paul's thought and practice in the letters. The model pertains most directly to Paul's 'anthropology' and 'ethics'. It expresses the basic logical shape of that— as well as of Stoic 'anthropology' and 'ethics'.

It is important to realize from the start the heuristic character of the model. It is an abstraction, drawn from the particularities of Paul's thought in three of his letters and from Stoicism in the many forms in which we know it. It is identical with neither. It leaves something out of both bodies of thought, while focusing attention on other things. But it also includes an extensive area of overlap between Stoic and Pauline 'anthropology' and 'ethics'. While the shape of this specific area is most extensively worked out in Stoicism, there are enough indications in Paul to show that there *is* an overlap. The asymmetry in this relationship is in itself quite unsurprising. After all, Stoicism was a philosophy and hence a discipline whose *raison d'être* (though not its only task) was precisely to develop the concepts needed to define an 'anthropology' and 'ethics'. What matters is that there is in fact material enough in Paul to show that he himself shared that 'anthropology' and 'ethics'.

The model has no *independent* value. In particular, it should not be considered on its own as stating what amounts to a shorthand reduction of either Pauline or Stoic thought. Rather, it functions as a map of reading the two bodies of thought in their *own* particularity. It should not be understood as directing attention away from the text itself, but rather towards it. Thus its immediate value lies in its ability to bring a sufficient amount of order to the complexities of each body of thought taken in its entirety and on its own. As we saw in the previous chapter, the comparison of Paul with the Stoics has *this* particular *exegetical* purpose, not just that of a basic stocktaking of 'similarities' and 'differences'. At

33

the same time, just because of its abstract character the model will be of value in helping readers of Paul to do the kind of analysis from the outside that is part of our agenda.

It is this abstract function of the model as a map of reading that will also finally vindicate it. If it helps to produce readings of Paul (and for that matter of Stoicism) that will command agreement among scholars *as* readings (that is, by appearing illuminating, helping to solve interpretive problems and the like), then we may also claim that the model does highlight a basic similarity between Paul and the Stoics.

The model

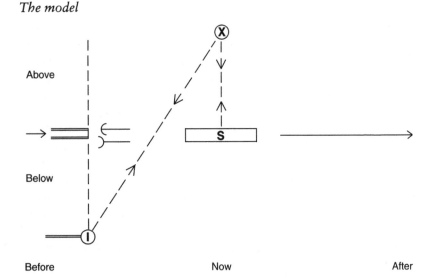

Reading the model: From I to We

The model depicts a change that may occur in the perception of individuals of their own identity and what has value for them. At the I-stage the individual person (i) perceives him- or herself as an embodied individual, the one who may say 'I' of him- or herself, and (ii) is merely concerned about fulfilling the desires of that individual. Then a shift may occur, which leads the person to the S-stage. Here the individual person (i) still perceives him- or herself as an embodied individual, but now also as one of the others so that the person may now include him- or herself in a social 'We'. Correspondingly, (ii) the person will now be concerned about fulfilling the desires of that 'We'. The model is frankly normative. What lies 'Before' and 'Below' is bad. And what lies from 'Now' to

'After' and 'Above' is good. The model is also dynamic. An earlier, bad state of an individual is exchanged for a new and good one.

The change in the individual perception of the person's own identity—in his or her self-understanding—has two elements. First, the individual is 'struck' by what figures at the X-level. In Paul X stands for God and Christ, in Stoicism for reason, which is also God (though certainly a different kind of God). X is different from the individual seen as under I. But X is also so related to the individual person that he or she may come to identify with it. The person may come to see him- or herself as *belonging* to X, which now expresses what the person takes him- or herself to *be*. This change is expressed in the model by the two arrows between I and X. The new experience of belonging at the X-level (↑) is a result of being 'struck' (↓) by something from that level.

Second, this transference of identity from I to X also has the direct result of bringing the individual from the I- to the S-stage. This is due to the specific content of what the individual has identified with at the X-level. In Paul that content comes out in the Christ event, in Stoicism in the special character of reason. In both, the result of identifying with precisely this is an understanding of oneself as one among the others, one of *all* those who *share* in participating in X, which is taken by all to identify themselves. This relationship between the X- and the S-levels is again expressed in the model by two arrows. Here the downward arrow, X→S, summarizes the downward and upward relationship between I and X, indicating that that relationship, which began from above (↓) and was then followed by the reverse movement (↑), results precisely in bringing the individual *over* to the S-level. Conversely, the upward arrow S→X indicates that the S-level is defined by the same relationship with X which to begin with brought the person away from the I-stage—compare the upward arrow I→X.

Note that the downward arrows in both cases stand for the relation of 'being struck' by something. This means that all four arrows express different types of intentional relatedness 'from *below*'. It is certainly possible to correlate the downward arrows with some explicit *action* initiated from above. That is what Paul does in his specifically 'theological' talk of God's act in the Christ event. But that act itself should be understood as lying outside the model—which is about 'anthropology' and 'ethics'. *Within* the model even the downward arrows stand for a type of relatedness from below, though one that is quite distinct from the type indicated by the upward arrow: the experience of being 'struck' by X *explains* the other experience of identifying with X by 'stretching upwards' towards it.

As presented here, the model calls for a temporal reading: it depicts the phenomenon of conversion conceptualized as a story. However, it is also possible to read it in a non-temporal way as picturing the relationship in a human being between egoism or a prudential stance (the I-level) and altruism or a moral stance (the S-level). Such a reading considerably reduces the model's forcefulness since the element of change from one thing to the other is now explicitly left out. Nor is it a reading that fits either Paul or the Stoics, who were concerned precisely with the idea of a genuine change *from* one thing *to* another. It is more congenial to a modern ethical perspective—or to Luther's idea of being *simul iustus et peccator*, when this is given a proper, naturalistic interpretation: that a human being will belong simultaneously at both the I- and S-levels.

But is there not something corresponding to this in Paul and the Stoics too, namely the idea of belonging at the S-level 'already—but not yet *quite*'? Not really. For the strongly dynamic quality that is also expressed in the model renders such a Pauline and Stoic sense of 'simultaneity' very different from a modern one. In the ancient reading the simultaneity is only an intermediate phenomenon as part of the dynamic movement of *progression* that may in principle be overcome already in this life. In the modern reading, by contrast, it will be an ineluctable fact about life in this world.

There is a final element in the model that concerns the relationship between life in the group at the S-level and life outside the group (or the group's own life in its pre-conversion state). In the new state we find both exclusion and inclusion of elements from the earlier state. For of course the group's new life will neither be completely new nor take over completely all that it has left behind. Thus there is an intricate relationship across the 'Before'–'Now' boundary line. What governs this is the extent to which elements in the pre-conversion state may be seen to correspond with, or to be reinterpretable in the light of, the new basic experience that constitutes the new group.

The basic interpretation of Paul expressed in the model

What overall profile will Paul's thought obtain once we look at it in terms of the I→X→S-model? What will it basically be about? Several answers spring to mind, which we may present here without argument merely to make clear the kind of overall understanding of Paul that underlies this book.

The first is this: it is about joining the group of Christ-believers, one that has a quite specific character *as* a group. One thing the model depicts is the move from being outside the S-group and coming to be a member of it. The model offers a special interpretation of the state of being outside the group, no matter which of the innumerable outside ways of living one might think of. That state, it claims, is an I-state, one at which the individual is in fact merely concerned about fulfilling his or her own desires, no matter how much he or she will also belong to some group or other. This is a stark claim, to which we shall return. Before that we must emphasize the basic, community-oriented feature of the model: that it depicts joining a group that is, as it were, the quintessential group, one that is constituted by nothing other than a 'We'.

There are at least two reasons why this is important. One is that it makes the model fit what is intuitively one of the absolutely basic facts about Paul's work. Paul was a missionary, but his missionary work took the quite specific form of creating congregations, groups of people engaged in a shared form of life in which the point of Paul's mission would and should display itself. Another is that precisely the community-oriented point of the model brings Paul in close proximity with Stoicism. But does not Stoicism rather differ from Paul by being wholly oriented towards the individual and his or her personal happiness? Absolutely not. As we shall see in the next chapter, Stoic ethics is just as community-oriented as anything to be found in Paul. It directly issues in a 'political' vision. There is and remains the important difference that whereas Paul's work resulted in actual communities being set up, the thought of the various Stoics did not, at least not in the same way. Indeed, as became clear with Roman Stoics like Seneca and Marcus Aurelius, it was possible to be a very individualistic Stoic, a Stoic more or less for oneself. (In fact, however, such a description does little justice even to this late Stoicism.) Important as the difference is, it does not, however, touch the basic community-orientation of Stoicism, which is as much in evidence in Seneca and Marcus Aurelius as anywhere else. Thus the model brings out very sharply the first of three basic features of Paul's thought that are common to him and Stoicism and distinguishes him when he is viewed from the philosophical perspective adopted in this book. It is the *social* and '*political*' feature.

As noted, the model also offers a special interpretation of the state outside the group and correspondingly of the form of life that constitutes life within the group. This interpretation is a *moral* one. It constitutes the second basic feature of Paul's thought viewed philosophically. It builds the basic distinction between inside and outside on the contrast between egoism and altruism, between a form of valuation which is based on and constantly refers back to the desires of the individual him- or herself and only gives secondary thought to those of others—and another form which sees the individual him- or herself as no more than one among the others and for that reason gives primary thought to the desires of all those involved. This contrast constitutes the essence of what Paul has to say about 'sin' (*hamartia*), the various moral vices that fall under it and the resulting 'fleshly acts' (*erga tēs sarkos*)—as it does of what the Stoics have to say about moral stupidity (*mōria*), vice (*kakia*) and the resulting 'errors' (*hamartēmata*). There is agreement on the other side too, in what Paul says of the life of the just and holy ones (*dikaiōthentes* and *hagioi*) and the Stoics of the wise and good (*sophoi* and *agathoi*). There also is a further agreement in the way both Paul and the Stoics conceptualize the move from the I-state to the S-state as a matter of progression (*prokopē*) from a childlike state to a mature state where the person is no longer a child (*nēpios*) but has reached perfection (is *teleios*, Paul) or again has left behind the kind of valuation that is natural to children (and people as they mostly are) in order to reach the grasp of the fully grown-up person (as in Stoicism).

This leads into the third area that the model is about and the third feature that distinguishes Paul's thought viewed philosophically: that of *moral psychology and anthropology*. There are a number of elements to this. In Paul no less than the Stoics there is an idea that the human being has two sides to it. One is tied to the physical body and the individual, the one who says 'I' of him- or herself, as thus embodied. It is this aspect of the human being which grounds the moral talk of an I-state. When a person is in the I-state, the embodied I is in charge of the moral valuation of that person, either exclusively or in the final account. The other side is tied to something which is both different from the human being as a whole and also present in it. In Paul this is spirit (*pneuma*), in Stoicism reason (*logos*). This is the aspect of the human being which grounds the moral talk of an S-state. When a person is in that state, it is this side of the human being which is in charge, and completely so. Indeed Paul and the Stoics share the belief that being in the S-state is—in principle at least—an all or nothing affair. If a person is really in it, then he or she is filled and led by the spirit or reason in such a way that there is no possibility of acting against either.

Another element in the shared moral psychology and anthropology is the fact that whether a person is in the I-state or in the S-state is all through a matter of belief and understanding, a cognitive as opposed to a desiderative matter. Desire is certainly involved. But whether a person has one set of desires or another is dependent on his or her understanding. We already know what that understanding is about and again in a way that is common to Paul and the Stoics: the person's own identity. They also agree on the form of this self-understanding. It is a matter of taking certain things outside oneself to 'belong' to one in the sense of being directly commensurate with oneself—or conversely of taking oneself to belong *with* those other things. Either way a person understands him- or herself by having him- or herself located in relation to things outside the person. One should not miss the normative character of this kind of having oneself 'located' in relation to other things or seeing oneself to 'belong' with them. But it is not immediately a state of desire. In itself it is cognitive—but such as also to give rise to desire.

There is a further element of moral psychology shared by Paul and the Stoics. In both, the desire that arises from the given self-understanding may take two forms, as general desiderative states, such as virtues and vices, and as particular desires and the acts triggered off by them. The distinction was crucial from Aristotle onwards in the ancient Greek ethical tradition to which Stoicism belonged. It is very important in Paul too, who was also more concerned about the inner states than the outward acts. He was certainly also very much concerned about the latter. But the states were considered by him a necessary precondition of the acts. Here too he agreed with the Stoics.

Thus the model is about three areas: a social and 'political' one, a moral one and a moral psychological and anthropological one. We need to keep them separate in order to be able to focus on the various distinctions that are made within them. In the final account, however, they should not be kept apart. Rather, we should see them as so many ways of articulating a single vision, a vision of the good for human beings. In Paul and the Stoics this vision is *justified* in quite different ways. In Stoicism it is grounded in a naturalistic understanding of the human being—but one that is also fully normative. Is it also a religious one? That depends entirely on the definition. The Stoics would themselves answer Yes (in a way that did not go against the correctness of also speaking of a naturalistic understanding). We may ourselves go either way—and we *will* answer No once we apply a *Christianized* notion of a religious understanding. In Paul, by contrast, the vision is definitely grounded in a religious understanding. For here it is justified by being referred directly to an act of God. Still, this difference does nothing to change the basic similarity of the content of the vision. The fact that Paul as distinct from the Stoics would speak of a vision of 'salvation' (*sōtēria*) is of little import here. For that term belongs to the 'theological' level of Paul's discourse, with which we are not here directly concerned.

Readers of Paul will probably agree that there is such a single vision in Paul, though hardly that it should be articulated in the way I have done it here by means of the I→X→S-model. But it is worth pointing out that on the Stoic side too the different sets of concepts are intended to articulate a single vision. It is separated out in those different sets because they do have a certain relative independence, with distinctions to be drawn within each set that have no direct counterpart in the other sets. Still, as the Stoics actually handled the three areas, they did mean to bring them together in a single vision. Nor is that at all surprising. For the Stoic conceptuality had its philosophical roots in Plato's account in the first books of the *Republic* of the good life for human beings. And here Plato had explicitly developed both a social and political philosophy and a moral psychology or anthropology *with a view to* answering the question about the (morally) good life. That, in essence, is what the I→X→S-model is about: a specific vision of the good life for human beings.

Let us finally note this. The fact that the model charts a vision is connected with the idea we saw to be common to Paul and the Stoics: that being in the S-state is—in principle—an all or nothing affair. The model charts a change and a change in self-understanding. Such a change certainly need not in itself be an all or nothing affair. But the model charts a special vision of that change. The vision is that of being *taken over* by something 'outside', 'over' and 'above' oneself (be it God, Christ or reason), though certainly, as we saw, something that also has its counterpart *in* oneself. Correspondingly, the vision is that of *giving up* 'oneself', the self that is precisely being taken over by the other thing. Viewed in that light, for the change to have come about at all, it must be an all or nothing affair. It is hard to see how a thing, A, may be said to be 'taken over' by another thing, B, if A or parts of A are still independently there after the change.

But is there not a problem here? Can we have an idea of a takeover and an all or nothing affair—and also one of 'already—but not yet quite'? Indeed we can. And that points to one of the most basic features of Paul's letters: that they are letters of *parenesis*. It raises particularly sharply the issue of the logic of *parenesis* to which we shall repeatedly return. Here too we shall see Paul to be in company with the Stoics.

Warding off criticism

It may be hoped that readers of Paul will intuitively feel that the I→X→S-model captures something that is reasonably central in Paul's thought world. But criticism is also to be expected. We may try to defuse some of this already here in order to prevent it from blinding potential critics to the usefulness of the model in the analysis of Paul.

The most pervasive criticism will probably be that the I→X→S-model is far too *individualistic* for it to have any real correspondence in Paul. This criticism derives its force from several sources. Thus scholars rightly object to finding any direct basis in Paul for the concern about the individual and his or her soul that came to be characteristic of much later pietism. Is not the 'introspective conscience of the West' and, more generally, modern individualism as a basic normative perspective a far more recent phenomenon, with roots that will in any case hardly go back beyond Augustine? And was it not precisely the individualistic tone of Rudolf Bultmann's existentialist project of reinterpreting Paul that showed its anachronistic character and doomed it to failure?

Many of these points are well taken, general as they are. But they do not touch the present project. For one thing, it is sufficient to refer to the realization in late Foucault that something like the idea of a *care of the self* was in fact being developed in Hellenistic thought. Here too belongs the late Epicurean material on *psychagogy*, e.g. in the philosopher Philodemus, that is in these years being made available to scholars and brought into contact with Paul.

For another thing, all this Hellenistic material only reflects the far more fundamental fact that ancient Greek ethics since Socrates took its formal or logical starting point from the question of the good life *as pertaining to the individual person*. Whether one likes it or not, that is what the question about 'happiness' (*eudaimonia*) is all about—in Aristotle, who gave the basic logical analysis of it, and in the succeeding ethicists, who took it over from him: What is the comprehensive end, over a whole lifetime, of the individual person? What is that kind of life—and it is after all only individuals who *can* 'lead a life'—that qualifies as the 'happy' one? Thus there is no getting around the fact that even centuries before Paul there was quite enough awareness and conceptualization of the individual for thought like that depicted in the I→X→S-model to fit smoothly into that context.

This argument is strengthened when one sees how the I→X→S-model also fits into the same tradition with respect to its other, social side. In Aristotle and Stoicism and in Epicurus too—in short, in the ancient Greek ethical tradition as a whole—while the *formal* starting point was a question about the individual's own life, the answer regarding the substance of that life invariably referred to the group. When it came to answering in substantive terms what the good life for the individual *consisted in*, any answer in the ancient ethical tradition would find a central place for the virtues, including the most important of these, justice—and thus for a type of behaviour that was essentially other-regarding. In its formal starting point, ancient thought on this matter *was* 'individualistic' (and very sensibly so), but in its substantive outcome it was quite the opposite. Here it was definitely social. Indeed, the very point of the Socratic tradition was to connect an 'individualistic' starting point with a social outcome. The good life (for the individual) is the *just* life. The I→X→S-model merely reflects this picture.

By the same token, although an objection to finding Bultmann's existentialist individualism in Paul is very well taken, the objection does not in the least touch the element of formal 'individualism' contained in the I→X→S-model. I emphasize this because for a variety of reasons there is such a strong trend at present against finding in Paul any interest whatsoever in the individual person. If this trend is based on any of the considerations given above, it builds upon sand.

Another way of making this point is the following. We saw that the logical starting point of the search for the good life is the formal notion of an 'I'. But as this I figures in the I→X→S-model, it does not just introduce an individual person. As we noted, the I of the model may very well be seen as a member of this or the other group and hence not just as an individual. What happens when he or she is seen in the light of the model is only that the person is now claimed to be normatively concerned only with him- or herself and not, or at least only derivatively, with the other members of the group. Now such an attitude of egoistic and prudential self-concern is not a particularly modern form of 'individualism'. It is the central target of all ancient ethics since Socrates and his rejection (in Plato) of the ethics of the Sophists. Paul belongs squarely within this tradition and it is this particular reading of the I-state that is reflected in the model.

There is a somewhat different set of considerations regarding Paul's handling of the I which has been advanced in various forms during the twentieth century. Objections have repeatedly been made to taking Paul to be talking about his own autobiographical and experiential I when he speaks in the first person singular. Instead, he will be using a generic I (W. G. Kümmel) or a diatribal one (S. K. Stowers)—and in any case Paul was only constructing after the event and in the light of the Christ event 'experiences' with life outside Christ (Stendahl, Sanders), not recounting any such actual experiences. Again, the point is well taken that we must not immediately adopt an autobiographical reading of Paul (except, of course, where he is unmistakably autobiographical like in Gal 1:12 ff). But again it does not touch the I→X→S-model. For although in one of its readings it is a model of conversion, it is not to be understood as literally depicting a psychological process, either autobiographically (in oneself) or in anybody else. It should be taken to give nothing more than the logical form and content of such a process. What actually happens in that process is a different question. And so the I→X→S-model is itself quite open to a number of different applications: as the description of a psychological process that is under way (if such a thing could ever be grasped) *or* as the description of a reconstruction of such a process after the event.

This ties in with what one may call the rhetorical function of the model. When Paul makes use of motifs that may be connected with the model, what he does is *offer his addressees an understanding* of where they themselves belong within the picture drawn in the model. How they may individually have come to be there, from what starting point and by what route, are questions that lie outside Paul's immediate interest. Here as elsewhere he is offering them a way of understanding themselves as part of presenting them with a vision of a specific form of life that he aims to draw them into.

Thus, neither does the I→X→S-model saddle Paul with a form of individualism which either could not be his or is unlikely to have been it, nor does it imply any return to the naive, directly (auto)biographical and psychological readings of an earlier age.

Criticism to the effect that the reading of Paul in terms of the I→X→S-model is insufficiently theological need not concern us at this point.

Using the model

As noted, the I→X→S-model has been arrived at by abstraction from both Paul and the Stoics. It is meant to be used here by being brought back into contact with either. In what follows we shall do this first for Stoicism. Here we shall focus exclusively on ideas: those that flesh out the model in its Stoic form, which are also the ideas that constitute the essence of Stoic ethics. One might have done much more in addition. Most importantly, one might have studied the ways in which the I→X→S-model informs the practices of Stoic philosophers when they did not just develop ideas at an exclusively philosophical level and out of a purely theoretical concern, but doing something else: using the ideas to bring about conversion in some person to whom they were addressing themselves. In thus studying, for instance, Seneca's letters, one might show how he, the philosopher, mentor and 'sage', takes up the position at point X in the model and attempts to bring his still non-sage addressee (Lucilius) from the I-state to the S-state. One might also look at the very many different means by which Seneca seeks to achieve this result: by appealing to perceptions on the part of Lucilius which connect him with Seneca, by setting him off from outside perceptions, by acting in a philophronetic way (e.g. by pedagogically 'bending down' towards him) and so forth.

There is almost no end to the whole range of psychagogy that one might study here. Scholars influenced by the seminal work of Malherbe in this area have done much to bring out this dimension of 'practical Stoicism' and connect it with Paul. Nothing could be better. Here, however, the suggestion is that underlying this highly variegated practice there is a basic pattern, the one charted in the I→X→S-model. What the Stoic practice is basically about is generating the change from the I-state to the S-state, with the philosopher or sage himself occupying the position in this process which in other applications of the model is taken up by reason or God (X).

With the Stoics, then, we shall stay with the ideas. The reason is mainly practical: that I do not wish to load the book with material that is not strictly necessary. Looking at the Stoic ideas, by contrast, is absolutely necessary. For here we shall become able to flesh out the bare bones of the I→X→S-model in a manner that will bring out its genuine attractiveness—to us potentially and to Paul historically.

When we next turn to Paul, the use of the model will become more complicated and flexible. Here we shall let ourselves be guided by the letters themselves and the questions they raise. In responding to this, we shall bring in the I→X→S-model over a whole range of very different areas, not just the 'anthropological' and 'ethical' ones. The criterion of success for this enterprise—and indeed for the book as a whole—is the extent to which it becomes possible in the light of the I→X→S-model to see *connections* between three fundamental levels of discourse in the Pauline letters that we shall distinguish, and indeed to bring out a sufficient degree of coherence between those levels: between a 'theological' one, the 'anthropological' and 'ethical' one and a 'practical' one. If we succeed here, through the use of a model that is related to Paul and Stoicism in the way we have seen in this chapter, then we shall also have succeeded in laying bare a central area of overlap between Paul and Stoicism.

In short, whereas with Stoicism we shall stick to the basic set of ideas, in Paul's case we shall use the I→X→S-model over a broad range of material and try to bring out how, in the form it shares with Stoicism, it underlies the whole of Paul, as in a palimpsest the old writing is glimpsed underneath the new.

3

The Stoics

How was the I→X→S-model fleshed out by the Stoics? In discussing this, we shall have two aims. One is to focus on the features which are central to the Stoic ethical system when looked at in its own terms. We want to obtain a sure grasp of Stoic ethics as a whole, not just to look at individual motifs. This is partly because what we are after is 'a comparison of (whole) patterns of thought' (to paraphrase E. P. Sanders), partly because in this way we may fill in a gap in present-day New Testament scholarship. Most scholars have heard of, say, the Stoic wise man (*sophos*), the 'indifferents' (*adiaphora*) or Stoic 'freedom' (*eleutheria*), but few have studied Stoic ethics as a comprehensive philosophical system.[1] Nor is that strange. For although Stoicism has been alive all through history, and also in historical critical scholarship on the New Testament since the beginning of that, it is only within the last 20 to 30 years that scholars of ancient philosophy have engaged in a philosophically sophisticated study of this philosophy.[2] We must consider the basic features of Stoic ethical thought in its own right and we must study it as a comprehensive philosophical system. This agenda should not put off New Testament scholars. After all, together with Aristotle the Stoics formulated a comprehensive way of thinking about human life that has had enormous influence on European thought—running alongside Christianity—from the Church Fathers through Aquinas to Kant and beyond.[3]

The other aim is to focus on features that will turn out to be directly relevant to the study of Paul. In spite of any intrinsic interest they may have, we will not allow ourselves to discuss details of the Stoic system merely for their own sake. Thus the reader should constantly bear in mind that all Stoic themes discussed in this chapter will in principle come up again in the reading of Paul, unlikely as it may seem before the connections have been made. The reason why it is possible to fulfil both aims at the same time lies at hand. A discussion that focuses on the basic features of Stoic ethics will also bring out what is directly relevant to the study of Paul.

As a basic text, I have chosen Book III of Cicero's treatise *De Finibus Bonorum et Malorum* ('On Ends'), which is the best systematic statement of Stoic ethics that we have.[4] The provenance of the Stoic material in this book is unknown, but the material most likely goes back at least to the last representative of early Stoicism, Antipater of Tarsus (early second century BCE). It may thus fairly be taken to represent the fully developed ethical doctrine of early Stoicism, whose towering figure was Chrysippus (c. 280–207 BCE). There also is a comprehensive sketch of what appears to be basically Chrysippean ethics in Diogenes Laertius, *Lives of Eminent Philosophers* 7.84–131.[5] And of course there are the fragments as collected by Hans von Arnim in *Stoicorum Veterum Fragmenta*.[6] I have chosen Cicero as our basic text partly because his account is the most systematic one and partly because he brings out better than any others certain features of Stoic ethics that are at the heart of the I→X→S model.[7]

Why go back to Chrysippean ethics for a comparison of Stoicism with Paul? Why not concentrate instead on late Stoicism, much of which was contemporary with Paul (Seneca, Musonius Rufus) or not much later (Dio Chrysostom, Epictetus)? There are two connected reasons. First, it is gradually becoming clear that late Stoicism, in which we must also include Marcus Aurelius, represents something of a return to early Stoicism across the developments that took place in the middle Stoicism of philosophers like Panaetius (2nd century BCE) and his pupil Posidonius (2nd–1st century BCE).[8] In spite of the impact made, for instance, by Posidonius, Chrysippus remained the basic Stoic authority. Thus, going back to Chrysippus is not going against Paul's Stoic contemporaries. Second, where the late Stoics offer a very rich mixture of what may best be called applied philosophy, they presupposed an underlying theoretical framework, which was precisely the Chrysippean one. That is our theme here. For it is this framework that was used or applied by Paul too, in the way it was also applied by his Stoic contemporaries.

This point cannot be emphasized sufficiently. The argument of this book is that it is the basic structure of Stoic ethics that is in the end most directly relevant to a comparison with Paul, not just the individual motifs or *topoi* that get their meaning within Stoicism *from* the basic structure. This is not to deny, of course, that the individual motifs or *topoi* are relevant too. They obviously are. But the aim is to show that they are relevant *because* they 'sit', in their various specific ways, on the basic structure—which is also the one within which Paul is basically operating.

This particular focus is also the reason why in this chapter we shall consider in some detail the connection between the essential features of the basic structure within Stoic ethics itself. Here the philosophical language and ideas themselves will not always immediately strike a bell of recognition in the Pauline scholar. To take a trivial example, where the Stoics spoke of rationality and reason (though also identifying this with God), Paul speaks of God and Christ. Still, the claim is that it is the same basic structure that holds together Stoic ethics and Paul's comprehensive theologizing. Only, where they set forth the structure in its transparent nakedness, Paul made *use* of the *same* structure, but in a welter of ways of speaking that were partly philosophical and partly metaphorical (though Paul himself probably considered them eminently 'realistic' and directly referential).

The following account will highlight a number of central features of the basic structure as they enter into the Stoic reading of the I→X→S-model. There is first an account of what the model is all about. The answer is: human thought about the 'end' (*telos*) of human life, which is 'happiness' (*eudaimonia*). That may already seem widely different from Paul, who was not at all concerned about 'happiness'. In fact it is not. In his 'theologizing', that is, when Paul did 'theology' and 'ethics', he too was thinking about the general shape of the best form of human living, trying to develop a general scheme of its content and structure. Second, there is the Stoic account of the value system of a person (a child or an unreformed adult) who is living at the I-pole of the model. Is there anything comparable in Paul? Indeed, yes: the 'value system' that finds expression in *hamartia* ('sin'). Next there is an account of a sort of conversion to the new value system of the person who is living at the X-pole and a further analysis of how he or she will relate to the fact that as individual, bodily human beings they will also continue to live at the I-pole. That too is surely directly relevant to Paul since it serves to define the field within which he is operating when he engages in that most central activity of his: parenesis. Next there is the Stoic account of how living at the X-pole also directly implies living at the S-pole and thus how a person is brought over—via his or her relationship with X—*from* I *to* S. With the values we should give to I and S in Paul, that too is directly relevant to him. Finally, there is an account of a number of concepts in Stoic ethics that fill in the I→X→S-model at various points: 'progression' (*prokopē*); 'appropriate acts' or 'duties' (*kathēkonta*) as distinct from '(*actually*) right acts' (*katorthōmata*); 'passions' (*pathē*), 'freedom from passion' (*apatheia*) and 'good emotions' (*eupatheiai*) such as, e.g. joy (*chara*). As is generally recognized, most of these concepts (and indeed, most of the very terms) do figure in Paul. The only question is: how importantly? We shall see that the correct answer is: at the heart of his theologizing.

The basic framework: striving for the telos (Aristotle)

Stoic ethics presupposes a number of key concepts in the ancient ethical tradition that had been most thoroughly developed by Aristotle (384–322 BCE) a generation before Zeno (335–263 BCE), the founder of Stoicism. The most important is the notion of the *telos* (end), which Aristotle had spoken of as *eudaimonia* ('happiness'). We must recall a few features from Aristotle's analysis. They help to articulate what the I→X→S-model on its Stoic reading is all about. In so doing they will also tell us much about Paul.[9]

Book I of Aristotle's *Nicomachean Ethics* begins like this (I.i.1, 1094a1–3): 'Every art and every inquiry, and similarly every action and pursuit, is thought to aim at some good; and for this reason the good has rightly been declared to be that at which all things aim.' Aristotle then uses the whole of Book I to develop what 'the good at which all things aim' should be understood to be. One name for it is *eudaimonia*, but that is precisely only a name, something everybody will agree on in the abstract, but on whose specific content they will disagree. This sets the scene for Aristotle's two main aims in the treatise as a whole. He first (Book I) aims to analyse the logical form of that concept of 'the good' or *eudaimonia* on whose meaning all appear to agree. Next (the remaining books) he will describe what the proper substantive content is of that concept, what is rightly said to fall under it or fill it in; in other words, he intends to state and spell out what kind of life qualifies as the happy one. It is only the first task that need concern us at present. Here Aristotle's analysis was taken over wholesale by the Stoics.

The good or *eudaimonia*, Aristotle states, is something 'perfect' or 'final' (*teleion*), indeed the most perfect thing (*teleiotaton*). It is also something 'self-sufficient' (*autarkes*), which Aristotle defines as 'that which when isolated makes life desirable and lacking in nothing' (I.vii.7, 1097b14–15). And he concludes (I.vii.8, 1097b20–21): 'Thus happiness [*eudaimonia*] appears to be something perfect and self-sufficient, being the end [*telos*] of action.'

On this conception, *eudaimonia* is closely tied to action and therefore also to practical deliberation, which precedes action. It is not a thing, not a particular object or state to be reached through action. Rather, *eudaimonia* stands for the abstract state of a person's whole life in which all the individual objectives that a person may have for his acts have been reached. Nor is *eudaimonia* a feeling or at all a state of mind. It is rather a sort of limiting concept, an *abstract* state that constitutes the overall and all-comprehending point (*telos*) of *all* a person's acts and subsumes any particular ends of acts under itself. If you want something for itself and act in order to get it, you may 'justify' your act by saying that you want its end 'for itself'. But you may also add: 'I want it for the sake of *eudaimonia*', that is, as one of those things which *together make up* (what you consider to be) 'the happy life'. Then you have further 'rationalized' your wish for the end. It is now no longer just some particular end that you may want for itself more or less haphazardly. Rather, it is stated to belong somewhere within a comprehensive pattern. Note that it is precisely this formal, logical character of the concept that allows for the universal agreement on 'the name' from which Aristotle started: that the good and the best is—*eudaimonia*. People may agree on 'the name' even when they disagree about what falls under it. For there is no substantive content to 'the name', only a specific logical definition.

That definition, however, is immensely important. For it immediately shows what the theme is of Aristotle's ethical treatise as a whole—and by implication of the I→X→S-model on its Stoic reading: thought about the best overall shape of human life and behaviour. Thus if we can show that the I→X→S-model captures something central in Paul too, we will know that he too is engaged in that same exercise. And indeed, he of course is. What matters is only that we recognize this and recognize it fully. In addition to the other things that went into Paul's thought, he was intensely engaged in thought about the best, indeed, the only right, overall shape of human life and behaviour (in this world).

This is not to deny the vital differences. For instance, with the concept of *eudaimonia* and the *telos* as the basic one, Aristotelian and Stoic ethics were exclusively concerned with a this-worldly good, the end of all a person's acts in this present life and no more than that. That obviously does not hold of Paul. But that fact does not remove the similarity where the two bodies of thought do overlap. To spell out the point just made, the concern of Aristotelian and Stoic ethics with *eudaimonia* and the *telos* meant that both were strongly focused on reason, namely *practical* reason, reason as involved in practical deliberation. By its logical form, *eudaimonia* brings in the idea of *ordering* one's life and seeing how the many particular ends of acts may be held together by reason in a single grasp of an individual's happiness. It also brings in the idea of engaging in practical deliberation about particular decisions *in the light of* such a single grasp. Thus it contains both an element of 'upward' movement from individual ends to the comprehensive grasp and of 'downward' movement to particular decisions. Nor is there anything mechanical here or any easy answers. How one will order one's immediate ends and how one will decide in particular situations are questions the answers to which will influence one another. The decision in these matters requires an exercise of reason too. The overall point, however, is that this whole description will be true of Paul too—and should immediately appear so to people acquainted with his letters. Paul too, no less than his Aristotelian and Stoic predecessors, was engaged in *practical thought*.[10]

There is another feature common to Aristotelian and Stoic ethics which also reflects the basic 'eudaimonistic' set-up. This type of ethics is tied to the individual in its basic logic—but definitely not in its substantive content. It is important to be clear on the two sides of this because there are so many errors involved in the traditional understanding of 'eudaimonism'. First, in terms of its logic as a self-sufficient, abstract state, *eudaimonia* is the state which 'when isolated makes life desirable and lacking in nothing' *for the individual whose life it is*. As an end of all a person's acts in *his* or *her* life, *eudaimonia* is logically tied to that individual person him- or herself. It is true that just before he defines the self-sufficiency of *eudaimonia* in this way, Aristotle has extended the range of the self involved in self-sufficiency to cover not just the individual but also his or her family and wider relations. He says (I.vii.6–7, 1097b8–14):

> Now by self-sufficient we do not mean that which is sufficient for a man by himself, for one who lives a solitary life, but also for parents, children, wife, and in general for his friends and fellow citizens, since man is born for citizenship. But some limit must be set to this; for if we extend our requirement to ancestors and descendants and friends' friends we are in for an infinite series. Let us examine this question, however, on another occasion.

This is an important qualification. But what Aristotle is talking about here is the *content* of self-sufficiency, what falls under the concept and must be present in order to make the individual's life 'desirable and lacking in nothing'. In terms of the concept's own logic, *eudaimonia* as a self-sufficient state is tied to the individual him- or herself. That logical feature also holds of the Stoic talk of the concept and role of the *telos*—and of Paul's talk of the self-understanding of an 'I'.

It is entirely different when we move to the substantive content of *eudaimonia*. Aristotle's basic view was that the good consists in the moral virtues and acts that reflect the virtues (I.viii). First among these virtues was justice (Book V). Others include moderation, courage, magnanimity and more (III.vi–IV). Thus we are evidently very far from 'eudaimonism' in the mistaken sense of a theory that is basically directed towards discovering the road to what is merely one's own short- or long-term satisfaction. There is plenty of room for other-regardingness, even altruism, in Aristotle's 'eudaimonistic' theory (and even more in Stoicism). But the tie with the individual is maintained. It is 'my own' good that consists in morally virtuous acts, *including* genuinely altruistic ones.[11]

Among the virtues that fill in *eudamonia* in Aristotle we should also include a so-called intellectual virtue, *phronēsis* (moral insight). This is the practical counterpart of the other, theoretical branch of intellectual virtue, *sophia* (science). *Phronēsis* is closely connected with the moral virtues. It constitutes the rational content *of* these virtues which turns them from being merely inborn or habituated states of desire and perception into fully rationalized moral virtues proper. As Aristotle analyses *phronēsis* in Book VI of the *Nicomachean Ethics*, this practical and intellectual virtue contains both a grasp of the proper ends of action (and thus of the actual content of *eudaimonia*) and also an ability to see correctly what needs to be done in the particular situations in the light of that other grasp. From Aristotle's whole way of setting up his ethics, we can see that even though he attaches great importance to the moral virtues viewed as so many attitudes of emotion and desire, it is the rational element in them, *phronēsis*, that has paramount importance. For it is this virtue which *articulates* the actual content of the end, of *eudaimonia*.[12] Aristotelian *phronēsis* is the good state of the kind of practical thought that we saw to be the theme of Aristotle himself, of the Stoics *and* of Paul.

Speaking of the virtues, we should also mention that it was Aristotle who provided the ontological categorization of a virtue (II.v) that came to be orthodox knowledge in Stoicism too (and de facto, as we shall see much later, in Paul). A virtue is a state (*hexis*) of mind, one that need not always be active but may precisely be activated in the appropriate circumstances in an 'actualization' or 'activity' (*energeia*—an idea that points directly forward to Paul's claim in Gal 5:6 that the only thing that matters in Christ is faith that 'is active', *energoumenē*, through love). That also explains why Aristotelian *eudaimonia* may be said to consist in the moral virtues and those acts that reflect them. A moral virtue may be activated in a *mental* 'activity' (*energeia*) and if nothing prevents, such an activity may turn into an 'external' act proper, a *praxis* (cf. I.vii.14–15, 1098a7–17). That fits the account of *eudaimonia*. As we saw, *eudaimonia* is the universal end of (external) *acts*.

Aristotle also was the first to give an extended analysis of a phenomenon that belongs under the theory of virtue: that of weakness of will (*akrasia*, VII.i–x). A full virtue (what Aristotle called *hē kyria aretē*, VI.xiii.2, 1144b16) is a state of desire and understanding that leaves no room for a divided mind. By definition, therefore, a fully virtuous person will always do what is required. He or she both sees what is to be done and wishes to do it—and wishes nothing else. As we shall see, this idea is crucial for a proper understanding of Paul on Christ and the law. Comparing the state of desire of the 'self-controlled' person (*ho enkratēs*) with that of the fully virtuous person, Aristotle says this (I.xiii.17, 1102b26–28):

> That of the self-controlled person obeys [*peitharchei*] reason—but perhaps that of the moderate and courageous person is even more obedient [*euē-koōteron*, that is, '*listens* even better']. For it is all through in *agreement* with [*homophōnei*, '*speaks* the same as'] reason.

The same idea of a total agreement between desire and reason is stated in VII.viii.4, 1151a11–20—in the middle of Aristotle's discussion of *enkrateia* and *akrasia*. For it serves to define these two other types of people, who are not fully virtuous. There is first the *enkratēs*, who sees what is to be done and wishes to do it—but who also has countervening desires. However, since he or she is more strongly bent towards the virtuous action, they manage to control themselves and do what is to be done—or avoid doing what must not be done. The 'weak-willed' person (*ho akratēs*), by contrast, is also divided. But here there is a stronger tendency towards the wrong act and this person gives in to the tendency.

Aristotle's theory of *akrasia*, including his attempt to explain how a person can act against his or her own understanding of what is best for them to do, immediately set the scene for his successors. In particular, it was taken up by the Stoics in their (different) account of 'passions' (*pathē*), which they basically understood as cases of weakness of will. It goes without saying that this is all highly relevant to the Paul who wrote, for instance, Romans 7.

From Aristotle the Stoics took over completely the analysis of the logical form of the good conceived as *eudaimonia* or the *telos* (the preferred Stoic term).[13] They also agreed with his account of the substantive content of the end, but in a sharpened form. Aristotle had said: the moral virtues and virtuous acts. But he had also included—in a manner that rendered his theory somewhat unstable—a sufficient amount of so-called external goods (cf. I.viii.15–17 and x), the ordinary material and natural goods that are needed to sustain life and are those that, as

Aristotle says, are 'fought about by the many' (IX.viii.4, 1168b19; 9, 1169a21). Some, at least, of these had to be present, Aristotle felt, for a life to qualify as a happy one. In Stoicism, by contrast, the end consists in *nothing but* moral virtue and virtuous acts. This raises very sharply the question of how a Stoic wise and good person will relate to ordinary natural goods. That question, as we shall see, is at the centre of Stoic ethics. In conformity with Aristotle, however, the Stoics insisted that it is one's own, individual good that consists in morally virtuous acts (and nothing else), including genuinely altruistic ones. Thus the Stoic theory too is very far from being merely a self-regarding form of 'eudaimonism', indeed even further from this than Aristotle's.

The Stoics also sharpened the account of moral knowledge (*phronēsis* in Aristotle). To them moral, practical knowledge was not different from theoretical knowledge (*sophia*). Nor was it different from moral virtue. The *cognitive* emphasis is very strong in Stoicism, a fact that has immediate repercussions on their analysis of weakness of will. Everything hangs on coming to *see* the good, on getting a proper rational grasp of it. Then all 'passions' will be blotted out. There will be no weakness of will. And one will always and only *act* upon one's (new) insight. That is why the basic structure in Stoic ethics comes very close to describing a case of conversion. And that is one further reason why it is particularly relevant to Paul. Let us study how.

Oikeiōsis I: stage 1 (the I-level)

Cicero begins his account of Stoic ethics in *De Finibus* Book III with a careful statement of the theory that constitutes its centre, the theory of *oikeiōsis*. The theory is about how a person will or may undergo a change in his or her understanding of the good, from taking it to be constituted by what basically amounts to possession of ordinary, material goods on the part of the individual him- or herself to a quite different understanding of it.[14]

The change turns on what things in the world a person considers to 'belong' to him- or herself as the being that he or she takes him- or herself to be. The logical starting point is awareness of oneself and (*through* that) love of self and thirdly an understanding of one's own identity (who and what one oneself is) which gives rise to dividing up things in the world outside the self as either 'belonging' or being 'alien' to the self— things *oikeia* and things *allotria* in the Greek that underlies Cicero's account. *Because* the self, with which one stands in the relationship of self-awareness and self-love, is taken to be this or that, *therefore* certain things outside the self are seen to 'belong' to one or be 'alien' to one. Against this background, the change that we shall eventually consider is essentially the result of a development in the understanding of one's own identity (who and *what* the self is) with a concomitant change in the perception of what particular things 'belong' or are 'alien' to one. That development and change constitutes the essence of the process of *oikeiōsis*, which one may translate as 'familiarization'. In the present section we shall consider the initial stage of the process in some detail since it has a shape that is highly relevant to Paul.

Here is Cicero's account (*De Finibus* 3.16, tr. Rackham, with some changes and Latin keywords added):

> It is the view of those whose system I adopt [the Stoic one] that immediately upon birth (for that is the proper point to start from) a living creature feels an attachment for itself [*ipsum sibi conciliari*], and a commendation [*commendari*] towards preserving itself and loving [*diligere*][15] its own constitution [status] and those things which tend to preserve that constitution; while on the other hand it conceives an antipathy [*alienari*] to destruction and to those things which appear to threaten destruction. In proof of this they urge that infants desire [*appetere*] things conducive to their health and reject things that are the opposite before they have ever felt pleasure or pain; this would not be the case, unless they felt love for [*diligere*] their own constitution and were afraid of destruction. But it would be impossible that they should feel desire at all [*appetere*] unless they possessed awareness of self [*sensus sui*] and as result of this [*eoque*] loved themselves [*diligere se*]. This leads to the conclusion that it is love of self [*se diligere*] which supplies the starting point.

This passage describes a number of aspects of what it is like to find oneself at the I-pole of the I→X→S-model on its Stoic interpretation. One point is that it is very clearly concerned with an individual, and moreover with the perspective *of* an individual person on the world around him- or herself. What is described is how the world around the individual is seen *from within*, from the perspective of an individual person who says 'I' and 'me' about him- or herself. This element is of fundamental importance to the theory. For as Cicero says, it is the element of (1) self-awareness (*sensus sui*) which *provides* that (2) self-love which grounds and explains (3) *desire* itself and so also (4) *action* directed towards acquiring things outside the self. There is every reason, therefore, to speak of an I-pole proper in connection with Stoicism. And this remains basic. The Stoic theory is about a change in the *content* of a basic I- or self-awareness that remains in place all through the process and continues to ground and explain the very possibility of desire and action. That is the first basic point to be noted. It will turn out to be highly relevant to the Paul who wrote Gal 2:19–20. He too operates with a change in the perception of one's identity, but it is the content of the identity that changes, not the I-person who undergoes the change. In order for it to be possible to speak of a change of identity, there must be *someone* who undergoes it. That point is explicitly made in Stoicism and presupposed in Paul.

The passage in Cicero yields another point of the highest relevance to Paul, which is that we are quite justified in using, as I have already repeatedly done, the term identity (in the sense of 'self-identity', a sense of one's own identity) when speaking of the Stoics and of Paul. The term itself is certainly a modern one. But the idea is equally certainly ancient.[16] It is expressed in the Cicero passage in the combination of ideas that it formulates: that of self-awareness, that of awareness of what the self is (its 'constitution') and that of dividing up the world on the basis of those two forms of awareness into things that 'belong' to one and things that are 'alien' to one.

This whole set of conceptual elements is articulated in the passage when it shows that the logical basis of desire and action is not just self-awareness and self-love, but also an understanding of what the self *is*, its 'constitution', which in the present context includes its bodily structure. This helps to explain, not now just formally desire and action as such, but also substantively desire for this or the other particular thing that is taken to 'belong' to one and action to get *that*—here the particular objects that help to maintain and preserve the bodily structure. What the Stoics have in mind are things like food, shelter and so forth. This already points in the direction of what it is basically like to be at the I-pole, on the Stoic understanding. It is to lead a life that reflects nothing but the self-based perspective on the good and the bad that is tied to the individual and is in this sense 'subjective'. Such a life is directed towards obtaining ordinary goods for the bodily individual him- or herself. In that life there is a complete symbiosis of self-awareness and this particular bodily 'constitution'. That symbiosis constitutes the natural, subjective attitude of the child—or of the unreformed or unconverted adult as described by Paul in Rom 1:18–32. What the Stoics aim to identify in this way is the basis and essence of self-centredness. But their ultimate theme is how that whole attitude may then later be overcome.

It is worth emphasizing here that although the text clearly takes the I-pole to be defined by the individual's grasp of his or her own 'constitution' on a very narrow conception of this as his or her bodily structure, nothing prevents a person from including other people under it, e.g. one's close family or friends. Indeed, we shall see that there is even room for certain forms of altruism here. But it is always altruism towards others because they are seen to belong to the closed sphere of oneself taken as this particular bodily individual. They too may be viewed as *particularly one's own*. And so one may come to wish that they too will acquire ordinary goods for themselves. There is no logical change in such a wish nor any real development in one's desiderative attitude to the world. Obtaining goods for one's close relatives is merely an extended form of obtaining goods for oneself.[17]

It is very important to see that this whole kind of valuation is not in itself wrong. A few sections after the one we have quoted, Cicero provides a definition of the term 'valuable' which runs as follows (*De Finibus* 3.20):

> They [the Stoics] term 'valuable' [*aestimabile*] ... what is either itself in accordance with nature or produces something that is, in such a way that it is deserving of selection [*selectio*] due to its having a certain weight that is deserving of valuation [*aestimatio*—the Stoic *axia*]; and as against this they term 'valueless' what is contrary to the former.

When Cicero here speaks of 'deserving of selection' and 'deserving of valuation', he is applying the subjective perspective that he has developed in the earlier passage. It is the person who does the valuation who determines whether to see something as deserving of selection, namely by himself, and of having value ascribed to it, namely by himself. But Cicero also defines 'valuable' in terms of whether something is *in fact* in accordance with a thing's nature or not. The reason is that the Stoics took the kind of perception described in the earlier passage—a perception that consisted in ascribing value to certain things on the basis of an understanding of one's own nature—to be basically veridical. The immediate perception of one's own identity and what 'belongs' to it is in principle correct, even in the human child. But then we may also say that what is *found* valuable as being in accordance with one's own nature is also *in fact* valuable *and* in accordance with one's nature. If we then adopt a perspective from the outside, we may also directly say that what is 'valuable' is what is in accordance with a thing's nature. Then we have moved outside the charmed circle of the perspective of the person who does the valuation. But this is something we can do because his or her perception is from the very start taken to be veridical. I emphasize the validity of this move here—from what is *taken* to be in accordance with one's nature to what *is*. For we will later need the thought that the kind of valuation that goes into living at the I-pole is not by itself totally wrong. In Stoicism, ordinary goods are *in fact* valuable for human beings as the beings they are. Still, the essence of the theory of *oikeiōsis* is that a change in understanding may occur that places this immediate valuation in a quite different light. Let us now turn to this.

Oikeiōsis I: stage 2 (the X-level)

Immediately after the section on the term 'valuable' Cicero states the following (*De Finibus* 3.20):

> Next, on the basis of the principle that has been established, that things that are in accordance with nature are to be taken for their own sake and their opposites similarly to be rejected, the first appropriate act [*officium*]— for so I translate *kathēkon*—will be to preserve oneself in one's natural constitution,[18] the next to obtain the things in accordance with nature and to repel their opposites; when this [type of] selection and similarly rejection has been discovered, there follows next selection guided by a conception of appropriate acts [*cum officio selectio*], then such selection performed continuously and then finally selection that is consistent [*constans*] and in accordance with nature [*consentanea naturae*], which is the point at which the good properly so called first starts to be present and to be understood in its true nature.

The aim of this passage is to bring us from *oikeiōsis* as described in the first passage to *oikeiōsis* as it operates in adult human beings, ending in an understanding of what is genuinely good. The general direction of the five stages in the development described by Cicero is clearly that each stage should be understood as expressing a growing consciousness about how to act on the part of the person who undergoes the development. This is the process of *prokopē* (progression), which played an important role in Stoic ethics—and indeed in Paul (cf. Phil 1:26). More on this below. First we must consider the end point of the process, which is a grasp of the good properly so called. What is that good? How does a person grasp it? And why is only this a 'good properly so called'? We need to consider these questions in some philosophical detail since the answers will help us to identify how a person who takes him- or herself to belong at the X-level will relate to the world. As we shall see, such a person (the Stoic wise man) is a being who is both 'worldly' and 'outworldly'. That topic is directly relevant to Paul.

This similarity is justification enough for going into those questions. In particular, we should not let ourselves be distracted by the fact that Paulinists will balk at the idea of a gradual *development* towards the ultimate grasp (as opposed, for instance, to having it *revealed* to one). In Stoicism too one may ultimately speak of a 'sudden' grasp (though

obviously not a revealed one in a Christian sense). The talk of a 'development' mainly serves to show what *kind* of grasp the Stoics had in mind:
that it is one of the understanding. But *that* holds for Paul too.

Cicero helps us to answer some of the questions we raised (*De Finibus*
3.21):

> For man's first attachment is to the things in accordance with nature. But
> as soon as he acquires understanding [*intellegentia*] or rather, perhaps, the
> capacity to form concepts [*notio*], i.e. what the Stoics call *ennoia*, and sees
> the order [*ordo*] and so to speak harmony [*concordia*] of acts [*rerum
> agendarum*],[19] he values this [viz. order and harmony] far more highly
> than all those earlier objects of his love, and he concludes by rational
> argument [*cognitione et ratione colligere*] that in this [i.e. in this order
> and harmony] lies that something which is praiseworthy and choiceworthy
> for its own sake—the good for man; this [good], since it consists in what
> the Stoics call *homologia* and we may call conformity [viz. with the
> order and harmony mentioned]—since in this [i.e. in conformity with the
> order and harmony] resides that good to which everything must be referred,
> noble acts and the noble itself, which alone is counted among things
> good, therefore though of subsequent development, still that [viz. the
> conformity mentioned] is the only thing choiceworthy in and for itself,
> whereas among the first objects of nature none is choiceworthy for its
> own sake.

In this extremely condensed passage Cicero describes the rise from I
to X in the I→X→S-model on its Stoic interpretation. He clearly refers
the change in understanding of the good to a new cognitive capacity,
reason. At first (the I-level), what was taken to be good were the things
that were immediately seen as being in accordance with one's own bodily
nature. With the development of reason a person comes to find the good
elsewhere. It is clear from Cicero's description that a person will now
also begin to operate with the notion of a final end (*telos*) in the sense
that the Stoics had inherited from Aristotle. For the description of the
good as what is 'praiseworthy and choiceworthy for its own sake',
something 'to which everything [else] must be referred' directly reflects
the logical meaning that Aristotle had given to his concept of *eudaimonia*.
But that pertains only to the formal side. What is the substantive content
of the Stoic *telos* as described in this passage? And why is that to be
understood as the only good?

Cicero provides two answers which are also the two answers given in
Stoicism generally. The end is '*homologia*' (*convenientia* in Cicero's
Latin, 'conformity'). And the end is 'noble acts and the noble itself'. In
other words, 'life in accordance with nature' and 'moral virtue and
virtuous acts'. It is a crucial idea in Stoicism that these two specifications

amount to the same thing. How could they claim that? Let us first consider *homologia*. What the Stoics meant by this is: conformity of the human mind (reason, *logos*) to the way things actually are in the world. *Homologia* is *homo-logia*, the state in which *logos* is shaped in accordance with (*homo-*) the world. Now we saw that even the perception of a child regarding its own nature and what 'belongs' to that is in principle veridical. So what is added when the child grows up and acquires reason? This: the adult person now sees that because one is oneself a rational being—that is *now* seen as the most important feature in one's 'constitution'—therefore what 'belongs' to one is not so much this or the other particular object that one might attempt to acquire, but *using one's reason* for the purposes for which it is designed, that is, for reaching *truth about* the world. The child took a range of *first*-order things to be valuable because they were seen to 'belong' to the child itself as a being with that particular 'constitution'. They were things that helped to preserve the child's *bodily* 'constitution'. The adult takes an entirely different, *second*-order thing to be the basic and crucially valuable thing: being right about the world, *including* about what particular things in it are valuable for oneself. *That* is what 'preserves' one's *new, rational* 'constitution'. (A striking thought!)

Later Stoics, e.g. Marcus Aurelius, coined a phrase that helps to bring out the precise character of the new valuation. They spoke of the wise man—the person who has grasped the true human good—as a person who has adopted a 'view from above' (*Meditations* 7.48, 9.30, 12.24.3), that is, the perspective of a person who *as it were* occupies a position in that heaven where Paul will *literally* place both himself and his 'fellow-citizens of heaven' (Phil 3:20).[20] This fits the I→X→S-model. The wise man looks down from X on the world as a whole and is concerned about getting the *correct* description of that world. What he sees from above includes his own position at I. For in addition to having adopted the view from above, the wise man of course remains a bodily individual. In trying to reach the correct description of the world, he will therefore also consider the question of what things are objectively valuable *for* himself (not just subjectively *to* himself) as a being who also lives 'down there'. But his own *good*, the basic thing that is of crucial value both for and to himself, is no longer getting for himself any of the particular valuable things—those that present themselves *to* the person who finds himself at the I-level alone as the only things that matter. The wise man's good lies elsewhere, at the X-level itself, and consists in understanding the world correctly, which includes seeing correctly what things are valuable for himself (and indeed for others).

The character of this change as the Stoics developed it may be brought out by speaking of a change from subjectivity to objectivity. A person who belongs at the I-level is concerned about his own subjective interests because he constantly relates what 'belongs' to the particular, bounded individual that he himself is. By contrast, the interests of the person who belongs at the X-level are not in this way restricted to any particular I-level individual, including himself. Instead, one might say, they are the interests of the perspective from above *itself*, which the wise man has adopted. As a rational perspective, that perspective is by definition also unbounded and unrestricted. It is objective. It pays no *special* attention to any given individual and his or her interests just because they are those of that particular individual.

It is true that in human beings the perspective from above is a perspective adopted *by* a bodily individual, a person who to some extent continues to stay at the I-level. That feature does not change. Otherwise adopting it would explode completely the basic 'eudaimonistic' framework of the whole theory based, as it is, on the *formal* I-perspective that remains in place all through (as we saw). Adopting the perspective from above is and remains something done by an individual. It is what constitutes *his* or *her* good. But this formal basis at the I-level does not in any way restrict the radical character of the change from the I- to the X-level. It is the radicality of this change that makes the Stoic conception—and that alone among representatives of the ancient ethical tradition—directly relevant to Paul.

It is also true that the wise man, who belongs at the X-level in terms of what he takes himself to *be*, will *remain* concerned with the question of what is valuable for himself *too* (though as objectively seen from above and in fact no *more* than for others). For as we know, he is still an individual at the I-level with a bodily 'constitution' and everything that goes with that. The wise man does look down *upon* the world, *including* himself (and others) as belonging to the I-level, aiming to handle valuable things *in* that world. Still, by rising to the second-order level, he has dissociated himself from what actually *happens* to *himself as* a being who belongs at the I-level. *He* belongs elsewhere, at the X-level. He will of course look with interest from above on what happens to himself at the I-level, but he will in principle have no greater interest in that than in what happens to everybody else 'down there'.

This explains the last point in the passage from Cicero. The wise man sees *homologia* as 'the *only* thing choiceworthy in and for itself, whereas among the first objects of nature *none* is choiceworthy for its own sake'. Objects of choice at the I-level may be taken to be 'valuable'. Indeed, as we know, some of them *are* valuable, as even children *rightly* took them to be. To the person who belongs at the X-level, however, they are no longer *immediately* valuable *for themselves*, in the way they were taken by children. If they also *are* valuable now, it is *because* they are in accordance with the nature of the being in question as seen objectively from above. They are no longer just choiceworthy for their *own* sake as seen from the local perspective of the I-level. What is choiceworthy for its own sake is something different: *being right* in one's understanding of *the world, including* what is valuable for oneself (and others).

This answers one of our questions: why there is only one thing that is good. Immediate, particular objects of action at the I-level may be valuable and will continue to be so. But the Stoics no longer accepted that they should be called *good*. There is only one thing that may properly be called good: *homologia*, getting things right about the world. For that alone has the character that qualifies it for being what the *telos* consists in, the character of self-sufficiency. If you have grasped that the human *telos* is *homologia*, then you are in possession of a 'valuable thing' to which nothing can be added and from which nothing can be removed. Indeed, it is a valuable thing that in a sense 'includes' all other particular valuable things under it because it alone *determines* their value. A valuable thing with such a character is so special that one may reasonably see it as *the* valuable thing. Let us then reserve the term 'good' for that thing alone. Looking down from above, the Stoic wise man is in possession of *the* valuable thing, the good. Although Paul obviously does not employ this particular terminology, the basic conception is the same: the grasp of Jesus as the Christ and Lord (with *all* that this in effect means) is the *only* thing of ultimate importance.

Thus the Stoic wise man is both a worldly being and, in a sense, an outworldly one. He is worldly because he remains a bodily individual who belongs at the I-level and because when he looks down on the world from above, he is concerned about grasping *that* world. But he is also outwordly because he has found his own identity (the new character of his 'constitution') in something that has a second-order status in relation to the world: reason, the grasp *of* the world, *as it were* from an Archimedean point outside and above it. *That* is where he belongs.

How does he manage to get there? As Cicero describes the process, it is a matter of reaching rational adulthood. But are all adults wise? Far from it. In fact, it is a very real question whether the Stoics thought that there was even a single person who had reached wisdom.[21] We should probably divide the issue up into two. A human being who reaches adulthood may well realize that the true human good is *homologia*. This may be done through reflection on one's own acts and those of others. This is probably what Cicero refers to when he speaks of 'seeing the order and so to speak harmony of acts'. What a person will see is the pattern of action that the Stoics themselves had discovered behind even the acts of children, the pattern described by Cicero in *De Finibus* 3.16. For the Stoics would of course claim that the system they had discovered to explain desire and action was in fact to be found underlying all human behaviour. Thus with a little help from Stoic philosophers, many human beings might come to realize that the human good is *homologia*. The Stoics also tried to explain why some people did *not* realize this at all, or at least not sufficiently to act on it. They spoke partly of the influence of childhood experiences of the immediate impact of ordinary goods, partly of misunderstandings induced in the child by those responsible for its socialization (nannies and the like!).[22] Thus there was plenty of room for not arriving at a sufficiently clear grasp of the human good as *homologia*.

But the Stoics also had a stronger conception of that grasp, which meant that the wise man was perhaps just as rare as the Phoenix.[23] On this conception, not only must one have the single grasp that the human good is *homologia*: one must also be able to *see in each and every particular situation* exactly what is in fact 'in accordance with nature'. Such an understanding is evidently far outside the range of human beings. And the wise man who would have it, so they said, would not be much different from God understood as the rationality of the world itself. That kind of sage was as rare as the Phoenix and we need not worry about how a person might get into that kind of cognitive state. It must be emphasized, however, that on the Stoic view the two forms of understanding are not different in kind. Rather, the all-comprehending grasp enjoyed by the godlike sage represents a deepening—albeit an enormously comprehensive one—of the other grasp, that the human good is *homologia*. That grasp may be reached by many. It should be immediately clear to readers of Paul that this distinction too between two kinds of grasp is directly relevant to him. Compare, for instance, the contrast he draws in 1 Cor 1–2 between an initial faith and the final, complete wisdom, a contrast that reflects *his* distinction (1 Cor 3:1–3) between 'babyhood' and adulthood (the latter only by implication).

The grasp of the good and morality

We have not answered a second question that we raised: why the human good may be said to consist in moral virtue and virtuous acts no less than in *homologia*, in other words, why the two specifications come to the same thing. Consider some remarks of Cicero's about wisdom itself, that is, the mental, cognitive state of having grasped what the human good is. In a section in which Cicero compares wisdom with certain forms of technical expertise ('arts') like medicine and navigation, he says the following (*De Finibus* 3.25):

> Wisdom comprises both magnanimity and justice and judging everything that may happen to a man to be beneath one [*infra se*], which is not the case with the other arts. But no one can possess those same virtues that I have just mentioned unless he has decided that there is nothing that makes any difference or distinction between things apart from what is noble [*honesta*, that is, the sign of moral virtue] and base [*turpia*].

On a reasonable interpretation of this passage, Cicero is suggesting that there are two especially important moral virtues, magnanimity and justice, that share a feature for which wisdom is responsible, that of taking anything that may happen to a man to be beneath him. Indeed, it seems likely that we should take the shared feature to be what *makes* the two virtues what they are: those two ordinary moral virtues. In other words, Cicero apparently aims to identify what goes into a moral virtue and claims this to be the insight that is part of the intellectual virtue of wisdom. That insight is of course identical with the grasp of the human good as *homologia*. For that grasp resulted precisely in taking anything that may happen to a man to be beneath him—almost literally so: *infra se*. In that case the two specifications of the human good come to the same thing.

Were the Stoics right here? Would an ordinary Greek who thought he knew what a moral virtue was agree with the Stoic analysis of moral virtue to the effect that moral virtue is defined by the kind of wisdom had by a person who has adopted the view from above? Perhaps he would. The Stoics might actually be right in claiming that moral virtues as ordinarily understood did contain something like the step from subjectivity to objectivity that makes one 'judge that everything that may happen to a man is beneath one'. One's concern as the possessor of any of the moral virtues—so they might reasonably claim—is not directly with certain objects in the world and the attraction they may have to oneself, but rather with the moral principle itself (the view from above) that governs one's handling of those objects.

We may support this idea by looking again at the two moral virtues, magnanimity and justice. It is unlikely that they were chosen by Cicero merely at random. As we shall see in a moment, the Stoics spoke of *oikeiōsis* not once but twice in their general theory. The second time, *oikeiōsis* is specifically connected with a person's relation with others. Here the insight that is gained is the one that goes into the virtue of justice. Perhaps, then, we should understand the present text as implying that corresponding to the fact that the Stoics spoke of *oikeiōsis* in two contexts, the one we have considered so far and the one that issues in justice, they also tried to place all ordinary moral virtues in two 'columns', one entitled 'magnanimity' and the other 'justice'. Magnanimity is in fact quite fit for this role. Elsewhere it is defined by the Stoics as 'knowledge or a state that makes a man superior to what may happen to morally good and bad people alike' (*SVF* 3.264 and 265). In other words, Cicero's point about judging everything that may happen to a man to be beneath one is itself part of the definition of magnanimity. In addition, there is a precedent in Aristotelian ethics for taking magnanimity to be a sort of 'crown of the virtues'.[24]

Suppose we distinguish in this way between two general types of moral virtue. One, headed by magnanimity, will concern only the individual person himself and his or her relationship with everything outside him- or herself. In this column we will find moral virtues like courage, temperance and the like, where these virtues do not touch on one's relationship with others. What characterizes the morally virtuous person here is a capacity to apply nothing but the view from above on oneself and a consequent complete detachment from oneself as that particular individual. The other type is headed by justice and concerns those moral virtues, or aspects of them, that directly relate to others. The basic Stoic claim will then be that it is the feature of objectivity shared by both types of moral virtue that turns them into types of moral virtue proper and so ties them together in spite of their different fields of operation. Both 'judge that everything that may happen to a man is beneath one'.

This reading helps us to see how in the Stoic theory one and the same insight at the X-level governs the relationship of the individual person him- or herself both to the world around the person and also to other human beings. The first relationship is captured in the wise man's 'downward' movement X→I (as a result of I→X), the second in that of X→S (again as a result of I→X). But it is the same basic insight that is applied in either case, the one that expresses a person's sense of *belonging* at the X-level and looking down *from* there. Once more it should be immediately clear that this is directly relevant to Paul too, where the same basic insight—of belonging to Christ—governs a person's relationship both with the world at large (including one's own, individual relationship with the world) and with others.

Summary so far

For the sake of clarity, let us summarize some of the crucial features of the Stoic version of the change from **I** to **X** in the model:

(i)   The basic framework within which the change occurs consists of the individual person's understanding of his or her own identity. All through it is a question of who *I* am and where *I* belong. Scholars of antiquity who object (rightly) to reading features of modern 'individualism' into the ancient material may dislike this result. But they cannot avoid it. Both the basic notion of the *telos* and *eudaimonia*, which the Stoics took over wholesale from Aristotle, and also the Stoic innovation of going back to consider the development of the individual from childhood to adulthood belong squarely within a framework that works with an individual person's understanding of his or her own identity.

(ii)   The change from **I** to **X** is all through a change in the understanding (in Stoicism, which differs on this point from Aristotle). It is a matter of understanding in this or the other way what one oneself is and what consequently belongs to one among things outside oneself. The Stoic theory explains—in ways we have not gone into—how such an understanding may give rise to desire and action.[25] But the basic category is a cognitive one. Even self-love was explained by being referred back to self-*awareness*. It is the radically cognitive (in the scholarly jargon, 'monistic') construction of the human mind in Stoicism together with their focus on identity ('*self*-cognition') that constituted the framework for Paul's thought about the Christ event and its consequences.

(iii)   The change itself from **I** to **X** is one from subjectivity to objectivity. Its character is quite radical. The framework—including the cognitive category—of course remains the same. Within that framework, however, there is a complete change from relating everything subjectively to the individual that one oneself is—to relating it to the objective perspective of rationality itself, a view from above the individual that the individual may him- or herself come to occupy.

(iv)   The change from **I** to **X** results in a grasp of the single, unified concept under which any valuation, desire and act will fall, the concept of the good. This concept is understood as being identical with that of the final end (*telos*) and thus to have the logical features that Aristotle had developed in his account of the logic of the concept of *eudaimonia*.

The change from I to X also results in a grasp of the substantive content of the good: that it is *homologia*. The human good is understanding the world correctly, in theory and in practice. As the substantive content of the good, *homologia* fulfils the formal requirements for being what the *telos* and the good consists in, those of being final and self-sufficient in the senses used by Aristotle. *Homologia* is therefore choiceworthy in itself and never for the sake of anything else. And nothing but *homologia* matters. In two respects, therefore, the change from I to X is a distinctly 'upward' movement that consists in turning one's back on the I-level. Both the grasp of the formal concept of the good and that of its substantive content belong at the X-level. Another name for the mental state that results in *homologia* is wisdom. Wisdom is basically defined as the attitude that considers anything that may happen to a man to be 'beneath' one. Viewed in this way, wisdom too consists in turning one's back on the I-level. Thus the change from I to X intrinsically leaves the world behind—it has an outworldly dimension.

(v)   In spite of this, there also is a kind of 'downward' movement from X to I. Since *homologia* is a matter of understanding *the world*, which is found at the I-level, X-level wisdom also relates to the I-level. It includes seeing what acts in the world are 'in accordance with nature', that is, in accordance with what the world (including oneself and others) is actually like. Similarly, even if the good itself belongs exclusively at the X-level, there remain objects at the I-level that are rightly considered 'valuable' for human beings. For that is the verdict of wisdom itself when it considers objects in the world from above.

(vi)   Finally, there is moral virtue. That is another name for wisdom and it is defined by the same basic feature as that. One general type of moral virtue, headed by magnanimity, is merely another name for wisdom applied to the areas that relate specifically to the individual him- or herself at the I-level. Another type is headed by justice, which is another name for wisdom applied to areas that relate specifically to others and concern the mutual relationship between the individual him- or herself and the others. This type requires closer consideration. It is the type of moral virtue that will finally bring us from I via X to S.

Oikeiōsis II (the S-level)

As we have considered the wise man so far (I→X), he will (in spite of any impression we may have given to the contrary) remain self-centred—in practice, but certainly not in principle. For so far he will only apply his new grasp (*from* the X-level) to *himself* (as the I-level individual that he is and remains). In relation to the grasp itself that is purely accidental (since the grasp precisely *transcends* the subjective view *from* the I-level), but it remains the case in fact. For it will in practice be the subjective I-level perspective that *states the issues* that he will then solve *by* looking down upon them from above. In practice, therefore, he will continue to act on his own behalf—where that is allowed for by the perspective from above. Reason has of course provided him with no *more* justification for acting on his own behalf than for acting on behalf of any other individual, but neither has it provided him with any *positive* justification for acting on behalf of any of *them*. He just goes for what is objectively valuable, but since his starting point was concern for himself, it will remain so, even if only accidentally, until some other perspective has been brought in. And so, if he is to act directly on behalf of others (and the Stoics reasonably took it that one does precisely that, at least when one acts out of the moral virtue of *justice*), some further account must be given of why one should do that and how one may come to see that one should. So how does one get from the substantive self-love that was at the centre of *oikeiōsis* at stage 1 of its first version, and has remained so in actual fact (though only accidentally) at stage 2, to a form of genuine care for others?

The Stoics attempted to elucidate this basic step away from a natural self-centredness by bringing in *oikeiōsis* a second time. This move finally brings them to the S-pole of the model. Once more we must consider the logic of the move in some detail in order to grasp a striking, formal similarity with Paul. In spite of what we have just said about the possibility of staying self-centred (in practice, that is), we shall see that the step to S is in fact already logically contained in the one from I to X. Or more sharply: the step to S is already contained in the '*figure*', X, which constitutes the end of the first step. That 'figure', of course, is rationality and reason in the Stoics and Christ in Paul. But the formal role of either is exactly the same in the present, very important respect too.

Cicero says the following (*De Finibus* 3.62–63):

> They believe that it is relevant to the matter discussed to see that it happens by nature that children are loved by their parents. From this starting point we derive and explain the universal community of the human race. This must be clear already from the shape and members of the body, which by themselves make it clear that nature has arranged for the procreation of offspring. Nor could it be mutually consistent that nature should want offspring to be procreated and should not take care that the offspring be

loved. Even in animals the power of nature can be seen: when we see their labour in bearing and rearing their young, we seem to be listening to nature's own voice. Therefore, just as it is evident that we shrink from pain by nature, so it is clear that we are impelled by nature itself to love those to whom we have given birth.[26] From this arises a natural, shared attachment of man to man, so that just because he is a man, a man must be considered not alien by another man.

The first part of this passage argues for a basic love that parents have for their offspring, and the last sentence speaks of the extension of such love to one of humans for humans as such. Here too the vocabulary of *oikeiōsis* is explicitly brought in: 'attachment' (*commendatio*), 'alien' (*alienum*). We need only consider two points in Cicero's account. What is the role of parental love? And by what mechanism does the final 'natural, shared attachment of man to man' come into being?

Consider the first point. Love for one's offspring may at one and the same time explain two things about the first step towards a more pervasive altruism that is the Stoics' theme. It explains how the step may be taken at all—for one's offspring is in a quite concrete sense an extension of oneself. One can therefore understand people's loving their offspring as an extension of their basic self-love. At the same time love for one's offspring is also genuinely other-regarding: it is loving one's children for *their* sake and as *other* selves or beings than oneself. So love for one's offspring seems eminently suited to explain how a step towards a genuinely other-regarding attitude is at all possible. Secondly, love for one's offspring also has the advantage of being a pervasive natural fact— in the same way as the self-love from which *oikeiōsis* in its first version began.

Then the mechanism. Is it not strange to fix on a feature about *adults* (parents) in order to explain the genesis of an altruistic stance? Perhaps not. Parents love their children for the children's own sake. Conversely the children are loved for their own sake—by the parents. Furthermore, all children have had parents. So all children have been influenced in a way that makes it possible that they should *themselves* step out of the circle of self-centredness—in relation to the parents *or* in some other relation (to close relatives, friends and the like). Such attitudes, then, are to be understood as *acquired* ones that arise as a result of the influence of parents on their children. As opposed to this, love for one's offspring is a basic attitude, precisely a 'natural' one that is not acquired. And it is one that may account for those other attitudes.

Then we may bring in the basic mechanism of *oikeiōsis* once more. Consider a child who has been living in surroundings that are structured by other-regarding attitudes of various kinds stemming from the basic love that children have received from their parents. When such a child acquires reason, he or she will self-reflectively notice that all along one has oneself been caring for other beings for their sake, but always because they in some way 'belonged' to one as the particular individual one is: they were one's *own* parents or one's *own* associates in other ways. But the grown-up person now also sees him- or herself as a rational being, with the consequence that whatever else is rational will 'belong' to him or her too and be theirs just as much as, indeed even more than, the individual people who have formed part of their immediate surroundings. So one's basic, other-regarding attitude of care (for their own sake) for other individuals who were seen to belong to one will necessarily be extended to cover all rational beings. *They* are now seen to belong to one to the highest degree, since in so far as they partake of rationality, which is common to them all, they are identical with oneself in the respect which has by far the most important role to play in determining what one oneself is (that is, in determining one's 'constitution', as we know it from *De Finibus* 3.16).

Nowhere in our sources is the precise role made clear that rationality has in bringing about this result, but there can be little doubt that it is the one just given. For it is a mere application of the basic idea of *oikeiōsis* in its first version, and furthermore, it directly accounts for the strongly Kantian flavour of a passage like the following one, in which Cicero spells out the bond between human beings (*De Finibus* 3.64):

> They believe that the universe is governed by divine will, and that it is a sort of city and state shared by men and gods [*quasi communis urbs et civitas hominum et deorum*], and that each of us is a part of this universe; from which it follows by nature that we set the common advantage [*utilitas*] before our own. For just as the laws set the safety of all before the safety of individuals, so a man who is good, wise, law-abiding and conscious of his civic duty will care for the advantage of all more than of some single individual—or himself.

The universe that each human being is here said to be a part of is the universe of reason, and it is the fact that each human being may come to see others as belonging to him- or herself because they all share in reason, that explains how *oikeiōsis* in its second version may produce justice, or at least the basic attitude underlying justice, of genuinely other-regarding concern for others for their own sake.

Then we have filled the I→X→S-model in as the Stoics intended it to be done. From the I-level we were first brought to the basic grasp of the human good at the X-level which is also Stoic wisdom. That wisdom was also seen to underlie moral virtue. At first, however, it was moral virtue primarily as a matter of detachment from the world and the obsession to acquire worldly, natural goods for oneself, in other words, as a detachment from the immediate, self-regarding attitude of the child. It is only now that we can see wisdom to underlie also the other type of moral virtue, which is genuinely other-regarding. This too comes about as a result of a development of the original valuations of the child, in this case its immediate and local attachments to others for their sake. But it is only through the process of *oikeiōsis* that these immediate attachments are now transformed into proper, other-regarding moral virtues.

The crucial point in this for the comparison with Paul is the one we have already noted. In Stoicism it is the same cognitive mechanism—of self-identification with reason—that explains both types of moral virtue: that of detachment from ordinary, self-related goods (compare magnanimity) and that of genuine care for others (compare justice). Both types of virtue result from the same movement from I to X. Both pivot on the self-identification with the 'figure' that defines the X-level, reason. With *oikeiōsis* in its second version, however, it has been shown exactly how this self-identification brings a person the whole way from I to S via the content of the 'figure' X. The same picture is found in Paul. Here too it is one and the same cognitive mechanism—of self-identification with Christ—that brings a person the whole way from I to S via the content of the X-figure, Christ.

Corollaries: prokopē, kathēkonta and katorthōmata; pathē, apatheia and eupatheiai (e.g. chara)

With the I→X→S-model in place for the Stoics, we may consider certain subsidiary themes in their ethics which are also directly relevant to the study of Paul.

One concept we have already met: that of *prokopē* (progression).[27] It is likely that one should understand it in two ways. Consider a person who has not yet reached the final grasp of the good. Basically, he belongs at the I-level, but he may be on his way 'up'. That is the case described by Cicero in the passage we discussed earlier (*De Finibus* 3.20). It is well known that the Stoics distinguished sharply between the person who has reached the grasp of the good and the one who has not. The former is wise (*sophos*), *all* others are stupid (*mōroi*). Viewed in that light, the person who is progressing (the *prokoptōn*) remains stupid—though possibly *less* stupid than other stupid people! Wisdom (*sophia*) is an all or nothing affair. You either have it—and then in principle to the full—

or else you don't. And having it is the only thing that matters. As we shall see, that 'absolutist' conception is directly relevant to Paul. In Paul, if you have been 'grasped by Christ', you are in principle totally 'in'.

Put the Stoic picture like this:

– – – – – – *prokopē* – – – – – – I wisdom.

However, we saw that there may be two different types of wise man, one who knows everything and another who does not, but *has* acquired the one insight into the good that really matters. Then we may construct a different, more advanced type of *prokoptōn*. That is the person who has in fact acquired the one insight that matters, but still needs to know more in order to see what it concretely means in any particular situation. In one sense, he will have reached the X-level, in another not. Will he be stupid or wise? Either answer seems possible. And so, even though wisdom is in principle an all or nothing affair, it also seems possible to take some person to be *basically* wise (he *has* grasped what genuinely matters)—but perhaps not *quite* so. That distinction too is highly relevant to Paul, in whom there is faith—and faith that is 'weak'.

Put the new picture like this:

– – – – – – I (wisdom) – – – – – – *prokopē* – – – – – – wisdom.

The possibility that we should work with two different types of *prokopē* may also be formulated in terms of the two concepts of *kathē-konta* ('duties') and *katorthōmata* (right acts).[28] The former are act-types of such a kind that, taken generally, they should be put into practice, even though the concrete result may not always be a 'right act'. Example: one should take care of one's health. *Kathēkonta* are those acts that a non-wise person will do, no matter whether he is only on his way ('upwards') towards the basic grasp of the good or whether he *has* grasped it but without being *quite* able to see what the good actually means (moving 'downwards') in the particular situation. By contrast, a person who is through and through wise will always and only do 'right acts'—e.g. of *neglecting* one's health in a specific situation where *that* is called for by one's basic grasp of the good. Even where the wise man neglects or sidesteps a *kathēkon* rule that less wise people will choose to act on in the given situation, his act will be just right. For *he* is able to see aright in any particular situation. Once more, we note that wisdom is in principle an all or nothing affair—the wise man always and only performs *katorthōmata*. But again, it is also clear that there may be less perfect forms of a grasp and insight that may in principle still qualify as wisdom.

To summarize on *prokopē* and *kathēkonta*, Stoic wisdom is such a thing that you either have it completely—then everybody else is just stupid—or else you have the basic grasp but without being always able to implement it in every detail. In the former case you are 'out' if you do not have it. But you may of course be on your way towards both acquiring the basic grasp and seeing how to implement it. You will then be progressing in the first sense and be a person who generally performs *kathēkonta*. In the latter case you are basically 'in'. But you will still be in need of having your grasp deepened so as always to issue in right acts. Still, you will hopefully be progressing—*within* the framework of being 'in'—and will generally perform *kathēkonta* too. In spite of the material similarity, however, between the two kinds of people, the latter person has an all-important advantage over the former: that of already possessing the basic grasp. It should be immediately clear that this latter kind of figure is directly relevant to Paul. It pinpoints the logic that underlies Pauline parenesis.

In another area the Stoics were more rigid in maintaining that wisdom is an all or nothing affair. Passions (*pathē*) are completely eradicated in the wise man, whose state of mind will therefore be marked by *apatheia* (lack of passions).[29] In the same way, Paul 'and those generally who belong to Christ' have 'crucified the flesh' with its 'passions' (*pathēmata*) and 'desires' (*epithymiai*), according to Gal 5:24. This certainly does not mean, however, that the Stoic wise man will have no emotional reactions to the world whatever. As we shall see in a moment, there are three types of 'good emotions' (*eupatheiai*) that the wise man will have. What he will not have at all are 'passions' understood as either minor relapses, that is, cases of weakness of will relative to an adult grasp of the good that he *has* acquired, or else pathological fixations in an altogether childish form of reaction. The wise man is completely convinced (he is said to *pisteuein*)[30] by his grasp of the good and he remains steadfast in it (it is said to be unshakeable and 'immovable by reason'—because it is through and through rational)[31] even in cases where weaker people might be tempted to loosen it. Conviction (*pistis*) and steadfastness are of course central concerns of Paul's too. It is true that the wise man's conviction and steadfastness do not prevent him from *remembering* what it felt like to be in such a situation before he reached his new grasp. Thus he may well feel the kind of regret that finds expression in the thought that it *would* have been nicer to be without the present experience, had that been possible. He is not at all insensitive to what happens to him. But such a feeling will never become more than 'counterfactual'. It will never become so real as to enter into direct confrontation with that other basic emotional attitude of his which reflects his basic grasp, including the fact that he understands—in the distancing view from above—everything that happens and sees its intrinsic, objective meaning.

That basic emotional attitude is the one of *chara* (joy), which is the one 'good emotion' that concerns the present.[32] It goes without saying that *chara* is a central concept in Paul too, not least in Philippians. With regard to the future, there are two paired 'good emotions' in Stoicism, 'wish' (*boulēsis*) and 'caution' (*eulabeia*). The former corresponds with the irrational passion of 'desire' (*epithymia*), the latter with the equally irrational passion of 'fear' (*phobos*). But wish and caution are not irrational, but rational. They are emotional states of the wise man who *has* grasped that the presence or absence of ordinary goods and evils for himself is a matter of no consequence for his living the truly good life—but who would still *rather* have those goods and avoid those evils *if that is possible* (and if it does not conflict with other considerations and so forth). If the result then is that he does not avoid the evils or does not obtain the goods, he will not feel pain, but at most the kind of regret we noticed. For in Stoicism there is no 'good emotion' for the present corresponding to caution for the future—a sort of qualified 'pain'. In the present, the wise man will be filled by one emotion only, that of joy. Again, the point is directly relevant to Paul.

What is it that makes the wise man rejoice no matter what happens to him in the present? His joy is generated by his sense of possessing a perspective on whatever happens in the world that makes it fall into place and fit in. No matter what happens to him, it can be explained, it fits into his comprehensive understanding of what the world is objectively like. Moreover, as we know, he himself does not just belong in the particular situation (at the I-level) in which something untoward may concretely happen to him. Basically, he belongs elsewhere. Having moved from I to X, he has also been placed above particular situations. By identifying with reason, he has adopted an exalted position and perspective *from* which he may look down on the world and understand it. The sense of belonging there gives him joy, and this feeling is not the least diminished by whatever happens to him at the I-level. On the contrary, since he always understands what happens down there, the joy he obtains from belonging at the X-level will only be all the more marked.[33]

Ethics and politics: a Utopian form of life

Ethics in the ancient ethical tradition never concerned only the individual and his or her immediate relations with others. In Plato and Aristotle ethics was intimately connected with the social and political community, the *polis*. That is obvious, for instance, in the case of Plato's *Republic*, which explicitly construes the good life for the individual and the good political community as two sides of the same thing. In Aristotle too the connection is intimate. Thus on the second page of his *Nicomachean Ethics* Aristotle identifies his theme, the human good, as falling under 'political science' (I.ii.8, 1094b7–11):

> Even if the end is the same for a single man and for a *polis* [city state], that of the *polis* seems at all events something greater and more complete whether to attain or to preserve; though it is worth while to attain the end merely for one man, it is finer and more godlike to attain it for a people [*ethnos*] or for city states. These, then, are the ends at which our inquiry aims, since it is political science, in one sense of that term.

Aristotle also concludes the last book of the *Nicomachean Ethics* with a long chapter (X.ix, 1179a33–1181b23) that leads directly over to his *Politics*: compare, for instance, the following remark towards the very end (X.xi.22, 1181b12–15):

> Now our predecessors have left the subject of legislation [*nomothesia*] to us unexamined; it is perhaps best, therefore, that we should ourselves study it, and in general study the question of the constitution [*politeia*], in order to complete to the best of our ability our philosophy of human affairs [*hē peri ta anthrōpeia philosophia*].

Another sign of this orientation is the fact that Aristotle uses two whole books of his *Ethics* (VIII–IX: a fifth of the whole work) on the topic of friendship, aiming to show that the good and happy life will only be found in a friendship among virtuous people. Both the political direction towards the *polis* and the more private, *social* direction towards friendship are highly relevant to the study of Paul. This direction was even sharpened by the Stoics, who construed the political direction of their ethics in such a way that friendship and the political community became two sides of the same thing. We may see this most clearly in Chrysippus' version of the ideal community. But first we need to consider the character of the ideal community that had been sketched by Zeno, the founder of Stoicism, in his *Republic*.[34]

Unfortunately very few indications of the content of that work have been left to us and these mainly in sources that are hostile to the work. In the most substantial report (given by Diogenes Laertius, *Lives* 7.32–4) we hear that Zeno was criticized by some (even some Stoics, it appears, 7.34) for declaring the 'all-round education' (*enkyklios paideia*) useless, for claiming that 'all people who are not morally good (*spoudaioi*) are hostile to each other, enemies, slaves and aliens to one another (even parents to children, brothers to brothers, friends to friends)', whereas 'only the morally good are citizens, friends, kindred, free'. As has long been recognized, these ideas immediately bring the Stoics into contact with Paul.[35] Zeno also decreed community of women (not a Pauline concern!) and declared that 'no temples, lawcourts or gymnasia should be built in the cities', nor need any currency be introduced either for purposes of trade or for traveling abroad.

There has been much discussion about the precise character of Zeno's projected republic.[36] It evidently stands in the tradition of Plato's *Republic* and shares with that the character of being an ideal community or (as Plutarch terms it) 'as it were a dream or mental image of a philosopher's well-ordered constitution'.[37] There can be little doubt, however, that what Zeno envisaged was what has aptly been called an anarcho-syndicalist state,[38] or rather not exactly a state; for the point of abolishing temples, lawcourts, gymnasia, currency and the institution of marriage seems precisely to have been that there should no longer *be* a state. Instead, there apparently would be cities of some sort, probably communities at a very low level scattered in a landscape of no very clear limits. This is all rather fanciful, no doubt reflecting the fact that Zeno had more marked leanings towards Cynicism than some of his Stoic successors. But it belongs squarely within the ancient Greek Utopian tradition. Moreover, in spite of the obvious differences between Zeno's conception and Paul's idea of a Christ-believing congregation—one more or less a dream, the other very much a reality—the way they relate to the rest of society is closely similar. Both are, basically, outworldly entities.

How would Zeno's republic be governed? In accordance with its anarcho-syndicalist character, there would be next to no form of political rule. Instead, the 'cities' envisaged by Zeno would be characterized by three concepts that Zeno is known to have highlighted together: *homonoia* (oneness of mind, unanimity, concord), *philia* (friendship) and *eleutheria* (freedom, SVF 1.263). Similarly, Chrysippus declared that only the morally good man is capable of both governing and being governed. In fact, he alone does govern (*archein*)—if not actually then at all events dispositionally. And he alone is 'obedient to authority' (*peitharchikos*), since he 'follows one who governs' (is *akolouthētikos archonti, SVF* 3.615). It does not matter whether he does one thing or the other since the content of what he determines should be done (if he is the one who governs) or decides in obedience to do (if he is the one who is governed) is the same. He just *wills* the good. There is a basic idea here which will prove crucial to a proper understanding of Paul: although one may well speak in Stoicism of 'obedience to authority', there is no room for any idea of force being applied on anybody's part; on the contrary, the 'obedience' is through and through self-willed since it springs from a grasp that one has oneself acquired. That idea provides the key to a proper understanding of such an important term in Paul as 'obedience of faith' (*hypakoē pisteōs*).

In short, Zeno appears to have envisaged an ideal community where all social institutions, all socially based distinctions between people, possibly also all distinctions based on gender and finally all political distinctions have been abolished. There would be no hierarchies whatever, no subordination, since the only thing that would count was moral goodness or the lack of it. In this community there would be total *freedom*, which the Stoics defined as the right to independent action (*exousia autopragias*), as opposed to slavery (*douleia*), which is privation of the same (*sterēsis autopragias*, Diogenes Laertius *Lives* 7.121). For the wise man does all things well (*panta eu poiein ton sophon*) and all things belong to the wise (*tōn sophōn panta einai*, Diogenes Laertius *Lives* 7.125). The similarity with Paul is well known—and of crucial importance.

After Zeno, we find two changes in the conception of the Stoic ideal community. First, there is a change away from the strongly Cynic flavour of Zeno's original conception in the direction of removing from it anything that smacked of Cynicism. (Zeno, of course, began as a Cynic, and Stoic ethics and politics may to a large extent be seen as a theoretical superstructure on the Cynic practice.) This change is reflected in the story about the 1st-century BCE Stoic Athenodorus, who while in charge of the library in Pergamon literally excised from Zeno's works 'what the Stoics considered badly said in them' (Diogenes Laertius *Lives* 7.34), in fact most likely some of the points mentioned above. It is also reflected in the way in which the 2nd-century BCE Stoic Panaetius of Rhodes specifically repudiated the Cynic links, which he found distasteful.[39] This change might be of minor importance, but it probably is not. For it seems closely connected with the other change, which is of major importance.

This is a change in the understanding of the kind of thing that Zeno's ideal community is. In spite of its apparently Utopian, 'dreamlike' character, it was probably conceived by Zeno himself fairly concretely as a kind of recipe for social and political innovation, or even revolution. It constituted a model or matrix, elements of which any Greek city might put into practice should it so decide.[40] For it was in a sense Cynicism writ large (and backed philosophically), and in Zeno's time practising Cynics could be found wherever one looked. By applying Zeno's idea in practice one would just follow the lead of those Cynics who were practising what they preached and do it in the very same direction of breaking down conventional hierarchies whether social, political or gender-based.

In Chrysippus, however, the character of the ideal community changes. Now it appears as a community of all those people who are morally good wherever they live on the earth. They all belong to the same community (so there is only one such community) just by being morally good. Indeed, they, and they alone, are friends with one another in the full and proper sense of friendship. This conception was faithfully reflected by Clement of Alexandria in the following definition of the Stoic 'city' (*SVF* 3.327):

> The Stoics say that the universe [*ouranos*] is in the proper sense a city [*polis*], but those here on earth are no longer cities. They are called so, but are not really. For a city is something morally good and a people [*dēmos*] is some kind of refined organization or group of people that is governed by law.

And here too, of course, belongs Cicero's version of the ideal community that we have already encountered: that of the universe as governed by divine will and as a sort of city and state shared by men and gods (*De Finibus* 3.64).

On such a conception, the ideal community will probably not have been understood by Chrysippus as a recipe for direct social and political action. Rather, he will have seen it as a kind of limiting construct, which might then be put to use in actual social and political practice in a number of ways. It is noteworthy, however, that in his political thought Chrysippus kept those Cynic links (cf. Diogenes Laertius *Lives* 7.187–9) that Panaetius repudiated a hundred years later. This probably means that Chrysippus maintained the radically anti-hierarchical content of Zeno's original conception. The fragment referred to above which states that the morally good man will both govern and be governed points in the same direction. Here the Cynic links served the purpose of doing away with conventional social and political distinctions and so making room for the idea of what remains an an-archic, radically non-hierarchical community which ran directly counter to all ordinary societies.

In Chrysippus, then, the ideal community was a limiting construct which was neither a direct recipe for political practice (as in Zeno) nor the kind of relatively inconsequential 'moral ideal' that it appears to have become in Panaetius—who by severing the Cynic links undercut both the idea of genuinely trying to put the ideal into practice and also its original, anti-conventional character. It is Chrysippus' conception, combined with something like the original Zenonic concern about concrete practice, which is immediately relevant to Paul.

How was the old Stoic idea of the ideal community understood by
Stoics in Paul's own day? The question is complex. On the one hand, we
may note a kind of celebration of Cynicism in Stoics like Seneca and
Epictetus: in the description of Seneca's friend, Demetrius, and in
Epictetus' portrait of what is usually referred to as the 'ideal Cynic'.[41]
This return to the Cynic roots of Stoicism coincides with a Cynic revival
in the two first centuries BCE.[42] Cynics, one feels, were to be encountered
almost anywhere in the Mediterranean (witness: Dio Chrysostom). Thus
there certainly was an emphasis in this period on practice. The same
emphasis is found in another contemporary Stoic, Musonius Rufus.[43]
None of these Stoics, however, went so far as ever to consider practising
Stoicism as a communitarian project. Their Stoicism remained more or
less 'individualistic'. Some of them, it is true, had contact with the group
of senators in 1st-century Rome who constituted a 'Stoic opposition' to
the emperors. Here we do see some reflection of the political potential of
Stoicism. But to speak of a communitarian project of the kind envisaged
directly by Zeno and indirectly by Chrysippus would be wrong. It is easy
to explain this lack of any attempt to realize the full ethico-political
potential of Stoicism. For all the people referred to belonged at the
uppermost levels of society. They will not have been prepared to turn
their backs on society in actual practice. This also holds of the former
slave Epictetus, who had after all received the highest training as a
member of the imperial household. Even banishment from Rome could
not dislodge him from his (acquired) roots among the upper classes. As a
teacher away from Rome, he precisely taught young men *from* those
classes.[44]

Do we not find any attempt in Paul's day to practise Stoicism as a
communitarian project? Yes. With all the necessary qualifications: Paul's
own community-creating project is just such an attempt.

Conclusion: a set of ideas and a form of life

Stoicism is a philosophy. It is an attempt to provide a true and coherent
picture of the human world: the human access to the world (in logic and
epistemology), the basic comprehensive shape of the world as human
beings may understand it (ontology and natural philosophy), and the
best shape human beings may give to their lives in the world (ethics and
politics). The character of this attempt, however, must be correctly understood, no matter whether the Stoics would themselves have agreed with
this characterization or not. All through, Stoicism was very far from
providing a non-normative, *merely* descriptive account. In particular, the

Stoic analysis of the good life for human beings is frankly normative. Put another way, Stoic ethics was an attempt to provide a coherent account of a *specific form of life* that was seen (for various reasons, *including* 'philosophical' ones) to be the best one. Thus understood, Stoicism was not just a piece of 'philosophy' or a set of 'ideas' that might occupy the leisured classes in idle moments of theoretical interest. It was something far more serious: an attempt to give shape, and indeed a new kind of shape, to the concrete lives of human beings. Stoicism strove to articulate a *better way of living.*

It accords with this that what the Stoics were offering in their analysis of this form of life was intended to *appeal* to those it might reach and to convince them that the Stoic way of life and the Stoic ideal community were in fact the best ones. This appeal could take many forms. But since the Stoics were philosophers, their favoured procedure was to show that 'rightly understood' the *ordinary* perception of good and bad could be seen to point in the direction of their own view. *Their* view was the one that would surface as soon as one got to the heart of the ordinary perception. The Stoics might well be wrong here. Indeed, to the extent that they were trying to articulate a highly *specific* form of 'best life' out of the many possible ones, they certainly *were* wrong. What matters is seeing the two things they were *trying* to do: articulating a better way of living by providing a coherent, fully thought through picture of a highly specific form of the 'best life'—and at the same time also relating that conception to the ordinary understanding of the good and the bad. It is this fundamental, double concern—combined with the specific, distinctly outworldly shape the Stoics gave to their new picture as captured in the I→X→S-model and as set out in this chapter—that made Stoicism such an attractive repository of ideas for Paul when he set out to do in his own way what they had also done: to formulate *his* picture of the best form of life.

4

Philippians I
The Problem and the Beginning of a Solution

The issue of structure and overall meaning

In this chapter we shall begin the direct study of Paul by looking at his letter to the Philippians. The task is to show that the I→X→S-model helps to elucidate this Pauline text when it is allowed to bring in a number of ideas that go with it in its specifically Stoic form. The fundamental aim is to elucidate Paul. One can only justify the claim that one should (also) read Paul in the light of Stoicism and the I→X→S-model Stoically understood if the result of such a reading genuinely adds to the understanding of the Pauline text seen, as it were, on its own. The text must 'itself' become better understood when read from a specific perspective— in this case, a Stoic one—for that perspective to be vindicated. (As always, however, there will be other perspectives too that may be applied to the same effect.) I begin from setting aside a number of traditional, mainly historical issues in the reading of the letter. It is not that they are unimportant. But they have been extensively discussed. And even if they were finally solved, that would not in the least end serious work on the letter. On the contrary, I aim here to bring us forward to the further question of the overall meaning of the letter in a more comprehensive sense to be specified. It is here that the Stoic thesis will show its fruitfulness.

There are quite a number of unsolved problems in Philippians, some of which may even be unsolvable.[1] For instance, the wish for a wholly specific answer to the question of Paul's aim or aims in writing the letter is likely to remain unfulfilled. It seems clear that he is sending the letter (if indeed it is a single one, see below) back to Philippi together with Epaphroditus (i) with thanks for a recent gift of money that he had brought from them to Paul while he was in prison (in Ephesus, as I shall take it) and (ii) in order to recommend him to them: see 2:25–30 together with 4:10–20.[2] It is less clear whether—as has recently been suggested—the specific wish to settle the apparent conflict between Paul's old fellow workers (in Philippi?), Euodia and Syntyche (4:2–3), was also a direct factor behind Paul's writing.[3] It is even less clear—an old question here—how one should understand Paul's references to opponents of his own teaching (3:2–11, 17–21) and of the Philippians (1:27–30). First, who were they? Non-Christ-believing Jews? Or Christ-believers of a more strongly Jewish persuasion than Paul's? Were they basically the same kind of people or different groups?[4] Second, did they represent such a serious threat that we should see it as a primary concern on Paul's part to rebut them in order to secure the Philippians for his own cause (like in Galatians)? Or should we rather see his references to them mainly as a negative rhetorical foil—possibly within the *topos* of friendship—for statements that are really only positively concerned with the Philippians themselves?[5] Finally, if—with a recent trend—we read the letter as one of friendship, it is not quite clear how we should construe the friendly relationship between Paul and the Philippians. Was it of a more or less contractual kind? Did the Philippians think that Paul had broken his contract with them?[6] Or did Paul attempt to change their misconceived understanding of friendship onto a different plane?[7] All in all, the exact circumstances and Paul's exact aims in writing the letter to some extent remain in the dark. Moreover, they will probably continue to do so. For as soon as scholars come up with wholly specific answers to questions of this kind, they are likely to overemphasize some elements in the text to the detriment of others. And so they will soon be corrected by fellow scholars.

Another traditional issue concerns the letter's integrity. It is still not unusual to find scholars insisting that what we have is not a single, complete letter deriving directly from Paul, but rather two or three letters or letter fragments that have been put together by some other hand.[8] Here too, unequivocal answers may not be forthcoming. However, the recent trend—in English-language, though hardly in German scholarship—is towards unity. I think this is right and that it is not just a trend that may move in the other direction in ten years. What we find here in scholarship is a healthy reaction to overconfidence in scholars with regard to the possibility of reconstruction in history, in short, a healthy reaction to the urge towards speculation. A critical attitude to this urge dictates caution towards trusting that one has discovered a highly specific truth *behind* the text. Such caution implies acceptance that there are questions one cannot finally answer—like those of the exact letter situation we rehearsed or—with the present issue—acceptance that the supposed 'problems' of the text lie within the horizon of acceptability. At the present juncture of historical-critical scholarship we have *learned* something from the attempts of earlier scholars, namely, that the search for highly specific answers behind the text is quite often likely to be in vain. In this light, it is worth presenting here one hitherto unnoticed structural consideration which speaks fairly strongly for unity and hence for letting the text stand as it is. This will lead us to formulating the question that the following discussion is intended to answer.

There are no real problems with the structure of the letter up until 3:1. The initial greetings and thanksgiving section (1:1–11) is structurally unproblematic. The following section (1:12–26) on Paul's own troublesome situation in prison ends with a declaration of confidence that he will overcome it and become able to visit the Philippians again. This leads naturally on to a section (1:27–30) in which he exhorts the Philippians to steadfast unity in the face of certain opponents and a parallel section of paraklesis (2:1–4) dealing with the Philippians' internal attitude and behaviour. The Christ hymn that follows (2:5–11) is intended to support the paraklesis and is again followed quite naturally by another section (2:12–18) of direct exhortation of the Philippians. All in all, there is a clear development in Paul's thought: from his own situation to that of the Philippians ending with a look ahead that places them, somewhat proleptically, in a position with distinctly eschatological colours—they are (or should be) shining like stars in heaven (2:15). The two sections that follow are of a more immediately practical character: a statement (2:19–24) about Paul's future travel plans to the Philippians for Timothy and himself, and a covering-letter statement (2:25–30) about the background to Epaphroditus' travel home to the Philippians. These two sections too fall easily into place on the supposition that Paul is beginning to wind up the letter. But that, of course, is where the problems begin. Paul has much more to say. In 3:2 he embarks on a long warning against certain opponents (3:2–21) followed by renewed exhortation to stand fast (4:1) and renewed paraklesis (4:2–9). To complicate matters even further, he ends with a separate section of thanks (4:10–20) for the money gift that had already been mentioned in 2:25–30. Against this background, the three final verses of farewell greetings (4:21–23) are insufficient to render immediately transparent the overall structure of the letter as we have it.

Here is the observation I promised. It concerns the meaning of 3:1, the verse that stands exactly where the letter structure begins to crack up.[9] Paul says: 'As for the rest, my brothers, rejoice in the Lord. To write the same to you (once more) gives me no cause for hesitation, and for you it provides security against stumbling.'[10] The latter half of this (3:1b) is clearly meant as a conventional half-apology for a piece of repetition of something that has already been said. Where does this repetition occur? The obvious answer is: in the immediately preceding injunction to rejoice (3:1a). For this directly repeats 2:18.[11] Moreover, when Paul later repeats this injunction (4:4), he even adds this: 'I will say it again: rejoice!' But is Paul only apologizing for repeating this one word? Could it be that his apology in 3:1b is also meant as an apology for a far more substantial piece of repetition that he is now going to *embark* upon? That is the possibility we should explore.[12]

There are in fact some quite noteworthy—and well-known—repetitions in 3:2 ff.[13] The basic one is this: (i) 3:2–21 begins from Paul (3:4–14), moves on to the Philippians (3:14 ff) and ends with an eschatological look ahead (3:20–21). In this it repeats the basic structure just given of 1:12–2:18 as a whole. 3:4–14 corresponds with 1:12–26 and 3:14 ff with 1:27–2:18, ending (2:15) in the eschatological look ahead that is then repeated in 3:20–21. (ii) In his remarks about the opponents in 3:18–19 there is repetition too when Paul speaks (3:19 and 1:28) of their prospective 'destruction' (*apōleia*) as opposed to the Philippians' 'salvation' (*sōtēria*, cf. 3:20).[14] (iii) Further, in 1:21 Paul states that for himself dying (namely with Christ) would be a 'gain' (*kerdos*). The same (quite unusual) term of course plays an important role in his account in 3:7–8 of his own call. And there is more: (iv) 4:1 repeats the exhortation to steadfastness from 1:27, and (v) 4:2 turns to paraklesis like 2:2 did. All in all, it appears that Philippians is made up of two closely comparable portions of text: 1:12–2:18 and 3:2–4:9, where the latter should be understood as a repetition of the former, a repetition, moreover, that Paul himself announces.[15]

Can we also make structural sense of 4:10 ff? First, by beginning with an emphatic 'I rejoiced' (*Echarēn*) it is obviously tied closely in with what precedes (4:4). Also, it fits well with Paul's reference to himself as a model in the immediately preceding verse (4:9). The Philippians should now do what they have previously seen in him (4:9). Similarly, just as he now rejoices (4:10), they too should rejoice (as he has stated so many times). Thus if we take 3:2–4:9 to repeat 1:12–2:18, we may see 4:10 ff as taking up thematically 2:25–30 immediately before the repetition—but also as being closely connected with 4:9. Viewed in this way, 4:10–20 provides a fitting conclusion to the letter. Paul does not now dwell on the risks, suffering and near-death that Epaphroditus underwent when he brought him (what was lacking in, cf. 2:30)[16] their gift to him, or on his own suffering in that context (2:25–30). Instead, he expresses the joy he gets from seeing their gift (when it did arrive, cf. 4:10–11)[17] as a token of the Philippians' own attitude towards him. He is himself now 'full' through their intervention (4:18) and he is confident that 'his' God will eventually make *them* 'full' in return (4:19). Thus Paul concludes the letter with a happy promise on an upbeat note.

According to this proposal the basic structure of Philippians is that of two halves that mirror one another with 3:1 acting as pivot.[18] I have not argued properly for the proposal. In particular, is there any indication that we should understand Paul's reference to 'writing the same' in 3:1b more broadly—and in a forward-looking manner too—than as referring to the mere repetition of his exhortation to rejoice? I do not intend to argue the case in detail here. But in response to the question just raised it is at least worth pointing out the following: (i) Paul speaks of 'writing the same *things*' in the plural, not just the same thing.[19] (ii) 3:1b seems a very long apology for merely repeating the one-word exhortation to rejoice. (iii) While one *might* perhaps just take it like that, the effect would be to make the transition from 3:1 to 3:2 exceedingly abrupt, indeed almost wholly inexplicable, no matter whether one ascribes this to Paul himself *or to a redactor*. It is far more natural to take 3:1 as a whole to *introduce* what follows.[20] But in that case 'writing the same things' will not refer merely to the exhortation to rejoice.

More considerations might be adduced[21] and more counter-observations made. But let this suffice here. Let it just be noted that if the proposal is accepted, it should end all further discussion of the letter's overall structure and of its unity. If in 3:1 Paul himself *announces* that he will now proceed to repeat more extensively what he has already said, it becomes a futile exercise to go on asking about the letter's unity. Personally I accept this argument, but the following discussion will not rely on it in detail.

For the point is this. Even if the proposal be accepted, that does not in the least close all larger issues of interpretation concerning the thought structure of the letter. It is one thing to see an overall structure that makes sense at the uppermost level of the letter. It is quite another to be able to fit the many smaller motifs that constitute the texture of the letter (for example suffering, joy, unanimity, partnership and so forth) together and see them as having each their specific place in some comprehensive, coherent and indeed 'underlying' scheme. Do we know that there *must* be such a scheme? No. Paul might in principle have wanted to do nothing more in the letter than first to describe his own situation, then turn to the Philippians, then provide some exhortation of them, then bring in the figure of Christ and so forth. If a reader thinks that this is all there is to the letter, one cannot *prove* him or her wrong.

In actual fact, however, this will hardly do. Not even the most cursory reading can fail to note how keen Paul is on bringing out *intrinsic connections* between all the things he says, on tying them together in a tightly woven web of meaning. Scholars have generally realized this and they have therefore aimed to get at what I called an underlying scheme by trying to identify a single overarching theme of the letter. Often this search has been combined with asking about Paul's direct and immediate aim or aims in writing the letter. But we know that this search is likely to be in vain. Similarly, there is little agreement on any specific formulation of a single overarching theme. The problem seems to be this: either a scholar will fix on a fairly restricted motif as *the* theme of the letter—but then too many things will be left out; or else the scholar will include many specific motifs—then the problem becomes that of seeing how they on their side are to be combined; a final possibility is to fix on a single, specific, but very general motif (like 'the gospel'), which may hopefully cover everything else—but that only leaves the scholar with the further task of spelling out exactly how it does cover all the rest.

There are two ways out of this quandary. One is to let oneself be influenced by modern, literary and narrative perspectives and try to develop a sort of *story* that will allow the many motifs in the letter to be fitted in at various points.[22] This approach has several advantages. First, a whole, comprehensive story seems admirably suited to give coherence to a large number of individual motifs. Second, the approach intuitively seems to fit the text itself well. Right from the beginning (1:5–6) Paul brings out a very strong temporal framework for the letter when he speaks of the Philippians' sharing in the gospel 'from the first day' (presumably of their call) 'until now' and further on 'until the day of Christ Jesus'. What a story of this kind will express is the comprehensive worldview of the Christ-believing form of life in its dynamic aspect: once–now–then.

Seen from my perspective, however, this approach will have the drawback of staying too closely with Paul's own vocabulary. We need to face the fact that such an account will not describe the Christ-believing form of life sufficiently from the outside in a vocabulary that makes direct sense to us. For one thing, taken literally such a temporal story is just wrong: no 'then' in the immediate future materialized in the way this was conceived by Paul. For another thing, the temporal story is tied far too closely to a spatial understanding of the *kosmos* that we cannot share. Constructing a story on Paul's behalf is not of course wrong. Indeed it might be wholly apposite if only one could keep securely in mind that whereas for Paul and (presumably) his addressees it was a story that tells wholly realistically of facts about the world, it cannot be this for us. For us it can at most be a story of the kind that is analysed in those distinctly literary approaches to the New Testament texts. As long as this distinction is kept clearly in mind one should have no quarrel with the first approach.

But then one may just as well take the whole step outside Paul's own manner of thinking. The other way out of the quandary aims to do just that. It does it by, as it were, freezing the dynamic story into a single model devoid of its dependence on time and space, and by situating the various motifs voiced throughout the letter within such a model. The model will have its dynamic aspect too, but only intrinsically and in the abstract. The basic difference between the two approaches is between imaginatively entering the world-view that Paul is articulating—and watching it from the outside. The former operation will place the on-looker, who tends to become a quasi-participant, at a specific point of time in the story, namely at point *now* as seen from *Paul's* perspective. The latter will leave him or her where they actually are, in the modern present.

This sets our task: first to take stock of the many different motifs that Paul broaches throughout the letter, and then to see whether they can be fitted into a model that holds the web of meaning together in the second way indicated. It is the latter half of this task that calls for interpretation proper. The aim is to articulate the coherent picture of the Christ-believing form of life that one intuitively feels underlies the many things Paul says and does in his text, to lay bare the logic of that form of life, but doing it from the outside in the manner I have suggested. Here as always the criterion of success will be whether as a result of working on the text along such lines the interpreter obtains a sense of having acquired a more coherent, more comprehensive and indeed, a deeper understanding of the text.

A plethora of motifs

In order to bring out more concretely the need for this kind of logical analysis, we must engage in the somewhat laborious task of lining up some of the major motifs that make their appearance in various parts of the letter. We shall mention them as they turn up for the first time in the thanksgiving section but also include references to their later appearances. It will unfortunately be insufficient just to mention the relevant verses. In order to be able later to situate each motif in relation to the other motifs, we need to remind ourselves of the near context in which each motif shows up.

A major motif is introduced in 1:4: that of joy (*chara*), in this case

Paul's joyful prayer on behalf of the Philippians. In 1:18 Paul's joy is based on his conviction that he will overcome his emprisonment through the Philippians' prayer and their supplying the spirit of Christ Jesus. 1:25 speaks of the Philippians' joy in the faith and combines it with the idea of their progression (*prokopē*) in the faith. In 2:2 Paul urges them to fill up his own joy by their attitude to him and to one another. In 2:17 he states his joy, which he wishes to share with them, in spite of being faced with the prospect of dying. And in 2:18, as we know, he exhorts the Philippians to feel joy in the same way and to feel it together with Paul. Their joy is also part of his motivation for sending back Epaphroditus to them (2:28). Indeed, as he insists (3:1), they must rejoice in the Lord. If they stand fast in the Lord, they will be Paul's joy and crown of victory (4:1). They must themselves always rejoice in the Lord (4:4). And he repeats it: rejoice! Finally, Paul himself rejoiced (4:10) when they shared with him in his suffering (4:14). We may conclude, provisionally and unsurprisingly, that Philippians is shot through with references to joy. It is a 'letter of joy'! We may also note how Paul moves back and forth between speaking of his own joy and that of the Philippians, and indeed of their shared joy. We should ask: Exactly how do these various references to joy hang together both with one another and with the other motifs that come up in this context? Can we identify a set of ideas that describes a form of life within which this kind of multi-faceted joy makes sense?[23]

The motif of suffering and affliction is also brought in quite early when Paul refers to his 'chains' (*desmoi*, 1:7, cf. 1:13, 14, 17).[24] Again we should note the exact context for Paul's talk about suffering and affliction.[25] His chains are connected with his present task of 'defending' (*apologia*) the gospel (1:7, 16), a task that he expects to fulfil in such a way that he will not be brought to shame but will instead behave with all frankness (of speech and presumably also action) and so extol Christ in his own body, through life or through death (1:20). This connects the motif of affliction with Paul himself and indeed situates it near the centre of Paul's own personal experience of Christ. But there are also connections with the other parties within Paul's letter horizon. The whole section 1:12–26 is relevant here. Paul's affliction (*thlipsis*, 1:17) is partly due to internal opposition among Christ-believers in Ephesus (1:14–18), partly to his present imprisonment, that is, to external opposition. With regard to the latter he speculates about his chances and what he would himself prefer (to live on or to die and be with Christ), but ends on a note of conviction that he will survive—for the sake of *the Philippians* (1:18–26). The same idea is given striking expression in 2:16–17. It does not matter, says Paul, whether he should be poured out as a drink-offering in making his provision for bringing the Philippians' faith as an offering to God! External affliction is also mentioned in 1:28–30. Here it is first that of the Philippians (1:28–29), but Paul then parallels their present suffering with his own earlier suffering when he was with them and his present suffering in prison (1:30). Finally, suffering is also the theme of his remarks about Timothy and Epaphroditus. In the case of Timothy, the issue is internal suffering on Paul's part: apart from Timothy, there is nobody in Paul's entourage who genuinely cares for the Philippians (2:20); 'for they all seek their own and not that of Jesus Christ' (2:21). In the case of Epaphroditus (2:25–30), it is a matter of illness and risk-taking on Epaphroditus' part which has generated suffering among both Paul and the Philippians, a suffering which should now, as we know, be exchanged for joy.

It is noteworthy that the motif of suffering is not emphasized in chapters 3 and 4.[26] Here Paul rather paints a picture of opposition that has been conquered. He does speak of 'knowing . . . the partnership with the sufferings of Christ' and of 'being shaped together with him in his death' (3:10). As we know, this partly repeats motifs already broached in 1:12–26. But here in chapter 3 it is not so much the suffering itself that is in focus. Rather, the suffering with Christ is to be understood as an entry into the resurrection (3:11, 12–14) and the future experience of being gathered up with Christ on his return (3:20–21). Similarly, when he refers to his occasional lack of material means (4:12), Paul's aim is to bring out that he is himself precisely *above* being afflicted by it: he is 'self-sufficient' (*autarkēs*, 4:11, cf. 4:13, 17). We should ask: What is the role of emphasizing the suffering of all involved in the first letter-half? And why does Paul end on a note that is rather more triumphant?

Another major motif is also introduced very early on (1:5): that of partnership (*koinōnia*). At first the reference is to the Philippians' partnership (presumably with Paul) with regard to the gospel. A few verses later (1:7) it is to their partnership (and here explicitly with Paul) in grace, which they have shown when he was in prison and working to defend and secure the gospel. In the paraklesis that begins chapter 2, it is a partnership (and again clearly with Paul) in the spirit (2:1, cf. 1:19). In 3:10, by contrast, it is Paul's own partnership with the sufferings of Christ —and in 4:14 the Philippians' partnership with Paul in *his* affliction, a partnership with a very specific, pecuniary character (4:16).[27] In addition to these uses of the *koinōnia* root, there are many other expressions of partnership, e.g. those playing on the prefix *syn-* (together with). Some of these will concern us later. What matters here is only to note the motif

itself and its immediate ramifications. One thing at least is already striking: the extent to which the motif of partnership takes up and formulates
the idea of *sharing* in joy and affliction that we noted in connection with
those motifs. Can we discover a deeper logic behind these expressions of
actual and enjoined experiences on the part of Paul himself and his
addressees?

Then there is a quite different motif, which plays a major role in the
thanksgiving section: the dynamic idea of progression towards a goal.
We have already noted 1:5–6 where Paul speaks of the 'first day' of the
Philippians' call (cf. 3:14 for the notion of call, *klēsis*), of the period
between then and now and also of the future span between now and 'the
day of Jesus Christ'. In 1:9–11 this span is in view too when Paul prays
that the Philippians' love may grow in insight so that they may be flawless
and without blame 'toward' (*eis*) the day of Christ. Later (1:25) Paul
employs the technical Stoic term of progression (*prokopē*) for what he
has in mind.[28] In 2:12 the idea is that the Philippians must 'work with
fear and trembling on their own salvation [*sōtēria*]'—again in order that
they may be blameless and faultless (2:15) ... on the day of Christ (2:16).
Finally, in 3:12–16 Paul describes his own striving to grasp the goal,
which he does not himself claim to have grasped. The goal (*skopos*) is
the prize (*brabeion*) of God's upward call in Christ Jesus. And Paul clearly
recognizes that there may be differences among Christ-believers with
regard to how far each has gone on the road towards that goal. We thus
have joy, suffering, partnership and progression towards a goal: exactly
how do these various motifs hang together?

What Paul means by the 'upward' call is made clear a little later when
he speaks of the 'citizen body' (*politeuma*)[29] of Christ-believers as being
in heaven, from where their saviour (*sōtēr*), the Lord Jesus Christ, will
come (3:20) and to which he will bring them back (3:21). Clearly, the
temporal line *once–now–then* has a very definite end point, which Paul
understands in wholly realistic spatial terms as lying in another, heavenly
world. Thus the motif of dynamic progression towards a goal is supplemented by that of the goal itself, 'the day of Christ'. What falls under
this term is probably (i) the return of Christ from above (3:20), (ii) Christ-
believers being brought to heaven by Christ once he has changed their
lowly bodies into a shape that corresponds with his own exalted body
(3:21), (iii) and finally, Christ-believers standing (hopefully) unstained
and blameless before the tribunal of Christ and God (1:10, 2:15–16).
There is an important set of (partly traditional theological) problems
here: What is the logical relationship between progression (*prokopē*)
and salvation (*sōtēria*)? Between the doings of the Philippians here on

earth and that of Christ and God? Between growing in faith, love and insight and being in the heavenly state? A subsidiary motif is just voiced at the end of the thanksgiving section: the Philippians should be 'filled with the fruit of righteousness' (1:11). This undoubtedly points forward to Paul's contrast in 3:6–9 between righteousness by the law and righteousness through Christ faith. How does that motif cohere with the rest, that is, with joy, suffering, partnership and progression towards the goal of the day of Christ?

A further motif is introduced in 1:8 when Paul says that he is longing for the Philippians 'with the yearning (*splanchna*) of Christ Jesus'. The motif that is broached here crops up all through the letter in a range of guises. One version is the idea of Paul himself as (in some sense isomorphic with) Christ. At least, Paul has Christ's own yearning. Also, Christ will be extolled in Paul's own body (1:20). And living 'is for me Christ' (1:21), whatever that exactly means. Further, the Philippians' pride or joy will hopefully grow 'in Christ Jesus in me' through Paul's renewed presence with them (1:26). More generally, Paul clearly describes himself and his own possible fate (1:18–26, 2:17) on the model of Christ's (2:6–11) and even plays on his own absence and presence with the Philippians in the light of the same model (1:26–27, 2:12). In his more triumphant mood too he places himself more or less directly in the role of the risen Christ (4:18–19). The other version of the motif is that of Christ himself as a model for the Philippians. Here the Christ 'hymn' is of course relevant (cf. 2:5).

If we put the two versions together, what we get is the motif that is perhaps the most powerful one that Paul employs in the letter, that of *Paul modelling Christ to the Philippians*, that is, Paul himself being modelled *on* Christ *and* acting in that function as a model *for* the Philippians.[30] The most explicit formulations of this motif are these: (i) the reference to the Philippians' present suffering, which is the same as Paul's own earlier suffering—and also as his present one (1:29–30), which he has just described (1:18–26) on the model of Christ; (ii) Christ (2:6–11) as a model for the Philippians (2:5)—but with Paul himself as an intermediary (2:12) who himself wears the colours of the suffering Christ (2:17); (iii) finally, and most importantly, the description of Paul's own call (3:4–11), which made him 'symmorphic' with Christ in his death (3:10), of his own striving upwards for the prize of that call in Christ Jesus (3:14) corresponding to the fact that he has himself been grasped by Christ (3:12), and his concluding exhortation that the Philippians imitate him *together with* himself, presumably in a shared striving upwards.

Joy, suffering, partnership, progression, an eschatological goal, righteousness, identity with Christ and Christ as model: these are some of the
most important overlapping motifs that make their appearance throughout the letter. I have recalled them here in all their concreteness. But how
do they hang together? We can almost immediately see that were one to
fit them into a coherent picture that would directly reflect Paul's own
formulation of them, the best candidate would be a story that tells of
experiences Paul and the Philippians have had and a set of wholly realistic
expectations about different times and places. But is it also possible to
take one step further back and discover a different kind of underlying
logic behind them? Or must we stay at Paul's own level of discourse,
sensing a kind of unity to what by our lights appears as a colourful
variety of motifs and metaphors, but unable to formulate that unity in a
less picturesque vocabulary that is directly accessible to us? It is here the
task of interpretation must begin.

Paul himself: the call

In the rest of this and the next chapter I propose to show how a flexible,
philosophically enlightened use of the I→X→S-model in its Stoic shape
may help to answer this question. Let us first forget about Paul's
addressees, the Philippians, and apply the model only to what he says of
himself. Three motifs should engage us here, two of which we have only
touched upon briefly: Paul's call, his joy (*chara*) and his self-sufficiency
(*autarkeia*).

It will be helpful to begin from the account Paul gives in 3:4–14 of his
call. This account may be developed in such a way that it gives us a basic
feature in the underlying logical structure of Paul's thought throughout
the letter. It is no problem that the passage comes so relatively late in the
letter. For its content has been broached in different ways already earlier
in remarks about Paul himself (1:12–26) and about Christ (2:5–11). As
described in 3:4–14, the essence of Paul's call is that he has turned his
back on and left behind those values which before his encounter with
Christ he considered the most important ones. They now belong to the
flesh (*sarx*, 3:3–8), which Paul contrasts with the spirit (3:3). They *were*
forms of 'gain' (*kerdē*, 3:7), but Paul now considers them so many forms
of 'loss' (*zēmia*, 3:7–8). He even considers them refuse (*skybala*) 'in order
that' he may 'gain' Christ and be 'found in' him (3:8–9). Here we have
another load of metaphors. What is Paul talking about? Can we bring
this out in a less picturesque and better defined conceptual vocabulary?

An obvious answer is to say that he is describing a change in his perception of his own identity, of who he, Paul, is. The kind of self-identification that is involved here is a thoroughly normative one. It is not merely a case of taking note, as it were from the outside, of what properties one may ascribe to oneself, but of assigning a value to the properties one takes oneself to have. Identification of what one values serves to identify 'who one is' as seen from within, the kind of being one *wishes* to be. Paul did not, of course, stop to be 'circumcised on the eighth day, an Israelite by birth' etc. (3:5–6). But he stopped, so he says, ascribing any value whatever to those properties (3:7–8). Indeed, he stopped ascribing any value to 'himself'. Instead, he came to wish that he might himself be 'found in' Christ (3:9). This last twist only confirms what he has said in the immediately preceding verses. If he no longer ascribes any value to those earlier highly valued properties that continued to be his (the most valuable a Jew would normally aspire to), then he 'himself'—understood as the individual who defines himself by those properties—no longer matters to him. Instead, he now finds his normative identity outside himself, in Christ. He has become a 'Christ person'.

This Pauline account of a case of personal reidentification—a complete change in his perception of 'who he himself is' (normatively understood)—is closely similar to the change of self-understanding that goes into the Stoic account of acquiring the proper grasp of the good. It goes without saying that the 'figure' that functions as a target in either case is in itself widely different: in Paul it is Christ, in Stoicism reason. But the starting and end points of the change are closely similar. The starting point is the immediate, and probably natural, self-identification of an individual human being, which consists in an intricate interplay between two things: (*a*) the subjective sense of being 'oneself' (a sense which in the Stoic theory, as we saw, includes self-love) and (*b*) seeing that self ('oneself') as being defined by one's striving to obtain so-called natural goods for oneself, including the socially recognized ones, those representing the ordinary values within society. *I am* the person who strives to obtain for myself this or the other natural and social good. That kind of self-identification grounds what we may call the subjective perspective on the world. But the end point of the change is also similar in that it is derived from something that is taken to have an external or objective status in relation to the individual. Christ is obviously such a thing. But so is reason, on the Stoic understanding. The rise to a rational understanding is precisely a rise to an objective perspective which decisively relativizes the earlier, subjective perspective. In identifying with Christ *or* with reason, one comes to look 'down upon' one's previous individual self 'from above'.[31] That is, one loses one's grip on the values that previously went into one's self-understanding as reflected in the subjective perspective on the world. One now sees oneself not as that particular person who strives for natural and socially recognized goods for him- or herself, but as a person characterized first and foremost by having a share in the external, objective entity: as a Christ person or a rational being.

Thus the change described by Paul in these verses is so close to the one found in the Stoic theory that we may safely claim to be able to capture Paul's account by referring it to the I→X part of the I→X→S-model on its specifically Stoic interpretation. Paul is developing a *logic of the call* in terms that translate directly into those of normative self-identification as we know this from the I→X→S-model on its Stoic interpretation.

Against this background we can also see the stark character of the Stoic and Pauline idea of a change that leaves the very powerful subjective perspective completely behind. What they are saying is that this specific perspective is given up altogether at the other pole, when a person sees him- or herself at the X-pole of the model, as belonging to Christ or reason. Then the merely subjective 'I' of the I-pole no longer exists. It has been put out of action, and the person (*another* 'I'!) now finds him- or herself as it were *outside* (or 'above') him- or herself.

How are we in fact to understand this? *Can* the subjective perspective at all be left behind? If there is still a person left who can say '*I* am a Christ person', then the subjective perspective has not, it appears, been totally eradicated. So how should we conceive of the new state? We shall return to this question in the next chapter in connection with Gal 2:19–20. Here let it just be said that it is a problem that arises for Paul no less than the Stoics. Similarly, as we shall see, it is solved in the same way by both.

It is noteworthy how emphatically Paul speaks in the present passage of this transfer, for instance in 3:8 when he refers to the '*overpowering* quality of knowing Christ Jesus my Lord' (*to hyperechon tēs gnōseōs*). 'Christ Jesus as Lord' is the content of the universal confession that Paul envisages at the end of the hymn (2:11). It also probably constitutes the content of the 'word of life' (*logos zōēs*) that he urges the Philippians to embrace (2:16) when they shine like stars in the firmament (2:15). In 3:8, however, it has an altogether more personal character. Here it is Christ Jesus *my* Lord, a person whom Paul has encountered in an act of 'knowing' that has the character of knowledge by direct acquaintance: a 'takeover' (cf. 3:12: 'I was grasped or taken over [*katelēmphthēn*] by Christ').[32] How are we to understand and handle such a notion? Does it go against the close similarity with Stoicism that we have seen? Not in the least. There is no reason to deny that Paul is speaking of a personal experience. On the contrary, there is every reason to insist on it. In view of other passages in the letters (e.g. Gal 1:16; 2 Cor 4:6), it is even likely that he is referring to some kind of direct vision. But his interest in recounting this experience here is not just 'personal' or 'psychological' as if he were merely telling about his own experience to whoever might be interested in *that*. Rather, he is using his own case as a model for a kind of normative change and transfer that has universal application (as he claims): the change from a normative self-understanding tied to ordinary natural and social goods to be acquired by the individual for *him- or herself*—to one that, as it were, places the individual *outside* him- or herself. Such a change apparently requires that one is, as it were, 'struck' by something which one experiences as having an 'overpowering' character in relation to one's previous self. But that is not at all special to Paul. The Stoics would have agreed.[33]

It fits very closely with the Stoic link that Paul talks in explicitly cognitive terms of *knowing* Christ Jesus my Lord. As we saw in the last chapter, in Stoicism too the move from I to X was wholly a cognitive matter of coming to see oneself (normatively) as a rational being and to understand the specific relation to the world that follows from this. It goes without saying that the two forms of 'knowing' are not identical. In Stoicism it is 'propositional knowledge', knowledge *that*,[34] whereas, as we saw, in Paul it is—so far—one of knowledge 'by acquaintance'. Also, nothing prevents us from stressing the revealed character of the kind of knowledge that Paul speaks of. It remains true, however, that in both cases the change is a cognitive one and one in normative self-identification.

With such an understanding of Paul's account of his own call, the other passages in the letter in which he states his identification with Christ fall easily into line. For instance, when Paul claims to be certain that 'Christ will be extolled in his body' (1:20) and supports this by saying that to him 'living is Christ and dying is a gain' (1:21), the reason is that he has stopped ascribing any value whatever to his body understood as something that is peculiarly his own. Paul's body, his whole individual being has been (normatively) taken over by Christ. No property that belongs to him as a bodily individual being has any value to him when it does not serve the cause of Christ. As for Christ, he of course differs from Paul taken as the bodily individual that Paul is (and remains). Thus Paul is very clearly talking of a radical form of normative self-identification, of normatively 'locating' himself in something outside himself. The bodily individual remains objectively there. Subjectively, however, it has been completely transcended. Again this translates immediately into Stoicism, namely into the complex relationship that the Stoic sage will have to his body and his previous self. Moreover, the specific relationship between the self as placed outside the individual bodily being and the self *as* that being is one that was *only* developed to this degree in Stoicism.

So far we have established what will turn out to be a central element in the logical scheme we have been looking for. We have done this by analysing Paul's account in 3:4–14 of his call in the light of the I→X→S-model in its Stoic form. The claim has been that this particular model clarifies conceptually what Paul has stated in his own more metaphorical way. To the extent that we have succeeded in genuinely illuminating the latter by means of the former, we may also claim to have established an I→X line in an underlying *Pauline* scheme. In the rest of this chapter we shall attempt to fill this particular line in further.

Paul himself: joy and suffering

There is another passage in the letter that connects closely with Paul's self-identification with Christ but also adds our next motif, that of joy. We now move back—across the pivotal verse 3:1—from the second letter-half to the first, where we saw the motif of joy to be most thoroughly developed. In 2:17, where Paul entertains the possibility that he may himself be 'spent as a drink-offering' for the benefit of the Philippians, he clearly identifies with Christ and says that his own individual being does not matter at all. The only thing that matters is that he himself does the job that was also Christ's. And in that he rejoices. This allows us to connect Paul's use of the notion of joy with the I→X→S-model Stoically understood. In Stoicism, as we know, joy was a name for the attitude of positive affirmation that follows from having undergone the change from taking what matters to be one's own, subjective fate—as an individual and with regard to ordinary values—to taking it rather to be one's fate or individual situation as seen in the objectifying light thrown on it from above (in this case, the light of reason). Apparently Paul has the same idea. In other words, Pauline joy goes with being at the X-pole as we have established that for Paul. But in Paul joy is also closely connected with yet another of our motifs, that of suffering. That motif too we saw to be most thoroughly developed in the first letter-half. Joy is the proper *response* to suffering. So how does that motif fit in? How does it hang together with the other two?

Here is the answer. Joy is the emotional side of one's new normative self-identification as a being who is primarily, indeed exclusively, defined as one who belongs to Christ at the X-pole (the result of the call). It is the emotional affirmation *of* that self-identification. But it is this in response to suffering. The joyful response is generated by one's perception that there is a person who is suffering, namely oneself (the I at the I-pole), but that this person is *not* the being that one oneself centrally is. Joy contains an implicit claim that what *would* have been a case of suffering *and nothing but that* (to oneself as belonging at the I-pole) is in fact decisively relativized by that 'overpowering quality of knowing Christ Jesus my Lord'. This reading makes striking sense of Paul's initially somewhat bewildering claims about feeling joy and pain at the same time (e.g. 1:17–18), and sometimes almost even joy *at* being pained (e.g. 2:17). It does it by drawing directly on the way the Stoics had thought through the relationship between placing the self 'outside' the ordinary world—to which one nevertheless belongs—and being in that world.

It is interesting to speculate whether in spite of the similarity with Stoicism there remains a difference of logic in Paul's handling of joy compared with the Stoic one. In Stoicism one finds nothing but joy in the sage. The actual experience of pain (*lypē*) is excluded. Paul, by contrast, distinctly suffers. Indeed, he may speak of himself as having suffered 'pain upon pain' (*lypē epi lypēn*, 2:27), even though God has so far saved him from the final *coup de grâce* and may hopefully leave him with *less* pain (*alypoteros*, 2:28). If there is a difference here, one might even propose to explain it by pointing out that the Stoic system is intended to formulate an attitude that is and remains an attitude to the present world. It is all a matter of applying different perspectives on the present world. But is Paul not different? Is his view not that pain goes with the present world but joy with an altogether different one, the one to which Christ-believers already belong—though somewhat proleptically—and to which they will eventually—and finally—depart? To put the point differently, do we not here find a reflex of the crucial difference between the 'static' Stoic world-view and the essentially 'dynamic', forward-looking Pauline one?

Such a distinction will hardly do. When Paul speaks of his pain and affliction, he is certainly referring to his experiences with the present world. But the same in fact holds for his talk about joy. For him to 'live', in the sense of living *in* the *present* world, *is* Christ (1:21). And that is what makes him rejoice. It is certainly true too that this joy has its basis outside the present world, in the heavenly world where Christ resides and to which Paul wishes to go. But his joy expresses, as it were, the influx *from* that world *into* the present one. It is a joy that *reflects* the present painful affliction but then turns it into something quite different: an occasion for joy due to one's sense of belonging elsewhere *now*.

What then about the fact that Paul does experience pain (cf. the references above)? Does this distinguish the Stoic view from Paul's? Or should we just say that Paul has not (yet?) achieved Stoic wisdom? However, note the context. Paul's pain is, as it were, a rhetorical one, one that has first and foremost to do with his relationship with his addressees (cf. for instance 2:19 and 28). When he does not have their troublesome situation directly in mind, but is rather speaking of his own fate (as in 1:12–26 or 2:17), he is anything but pained. On the contrary, should he even be spent as a drink-offering on their behalf, he rejoices (2:17)! When he is on his own, Paul is wholly like the Stoic sage.[35]

We may conclude as follows on the call, joy and suffering. Paul's talk of joy logically presupposes the earlier motif of his normative self-identification with Christ, outside the ordinary normativity that goes with the present world. In the letter to the Philippians, that motif was spelled out with full force only in the second letter-half, in 3:4 ff. But it has been adumbrated already in 1:20–21—in the middle of the joy section of chapter 1 (1:18–26)—with sufficient clarity to render the connection between the two motifs perspicuous. *Because* Paul identifies with Christ, *therefore* he may also rejoice when faced with the tribulations of the present world. His new self-identification has brought him from I to X on the I→X line, and being now at X he may look down with joy on everything that happens to him as a being who physically, of course, remains at the I-level—but only physically. Joy, as I said, is the emotional side of being at X, but it relates to what happens to the person at the I-level.

Paul himself: otherworldliness, self-sufficiency and a summary

I began discussing Paul's account of his call in 3:4–14 and then turned to the motifs of joy and suffering as present mainly in chapters 1–2. In terms of the I→X→S-model the first motif is about I→X, the two others rather about X→I. That, of course, was why I began from chapter 3: we needed to have I→X before we could introduce X→I. Now, however, we can reverse the sequence in order to do justice to the fact that Paul himself does begin from X→I. What does this show us about the letter? In particular, why has Paul chosen to spell out the I→X line only relatively late, after the pivotal announcement of repetition in 3:1?

The I→X→S-model itself helps us to find the answer. The first letter-half is mainly concerned with how to handle the present world, which gives rise to suffering, in the light of one's sense of belonging in the other world, but *focusing* on life in the present one, in short X→I. We do not quite know to what extent Paul is here reflecting the actual situation of the Philippians. 1:27–30 suggests that, to some extent at least, he is. But there can be no doubt that he has also rhetorically magnified the motif of suffering—in himself and in them—in order to be able to impress on his readers that other side of it: joy. Still, the overall theme that he treats in this way is this: how to handle the *present* world when one *really* belongs elsewhere. In other words, his theme is the interplay *at the I-level* between an emotional attitude based in a sense of belonging at the X-level and a straightforward I-level-based perception of the world. His gaze is directed towards the present world, his own present situation and that of the Philippians.

In the second letter-half, by contrast, Paul to some extent leaves behind life in the present world. Here the general drift is towards pointing very strongly in the direction of the other world. Now the move is clearly from the I-level to the X-level, the move which we saw Paul to spell out in 3:4–11. Paul even adds a special section (3:12–16) that develops how he is himself pushing ardently forward (*diōkein* in 3:12 and 14), forgetting what lies behind and stretching out towards what lies in front (3:13): the goal that consists in the prize of God's upward call in Christ Jesus (3:14). His aim with this section is clearly to make the Philippians follow the same course (3:15 ff). Finally, he produces his enticing sketch of the heavenly homeland (*politeuma*) where Christ-believers will live in glory (3:20–21). The mention of present-world opponents (3:2–3, 18–19) only serves to underscore this direction of the argument, since no matter to what extent Paul aimed to warn directly against them, he also seems to have treated them as a springboard for elaborating the image of that *other* world to which Christ-believers belong—in contrast with the opponents, whose final end will rather be destruction (3:19).

It is true that he goes immediately on to give advice (4:5–9) that reflects the fact that his Christ-believers do live in the present world (cf. especially 4:5a and 8). But even here the text is shot through with forward-looking references—to the co-workers whose names are written in 'the book of life' (4:3), to the Lord whose nearness (4:5b) means that the Philippians need not worry about anything but may direct their prayers and petitions to God with complete confidence (4:6), finally to that God himself who is one of (eschatological) peace (4:7, 9). Even Paul's exhortation in 4:1 to steadfastness should be understood within this strongly forward-looking perspective. First, it is said to *follow* directly (cf. *hōste*) on his celebration of the eschatological future in the immediately preceding verses. Second, it is an exhortation to stand fast in the Lord 'in that way' (*houtōs*), meaning presumably in the way Paul has described for them in 3:4–21. And third, Paul addresses the Philippians as his joy and 'crown of victory' (*stephanos*), which immediately brings in the idea of the day of Christ (cf. 2:16) when Paul may hopefully boast of them to the Lord and put their presence in the heavenly *politeuma* down as his own claim to victory.

We should conclude that there is a marked, but still relative difference and development between the two letter-halves: from concern with *this* world to directedness towards the *other* world. Moreover, there is a letter-writing strategy here which is obviously highly effective rhetorically and which makes immediate sense—once one has seen it. But—and this is the point—it has taken the I→X→S-model to *make* us see it.[36]

Then we can also see how 4:10–20 fits into Paul's line, in particular Paul's reference to his self-sufficiency (*autarkeia*, 4:11–13). This section has received much attention from scholars over the last decade, not least in readings of the letter that focus on the topic of friendship.[37] Scholars have emphasized the heavy use of commercial language (4:15, 17–18) and they have attempted to situate a great deal of the specific motifs that go into Paul's text under the topic of friendship (in 4:10–12, 14–19).[38] What kind of partnership should we reckon with for Paul and the Philippians? And what was their mutual relationship considered as friends? I have already expressed my doubt that we shall ever be able to arrive at any very precise answers to these questions that will also be generally persuasive. What we can see is that Paul is intent on doing two things: to thank and give praise to the Philippians in a manner that will be gratifying to them[39]—and also to reserve a position of independence for himself. The first line is clearly in evidence in 4:10. Paul rejoices greatly that they have 'bloomed with respect to their concern for him'.[40] And even though there had apparently been some delay (cf. *ēdē pote*, 'now at last'),[41] he hastens to add (at the end of the verse) that they did have that concern earlier—but not the opportunity. In spite of this, however, the intimation remains that the gift did arrive somewhat late. Also, it is at least noteworthy that Paul's great joy is 'in the Lord'. By this phrase he may be pointing forward to what will be his general line in the section as a whole: that even though the Philippians did well in sending the gift and even though Paul rejoiced in getting it, the reason was not that he, Paul, stood in any special need of it.

That idea constitutes the second line. 4:11: when Paul rejoices in the gift (4:10), it is *not*, as he hastens to add, because he was himself lacking in anything. For he has learned to be self-sufficient (*autarkēs*).

Traditionally, this has been connected with the Stoic notion of *autarkeia*.[42] Recently, however, it has been suggested that a (moderate) Cynic or even Pythagorean understanding of self-sufficiency is more relevant.[43] I am reluctant to see any contrast here. It was Aristotle who placed the concept on the philosophical map when he introduced the term *autarkēs* as a defining property of the final good, which is also happiness (*eudaimonia*).[44] And it does not appear to have changed its meaning even when it became a part of educated vocabulary more broadly conceived. However, what we do see in Stoicism in particular is a further *elaboration* of that *shared* content of the concept: that apart from the something—whatever it may be—that *constitutes* a person's *autarkeia* everything *else* is of no consequence whatever. It is *adiaphoron*, as *the Stoics* and no one else formulated it.

Now that is precisely the idea that Paul uses too. When he states that he has been 'initiated into' richness and poverty and so forth, what he means is that neither thing *matters*. And he himself explains why: he has *strength* (*ischyein*) through the one (presumably, God) who *empowers* him to take up such a stance. Translate that into a less colourful language and it means this. Paul is self-sufficient; his personal situation with regard to material goods is a matter of complete indifference to him; for he has a kind of strength—and why not call it an *inner* strength?[45]—that comes from his sense of belonging *elsewhere*, *with* the one who gives him strength and power. Or again: Paul is self-sufficient, that is, he belongs at the X-pole; whatever may happen to him at the I-pole is of no concern to him; for he is not *alone* at the X-pole: there is somebody there with whom he belongs, and indeed identifies, and who gives him the strength that goes with his sense of belonging there.

We should conclude that it is in fact the Stoic, most sharply developed understanding of self-sufficiency that Paul is drawing on in these verses. We should also note for later use how exceedingly close a connection Paul depicts between himself and God: 'I have strength in every situation through the one [God] who empowers *me*' (4:13)!

Following on from this very strong play on the I→X-line, Paul quickly calls himself back to the first thematic line: praise for the Philippians (4:14). One can easily understand why he needs a strong *plēn* ('nevertheless', 'but still') to bring that change of direction off. Has he not stressed his self-sufficiency 'to such a degree that the value of the gift could be put in question'?[46] His renewed praise, however, is unfeigned and genuine (4:14–16). But curiously, it is once more (4:17) broken off by Paul, who hastens (cf. *ouch hoti* in 4:17 like in 4:11) to add that it is not that he seeks the gift (itself or *for him*self); instead, what he seeks is something that will benefit *them*. Next he does provide a sort of receipt (4:18), but again in a curiously double-sided way. He has received it all, he says, or he has it all more than to the full (*apechein*)—where 'all' reminds one of 'all' those things he has learned to *neglect* (4:12–13); he is 'abundantly rich' (*perisseuein*)—again with a clear reference back to 4:12; indeed, he is 'full up' from having received their gift through the hands of Epaphroditus—but because that gift is well-pleasing to God (*not*, that is, as something that matters directly to *Paul*). In short, Paul seems clearly intent on effecting a 'displacement' of the gift from being of any straightforward concern to *himself*. That aim is finally reached when he states that '*his*' (!) God will repay them (4:19).

In conclusion, Paul is not just being 'positive' to the Philippians. He is out to do something more than fit a point about the self-sufficient virtuous person (himself) into a general, philophronetic celebration of his and the Philippians' friendship. Nor is he just being 'negative'. Again he is out to something more than merely acknowledging their gift in a manner that might, at least, be construed as a piece of rather 'thankless thanks' for their gift.[47] He is doing two things at the same time (not an unusual thing in Paul): thanking and praising the Philippians, drawing them *in*—and placing himself *above* them, at one with 'his' God. It is in order to reach this last aim that he begins to speak of his self-sufficiency—and in a distinctly Stoic way. But then we can also see how this whole section fits into the second letter-half. For what it does is to describe Paul in exactly the same way as he has himself explicitly done it in 3:12–14: as one who pushes ardently forward without (really) looking back—even at the Philippians. Paul's God empowers him to stay securely at the X-pole with his back turned completely on everything 'earthly' (cf. 3:19), everything that may happen to him at the I-level (4:11–13). Still, of course, it was certainly very nice of the Philippians to send their gift, and very beneficial too—to themselves. Paul's God will see to that.

Summarizing, we may reasonably claim that the three initially independent motifs we have discussed—the call, joy and suffering, and self-sufficiency—fit completely into an I→X line of the I→X→S-model on its Stoic interpretation. They do this in Paul's own way and by means of that immensely variegated and in part strongly metaphorical vocabulary which is his. But they also do it in such a way that we are justified in claiming that the I→X→S-model in its Stoic form—though only so far its first half—gives us the best conceptual means of holding together Paul's own vocabulary in a manner that engages directly with them, but also does it from the outside to such an extent that they make immediate sense to *us*. Paul is obviously not speaking of the same *things* as the

Stoics. Where he speaks of Christ, they speak of reason. Where he works with the notion of another world in the most massively concrete sense of this that one can imagine, the Stoics definitely did not. But Paul speaks *of* these things in a manner that is closely similar to the way in which the Stoics spoke of theirs. What binds the two systems together is a shared interest in what we might call the 'anthropology' of either system, what the two different forms of life (different as they evidently are) actually mean for human beings living in the present world—in terms of their normative self-identification and their concomitant attitude towards the present world. In this particular area, the shared interest and the similarity in the ideas through which it is expressed are so extensive that one should allow for the possibility of some (probably indirect) historical influence. But the more important conclusion is that the I→X→S-model on its Stoic interpretation has helped us to fit a number of motifs in Paul's letter into a logical structure that we may reasonably claim underlies Paul's own highly variegated discourse. So far, this structure only pertains to the line from I to X and the three or four motifs of the call, joy and suffering, and self-sufficiency. But the result is nevertheless important since it provides the first instance of the kind of logic I am arguing underlies Paul's variegated talk.

We have now analysed Paul's account of his own movement from I to X and its implications for his attitude to the present world. In the next chapter we shall look more closely at the way he uses that account directly in his dealings with the Philippians. Here we turn from looking merely at what he says about himself to what he does by saying it. But here too the I→X→S-model and the comparison with Stoicism will help us understand better what is actually going on.

5

Philippians II
The Solution Developed

Paul's turning towards the Philippians: the logic of paraklesis

Joy, suffering, partnership, progression, an eschatological goal, righteousness, identity with Christ and Christ as model: in the previous chapter we considered only some of these recurrent motifs. Discussion of the eschatological goal and righteousness will be reserved for the end of the present one. Before that we shall consider the rest: partnership, progression, identity with Christ and Christ as model. The argument will be that they can all be brought together under the idea of Paul—the 'sage' and 'teacher', the one who *knows*—'bending down' to the Philippians—to be understood as his 'quasi-pupils', who know less, but *are* progressing in knowledge—in order to make them 'move up' by their own means to his own level of insight. Furthermore, it will be claimed that this idea defines Paul's own notion of *paraklēsis*—and that Philippians *is*, first and foremost, a letter of paraklesis.

Three points should be noted in the notion of paraklesis as so defined: (i) that it operates within a field of understanding and knowledge of a special kind, (ii) the specific point of speaking of 'bending down' and 'moving up', and (iii) the point of saying that the quasi-pupils should move up 'by their own means'. The three points go very closely together. They are to be understood, as I shall show, within the framework of the I→X and X→I lines as we established these for Paul in the previous chapter. Only now we must add that the change in normative self-identification not only results from getting to know Christ by acquaintance. It is also a matter of acquiring a new form of *propositional* knowledge: a piece of normative knowledge that defines the X-pole with which one identifies oneself, one for which Christ, as it were, stands. It is *because* Paul has acquired that kind of knowledge that he pursues his paraklesis the way he does.

(i)   Paul himself clarifies the content of this knowledge, as we may see
by moving back from 3:8 to the Christ 'hymn'. Through his call, as we
saw in the previous chapter, Paul has reached the state at the X-level of
knowing 'Christ Jesus my Lord' (3:8). That was, to begin with, a matter
of knowledge by acquaintance and we drew on it in speaking of a new
self-identification. However, there was also something *that* Paul came to
know. We saw that the reference to 'Christ Jesus my Lord' contains the
idea of Christ Jesus *as* Lord. Now this captures the confession that Paul
speaks of in 2:11: 'Christ Jesus is Lord'. And the content of that confession is expressed in the Christ 'hymn'. Thus knowledge of Christ Jesus
as Lord also includes an *understanding* of the Christ event as described
in the 'hymn': what Christ did (and what then happened to him), and
furthermore, the *meaning* of what Christ did as reflected in Christ's
mindset: his own normative understanding (cf. 2:5–6) of his action (2:7–
8), the understanding expressed *in* it. Moving further back we can see
that this understanding is stated already in 2:4 immediately before the
transition (2:5) to the 'hymn' (2:6 ff), a transition that precisely bridges
between 2:4 and 2:6 ff.[1] 2:4 states a principle of action (to the Philippians)
which I shall call *Paul's maxim*: do not consider your own interest, but
that of others.[2] 2:5 next states that the Philippians must 'think' (*phronein*)
the same as is to be found in Christ Jesus. And 2:6 then states what
Christ did think and do in the Christ event, namely, as it turns out,
something that accords closely with Paul's maxim. Thus the maxim and
the Christ event as described in the 'hymn' together express a piece of
normative knowledge: that the correct normative attitude and principle
of action lies in not looking to one's own interest (cf. 2:4; in Christ's
case that of his own divine status, 2:6) but instead to that of others (cf.
2:4; in Christ's case that of humankind, 2:7–8). That piece of normative
knowledge, then, is one that Paul acquired too when he changed in self-
identification and moved from I to X. In getting to know 'Christ Jesus
my Lord' by direct acquaintance—thereby also getting to see himself as
a 'Christ person'—he also got to know *that* the Christ event expresses
the normative truth we have identified.

(ii) However, instead of merely staying for himself at the level of his
new knowledge or of looking joyfully down for his own sake at his own
earlier (and still partial) existence at the I-pole or at others' present
existence there, he actively turns or bends down towards them, leaving
behind his own exalted state of knowledge, addressing *them* at the level
to which *they* belong and aiming in this way to make them move up to
his own level. In accordance with the way we have just spelt out Paul's

knowledge at X, this act was seen by himself as a kind of recapitulation of Christ's saving act as described in the 'hymn'. Christ left behind his own exalted position (2:6) and reached down to human beings (2:7–8, X→I). Christ also caught hold of Paul (cf. 3:12) at the I-pole by making him acquire Christ's own knowledge (cf. 3:8). And Paul now repeats the same movement (X→I) on behalf of the Philippians, trying to make *them* undergo the change from I to X which he has himself already undergone. If we may risk the pun, what Paul does to the Philippians in his *paraklēsis* (exhortation) is what God did to Paul himself through Christ in God's *klēsis* (call) of him.

(iii)   But precisely because being at the X-level is a matter of understanding, the only way in which Paul may reach his aim with regard to the Philippians is by speaking and acting in ways that will make them *themselves* move up to his level. He cannot just order them to do it since no matter how much they may wish to comply, if they do not themselves *see what he sees*, they will remain at the I-pole. And so all of Paul's parakletic practices are held together by his aim of making them see *for themselves* what they *should* see. This feature will actually be common both to God's original call of the Philippians as transmitted by Paul and to his present paraklesis of them. But it is particularly apposite for the latter operation, which presupposes that they have already seen some part of the truth and are in a state of progression towards a fuller grasp of it.

In all this Paul is speaking and acting as a teacher in relation to his pupils in the way of the Stoic sage. He too will attempt to make others travel the same route that he has himself gone instead of merely keeping the insight he has acquired to himself. As an example, one might mention the highly complex relationship between the philosopher Seneca and his pupil Lucilius as reflected in Seneca's letters. A catalogue of actual pedagogical practices combined with the many indications of Seneca's own awareness of his pedagogical practice would reveal a large number of significant similarities with Paul's practice in his letter to the Philippians. Setting this out in detail would require an investigation of its own.[3] What matters here is the basic point that the line X→I—the sage's bending down to other people in order to bring them up by their own means to his own level of insight—constitutes what I suggest is *the* logical form of all those various practices. The sage has reached an all-comprehending insight that he wishes to impart to his pupils. But he aims to make them acquire it as it were for themselves. Otherwise, it will not be theirs in the way he intends: as understood by them in such a way that they will use it for themselves in their own practice and 'live' it as their own form of life.

It should be immediately obvious that this is directly relevant to Paul's letter to the Philippians. For more than perhaps any other Pauline letter (apart from 1 Thessalonians) this one appears to have as its primary aim to bring the addressees forward on a line on which they are already settled, as Paul is confident (cf. 1:5–6), though without having gone so far as Paul himself (cf. 3:15–16). If I am right that this is also the specific situation that is presupposed in paraklesis, one would expect to find Paul too adopting in Philippians a number of parakletic practices of the bending down type. Before investigating this further, however, we should note that the letter is in fact identified by Paul himself as one of paraklesis.[4]

That is shown by the exact place where the words *paraklēsis* and *parakalō* make their appearance in the two letter-halves. In the first half, *paraklēsis* is referred to in 2:1 together with the kind of resumptive *oun* that is sometimes combined with *parakalō* (and quite often with other parenetic markers) to introduce a section of exhortation.[5] We saw that Paul's line was: a section about himself (1:12–26), exhortation of the Philippians to remain steadfast (1:27–30, cf. especially 1:27) and then paraklesis, which extends as far as 2:18. Clearly, the paraklesis section proper constitutes the end point of Paul's line of argument from 1:12 onwards. It is what he is driving towards from the very beginning. And it is itself amplified when Paul in 2:5–11 brings in Christ himself as a model that far outdoes his own example, from which he had otherwise begun.

Similarly in the second half, the term *parakalō* is introduced in 4:2 and soon followed by Paul's repeated exhortation that the Philippians rejoice (4:4). This connects the present paraklesis section directly—via the pivotal verse 3:1—with the conclusion of the previous one (2:18), where Paul also exhorted to rejoicing. In the second half too, as we saw, Paul's line begins from Paul himself (3:4–14), gradually includes the Philippians (3:15–21) and ends with an emphatic concluding exhortation that the Philippians remain steadfast in the Lord (4:1). And then we again have the paraklesis section (4:2–9). It is true that if one were asked to identify the point Paul is driving at in 3:2–4:9 as a whole without glancing at other sections of the letter, one would probably come up with 4:1, the emphatic exhortation to steadfastness.[6] But that observation does not really counter the claim for the role of paraklesis in the letter. For in the first half too, there is an especially close connection between the exhortation to steadfastness (1:27–30) and the paraklesis proper (2:1 ff). It is also true that 4:2–9 is far more conventional than 2:1–18.

But that does not necessarily make it less important. In fact, Paul ends the section on a note that ably summarizes the basic line of thought in the letter as a whole: 'What you learned, received, heard and saw *in me, do* that!' (4:9).[7]

We should conclude that the letter to the Philippians is *through and through* a letter of paraklesis. Let us now consider some ways in which Paul makes use of what I suggested is his basic parakletic idea of bending down from the X-level to his addressees in order to bring them up to the same level of insight. Consideration of these ways will show that it is in fact the idea of bending down, with the three features I highlighted, that lies behind and holds together Paul's highly variegated practice. In the section that follows we shall then consider whether we can be certain that this bending down is also specifically Stoic in form.

Paul's turning towards the Philippians: progression, partnership, Paul as model, Christ as model

The first separate motif that is relevant is that of the Philippians' 'progression' (*prokopē*). The term itself was used with this meaning in 1:25. But the idea was strongly present already in the thanksgiving section (1:6, 9–11). And it is presupposed in 3:15–16 too. 1:9–11 reveals particularly clearly that Paul understood progression in cognitive terms. The first half of the three verses (1:9–10a) refers to Paul's prayer on behalf of the Philippians that their *love* (*agapē*) may abound more and more, but not just in a vague and emotional sense, rather 'in discernment' (*epignōsis*) and 'every form of appreciation' (*pasa aisthēsis*) so that they may 'scrutinize' (*dokimazein*) the 'differences' (*ta diapheronta*). Later, as we know, Paul will say that love itself stands for a normative principle of action—Paul's maxim—that reflects Christ's own mindset (2:1–6), that is, a piece of normative knowledge. Thus progression is a cognitive phenomenon that consists in getting an ever better grasp of Paul's maxim and seeing more and more clearly how it should be applied in particular situations. That is the only thing that matters (the only true *diapheron*).[8] The rest does *not* matter (but is an *a-diaphoron*).[8] Understood in this way progression completely fits into the I→X line Stoically conceived. It is all a matter of growth in understanding through an application of what one *already* knows.

That point had to do with progression on the part of the Philippians. It is noteworthy, however, that in all four passages referred to (1:6, 9–11, 25 and 3:15–16) there is a specific practical pattern in the way Paul, on his side, aims to *bring about* this progression. His strategy is twofold. He either (*x*) appeals to the already established partnership between himself and the Philippians or else (*y*) uses himself as a model for them. These are not just rhetorically effective means on Paul's part. On the contrary, the two practices together constitute a specific practical pattern which fits closely into the logic of paraklesis that we developed.

The pattern is this: (*a*) *Paul*, on his side, *does* something to the Philippians (which *reflects* a *knowledge* that is *his*), (*b*) in order to make *them*, on their side, *do* the same, (*c*) so that *they* will thereby acquire the *knowledge* that was his. Paul's twofold rhetorical strategy falls under this pattern. (*x*) We shall see that this holds of his appeals to partnership. Here Paul does refer to his *own* sense of partnership. That sense does reflect his own *knowledge*. The appeal does aim at making the Philippians, on their side, have the *same* sense of partnership. And Paul does act in this way in order to make *them* acquire his own *knowledge*. (*y*) But can a strategy of presenting oneself as a model to others be understood in the same way? Yes. For Paul gives his act of modelling himself to the Philippians the specific form of 'bending down' to them, of trying to 'meet' them at their own level. That act *can* be reciprocated by the Philippians once they, on their side, try to 'meet' *him*. And here too we shall see that Paul's acting in this particular way itself *reflects* a piece of knowledge on his part and is also geared to making the Philippians on their side *acquire* the same knowledge.

The connection between this pattern of Paul's rhetorical practice and the three features of paraklesis that we highlighted is as follows. The first feature: As just stated, the two rhetorical strategies are understood by Paul as both reflecting (on Paul's part) and issuing in (for the Philippians) a state of normative knowledge. The second feature: As just noted too, the two rhetorical strategies come together in the notions of Paul's 'bending down' and the Philippians' 'moving up', in other words, in their mutual willingness to 'meet' one another. And the third feature: It is precisely within a partnership of the kind to which Paul appeals that he as a teacher may hope to change or genuinely develop his pupils in the *indirect* way of presenting himself as a model, that is, in a manner that leaves the actual progression to *them*. I now propose to go through some of the most important passages in the letter in order to show that Paul does operate within the practical pattern I have identified—and hence also in conformity with the logic of paraklesis that we highlighted. The passages are 1:6–11 and 2:1–4; 1:12–26 and 3:2–16.

The first of Paul's two strategies—appeal to an already established partnership—plays a central role already in the thanksgiving section. Paul backs his declaration of confidence that they will make progress

(1:6)—another rhetorical practice of bending down to them—on his appreciation of their partnership (with himself) in the gospel from the first day up to the present. Similarly, his prayer that their love will grow (1:9–11) is backed by the declaration of his love for them (1:7–8) based on their partnership with him in grace (end of 1:7). The underlying idea is evidently that the love of mutual partnership that *already* binds them together—*as it were* already at the X-level—will hopefully increase in them now that Paul has affirmed its presence and strength in himself. But what kind of partnership? Obviously one of love—but also of knowledge, the eventual goal. For what Paul will do at later points in the letter is to develop the content of this partnership as he has appealed to it in the thanksgiving section. Partnership in the gospel will then become a partnership in the shared self-identification that he will describe to them in chapter 3 (see in particular 3:12–16 in the light of 3:4–11). And partnership in grace will become a partnership in the shared normative knowledge of the Christ event and its meaning that he will set out to them in chapter 2 (2:1–5, 11 in particular). We have already seen that his use of cognitive terms in 1:9–10a points forward to that.

Note then that what Paul aims to bring about in 1:9–11 is a growth of love among the Philippians *themselves* (at the I-level or wherever they may eventually find themselves)—as a result of their partnership of love with Paul (proleptically, as it were, at the X-level) and his explicit declaration of the same for them (X→I). Thus the theme of Paul's bending down to his pupils in love is matched by the idea that what will hopefully come out of this is the same attitude of love among the Philippians *themselves*—as a *result* of their positive response of love in relation to Paul. There is a complex theory here of the logic of 'mutual love': X→I (Paul's doing something to the Philippians) eliciting and hopefully resulting in I→X (the Philippians' doing something to Paul)—but also, as a result of this, in love *among* those who previously belonged at the I-pole. In itself there is nothing strange in this added twist. For if the eventual goal of the whole exercise is that the Philippians are brought up to Paul's own state of knowledge (at X), then they will also automatically begin to apply that knowledge in their own *mutual* relationship. And that is precisely the point. The ultimate goal of Paul's hortatory practice is that the Philippians *themselves* begin to *act* on the *knowledge* that Paul aims to make theirs.

Where *will* the Philippians belong if Paul's parakletic practice proves successful in this way? At the S-pole! As we know that pole from the I→X→S-model on its Stoic interpretation, it is peopled with individuals who via their realized relationship with X (in this case, reason) have left the I-pole completely behind and are now able to engage with one another in the manner of sages. Similarly in Paul there is an S-pole that is peopled with individuals who, via the relationship with Christ that is prefigured in their relationship with Paul, have in fact left the I-pole behind in the way Paul himself did this and have now become able to engage with one another in the manner shown to them by Paul. Thus Paul's call for mutual love among the Philippians *themselves* points directly forward to a *social* completion of the I→X→S-model: the move from I via X to S.

So, by doing something to the Philippians *within* a stated framework of partnership and eliciting a converse response from them within the same framework, Paul hopes to bring them up to the level of knowledge that lies behind and informs his own action. If he succeeds, they will continue to act on that knowledge also among themselves. Thus the practical pattern I set out is fully present already here.

The appeal to an already established partnership between Paul and the Philippians finds striking expression in 2:1–4 too, that is, at the emphatic beginning of the paraklesis section of the first letter-half. Paul begins by appealing to the very idea of *paraklēsis* in Christ, to the encouraging consolation (*paramythion*) of love, to partnership in the spirit, and to the deep feelings of love and compassion (2:1). On this very strong basis of emotional solidarity, he then addresses the Philippians with a direct piece of exhortation (2:2)—that they do what? That they 'fulfil his own joy' by 'thinking the same' (presumably as himself), by having the same love (again presumably as himself)—and by being of one mind and so forth, namely *among each other* (2:2).[9] They must do nothing from selfishness (*eritheia*). Instead, they must see the others as above themselves (2:3) and must not look to their own interests but to those of the others (2:4). Once more Paul is appealing to the already established partnership of love (2:1) between himself and the Philippians (as it were, already at the X-level) and using an affirmation of his own love for them (X→I) as a basis for exhorting them to respond to him (I→X, 2:2 'fulfil my own joy' and so forth). But here too we see that the ultimate goal is that the Philippians themselves acquire the piece of normative knowledge formulated in Paul's maxim so that they will come to practise it in their own mutual relationship, not just in relation to Paul.

That Paul wishes them to acquire such a piece of knowledge needs little argument. It is generally recognized that Paul uses the Greek root *phronein* ('think') more often in this letter than anywhere else.[10] And the present passage contains a particularly strong representation of it. The term reminds one of Aristotle's use of *phronēsis* as *the* term for practical, moral 'insight'. Why does Paul not speak of 'knowledge' (*sophia*), which would be the proper term in Stoicism? Several explanations are possible. For one thing, he probably wanted to dissociate himself from the philosophers of his time.[11] What he was talking about was not just 'knowledge', but 'knowledge in Christ'. For another, the term *phronein* points to the active sense of 'appreciation', 'application of an insight' and the like. And that probably suited Paul better than the more static sense of knowledge had. In spite of this, however, it is quite clear that what Paul wanted the Philippians to acquire is a piece of normative knowledge, the content of Christ's own mindset as formulated in Paul's maxim.

Then it follows directly that the eventual goal of Paul's exhortation is that the Philippians acquire and practise this knowledge in their own, mutual relationship too. That last extension is in fact the explicit point of Paul's whole argument. This is made clear in a striking manner in 2:2 when he moves from speaking of 'thinking the same', namely as *himself*, to 'thinking one thing', namely among *themselves*. It is through responding (I→X) to Paul's declaration of love (X→I) and by honouring the already established partnership with him that they will hopefully *also* come to lead the kind of life that Paul aims to bring about in them: the life of *mutual* love. Here again the X→I / I→X relationship points directly forward to the social completion of the I→X→S-model: the move from I via X to S. It is at the S-pole that the Philippians will lead the life of mutual love. Note then the following point. Rhetorically, as we saw, the paraklesis section (2:1–18) is what Paul is driving towards in the first letter-half. It follows that what he is driving at in terms of content and ideas is in fact the social completion of the I→X→S-model. That fits closely with a Stoic reading.

It is noteworthy that Paul begins to speak of *joy* in this same connection (2:2). What he appears to be saying is that by responding to his appeal (his bending down and the declaration of his love), the Philippians will make *his* joy complete. One might certainly see this as no more than a rhetorical statement. Is Paul's joy, as we analysed it in the previous chapter, not complete no matter how the Philippians behaved? Well, perhaps not. Perhaps joy of this kind presupposes not just the kind of partnership that Paul has with Christ but also the kind of inter-human partnership that he is exhorting the Philippians to maintain and bring to completion in relation to himself. How will they do that? Presumably by moving up to the position at the X-pole (and hence to the S-pole) where Paul is himself situated, a position where one models oneself on Christ and his knowledge. For that is in effect what Paul is exhorting them to do in 2:2–4 and 2:5 ff, in the former passage by exhorting them to the strikingly disinterested form of mutual love formulated in Paul's maxim and in the latter by grounding that attitude in the mindset directly shown by Christ himself in the Christ event. Thus the Pauline feeling of joy may actually presuppose the kind of disinterested inter-human partnership and love which is only found where a *group* of people have together left the I-level completely behind and have become able to look down on it from above in the way prefigured to them by Paul himself and by Christ. Or again, in spite of what we have said so far, Pauline joy may actually be a *social* emotion. Once more, Paul seems to point forward to the S-pole of the I→X→S-model.

In summarizing these observations on partnership, we can see that Paul's reference to an already existing partnership is not just a rhetorically effective tool in his arsenal. It is that. But it is also two other things. First, it is an appeal to what the whole thing is about, the eventual, ultimate *goal* of Paul's paraklesis, namely, practice of Paul's maxim. For that is the essential content of true partnership. Second—and of more immediate importance—it is a more or less explicitly conceptualized claim that practice of Paul's maxim is something that *informs* Paul's own parakletic practice and gives it its special shape. In practising paraklesis the way he does, Paul on his side is practising on the Philippians the kind of partnership that he is attempting to bring to full flourishing in them.

The second of Paul's two strategies—presenting himself as a model—is basic in two important sections: 1:12–26, where it leads up to the explicit talk of the Philippians' progression, and 3:2–16, where it issues in Paul's explicit exhortation (3:17) that the Philippians become (co-) imitators of him (*symmimētai mou*), that is, imitators *of* him who *join with* him in what he is himself imitating, and that they take him as their model (*typos*).

In the first section, as we know, Paul's line is to develop and amplify his own very difficult situation of both internal opposition (1:14–18) and external threats to his life (1:18–26) and to state his own reaction of joy to it—and then to suggest that *the Philippians* now find themselves in a closely *similar* situation (1:27–30), which includes having to do with external opponents (1:28) in relation to whom they must be steadfast (1:27) and respond with complete internal unanimity (again 1:27 and 2:1–4). What Paul does here is in complete conformity with the practical pattern we formulated. He works out his *own* situation and pattern of behaviour in it, which reflects his knowledge at the X-pole, in order to make the Philippians see for themselves that *their* situation is closely analogous to Paul's and then to transfer to their own situation the image he presents of his own complex attitude to *his* situation: *they* should relate to their own situation in the way *Paul*, their cherished figurehead, relates to *his*. But the ultimate goal is that they will then also acquire the knowledge that is his and on which he acts.

In the second section (3:2–16) Paul writes out as emphatically as possible the complete change that his call meant for his own self-understanding—in order to present himself *explicitly* as a model for the Philippians. That virtually *states* what he is doing: describing his own experience to them so that they on their side may have the same experience and so reach the knowledge that went into Paul's own original change in self-understanding. Note then also the specific turn Paul gives his self-description here. He has *not* himself reached the goal, he says, but is only striving towards it, though of course ardently (3:12–14); and they must do the same (3:15–16). Paul's aim with this is clearly the one we noted earlier of narrowing the gap between himself and his addressees while also keeping his own role as a model. The effect will be that the Philippians, on their side, are brought closer to the goal. Here is another—rhetorically highly effective—way in which Paul 'bends down' to his addressees. But it is not *just* a matter of rhetoric. On the contrary, it reflects Paul's own knowledge as expressed in his maxim and aims at bringing the Philippians up to the same level of having grasped and being grasped by Christ (cf. 3:12). Thus Paul's second rhetorical strategy too is ultimately based in his knowledge and aims to bring the Philippians up to the same level of knowledge. And it *shows* him *practising* his knowledge.

Then we may bring in the last important motif that belongs under Paul's turning towards the Philippians. It is one that in a way combines the two others—of Paul's appeal to the partnership of love and of his acting as a model. Like them it ultimately reflects the possession on Paul's part of the knowledge expressed in his maxim. I am referring to a motif that has come up a number of times: Paul's presentation of himself as standing in relation to the Philippians in the role of Christ. We know the passages. In 1:8 Paul states that he is longing for the Philippians with the yearning of Christ Jesus himself. Further, though himself suffering and possibly preferring to die in order to be with Christ, he will remain alive for the Philippians' sake (1:24–26). Finally, he feels nothing but joy at the prospect of dying while working on behalf of the Philippians' faith (2:17). These striking and almost hyperbolic self-descriptions fit directly into the pattern of Paul's paraklesis understood as an activity of the bending-down type. Behind the already established partnership between Paul and the Philippians and behind Paul's own acting as a model stands another model: Christ. The partnership is one 'in Christ' and Paul acts as a model within that partnership. But how? How does Christ inform those two rhetorical strategies? Answer: 'Christ' stands for the experience of Christ that Paul describes in direct, experiential terms in 3:4–14 as a matter of knowledge by acquaintance and *spells out* more discursively in 2:4–6 as a matter of normative, propositional knowledge. And as we have seen, these two things—and not least the latter—do inform Paul's rhetorical practice. When Paul appeals to an already established partnership and presents himself as a model of the bending-down type, he is *applying* his own knowledge of Christ. It is this that allows him to present himself, more or less, *as* Christ. Christ and his mindset is the ultimate model for Paul's own downward movement from X to I. Or as we said: Christ's bending down to humankind in God's call (*klēsis*) of them is directly reflected in Paul's bending down to the Philippians in his *paraklēsis*.

We may conclude that behind the three practices we have considered— Paul's appeal to an already existing partnership between himself and the Philippians, his acting as a model, and his virtual impersonification of Christ—there lies the idea that these practices express, flow and follow from a state of knowledge, a normative, cognitive grasp—the first feature in the logic of paraklesis. Further, the ultimate aim of all Paul's practices is to bring the Philippians up (compare the second feature) by their own grasp and understanding (compare the third feature) to the same level of knowledge as Paul's. When that has been achieved and they too find themselves at the X-pole, then they may also *practise* this knowledge in their mutual relationship at the S-pole. If that is in fact the picture we should operate with, then we may also conclude that it is the I→X→S-model Stoically conceived that constitutes the ultimate logical scheme behind Paul's hortatory practice.

Paul's turning towards the Philippians: is it specifically Stoic?

But are there not other possibilities? If we are prepared to go outside Paul's own immediate horizon, might we not explain his hortatory practice in terms of mere rhetorical strategy or else of the theory of pedagogical psychagogy cultivated, for instance, by contemporary Epicureans?[12] If instead we choose to stay within Paul's own immediate horizon, is the Christ event itself not sufficient to explain Paul's hortatory practice? Why do we need to bring in the I→X→S-model on its specifically Stoic interpretation?

The answer is this: The Christ event might certainly suffice as a model for Paul in the way we have already seen, but only once it has received an interpretation which will in effect fit *that* into the I→X→S-model on its Stoic interpretation. Epicurean psychagogy or rhetorical technique might also in themselves suffice to explain Paul's actual practice. But neither would explain a feature that we have seen to be central to Paul's turning towards the Philippians: that this turn should be *understood* as a direct *application* of an insight that he has himself acquired. Paul has been overwhelmed by his knowledge of 'Christ Jesus my Lord' in such a manner that he has given up his former self in the way we spelt this out: he has moved from I to X. At the same time he has also realized *that* this movement constitutes the essence of the Christ event. Only there it went the other way, from X to I: Christ gave up his own self in order to move *down* to the level of human beings, but with the ultimate aim of making them move up to his own level. Fortified with this knowledge of the meaning of the Christ event, what Paul now does in relation to the Philippians is to *repeat* in his own person that same downward movement as an application of his knowledge. I have restated this particular, very tight nexus of ideas here because it reflects a specifically Stoic feature that does, however, come out far more flatly in Stoicism. The Stoic sage realizes his own identity as a rational being and it *follows* from this that he will next reach out to *other* rational beings and try to bring them up to his own level. Similarly, Paul has come to *know* Christ Jesus *as* one who bent down towards humankind and it *follows* from this that he will next himself do the same. Thus Paul's bending down is a direct application of the actual content of his new insight, as it is in Stoicism. To say that it is a merely technical operation of rhetoric or Epicurean psychagogy would be to miss completely the way it is *directly* tied to the very content of the form of life that Paul is developing and presenting to his addressees. Indeed, it is a basic point of the I→X→S-model to bring this out. There is an exceedingly tight connection in Paul between his 'theological', 'social' and 'ethical' construction of a world-view—and his actual practice.

Is it not then, after all, just the Christ event itself (*Christ's* bending down) that provides the explanation for Paul's hortatory practice that we are after? No. It is the Christ event *on that interpretation*. And that is precisely a Stoicizing one. It is an interpretation of Christ as having had a certain *mindset* which *made* him bend down towards humankind—just as the Stoic wise man would necessarily bend down towards his fellow human beings as a result of having acquired *his* characteristic mindset. I am suggesting here that Paul in practice construed the Christ event along the lines of the I→X→S-model on its specifically Stoic interpretation. This will seem a particularly stark claim.[13] But note the special way in which he describes Christ's mindset in the 'hymn'. Christ did not hold on to that which was otherwise undoubtedly his particular property:

his divine status (2:6–7). Instead, he gave it up, if only momentarily. Thus Christ did, at his X-level (2:6), what Paul will go on to say that he has himself done, at *his* I-level: give up everything that distinguished him as that particular individual. Or in other words: Christ may serve as a model *because* he did something that Paul will also describe in specifically Stoic terms. Thus the reason why we must invoke the I→X→S-model in its specifically Stoic form to explain Paul's hortatory practice is that this practice must be understood as flowing directly from his own under- standing of the Christ event and that understanding itself built directly upon the Stoic model: that Christ's downward movement reflected a mindset on his part that consisted in giving up 'his own'.

This piece of reasoning will not seem initially persuasive to many. For one thing, is it not generally recognized that the Philippians 'hymn' is pre-Pauline?[14] So did *they* think along Stoic lines too? For another, what has a piece of Stoic anthropological reasoning to do with Paul's con- struction of *the* crucial, most exalted and striking *religious* idea in his arsenal: the meaning of the Christ event? Several answers are possible. (i) We do not actually know that the Philippians 'hymn' is pre-Pauline.[15] (ii) But even if it is, we do not know that an early Christian construction of Christ's death as a 'noble death' could not have drawn on ideas like the one that is particularly sharply spelt out in Stoicism: that of giving up one's own, including one's life, for the sake of others.[16] In fact, already in Aristotle that comes out as the highest sign of moral virtue.[17] And it is well known that the idea played an important role in the Jewish, post-Maccabean martyr tradition. (iii) Nor should we at all accept the implied contrast between anthropological and religious reasoning. If anything is certain about Paul, it is that he strove ardently to bring together his accounts of the specifically 'religious' side of his world- view—to the extent that we can identify such a side—and the specifically 'anthropological', 'social' and 'moral' side. We do not know in advance that the connections he saw went *only* from the former side to the latter one. For all we know, they might very well go both ways. (iv) Finally, even if we cannot settle the question of the genesis of Paul's ideas as they are set forth in the letter (who, in fact, can tell?), we are fully entitled to use the Stoic perspective in the way we have done as *our* tool for making transparent the connections between Paul's many ways of speak- ing—as long as it works for that purpose without unduly distorting his text.

The whole issue is obviously both extremely important and very difficult. But enough has been said to ensure that the reading suggested here cannot be written off just like that. On the contrary, that reading alone, I suggest, allows us to hold together in a single grasp the many different ideas and practices that go into Paul's paraklesis as practised in his letter to the Philippians.

It is time to summarize this nucleus of ideas. In coming to see himself as a 'Christ person' (I→X) Paul has also acquired a certain normative knowledge (at X) that he states in his maxim. He then applies this knowledge in bending down again (X→I) to the level of the Philippians trying to make *them* progress and move up to his own level (I→X). His strategy in doing this—appealing to an already existing partnership and presenting himself as a model—is both rhetorically effective but also, and more importantly, governed by the thought that since it is all a matter of progression in understanding and knowledge, he can only appeal to his addressees to make them see on their own what they should see. To reach this aim he brings the Christ figure directly in: firstly, in the 'hymn'; secondly, when he presents himself to them as a model who carries the colours of Christ himself; and thirdly, in his invocation of a partnership between himself and the Philippians which *already* stands under the figure of Christ. This is all directed towards bringing the Christ dimension of the X-pole to bear on the Philippians as strongly as possible. The final aim of Paul's efforts is that the Philippians acquire the full normative knowledge (at X) that set himself going in his dealings with them. *If* they do this, then Paul's own role will be fulfilled. Then they will no longer have a special relationship with *him* but will be able to practise their new knowledge (as expressed in Paul's maxim and prefigured for them in the Christ event) in relation to *everybody* (within the group). And so they will finally have reached the S-pole. That is where Paul aims to bring them.

The Philippians: the goal

I have argued that the I→X→S-model in its Stoic form lies directly behind Paul's account of his own call, his joy and his self-sufficiency. I have also argued that it is specifically this model that constitutes the logical form of all of Paul's highly variegated hortatory practice. We must now consider a third question of what the goal is that the Philippians should be striving towards—and that Paul himself is apparently also striving towards (3:12).

Hitherto we have taken this goal to be a state of full knowledge: the final 'grasp' of Christ Jesus (3:12) which will also be the complete knowledge (*gnōsis*) of 'Christ Jesus my Lord' (3:8). That is what Paul presents to the Philippians as the end point for their movement from I to X: being in full possession of the new normative knowledge that matches their new self-identification. However, since the content of this knowledge is what is expressed in Paul's maxim (2:4), when they bring the movement from I to X to completion, the Philippians will in fact also have been brought the whole way from I via X to S. Here they will *live* in accordance with their new knowledge, *practising* it in relation to one another. In short, the Philippians' goal is a state of mind (a piece of knowledge) and the practising of it.

However, Paul also provides other, quite different descriptions of the goal. We must consider how they cohere with what we have already learned, and for the following special reason. Some of these descriptions are so utterly different in logical category that they tend to throw serious doubt over whether what we have hitherto said about the goal can at all be correct, namely that it consists in being at the S-pole of the I→X→S-model Stoically conceived. Should the goal be understood as a state of mind or in logically quite different ways? If the latter answer proves to be correct, then we can no longer claim that Paul relies on the I→X→S-model Stoically understood, at least not as regards his account of the eventual goal. For in Stoicism the goal is through and through a matter of states of mind, it is wholly cognitive. Very much is at issue here, which is why the question needs to be pressed in spite of the somewhat speculative character of parts of the ensuing discussion. In addition, we here meet for the first time head-on a problem that will continue to keep us engaged: that Paul thinks *partly* in logical categories that are quite different from Stoic, philosophical ones. We need to consider this problem very carefully from case to case. Since Paul also does think in philosophical categories, we cannot just write the problem off by placing him altogether outside a philosophical context.

There is one way of conceiving the Philippians' goal which is very clearly in evidence throughout the letter. That is the idea of the Philippians standing blameless and spotless, probably before God's tribunal, on the day of Christ, filled with the fruit of righteousness (1:10–11, cf. also 1:6 and 2:15–16). It is not quite clear exactly how this connects, at the basic level of story, with the motif of Christ's return and his establishing Christ-believers in the heavenly 'citizen body' (*politeuma*, 3:20–21), but the connection is probably very close. For Christ will make his appearance as their saviour (*sōtēr*, 3:20) and when the Philippians act on earth in order to become blameless and spotless (2:14–15), they are themselves working on their own salvation (*sōtēria*, 2:12). This raises our question in one of its forms. How does Paul conceive of the Philippians' goal when he describes it as their 'salvation'? And what is the exact relationship between that goal and the more immediate goal that they come to be blameless and spotless?

The first part of this question might seem to be very easily answered. Salvation appears to stand for the future goal of all Christ-believers, their stay in the heavenly *politeuma* when Christ will have changed their lowly bodies and made them symmorphic with his own body of glory (3:20–21). I take it that this should be understood in a quite straight-forward, 'physical' sense, as we use the term 'physical'. But exactly how will that conception of the final goal then be related to what appears to be the entirely 'moral' state of the Philippians and other Christ-believers standing blameless and spotless before God's tribunal—where the term 'moral' is used to indicate something that has to do with their mindset? Before attempting to answer the question about the relationship between these two things (being, physically, in the heavenly *politeuma* and having, 'morally', the proper mindset), let us note that the two types of account, which superficially appear to belong to two quite different logical categories, make their appearance all through the letter. In some passages, they even appear to be closely connected, a fact that only serves to raise our question particularly clearly.

For instance, whereas in 2:12 ff Paul first speaks of the Philippians as working on their own salvation (2:12) and then (apparently) of the end of that work, namely that they become ('morally') blameless and spotless (2:15), he immediately goes on to say that they already *are* 'unblemished children of God who shine like stars in the firmament in the midst of a crooked and perverted generation' (2:15) and suggests that this fact will later *become* something for Paul to delight in, namely on the day of Christ (2:16). He is certainly not saying that they already *are* stars. Still, he is drawing on this physical conception (presumably because he also speaks of salvation and the day of Christ) and bringing it into very close connection with the 'moral' idea of being blameless and spotless.

Another example: In 3:11 Paul states his hope to be able to arrive at the resurrection. In view of the way he ends (3:20–21) this whole section of the letter, it seems clear that already in 3:11 he has the later physical idea in mind. In 3:12, however, he adds that he 'has not yet grasped it', meaning, presumably, the resurrection but is only striving towards it (and of course ardently). But how can he at all entertain the idea of *having reached* the resurrection, which appears to be both a heavenly and a physical state, while still being here on earth? Something seems to be jarring violently here.[18] Again, the question becomes: how are the two types of description meant to cohere?

There is one solution that initially looks quite straightforward and for that reason rather attractive. The question still concerns the logical relationship between the physical change to life in the heavenly abode and the 'moral' mindset that Christ-believers should have, both in their present and immediately future earthly existence (2:1–5, 15) and also on the day of Christ (1:10–11, 2:16). Should we not just say that the physical transfiguration is to be understood as a *result* of the moral 'transfiguration', indeed as a reward for it, an added boon that is external to the mindset on whose presence it is based? Indeed, since Paul also speaks of righteousness (1:11 and 3:6–9) and apparently thinks that the Philippians will on the day of Christ stand before God's tribunal (which is when they should hopefully be completely blameless and spotless), we may also include a 'juridical' dimension under the 'moral' category: when the Philippians are blameless and spotless, they will be declared righteous by God. So, will their transportation to the heavenly *politeuma*, or possibly their eternal stay there, not have to be understood simply as the ('physical') reward for their 'moral' state as formally recognized by God?[19]

As I said, this solution has the virtue of being quite straightforward. Some will find it intrinsically or theologically very unattractive.[20] But that is of course no reason for saying that it was not Paul's. Indeed, there is one misreading of Paul that must *not* be advanced against it. Some (indeed, quite a number of) people will say: To say that Paul might think of Christ-believers as working for their own salvation by trying to become morally good, or indeed that he might even enjoin them to do so, mistakes fundamental ideas in Paul on grace, 'works' and the like. However, there is here what I consider to be a ghost of a traditional, theological kind that should be laid quickly to rest. Consider Paul's exhortation in 2:12–13: 'work with fear and trembling on your own salvation. For it is God who is active in you'. Should we take Paul to be saying here that the Philippians should *themselves* 'produce' their own salvation? Both yes and no. No, if this is understood to mean that they should do something for which they can *themselves* take credit as *opposed* to giving credit to God. Paul simply does not entertain any such idea. In 2:13 he *supports* his injunction that they work on their own salvation (2:12) by saying that it is God who makes them both wish and do whatever they do. He is not thinking here of any contrast between 'their own doing' and 'God's doing', but making the entirely different point that in working on their own salvation along the lines set out by Paul, they are doing the *right* thing since it is God himself who makes them both wish and do it. How does God do that? A reasonable guess is: through the Christ event and the way it helps (with Paul as an intermediary) to (re)form the

Philippians' minds. But also yes. Paul of course means what he says: that they should themselves now certainly work on their own salvation, precisely because they will then be doing something that God has himself *made* them do. Again, how must they do that 'work'? Again a reasonable guess is: by grasping and understanding what Paul is saying; by seeing the meaning of the Christ event and letting it inform their minds. There is nothing intrinsically wrong, therefore, with entertaining the idea that Paul saw salvation as something one might work to bring about.

So, is the solution to our question simply that the 'physical' account of the goal refers to the *final* goal, which constitutes a *reward* for the more intermediate, 'moral' goal of a blameless and spotless moral stance? In spite of everything that has been said so far, I have strong doubts about this solution. It would mean that both progression towards the goal of the kind Paul is aiming to bring about in the Philippians and also his own converted mindset as he expresses it in so many ways throughout the letter—indeed, the whole kind of knowledge and understanding that the letter is so centrally concerned to further—would have a status as nothing but a set of external means. They would be means to the eventual goal of standing blameless and spotless before God's tribunal and that standing would itself be an external means to the reward of getting eternal life in a physical guise. That cannot be right. It just seems impossible to reconcile such a conception with the actual way in which Paul describes both the Philippians' progression, his own grasp and mindset and the mindset of all Christ-believers if or when they stand blameless and spotless before God's tribunal.[21] All these things Paul describes in ways that make them come out very definitely as *ends in themselves* (for the two latter things) or as intrinsically directed towards *ends in themselves* (for the Philippians' progression). To take an example, what kind of goal is Paul operating with in 3:4–14? We could of course say: resurrection from the dead (3:11), that is, the physical goal. We could also say, more vaguely: 'the prize of God's upward call in Christ Jesus' (3:14). But we could certainly also say: that Paul 'gain' Christ (3:8), that he be 'found in' him (3:9), that he finally and completely 'grasp' Christ the way he has been grasped by him (3:12). We have interpreted these expressions as standing for cognitive phenomena. They are so many ways of expressing the basic, direct knowledge-by-acquaintance of 'Christ Jesus my Lord' that Paul celebrates in 3:8. But could we then also say that this kind of knowledge and self-understanding is merely to be understood as an external means to something quite different, the physical transformation into a body of glory, eternal life in such a body or something similar? It seems to me that if we did, we would have left the actual cognitive and 'moral' level at which Paul is operating throughout the letter so far behind that it is no longer clear that we would really be speaking about *that*. The basic argument against the means–end picture is therefore that it seems impossible to end up saying that what Paul is generally talking about in the letter (his own mindset as called, the partnership of totally disinterested mutual love and so forth) has value *only* as an external means to something that is logically entirely different.

How then should we solve our problem? There is one alternative possibility, which is not after all too difficult. We could ascribe to Paul a dual conception of the goal as being both physical and 'moral'. On such a conception the final goal will be both the resurrection from the dead as Paul describes it in 3:20–21: a total physical change from an earthly body to a heavenly body that is isomorphic with Christ's own body of glory—and also a concomitant, but in principle distinguishable state of 'moral' perfection: the state of standing totally blameless and spotless before God, but now as *part* of the resurrection. The idea would be that Paul might well have had a dual way of conceiving the goal without necessarily experiencing any conflict between them. This solution is attractive since it makes immediate sense of 3:11–12 where Paul appears to be talking indiscriminately about the resurrection and 'moral' perfection. It may also be strengthened by the observation that this solution does not even exclude seeing the future stay in the heavenly *politeuma* as in fact some kind of reward. For the 'moral' state of perfection may of course quite well be seen as *both* an end in itself *and* a means to the end of staying in the heavenly *politeuma*. What matters is only that it be not seen as such a means *only*.

There is another possibility which we might at least briefly entertain. It consists in taking quite seriously the idea of a dual conception of the (final) goal itself. Thus one *might* attempt to see the physical change as the *physical manifestation of* a mindset, *both* of which might in fact, to some extent at least, be present already now but would also hopefully be completely present in the future. In support of this one might refer to 2:15 and Paul's talk of the Philippians as already now shining like stars in the firmament. It is true that he only says that they shine *as if they were* (*hōs*) stars. But even that might be enough. Thus we could perhaps ascribe to Paul the idea that the hoped-for physical change that he envisaged for the future had, in a way, already begun. In that case the physical and the 'moral' dimensions might run entirely side by side both now and in the future world. That is all very speculative, of course. We should probably admit that certainty about what Paul thought on this issue may in the end be outside our grasp. But we should also insist that any solution that turns the 'moral' dimension (including the basic attitude to God that Paul develops in the letter in so many ways) into a *merely* external means to something entirely different must be inadequate.

What all this points to is the conclusion that the final goal towards which Paul is himself striving and aiming to make the Philippians strive is not merely the state of being present in the heavenly *politeuma* (3:20) conceived in some physical form (3:21). It certainly is that. But it is also the state of belonging to a group of people (no doubt to be found in heaven) who are all characterized by the mindset of those who have reached the S-pole of the I→X→S-model in its Stoic form. We have seen that the *earthly* goal to which Paul aims to bring the Philippians is the life of mutual love and 'self-abasement' (*tapeinophrosynē*) described in 2:1–5, the life that consists in leaving behind everything that is connected with one's own individual self. We may add that this kind of life apparently constitutes the precise content of what the Philippians must do in order to 'live in a *politeuma*' in the proper way *here on earth* too (1:27, where Paul precisely uses—and here alone—the term *politeuesthai*, which he will then take up again in 3:20 in his remark about the *politeuma* that lies in wait for the Philippians in *heaven* and in the *future*). This explicit, linguistic connection almost forces us to conclude that the resurrected (cf. 3:11) life in the heavenly *politeuma* too will be one of mutual love, only now a life that has been brought to its final 'moral' perfection (3:12). And indeed, Paul more or less explicitly refers back in 3:21 to the earlier idea of self-abasement when he speaks of the change that will happen to 'our *lowly* body': to everything in our individual, bodily being that needs to be left behind. Apparently, life in the heavenly *politeuma* will be one of—literally—transfigured self-abasement. Thus whether or not we should think that in Paul's view the physical transfiguration had already begun in Christ-believers here on earth, we may safely conclude the converse point that the physical life in the heavenly *politeuma* will also be characterized by a certain mindset in its participants. And so we are in fact back with the I→X→S-model on its Stoic interpretation.

In the end, the connection with Stoicism that we find here is not at all strange. For if there is a close similarity with Stoicism in Paul's account of his call, of his joy and of his self-sufficiency; if the same is also true of his whole parakletic practice; then it is also to be expected that there should be a close similarity in his picture of the eventual goal of it all. It should come as no surprise, therefore, that we may draw a picture of

the 'moral' side of Paul's heavenly *politeuma* that renders it almost indis-
tinguishable from that of the Stoic Utopian community of sages.

The logic of community formation

It is time to look back. There is a range of topics in Philippians that we
have not discussed. Let me mention a few examples.

(i) Paul's specific way of contrasting righteousness in accordance with
the Jewish law with righteousness through Christ faith (3:6–9) deserves
more careful consideration than we have given it. The issue itself will
come up in later chapters. Here we may just note how easily Paul's reference to '*my own* righteousness, the one from the law' fits into the picture
we have drawn of Paul ceasing to attach any normative significance to
properties that defined his own, individual being, e.g. those that had to
do with his status under the law. Paul was not necessarily against the
Jewish law at all, only he had normatively given up his own self, which
was *in fact* defined by the Jewish law, in order to become a 'Christ person'
and nothing but that. Any kind of righteousness that he would henceforth
have would belong to him as a 'Christ person'.[22]

(ii) Nor have we spent much time on friendship as a category that
informs much of the relationship between Paul and the Philippians as
witnessed in the letter. That is certainly not because I consider the recent
emphasis on this to be wrong. On the contrary, it is right and important.
But it needs to be supplemented by the picture I have drawn. This can be
done quite easily. Basically, the topic of friendship has two sides to it
that we shall do well to separate. One is friendship as a social convention
and as actually practised. This side of the topic is accessible to any kind
of modern analysis, for instance one that connects friendship with the
ancient system of patronage.[23] The ancients themselves did not make
that specific connection, even though they did speak of various 'lower'
types of friendship, e.g. of utility or of pleasure. The other side of friendship is the one on which the ancient philosophers themselves focused:
friendship of virtue, which was the true form of friendship. This kind of
friendship represents an ideal. Seen from the perspective of a modern
hermeneutics of suspicion, a discourse that operates within such a framework will be open to all kinds of ideological use of language. That is
highly relevant to Paul too. Thus a full analysis of his letter to the Philippians in terms of friendship would focus on *both* sides. That implies,
however, that it remains necessary to analyse the letter *also* as operating

within the discourse of the ideal friendship of virtue that was in primary focus for the ancients themselves. And that is where the analysis I have conducted overlaps with an analysis in terms of friendship. For the kind of community to which all of Paul's *paraklesis* is *directed* (on my reading) is nothing but an ideal community of friends, as the philosophers conceived of this. Furthermore, it is within such a community that the special kind of *practice* of paraklesis that I have ascribed to Paul finds its proper place.[24]

(iii) Other themes might have been discussed too, e.g. an intriguing tension throughout the letter in Paul's attitude to his addressees. On the one hand, he appears to place himself on the same level as them. That happens in the group of motifs whose logic we have identified as falling under his bending down to the Philippians. On the other hand, he also from time to time adopts a far more authoritative tone which presupposes his sense of a clearly defined hierarchy: Christ–Paul–Epaphroditus/Timothy–the Philippians. How these two positions may be related is a question that I shall pass over here.[25]

Here my aim has been to ask about the unity of the letter as an exercise in thought: Paul's own thought—to the extent that it is also directly accessible to us. My answer has been that this unity is to be found in Paul's *presentation* and *use* of the various elements that go into the I→X→S-model on its Stoic interpretation. It may be useful in conclusion to bring out three senses—a formal, a substantive and a methodological one—in which this model should be understood as answering the question about unity and overall meaning.

The formal sense may be described as follows. We began from a more superficial question of unity at the uppermost level of discourse. What was Paul's aim or aims in writing? Can we fit everything he says into any particular answer to this question? Or what main theme or themes should we see him as trying to articulate? Can we fit everything he says into any particular answer to *that* question? That is the direction modern scholarship has by and large been taking. For the reasons I gave there is little hope that this way of asking for unity will provide any definite answer that may generate a consensus. Thus we must dig somewhat deeper to a level where we may speak of the overall form of life that Paul is both reflecting and articulating in his letter. We noted two different ways of discovering some degree of unity at this level: as a story and in the form for which I eventually settled. What we were looking for here was a closely connected *pattern* of ideas that would be sufficiently distinctly defined to qualify as philosophical—but which might then also be seen as *informing* and *explaining* Paul's actual use of ideas, metaphors, symbols and so forth at the uppermost level of discourse. Put differently, we were looking for the *logic* of Paul's discourse. Understood in that way the task may be said to have drawn vaguely on the familiar distinction in linguistics between *langue* and *parole*. But only vaguely. For I do not in the end wish to operate with a clear-cut distinction of levels. To the extent that there are at all two levels here, they should be understood as lying on a single continuous line from the *more* metaphorical to the *more* philosophical. There are a number of reasons for that. One is that it would in fact be false to claim that the logical pattern I have presented has been defined with full philosophical rigour. Another is that I have not really been looking for that kind of thing. Rather, the search was for a kind of logical pattern that would be both sufficiently close to Paul's own level of discourse for it to avoid *reducing* the Pauline text unduly and also *sufficiently removed* from it for it genuinely to *illuminate to us* what is being said and done in the Pauline text. The argument has been that this pattern is to be found in the I→X→S-model on its Stoic interpretation.

Viewed in substantive terms, the same model provides an answer to the question about unity in the following way. In addition to discussing Paul's aim or aims in writing the letter or its theme or themes, modern scholarship has also made a broader—and for that reason much more successful—suggestion to the effect that the letter is basically an exercise in community formation.[26] That seems quite right. But then the question very soon becomes: *how* did Paul do it? How did he achieve that comprehensive aim by writing the letter the way he did? The reply we may now give is this: by trying to make the Philippians see themselves in the light of the I→X→S-model. The I→X→S-model itself virtually has the character of a 'theory' of community formation: leave your individual selves behind (I→X) in responding to me and to Christ (X→I)—and the result will be the Christ *community* (S), where the mutual attitude and relationship stated in the maxim of 2:4 will be put completely into practice. What Paul then did to achieve his community-formative aim was two things: state the (various elements of the) model in order to make the Philippians *understand* the 'theory' implied in it and *use* or *apply* the model in his dealings with them so as to make them *feel* it. In both cases the ultimate aim was that they should themselves fully acquire the self-understanding that the model is all about: the self-identification and the normative knowledge that goes with this. For then they would also practise it. And then the projected Christ community would in fact be formed.

Finally, there is the methodological issue. Once more: Paul attempts to make his addressees *understand* the model and *feel* it. It is this double aspect of his use of it that explains why one may experience a certain lack of immediate clarity concerning the relationship between the model and parts of Paul's text. I have had no difficulty in showing that Paul does state the different components of the model—though not in quite those words—in different parts of the letter, for instance the I→X line in 3:4–14 and the (I→X)→S line in 2:1–4. Moreover, the fact that he speaks of himself—in the way he has described himself in 3:4–14—as a *typos* for the Philippians is virtually identical with having him say: look, this self-description of mine constitutes a model for your own self-understanding and practice. In addition to that, however, Paul also *uses* the model somewhat more implicitly, e.g. when in 1:12–30 he plays out, even *acts*, his own bending down to the Philippians. It is this double use of the model, I suggest, that from time to time makes its relation to Paul's own text less than wholly transparent. One simply cannot always see immediately and at a single glance exactly how the model informs Paul's text.

That should not, however, confuse us. On the contrary, I am proposing that if we are looking for unity in the letter of the kind I have identified, then the I→X→S-model provides *the* methodological key to the question. What we should try to do, therefore, is constantly to apply the model in detailed analysis and see whether it does not in the end allow a given text to fall into place.

Let me end by giving a single example. Paul at one point complains that apart from Timothy, there is nobody in his entourage who genuinely cares for the Philippians (2:20); 'for they all seek their own and not that of Jesus Christ' (2:21). What is going on here? Is Paul just informing the Philippians about his views on Timothy and the others? Or may we spell out what he is saying and doing in such a way that we may hold it together with the *other* things he also says and does? Well, Paul is *saying* that apart from Timothy (and himself) there is nobody in his entourage who has the proper S-relationship with the Philippians, and explaining this by saying that the others have *not* moved *from* I *to* X; on the contrary, they have *stayed at* I and do not therefore act on Paul's maxim as stated in 2:4. But Paul is also *doing* something: defining a space (S) for himself (as being *different* from those who only seek their own), for Timothy (as one who precisely belongs with Paul in that space)—*and for the Philippians* (if, as Paul hopes, they will in fact respond to Paul's declaration of his and Timothy's care for them). In other words, in these few remarks Paul is both *stating* the crucial elements in the I→X→S-

model and *using* them to bring into existence what he is ultimately concerned to achieve through the whole of the letter: the complete Christ
community in Philippi.

6

Galatians I
The Problem and the Beginning of a Solution

This and the next chapter are intended to show that with regard to Paul's letter to the Galatians too, we shall obtain the best grasp of what the letter is ultimately about by bringing in the I→X→S-model in its Stoic form. The discussion will be focused around a specific section of the letter, 5:13–26, and the question of how this so-called 'parenetical' section fits into the letter as a whole. The argument will be that this section constitutes the culmination of Paul's argument and that it brings out a number of altogether crucial features in Paul's picture of the genuinely Christ-believing form of life. As always, our ultimate concern will be to grasp the basic features of this picture, the underlying logical structure of the Christ-believing form of life as presented in Galatians.

Like we did in the case of Philippians, we shall begin by considering the formal structure of the letter, in this case from placing 5:13–26 (or 5:13–6:10) within that. Next I shall define three different 'levels' of discourse in the Pauline text in order to give us some tools for handling the concepts of 'theology', 'ethics' and 'parenesis'. With these preliminary issues out of the way, we shall address the central task of the two chapters: to provide a reading of the letter as a whole that aims to bring out the basic pillars supporting the form of life that Paul wished his Galatian addressees to adopt. As might be expected, these pillars consist of a number of beliefs about God and his acts, about Christ and about the relationship of the Christ-believer with God and Christ and with others. We shall see, however, that these beliefs all come together in a coherent picture centred on the question of personal identity and self-identification, of how the Christ-believing *I* sees him- or herself. That theme will engage us in the rest of this chapter. In the next chapter we shall then turn directly to 5:13–26 and provide a reading of that section that will display its culminating role and show the *social* dimension of Christ-believing self-identification.

5:13–26 *within the letter structure*

Paul's purpose in the letter is very clear. Faced with a crisis among the Galatian churches whose background we need not go into, Paul aims to persuade his non-Jewish addressees that they should not let themselves be circumcised or in other similar ways enter under the Jewish law. Against this he places the Christ faith as the only thing that matters.[1] He does not explicitly forbid Christ-believing Jews continuing to apply the law, but insists that for them too the only thing that really matters lies elsewhere. Neither circumcision nor uncircumcision 'has any force' or 'is anything', only 'faith that is active through love' or 'a new creation' (5:6 and 6:15 respectively).

For the major part, the formal structure of the letter is clear too.[2] It need not detain us up until 4:21. Before that, Paul's argument has flowed quite easily with a greeting (1:1–5) and statement of the letter situation (1:6–9), an account in three stages of Paul's own earlier relationship with the Jerusalem apostles (1:10–2:21) and a sustained argument based on scripture to the effect that Christ-believers, whether Jewish or not, are the true sons and heirs of Abraham (3:6–4:7). That argument is surrounded by three connected sections (3:1–5, 4:8–11 and 4:12–20) that recall the Galatians' own experience and behaviour when they were converted by Paul's original teaching and contrast it with their later behaviour.[3]

With 4:21, however, problems begin to creep in. We must consider the letter structure from 4:21 onwards in some detail since it raises the basic, structural issue of what these final pages of the letter, and in particular 5:13–26, add to Paul's message to the Galatians.[4] Are they only meant to summarize (5:1–12 and 6:11–18) what has gone before and to supplement it, and indeed 'parenetically', by making an addition (5:13–26 and 6:1–10) to an argument that has reached its intrinsic conclusion already before these pages? Or should we take them in the opposite way as intended to formulate what is actually the conclusion to Paul's general argument, an argument that would have been genuinely truncated were it not for these final pages? The issue is a classic one.[5] Important steps have recently been taken to solve it.[6] I shall build on this and argue here for the latter option in a sharpened form. Put briefly, Paul is saying this (from 4:21 onwards): 'I have argued *negatively against* your sense that you need to enter under the law of Moses. For the Christ event and faith has brought *freedom* from the law. Then stick to that (5:1). And here is what is *meant* by that freedom, which by the earlier scriptural and experiential arguments is yours: ... [5:6b, 13 ff].

That is the form of life I have (implicitly) been *positively* arguing *for* all through. It is one that can *only* be lived with Christ as the exclusive focus.' Let us consider the details of the letter structure from 4:21 onwards.

The section 4:21–31 is somewhat difficult structurally. Why is it placed exactly here?[7] The best solution seems to be that Paul is here moving towards formulating his message to the Galatians explicitly in terms of the positive notion of freedom (from the law: 5:1)—as opposed to the merely negative one of slavery (under it) that he was earlier relying on (see below). For that purpose he draws out of his earlier argument about Abraham and the law (3:6–4:7) both a literary motif and a specific idea. The motif is the story of the women partners and sons of Abraham— one couple free and one enslaved—and their mutual relationship, which foreshadows the relationship between Christ-believing non-Jews endowed with the spirit and non-Christ-believing Jews in the flesh. And the idea is the one introduced in a number of ways in 3:22–24 and 4:1–5 to the effect that Jews living under the law will (or should) experience that life as some form of slavery. That idea was not spelled out in so many words in 3:22–24 and 4:1–5, but Paul now makes use of his earlier hints about what it felt (or should feel) like to be under the law: as being in a prison (3:22–23), under a pedagogue or male chaperon (3:24), under guardians and stewards (4:2). He now suggests—with a perverse daring that will have appalled Jews—that just because of this element of slavery in life under the law, Jews in the flesh (who of course do live under the law) represent the *il*legitimate succession from Abraham, the one inaugurated by the slave-woman Hagar and her son Ismael, whereas Christ-believers, including non-Jewish ones, represent the legitimate succession from Abraham, the one derived from the free woman Sara and her son Isaac, who was generated in a non-fleshly way by the spirit. Thus on one side we have the law, *slavery*, the illegitimate succession and non-Christ-believing Jews in the flesh—and on the other the spirit, *freedom*, the legitimate succession and Christ-believers, including non-Jews.

There is every reason to be sceptical about this argument, which is both wilful and sophistic.[8] But what matters here are two things. First, Paul is gathering up his previous argument in terms of the precise notion of freedom (from the law). This on the one hand serves as a highly suitable entry into 5:2–12, in which (see below) Paul summarizes the negative thrust of his whole argument so far: *not* the law (but Christ faith); that is, *freedom from* the law, circumcision and the rest. But since the notion of freedom is also taken up in 5:13, 4:21–31 also serves as a pointed entry into the 'parenetic' section of 5:13–6:10: freedom *from* the law, all right—but also freedom employed *for* this and that. Even more important is the fact that the two triads of law, flesh and slavery versus Christ faith, spirit and freedom will be developed *with regard to their internal, logical connection* in the 'parenetic' section. In addition to providing exhortation of the Galatians, which it does do, that section also spells out *exactly how* it makes sense to connect the three items in either triad. Overall, therefore, Paul is doing far more in 4:21–31 than being merely sophistic. He is drawing out of his previous argument the notion of freedom for the dual purpose we have identified, including that of giving in 5:13 ff a full account of what he is positively arguing for.[9] Let us consider the manner in which he moves from 4:21–31 to the 'parenetic' section.

Fortified with the notion of freedom from the law, which he now (5:1) also explicitly contrasts with that of living under the 'yoke of slavery' of the law, Paul summarizes his point in an exhortation that they remain fixed (also 5:1) in that freedom.[10] He then adds an emphatic section (5:2–6) that brings the whole earlier argument to the crunch. There is first a direct appeal to Paul's own act of addressing the Galatians here and now through the letter. His aim is clearly to state the negative part of his message as sharply as possible: they must *not* let themselves be circumcised and so move in under the law. In view of the similarity with 6:11, where Paul also refers to his own act of writing, one is tempted to see him as beginning to wind up the letter already by 5:2. In a way he probably is. But that only raises even more sharply our question about the purpose of the section that lies between 5:2 and 6:11, in particular the 'parenetic' one of 5:13–6:10. Next, Paul for the first time explicitly mentions the issue of circumcision (5:2–3), which as 6:12–13 makes clear, was the most immediate bone of contention between himself and his opponents. He then repeats his basic view of the law, righteousness, grace and faith (5:4–5), which he had already introduced in 2:14–21 before beginning his Abraham argument. And finally, he formulates a catchphrase for his negative position: that circumcision or uncircumcision are wholly indifferent (5:6a)—and then ends with the *positive* idea to which he will turn in the 'parenetic' section: of having faith which is active through love (5:6b). In short, apart from the final four words of 5:6, 5:2–6 constitutes a very forceful summary of the negative thrust of Paul's whole argument so far, prepared for by the rhetorically highly effective formulation of the same idea in *positive* terms in 5:1: you *are* in *freedom* (the positive formulation); therefore do *not fall back* under slavery (summary of the negative point, cf. e.g. 4:9).

One's impression that Paul has begun to wind up the letter from 5:2 onwards is supported by the fact that he now goes on to address his opponents head on (5:7–12, though still without actually naming them)— in a manner that recalls 1:6–9. Thus the best structural account of 5:1–12 goes like this. In one way, 5:1–12 is backward-looking. 5:1 constitutes the conclusion of 4:21–31, which itself develops motifs from 3:6 – 4:11. 5:2–6 reaches even further back to 2:14–4:11 in a summary which states to the Galatians with unsurpassable sharpness the essence of Paul's negative thesis. Finally, 5:7–12 reaches as far back as 1:6–9 to the kind of third person, indirect reference to Paul's opponents that was used there. Thus 5:1–12 as a whole constitutes an exceedingly pointed summary of the main, negative message given in the letter so far. Put it like this:

4:21–31 (3:6–4:11)	← 5:1
2:14–4:11	← 5:2–6
1:6–9	← 5:7–12

But 5:1–12 also points forward. 5:2 is clearly taken up again in 6:11. And the references to circumcision and the opponents in 5:2–12 are similarly taken up again in 6:12–13. In addition, Paul's catchphrase for his negative position in 5:6a is almost literally repeated in 6:15a. Whereas 5:2-12 are thus unequivocally connected with 6:11 ff, 5:1 rather points forward to the section that comes in between 5:12 and 6:11, in particular, of course, to 5:13. Similarly, 5:6b constitutes, as we shall see, a very pointed preview of what Paul is going to develop in 5:13–26. We may schematize it as follows:

5:1	→ 5:13–26 (or –6:10)
5:2–12	→ 6:11 ff
(5:2	→ 6:11
5:2.11–12	→ 6:12–13
5:6a	→ 6:15a)
5:6b	→ 5:13–26

These structural considerations already show that 5:13 ff must not be seen as a sort of parenetic afterthought intended to serve one or more of the following functions: to restrict the moral freedom with which freedom from the law might be taken to leave Christ-believers; to defend Paul against attacks for such permissiveness; to bring the Galatians to order morally; and more.[11] It has been carefully prepared for by the reference to freedom in 5:1 and to faith that is active through love in 5:6b. Indeed, putting 5:1 and 5:6 together we may say that these two verses capture the essential thought structure that Paul is operating with from 4:21 onwards: there is freedom *from* the law—in other words, circumcision is *in*different (the negative thesis); *instead*, what matters is Christ faith that is *active through love* (the positive thesis). Perhaps one might make the point like this. The freedom of which Paul speaks in 5:1 is a freedom *from* something and to that extent primarily a state that is formulated in negative terms. In itself, however, the term freedom *also* has those distinctly positive connotations that we mentioned before. So freedom from the law is also freedom *for* something. And that something is precisely what Paul then goes on to spell out in 5:6b—and 5:13 ff. Thus the so-called parenetic section, which is introduced in this way, constitutes a vital part of the letter since it provides the most comprehensive description of the form of life that Paul aims to present to his Galatian addressees as *the true, positive alternative* to the kind of life enjoined by his opponents. It is true and important that Paul's effort to bring this out is witnessed throughout the letter whenever he says 'not the law, *but Christ*', e.g. in 2:19–20. Still, 5:13–26 plays *the* crucial role here by finally spelling out far more comprehensively what has been implied all through: life in Christ on the part of Christ-believers means just what 5:13–26 says it is. *That*, then, is, positively stated, the form of life that the Galatians should adopt when they turn *away* from the form that Paul has been arguing *against*. There is freedom *from* the law, which is also a freedom *for* something, namely, for *fulfilling* the law.[12]

Three levels of discourse and the concepts of 'theology', 'ethics' and 'parenesis'

Why have modern scholars mostly been unable to see that 5:13–26 has this specific function within the letter structure? The answer probably lies in a set of modern misunderstandings revolving around the concepts of 'ethics', 'parenesis' and 'theology'. These misunderstandings make scholars take 5:13 ff to be about 'ethics' as something that is distinct from the 'theology' that Paul has treated earlier in the letter—and about 'parenesis' as something distinct from the earlier account of certain 'indicative' facts. In order to get a grip on these misunderstandings, I shall supplement the I→X→S-model as we know it with the following distinction between three different 'levels' (or fields) of discourse.

We need to separate Paul's talk of God and Christ and his talk about human beings. Think of the first field as belonging at an **A**-level and the second as belonging at a **B**-level. When Paul speaks of God's relationship with human beings (from 'above'), he is speaking at the **A**-level. When he speaks of the relationship of human beings with God or Christ (from 'below'), he is speaking at the B-level, though indeed in relation to the A-level. Call this latter kind of talk **Ba**. Then we may add another kind which is about the relationship of human beings with one another, 'horizontally', as it were. Call this **Bb**. In addition, we need one more level: **C**. Where the two other levels are about intentional relationships between God, Christ and human beings, that is, types of cognitive attitude, this level is about practice. It is about human beings practising their beliefs and attitudes, those reflecting and expressing their relationships at the B-level to God (**Ba**) and to one another (**Bb**). Then connect this with the I→X→S-model. The relationship X→I belongs at the A-level, the opposite one (I→X) at the B-level: **Ba**. I(→X)→S and S→S also belong at the B-level: **Bb**. The C-level of actual practice, by contrast, does not stand for any special relationship. Instead, it comes in at both the I-pole and the S-pole. It is the practical dimension of what it is like to be cognitively at either pole.[13]

Apply this now to the question of the relationship between 'theology' and 'ethics' in Paul. It will obviously be possible to say that when he operates at the A-level, Paul is speaking 'theology'. Similarly, when he operates at the **Bb**- and C-levels, he is speaking 'ethics'. But the aim of distinguishing between the three levels is to achieve greater precision. For instance, there are at least two types of 'ethical' talk that need to be distinguished: those captured under **Bb** and **C** respectively. In addition, just to talk of 'theology' and 'ethics' will be seriously deficient since it does not find room for **Ba**. But as we already know from our discussion of the letter to the Philippians, **Ba** is a crucial category. Even more: the I→X→S-model shows us that **Ba** (that is, I→X) is precisely *the* crucial relationship which ties the 'theology' (represented by X→I) together with the 'ethics' (represented now by S→S). For the movement from I to S goes *via* X. It is I→X→S. This already shows that what Paul is talking about are not two different things, 'theology' and 'ethics'. Rather, 'theology' (represented here by **A**) and 'ethics' (represented here by **Bb**) are two sides of the same coin, bound together *by* the **Ba** relationship. Thus we may *at most* say that in Gal 5:13–26 Paul turns to the **Bb**-*side* of that same coin: to spell out in greater detail than he has hitherto done what the Christ event means—with respect to that particular side of it. Indeed, we may take one step further. Once we give the arrows of the I→X→S-model the role they are intended to have, we will have to say that setting forth the S- or **Bb**-side of the single coin amounts to nothing less than at long last stating what the Christ event is in the end *all about*: the **Bb**-relationship that *results from* the **Ba**-relationship that has been *brought about* by

God's intervention from above (X→I). To see the topic of 5:13–26 as just a matter of 'ethics' or something that has only a secondary importance misses the point altogether. On the contrary, as we said, in 5:13 ff Paul finally spells out with full comprehensiveness what it is that he in his previous mainly negative argument has been arguing *for*. That cannot just be an exercise in 'ethics' as something that is distinct from 'theology'.

Consider then the notion of 'parenesis'. We know from our discussion of Philippians that Pauline parenesis has the logical form of Paul 'bending down' towards his addressees. Paul presupposes a kind of community of knowledge between himself and his addressees reflecting the fact that they are already 'in' and have already in principle grasped what he has to offer them. His aim is not to convert them in the first place. Still, within that community of knowledge he reaches down to their position, which after all remains somewhat lower than his own, in order to bring them the whole way up to his own position. What he does is either to remind them of what they *already* know or to spell out further what that something concretely *consists* in. And his bending down constitutes the framework for issuing an appeal to them to practise what they have now been reminded of or come to see for the first time in all its concreteness. Thus Pauline parenesis is much more than merely ('moral') *exhortation* in an unspecific sense. It rather consists in (*a*) *spelling out* the normative knowledge that goes into the Christ faith, thereby (*b*) *reminding* the addressees of this (as of something they *already* know) and finally in (*c*) *appealing* to them to put that *previous* knowledge of theirs into *practice*. There is a sort of continuum here in terms of the speech acts that are involved: *spelling out* further to the addressees something that they are already taken to know basically, thereby also *reminding* them of it— and doing both things in the form of an *appeal*, the aim of which is to make them *themselves practise* that revived and completed knowledge of theirs.

Now if that is the form of Pauline parenesis, it follows that when Paul engages in parenesis, he will also be doing 'theology'. He is either repeating or spelling out further, that is, developing, the normative knowledge reflected in the Christ event and encapsulated in the faith that it generates. But repeating or developing something cannot be changing the subject. In addition, in his parenesis Paul reveals his view that the ultimate purpose of the Christ event and faith lies in *practice*, namely of the specific kind he spells out to his addressees. But again, stating that the ultimate purpose of something consists in a certain practice cannot be changing the subject. There are two elements in Paul's parenesis, however, that are not directly a statement of 'theology': (*b*) *reminding* the addressees and (*c*) *appealing* to them, in short the various features that are directly geared to making the addressees themselves do the things that, on Paul's understanding of the Christ event, *should* be done. These 'illocutionary' elements in Paul's parenesis do not constitute an intrinsic element of Paul's 'theology' considered as a set of (implicit or explicit) beliefs, whereas the rest of the parenesis is precisely that.[14] Further, it is obviously the existence of the illocutionary elements in Paul's parenesis that both sets it off from being *merely* a statement of his 'theology' and also accounts for his use of mutual exhortation and even direct imperatives. But that does not of course change the fact that *the rest* of Paul's parenesis does form part of the statement of his 'theology': the spelling out, the reminding of something they *already know*, the appeal to their *previous knowledge*.[15]

What has been said so far about 'ethics' and 'parenesis' in relation to 'theology' may be seen more clearly if we bring in the C-level with full force. In the remarks about 'ethics' we spoke about the **Bb**-relationship at the S-pole. But as we shall see, Gal 5:13–26 also brings in the C-level and the point about practice. Thus what Paul took the Christ event to be all about was not just (i) the **Bb**-relationship at the S-pole, but (ii) that relationship as *practised* and *lived*. The final goal of the I→X→S-model is the special way of (actual) *living* that reflects the model taken as a whole. But that, as we saw, is just what is shown by Paul's 'parenesis' too. It is as if Paul were saying this: '*Practising* the I→X→S-model is what the Christ event is all about (cf. (*a*) above). We who have become part of that event *already* belong under the model (cf. (*b*) above). So, to the extent that we do *not* already *do* it, *let us* (then, finally) do it (cf. (*c*) above).'[16]

Overview: the central task

Let us now turn to the central task of bringing out the main pillars in the Christ-believing form of life that Paul wished his Galatian addressees to adopt. In the rest of this chapter we shall discuss a range of passages in the letter that adopt the perspective of the Christ-believing *I* as seen from within. The argument will be that the best way to obtain a satisfactory understanding of this particular perspective is by bringing in the I→X→S-model in its Stoic form. We shall focus on a fairly restricted set of passages that speak directly, though in different ways, to this theme: 1:4–5, 2:19–20, 3:10–14, 3:19–29, 4:14–15, 5:13–26 and 6:14–15. Our first topic will be that of God's plan with human beings, his aim with the

Christ event: to wrench them out of the present evil world (1:4).[17] This topic is about an X→I relationship which in a manner of speaking lies outside and before the I→X→S-model proper. Paul has stated this topic as part of a comprehensive framework for the letter as a whole. Thus the apocalyptic idea of being wrenched out of the present evil world receives its framing counterpart at the end of the letter when Paul speaks of himself as being 'crucified to the *kosmos*' (6:14). The movement from speaking of God's *plan* to stating its actual result in Paul is noteworthy. In a way, the overall theme of the letter is precisely this: to show *how* this result is achieved, *how* God's plan is executed. Our next topic will be the Christ event itself: exactly how that helps to achieve God's aim. Under this topic too we shall come across an X→I relationship, when Paul speaks specifically of the Christ event—in a manner that we already know well from Philippians—as Christ's act on behalf of human beings (1:4, 2:20, 3:13). But here the opposite relationship, I→X, comes out as being of even more central interest to Paul. That constitutes our third topic. We need to investigate all traces of how Paul understood this relationship. In fact, it will be my contention that we must understand the whole of Paul's construction of the X→I relationships (God's and Christ's with human beings) as being geared towards what he says about the I→X relationship.

Having clarified these three issues in the present chapter—the character of God's and Christ's intervention and the character of the individual human response—we shall turn in the next to a closer analysis of 5:13–26. We need to consider in detail the argument by which Paul makes the two points noted earlier: (i) that the Christ-believing form of life is directly a matter of relating to others in certain specific ways and (ii) that it is a matter of practice, of actually doing what one knows should be done. This evidently concerns the S-pole of the I→X→S-model, and indeed, in its Stoic form. Thus 5:13–26 at last brings out that it is the complete I→X→S-model that captures the Christ-believing form of life that Paul wished his Galatian addressees to adopt. In the last resort, it is by being at the S-pole—as Paul himself in fact is in relation to the Galatians (cf. e.g. 4:12–20)—that Christ-believers will be wrenched out of the present evil world and crucified to the *kosmos* as this has been prefigured to the Galatians by Paul. I have mentioned already here that this is where we shall eventually end. Otherwise readers might draw the completely erroneous conclusion from our discussion in the present chapter that Paul's Christ faith is only a relationship between an individual and 'his' or 'her' God. Nothing could be more false.

God's purpose with the Christ event, his graceful intervention and the specific role of Christ

In 1:4–5 Paul takes the occasion to state the basic framework within which he wishes everything else to be understood: the Christ event as seen from the perspectives of God and Christ himself. This clearly belongs at the A-level we distinguished. A careful look will reveal, however, that all events at the A-level, as construed by Paul, are exceedingly closely connected with things that take place at the B-level. God's and Christ's acts have definite consequences for what it is, as it were, like to be at the B-level. This close connection is a central feature of the overall picture of the form of life Paul is depicting in the letter. Our discussion in this section will be focused on bringing that out.

In 1:4–5 Paul describes Christ's own purpose with the Christ event— to 'wrench us out of the present evil world'. But he also adds that it all happened in accordance with God's will and concludes with a doxology of God. So, the Christ event as a whole was part of God's plan. We may therefore ascribe the saving aim to God too. Keeping in mind the contrast Paul draws at the end of the letter with the *kosmos* as a whole, we may also say that God's purpose with the Christ event was to bring human beings into an 'outwordly' state. How was this state understood by Paul? Exclusively as seen from above (example: God would note that human beings had reacted to the Christ event with *faith*)? Or also from below? Is the 'outwordly' state also a state in which human beings understand themselves (and others) differently, feel differently, act differently? When they are in the 'outwordly' state, has anything happened, not just *to* them, but *with* them *at* the B-level where they find themselves?

Paul also identifies God's purpose in a different way as being that of leading human beings to 'life'. When Paul himself 'died to the law' by being 'crucified together with Christ', the aim was that he should come to 'live for God' (2:19). By contrast, against all previous Jewish expectations, the law could not 'make alive' (3:21). Thus, in the Christ event God aimed at 'life' for human beings, a life which would also be a 'life for' God. It should come as no surprise, therefore, that Paul's description of himself as being 'dead [again 'crucified'] to the world [*kosmos*]' is also meant as a description of something he calls a 'new creation' (*kainē ktisis*, 6:14–15). For whatever else this may mean, a new creation will of course also imply a new form of *life* for human beings. But how are we to understand this 'life'? Once more, is it a state that Paul aimed to identify exclusively from the perspective of the A-level? Or did he (also) see it as having definite and concrete consequences for what it is like to be at the **B**-level? There is not much direct material in Galatians on which to base an answer to this question. Still, the fact that in 2:19 Paul does speak in strongly experiential terms of his own coming to 'live for God' suggests that he *also* saw this (present or future) life as having a definite shape at the B-level, as a state of existence in which human beings might find themselves, not just a state that would be unilaterally 'observed' from above. Not only was the Christ event *aimed at* human beings as being intended to do something *to* and *for* them: even more, the 'life' that Paul speaks of appears to be not just an 'eschatological' something whose only known property is that it is given by God; it is a way of existence *for human beings*, one in which they can find themselves, at present or in the future. In this sense, then, when Paul speaks at the **A**-level (of God's plan and the like), he also does it very much from within the perspective of the B-level, thinking of what kind of direct impact God's plan will have *on* human beings if it succeeds.

If we may provisionally take it that it was part of God's plan, as Paul understood it, to make things happen *with* human beings, this also has consequences for his claim that the Christ event was due to an inter-vention on God's part that had the special property of expressing God's grace (*charis*, 2:21). It is probable that this connects with the idea that the Christ event took place *for the sake of* (*hyper*) human sins (1:4) and human beings (cf. 2:20 and 3:13). The idea is probably the one that Paul will make much of in Romans: that before the Christ event, human beings were sinners and hence in need of a free and entirely un-'deserved' act on God's part by which he would finally achieve his ultimate purpose of bringing human beings to life, including life 'for' God himself. The Christ event *is* that act of God's grace, set going by God in order to *help* human beings *out of* their sins. And how? By *changing* them so that they no longer *will* sin. Here too, when Paul speaks at the A-level, he is at the same time very much concerned about the intended effects on human beings at the B-level, how it changes *them*: their understanding of them-selves and others, their feelings and their actions. What, in short, is it that God has done *to us*—and here to our sinning?

The idea of God's graceful intervention presumably also lies behind Paul's claim that Christ bought human beings *free* from the *curse* of the law (3:13, cf. 4:4–5). This is another idea that is very much about the effects on human beings of God's and Christ's doings. Living under the law, human beings (and here evidently specifically Jews, whose 'identity is derived from observance of the law') would also be living 'under' a (potential) curse, the one actually uttered *in* the law against those who might transgress it (3:10, 13).[18] Since by the peculiar form of his death

Christ actualized the potential curse and since Christ came to function as a stand-in for those human beings who came to belong to him, these people too would be removed from the curse of the law.[19] To the extent that living 'under' the curse of the law would also be felt as burdensome and that Jews would have continued to live like that if nothing had happened, Christ's 'buying off' Jews from the curse was an expression of God's grace too. Here Jews were concretely benefited by an intervention that was wholly God's. We shall return to the issue of the law. The suggestion is not that Jews had *actually* felt the law to be burdensome. Paul's account is a construction after the event.[20] But this entirely correct point should not prevent us from seeing that (after the event) he does read the effect of the law in *experiential* terms from within the perspective of the B-level: as burdensome and placing human beings as if in a prison (cf. 3:22–23). That is what he brings out through his repeated use of the locution of living (or the like) *'under'* the curse (of the law), sin or the law (3:10, 12–23).[21] God's graceful intervention with the Christ event *removed* them from that state and brought them into a different one.

Summarizing so far about the overall framework, we should see Paul's talk of God's grace as expressing the idea of God's completely autonomous intervention with the Christ event for the distinct and concrete benefit of human beings: to bring them out of a state that was both negative (as being filled by sin) and burdensome (of being under the law)—and to bring them to a new form of 'life' that is in some sense 'outworldly'. This was all part of God's plan, as stated at Paul's A-level of discourse. But we have emphasized the extent to which Paul construed the plan as being intended to have direct and concrete consequences on matters that belong at the B-level, not just with respect to the negative state before God's intervention but also to the positive one that God appears to have had in mind. Apparently, God aimed to effect a real change in human beings from one concrete state to another. God acted to make an *impact on* human beings. The crucial question that will gradually come more and more into focus is then *how* that aim was achieved.

Another motif that belongs here is that God's grace also shows itself in the fact that he has *called* human beings to enter into the gospel of the Christ event. Taken materially God's call is presumably identical with the Christ event itself. But Paul also speaks somewhat more specifically about the precise manner in which God's graceful intervention with the Christ event might in fact reach its destined purpose in human beings. God's call was addressed both to the Galatians (1:6) and to Paul himself (1:15, 2:9). Note then how the call was made: not, Paul says, through

some human tradition or teaching, but by a direct revelation of Christ
(1:12 and 15–16, cf. 1:1). In fact, just as Paul had had Christ revealed
'in him' (1:16), when God called him through his grace (1:15), so the
Galatians have had the crucified Christ drawn to their very eyes (3:1)
when Paul proclaimed the gospel to them for the first time (4:13–14).[22]
Apparently, the Christ event was transmitted by God in the special way
that the figure of the crucified Christ was revealed to human beings in a
sort of *direct vision*. Paul may thus have understood the visualized figure
of Christ as directly mediating between God and human beings, in other
words as a figure who enables God (from above) and human beings
(from below) to 'meet'. In order to explore further this mediating role of
Christ, let us consider the Christ event as it were from the perspective of
Christ himself as distinct from God.

Paul is very careful to give an active role to Christ too, in a manner
that is wholly in line with what we saw at the beginning of the Christ
'hymn' in Philippians. Thus Christ 'gave *himself* [*heauton*] up for the
sake of [*hyper*] our sins' (1:4). And he 'felt love for me and gave *himself*
[*heauton*] up for my sake [*hyper*]' (2:20). Also, it was Christ who 'bought
us off from the curse of the law by becoming a curse for our sake [*hyper*]'
(3:13). Indeed, God sent out his son in order that *he* might buy those
under the law off from it so that *they* 'might receive the status of sons [of
God]' (4:5). And when that had come to pass, God also sent out *his
son's* spirit into our hearts (4:6). Why this emphasis on Christ and his
close relationship with believers?

Let us consider a little more closely the exact force of Paul's repeated
use of the term 'for the sake of' (*hyper*) that we already noted.[23] It has
several sides to it. In 1:4 ('for the sake of our sins') it initially seems to
have the neutral sense of 'concerning' or 'because of'.[24] However, it also
seems to include the more distinctly positive sense of 'bringing help'.[25]
Thus the least loaded, but sufficiently full meaning of the phrase will be
that Christ gave himself up *in order to bring help* to human beings
because of their sins. How, then, would Christ's act help human beings?
Fortunately, there is no need here to go into any detailed discussion of
this. For the final clause that immediately follows ('in order to wrench us
out of the present evil world') shows with sufficient clarity that the help
given by Christ's act was to remove human beings from the realm of sin,
in other words, to *prevent* them from any further sinning.[26] In 2:20 ('for
my sake') the sense of *hyper* is clearly the positive one of 'bringing help'.[27]
The same meaning is implied in 3:13 ('becoming a curse for our sake').
But here there is also the further idea of things happening 'vicariously',
'instead of' others.[28]

What all this points to is the idea that Christ had the very specific role in the Christ event of *enabling* human beings to *respond* to the event *in the way they were meant to by God*. When Christ, the mediator, bent down in love and gave *him*self up 'for *my* sake' (2:20), that is, by *his* suffering (vicariously) in order to bring '*me*' help in a situation which was negative for '*me*' (compare 1:4 and 3:13), then 'I' *responded in kind* and through that response came to live for God and so 'live'. This specific role of Christ in the Christ event brings out very clearly the extent to which this event was very far from being merely an 'objective' one which had intrinsically nothing to do with how human beings would respond to it. On the contrary, it was precisely *geared by God, through* Christ, *towards* a human response. In other words, what Paul says at the A-level of discourse has *immediate implications* for what he will say at the B-level. God acted in order to effect a genuine change in human beings.

In this way the two sides of God's graceful intervention (the Christ event and the call) hang exceedingly closely together. God intervened with the Christ event on his own good initiative in order to bring human beings out of a state that was both negative (as filled by sin) and burdensome (as being under the law). He also intervened by revealing the crucified Christ to (some) human beings. The two points hang together. For as we shall see, it is precisely *by* having the crucified Christ revealed to them that Christ-believers *are* brought out of the negative and burdensome state into an 'outwordly' life for God. How this is so becomes clear when we bring in with full force the human perspective from below and look at the matter from within the I→X→S-model. We shall see: when Christ-believers are brought into the I→X-relationship with that figure of Christ (X) who has himself bent down (X→I) to bring them out of their negative and burdensome state, then just by leaving the I-pole behind they are in fact brought out of the sinful state of (merely) living under the law. Thus the Christ event *works* (and was intended by God to work) through a self-*identification* (I→X) on the part of the human being with the Christ who, on his side, 'gave himself up for me' (X→I). It is I→X in *response* to X→I.[29]

Before looking more closely at this from the perspective of the I→X→S-model and the individual Christ-believer, we should note that as soon as we consider the Christ event from the perspective of Christ, the vexing issue of how to construe Paul's references to *pistis* (faith or faithfulness) immediately raises its head. This is not the place to go into detail on this.[30] Suffice it to say that there is a hitherto unnoticed linguistic argument in Galatians for finding here the notion of Christ's faithfulness (towards God). I have in mind verse 2:20 in which Paul states that to the extent that he continues to live in the flesh, he lives *en pistei . . . tēi tou hyiou tou theou tou ktl.* If Paul had meant to say that he lived 'in faith of the son of God etc.', he should have left out the *tēi.* Instead, his meaning comes out correctly in the Authorized Version: 'I live by [or perhaps rather, in] the faith [that is, the faithfulness] *of* the Son of God, who'.[31] Christ was faithful to God in giving himself up for human beings. In the same way human beings come to live for God by living in that faithfulness which was Christ's. And how? As we know: by *identifying* with the Christ who in the Christ event had, as it were, identified with human beings.[32]

We have discussed a number of central features in Paul's 'theological' picture (as seen from above: the A-level) of the world-view that goes into the Christ-believing form of life. But we have also seen how this picture is directly geared to making certain specific things happen at the B-level, where the perspective is one from below. We now turn directly to the latter perspective, which focuses on the issue of identification and identity.

Identification with Christ, I: 2:19–20

There are a number of passages interspersed throughout the letter which indicate how Paul saw the effect of the Christ event on human beings: 1:16, 2:19–20, 3:26–29, 4:6, 4:14–15, 5:24, 6:14. The metaphorical terminology in many of these passages is quite striking and it is obvious that they are attempts on Paul's part to express a key experiential side of his thought. In view of the metaphorical character of the writing, there is an urgent need to try to advance to at least some clarity about what is Paul actually talking about. Thus we need some kind of translation. One term that has been used to provide this is 'participation'.[33] It is helpful in many ways, but that term is of course in need of clarification too. Here I shall show that the best terminology is once more that of self-identification and identity as captured in the I→X→S-model in its Stoic form: seeing oneself as a being whose normative identity is to be found in something one belongs to outside one's more immediate, individual self.

1:16 ('revealing his son in me') may stand as a headline for what Paul aims to say. It is not very specific. Still, even though the sense of the preposition *en* ('in') in Paul's Greek is notoriously somewhat fluid, it seems certain that he did not merely wish to say here that Christ was revealed *to* him. In some sense Christ was revealed *in* him.[34] The same idea is taken up in 2:19–20 when he says: 'I no longer live, but Christ lives in me'. But this passage gives us far more to go on. First, the fact that Paul speaks not just in the first person singular but with a marked *egō* ('I') already shows that he is working with the kind of heightened awareness of the 'self' which goes with any kind of reflection on a person's own identity. Second, it is noteworthy that Paul speaks in a somewhat different manner of his relationship with the law and with God on the one hand and his relationship with Christ on the other. He has died *to* the law in order that he might come to live *for* God. This appears to be a statement about two things that figure at the opposite ends of a 'scale of positive value'. The law no longer has any positive value for Paul. God, by contrast, has ultimate value for him. Indeed, God and what he stands for is the *only* thing to which Paul ascribes any value. Theologians often object to using the terminology of 'value', believing that it implies that a person who ascribes value to something must be taken to be in some ultimate sense him- or herself responsible for the valuation. It is *his* or *her* (own) *deed*. That seems a complete mistake. One may certainly speak of value and valuation in a neutral way which has no implications whatever for the question of ultimate responsibility. So, Paul wishes to 'live for God' in the sense that he ascribes ultimate value to one thing alone: God.

His relationship with Christ is different. Paul immediately goes on to describe this in support of his claim about God. In other words, the *way in which* he has come to 'live for God' is by obtaining a certain relationship with *Christ*.[35] In his description of this he no longer uses the terminology of 'my-living-*for*'. Instead the claim is the even stronger one that 'I' am altogether *dead* and *Christ* lives—*in* 'me'. We may certainly speak here of some form of 'participation'. But what should that mean? And is the term sufficiently strong? 'Mysticism', then? But what is that? A far better *translation*—on the supposition that we are looking for that kind of thing—is to see Paul as talking of self-identification. The 'I' will be dead in the sense that there is *nothing whatever* in the individual person whose self-reflection is here being described with which he wishes to *identify normatively*. Literally, of course, he is not dead. But as normatively seen by himself, he no longer *is* that individual person (Paul himself with all his individualizing traits). That person is normatively 'dead' and gone. He has *no* value for Paul. Instead, *Christ* lives 'in me'. That is, Paul sees and identifies himself normatively as *nothing but* a 'Christ person'.

Paul immediately goes on to explain this further. Even though, as he admits, the self-identifying person after all remains alive as a person with individualizing traits (what Paul describes as 'living in the flesh'), nevertheless, the way he does live is 'in the *pistis*-relationship of the son of God who felt love for me and gave himself up for my sake' (still 2:20). The idea will be this. Just as Christ in his *pistis*-relationship of faithfulness

towards God gave *himself* up in the downward movement (X→I) towards helping Paul the human being, so conversely Paul gives *him*self up
(I→X) in the *pistis*-relationship of *his* faithfulness (towards God), which
has come about when in response to the Christ event Paul identified in an
up-ward movement with *Christ*.[36] As we said: It is I→X in *response* to
X→I.

We should conclude that in these crucial remarks about Paul's own
relationship with Christ, he is talking about nothing other than the
I→X relationship of the I→X→S-model in its Stoic form. And indeed,
quite specifically in its Stoic form. For the movement away from the
I-pole is clearly understood by Paul as normatively leaving behind everything that *individualizes* the self-identifying person. What is left behind
is precisely the 'I' (*egō*), that is, whatever makes a person *that particular
individual* as whom he would previously identify himself and to whom
he would ascribe value. No substantive individual remains as the target
for this kind of normative self-identification. What there is, is only a
hollow shell: the formal self or self-identifying 'I' (the one who does the
self-identification) who is now filled with a new substantive content that
he in fact shares with others—and who normatively identifies himself in
relation to nothing but that, as a Christ person. The formal similarity of
this with the change that is described in the Stoic theory of *oikeiōsis* is so
close that it cannot be accidental. There too it was a change from seeing
oneself as that particular individual and ascribing value to that—to seeing
oneself normatively as something altogether different, something that
one in fact shared with all others of the same kind: a rational being, a
person of reason. And there too we met the curious, but certainly
intelligible, idea that the individual perspective is left completely behind
as understood in substantive terms, but that it also remains in place in
formal terms. There is and remains an I—the self-identifying I: call this
I[1]—who can say that he or she—I[2]: what the I *stood* for in substantive
terms—has been left completely behind. In Gal 2:19–20 Paul employs
exactly the same logical idea as the Stoics, an idea that also lies behind
his self-description in Phil 3:7–9.

I submit that this gives a far better formal understanding of the
meaning of these verses than merely to speak of 'participation' (not to
say 'mysticism'). But still only a formal meaning. Thus it remains unclear
so far what being a Christ person will concretely mean. One may guess
that the answer should in some way be extrapolated from the Christ
event itself. Indeed, on the basis of what we learned from Philippians
(not least from the 'hymn'), one would suppose that the answer is to be
found in Paul's claim here in Galatians (2:20) that he lives in the *pistis*-

relationship (towards God) of the son of God *who 'gave himself up'* and so forth (cf. Phil 2:6–8). But whereas in Philippians Paul had formulated his maxim just before the 'hymn', in Galatians he has not yet stated comprehensively and in substantive terms what it means to live in such a relationship. That only comes later—in 5:13 ff.

Identification with Christ, II: 3:26–29

This is another passage that is best understood in terms of self-identification of the kind that goes into the I→X→S-model. Initially, however, it appears to make use of a terminology that reflects a very substantive notion of participation in Christ as in a body. Paul's ostensive point is that with the coming of Christ, his addressees have themselves become 'sons of God' (3:26), as opposed to being under a male chaperon, as Jews under the law had previously been (3:25). This has apparently happened through their coming to be *in* (*en*) Christ Jesus (3:26, again 28). And the way this has come about is through baptism, in which they have *put on* Christ as their new garment (*endysasthai*, 3:27). Here we meet for the first time a problem in the interpretation of Paul that will engage us repeatedly. Is Paul's talk of 'being in Christ' and 'putting him on' figurative language or is it meant in a non-figurative way? It is difficult to decide. The difficulty is this. If a modern scholar claims that Paul's language is not to be understood figuratively, it is both unclear what claim is actually being made and also impossible to reject it. Often the claim is made in a somewhat self-protective way. Christ-believers *really* put on Christ as a new garment—but of course not *literally* so. What claim is then being made? On the other hand, if we are in fact up against the boundaries of sense (to us), it is also impossible for us to reject the suggestion out of hand. Let us therefore accept that Paul may have found more things 'real' than we are prepared to do. And let us keep that possibility in mind all through. But let us *also* hunt for indications of other, supplementary ways of understanding that are more accessible to us.

Two features about 3:26–29 give us something to go on. The first lies in Paul's reference in v. 26 to faith. In view of what precedes, the reference to 'the' faith here is likely to include both Christ's own faithfulness in the Christ event (cf. 3:22 and the repeated reference to the 'coming' and 'revelation' of 'the' faith, 3:23 and 26) and that faith with which human beings respond to the Christ event (cf. 3:22 and 24). Thus the idea appears to be that it is primarily (*a*) *through the faith* that Paul's addressees have themselves come to be (*b*) sons of God, not just by being 'in' Christ. This reading is supported by the fact that 3:27 (cf. *enedysasthe*) is meant to argue for (*c*) their being 'in Christ Jesus' (end of 3:26) in a *new* way, namely, by bringing in baptism. But already in 3:14 and again in 4:6 Paul implies a precise chronological relationship between faith (and sonship, 4:6) and reception of the spirit in baptism. Faith comes first.[37] In that case the reference to faith in 3:26 genuinely adds to the picture of participation in Christ as a body, which is tied to baptism and reception of the spirit. *Before* Christ-believers come to be in Christ through baptism (3:26–28) and *before* they come to receive the spirit in baptism (4:6 and 3:14), they have obtained a faith relationship with Christ and God which reflects Christ's own relationship of faithfulness towards God. Thus if we are on the right track here, we may spell out the meaning of 3:26 as follows: For you are all sons of God through the faith <so as to be> in Christ Jesus.

The other feature has to do with 3:28. Paul's claim that among his addressees there is neither Jew nor Greek, neither slave nor free, neither male nor female is striking in our context. For it has obviously to do with self-identification. Being a Jew (etc.) is of course a socially ascribed property. But it is also something that enters into a person's understanding of him- or herself. Therefore, when Paul says that 'there is' no Jew (etc.) among them, but they are all one in Christ Jesus, the point mus be that even though there certainly remain Jews (etc.) among them *as viewed from the exterior*, they will no longer let these properties play any normative role whatever in their own self-definition. Instead, they will see themselves as *all one*—in Christ Jesus. That is, for their normative self-identification they will focus on no other self-defining characteristic than the one which they all equally share, that of being 'in Christ Jesus'. With such a reading, what Paul is talking about is not *just* being 'in' Christ in some supposedly real sense. It is also *seeing oneself as* being 'in' Christ, taking that to be a defining, normative property of oneself, indeed the only such property. In other words, the being-in-Christ terminology may itself be *interpreted* in terms of normative self-identification. Or again, it looks as if Paul's participationist language may itself be understood in terms of the I→X→S-model, and even in its Stoic form.

This is the only reading that will give proper sense to v. 28. What Paul needs for his argument is the idea that his addressees are all in some way identical with Christ. For only then will they be that 'seed of Abraham' (3:29) which he has earlier identified as Christ (3:16). But how may a group of people—and even people with marked individualizing differences—be 'identical with Christ'? First, they must be in some way identical with one another, they must be one. And second, being one they must be related to Christ in a way that may count as a case of identity. How may they do these two things if the individualizing differences remain objectively in place, as they evidently do? Only one answer seems possible: by *giving the differences no role* in the process in which they would otherwise precisely have had a role—that of normative self-identification. Instead, Paul's addressees will all be at one in singling out an entirely different individualizing normative property from those through which they would formerly identify themselves: that of being (through baptism and reception of the spirit) 'Christ people' ('in' Christ Jesus). What defines them, *as they would themselves see it*, is finding themselves 'in' Christ, as we too say by a *metaphorical, figurative* use of 'in'.

It agrees with this that Paul should immediately (3:29) go on to say of his addressees that they 'are Christ's' in the sense of belonging to Christ. For on an ancient perception of ownership, e.g. as expressed in the master–slave relationship, what *defines* the thing or person who is owned (e.g. the slave) is precisely the owner (or master). What Paul is talking about, therefore, is self-identification of the following type: finding what one takes to identify oneself normatively *outside* oneself, but in something to which one belongs.

We should conclude that 3:26–29 is best understood in terms of normative self-identification and the I→X→S-model. Paul is talking about the kind of self-definition which locates the self in something outside one's individual self, something one shares with (the relevant) others. He is talking of the I→X- and **Ba**-relationship.

Should we also find in 3:26–29 hints of the substantive way of filling out the I→X→S-model that we already know from Philippians, the one that brings us to the S-pole and the **Bb**-relationship? It is very tempting to do so on the basis of 3:28. However, the role of this verse is rather to bring out that the **Ba**-relationship that Paul has set forth in 2:19–20 as pertaining to himself holds indiscriminately for all baptized Christ-believers. For that is what directly explains the point towards which he is driving: that they are all *one* (namely, *by* having left their individualizing traits behind). And that is the point he needs in order to make them all one *with Christ* (and so heirs to the blessing of Abraham 'and his seed'). Thus 3:26–29 does not bring us the whole way to the S-pole in the sense of the **Bb**-relationship. It does bring us to the S-pole, but only in so far as that is characterized too by a **Ba**-relationship, namely S→X (which is just another form of I→X on the part of those living in a *group* of Christ-believers). The possible consequence of this for the direct relationship between Ss at the S-pole is not yet in view.

Identification with Christ, III—and the flesh and boasting: 4:14–15,
5:24, 6:13–14

There are a few more passages in the letter that work with the notion of
normative self-identification. We may rehearse them briefly in order to
strengthen our case. In 4:14–15 Paul recalls his first reception by the
Galatians. (*a*) They might well have rejected him (for reasons connected
with Paul's health that must remain unclear), but instead they received
him as an angel of God, indeed as Christ Jesus himself. In other words,
the Galatians saw him, so Paul suggests, as (more or less) identical with
Christ himself. (*b*) What is more, they were also prepared to give him
their most precious belongings: to dig out their own eyes and hand them
over to him. Once more the idea is one of giving up everything that from
a normal perspective is closest to what one oneself is. Putting both points
together we may say that they had come to identify, normatively and
completely, (*a*) with Christ (*b*) through Paul.

The idea of normative identification with Christ is brought in again in
5:24 and here too by means of the terminology of death and crucifixion.
Those who belong to Christ, says Paul, have crucified their flesh together
with its passions and desires. Three points are worth noting. First, when
Paul speaks of 'belonging to Christ' (literally, 'being Christ's'), what he
has in mind will be the idea of being a Christ person in the sense we have
spoken of: taking one's relationship with Christ to be the only thing that
goes into defining who and what one oneself is as seen from the perspective of normative self-identification. Second, the point that Christ
people have 'crucified the flesh' will be that they have come to leave out
of consideration completely—as what defines themselves and has value—
anything that goes into the flesh. Third, the fact that Paul connects the
flesh with passions and desires is of great importance for spelling out the
meaning of his notion of the flesh throughout the letter. We have from
time to time spoken of the flesh and connected it with the I→X→S-
model. It is time we looked a little more comprehensively at its overall
meaning in Paul, at least as reflected in Galatians.[38]

There are two sides to this meaning. In one use, the flesh serves as a
broad term for the bodily existence of an individual. Thus in 2:20 Paul
spoke of his (own) present life in the flesh and in 4:13–14 he refers to a
weakness of his own flesh (probably an illness) when he was with the
Galatians for the first time. The same idea of natural bodily existence
is involved when Paul speaks of Ismael as having been begotten in a
fleshly manner (*kata sarka*, 4:23, 29). But then there is another use,
which comes to the fore in 5:13 ff, the passage to which 5:24 belongs.

Here the flesh is described very much as an active force (5:13, 16, 17, 19) with a definite, normative content. The flesh has desires of its own (5:16) and generates acts (*erga*) of the types given in the long and impressive vice list of 5:19–21. (The use of *sarx* in 3:3 and 6:13 lies between the two basic uses.)

These two sides of the meaning of the flesh bring into focus the normative dimension that is a vital part of all of Paul's talk of self-identification: the idea that any features that will be mentioned in a case of self-identification also have a normative role to play that is directly connected with desire and action. Flesh as bodily existence is a feature of the human being that may, or indeed may not, figure in an identification of one's own *essence*, of who and what one oneself *primarily* is. *If* it is allotted such a role, it will also be given a normative role and the flesh as an active force may then be allowed free rein.

It is very important to see, however, that the flesh does not merely stand for bodily existence. This follows from the fact that Paul's theme is precisely self-identification and the normative role of that. For it is certainly not the body alone that may figure in such a context. Rather, the flesh will stand for any feature that an individual may single out as being specific to him- or herself as that particular individual—over against any features that he or she will share with others. Foremost among the former type will of course be features of the body. For the body is necessarily individual in the required sense. But the flesh is not coextensive with the body, but covers *any* feature—bodily *or* non-bodily—that belongs to *the individual* (who is also a bodily being) and is singled out as having a normative role to play. Thus, if one took *oneself* to have some special *non*-bodily quality which one would consider important—like being blameless with respect to righteousness in accordance with the Jewish law!—that quality too would be part of one's 'flesh' precisely in so far as one would take it to be part of one's own essence and ascribe value to it.[39]

This reading of the flesh is strongly supported by the actual content of Paul's vice list in 5:19–21, the one that states what the 'acts of the flesh' are. For here there are two main types of vice. One has to do distinctly with the body (compare 'adultery', 'uncleanness', 'wantonness', etc.). But there also is another type, which has no special basis in the body: enmities, strife, emulation, fits of anger, selfish intrigues, etc. What characterizes this type is only that it is quite generally based on selfishness no matter what feature of the self may serve as its basis. Here any individual feature will do—as long as it is taken to be specifically one's own and to have value.

We should conclude that when those who belong to Christ have 'crucified the flesh with its passions and desires', what they have done is give
up identifying themselves by any feature which is specifically their own
(this already goes into coming to belong to Christ) and stop attaching
any normative significance to any such feature. It will be immediately
clear that this connects Paul's use of the flesh directly with the I→X→S-
model, and indeed on its specifically Stoic interpretation.

Finally, there is 6:13–14, where Paul contrasts himself directly with
his opponents in Galatia. Where they make their demand for circumcision, as Paul says, in order to become able to boast (to other Jews?) by
pointing to something they have brought about on the Galatians' flesh
(that is, their body), Paul wishes to boast of one thing alone, the cross of
Christ, through which the world has been crucified to Paul and he to it.
The contrast here between the flesh and the cross continues Paul's use of
the same contrast in the immediately preceding verse (6:12) and of course
also recalls 5:24. What is new and interesting is the idea of boasting
about either thing. That idea too has to do with self-identification. Let
us consider how.[40]

Phenomenologically, the idea of boasting has two elements, that of
relating to some feature of one's own that one takes to distinguish oneself
from others, and that of explicitly drawing attention to that feature in
an attempt to aggrandize oneself at their expense. Correspondingly, what
Paul criticizes in his opponents is self-aggrandizement—which is bad
enough in itself: it consists in giving normative force to some special
feature of oneself. But even more, it is self-aggrandizement based on
such an insignificant feature as having (hopefully) brought something
about on (of all things) the Galatians' body. Clearly, Paul is working
centrally here with the notion of self-identification (as part of the notion
of boasting),[41] with a self-identification that is wrong-headed by being
based on insignificant features of the self and finally with a correspondingly mistaken normative stance, that of self-aggrandizement.

Against this stands Paul's own boasting. Its occasion, the cross of Christ,
is such a special one that it completely changes the character of the boasting.[42] Paul is not boasting *of* any feature of himself as that particular
being. For as he goes on to say, the *kosmos*, which includes anything
fleshly, has been crucified in relation to him and he to the *kosmos*. As we
recall from 2:20, *he*—the substantive individual—no longer lives or plays
any normative role (−I), but Christ lives in him: Christ is the only thing
that matters to him (I→X). Nor will he be boasting *to* anybody. For that
presupposes the worldly picture of boasting according to which one oneself
possesses something that one may refer to at the expense of others; and

Paul will have none of that. In addition, it pre-supposes that what one might point to as a reason for boasting is something that stands high in the scale of worldly values; and the cross of Christ evidently does not. The fact is that Paul's boasting is no real boasting at all.[43] On the other side of being crucified with Christ to the world there is no ordinary *boasting*. Instead, there is another kind of intentional stance: the attitude of directedness towards Christ and God which reflects that one has turned one's back on the world and its normal values. As we know, this directedness consists in having placed one's own identity in Christ. What is brought in by speaking of 'boasting' in this particular context is an emotional element that reflects the normative side of *this* self-identification. The sense of belonging with Christ and having turned one's back on the world makes one *rejoice* in the cross of Christ. Thus the translation that best brings out the actual meaning of *kauchasthai* in this particular context is that of 'rejoicing'.[44] Paul wishes that he may *not* actually *boast* in anything whatever. Instead, he will *rejoice* in the cross. Looking back to Philippians, we might say that in Paul's use *chairein* and *kauchasthai* express much the same intentional stance, with the slight difference that the former looks rather more backwards: it is joy in a situation of worldly affliction. The latter, by contrast, looks very strongly forward. The person who rejoices (*kauchatai*) in the cross of Christ has left the present *kosmos* and his own individual self completely behind and is filled with the positive sense of belonging to Christ, in another world.

I conclude that all through his talk about being dead to one thing and living for another Paul is talking about self-identification and the normative force that goes with seeing oneself as either this or that. His use of the notions of flesh and boasting spells this out. With these points settled we are ready to look at 5:13–26 and the precise manner in which Paul will here bring the I→X→S-model to completion in his analysis of the particular shape of the Christ-believing form of life that he wishes his addressees to adopt.

7

Galatians II
The Solution Developed

Other-directedness: the spirit and love in 5:13–26—with a prelude on
5:5–6

In the previous chapter we saw that a number of apparently quite
important passages in Galatians are best elucidated in terms of self-
identification and the I→X- and Ba-relationship of the I→X→S-model
in its Stoic form. It is now time to turn to our primary passage, 5:13–26.
The aim is to show that here too the I→X→S-model in its Stoic form will
help us, and now not only to understand better what Paul is at all talking
about seen a little from above, but also to analyse his argument better at
the direct, textual level. We shall see that the passage is basically about
two things: (i) the **Bb**-relationship at the S-pole of the model (S→S), that
is, other-directedness, and (ii) a mental attitude that will issue in
expressing one's relatedness to Christ (S→X) and to the others (S→S) in
actual practice (at the C-level that we distinguished). Both themes have
been introduced by Paul with inimitable terseness in 5:6, when he stated
that the only thing that matters in Christ Jesus is faith that is '[ii] active
[i] in love'. We shall discuss other-directedness in this section and practice
in the next.

First, however, it is worth asking how *pistis* (faith and faithfulness)
and the *pneuma* (spirit) should be placed in relation to one another within
the model. For whereas we have hitherto been mainly concerned with
pistis, the *pneuma* takes centre stage in 5:13–26. A traditional reading of
Paul will say that *pistis* is a term for the I→X relationship and therefore
specifically connected with the 'theological' theme of a person's standing
in relation to God, including the issue of justification and righteousness.
The *pneuma* may then be taken to refer rather to the I→S or S→S
relationship and thus to be specifically connected with the 'ethical' part
of the system. Versions of this position have been dominant in 20th-

century readings of Paul before and after Dialectical Theology.[1] In support of this position one might point to two passages in the letter. In 2:19–20 Paul spells out the comprehensive meaning of *pistis* in connection with the theme of justification by faith (2:15 ff), but does not in that connection refer to the *pneuma*. Conversely, in 5:13–26, where he is speaking of the supposedly 'ethical' side, the *pneuma* plays a very important role and *pistis* virtually none.

We have already rejected the contrast between 'theology' and 'ethics' that is presupposed here. But exegetically too, the proposed separation will not do. In 5:5–6, for instance, Paul *first* connects the *pneuma* (though certainly *pneuma* 'on the basis of' *pistis*: *ek pisteōs*) with the confident and hopeful expectation of future *justification* and *then* introduces the *'ethical'* theme—in terms of *pistis*! On the other hand, we have already seen that Paul is nevertheless quite careful in places to clarify the relationship between the two. Thus 3:2, 5, 14 and 4:5–6 (taken together with 3:26) show that *pistis* literally comes first. There is first a 'faith-hearing' (*akoē pisteōs*, 3:2, 5), that is, a grasp and understanding of the gospel that presumably involves taking it to be true.[2] On the basis of this (and probably connected with the ensuing baptism), there is reception of the spirit.

We have two things on our hands, then: a breakdown of a sharp distinction between *pistis* and the *pneuma*; but also some kind of chronological sequence. A resolution might go like this: *pistis* is primarily a term for the basic grasp and conviction that goes into the initial call and conversion to the Christ gospel. In this use it is an occurrent phenomenon that has to do with entering the group. *Pistis* is of course also something that continues to be there (cf. S→X in the model). That is why Paul may use it in 5:6 to introduce the theme of 'ethics' *within* the group, that is, once a person *has* entered it. Still, *pistis* apparently has its primary logical place—one might even say its missionary *Sitz im Leben*—in connection with conversion and entering the group. The *pneuma* by contrast is an entity that is primarily connected with being in the group. It highlights a certain stable state of the believer. For that reason it is a particularly appropriate term to use when Paul aims to discuss the mutual relationship of those who belong in the group, that is, 'ethics' or the **Bb**-relationship (S→S). But—and this is the point—there is no new and different *content* to having the *pneuma* than what already went into having *pistis*. To insist on that is indeed the point of the I→X→S-model as a whole. The relationships of I→X (for *pistis*) and S→S (for the *pneuma*) cannot be separated from one another.

All sides of this solution are in fact contained in 5:5–6. *Pistis* comes first (cf. 5:5: *pneumati ek pisteōs*) and will thus refer to the initial act of conversion.[3] But Paul brings in the *pneuma* already in connection with this because he aims to speak of the *expectation* of (final) justification, which is a *continual* state that believers are in. With regard to the content itself of having the *pneuma*, however, there will be no difference. For 5:5 connects the *pneuma* with justification, which is normally connected with *pistis*. Turning then to *pistis*, we see from 5:6 that this term may apparently also stand for a stable state: the one which (constantly) issues in acts of love. Why does Paul not speak here of the *pneuma* if he aims to identify a certain stable state? Presumably because he now wishes to remind his readers of the constant *background* to the state they are in, the fact that they have undergone, and as it were continue to undergo, the I→X movement. On the other hand, it makes excellent sense that in 5:13–26 Paul should focus on the *pneuma* instead of *pistis*. For here he goes more deeply into the state he has only briefly introduced in 5:6 and discusses the state itself as opposed to merely indicating how it has been *generated*.

The upshot is that *pistis* and the *pneuma* may after all be distinguished in the way I have suggested: that *pistis* has it primary role in connection with the occurrent event of entering the group and the *pneuma* in connection with the stable state of being in it. But they are also so closely connected by Paul that it would be totally false to see the one as 'theological' and the other as 'ethical'. Once again, the various parts of the I→X→S-model must not be torn apart.[4]

Let us now look more closely at the overall argument of 5:13–26 and what role it assigns to the *pneuma*. If for the moment we leave out of consideration everything in the passage that has to do with the law (5:14, 18, 23), we may summarize its contents as follows. The freedom (from the law) that Paul has established for his Christ-believing addressees (5:1) is one that should be *used* in slavery in *love* for one another instead of as a base of operations for the flesh; Paul therefore exhorts the Galatians to behave in accordance with this (5:13). More specifically, and in order to do that, they must walk by the *spirit* (5:16), let themselves be guided by *that* (5:18) and agree with *that* in their acts (5:25). For the 'fruit', that is, the outcome,[5] of the spirit is precisely that special kind of attitude: *love*—plus joy, peacefulness, magnanimity, kindness, goodness, loyalty (*pistis*, trustfulness), mildness, self-control (5:22–23). Since the Galatians live and have life by the spirit (as Paul assumes), they should conform their concrete acts with it and hence *apply* the attitudes that constitute its fruit in practice (5:25): actually love one another—and therefore refrain from various forms of rivalry (5:15, 26). When they do that, as we may conclude the argument, they will employ their freedom (from the law) *in*

the way in which it was intended. That—positively stated—is what the
Christ event (with all its implications) was intended to bring about.[6]

There are two points to be made about the *pneuma* on the basis of
this argument, one connecting it with other-directedness and one with
moral virtue. The first is that the *pneuma* is responsible for the **Bb**-
relationship that Paul identifies as (inter-human) love, that is, genuine
human other-directedness (S→S). Thus life in the spirit will stand for life
at the S-pole of the I→X→S-model. Paul's list in 5:22–23 of the 'fruit' of
the spirit spells out this specific feature of the *pneuma* with all clarity,
since what it gives are attitudes that are all specifically other-directed.[7]
Looking back to Philippians, we may say that in Gal 5:22–23 Paul brings
out the set of attitudes that will find expression in the kind of behaviour
he stated in his maxim in the other letter (Phil 2:4). That combination is
not in the least far-fetched. For in Philippians too, the *pneuma* turns up
in this very context—in 2:1, where Paul invokes his own partnership
(*koinōnia*) with the Philippians in the spirit. Conversely, Galatians too
has a version of Paul's maxim—in 5:13, when Paul exhorts the Galatians
to act as slaves to one another through love, and in 5:14, when he
supports this by quoting scripture: Thou shalt love they neighbour as
thyself. All through, the theme is that of other-directedness of the radical
kind that Paul formulates in his maxim in Phil 2:4.[8]

The other point is that Paul saw the *pneuma* as issuing in something
that had the ontological character of a mental attitude, a state of mind.
Not only is the *pneuma* invoked, as we expected, as being responsible
for the general state that Christ-believers are in when they have entered
the charmed circle of being in Christ. But far more distinctly, it is stated
to be responsible for certain states *of mind*, namely *mental attitudes*, in
fact for nothing other than the virtues in the Greek philosophical
tradition. This is something we should be able to see on its own, since
5:22–23 is in principle an ordinary Greek virtue list.[9] Also, as we shall
see, Paul intends to contrast the fruit of the spirit considered precisely
as a set of mental attitudes with those *act(-type)s* (of the flesh) that
one constantly risks doing when one is living under the law (cf. 5:19–
21). But the point is far more easily grasped once we bring in the
I→X→S-model in its Stoic form. For here the attitude aspect of being at
the S-pole, its character of consisting in having all the *virtues*, is of crucial
importance. It is what explains a fundamental point in the ancient ethical
tradition that came out with particular clarity and forcefulness in
Stoicism: that being in the proper moral state or having a moral virtue
meant that one will also always and everywhere *act* in the proper way.[10]
We shall see in a moment that this specific piece of theory plays a central

role in the present passage too in the contrast Paul draws between living in the spirit and living under the law. This point presupposes that the fruit of the spirit consists precisely in that set of mental attitudes, the virtues.

In short, as invoked in 5:13–26 the *pneuma* is responsible for a set of mental attitudes, which are, moreover, genuinely other-directed: the virtues.

Practice: the spirit and the law in 5:13–26

So far we have considered the positive content of 5:13–26, those parts of the passage in which Paul develops his terse identification in 5:6 of what being in Christ Jesus positively consists in: faith that is active through love. But Paul also wanted to show that the kind of life whose positive form and content he was spelling out could be related in a specific way to the kind of life under the law that he had previously argued so strongly *against*. And so he again brought in the law. Here his basic claim was this: it is *precisely* life in the spirit and Christ Jesus, a life of *freedom* from the law, that *fulfils* the law! In other words, *if* the Galatians really wanted to do the law—then they should stick to the *pneuma* and Christ! If this was seriously meant by Paul, as it no doubt was, we may once more note how closely 5:13 ff hangs together with the rest of the letter: *Not* the law, but Christ (the negative claim). Indeed, *if* the law—then *Christ*, in the way I (Paul) shall now show (the positive claim)! We must look carefully at how Paul aims to support this claim. Once more the I→X→S-model will provide the key.

Paul has two things to say here. First, against his opponents' belief to be acting as spokesmen for the Mosaic law, he claims that what he was himself bringing (Christ, faith and love) in fact constitutes the essence of that same law. The law is fulfilled in the love command (5:14, cf. also 6:2). And love as the only valid principle of action constitutes the ultimate message of the Christ event. To a large extent this looks like an ingenious *argumentum ad hominem*, which trades on the inherently vague notion of 'fulfilling' the law.[11] But Paul no doubt meant it quite seriously. In Christ-believers, being *free* from the law is one side of a coin the other side of which displays another kind of *servitude*, servitude in *love*. And this particular kind of servitude, as Paul is happy to claim, actually fulfils the law: it is what the law is all about! It would certainly have been possible for Paul to develop this line of thought by connecting the idea of servitude in love with ideas like those we encountered in and around the Philippians 'hymn': of Christ's servitude to God resulting in servitude on the part of human beings to Christ and hence also to one another. But Paul chooses another tack in 5:16 ff. It leads to his second mention of the law, which initially looks even more intriguing (5:18–19). Paul here almost explicitly connects the law with—the flesh: if the Galatians are led by the *pneuma*, they are not under the law; and here is a list of the 'works' (*erga*)—of the flesh: . . .! What does he have in mind? We need to consider 5:16–25 in some detail. The passage is complex and I do not think that all its riddles have been solved. For a good reason: scholars have not realized that Paul is trading here on the theme of the relationship between a mental attitude (*hexis*) and actual practice (*energeia*) that played such an important role in the ancient ethical tradition generally. The reading that follows is an attempt to set this deficit right. In achieving this, we shall reach another sense in which a Christ person will 'fulfil' the law: by doing it.

5:16–25 should be seen as constituting a single argument for an exhortation and a claim that Paul makes in 5:16. This verse is introduced in explanation (cf. 'What I mean is this: . . .') of the immediately preceding exhortation that the Galatians stop fighting with one another. And that exhortation is in its turn introduced as the negative counterpart of the immediately preceding exhortation that they exercise love towards one another. Thus the explanatory force of the exhortation and claim made in 5:16 will be this: 'I have urged you to practise love towards one another [5:13–14] and not do the opposite thing of fighting one another [5:15]. Let me put it like this [*Legō de* . . .]: walk in the *spirit*; then you *will* not act in a non-loving way [5:16].' Then follows the argument proper which is intended to support the claim made in the second half of 5:16.[12]

The argument begins with a new point about the mutual relationship between the flesh and the spirit (5:17): the flesh desires against the spirit and vice versa; the two stand against and oppose one another 'in order that you may not do whatever you wish'. The quoted words from 5:17 allow a range of different interpretations.[13] Since the verse is introduced by *gar* ('for'), we should settle for an interpretation that will make it come out as a real explanation of the claim made in 5:16. Superficially that is not so easy. The first half of 5:17 up to the quoted words easily fall into place. If the desires of the flesh are directly opposed to those of the spirit and vice versa, then the claim made in 5:16 is vindicated: if the Galatians do walk in accordance with the spirit, they will not, indeed cannot, fulfil any desire of the flesh. But what about the quoted words themselves? How will they help to explain 5:16?

Not if we locate the battle of forces in the individual soul as a battle that is actually and concretely being waged there. Then the quoted words will actually work against the claim made in v. 16. If the flesh is active in the individual soul aiming to prevent the person from putting his spirit-based wishes into practice, then the Galatians can*not* be certain that if they do walk by the spirit, they will not fulfil any desire of the flesh.[14] Thus Paul must have something different in mind.

I suggest that he is speaking of a battle of forces at a more general, 'mythical' level, though certainly one that has direct implications for individual souls. *Generally*, the two 'mythical' forces of spirit and flesh aim to prevent human beings from putting wishes based on the other force into practice. They aim to prevent the one thing with which Paul is really concerned here: wishing *and doing*, not just wishing, but wishing of the complete kind that invariably leads to doing. The two forces are at loggerheads. They try, as Paul suggests, to insinuate themselves in individual souls that are in principle taken up by the *other* force in order to prevent the complete success of their opponent. However, they will only manage to do this *if the individual person lets them do it*. As Paul had already said in 5:15: if the Galatians practise unloving acts towards one another, they *risk being consumed altogether* by that unloving relationship. And that is just the point. The general account is designed to leave it *up to those individuals* whom Paul is addressing whether *they* will let 'the other force' have its way or not. If *they* decide to stick to the force which is responsible for their wishes, then they can be certain that they will both wish *and act* in accordance with *that*. And so, if they will in fact let themselves be led by the spirit, they *will* resist any attacks by the flesh. By allowing themselves to be taken over completely by the spirit, they will bring themselves into the position that interests Paul: that of both wishing *and acting* in accordance with the wish. It is the point about acting that is in focus—and that is what the *final* clause of the verse is in fact talking about: 'in order that you may not *do* what you *wish*'.[15]

This reading has the advantage of helping us to see why Paul so suddenly brings in the law in 5:18: 'If you are led [that is, *let yourselves be* led] by the spirit, then you are not—under the law.' Paul's idea is this. If people let themselves be led or 'driven' by the spirit, then, by the argument of 5:16–17, *the flesh will have lost* in the general battle Paul describes there. It will have been put out of action (in relation to these particular people, that is), and completely so. But then, *neither* will these people be under that *law* which tells them *not to do any acts of the flesh*. There no longer is any *need* for such a law.[16] It was different when it was the law that took the side which in Christ-believers is now (hopefully and in principle) being taken by the spirit. In a person who has not obtained the spirit, the flesh will still be active. If the person is a Jew, he or she will also be under the law. The law may then issue its commands against acts of the flesh. But they will not *always* be obeyed. If the two opposing factors are the law and the flesh, it is only too well known that sometimes, at least, the winner will be the flesh. With respect to people who are under the law, therefore, it is entirely appropriate to list 'acts of the flesh' that they will from time to time regrettably perpetrate *against* the commands of the law: adultery, uncleanness, etc. The flesh and the law do not, unfortunately, stand in the kind of direct confrontation with one another that we encountered in the case of the spirit. Why not? Paul does not say so, but we may venture a guess. No matter how much a person may wish to surrender himself to the law, he will never succeed completely. The law is just not the kind of thing that *can* generate *this* kind of commitment. (We shall return later in this chapter to the theme of the inadequacy of the law.)

Again, why not? Fortunately, the answer becomes clear when Paul introduces a little later the fruit of the spirit: love, joy and so forth. These things, he says, fall outside the sphere of the law; the law is in no way 'about' them (5:22).[17] How so? Has Paul not just quoted the love commandment from Leviticus itself (5:14)? Yes, but there is a vital difference. The law may issue *commands*, as when it says that one must love one's neighbour or must not do this or the other type of thing. The law is then concerned with act-types (*erga*) of the same logical *kind* as those for which the flesh is responsible: behave in this way (type); do not behave in this way (again type). The law and the flesh share this concern about *act-types* (as opposed to states of mind).[18] But as Paul says, the law is not 'about' *attitudes*, in the sense of being able to bring into existence *that* kind of thing. For that, something entirely different was necessary: the Christ event. That event generated the whole change in a person that is captured in the I→X→S-model in its Stoicizing form, the complete restructuring of a person's self-understanding which meant that the very basis for all fleshly desires at the I-pole was left completely behind. What was generated in this way was precisely the set of attitudes that Paul has identified as the fruit of the spirit, those that a person will have who has arrived at the S-pole. And attitudes of this kind have the special character that they will *invariably* issue in the corresponding acts. Here it is not just a matter of more or less idly wanting to do the proper thing, e.g. because one wants to follow the law. Rather, it is a matter of singlemindedly wanting *and* doing.[19]

We can now see the whole extent of Paul's indebtedness in this important section to Greek philosophical theory and to Stoicism in particular, which was the only school in the ancient ethical tradition that entertained a similarly radical conception of a complete change from **I** via **X** to **S**. In Paul, a total self-identification with Christ (something outside the individual person, to which he or she now sees him- or herself as belonging) results in a complete restructuring of the mind which means that the mind is now taken up by a single set of attitudes that will always and everywhere make the person do the proper acts. In being in this way taken over by Christ, a person will no longer even be tempted to do any acts of the flesh, and so he or she will no longer either be under the law. What we have here is (ancient philosophical) *virtue ethics* in its starkest form.

It is reassuring to see that Paul himself spells out, in 5:24, a crucial part of this theory with all precision. What was required was the Christ event with its consequence that human beings came (through faith) to see themselves as 'belonging to Christ' and so also as being completely dead to (indeed, to have 'crucified') what otherwise constituted a constant threat to the demands of the law—the individual's own 'flesh *with its passions [pathēmata] and desires [epithymiai]*', that is, his individuality seen as a normative factor. The Christ event destroys the flesh in believers. It puts it entirely out of action, resulting instead in the completely stable and unalterable set of other-directed attitudes that constitute the fruit of the spirit.[20]

What Paul gives us in this verse is an explication of the ('theological') transferral of the individual into Christ in the initiating faith (cf. 2:19–20) in a terminology that shows its *immediate, 'ethical' and practical implications*, in other words brings us from **I** *the whole way* to **S** with regard to the two basic themes we have identified in 5:13–26 as a whole: (i) the other-directed **Bb**-relationship at the S-pole (S→S) that *follows directly from* leaving **I** behind in directedness towards Christ (I→X) and (ii) the idea at the **C**-level of actually practising what one knows should be done.

Paul concludes his argument in 5:25 with a piece of exhortation to which we shall return in a moment. Here we may summarize the logic of the proposed reading of 5:16–25 in the following paraphrase:

16   Headline: Actualize the spirit (walk by it); then you may be certain not to fulfil the desire of the flesh.

17   *For:*
        The flesh desires against the spirit and vice versa.
        Being directly opposed to one another, they seek—by attempting to generate internal dividedness—to prevent people from doing what they wish to do.

But if *you* let yourselves be led by the spirit,

(*A1*) then you are not (any longer)—under the *law* (18).

(*A2*) Here belongs the *flesh*, i.e. the 'works' or *acts* (type) of the flesh (19–21).

(*B2*) Contrast this with the fruit of the *spirit*, which consists in *attitudes* (22–23a).

(*B1*) Such things the *law* is not concerned with (23b).

Those who belong to Christ (as opposed to those under the law) have 'crucified', that is, done completely away with, the flesh with its passions and desires (24).

25   *Therefore: If* we live by the spirit (compare 22–24), then let us also actualize it in practice (compare 16a).[21]

In short, 5:13–26 shows that (*x*) directedness towards Christ (I→X, 5:24) necessarily results in (i) directedness towards other human beings (I→S, 5:13–15, 26), (ii) which shows itself invariably in one's practice (5:16–25). To put it differently, the Christ event generates exactly what Paul had said in 5:6: (*x*) faith (I→X) that is (ii) active (i) in love. *Through faith the Christ event generates the proper other-directed practice.* And that, as we may suspect from far back, was God's whole purpose with it.

The logic of parenesis in Galatians: 5:13–26

I now turn to two corollaries of the understanding we have reached of 5:13–26 in relation to the rest of the letter. One is about the logic of parenesis. The other is about the inadequacy of the law.

Consider the famous verse 5:25 in relation to the question of the logical form of Paul's parenesis. I suggested earlier that in his parenesis Paul presupposes that his addressees belong within the group of Christ-believers and then bends down to them in an appeal that consists in *spelling out* what they in a way already know and *reminding* them of it. It is in complete accordance with this that 5:25 does not contain any imperative at all,[22] but employs instead the subjunctive of mutual exhortation: *if*, in the sense of *in as much as*, we (already) live by the spirit, then *let us* also show it in practice. There is no question that 5:25—and as we have seen, 5:13–26 as a whole—*is* 'parenetic', but Paul's parenesis has the precise form I have indicated.

Then we need to address explicitly a problem that could only be raised once we had seen what Paul *also* aims to say in 5:13–26 as a whole, specifically the basic point for which he sets up his whole argument: that if Christ-believers let themselves be led by the spirit, they can be certain of not fulfilling the desires of the flesh, indeed, they *cannot* act improperly. The problem is this: if that is what the proper response to the Christ event means, as Paul has now spelled out to his readers, then why is there still a need for exhortation? If Christ faith *means* that Christ-believers *will* act properly (or as we may say, be actually sinless in their acts), then why do they still need to be *exhorted* to do so? The problem is famous and will engage us again in connection with Romans.[23] In relation to Gal 5:13–26, there is a very clear solution. It trades on our reading of 5:16–25 in terms of the I→X→S-model. And it is a solution that seems to have the potential for solving the 'problem of Paul's parenesis' once and for all.

In essence the solution goes like this. Whether Christ-believers will act properly or not depends on whether they will *let themselves* be 'led by the spirit'. But they will not be able to do this unless they have grasped and understood that acting properly constitutes the actual content of being 'led by the spirit'. In his parenesis, Paul therefore spells this out to them. He aims to *make them see* that living in the spirit consists in having the other-directed mental states (as opposed to being commanded by the law to do or not-do certain act-types) and acting on them—and that this *total* 'crucifixion of the flesh' constitutes the true content of having come to belong to Christ. However, as we also know, his activity of spelling this out has the form of reminding them of something they in a way *already know* and appealing to them to *remember* it. For Paul presupposes all through that they in some way do 'live in the spirit' and basically do see themselves as belonging to Christ. The rationale for his use of parenesis understood in this way is therefore that if they come to see and grasp that what Paul has spelled out to them constitutes the actual content of belonging where they *already* belong, then they *will* let themselves be 'led by the spirit' in the way Paul has described this; and *then* they no longer will, indeed no longer *can*, act improperly.

But neither will there *then* be any need for exhortation. The secret here is that the supposed 'problem' of Paul's parenesis gets things in the wrong order. The problem ran: if Christ faith means actual sinlessness, then why is there still a need for exhortation? We can now answer: There is Christ faith and Christ faith. Paul's parenesis aims to *bring home* to his addressees *that* the Christ faith that they do have means actual sinlessness. If they do see that and so let themselves be led by the spirit, *then* they *will* be actually sinless. And *then* there will *no longer* be any need for exhortation. Thus Christ faith does mean actual sinlessness. But Paul's addressees have not yet (quite) arrived *there*. They do have

Christ faith (to a certain degree), but not yet one that is fully realized—
in the *two* senses of 'realize'.²⁴

This understanding of the logic of Paul's parenesis relies crucially on
the idea we found behind Gal 5:16–18 that it is up to Paul's addressees
whether to let themselves be led by the spirit or not. It is within this
framework alone that it makes sense, and very good sense, to do what
Paul does: to spell out and explain what the Christ faith actually consists
in and to appeal to their sense of already belonging with Christ. We may
make the point in the following alternative fashion. The Christ faith
(with baptism and spirit reception) brings a person to do the proper acts
always and everywhere *if properly had*, that is, if the believer has in fact
undergone the changes in self-understanding and experience that Paul
takes to go into faith. But that is precisely why Paul *spells out* to his
addressees his own understanding of what goes into faith. He does this,
as we now know, in terms of the I→X→S-model. In other words, he
presents to them a (bit of) *theory*. He presupposes that they are and see
themselves as Christ-believers. But he then aims to bring them to *understand what* the change that they have already undergone (to whatever
precise extent) actually amounts to. If they do understand this, *then* (on
Paul's theory) they *will* act in accordance with it and so always and
everywhere do the proper acts. *So they had better come to understand it.*
Paul's parenesis aims to bring home to his addressees the *full* content of
the turn towards Christ that they have already undergone. It is not to be
understood as exhortation to bring something into *practice* that they are
taken already to *fully know*. Paul's parenesis addresses itself to the *understanding*.

With this construction of the logic of Pauline parenesis we again see
how close Paul is to the ancient ethical tradition, and here again very
specifically to Stoicism. For Stoicism was famous in antiquity for the
character of its psychology, which for want of a better word we may
term 'intellectualist'. As we know, every psychological phenomenon in a
human being was analysed by the Stoics as some form of understanding
or misunderstanding. And that included desires, wishes, passions and so
forth. It followed that any kind of psychic 'remedy', e.g. in the 'cure of
passion', would also have the form of an address to the understanding,
of spelling out to the person in need where his self-understanding was
deficient.²⁵ That is also what constitutes the very logic of parenesis in
Paul. Furthermore, what a Stoic teacher would quite often do is rehearse
once more to the deficient person the essential elements in the process of
oikeiōsis that the person would have already undergone, though insufficiently. Paul does exactly the same when throughout Galatians he presents

the various parts of the I→X→S-model to his addressees, culminating in the bit of theory he presents in 5:16–25 to show them that they (really) belong at the S-pole of the model and what that concretely means. In short, Paul's parenesis presupposes the specifically Stoic moral psychology. It addresses, not the 'will', but the understanding.[26]

The inadequacy of the law in relation to sin and righteousness

Then the other corollary. The passages we have considered hitherto present Paul's understanding of the new possibility for human beings generated by the Christ event, the new 'creation' (namely, *of* human beings) that it results in once that possibility has been fully affirmed in faith.[27] The new scholarly perspective on Paul has emphasized that it is in the light of this understanding of the new situation created by the Christ event that Paul's remarks about the inadequacy of the old situation must be understood.[28] That situation includes being under the law. If we presuppose Paul's 'solution' as we now understand it, how should we understand his account of the previous 'plight' of being under the law? In some way something must have been 'wrong' with the law: what? This whole issue has of course been thoroughly discussed for ages, not least during the last few decades of the paradigm shift away from the tradition-oriented, Protestant reading of Paul that formed a nucleus in Dialectical Theology.[29] The reason for going into it here is to show how the Stoically informed reading of Galatians that we have delineated may throw further light on this old question. The following remarks will presuppose much in the new paradigm, but also give a more coherent position to Paul on the respective roles of the law and Christ within some incipient form of salvation-historical scheme.[30]

We may take as our starting point here the account hinted at in 2:19–20 and 3:13 of how the Christ event removed Christ-believers from being under the law. Christ died, moreover he died accursed by the law. Both facts, and not least the latter one, have removed him from the sphere of operation of the law. There is, as it were, nothing more that the law can do with him. Christ-believers, by contrast, have not died physically. Nor have they necessarily been accursed by the law, at least not beyond the possibility of the kind of reintegration by atonement that was open to Jews who followed the law.[31] However, that possibility is not in view for Pauline Christ-believers. Instead, by 'dying together with' Christ, they too have died *to* the law (2:19) in the sense of being altogether removed from its sphere of operation. Since Christ-believers remain alive, what kind of 'dying together with' Christ is that? We know the answer. Dying with Christ is a matter of giving up oneself completely to Christ in the sense of losing one's substantive individuality—I→X in the model. And this comes about when the human being responds with faith to the Christ event and in particular to Christ's giving himself up for *our* sake (2:20, cf. 3:13)—X→I in the model. Since Christ has been placed outside the sphere of operation of the law, so will the person be who has now 'died together with' Christ. It therefore *just about* makes sense to say that the Christ-believer has died to the law *through* the law, meaning through the law that has placed *Christ* outside the law, Christ *together* with whom the believer too has died.[32]

This is all very technical. Has it any broader meaning which we may formulate by stepping back a little from the technical picture? In the present context the essence of the picture must be that Christ functions as a sort of focal or pivotal person around which two entities revolve: the sphere of operation of the law and the human being. Christ's function will be to help remove the human being *from* the sphere of operation of the law, where he or she would otherwise belong, to some other sphere. What does the new sphere look like? And why was it necessary to bring the human being over there? These questions are not difficult to answer on the basis of our discussion of 5:13–26. Indeed, it is of vital importance for understanding the letter as a whole to see that these questions receive their final and most comprehensive answer precisely in that passage. First, however, we must look at Paul's remarks about the law earlier in the letter and combine them with those in 5:13–26.

At this point a well-known question arises. If Christ's function was the one given, is the reason that there was something wrong with the law? If so, what? Basically, there are two possibilities. Either being under the law was intrinsically wrong-headed—the whole *direction* of the law was false. Or being under the law was, in a way, good enough; the direction was right, only the purpose that was achieved with the Christ event was not brought about by the law: it *could* not be this, perhaps the law was not even *intended* that way.

In spite of a long theological and scholarly tradition that has supported the former answer, we must settle firmly for the latter.[33] There is no indication in Galatians that Paul thought that the whole direction of the law was wrong. Rather, what he says is twofold. First, the law was *inadequate* if taken as a means to bringing about what the Christ event did bring about. In itself the law was fine (indeed, better than any law!), but it was inadequate for *that* particular purpose. 3:21 runs: 'If a [meaning: any] law had been given [but none has!] of such a kind that it could generate life [which of course is what the Christ event did], then righteousness would certainly (*ontōs*) have been brought about by the [*Mosaic*] law.'[34] Paul and his Jewish co-believers in Christ had realized this inadequacy of the law: 'that no human being may or can be justified from works of the law, but only through the faithfulness of Jesus Christ' (2:16). But second, the actual purpose of the law was not at all, Paul now claims, to generate this kind of 'life'. Instead, the law was meant to *keep down* transgressions until the arrival of Christ (3:19).[35] That function it fulfilled rather well, almost too well. At least the law managed to keep its supporters shut up as in a prison (3:22, 23). And it kept vigilant watch over them (3:23), acting as a pedagogue or male chaperon (3:24).

Thus the law was good for one task (to keep down transgressions), and that was its purpose. But it was inadequate for another task (to generate 'life'), and that, says Paul, was not its purpose either. Now the crucial point lies in realizing that the two tasks are not unrelated. On the contrary, they are both concerned with one and the same thing: sin. That this is so for transgressions is immediately clear. Transgressions (3:19) and acts of the flesh (5:19) are so many forms of sin. But 'life' too has to do with sin. That becomes clear if we note the way Paul connects 'life' and righteousness in 3:21 and combine this with their role in 2:15–21. Here too, of course, Paul's theme is righteousness (2:15–17, 21)—but also 'life' (2:19–20). But here it also becomes explicit that righteousness and 'life' are directly related to sin (*hamartia*, 2:15, 17–18)—as its opposite.

This realization suggests a distinct and simple understanding of life under the law in relation to the new life in Christ. Whereas life under the law is a life that still belongs within the sphere of operation of sin—a sphere where the law is good at *keeping down* transgressions, but *cannot eradicate* them altogether—the new life in Christ is a life where sin *has* been overcome and eradicated (cf. our reading of 5:13–26). A human being who has been incorporated into this life has become altogether *incapable* of doing those unlawful acts that the law, on its side, was designed to keep down (again 5:13–26)—if, that is, he or she *sees* this.

We asked about the broader meaning of the technical story about how the Christ event removed Christ-believers from the sphere of operation of the law. We can now formulate that meaning. It lies in a point about the Christ-believer, the two sides of which Paul spells out in 2:19–20 and 5:13–26. By identifying with Christ, the Christ-believer has died to his own individuality—2:19–20. But that means that he has also died not just to the law, but also to the thing which is, for obvious reasons, the sphere of operation of the law—as it were its *Sitz im Leben*: sin. This is the point that Paul spells out in 5:13–26 when he brings into the open that the substantive content of the new life is this: *practice* (C-level) shaped by love (the **Bb** relationship). Dying with Christ (in the specified sense) is dying *to* the *sin* and *sinning* that reflects *staying at the I-pole*—and *hence also* to the law, whose purpose it precisely is to *regulate* sin in a person who does stay there. Thus the most crucial thing that happened in the Christ event (and the proper human response to it) was that the Christ-believer was altogether removed from the sphere of operation of *sin*, the I-pole; *he became* (as we said) *sinless*—if, that is, he has *seen* this.

We can now see that everything Paul says about the law in 2:15–4:6 makes excellent sense in the light of this particular understanding of the *new* situation. The law was good enough and it had a fine purpose. It also behaved in the way a law should behave, by adding sanctions to its commands (3:10). Nor is it at all strange—or even problematic—that the law formulated commands about action (3:12) as opposed to being a matter of trustfulness (faith). For that is what a law does and should do. As we saw in connection with 5:18–19, the law is precisely concerned with *act-types*, which is also the sphere of operation of that sin which the law is given to prevent. The only thing that was 'wrong' with the law was that it could not (of course) do what the Christ event both could and did. It could not bring it about that human beings *always and invariably* do what they should do. With respect to that goal, the law was inadequate. For here something else was required: faith of the radical kind generated by the Christ event, the kind of faith which takes a person completely out of the sphere of operation of the flesh (his individuality: I), the sphere which is precisely also the sphere of sin where the law is operating.

Let us go back from here to the issue to which the whole of Paul's letter appears to respond. To judge from 2:15 ff, that issue was whether the Galatians could, as Paul insisted, become righteous without placing themselves under the law or whether, as his opponents claimed, they would have to place themselves under the law in addition to having Christ faith. Where was righteousness to be found? And where, conversely, would there still be sinning? That is what Paul and his more law-oriented Christ-believing compatriots were discussing. And that is the question that Paul was finally able to answer in 5:13–26 in his own favour.[36]

Then we can also see what Paul meant by righteousness. When he states that no human being is made righteous by works of the law, but instead by Christ faith, what he means by righteousness is this: God's declaration (possibly in the future, cf. 5:5) of the positive standing of a human being vis-à-vis God himself in recognition of the fact that the

Christ-believer *has now actually become sinless*. He has faith, of course, which is a relationship with God through Christ that matches the faithfulness of Abraham in relation to God which God set down to his account as qualifying for righteousness (3:6). But *he also has the inner structure generated* in his response to the Christ event, which means that he never lets himself do any acts of the type listed in the 'vice' list of chapter 5. On the contrary, he constantly acts in accordance with the set of attitudes which constitute the fruit of the spirit. Thus both in relation to God and to other human beings he is not just 'counted' righteous; he *is* righteous and will therefore also of course be *declared* righteous by God. Righteousness in Galatians means sinlessness in the most direct sense. It is something 'imputed', of course, but also something directly present. It is also something 'imparted', through God's gracious intervention with the Christ event and his call. But it is still also something directly present in the believer as a state of mind of his or hers.[37] The Christ-believer is an altogether 'new creation' in the fullest sense of this. And he or she has a correspondingly new 'life'. And just as the 'old creation' was manifest and present in the world as a sinner and his or her 'old life' as sinful life, so the 'new creation' is equally manifest and present in the world as a sinless being and his or her new 'life' as a sinless life—if, that is, they see and remember this.

Before leaving the law, we should note one point in Paul's account of life under the law which is of some significance in itself and also quite important in the light of what he will make of it in the letter to the Romans. We saw that Paul was not out to throw doubt on the general purposefulness of the law. Only it was not designed to generate 'life' and righteousness (3:21). In spite of drawing such a relatively positive picture, however, Paul also suggests that there was a side to the actual function of the law which was far less positive. This pertains to the way the law was experienced by those living under it: as a jailer or a male chaperon (3:22–24). It also pertains to Paul's hint that although the law was in itself good enough, it was not given directly by God himself, but only through certain intermediaries (3:19–20).[38]

There is no great mystery here. Paul is arguing against people who are advocating that the Galatians place themselves under the law. His primary move was to push back behind the law to the story of Abraham in order to place the law in a secondary position (cf. 3:15–18). But he also aimed to suggest, in a second move (3:19 ff), that although the law's role of keeping down transgressions was fine in itself, it had a somewhat overpowering effect on those living under it. We know that this picture is drawn from and based on Paul's sense of the new life in Christ. No

Jew need have felt life under the law in the way it was depicted by Paul, not even when one remembers that his reference to the 'yoke of slavery' (5:1) relies on a well-known Jewish locution ('the yoke of the law').[39] Still, it remains noteworthy that he does depict life under the law in such strikingly experiential terms. Is there a specific difference between life under the law and the new life in Christ that he aims to express in this particular way? If we recall the distinction he draws in 5:19–23 between act-types that are forbidden by the law and attitudes that are brought forth by the spirit, we may venture to see a real difference here that may be brought out by contrasting a 'thou shalt' or 'thou shalt not' with an 'I (or better: we) *will*'. In the new life in Christ there is a freedom from what Paul *retrospectively* describes as the prison of the law, a freedom that hangs on the fact that Christ-believers at long last *will for themselves* (and so *actually do*) what they have all along been *obliged* to do. The freedom that Paul celebrates in Galatians is therefore not just a freedom from the law, but by the same token also a freedom *from obligation*. That is what has been brought about by that completely new experience of theirs: a total self-identification with Christ. In the light of this, it is not at all strange that Paul should go on to speak of a completely 'new creation'. But note that this may not just be an ad hoc celebration on Paul's part of his own position compared with anyone else. At least, it does not seem quite fanciful to think that people who had faith in the Christ event, as Paul describes this, *may* also have experienced this in such a way that now at last any previous barriers in themselves to 'living for God' (cf. Gal 2:19) will have been removed. Thus it *may* be that in some cases, at least, the experience of Christ did have a real and new effect on people that the old, venerated law apparently could not have.

New creation and the character of Pauline outworldliness

We began our reading of Galatians in the previous chapter from Paul's initial statement about God's plan with the Christ event: to wrench human beings out of the present evil world (1:4). And we have ended with his notion of a new creation, which he introduces immediately after having stated that the world is crucified to him and he to the world (6:14–15). We may summarize a substantial part of our findings in the two chapters by considering the precise character of the kind of 'out-worldliness' implied in these remarks. There initially seem to be three options. First, Paul might consider the outworldliness he has in mind as a future state of being with Christ, in something like the heavenly *politeuma* that we have met in Philippians. Second, he might consider it both as that and also as a present state on the part of the individual who has faith and whose mind is therefore completely turned towards Christ and God. Third, he might consider it as both of these things and also as a state that not only pertains to the individual but also in an extensive way involves the lives of other Christ-believers in the present world. Which option should we choose? To answer this question we may look once more at 5:5–6.

5:5 is important here for two reasons. First, it brings in very explicitly the dimension of time: Christ-believers have a confident *hope for* justification, most likely on the final day of judgement, in any case in the future. That would initially point in the direction of the first kind of outworldliness identified above. Second, however, the verse also raises the question of what their *present* state will be like when, filled with the spirit on the basis of faith, they *stand in* the confident hope for justification. That points in the direction of what initially appears to be the second kind of outworldliness we noted. For what Paul has said in the letter up to 5:5 suggests that a present state of hoping with confidence for justification will be characterized by the following two features. If we go by 2:19–20 and 3:26–29, such a state will be a matter of directedness towards Christ on the part of the individual and him alone. That is what 2:19–20 is explicitly about (**I→X**) and we saw that 3:26–29 is about the same relationship as engaged in by each individual member of the group of Christ-believers (**Ss→X**). No genuinely social aspect (**S→S**) seemed involved. It was all a matter of the individual. The other feature is that the relationship with Christ that Paul speaks about in those passages appears to be a matter of pure self-understanding, of identifying oneself in a special way. Here the point is that nothing by way of action and practice seems involved. We might therefore conclude that the state of present expectation is indeed outworldly in the second sense identified above: as a matter of the individual person's self-identification with Christ and nothing else. One might add that it is precisely this picture of Christ-believing outworldliness that Paul pinpoints at the very end of the letter when he speaks of himself as being crucified to the world through his relationship with the cross of Christ.

That is a picture which may or may not be congenial to a modern sensibility. But it has nothing to do with Paul, who forces us instead to adopt the third option for understanding his peculiar form of Christ-believing outworldliness. The connection of 5:5 with 5:6 shows this, in particular the fact that 5:6 is given by Paul in support or explanation of 5:5: we have a confident expectation of future justification *because* (cf. *gar*) the only thing that matters in Christ is faith that is active through love. We know that the last few words here speak about the *present* life of believers, and also that they point directly forward to 5:13–6:10 where it is again the *present* life of Paul's Galatian addressees that is up for discussion. We also know that those words (and 5:13–26 as a whole) are directly about the following two things: first, the *mutual* relationship *among human beings* (5:6: 'through love') either within the group of believers (5:13–6:9) or even outside it (cf. 6:10)—and second, practice (5:6: 'being active'). Exactly how should 5:6 then be taken as support for 5:5? Is Paul saying that the present state of having a faith that is ('ethically') active through love is what *grounds* our confident expectation of God's future justification of believers? Is the former even a *condition* of the latter? To a Protestant ear that may sound almost heretical. Can one possibly get farther away from a Lutheran Paul?

There is a way around this, if one does wish to get around it. One could say that what supports 5:5 in 5:6 is everything up to and including *pistis* but excluding the words that follow: 'active through love'. These words, one might say, are merely tacked on to *pistis* in order to lead on to the *new* subject matter of 5:13 ff: ethics and parenesis. The solution is desperate. But neither is it at all necessary. What we should say is certainly not that Paul is basing a prediction about God's justificatory act (5:5) on a claim about the present proper 'ethical' behaviour of believers (5:6b) *as if faith and 'ethical' behaviour could be separated out*. That is precisely what cannot and must not be done. Furthermore, it is something one will only do if one distinguishes *beforehand* between 'theology' (**A** and **Ba**) and 'ethics' (**Bb** and **C**). But the connection that Paul himself makes between 5:5 and 5:6 precisely shows that one must not do that. God will justify (in the future) on the basis of faith *with all that this implies* (now). There is no faith which is *merely* a relationship with God (**Ba: I→X**). Nor, consequently, is there any justification on the basis of faith which does not presuppose the whole range of attitude and behaviour (including every single feature at the S-pole) which we have seen to be built into Paul's notion of faith. Thus what Paul does by means of his introductory *gar* in 5:6 is give support to a claim about confidence with respect to God's final justifying act by referring to that *one* thing, namely, faith-*the-set* or faith-*with-all-that-it-implies*. That *is* a presupposition, indeed a condition, of justification.

The conclusion to be drawn is that while it is certainly likely that Paul has added the phrase 'that is active through love' in anticipation of 5:13 ff, he is not thereby changing the subject. On the contrary, *against* the expectation we entertained a moment ago about how to understand the present state of hoping for future justification, we must insist that

Paul's addition in 5:6 merely spells out what was already there. What justifies is faith-that-is-active-through-love. Or to put it in our own terminology: what justifies is having gone through the I→X→S-model *in its entirety*. Thus just *before* 5:13 ff, in a passage that is intended to summarize what Paul has *up to that point* said about faith and justification, he brings in his *whole* theory. The proper 'theological' **Ba**-relationship and the proper 'ethical' **Bb**- and **C**-relationship belong together and must not be torn apart.

That conclusion also answers our question about the precise character of the kind of 'outworldliness' we should ascribe to Paul in Galatians. It is an outworldliness not just in the sense that a Christ-believer objectively belongs with and in a future state (of being justified by God on the day of judgement and taking up some kind of life in the heavenly *politeuma*), nor in the sense that he subjectively understands himself, for his own individual part alone, as belonging with Christ. No. It is also an outworldliness of the third kind we identified. It is one that shows itself *in* 'the present evil world' to which Paul *has* been crucified, namely, in a specific set of genuinely other-regarding mental attitudes towards other human beings (believers *and* non-believers) and in the practice of that set—in that world. It is a state of genuine, practised sinlessness in that world (if only the Christ-believer will *see* this).

That this constitutes the full content of the kind of 'new creation' that Paul refers to at the end is shown by a very simple fact: that his reference to the 'new creation' should be read quite straightforwardly as a *gloss* on 'faith that is active through love'. (Compare the almost identical wording of 5:6 and 6:15 apart from that change.) In *that* form of life (the positive account finally given in 5:13–26), says Paul to his Galatian addressees, and not in a life under the law (the negative point) lies the full meaning of the Christ event. That form of life too is the one that will give them the final verdict of righteousness (5:5–6 and 2:16). So let them stick to that (5:1 and 6:16).

8

Romans I
The Problem

The issue of structure, letter situation and overall meaning

The basic structure of Romans is not in itself very difficult to grasp. It need not be repeated here. More difficult—indeed a matter of almost perennial discussion—is the question of how the various parts of the letter contribute to its overall meaning and what that meaning is. One may certainly question the fruitfulness of the search for a 'single meaning'. On the other hand, looking for the overall meaning is not necessarily looking for one thing alone. The overall meaning of the letter may have many sides to it. The question will be whether we shall be able to hold them together as contributing to some logical and pragmatic whole.[1]

To a large degree the difficulties hang on the question of establishing the situation behind the letter. Recent scholarship has gradually moved away from the traditional way of reading the letter either as a kind of theological tractate or at least as a generalizing, summary statement of Paul's 'theology' almost completely unrelated to any supposed letter situation.[2] Instead, scholars rightly insist that the letter must be understood against some fairly specific reconstruction of the letter situation in the same way as this is done for the other Pauline letters.[3] It is true that in Romans Paul does not respond directly to questions from the congregation (like in 1 Corinthians) or to some new situation in it (like in Galatians). There is also the difference, which Paul himself does not in the least conceal (cf. 15:20), that he is here writing to congregations that he had not himself founded and that were largely unknown to him personally. One might therefore conclude that the side of the letter situation that is most immediately relevant to the letter is the one that has to do with its sender, Paul himself.[4] And indeed, it does look (e.g. in chapter 1, see 1:8–15) as if he is writing on his own initiative and for purposes of his own. Seeing this, one might take the letter to be basically one of *self-presentation.*[5] However, there is enough topical material in it specifically directed to its addressees in Rome (e.g. in chapters 13 and 14–15) to suggest that this side of the letter situation is relevant too. And so one might include in one's understanding of the letter an element of *intervention* in Roman affairs by Paul. The two views obviously do not exclude one another. Still, emphasis on the former perspective to some extent points back towards the traditional, universalizing reading of the letter as a sort of tractate,[6] whereas emphasis on the latter tends to suggest that the letter should be read in exactly the same topical manner as the other Pauline letters. In moving away from the traditional reading, recent scholarship has therefore gone as far as possible in the topical direction, stressing Paul's aim to intervene in Roman affairs. That basic framework will be adopted here too.

But of course, there is far from universal agreement on exactly how the letter situation should be reconstructed on its Roman side and how Paul may therefore have intended to intervene in Rome. That should give us pause for a certain amount of methodological reflection. By way of introduction, I shall state what I think we can know about the letter situation as a whole, on Paul's side and on that of the Romans. I shall then give a few examples of how we should go about fulfilling the central task of interpretation: showing how the different parts of the letter hang together with the others and how they together constitute Paul's response to the letter situation. The aim here is merely to introduce the comprehensive way of fulfilling this task that I suggest achieves it best. With that settled, we shall go to work.

The letter situation, I: why Paul wrote and to whom

Faced with the many different proposals that have been made regarding the letter situation, it is sound scholarly policy to adopt a minimalist interpretation: the understanding that appears absolutely necessary to make sufficiently coherent sense of the letter as a whole and that does not stray into speculations where scholars begin to disagree.[7] Such an understanding will necessarily be more general and less precise than most others that have been proposed. The reason is clear: it is when scholars make their proposals precise that they leave behind the area of scholarly agreement. It follows that if some general understanding will in fact be able to make satisfactory sense of the letter, then its very generality and lack of specificity will be a virtue, not the opposite. I repeat: generality will be a virtue. For the generality will then yield what we are looking for: a reading that makes sufficiently satisfactory sense—*and* that may command general agreement. There is a clear methodological lesson to be learned here. If a somewhat general, minimalist reading of this kind can be achieved, then that should suffice. And then one might also consider putting something like a ban on scholarly attempts to achieve *greater* specificity. For that may only be done at the cost of leaving behind the area where agreement is at all possible. Another methodological principle to which we should adhere is one that has recently been stated with great emphasis: that we must—in principle at least—reconstruct the letter situation only on the basis of evidence that is internal to the letter itself. The two points of method are not identical. But they do point in the direction of the same basic kind of reading, one that is not speculative, but sufficiently verifiable.

The reading I shall propose answers three questions: (1) why Paul wrote the letter, (2) to whom he wrote it, and (3) what basic message he wanted to convey to them.

1. *Why did Paul write the letter?* The answer will draw on the framing sections, 1:8–15 and 15:14–33, where Paul gives his most direct indications, and on how the intervening bulk of the letter may be connected with those indications. In this first round of discussion we shall basically stay with the answer suggested by the epistolary framework. The result is as follows:

1a. Paul wanted to prepare for a reasonably extended stay in Rome. This observation, though rather general and unspecific, is somewhat less banal than it might immediately appear. It derives from paying close attention to Paul's careful discourse in the framing sections.

The message of 1:8–15 is twofold. Paul partly states his long-standing *desire* to 'come to you' (1:10, 13a) and partly explains his projected *aims* with such a visit (1:11–12, 13b, 15). But he does not explicitly announce an immediately forthcoming visit. In 15:14–33 he refers to two *other* plans of his. One concerns a missionary journey to Spain (15:24, 28). It is first mentioned in a subsidiary clause ('when I would be travelling to Spain') that depends on a renewed statement of Paul's *desire* (indeed his 'longing') to 'come to you'. That statement is then broken off by another statement to the effect that Paul '*hopes*' to 'visit you' '*en route*' (namely to Spain), and indeed to 'be sped on my journey there [that is, *away* from Rome] by you' (15:24). Thus Paul has not yet even *announced* his visit with them. That only comes, but again somewhat indirectly, in 15:28: having done this and that (in Jerusalem), 'I will go away [namely *from* Jerusalem] *through you*—to Spain'. Paul's other plan concerns that trip to Jerusalem (15:25–28a), for which he asks for the Romans' spiritual support (15:30–32). What is striking in all this is that Paul does not even directly announce a visit to Rome, nor a fortiori does he declare that he plans a real stay in the city. But he does *suggest* both things with such clarity that nobody could be in doubt that that was what he planned. Indeed, it is quite noteworthy that at the very end of each of three sections in 15:22–33 in which he mentions his travel plans, he refers precisely to what looks like a real stay in Rome. That happens in 15:24 *fin.* ('once I have—to some degree (at least)—had *my fill* of you'), in 15:29 ('but I know that *when I come to you*, I *shall come* in the *fullness* of Christ's *blessing*'), which is presumably about the *reception* by the Romans that Paul 'knows', or rather, *hopes*, he will get—and finally in 15:32 ('in order that I may come to you in joy . . . and *relax in your company*'). In short, Paul wrote the letter in preparation for a reasonably extended stay in Rome, but he went about this in a most careful manner so as hopefully not to cause any anxiety among the Romans vis-à-vis such a stay.

There are other answers to our question that one would not be sufficiently warranted in making, for instance, that he really wrote a letter 'to Jerusalem' defending his understanding of the Christ event on the eve of his trip there, or that he had a specific plan of setting up the Roman congregations as a base for a western Mediterranean missionary enterprise in the direction of Spain.[8] These proposals point away from Rome itself either to the east or to the west. But there are two arguments against them. First, we have just seen that a close reading of Paul's careful discourse points unmistakably in the direction of the Roman visit itself as his primary target. Seen in that light, the two other proposals just let themselves be taken in by Paul's own slightly wily references to Jerusalem and Spain. Second, suggestive as those proposals are, they are more specific and one-sided than the simpler one we have given. That is also the reason why they will not command general agreement, indeed have not done so. But neither are they necessary, in as much as the more general and straightforward one is, so far at least, sufficient: Paul just wanted to prepare for a reasonably extended stay in Rome, with or without any specific connection with the further missionary plans that he of course *also* had. In addition, since they are not explicitly stated in the text, the other proposals look as if what we wanted to know was what went on in Paul's mind when he decided to write the letter. That is certainly not the case. Instead, we want to make sufficient sense of a text. When the question is viewed at the textual level, there does not seem to be much room for disagreement about the correct answer.

To state that Paul wanted to prepare for a reasonably extended stay in Rome does not of course say very much. So far it might fit, for instance, with seeing the letter as basically one of self-presentation. However, Paul is himself also somewhat more specific. We may add the following point:

1b. Paul wanted to admonish (*nouthetein*) his addressees and to remind (*epanamimnēskein*) them of the meaning of the Christ gospel. This observation too is based directly on Paul's own statement about his aims (15:14–15).[9] A question immediately arises: is this statement meant to cover the letter as a whole or only the preceding few chapters (e.g. from 12:1), which are indeed specifically parenetic?[10] Fortunately, the way Paul introduces the bulk of the letter, as it were at its other end (1:11–15), makes it clear that he saw the *whole* letter as an exercise in admonishing and reminding. Paul had long wanted to bring the Romans 'some spiritual gift in order to make them strong' (1:11), to 'achieve something' among them as he had been doing among the other gentiles (1:13), indeed to 'preach the gospel' (*euangelizesthai*) to them too (1:15). Then follows the bulk of the letter, after which Paul makes his statement about admonishing and reminding. He also adds that he may have been somewhat bold in doing this (15:15). The reason is clearly that he did not know them personally, that he was not their founding father, and that, as he goes on to say, he had always made it a point of principle to move on to 'preach the gospel' (*euangelizesthai*) where Christ had *not* been mentioned so as not to build on somebody else's foundation (15:20). The two facts that Paul apologizes for his boldness in 15:15 and that he introduces the letter in 1:15 by stating his 'readiness *on his side*' to do what he regularly does *not* do, namely 'preach the gospel' to people who have already heard it from somebody else, show unmistakably that Paul saw this letter itself as an exercise in just the kind of activity that he had normally adopted in his letters to those other congregations that he *had* himself founded. In short, *euangelizesthai* in 1:15, which introduces what is going to be said in the letter, refers to what Paul says in 15:14–15 *has* been going on: parenesis.[11] On Paul's own account, Romans is a letter of parenesis.[12]

This conclusion is far from banal. As Paul himself presents the letter, Romans will now no longer be primarily a letter of self-presentation. It will be directly geared towards its addressees since any kind of parenesis is necessarily that. It does not of course follow that the kind of intervention that the letter represents is also very specific. For instance, we cannot know that Paul aimed to intervene in an intra-Roman situation of conflict with a very specific shape. Paul is not himself sufficiently specific on this. Nor are we warranted in bringing in speculations about the shape of the Roman congregations based on outside information like Suetonius' reference to fighting among the Jews brought about by a certain 'Chrestus', the edict of Claudius, the possible 'return of the Jews' after AD 54 or the like. Once more, many of these proposals are suggestive in themselves. But the tie between the letter itself and the external snippets of supposed historical fact is too weak for us to *know* that they are right.[13]

In another respect, the observation that on Paul's own account Romans is a letter of parenesis raises a crucial question. Parenesis proper is found in chapters 12:1–15:13 of the letter, the final part of chapter 11 (from 11:13 onwards, cf. 11:25) and, as we shall see, chapters 6:1–8:13. What, then, about the other sections, which are descriptive rather than prescriptive? Will they too in some way fall under parenesis? To ask that question is to set the central task of interpretation of the letter—and indeed of definition of 'parenesis'. We shall return to this presently.

On the basis of Paul's own statements in the epistolary framework of the letter (in particular 1:8–15 and 15:14–33) we should for the time being stay with the two answers I have proposed to the question of why he wrote the letter: that he wanted to prepare for a reasonably extended stay in Rome and that he wanted to exhort the Roman congregations.

We may, however, just raise the following central question, which brings in also the bulk of the letter. Were Paul's two reasons for writing connected or were they independent of one another? These are not questions about what went on in Paul's mind but about what understanding provides the best overall reading. Seen in that light the former understanding immediately recommends itself. But then the question becomes this: why would a letter of exhortation be the best way of preparing for an extended stay in Rome? Can we see how writing a letter with that specific content might serve such a purpose? In short, can we see how the bulk of the letter (1:16–15:13) *functions* within the epistolary framework as we now understand it? The answer I shall be arguing for is this: if Paul succeeded in reaching the aim of his exhortation—briefly, to generate the kind of God- and Christ-oriented unanimity in the Roman congregations that he speaks of in 15:5–6—then he would also have prepared his own visit in the best possible way; for if *as a result of getting Paul's letter* the Romans would enter into the kind of unanimity for which Paul had been arguing in it, then they would certainly also be prepared to receive *him* 'with Christ's blessing' (15:29) and to enter into 'mutual encouragement' with *him* (1:12) in such a way that *he* might in fact 'come to them' 'with joy' and 'relax' in their company (15:32).

2. *To whom did Paul write? What is the profile of his addressees?* Once more the question should be answered exclusively in terms of the letter itself as a question about the encoded readers. Important steps have recently been taken towards reaching an answer in a manner that fits in with the minimalist approach.[14]

2a. Paul's addressees are to be identified as gentile Christ-believers. A number of passages where Paul speaks of 'You, brothers' positively suggest this: 1:5, 13, 9:3 ff, 10:1 f, 11:13, 23, 28, 31, 15:14-16. By contrast, passages that address some person in the singular ('You there', *sy*) make use of diatribe style to engage a fictive person imagined to be present, but not actually there. This holds, for instance, of 2:1-5, 2:17 ff, 8:2, 9:19, 14:4, 10. Some of these passages clearly refer to Jews: 2:17 ff, 8:2, 9:19. Others are more general, but in such a way that Jews may at least belong under those addressed in this way: 2:1-5 and 14:4 and 10. But Jews are not directly addressed in the letter.[15]

One passage might seem to go against this conclusion: 7:1-6. However, when Paul here (7:1) addresses the brothers in the second person plural, adding that he speaks to people who know the Jewish law, it is in fact more likely than not that he presupposes that they are *not* Jews. Why else make the addition? Similarly, when he states of his direct addressees (again 'You, my brothers', 7:4) that they have died to the Jewish law through the body of Christ, he seems engaged in the same exercise as in Gal 4:1-11 where he suggests that the effect on gentiles of the Christ event closely *parallels* its effect on Jews. This is supported by noting that in 7:5-6 Paul changes to a 'we' that includes the *Jew* that he himself was *and* his gentile immediate addressees.[16]

2b. This answer to the question of Paul's direct addressees must be qualified in the following way. If, as we shall see later, it remains most likely that the 'weak' people of whom Paul speaks in 14:1-15:6 are primarily Jews and the 'strong' primarily gentiles, then we must say that Paul's immediate addressees in the letter will at least have had direct *contact* with Jews, *within* the Christ-believing congregations in Rome. But this does not of course mean that the letter is *addressed* to those Jews. As we saw, *they* are accosted in the diatribal style of the second person singular. By contrast, the 'strong' are being directly addressed (14:13-23) or included in Paul's inclusive 'we' (15:1-6). (Even 15:7 need not be taken to imply that the 'weak' are actually being addressed.)[17]

The minimalist point is this: In the congregations to whom Paul is writing there will have been some Christ-believing Jews. But he did not necessarily write *to* them too. It is sufficient to see him as writing to the gentile Christ-believers in those congregations.

Similarly, in chapters 9–11 Paul is only writing to gentile Christ-believers. And when he enjoins them not to be haughty in relation to non-Christ-believing Jews (11:23), we need not even suppose that they had any direct, close and everyday contact with such Jews. They may well have had that and it would make excellent sense in itself if they had. But this extra point is not *required* to make sense of what Paul is saying. So we should not assert it.

The letter situation, II: Paul's basic message in the letter body

3. *What basic message did Paul intend to convey to his gentile Christ-believing addressees?* In a first round of discussion we must try to extract the gist of the various sections of the letter at the uppermost level of straightforward exegesis. That might seem a huge task were it not for the fact that we aim for the simplest picture that will make sufficient sense of the letter. Everything to be said here should immediately command general agreement. Where this condition does not obtain, I shall provide brief argument.[18]

3a. (1:18–4:25) Paul aims to 'remind' (cf. 15:15) his gentile addressees that *they have a share in God's righteousness on the same footing as the Jews:* through the Christ event and Christ faith (3:21–4:25)—just as *before* and *outside* the Christ faith they *shared* a life under *sin* with the Jews (1:18–3:20).[19]

There are two sides to the idea of the same footing. One is that Paul's emphasis on the Christ faith as both necessary and sufficient for righteousness means that what had recently and traditionally distinguished Jews from gentiles, namely the law, has become irrelevant for righteousness. Both Jews and gentiles gain righteousness through the Christ faith (cf. 3:30) and indeed, through that alone.[20] The other is that the Christ event and Christ faith constitute a sort of reversion to and culmination of a phenomenon *within Judaism* that was *more original* than the law and went back to the forefather of the Jews, Abraham: faith and the promises. There is a same footing, therefore, with regard to the more recent law. With regard to the roots, however, the Jews excel. Both sides are brought sharply to expression in Paul's repeated phrase 'for the Jew first and also, equally, for the Greek' (1:16, 2:9, 10).[21] The basic distinction here is between (Paul's construction of) *recent* Judaism with its emphasis on the law and *original* Judaism with its emphasis on God's promises and Abraham's trust in them. In a nutshell, gentiles have access on the same footing as the Jews, outside the law but through that Christ faith which is also the ticket of admission for Jews; however, what gentiles (and Jews) will thus obtain is something originally Jewish.

3b. (5:1–8:39) Paul aims to 'remind' his gentile addressees that *they now stand together with all Christ-believers in a shared state of righteousness that is also distinctly forward-looking* as characterized by hope for the final fulfilment (5:1–11 plus 8:14–39). His description of this, however, serves as a background to a section of parenesis (6:1–8:13) in which Paul admonishes his addressees to *display their new state in the actual practices that make up their lives before the final fulfilment.*

Two points in this account are not universally agreed upon, but in need of special defence: that 8:12–13 go with 6:1–8:11; and that 6:1–8:13 is basically parenetic. The two points hang together. They can only be properly defended once we turn to an actual reading of the passages. Here we may just note (*a*) that chapter 6 carries its parenetic character on its sleeves (cf. 6:11–13, 19), (*b*) that chapters 7 and 8 at least contain two pointed examples (7:4, 8:9) of the distinctly parenetic turn to the second person plural ('You too') that we find in explicitly parenetic form in 6:11, (*c*) that 8:12–13 constitutes an emphatic summary (cf. 8:12 'So then') of 8:1–11 (and indeed 7:7–25 too) with explicitly parenetic import ('So then ... we are obliged'), (*d*) that 8:12–13 speaks of flesh and spirit, death and life just like 8:1–11 does, (*e*) and finally that 8:14 introduces a quite new idea of sonship, which is central in 8:14–17 and continues into 8:18–39 (see 8:23).[22]

3c. (9:1–15:13) Paul also aims to 'admonish' his gentile addressees that *their present state of shared righteousness must show itself in certain more specific forms of practice*—of *respect* for the Jews outside the Christ-believing congregations (9:1–11:36) and of *unity* with those inside them (14:1–15:6), as well as among themselves (12:1–13:14). In the latter text Paul also exhorts his addressees to submission to external authorities (13:1–7) and to practising goodness towards outsiders generally (12:14–21).

In making this point in relation to the non-Christ-believing Jews (9:1–11:36), Paul first (9:6–10:13) repeats his claim from 1:18–4:25 that Jews outside the Christ faith have no present-day advantage over non-Jews with respect to righteousness and that within the Christ faith too both parties stand on the same footing (10:12). Once this has been established, however, he goes on (11:1–36) to insist *against* his gentile addressees that the Jews do have the original roots and that in terms of those, the gentiles are newcomers. Thus the same double relationship with Judaism holds as before: on the *same* footing with *contemporary* Jews, but grafted on to the *original* Jewish tree and drawing sustenance from *its* roots. There is all the more reason, therefore, for Paul's addressees to respect the Jews and see themselves as at least potentially one with them, namely once they on their side have come round to the Christ faith (end of chapter 11).

The parenetic section proper (from 12:1) has its most emphatic focus on unity within the Christ-believing congregations themselves: among Paul's immediate addressees (12:1–13, 13:8–14) and from their side in relation to Christ-believing Jews (14:1–15:6). The latter section stands out as being particularly important for two reasons. First, it comes after a passage (13:8–14) which brings the general parenesis begun at 12:1 to a fitting conclusion, focusing as it does on love (13:8–10) and (once more, cf. 8:14–39) the eschatological hope (13:11–14). Since 14:1 ff looks far more directly topical than this, it will immediately have attracted the attention of Paul's addressees. Second, 14:1 ff leads directly into a passage (15:8–13) which by common consent appears to summarize the letter as a whole.[23] But it does this by explicitly tying the specific topic of 14:1–15:6 into the final, comprehensive summary. That happens in 15:7. These two facts are obviously of great importance for reaching an adequate grasp of the overall meaning of the letter. If 14:1–15:6 is directly topical and prescriptive and also particularly closely connected by Paul with what he apparently summarizes as the *general* theme of the letter as stated in descriptive terms, there is every reason to consider the connection in more detail. We shall do that in a moment.

I have presupposed here that 14:1–15:6 is fundamentally about how Paul's gentile addressees should react to *Jews* (or gentiles with Jewish leanings) who had some residual trouble with a lawfree practice in relation to foods and festivals, kashrut and sabbath. As has recently been emphasized, such a reading is not exactly a minimalist one. Paul does not *say* this. And there are other possible readings that do not presuppose it.[24] I reply: an excellent case has recently been made for explaining *why* Paul should have been less than wholly explicit here.[25] That holds even if he did have in mind a mainly gentile–Jewish split. The basic point is that Paul aims to avoid bringing a more or less potential split into the open. It was better, then, to describe the conflict somewhat obliquely in a manner that made it possible for Paul's addressees to situate *themselves* wherever they felt they belonged in Paul's more general description. Then they would presumably be more willing to go along with Paul towards *overcoming* the split.

This reading fits closely with Paul's actual manner of arguing. In 14:1 he begins with an imperative directed at the 'strong'. Since this imperative is in the second person plural, the 'strong' should be identified as Paul's gentile addressees. So they are his real target. However, he goes on in 14:2–12 in a manner that appears directed at both the 'weak' and the 'strong'. But note that he here makes use of the second person singular diatribal style, which means that he is not necessarily speaking *to* anybody in particular.[26] In conformity with this, his argument has the special shape that *both* parties may be subject to the *same* criticism, which they may then *both* ward off by unanimously directing themselves towards the same thing, Christ. In 14:13–23, however, Paul returns to his prime target, the 'strong', urging *them* (cf. 14:13, 16) more specifically to abstain from eating meat and drinking wine if that causes problems to their 'weaker' brothers (14:21). But his advice, though clear enough, is still very gently given, by the way he includes himself among the 'strong' (14:14, 19, 15:1 ff), by his use here too of the diatribal second person *singular* (14:15, 20–22), which takes something out of the direct sting, and by the manner in which he raises the recommended behaviour of his immediate addressees into being in line with that of Christ himself (15:2–3, cf. 14:15) and with the kingdom of God (14:17).

In short, there are good grounds why Paul should not have brought the specific issue wholly into the open—if it is in fact a gentile–Jewish one. Paul did not want to consolidate two opposed fronts in relation to an issue which was obviously there, but rather to address it in an oblique manner that would enable his addressees to solve it for themselves. But was the issue a gentile–Jewish one? Since it is of great importance to get clear on this not quite minimalist reading, I supply the following considerations.

First, it is true that Paul does not explicitly speak of kashrut and the sabbath, but only refers to vegetables (14:2), 'days' (14:5–6) and meat and wine (14:21). It is obviously the food question that is the more important (14:13–23) and here it is clearly an issue of clean and unclean (14:14, 20). But then it is certainly noteworthy that abstention specifically from meat and wine is mentioned elsewhere as a Jewish practice in situations where the issue of clean and unclean had come up.[27] In addition, it should really go without saying that the purity or impurity of foods and festivals was not a pervasive problem in the Greco-Roman world, but one specifically tied to Judaism and the Jewish law.[28] Where the issue of foods and festivals came up in a context like the present one, it would *a priori* be taken to be specifically Jewish. And here it is Paul the Jew addressing it in a letter to gentiles! It seems very difficult to escape the obvious conclusion that Paul is in fact speaking of Jews and gentiles.

Second, there is the transition in 15:7 from 14:1–15:6 into 15:8–13. In 15:7 Paul says that his addressees must accept 'one another' (*allēlous*) just as Christ accepted them to the glory of God. In the light of 14:1 and 14:1—15:6 as a whole, the second person plural here in reality only covers the 'strong', whom we took to be gentiles. Paul's 'one another' is therefore another example of his oblique approach (cf. 14:23). That he is in fact addressing gentiles in particular is supported by the reference to 'glory' in the second half of the verse taken together with 15:9, where Paul again refers specifically to gentiles and connects them precisely with coming to 'glorify' God. In that case, what Paul is saying in 15:7 is that his gentile addressees should accept the 'weak' ones, just as Christ had accepted them into the glory of God. (For the comparison between the gentiles and Christ, see also 15:1–3.) Note then how Paul continues into the summary of the letter as a whole: *For what I mean* is that (*legō gar*) Christ became a 'servant of the Jewish people' with a view to making good the promises to the Jewish patriarchs (15:8) and to making the gentiles glorify God for his mercy (15:9).[29] What does the *legō gar* mean?[30] This: Paul's gentile addressees must accept the 'weak' brothers just as Christ has accepted themselves. *Indeed*, just as Christ became a servant to the Jews (for the two purposes that Paul goes on to spell out)—so the gentiles must be the same, in other words, servants *to the Jews*.[31] It seems impossible, therefore, not to conclude that the 'weak' brothers were precisely (basically) Jews.

We should conclude that the conflict that *underlies* 14:1–15:6—but is not, then, allowed to become wholly explicit—was a gentile–Jewish split over (mainly) food. We should also conclude that the summary of the whole letter that 15:7 leads into focuses on precisely the two basic points that Paul has made throughout the letter. Christ became a 'servant of the Jewish people' with a view to making good *the promises to the Jewish patriarchs* (15:8) and to making *the gentiles* glorify God for his mercy (15:9). That is, the gentiles have—through the Christ event—obtained cause to glorify God since they have been adopted into the promises on the same footing as the Jews, by circumventing the law. *But* the Christ event also meant that God made good his *original* promises to the Jews, including the part of the promises that had to do with gentiles. The last point is then supported by Paul by a series of Old Testament quotations that show that the *original* promises to the Jews precisely also referred to gentile participation in the blessing (15:9–13). But the crucial point is this: that gentiles were adopted by means of the Christ event (and as we know by circumventing the law) *into the Jewish promises*. That in itself wholly adequate summary of all the descriptive portions of the letter is brought in here (in 15:8 ff) *to support* (cf. *legō gar*) the prescription made in 15:7. Should we take this as an indicator of how the descriptive and the prescriptive parts of the letter hang together all through? Indeed yes. More on this in a moment.

3d. (16:17–20) Finally, Paul aims to *warn his gentile addressees against false teachers* who generate splits and lay snares for them (16:17–20). I shall take it without detailed argument that these opponents are Jews who try to convince Paul's gentile addressees that they need to follow the Jewish law. They differ from the Jews referred to in chapters 11 and 14:1–15:6. (i) The former were not described as being in any kind of engagement with Paul's Christ-believing addressees. (ii) The latter were, but they were not represented as trying to bring the addressees over to a law-observing form of Christ faith. Instead, they were in principle ready to adopt a lawfree form of life. Only, they were 'weak'. (iii) By contrast, the Jews of 16:17–20 are rather like Paul's opponents in Galatia who tried to bring his gentile addressees away from a lawfree form of Christ faith. Paul's reaction varies in accordance with these differences. (i) In relation to the Jews of chapter 11 he advocated respect. They were not Christ-believers. But neither were they represented as constituting a threat to the lawfree Christ faith of Paul's addressees. (ii) In relation to the Jews of 14:1–15:6, Paul exhorted his gentile addressees to a certain degree of self-denial. These Jews were both Christ-believers and not out to change the form of life of Paul's addressees. (iii) In relation to the Jews of 16:17–20, however, his reaction is quite different. They may or may not have believed in Christ. But what matters is that they were decidedly out to change the ways of Paul's addressees with regard to the law. And that was just as wrong here in Rome as elsewhere.

In short, Paul's basic message in the letter body is clear: to the Jews *first*, in fulfilment of the promises made *originally* to *them*, but also to the gentiles, and now *equally* and on the *same* footing, that is, by circumvention of the more recent Jewish law; and furthermore, *that* understanding should govern the behaviour of Paul's gentile addressees vis-à-vis Jews of various orientations.

The central task of interpretation, I: the relationship between description and prescription

We have stated Paul's basic message in the letter body at the uppermost level of straightforward exegesis. We have also earlier seen how such a

message might be taken to *function* in relation to Paul's most immediate
reason for writing as stated in the epistolary framework: that of preparing
for a reasonably extended stay in Rome. The idea was that if Paul could
get his basic message across to his Roman addressees in such a way that
they would themselves behave in accordance with it, then he would *eo
ipso* have prepared his own visit to them in the best imaginable way. If *as
a result of reading Paul's arguments* they would 'have the same thoughts'
among themselves (15:5) and *together* 'glorify God with one mind and
one mouth' (15:6), then they would certainly also be ready to receive
him in the way he wanted on his arrival.

At this point we shall move one step down from the uppermost level
of straightforward exegesis to a level of what we should consider as an
even more central task of interpretation. It pertains to an issue in the
letter body that has already surfaced: how the descriptive passages of
this section are connected with the prescriptive or parenetic ones. For we
saw that 1:18–4:25 plus 5:1–21 and 8:14–39 are basically descriptive,
but 6:1–8:13 is basically prescriptive. Again, 9:1–10:13 or even 11:12 is
basically descriptive, but 11:13–36 mixes the descriptive with the prescriptive. 12:1–15:7, however, is basically *pre*scriptive, but 15:8–13 reverts
to the descriptive mode. How should we hold all this together?

Logically there are three possibilities. We might say that Paul wanted
to do two separate things: describe—that is, spell out the overall content
of the Christ faith—and prescribe. The first thing might fall under his
declaration that he has wanted to 'remind' his addressees, presumably of
the content of the Christ faith. The other thing might then fall under his
stated wish to 'admonish' them. But we might also decline to accept the
separation of description and prescription. That has traditionally been
done by placing most emphasis on the description. The prescriptive parts
were then seen as mere practical 'consequences', important enough for
practice, but not for the fundamental theme: that of making clear God's
ways with the world. But there is of course a different possibility, which
is to place relatively more emphasis on the *pre*scriptive parts. Then one
will see the descriptive parts as providing the—vitally important—*premisses* for the conclusion, which will reside in Paul's explicit prescription
or indeed in his addressees' acting on it if they understand him and agree
with him.

To sharpen the picture of the two alternatives, let us consider how
one might spell out the *oun* ('so then') with which Paul begins his
parenesis proper in 12:1. We might paraphrase it as follows: 'With all
this settled, let us briefly consider what follows from this, and indeed
logically, with regard to your *practice*'. But we may also take it to mean:

'That being so, consider now what all this leads up to: a practice on your part with the *following* shape'.[32]

The latter picture immediately fits in with the direction in which most recent scholarship on Romans has been moving. If one generally seeks to read the letter as a whole against a particular situation, and if one even emphasizes the addressee-oriented side of this which focuses on intervention as opposed to the author-oriented side that works primarily with self-presentation, then for obvious reasons one will a priori be more attracted to the second reading of the relationship between description and prescription. We have already seen that the second reading in fact makes excellent sense of the whole letter at the uppermost level of straightforward exegesis. Moreover, by combining Paul's reason for writing as stated in the epistolary frame with his basic message as given in the letter body, this reading is also able to *combine* within the same picture a basic addressee-orientation with some degree of author-orientation. We are therefore justified in pressing on along this line of reading. Then the central task of interpretation becomes not just to show how the different parts of the letter hang together with the others and how they together constitute Paul's response to the letter situation (that we have already done), but more specifically this: to ascertain *exactly how* the descriptive parts of the letter may supply *premisses* for the content of the prescriptive parts. I have already indicated how the relationship between 15:8–13, 15:7 and 14:1–15:6 suggests an answer to this question. To clarify the project, however, let me give three further examples.

First, on the kind of intervention- and practice-oriented reading of Romans we are now considering one must be able to explain sufficiently how, for instance, 1:18–8:39 may provide premisses for the general parenetic section of 12:1–13:14. That may not be so difficult. For the parenetic section ends with (*a*) heavy emphasis on mutual *agapē* (13:8–10) (*b*) in the light of an approaching eschatological salvation (13:11–12) (*c*) that requires that Paul's addressees 'put on the Lord Jesus Christ and stop thinking on behalf of the flesh and its desires' (13:14). (*a*) Now the theme of mutual *agapē* may well be seen to have been prepared for in 1:18–8:39 when Paul showed that Christ-believing Jews and gentiles *share in* righteousness and salvation, just as before Christ they *shared in* living under sin. The point about sharing *backs* the claim about *agapē*. (*b*) The theme of the approaching eschatological salvation has of course also been extensively prepared for in 1:18–8:39. For instance, the Christ-believing Jews and gentiles of 5:1–11 and 8:14–39 stand together sharing the same hope for the eschatological fulfilment. (*c*) Finally, the theme of putting on Christ and putting fleshly desires behind one has been prepared for negatively in 1:18–32 and positively in chapter 6 and 8:1–13.

Nor would it be difficult to show how 1:18–8:39 may provide premisses for the more specific parenetic section of 14:1–15:6, on the reading we adopted of that. 14:1–15:6 ends with an exhortation (15:1–6) that Paul's gentile addressees take Christ as their model and adapt themselves to the Christ-believing, 'weak' Jews so that both parties may glorify God with one mind and voice. Now that piece of exhortation may well be seen to have been extensively prepared for in 1:18–8:39. If, by God's graceful act in Christ, gentiles have received a share in his righteousness and salvation on the same footing as the Jews, then it follows that they should themselves respond to their 'weaker' Jewish brothers in a manner that reflects that act of grace and allows *them* to share in the same glorification of God.

The second example concerns Paul's teaching on the law in 1:18–8:39. Does it make sense to claim a parenetic purpose for that too? Again, the answer should be positive. Throughout 1:18–8:39 Paul drops a number of hints about the function and place of the law: 3:20, 31, 4:15, 5:13, 20. These hints are then taken up in 7:7–25, where Paul provides as much of a reasoned and coherent account of the place of the law within his salvation-historical scheme as he was able to give. But is that parenetically relevant? Yes. For Paul's descriptive account in 7:7–25 of the function of the law is immediately followed by an account of life in the spirit. And that section (8:1–13) is basically parenetic, as we shall see in more detail, and ends up being explicitly directed to Paul's addressees (from 8:9: 'You, however, are not in the flesh, but in the spirit'). Thus Paul may well be seen to give his most reasoned account of the role and function of the law (7:7–25) not so much because of its intrinsic interest to himself or to his addressees, but *as a negative foil for* his positive—*and parenetic*—statement of where, by contrast, his addressees now find—*and should find*—themselves.

The third example concerns the structure of chapters 9–11. Why a long and substantial, descriptive section (9:1–11:12) explaining how and why Jews have not responded to God's call in Christ whereas gentiles have—if that section is only meant to lead up to a section that tells the gentiles to behave respectfully in relation to non-Christ-believing Jews (11:13 ff)? The answer is not difficult to find when one remembers the two connected points Paul makes throughout the letter about the gentiles in relation to recent Judaism (the law) and to original Judaism (the promises). Paul aims to tell his gentile addressees to respect those Jews who were the direct heirs to God's *original* promises—*but* who, for reasons best known to God, had *not* responded to God's act of making good those promises in the Christ event. But in order to be able to do that in a manner that could not be misunderstood to imply that the gentiles should also adopt the law, he needed to spell out once more—and with unprecedented sharpness—that the (merely) law-abiding, *non*-Christ-believing Jews were *wrong* and that Paul's addressees, who had been brought in *outside* the law, were *right*. It is only against this particular background, which has to do with *recent* Judaism, that he could go on to recommend the specific kind of respect for non-Christ-believing Jews that he derives from *original* Judaism.

These were only examples. With an intervention-oriented approach to Romans one will work along such lines towards obtaining an entirely clear grasp of the network of ties that binds together the comprehensive 'world-view' that Paul descriptively develops throughout the letter with the 'ethos' that he is also prescriptively exhorting his addressees to have and to practise. The final result of such an enterprise will be an ability to see exactly how the letter body may serve as an extensive plea for unity among all Christ-believers (including Jewish and gentile ones) and for respect, forthcomingness and submission on the part of his immediate gentile addressees in relation to, respectively, non-Christ-believing Jews, non-Christ-believers generally and the authorities. For not only is Romans a letter of parenesis; its parenesis is also specifically directed towards those objectives. Also, one will become able to see exactly how Paul's central message to which everything in the letter tends is summed up in the verses we have already quoted as concluding his most specific piece of exhortation (14:1–15:6): 'May God, [the source] of perseverance and [mutual] encouragement (*paraklēsis!*) grant that you may have *the same thoughts among one another* in accordance with Christ Jesus, / in order that you may *with one mind and one voice* praise the God and Father of our Lord Jesus Christ' (15:5–6). With this one may also connect the reference to 'righteousness, *peace* (*eirēnē*) and joy' (*chara*—a shared thing, as we know)[33] 'in the holy spirit' as what 'the kingdom of God' *consists in* (14:17) and the concluding wish that the God of hope may fill Paul's addressees with 'all joy and peace' (again *chara* and *eirēnē*) in their life of faith issuing in an overflow of hope brought about by 'the power of the holy spirit' (15:13).

That is where we should end.[34] And pursuing the exact ties between description and prescription at the level at which we have hitherto been operating would be an instructive task in itself. I shall argue, however, that in the *specific* way in which Paul sets up his 'world-view' and the changes brought about in it by the Christ event, he makes use of a wholly distinct set of ideas that point forward far more directly to his account of the Christian 'ethos' and indeed to his exhortation to bring that into practice. Furthermore, this is something the full impact of which one will only notice once one approaches Paul's text with the I→X→S-model in mind. The claim is that in addition to—and underlying—the many different connections between 'world-view' and 'ethos' that one may tease out throughout the letter, there is a single, basic connection that holds all the others together: the one expressed in the I→X→S-model.

The central task of interpretation, II: the I→X→S-model

As a way into the following more detailed analysis of the letter, I shall present how the various sections will look in the light of that model. The aim is not yet to argue the case but only to sketch the contours of the landscape over which we shall range in the more detailed analyses that follow.

1:18–3:20 aims to show that both non-Jews and Jews outside Christ have had (or at least risk having) a false relationship with God (**Ba**: –I→X) and for that reason also a false relationship with one another (**Bb**). Or at least, if they do have a proper one, they do not (always) put it into practice (**C**-level). All three features go into the claim that both non-Jews and Jews outside Christ are 'under sin' (3:9). Paul also shows that this whole sorry state has to do precisely with features that belong to the kind of being who may at all have some relationship or other with God: the individual human being viewed as an individual, precisely somebody who belongs at the **I**-pole of the model in the precise way this should be understood.

3:21–4:25 aims to show that the Christ event generated the proper relationship with God (**Ba**: I→X), that of Christ faith. In the light of the whole complex of ideas set forth in 1:18—3:20 the question immediately arises whether the proper **Ba**-relationship will also have implications for **Bb** and **C**. But Paul does not yet answer this question. Thus a very great deal is left hanging here of the complex that was introduced in 1:18–3:20. Indeed, it is precisely the aim of the rest of the letter body to spell out the precise implications *for* **Bb** and **C** of the proper **Ba**-relationship that the Christ event and faith have brought about. That, at a deeper level, is the logic that holds the letter together from 5:1 onwards.

5:1–21 and *8:14–39*, then, celebrate the new position of Christ-believers. After the backward-looking perspective of 1:18–3:20 and the perspective of 3:21–4:25 that focused on the *nyn* (cf. 3:21) of the Christ event and the resulting Christ faith, the perspective in 5:1 ff becomes distinctly forward-looking. Here Paul establishes the stance to which he will eventually appeal in 15:5–6 and 15:13: of present-day perseverance and hope for the future (e.g. 5:3–5, cf. 15:5 and 15:13 respectively) that should be matched by the unity and indeed unanimity that Paul aims to bring about among his addressees (15:5–6). In relation to the I→X→S-model and our three levels, we may note that Paul's focus here is very much on the B-level, on how *believers* now stand looking directly towards God—though of course as a result of God's graceful intervention (A-level: X→I—the theme of 3:21 ff) and their own response of faith (I→X, 3:31–4:25). We may also note that Paul's perspective on the believers is very much a collective one. It is constantly a matter of 'us' standing directed towards God in the confident hope that 'we' shall eventually reach his glory. In short, Paul is talking of the S→X relationship, once more the one with which he also ends in 15:5–6. The question remains, however, how this relates to **Bb** (S→S) and **C** ('ethical' practice). Can the S→X relationship that Paul celebrates in 5:1–21 and 8:14–39 stand alone? Or does it imply a specific version of **Bb** and **C**?

6:1–8:13 answers one half of this question, namely as applied to **C**. Here Paul argues that the Christ faith (I→X), as symbolically and ritually bodied forth in baptism, *implies* a practice which reflects the fact that a Christ-believer is no longer 'under sin'. (And therefore, as we know, *'you' should* no longer sin.) All through the passage Paul is very much concerned with the individual human being, and not with the **Bb** relationship. He claims that an individual who has responded to the Christ event with Christ faith (I→X) will also in concrete practice be outside the realm where sin is in command. In other words, in his concrete bodily practice he will do what he should do. Paul's account here harks explicitly back to the account given in 1:18–3:20. Thus in chapter 6 his point is that the baptized Christ-believer will now avoid doing (at the C-level) precisely what the non-Jews of 1:18 ff did do in their mistaken **Bb**-relationship, which reflected their equally mistaken **Ba**-relationship. And in 7:1–8:13 the basic point is that the Christ-believer will now do (again at the C-level) precisely what the Jew of 2:17 ff did not do: fulfil (8:4) the law, in the sense of actually doing it. In both cases we must evidently analyse how these happy results have (and should!) come about. What is the specific *theory* underlying Paul's various claims here?

9:1–11:36 takes up the second half of the question we raised, the half concerned with **Bb**. These chapters show that the radical directed-ness towards God (**Ba**: I→X) that the Christ event has generated has specific implications (namely, that there is no relevant distinction between

Christ-believing Jews and gentiles), which again has implications for the 'ethical' relationship of human beings towards one another: **Bb**—in this case from the side of Christ-believing non-Jews towards *non*-Christ-believing Jews. Being directed towards God, the former have no more reason to take pride (cf. 11:18) in their own happy fate with respect to righteousness and salvation over against the latter—than non-Christ-believing Jews had in relation to non-Christ-believing gentiles (cf. 2:17–24).

9:1–11:36, it may be said, argues for a special version of the proper **Bb**-relationship since it is about the relationship of Paul's addressees to *non*-Christ-believing Jews. But it is easy to see that this particular issue follows directly on the 'salvation-historical' story given in chapters 1–8. If Christ-believing Jews and gentiles stand together, by the end of 1:18–8:39, in the confident expectation of receiving God's glory, then how is it in fact with those Jews who have not (yet) turned to Christ, particularly when, as Paul insists (cf. 3:1–2, and indeed 9:1–5), the Jews in principle excel since the original promises were made to *them*? Even more to the point, the issue of gentile respect for the Jews leads specifically forward to the one treated in 14:1–15:7 when this is taken to concern the relationship of Paul's gentile addressees to Jews *within* the Roman churches. Indeed, one may even claim that it is this forward-looking, preparatory dimension that accounts for *why Paul has chosen to give his 'salvation-historical' sketch in the first place* from the very beginning of the letter (1:18 ff), focused as it is precisely on the relationship between Jews and gentiles in and outside of Christ. Still, in view of the manner Paul set up the discussion in 1:18 ff (cf. above), a more extensive discussion was required of the implications for life at the **Bb**-level of the Christ event and the human faith response. As we know, that is then the topic of chapters 12:1–15:13, where *12:1–13:14* basically gives general parenesis (though with 13:1–7 being somewhat more specific) and *14:1–15:6/7* quite specific and highly topical parenesis.

To put it all in schematic form:

1:18–3:20 sets up the whole complex problem with all its various components: a mistaken response to God (– **Ba**) based on an inability to leave the I-pole and resulting in a mistaken inter-human relationship (– **Bb**) and a lack of the required practice (– **C**).

3:21–4:25 introduces the solution to the problem: a proper response to God (+ **Ba**) that sets the movement from **I** to **X** (and **S**) going as something that results from God's gracious intervention with the Christ event (**X→I**).

5:1–21 and *8:14–39* celebrate the success of the solution in a manner that prefigures the concrete solution that Paul will eventually formulate in 15:5–6 to a concrete problem within the Roman churches: in effect a shared relationship upwards (S→X).

6:1–8:13 spells out and explains how the solution actually does solve the problem at the level of practice (+ C).

9:1–11:36 repeats the basic idea (of the Christ event and resulting Christ faith as the solution to the *whole* set that constitutes the problem) as applied to the specific problem of the relationship of Christ-believing non-Jews to non-Christ-believing Jews: + **Bb** in one specific relation.

12:1–13:14 spells out how the solution solves the initially formulated problem at the level of the inter-human relationship more broadly defined, within the group of Christ-believers (+ S→S) and in their external relationship: + **Bb** in several general relations.

Finally, *14:1—15:13* brings everything—that is, the Christ event as the solution to the *whole* set that constitutes the problem *and* the issue of the relationship between Jews and gentiles in terms of which Paul has presented both the problem and the solution—to bear on the question of the mutual relationship of Christ-believing Jews and non-Jews *within the Roman churches* (+ S→S): + **Bb** in another specific, highly *topical* relation.

If this is right—if, that is, we shall be able to show how the details of what Paul says fit into the I→X→S-model in the very specific form in which we understand it—then it is fair to say that the model formulates a comprehensive 'theory' of a problem and its solution, a theory that connects the various parts of the letter with one another and allows us to hold the whole letter tightly together. We may then take one further step and claim the following. In addition to making his addressees see the various connections we have noted so far, Paul will also have aimed to make them understand the comprehensive set of connections itself which is formulated in his theory. Here his idea will have been this: *if they saw it, then they would also act on it.* Thus the *theory* as captured in the I→X→S-model hangs exceedingly closely together with Paul's *parenetic* aim with the letter as a whole.

In the analysis that follows we shall go through some of the main themes that go into the story just given. Basically, there are three: (*a*) the theme of total directedness towards God (**Ba: I→X**), (*b*) the consequent removal of the I-pole that stands in the way of the proper inter-human relationship (**Bb**) and the proper practice (**C**), (*c*) and the resulting total openness towards others (**Bb: S→S**). The aim is to disclose the precise ways in which Paul's text connects these three themes and thereby to defend the claim that the I→X→S-model, which formulates these connections, underlies the whole letter and displays its essential unity. In accordance with the approach adopted in this book, we shall constantly allow ourselves to raise questions that concern the intrinsic meaningfulness and coherence of Paul's various claims at an empirical, phenomenological and philosophical level. As we go along, we shall also from time to time touch on a number of basic themes in traditional theological readings of the letter, but only in such a way as to show how they should be handled within the framework I am proposing. Perhaps the most important among these themes is the one that asks about the degree to which we may claim that Paul's own text allows us to analyse what he says in terms of what is the essence of the I→X→S-model: intentional relationships in the mind of the individual Christ-believer.

Directedness towards God and 'ethical' behaviour: 1:18–3:20

1:18–32 on non-Christ-believing gentiles sets out a closely knit connection between three themes that correspond to the three we noted: (*a*) a failure in the required directedness towards God, (*b*) a failure in 'ethical' behaviour and (*c*) the phenomenon that explains both, self-directedness. In the present section we shall consider only the first two, aiming all through these remarks to discover how Paul's various points are logically connected. The third theme will be taken up in the next section but one.

Paul is careful to spell out the special form of the ungodliness (*asebeia*, 1:18) that characterizes non-Christ-believing gentiles. They did know of God (1:19–21), but did not glorify and pay thanks to him (1:19) or think fit to recognize him (1:28). The eventual result was a growing darkening of their understanding (1:21), which showed itself in a change from what should have been the case—glorification of the eternal God—to a glorification of a 'god' in the form of mortal man or something further down the scale (1:23), in short of created things rather than the creator (1:25). This failed relationship with God (**Ba**) is clearly a mis-*understanding*, a lack of the proper intentional directedness towards God that would reflect the *truth* about him (1:18, 25), namely the grasp of 'his eternal power and divine majesty' (1:20). Non-Christ-believing gentiles are directly and indubitatively lacking in this, the proper form of the relationship with God (*a*).

But this failure at the **A/Ba**-level also shows itself at the 'ethical' level in a propensity in these gentiles for immoral behaviour (*b*). Paul three times (1:24, 26, 28) relates how God 'gave' the gentiles 'over' to immoral behaviour of various sorts in punishment for their lack of recognition of God. We must return to consider this in more detail (the next section but one). The fact itself that the punishment is meant to correspond in kind to the crime already suggests that there is an intrinsic connection that we need to articulate between the two types of failure. Let us just note here that the 'ethical' failure Paul has in mind is not a failure at the C-level of not doing what one knows should be done and in a way also wishes to do. It is true that these people do recognize God's negative attitude to their own favoured behaviour (cf. 1:32). But their problem is that they altogether neglect this insight. They forget about God, that is, they do not in fact have any relationship with him of the form that one should have: I→X.[35] Correspondingly, as we shall see, their 'ethical' failure is one that pertains to a person's relationship with *others*. It belongs at the Bb-level.

The general connection between lack of directedness towards God and 'ethical' failure is also found in the people described in 2:1–6. These people take God far more seriously than those described in 1:18–32, to the extent of even criticizing the latter for their neglect of God's just demands (2:1–3 with 1:32). But they also themselves act in the way they criticize in others (2:1, 3), apparently fancying that they will themselves escape from God's judgement (2:2, 3). This amounts to despising God's present forbearance and neglecting its purpose, which is to make people turn round (2:4). So these people too lack the required unambiguous directedness towards God. How should we understand their 'ethical' failure? Does it belong at the Bb-level or at the C-level? Clearly the latter. For in contrast with the people described in chapter 1, they do not just neglect God's demands. They acknowledge them and even try to enforce them—against others. So they *know* them full well and take them quite seriously. Their failure belongs at the C-level. It is a failure of *practice*.

Who are the people described in 2:1–6? The question is a thorny one.[36] However, we need not make a more specific decision here than is more or less immediately warranted by the text. These people are those who (i) have enough of a relationship with God for it to serve as an appropriate backing, as they themselves see it, for criticism of others, but also (ii) have an insufficiently focused relationship with God for them to apply that relationship to their own actions. They may therefore be those whom Paul is actually addressing in his letter—to the extent that the description he gives in 2:4–5 may still also apply to *them*. Such a reading could be said to be suggested by Paul's sudden diatribal turn to a second person type of address in 2:1.[37] Paul, one might say, aims to prevent his direct, gentile addressees from feeling too smug about themselves once they have heard his violent criticism in chapter 1 of their *non*-Christ-believing ethnic brothers. However, the traditional reading that the people addressed here are Jews who have not (yet) come round to the Christ faith also has something to be said for it, not least the similarity between the descriptions given in 2:1–3 and 2:17–24. The best solution is to reject the demand for precise specificity.[38] Instead, we may take it that Paul intends to speak, as he himself indeed says (2:1), of *every* (kind of) human being who judges others on the frail basis that he goes on to describe. This group probably includes, again in his own words, 'the Jew first and also, equally, the Greek' (cf. 2:9–10). What really matters is that these people have not (completely) turned round to God (2:4–5). That is what *explains* the special kind of wrong behaviour that is theirs.

On the basis of these remarks about 1:18–32 and 2:1–6 we may ask the following set of general questions that will keep us occupied: Is the connection between a failing directedness towards God and 'ethical' failure so close that it goes both ways? Does the former *imply* the latter? And conversely, can we deduce the former *from* the latter? Correspondingly, what about the *proper* kind of directedness towards God and 'ethical' behaviour? Does the former imply the latter? And can we deduce the former from the latter? We must return to these questions.

2:12–16 introduces a third and intriguing group of gentiles: non-Christ-believing gentiles who do the law (2:13) and have its content (*ergon*) written in their heart (2:15), but who, by definition, do not recognize the Jewish God.[39] These people reappear in 2:26–27. But are they real or are they merely introduced by Paul as a contrast to and foil for what he has to say about the Jew to whom he turns in 2:17?[40] The question pertains directly to the issue we noted. Could there according to Paul be a proper 'ethical' practice *without* the proper directedness towards (the Jewish) God? Or is successful 'ethical' practice *proof* of a proper relationship with God? We must consider the identity and character of the gentiles described in 2:12–16 a little more thoroughly.

The following considerations speak for taking these people as fictive. Could Paul in the end countenance the possibility of through and through righteous gentiles with no backing in a proper relationship with the Jewish God? Moreover, does it not go against what appears to be his overall strategy in chapters 1–3, of arguing that a false or non-existing relationship with God necessarily leads to improper 'ethical' behaviour? If the connection is of the logical kind so that a false relationship with God can be immediately read off improper 'ethical' behaviour, does the converse not hold? Should one not be able to read a proper relationship with (the Jewish) God off *proper* 'ethical' behaviour? But these non-Christ-believing gentiles obviously do *not* have a proper relationship with (the Jewish) God. So they are probably fictive.

On the other side are the following considerations. If Paul is arguing that God harbours no respect of persons between gentiles and Jews (2:11), it would be very odd if the first group that he then introduced, that of certain gentiles, was meant to be taken as entirely fictive. Similarly, it would be very odd for Paul to say that God will judge a fictive group (together with the rest of humankind) on the day of judgement (2:15–16).

There is a way out of this quandary, which will show us something important about the role of directedness towards God for 'ethical' behaviour. Whereas in 2:25–29 Paul begins from the similar figure of the law-fulfilling non-Christ-believing gentile (2:26–27), he ends up with a figure (in 2:29) who is, in effect, a Christ-believer. For the 'hidden Jew' is the one who has had circumcision performed on his heart *in the spirit* (*pneuma*). As Paul uses the term, possession of the spirit presupposes Christ faith and hence the proper Christ-based directedness towards God.[41] Will this help us with 2:12–16? Does Paul also mean to say here that in the end these people are Christ-believers? No. For they do what the law states *by nature* (*physei*).[42] Instead, note that although these people actually do the law, in testimony of the fact that they have its content written in their heart, what God sees on the day of judgement is an interior that is *divided*, with thoughts *accusing* and *excusing* (2:15–16). This may be taken to suggest that even though these non-Jews end up doing, at least often, what the law too demands, their action is not (literally) 'wholehearted'. And why? Could it be because their state of mind does *not* include the complete intentional directedness towards God that people do have when they have had circumcision performed on their heart in the spirit? In this way the people of 2:12–16 may actually differ from the gentiles of 2:25–29 as these are *eventually* described in 2:29, those whose possession of the spirit renders them fit objects for praise by God.

On this reading, the people of 2:12–16 will be gentiles who have the content of the law written in their heart and who for that reason do it (at least with some degree of regularity), but who may still lack the total directedness towards God that will ensure that their heart is completely undivided and that they will therefore *always* and *only* do what is written in their heart.[43] With this solution we save most of our original intuitions. The people of 2:12–16 are not just fictive. But neither is it the case that without having the proper relationship with God they are nevertheless able to engage, always and everywhere, in a completely proper 'ethical' behaviour. There remains something for the proper relationship with God to provide.

This solution is not much more than guesswork. It gives the best answer to the question of how Paul wanted his addressees to see the connection between the proper relationship with God and the proper 'ethical' behaviour. Paul does not raise this question in 1:18–2:29 in any explicit way or in the terms in which we have done it here. But what he actually says of the various groups he discusses will only make coherent sense if one takes it that he is implicitly addressing just this question. And the solution proposed here to the question of how we should understand the people described in 2:12–16 is sufficient to ensure that 2:12–16 may not be adduced as proof against the following contentions: Paul aims to show in 1:18–3:20 as a whole, and indeed as far as 4:25, that:

—one basic thing that is wrong with people outside the Christ faith is a failure of directedness towards God (the A/Ba-level);

—this is *shown* by their lack of the proper 'ethical' behaviour (the Bb- and C-levels);

—both kinds of failure go into their state of being 'under sin' (3:9);

—and more specifically, the gentiles of 2:12–16 and 2:26–27 (as *opposed* to 2:29) who lack the proper relationship with God, but nevertheless fulfil the law are not just fictive; there may be gentiles who *generally* do the content of the law, which they have written in their heart, even though they do not, by definition, have the proper relationship with (the Jewish) God.

A fifth point that has come out, if only somewhat tentatively at this stage, is that total directedness towards God may be required for *undivided*, 'wholehearted' and 'single-minded' fulfilment and doing of the (content of the) law. This idea will come up again with full force in connection with chapters 7–8.

Turning now to 2:17–24, do we also find the idea of a failing directedness towards God in connection with the Jew who is being addressed here? We do. In Paul's ironic description, this Jew takes pride in his relationship with God (2:17), but otherwise focuses on his knowledge of the law (2:18), which, as he himself sees it, makes him a light to blind gentiles (2:19–20). Clearly, whether justly or unjustly, Paul is drawing the picture of a Jew who misuses the law for other purposes than those for which it was given. Instead of applying it to himself and doing what it prescribes (2:21–22, the C-level), he uses it to enhance his status vis-à-vis gentiles. This attitude is in fact diametrically opposed to the one actually required by his knowledge of God. He should have been directed *towards God* in a proper form of *kauchēsis* ('boasting', 2:17), which consists in this: rejoicing in God with no side-glance towards others. Instead, he rejoices in *the law* (2:23) in an *im*proper form of *kauchēsis*, which takes pride in it over and against what blind, unenlightened, foolish and childish gentiles have to guide them (2:19–20), that is, in a comparison with the state of other human beings. He is not in fact sufficiently directed towards God nor, certainly, towards others, but rather against them.[44] Thus the Jew too of 2:17–24 is shown to be lacking somewhere in the proper directedness towards God. Like the people described in 2:1 ff, he is primarily directed against others. And here too this general failure at the A- and B-levels shows itself in a failure of practice (C-level), in not applying the law to oneself (cf. 2:1–3).[45]

Lack of directedness towards God is also true of the people described in *3:1–20*. For the first time since 1:16–17, Paul here introduces the central term for this lack: *apistia* or lack of trust in God (3:3). Otherwise the ideas in this passage (on Jews) are partly the same as in 1:18–32 (on gentiles). The Jews of chapter 3 might also very well be said to 'keep the truth (about God) down in injustice' (1:18, cf. 3:4, 7 on the 'truth of God' and 3:5 on 'our injustice'; and compare 3:4.7 on 'our falsity' with 1:25). In the *catena* of quotations from the Septuagint with which Paul concludes the section, he also makes explicit the point about a lack of directedness towards God: there is none who seeks after God (3:11). Throughout the passage it is also clear that this failure at the A/Ba-level has consequences at the Bb- and C-levels. This apparently holds of Jews no less than of gentiles.

Are all non-Christ-believing Greeks and Jews under sin (1:18–3:20)?

At this point a famous cluster of questions arises. We need to address them since they pertain directly to our basic decision to read Paul as making rationally and empirically verifiable truth claims. Paul's comprehensive aim with 1:18–3:20 is undoubtedly, as we should continue to see it, to 'accuse both Jews and Greeks of being all under sin' (3:9).[46] But we have also learned to see that this accusation and identification of the 'plight' of 'universal sin' is based on Paul's own, new view of the 'solution' in the Christ faith. Should we then take him to be saying that *all* Greeks and *all* Jews sinned in the various ways he has described? In particular, did *all* non-Jews (outside the Christ faith) sin in the way described in 1:18–32? If so, what about those described in 2:12–16, as we understood them? Similarly, did *all* Jews sin in the way described in

2:17–27 and 3:1–8 plus 3:10–20? Indeed, did *no* Jew have the proper directedness to the Jewish God? What a preposterous claim![47]

One way out of this quandary is to insist on the special perspective that lies behind Paul's claims here. Is Paul not just being rhetorical? Does he not merely presuppose his own new understanding of the proper relationship with God and accuse all others of whatever sins he can think of just because they did not stand in that relationship? In short, is this not just an unargued and unarguable assertion based on Paul's own preferred perspective and with no sense of responsibility towards how things actually were? We should resist this suggestion. We might certainly end up taking it to be correct, but since it would deprive what Paul says here of any independent, phenomenological interest, we should at least read carefully before opting for this solution.

It is noteworthy that the rhetorical, and indeed quite overtly psychologizing, reading just hinted at shares the feature of removing any analytical interest from Paul's words with another reading, which is in other respects sharply opposed to it, namely an explicitly theological one. On this traditional reading, the truth Paul aims to state is a metaphysical one to the effect that even though there might in fact be some Jews and Greeks who did not succumb to the specific sins described by Paul, nevertheless as members of 'fallen humanity' they are all sinners. Indeed, *we* all are! Thus Paul's claim that Jews and Greeks are *all* under sin should be taken literally. They (we) are *metaphysical* sinners even though it may not immediately appear so in each individual, e.g. in the law-fulfilling gentiles described in 2:12–16. Similarly, the suggestion in 3:4 that every human being might be false (to God) is not to be understood as an imagined possibility but as sheer fact. That is what human beings are, outside the Christ faith—and even within it.

We should attempt to steer a middle course between these two readings. Either view empties Paul's claim of any real-world interest. Instead, we should ask the following questions. Suppose Paul was aiming to describe the real world: what features of gentile and Jewish mentality outside the Christ faith did he fix on? What empirical difference would the Christ faith as he understood it make? Was there some feature in it which was not to be found anywhere else? And will this difference *explain* why gentiles and Jews outside the Christ faith might appear to Paul in the way they did? By asking such questions, we move away from the area of bald assertion into one of empirical analysis and argument. That is where we have decided to look for Paul.

A good way into this area goes via the observation that Paul's claim about Jews and Greeks in 3:9 may in fact be far from saying that *all* Jews and Greeks, in the sense of each and every one of them, were *actual sinners*. Consider Paul's use of 'all' (*pantas*). The way he takes this up again in 3:22–23 suggests that what he had in mind was 'all' in the sense of '*both* Jews *and* Greeks'. For in 3:23 'all' (*pantes*) is brought in to explicate the claim that there is no *distinction*, *namely* between Jews and Greeks. They 'all' sinned, that is, both Jews and Greeks sinned.[48] But what then about 3:10–12 with its repeated emphasis that there is *not one* who is just (v. 10), *not one* who does what is good (v. 12); instead, *all* (*pantes*) have missed the path? Observe, however, that this comes in a set of quotations. Since the point of the 'all' in 3:9, on the reading we are considering, is that Jews *too* are under sin,[49] is it not in fact quite effective for Paul to be able to bring in quotations from the Jewish scriptures that state that 'not even a single Jew' is just and so forth? Thus Paul *may* not have meant that each and every individual Jew outside the Christ faith actually sinned. Similarly, he may not have meant that each and every Greek outside the Christ faith actually sinned. And indeed, he suggested as much in 2:12–16. It remains the case that both Jews and Greeks might 'all' be under sin, as he has *paradigmatically* described them in 2:17–24 and 1:18–32 respectively.

However, this conclusion needs to be reformulated once we have addressed the idea of being 'under sin' (*hyph' hamartian*, 3:9). What this means is not necessarily 'to sin' or 'to be a sinner in such a way that one constantly or at least regularly sins'. To be 'under sin' may logically mean no more than this: that one *risks* sinning, *risks* doing actual sins. That is as close as one may come to having left sin completely behind. But if the risk is still there, one may well be said to remain 'under sin'. One still belongs within the 'realm' of sin (to speak, for once, a little *à la* Käsemann) and so at least risks sinning. This of course also allows that some of those who are said to be 'under sin' actually do sin as opposed to merely risking to do it. On such a reading, all who are 'under sin' may well be called 'sinners'. Also, one may well say that no one among them is just, that they have all missed the path and so forth. Here, then, we *may*, if we so wish, take the 'all' completely literally. *All* are 'under sin' in the sense of either doing it or risking to do it. At the same time, however, it may also be the case that some among them do not actually sin (at least not habitually). But the risk is always there.

This reading would account for the gentiles described in 2:12–16 who actually fulfil the law. Indeed, it would fit them perfectly. They know the law's content and they do it. But according to 2:16 they also have opposing thoughts. If they are able to keep these in check when they do the good, then they are people of the type which the ancient ethical tradition called 'self-controlled' or 'strong-willed' (*enkrateis*). But since such people do have the opposing thoughts, they are precisely also under the risk of *not* being able to control them. They constantly *risk* succumbing to those thoughts. *If* they do, then they will have become weak-willed, *akrateis*. And that is the kind of people Paul describes later, in chapter 7. (Incidentally, the proposed reading would even account for the claim Paul notoriously makes elsewhere about himself, that he was 'blameless with regard to righteousness according to the law' (Phil 3:8). For even somebody who was in fact blameless might still *risk* sinning. He would not necessarily be entirely out of sin's reach, but still 'under' it.)

This reading, as we shall gradually come to see, is on the right track. It relies on the crucial distinction in the ancient ethical tradition between the *akratēs* ('weak-willed person'), the *enkratēs* ('strong-willed person')—and the *spoudaios* (the wholly 'good' person), who never wavers. Paul appears to be playing on this very distinction in 2:15 (as we saw: the *enkratēs*)—and also in 2:29 when he speaks of a 'circumcision of the heart' (in the spirit) which will turn a person into the real, hidden Jew, the one who will always and everywhere *fulfil* the law (the *spoudaios*). We do not yet quite have the material that is required to spell out how 'risking to sin' should be further construed. That only comes with chapter 7. But it is at least clear from what Paul has said of all the different types of people described in 1:18–3:20 that what would account for such a constant risk is a failure in the proper directedness towards God.

By way of conclusion let us note the precise way in which Paul repeats, in 3:22–23, the general point he has been driving at all through 1:18–3:20: that 'all' (non-Christ-believing) Jews and Greeks are 'under sin'. What he says is that 'all have sinned' (in the *aorist*: all went wrong; not in the imperfect: all were regularly sinning) *and all fall short of the glory of God*. On the basis of 1:21, 23 and 2:23–24, this must primarily mean that all have 'fallen below' God's glory in the sense that through their sinning they have 'failed to do justice' to it or not 'lived up' to it. Only secondarily will it mean that (after the fall) they do not therefore (any longer) *possess* it.[50] Paul's basic point seems to be that before Christ, all, both Greeks and Jews, have been lacking in the proper directedness towards God which alone, *from* the human side, will do justice to the glory that is God's. That is a very neat summary of the basic thrust of 1:18–3:20: the failure in the proper **Ba** relationship on the part of 'all' Jews and Greeks. But we have also seen that throughout 1:18–3:20 Paul connects this failure (*a*) with a failure in 'ethical' behaviour (*b*). Both kinds of failure go into Paul's claim that Greeks and Jews outside Christ are all 'under sin'. We must now consider more closely the precise logic that connects (a) what Paul says about the **A/Ba**-level with (b) what we have seen him to be also saying about the **Bb**- and **C**-levels.

The bodily self as stumbling-block: (i) self-directedness (1:18–2:10/11)

What explains (a) the failure in directedness towards God on the part of gentile and Jew alike outside the Christ faith? And what explains (b) their concomitant 'ethical' failure? 1:18–32 hints at an answer—which will also bring us to our third theme (c), the lack of a total openness towards others.

In 1:18–32 Paul ascribes to gentiles two different types of mistaken attitude—one relating to God and one to 'ethical' practice—that involve a mistake in the understanding. The former is derived from the initial lack of recognition of God (1:19–21). But it develops. The gentiles gradually became 'vain' (*mataiousthai*) in their thoughts (*dialogismoi*), their hearts were 'darkened' (*skotizesthai*) into a total lack of understanding (they became *asynetoi*) and they became 'fools' (*mōrainesthai*) instead of wise (*sophoi*, 1:21–22). We saw how this development occurred. Instead of giving glory and thanks to God (1:21), they came to place the glory of the creator in things created by him (1:25), from man himself and downwards in the *scala naturae*—indeed quite literally so: in images of birds, beasts, reptiles (1:23). This, Paul seems to say, constitutes a sort of *category mistake*, an *intellectual error* of the first magnitude: keeping down the *truth* about God (1:18) and changing it into *falsity* (1:25). But how is it to be *explained*? 'Imagining themselves to be wise, they became fools' (1:22). Clearly, Paul suggests that gentiles took *themselves* and *their own* immediate perspective on the world as the yardstick for their views about the divine. Nothing above man (it would seem)! If God should not be imagined in the image of a man, then of something below him! As a criticism of pagan religion this is clearly not very perceptive. What matters here, however, is Paul's own viewpoint. To him pagan religion appeared to involve a central element of *self-directedness*. Gentiles understood God in their own image—or even further below.[51]

Now self-directedness is also the essence of the mistake of 'ethical' practice that Paul aims to identify. He initially characterizes in two ways the immoral behaviour with which God punished the gentiles' mistaken views about the divine. It is 'dishonourable' (24, 26), in the sense of socially stigmatized, and 'against nature' (26, 27). The latter point reflects Paul's, as we should say, naive use of 'nature' in support of traditional and social normative perceptions. Both points, however, fit closely with

seeing this kind of behaviour as a punishment for the failure in directedness towards God. For as Paul has already said, the proper directedness towards God is the *truly* 'natural' one (cf. 1:18–20) and it gives *true*
'glory' (another form of 'honour') where it belongs (cf. 1:21–3). Similarly,
then, the 'ethical' failure that constitutes God's punishment is 'against
nature' and 'dishonourable'.

However, the feature on which Paul places most emphasis is a certain
self-directedness of the behaviour he describes. It is probably because he
aims to identify this that Paul chooses same-sex relations as examples of
the kind of immoral behaviour he has in mind. They lent themselves,
within Paul's (mistaken) optic, to a description as being essentially self-
directed: not merely a case of desire (*epithymia*), which from Paul's perspective would be bad enough in itself, but of desire connected specifically
with the body (*ta sōmata*, 1:24) and moreover directed towards 'other
selves', namely others of the *same* sex. Here Paul's *ultimate* target, for
which he uses same-sex relations as an *example*, could be most strikingly
exposed: the immediate and, as *we* might say, 'natural' self-directedness
of the human bodily individual (irrespective of any sexual orientation)—
in fact precisely the self-directedness that defines the I-pole of the
I→X→S-model on its specifically Stoic interpretation. Once more, we
need not concern ourselves with the truth of Paul's contention concerning the character of same-sex relations. The important question for us is
what he intends to say by using this example.[52] That should be clear
enough. What lies behind and explains both the mistaken relationship
with God on the part of gentiles and their concomitant mistakes in
'ethical' practice is a single thing: taking as the basis of one's normative
understanding *oneself as a bodily individual* (I). That is the fundamental
stumbling-block that explains why gentiles outside the Christ faith were
invariably under sin.

Why this concern about desire (*epithymia*, 1:24), passions (*pathē*, 1:26)
and any form of appetency (*orexis*, 1:27)? Was Paul especially concerned
about the body and sex? Probably not. He goes directly on to give a long
vice list (1:28–31) which is wholly reticent on bodily vices. Instead, it
concentrates on a wide range of vices that are all basically social. Apparently Paul thought that there is a *single thing* that underlies *both* bodily
and social vices. That makes excellent sense in an ancient context. As we
know, philosophers tended to derive the social vices from the individual's
concern about his or her own body. The claim was not that every social
vice was *eo ipso* a bodily one and wrong for *that* reason. Rather, every
social vice was seen to be derived from concern of the individual for
him- or herself alone, to the exclusion of others for whom one might

also be concerned. And this kind of self-concern was seen as an *extension* of concern for one's own body. Material gains for oneself were gains in what was quite literally bodily goods or at least goods ministering to the body. And these were seen as a sort of focal example of social gains more widely understood. Viewed in this light it makes excellent sense that Paul should end with a list of social vices. Indeed, it is noteworthy that the first vice on the list, that of injustice (*adikia*, 1:29), was already introduced in 1:18 in Paul's headline for the whole section. Moreover, in the ancient ethical tradition injustice was the recognized paradigm of social vices, consisting as it does in not giving others their due, but trying to get as much as possible for oneself of whatever it is that one covets. But it also fits in very well that Paul should *prefix* his list of *social* vices with examples of distinctly *bodily* vices, and moreover vices which could be construed as being both bodily and in a heightened way self-directed. We see here that there is much more of a theory involved in such a passage as 1:18–32 than is usually recognized, a theory which claims that bodily and social vices are all derived from the same thing: a basic concern for oneself on the part of the individual bodily self. That theory is a vital element of the I→X→S-model on its Stoic interpretation too.

1:32 provides support for this reading. Paul here refers to certain people who not only do the things they *know* are liable, by God's just regulation, to punishment by death, but also commend *others* for doing them. His aim is to identify an attitude which, as he saw it, was a climax of self-directedness, self-directedness raised, as it were, to the second power—in spite of the fact that these people *know*. We may schematize it as follows: I→ . . . I! Paul may even have seen this attitude as containing an element of near-'perversion'. Commending others is intrinsically a form of openness towards others which leaves behind one's self-directedness (I→). But these people commend others for acts that precisely *express* self-directedness (I→I)! They aim to set up a group held together by selfless praise for self-directedness, I→ . . . I! Viewed in that way they form a close parallel with Paul's sex sinners. Both groups, within Paul's optic, were held together by an *appreciation* in each individual that the *other* individuals in the group had the same concern for their *own* individual self and body. To Paul this will have appeared a climax of 'group perversion': a group that is precisely not a real *group* (with all the *genuine* openness towards others that this implies).[53]

The note of 'perversion' is continued at the beginning of chapter 2 and in fact explains why Paul begins here with a 'therefore' (*dio*). As we know, he is here addressing people who, in a way rightly, criticize and judge those he has just mentioned. Thus they do know what is required by God—as the others in principle did too. In fact their case closely resembles that of those others. Where the earlier people *commended* those whose acts were directed against others, the new people of course *criticize* them—and rightly. *But* the people of neither group apply their insight on themselves. In the new case too the basic stumbling-block is self-directedness. Where the earlier people displayed a perverse form of *acceptance* of others, the new people display a form of *rejection* of others that is also somewhat 'perverse' or crooked since it is not followed by self-application. Both parties ought instead to concentrate on applying to themselves the understanding of God that they (to a varying extent) do have. That understanding alone will remove them from the kind of concern for themselves that underlies their apparently opposed behaviour.

It is in complete accordance with this that Paul may introduce in 2:7–10 the *mot juste* for the attitude that underlies everything he has said so far, that of *eritheia* ('selfishness', 2:8). His other terms in these verses are either precise but quite general (e.g. when he speaks of steadfastness in 'good work', 2:7, or in 'doing wrong' and 'doing good', 2:9–10) or else an apt recapitulation of the basic perspective from 1:18 onwards (e.g. when he speaks in 2:8 of people 'disobeying the truth' and 'obeying injustice', cf. already 1:18). The single addition that he makes is the one that introduces *eritheia*. That must be significant. Thus at the end of this first round of identification of what underlies the state of being 'under sin' (3:9), what Paul focuses on as the stumbling-block to 'obedience to the truth' and 'disobedience to injustice' (2:8) is this: selfishness. I have already indicated that this virtually cries out for being seen in terms of the I→X→S-model. Selfishness is the proper word for the kind of directedness towards the individual bodily self that goes with the I-pole when the required form of directedness towards God (I→X) has *not* been established.

The bodily self as stumbling-block: (ii) lack of internalization (2:11/12–29)

It is gradually being recognized that the major division in 1:18–2:29 lies, not at 2:1 but around 2:11 (with 2:11 itself acting as a 'Pauline bridge' between 2:9–10 and 2:12 ff).[54] And indeed, 2:12–29 brings in a new, highly significant element in Paul's identification of the stumbling-block. The new element is one that is meant to *explain* the difference with which Paul begins (2:13), between doing the law and merely 'hearing' it. That difference has to do with the issue of practice (the C-level), which was raised already in 2:1ff. But Paul of course introduces the difference as one that pertains to doing *the law*. Why does he now speak of the law? Superficially, his aim might seem clear enough. In chapter 1 he spoke of gentiles, but in 2:9–11 he has announced that the basic distinction between doing good and doing bad pertains to Jews no less than to Greeks, indeed to the Jew first—as well as to the Greek. There is every reason, therefore, why he should now turn to argue his case with respect to the Jews too. But that does mean speaking of the law. Thus understood, we should take it that 2:12 has Paul embark on a new, single theme: to develop (for the benefit of his gentile addressees) the failure of Jews to do what *they* should do—namely the law. What he does is to introduce first (2:12–16) a positive *counterpart* ('law'-doing *gentiles*), then (2:17–24) his negative target (*non*-law-fulfilling Jews) and then (2:25–29) to combine the two figures in order to make his ultimate point: that the true Jew, who is also the law-*fulfilling* gentile, is the person who is a *hidden* Jew (circumcised on the heart with the spirit)—the Christ-believer.

However, there is more to the passage than that. For what Paul also does is to bring in a new element that will *explain* the (at least outward) success of the gentiles (in relation to doing the law), the failure of Jews (in the same respect) and the (complete) success of Christ-believers. The new element makes its appearance in Paul's description of certain gentiles, who do not 'have' the law, but still do (at least regularly) what it enjoins. How? Why? What feature about them will explain this? Well, they have it written in their heart! Thus what matters, namely with a view to practice, is not just some external form of 'having' or 'hearing' the law, but having *internalized* it, as we would say. It is for this reason that Paul speaks so much in 2:12–16 about what takes place in the *forum internum* of the gentile. In 2:25–29 he repeats his strategy of using the gentile who acts rightly to bring into light the importance for external action of the inner psychic structure. Conversely, as we may conclude by reading back from 2:28–29 to 2:17–24, what is lacking in the Jew described in 2:17–24 is the same kind of thing: circumcision of the heart, a certain inner psychic structure. All this is entirely in accordance with the ancient ethical tradition. It is highly appropriate, therefore, that Paul should bring it in precisely in connection with gentiles (2:12–16). But it is also very significant that he feels able to use these originally Greek ideas in a description of the 'true' *Jew* (2:28–29), the one who is in fact also a believer in *Christ*. Here Paul fuses completely Greek and Jewish ideas to bring out certain crucial features of his own Christ-believing position.

How does the new element of internalization, as part of Paul's identification of what is wrong with Jews and gentiles outside Christ, relate to the earlier one of selfishness? Some connection there must be. For 2:12–16 and 25–29 surround a passage in which Paul does not speak directly of the inner prerequisite for doing the good, but instead depicts the Jew as one who, like the person described in 2:1 ff, knows what is right but does not put this knowledge into practice by applying it to himself. Furthermore, the reason why the Jew of 2:17–24 does not do this is that he is tainted by the same kind of selfishness as the person described in 2:1 ff. Both take themselves to be above *others*; both are concerned to bring *that* to expression instead of applying their knowledge to themselves. So, can we see a connection between selfishness vis-à-vis others and a lack of the internal structure described in 2:12–16 and 2:25–29?

The following answer suggests itself if one is accustomed to thinking along ancient Greek philosophical lines in the way Paul himself plainly does in 2:12–16. A person who has internalized the content of the law (or moral behaviour more broadly conceived) in the manner described in 2:12–16 will *want* to do it whenever the occasion arises. Internalization is a matter of coming to want to do something for oneself. This means that in relation to 'having' the law, one's main concern will be with the thing that the law *qua* law is actually and primarily for: being done. Doing the law (or rather: its content—*ergon*!) is what one has come to want for oneself. One will not, therefore, be particularly concerned about other sides of having the law, e.g. that it may serve to identify and enhance oneself over against others. One certainly could have such a concern, but only by adopting a viewpoint on having the law that is secondary in relation to its basic point: that one 'has' a law in order to do it. Conversely, as long as one primarily refers one's having the law to one's relationship with others, one has not properly internalized it or made it one's own. One's relationship with the law remains, as we will say, an 'external' one.

In all this Paul clearly presupposes a specific theory about the inner prerequisites for external action. In the ancient ethical tradition, no act was a moral act unless the agent basically himself willed it. But neither would it at all be done unless the agent himself willed it under some description or other. The ancient philosophers therefore directed their gaze inside the human being and constructed a fine-grained theory about different ways of willing an act. One of these is the one Paul invokes in 2:12–16 to the effect that an agent may with the stronger part of his mind himself will the content of the law. He has it written in his heart.

With another part he may also continue to will something else, which accounts for the divided mind that Paul describes in 2:16. Still, since he is self-controlled and strong-willed (*enkratēs*), what he will actually do (at least, generally) is the content of the law.

On this reading, the line of thought of 2:12–29 may be paraphrased as follows. (i: 2:12–16) Internalization, which leads to doing, (ii: 2:17–24) is lacking in the Jew; for his relationship with God (his 'boasting' of God, 2:17) retains an element of self-directedness (in his 'boasting' of *the law*, namely vis-à-vis non-Jews, 2:23), which explains why he does not (always) *do* the law (2:22–23); (iii: 2:25–29) the true Jew, by contrast, is circumcised on the heart (that is, he has internalized the law) through the spirit (that is, due to a relationship with God which means that his self-directedness has now been overcome); *he* therefore does (2:25) and keeps (2:26) the law.

We should conclude that 2:12–29 adds a significant element of moral psychological theory to the particular way we already saw Paul to be using the I→X→S-model. The basic stumbling-block that is overcome in the proper directedness towards God is self-directedness: to remain fixed at the I-pole and make the 'I' of the bodily individual the normative centre. But this stumbling-block will only be completely overcome in a person who has acquired a certain *inner state of mind*, one that ensures that he actually does what he knows needs doing because he (now) wishes to do it for himself. This idea will gain enormously in importance as we move on through the letter. Paul has chosen to introduce it already in chapter 2 in order to provide a full explanation of the failure of a Jew who does 'have' the law, but does not (always) act on it. The explanation he gives refers to a lack of internalization. And this failure is itself to be explained by the kind of self-directedness that is the other side of a failure in the proper directedness towards God. The Jew described here retains so much self-directedness that he wishes to use his 'having' the law as a springboard for pride in relation to others. He turns outward in misplaced self-assertion.[55] This attitude prevents him from coming to will the law for itself and for himself, that is, from internalizing it. To bring him there, his self-directedness would have to be erased. And for that, he would need a different kind of directedness towards God. Phenomenologically, as opposed to historically, there is much to be said for Paul's theory. Whether it also makes sense historically will depend on whether Paul could argue that there is a kind of law-fulfilment that is only possible on the basis of the new Christ faith and the new kind of relationship with God that it expresses. We shall return to this theme in the next chapter.

Conclusion: the problem for gentiles and Jews outside Christ

So far, we may fairly claim that Paul has managed in 1:18–3:20 to set up a closely knit set of themes which he suggests identifies the problem to which the Christ event and the Christ faith constituted the solution. The problem lies in a failure in the proper relationship with God (**Ba:** – I→X) which shows itself in a corresponding failure in 'ethical' behaviour. The latter may take the form either of distinctly body- and self-orientated, anti-social behaviour (**Bb:** in effect – I→S) or else in a failure to practise (at the C-level) the kind of moral behaviour that one knows should be done and in a way wishes to do. What lies behind this, not least the failing relationship with God, is an inordinate (or as we would probably say, quite 'natural') amount of self-directedness (failure to leave the I-pole behind). We also saw that Paul aimed to spell out in terms of a moral psychological theory how a half-*proper* relationship with God (namely, on the part of a Jew) might still fail to remove the amount of self-directedness that stood in the way of actually doing what one knows should be done and in a way wishes to do. To overcome this problem, he suggested, one's grasp of what should be done must be internalized and become a part of oneself and what one oneself wills. Basically, therefore, the problem that Paul has sketched is this: What kind of relationship with God is the fully proper one? How will it come about? And how will it generate the internalization of the law that will make people actually do it? Or to be more specific: How does the new relationship with God that has in fact been generated by the Christ event differ from the various ones that Paul has depicted in 1:18–3:20? And how will that new relationship generate the wish actually to do the kind of 'ethical' behaviour which qualifies as the moral one? These are the questions we shall address in the next two chapters.

9

Romans II
The Solution

In 1:18–3:20 Paul has identified a failure in directedness towards God as the fundamental problem that explains why all Jews and gentiles outside the Christ faith are 'under sin'. In 3:21–4:25 he presents the solution, which is of course to be found in faith in the God who has raised the Lord Jesus from the dead (4:24). Formally, 3:21 ff continues (well into chapter 4) the dialogue with a Jew that was begun in 2:17.[1] This Jew is now told the meaning of the Christ event (3:21–26), its consequences for Jewish *kauchēsis* vis-à-vis non-Jews (3:27–31) and how the particular kind of faith engendered by the Christ event has in fact been introduced already in the story of Abraham's faith (chapter 4). The net result is that just as Jews and gentiles outside the Christ faith shared the fate of being under sin (3:9, 22–23), so they also share in God's righteousness and with the same basis in Christ faith (3:30, 4:11–12, 16). We should ask about the phenomenology in this. How did Paul understand this kind of faith? And exactly how would this particular type of faith constitute a solution to the problem as set out in 1:18–3:20? 3:21–4:25 answers the first question, 6:1–8:13 the second. In showing this we shall make no attempt to provide a rigorous and detailed exegesis of these highly complex passages. Rather, we shall attempt to draw out of Paul's rich discourse the basic underlying points they make in relation to the problem he has set up in 1:18–3:20 and discuss to what extent they may be seen to operate within the framework of logical categories I am arguing we should apply to the analysis of Paul.

Total directedness towards God: 3:21–4:25 and onwards (5:1–11 and 8:14–39)

Two closely connected points are central in 3:21–4:25. First, God's intervention with the Christ event was totally gratuitous, totally undeserved, an act of grace (3:24). It was an expression of God's own righteousness in the face of human lack of faithfulness. God showed that he intended to stand by his covenant faithfulness (cf. 3:2–3) in spite of everything. He would act in such a way that human beings would get another chance (3:25–26). The theme of gratuitous grace is central in chapter 4 too.[2] Abraham was declared righteous for his trust in God, not for anything he had done, as might have been the case had he done acts of the (far later) law (4:2–5).[3] In relation to such acts he was ungodly (*asebēs*, 4:5). Still, God declared Abraham righteous merely for his trust. And David too has spoken of human beings whom God has declared righteous even though they had not done what the law required them to do (4:6–8).

Paul makes it quite clear why he stresses so much the gratuitous character of God's intervention. God, he claims, meant the story of Abraham to point directly forward to the present situation (cf. 4:23–25). In fact, God had the following specific purpose with making his promise to Abraham and his seed *not* on the basis of the law but through righteousness from *faith* (4:13–14): only then would it be clear that it would also *eventually* be realized through God's grace alone (as opposed to being tied to the law); and only then would the promise made to Abraham also be secure or guaranteed for *all* the seed, including in the present both (law-abiding) Jews *and gentiles* (4:16). But why, then, should God's promise be secure for *all* the seed? Or better, why should Abraham's seed include even gentiles? First, that was how God had originally made it (4:11, 17). And second, God saw, as Paul has himself earlier explained, that both Jews *and* gentiles were in need of some new act on God's part, one that would finally bring about what the law or anything like it had not been able to generate. Thus the first central point isolates the character of God's intervention seen in relation to the previous state of being 'under sin' that was shared by Jews and gentiles. In terms of the I→X→S-model what Paul brings out is the wholly gratuitous character of the movement X→I, triggered off as it was by a previous state in which both Jews and gentiles were basically to be found at the I-pole and nowhere else.

There is no hint in this that when Jews later than Abraham and Moses attempted to keep the law, they were in some way going against God's wishes, trying to 'earn salvation' by their own means or the like. That misunderstanding may safely be put to rest. What Paul says is merely this: that neither gentiles *nor in fact Jews* outside the Christ faith had *in fact* become righteous (in the sense we developed on the basis of 1:18–3:20: so as to be *completely* removed from the realm of even *risking* to sin); and that God intervened with the Christ event—quite gratuitously out of his mercy—in order to give human beings (Jews and gentiles alike) a *new* chance to become righteous, in other words, in order to *make* them righteous (3:26, cf. 4:25). That specific type of totally gratuitous intervention was precisely what was foretold in the story about Abraham.

The other central point in 3:21–4:25 has to do with the human reaction to God's gracious intervention, faith. What is the specific point of *the faith* that was generated *by* God's undeserved intervention—Abraham's and the Christ faith foreshadowed by that? Why, in Paul's view, did God attach such importance precisely to faith that he declared Abraham righteous specifically on the basis of his trust in the promise, to the exclusion, for instance, of circumcision, which came a little later (4:9–11), or even observance of the Mosaic law, which of course came much later? Here it is certainly possible to follow through the answer we suggested— in the last paragraph but one—to the question of why Paul emphasized that God's intervention was one of grace. We could say that Paul wished to bring out that God is the God of all, not just of Jews (cf. 3:29), and so he saw God as focusing on something that was in fact accessible to all, faith in God, trust that God is able to do whatever he has promised, be it ever so unlikely by human standards (cf. 4:17–22). Such an answer would of course tie in Paul's view here directly with his project of *mission* to *gentiles*.

However, the very fact that Paul develops Abraham's trust in God by emphasizing the *utter unlikelihood* of the object of that trust suggests that he wished to make a *phenomenological* point about faith in the God who has raised the Lord Jesus from the dead, a point that made it *appropriate* for God to intervene in a way that would generate precisely this kind of faith in human beings. *If* that faith then also became accessible to gentiles without requiring that they perform specifically Jewish practices like circumcision and observance of the Mosaic law, then that would be due to an independent property of the Christ faith—as prefigured in the story about Abraham—that would *explain* why God's righteousness (through faith) would (now) also be open to gentiles no less than to Jews.

To repeat the point, it is often said that Paul insisted on righteousness through faith as opposed to works of the law because he wanted access to God to be open to gentiles no less than to Jews, that is, as part of his missionary project. But it may be that Paul wished the direction of thought to go the other way. Access to God would then be open to all *because* it *had* to be based on faith of the kind Paul attempts to isolate. The idea is certainly not the old one that Paul felt that there was something wrong with the law or with trying to keep it. With regard to the law, the most we can say is that it had proved insufficient, as Paul had already claimed in Galatians and will again claim in Rom 7:7–8:1 ff. Instead, the idea will be that faith of the specific type that would result from the Christ event, *Christ* faith (but still also as prefigured in the story about Abraham), contains some special feature that, as Paul's God saw it, was required for righteousness. From that it will then *follow* that gentiles too would have access to God. For *Christ* faith was not tied specifically to the Jewish law (but to Christ).[4]

Against this background, it is difficult not to see it as a central aim of Paul's in 4:17–22 to bring out precisely a very special property of the kind of faith that he is talking about. He again and again stresses the *utter unlikelihood* by human standards that God might in fact bring about what he had promised Abraham. But still, against all reason Abraham adhered to his faith and trust in God. If this is what makes Abraham's faith paradigmatic of the Christ faith, then the feature that singles out faith as what in God's eyes qualifies to the status of right-eousness vis-à-vis God is this: *total* directedness towards God, *complete* trust in the God who may call into being things that are not, faith in the sense of 'hope against all hope' (4:18). And *then* we may well add: *that* particular kind of faith and trust will not be specifically tied to the Jewish law; it will be equally open to all.

Then we may go back to where we began. The problem identified by Paul in 1:18–3:20 was a failure in the relationship with God. The solu-tion, God's solution, as we have now seen, was an intervention through the Christ event that was completely undeserved and wholly an act of grace due to the previous failure in the relationship with God (the first central point), but was also intended to generate a new form of that very relationship, one that consisted in *total* directedness in faith towards God (the second central point). Presumably, then, it was *that* kind of relationship that was previously lacking. This new story (of the Christ event and the faith that it generates) was prefigured in the story of Abraham, who showed by his own example how all people *should* have been related to God. In fact they were not, not even Jews, to whom God's oracles (*logia*, 3:2) had otherwise been entrusted (*e-pisteuthēsan*). Some of them, at least, responded with lack of trust, faithfulness or faith (*a-pistia*, 3:3), namely of the radical kind wanted by God. Abraham, by contrast, had trusted in God even against hope (4:18). He had not become weak in faith (4:19). Nor had he been in two minds or wavered (*dia-krinesthai*) through lack of faith (again *a-pistia*, 4:20). He had been utterly convinced (4:21). In short, Abraham is the father of all who have *this particular, radical form of faith and trust* (4:11, 12, 16).

We should conclude that in 3:21–4:25, and particularly in chapter 4, Paul aimed to bring out a very special form of directedness towards God: one as total as the Christ faith that was prefigured in the story of Abraham's trust, in fact I→X in the I→X→S-model.

If we then ask about the relationship of this to what was said in 1:18–3:20, we are allowed to conclude that it was the lack of this special form of directedness towards God (I→X) that explains the various forms of failure of 'ethical' behaviour at the **Bb**- and **C**-levels that Paul spelled out in the earlier passage. Here we see very distinctly how Paul constructed his picture of those outside the Christ faith in the light of his understanding of that faith. This is shown almost literally by the fact that it is not in 1:18–3:20 itself but only later that Paul makes clear the specific character of the required relationship with God which *explains* what he has said in 1:18–3:20. In this way Paul's idea of a radical form of directedness towards God serves to explain the *negative* connections that he has stated in 1:18–3:20. It remains to be seen whether in Paul's view the *proper* kind of directedness towards God through Christ will also actually generate the *proper 'ethical'* behaviour, in other words, whether there is a comparable *positive* connection. That issue is only treated in 6:1–8:13. In 3:21–4:25 Paul addresses neither issue. Here he is only concerned to bring out the radical character of the new **Ba** relationship itself that Christ-believers stand in to God. That relationship constitutes the key feature of his whole theory. Do we need to add that in terms of logical form and function this relationship is identical with the I→X relationship in Stoicism and with that alone? Hardly. The Stoics alone conceived of the I→X relationship as, literally, a (cognitive, self-identificatory) takeover of the individual, bodily being by reason.

There is no need to rehearse in any great detail later passages in Romans where the idea of the total directedness towards God on the part of Christ-believers is again formulated. It is a major theme in 5:1–11 and 8:14–39. In the former passage, Paul (*a*) repeats his point about the Christ event occurring 'for the sake of the ungodly' (5:6). He also (*b*) introduces the new term of human 'reconciliation' with God (*katallagē*, 5:10–11) brought about by God through the Christ event. Both points again show that Paul has raised radically the stakes for the kind of relationship with God that is required to bring people away from being 'under sin'. They must (*a*) respond in the total manner that can only come about if against all 'natural' human inclinations they react positively to an act of God that is understood as having been directed in entirely undeserved grace to people who would otherwise fall completely outside of God's realm (the 'ungodly'). And they must (*b*) see themselves as having actually been just that: ungodly and in need of nothing less than a genuine 'reconciliation', no matter where they would otherwise have situated themselves on the spectrum of different types of relatedness to God that Paul has described in 1:18–3:20. By describing the character of God's intervention in this particular way, Paul shows how radically he understands the kind of directedness towards God that is required. Only total directedness towards God will at all do. Otherwise people will be nothing less than 'ungodly' and in need of 'reconciliation' with God.[5] We may note in passing that Paul here employs the term *kauchasthai* ('boasting') in a reinterpreted manner that almost makes it a term of art for the new relationship with God (5:2, 11). Christ-believers may now *rejoice* directly *in* God (I→X) in a manner that is entirely opposed to the way of the Jew of 2:17–24, whose *kauchēsis* was precisely criticized for being *in*sufficiently directed towards God and rather directed towards himself (I→I) and *against* other people (non-Jews). As against this, Christ-believers stand together in a singleminded, wholehearted directedness towards God. They do not *pride* themselves on *anything*, but *rejoice in* God.

As for 8:14–39, it is difficult to think of any more striking expressions of the total directedness towards God on the part of Christ-believers. They are 'sons of God' (8:14). Filled with the spirit, they have received the 'sonship' in which they stand crying 'Abba! Father!' (8:15). This forward-looking orientation towards God is only made all the more powerful by the fact that they live in present suffering (8:17–18) and under the frustration of all creation. Theirs is only a mode of hope (8:19–25)—but a mode in which the spirit (8:26–27) and God himself (8:28–30) actively intervene on their behalf. No wonder therefore that they have the sense that with God being for them, nothing can go against them (8:31–39). All through this text Paul piles metaphor upon metaphor. What he expresses is a sense of total directedness towards God on the part of Christ-believers.

Let us conclude on this topic by bringing entirely into the open how the motif of total directedness towards God as part of the I→X→S-model is connected with that other motif which provides the comprehensive framework for the whole of chapters 1–8 (and indeed of 9–11) from the moment it has been introduced (1:17): God's righteousness as expressed within a scheme of the history of salvation (cf. 1:16–17, 3:1–8, 3:21–26).[6] God is righteous (*dikaios*) and trustworthy or faithful (*pistos*, cf. 3:3). But human beings had all been 'under sin'. They did not have the totalizing kind of I→X relationship that was always meant as a part of God's covenantal relationship with his people. In response to this situation God did something, gratuitously. He staged the Christ event as a form of reaching down to human beings: X→I. The aim was to bring about the human relationship with God which had hitherto been lacking: I→X. And God succeeded. In the response of faith to the Christ event human beings reacted with a total directedness towards God which brought them into the covenantal relationship of mutual righteousness. They now *were* righteous in relation to God and so he could *declare* them righteous. God had, through the Christ event, made them part of his own righteousness.

However, this X→I / I→X theme, the one on which we have hitherto concentrated in this chapter, is only one strand in the story, though a very important one. Another concerns the wider consequences for human beings of having become completely directed towards God. Against the background of Paul's set-up in 1:18–3:20, we would expect him to be keenly interested in such consequences. We would expect him to answer questions such as these: How will Christ-believers who have left the I-pole behind and become completely directed towards God relate 'ethically' to other human beings (Bb)? Will they in fact be able to overcome the types of 'ethical' self-directedness exemplified in Paul's vice list in Romans 1? And how will they lead their lives concretely and 'practically' (C-level)? Will they be able to overcome the failure of practice that Paul has castigated in Romans 2? The last two questions are answered by Paul in 6:1–8:13, the first two only later. But then there is also this absolutely central question. Following Paul's lead we have hitherto (in this chapter and the previous one) developed his concerns in the terminology of intentional directedness, understanding and self-identification. Will these logical categories remain appropriate to Paul's discourse as we move on in the letter? This question will be very much in focus in the discussion of 6:1–8:13 to which we now turn.

Locating 6:1–8:13 within Paul's line of thought

6:1–8:13 is surrounded by texts that describe Christ-believers in their new state of righteousness, reconciliation with God and forward-looking hope for the 'freedom of the glory of the children of God' (8:21). The passage itself is about how they should concretely lead their lives in the present world before the return of Christ.[7] We may be a little more specific. The theme is not that of the form and content of 'ethical' relationships at the B-level between Christ-believers (Bb). That theme is only taken up later in the letter, in chapters 12 ff. Instead, the discussion in 6:1–8:13 pertains to the C-level and the question of putting into practice what one knows must be done. Thus Paul differentiates very clearly between the two types of 'ethical' issue that we have distinguished. In 6:1–8:13 the issue pertains to the C-level, as it did in chapter 2. In chapters 12 ff it pertains to **Bb**, as it did in 1:18–32. One can easily understand why Paul addresses the C-level issue here. After all, *practising* what one knows should be done is *more* difficult than getting to *see* what should be done. All the more reason, therefore, to show that with the new relationship with God, there is also the proper practice. The idea appears to be this: *not only* will believers see what should be done in their mutual relationship; they will also actually do it. Or again, with the new relationship with God, *all* the 'ethical' problems that Paul had developed in 1:18–3:20 will have been solved too.

In overtly literary terms, the function of 6:1–8:13 is to respond to the various questions that trigger off each section (e.g. 6:1, 6:15, 7:7). Underneath this, however, the function is, as we saw in the previous chapter, basically parenetic. What the passage does is to develop in the indicative mood (e.g. 6:1–10, 17–18, 8:1–11) how the earlier self-directedness that stood against the proper relationship with God has already been thrust aside and what difference this makes to the lives of Christ-believers—or else to state in the imperative mood (e.g. 6:11–13, 19, 8:12–13) that and how this change should finally come about. It is clear from the start that Paul in fact speaks in both moods and it is a famous question how he could do that: if the earlier self-directedness *has* been thrust aside, then why is there also a need for parenesis that it *be* thrust aside? We shall address this issue as we did in our discussion of Galatians, not so much for its own sake, but rather for the light it throws on the basic categories within which Paul's whole discussion is conducted. Once more we shall see that the so-called problem of the indicative and the imperative is no problem at all. It certainly does not require anything as elaborate by way of solution as it received, famously, in the hands of Rudolf Bultmann.

In this connection there is a specific issue that will engage us directly, particularly in the analysis of 6:1–23 and 8:1–13. Here Paul describes the change into the new relationship with God as a 'dying and rising with Christ' in baptism or else as a matter of having God's and Christ's spirit 'in' one. Should we understand this as referring to some form of substantive event, a real death now (if not yet the corresponding resurrection) and a substantive infusion and takeover by some external agent? Or should we take it that no matter what substantive ideas Paul may also have had, baptism and spirit-infusion were also, and centrally, seen by him as matters of the understanding and of self-identification?

The importance of the issue lies in the fact that it raises directly the question of what interpretive categories we should use for an adequate reading of Paul. In this book I am arguing that the categories provided by the ancient ethical tradition are in fact far more comprehensively in play in Paul than has normally been recognized. Within such a perspective, what appears superficially to be a rather massive form of substantive thinking in the sections on baptism and spirit-infusion needs to be carefully considered. We shall see that there is plenty of material in 6:1–8:13 that not only presupposes but even distinctly operates within a framework of understanding and self-identification. If Paul also had other types of ideas, then we must conclude that he himself did not see any intrinsic opposition between the use of either type.

The issue is also important since it pertains directly to the old question of how to relate what Paul says in 6:1–8:13 of the present 'ethical' life of Christ-believers based on baptism and spirit-reception with his understanding of their new 'religious' status as righteous through faith, which he ascribed to them in 3:21–5:21. Are there two completely different themes here that are treated in quite different logical categories: righteousness understood by Paul in cognitive, intentional and indeed 'forensic' categories (as 'justification'), and 'sanctification' treated by him in substantive and indeed 'participationist' categories? Or should the two themes be understood within the same logical framework, the cognitive one? Are they in fact *not* two different themes, but two sides of the same theme? If we end up concluding that Paul does operate, in the two groups of texts, with two distinct logical categories, then righteousness and 'sanctification' cannot be held together in a single theory. That is what older incisive interpreters like Albert Schweitzer have suggested.[8] If, by contrast, we find that even where he is using his most substantive and participationist language, Paul *also* thinks in cognitive terms, then we *may* be able to hold his talk about righteousness and 'sanctification' together in a single theory, and indeed to see them as two sides of the very same theme. Very much hangs, therefore, on whether we shall be able to understand the analysis of life in Christ that Paul gives in 6:1–23 and 8:1–13 within the cognitive, philosophical categories of the I→X→S-model. Let us turn to the first of these passages.

The bodily self removed, I: 6:1–23

As usual, our aim is not to provide any detailed and comprehensive exegesis.[9] We shall presuppose that and draw out of the text answers to the questions that concern us. They are the following: At the beginning of the chapter, Paul's ostensive point is that in baptism Christ-believers have altogether died to sin (6:2) and so, one supposes, cannot but 'walk in a new life' (6:4). The 'old man' has been crucified with Christ in order that the 'body of sin' be 'made inoperative' (*katargeisthai*, 6:6). (i) The first question asks specifically about how we should conceive of that 'old man' and 'body of sin' which is shed in baptism. In particular, does Paul understand it in the way the I→X→S-model would lead us to expect: as the individual, bodily being viewed, in its very individuality, as the locus of normativity? (ii) The second question asks more generally about the logical categories in which we should understand the whole process of baptism according to Paul. In particular, does he quite generally operate with the logical categories that go into the I→X→S-model, categories that have to do with understanding and self-identification? I shall argue that the answer should be positive in both cases. Paul is (at least *also*) talking about the cognitive movement I→X in the I→X→S-model, coming to identify oneself as belonging with God through Christ and to find the locus of normativity there and not at the I-pole. (iii) Then a third question will arise: does Paul think that Christ-believers who have been baptized have become sinless? Have they left sinning completely behind? In discussing this question we shall once more address the issue of the indicative and the imperative and develop our alternative understanding of that so-called problem. (iv) Finally we shall discuss two specific remarks of Paul's in the chapter, one relating to the addressees' conversion 'from the heart' (6:17) and the other to their continuing 'weakness of the flesh' (6:19). Here the aim is to show how these remarks contribute to enrich rather drastically Paul's picture of what it is like to live in the Christ faith as opposed, e.g. to living under the law.

(i) What is that 'old man' of ours who has been crucified in baptism? What is the 'body of sin' that has been made inoperative? To be more precise, is it something intrinsically tied to the individual? Is Paul talking of the 'old man' of each individual Christ-believer who in baptism has been crucified together with Christ? Is it the 'body of sin' of each individual Christ-believer that has been made inoperative? Or is he rather talking in more collective terms about the 'old man' of all those outside Christ taken collectively and of the 'body of sin' in some collective and more than individual sense? There is a strong exegetical tradition for understanding Paul in the latter sense.[10] We should not deny that he may have been thinking along such collective lines. But we should insist that he certainly *also* had the first type of thought. Here are some arguments:

When Paul speaks of a death, burial (6:2–4) and indeed crucifixion (6:6) together with Christ, it is very difficult not to be reminded of his claim in Gal 5:24 that those who belong to Christ Jesus have 'crucified the flesh together with its passions and desires'. That might just barely be taken in an exclusively collective way too. But within Galatians it clearly refers back to 2:19–20 where Paul spoke of his own death and crucifixion together with Christ, which gave him the possibility of coming to live for God (cf. Rom 6:11) even while he was still living in the flesh, that is, as an individual bodily being. Here Paul was unmistakably speaking of his own, individual experience, though certainly one he took to be a representative one. It is initially overwhelmingly likely that he is doing the same in Romans 6 though now as applied to each individual Christ-believer who has undergone baptism.

This point is strengthened by noting how consistently throughout Romans 6 Paul speaks of 'ours' and 'yours'. It is *our* 'old man' who has been crucified, not just a general one (6:6). It is *your* 'mortal body *(thnē-ton sōma)*' with *its* 'desires *(epithymiai)*' (6:12) that should now be out-side the kingdom of sin. It is *your* 'limbs *(melē)*' that *you* once presented as slaves to uncleanness (6:19), *your* 'limbs' that *you* must no longer present to sin as instruments of injustice (6:13), *your* 'limbs' that *you* must now present as slaves to righteousness (6:19). Similarly, when Paul speaks 'human talk' (6:19, more on this later), it is because of the weakness of *your* 'flesh *(sarx)*'. All through Paul appears consistently to be talking of whatever is connected with sinfulness in his addressees under-stood as so many individual participants in a group. When he addresses 'them', he addresses *each and every single one among* them. There is certainly no problem about also seeing sin as a general phenomenon, which may even rule over *(basileuein,* 6:12) the mortal bodies of Paul's addressees. But as he describes these matters in Romans 6, sin appears constantly to be working *through* the individual bodies of individual people.

This may again be strengthened by noting the specific way Paul contrasts the earlier slavery to sin on the part of his addressees with what happened to them when they moved away from sin: they obeyed 'from the heart' *(ek kardias)* the type of teaching to which they were given over (6:17). Surely, this can only refer to the heart of each individual person who has become a Christ-believer. We may take it, therefore, that all through he is thinking of what happens in baptism to individual Christ-believers taken as individuals. We should certainly add: in addition to whatever other ways he may have had of thinking of these matters. There is no exclusivity here. But it seems certain that the individual perspective is also there. To deny that is to commit the 'individualistic fallacy' of taking *any* kind of talk of the individual to have the meaning of *modern* 'individualism'.

We may take one step further. Paul says to his addressees: 'Do not present your limbs to sin as instruments of injustice; instead present *yourselves* to God as people who are alive after having been dead and (present) your *limbs* to God as instruments of justice' (6:13). By distinguishing in this way between the addressees 'themselves' and their 'limbs', Paul clearly presupposes the idea that there is an 'I' who is logically separate from the limbs (or generally, the body) *of* that 'I'. Furthermore, seen somewhat in the abstract this 'I' may be taken to have (or to have had) a choice between identifying with the 'mortal body' and so using its 'limbs' as instruments of injustice in subservience to sin—or of 'presenting itself to God' and so using its 'limbs' as instruments of justice in subservience to God. Thus what we find here is exactly the kind of understanding which we also found in Gal 2:19–20: of an 'I' who may choose to identify with him- or herself as the bodily being that he or she is and thus make that being its normative basis—or else to identify with Christ and through him with God. That choice, a choice that, as Paul sees it, has already been decided for his addressees, is what Romans 6 is all about. It should go without saying that it is the choice between staying at the I-pole of the I→X→S-model and moving up to X, and once again on a distinctly Stoic interpretation of this. So, whatever else Paul may have thought took place in baptism, he will also have seen this ritual as a celebration or sign of the movement of an individual 'I' away from identifying with the individual, bodily being that he or she (also) is and from making *that* the locus of normativity. Baptism is a sign of the 'removal' of the 'bodily self' as understood within the terms of the I→X→S-model on its Stoic interpretation.

(ii) This already goes a long way towards answering our second question too: within what categories should we more generally understand the whole process through which the bodily self, the 'old man' or the 'body of sin', is made inoperative in baptism? In particular, is it a process that does not essentially involve the understanding? Or does it rather do just that, no matter what else we must say of it? Let us consider this question by looking again a little more closely at 6:1–11.

It is often said that as Paul describes baptism here, the idea must be that the 'old man' has, in some sense, *really* been crucified and the 'body of sin' *really* been made inoperative.[11] If baptism is a death and a burial in some way homologous to those of Christ (6:3–5), then they must mean a real end to the body of sin. What is often missed, however, is that in setting this forth Paul is explicitly *reminding* his addressees of it: 'or are you unaware that ...?' (6:3); 'while realizing this that ...' (6:6); 'knowing that ...' (6:9). That is quite important. For it points directly forward to Paul's conclusion that his addressees should *think of themselves as* dead to sin and living for God in and through Christ Jesus (6:11). It follows that no matter how one may otherwise wish to describe what takes place in baptism, in Paul's view it was indeed also a matter of the understanding, in fact a piece of self-identification, on the part of the baptized person: coming to think of oneself as one who is dead to (the body of) sin and living for God in and through Christ Jesus (6:11), or for short, coming to think of oneself as a 'Christ person'—in fact, quite clearly I→X in the Stoic model. That is about the only feature of Paul's conception of baptism of which we can be quite certain.

It is possible to counter this argument in the following manner. The fact that Paul reminds his addressees of something that has happened to them does not in itself imply that what happened to them belongs to the same logical category as the act of reminding them. Similarly, the fact that he enjoins them to think of themselves as being dead does not imply that the state of being dead is itself to be understood as being a cognitive one. The objection is justified in principle, but not as applied to the case at hand. Suppose that being baptized was understood by Paul as an event that did not involve any cognitive component at all, like obtaining a different colour all through one's body—say, becoming blue instead of having people's accustomed colour! Suppose it was also at issue whether people who *had* become blue would continue to act in the ways that corresponded with their earlier colour. Such an issue would be very odd in itself. If they were blue, then they would of course do bluish things. But it would be even odder for somebody to *remind* such people that they were in fact blue—unless it was presupposed that this reminder should in fact be construed as an appeal to some pre-existing under-standing on the part of the blue people that there was an intrinsic connection between an *understanding* of theirs of what they themselves were and the kind of behaviour they would engage in. But in that case the original turning blue would not just be a matter of obtaining another colour. It would also involve a cognitive component that had to do with the self-understanding of these people. We should conclude that the fact that Paul appeals to the understanding of his addressees does allow us to infer that baptism, as he saw it, had a cognitive component.

It is worth repeating this reading of baptism from a slightly different angle. Paul's understanding of what happens in baptism may initially appear to be this. Christ died, literally and physically, and he is therefore now obviously also dead to sin, which was precisely tied to the body that died. Similarly, when the Christ-believer 'dies' and is 'buried' in baptism, the 'old man', including the 'body of sin', will participate in Christ's death: he too will die. However, this can really only be the beginning of the story. For one thing, it renders the need for parenesis inexplicable. If the 'old man' *is* dead, then why is there a continuing need for parenesis? This is of course one side of the old question about the relationship between the indicative and the imperative: the construal just given of the indicative renders Paul's turn to parenesis inexplicable. But 6:11–13 and 19 show that 6:1ff as a whole *is* basically parenetic, not just an announcement in the indicative that the body of sin is of course already dead. So there must be more to be said. For another thing, no matter how much dying takes place in baptism, it is certain that the body (of sin) of the baptized person, which we saw to be also the individual body of the individual person, does not in fact, literally and physically, die. We should certainly be open to the claim that Paul did not think of these locutions as 'mere' metaphors. Still, there must be *some* metaphorical element to them. And it is in fact noteworthy that Paul does speak, sensibly, of baptism as an *analogue* (*homoiōma*) to Christ's death (6:5). (Similarly, Paul says in 6:13 that his baptized addressees must present themselves to God *as if* they were living from dead.) We must find some understanding of the dying that takes place in baptism which will allow baptism to have its intended force while recognizing that in the case of baptized people, as *opposed* to that of Christ, there is no physical death of the body of sin.

6:10 provides what we need. Here it becomes clear that in Christ's case what happened was not just a death (and of course a resurrection) which put him outside the sphere of operation of sin, so that sin no longer had any legal claim on him (6:7). It also meant that he died *to* sin, once and for all, in such a way that in his resurrected life he now lives totally and exclusively *for* God (6:10). We should of course not begin to ask here whether before his death Christ did *not* live for God and in what sense he might be said to have lived then for sin. It is sufficient that Paul has tied these notions to the earthly existence of living with a body of sin. What matters, however, is that *these* notions of living or not living 'for' God and living or not living 'for' sin may be immediately transferred to the human being who in baptism experiences an analogue to Christ's physical death which is not itself a physical death. Living 'for' something is an intentional notion, it has to do with how one understands oneself, where—among things outside oneself—one places oneself, where one takes oneself to belong. In short, it is a term for the kind of 'directedness' and normative self-identification that we have been constantly talking about. It is a striking fact that after having described Christ in *these* terms Paul goes directly on to enjoin his addressees, as we saw, to think of themselves as 'dead *to*' sin and 'living *for*' God through Christ Jesus (6:11).

We asked what categories we should invoke to understand the process by which the 'body of sin' is made 'inoperative' in baptism. We can now say that no matter what ideas Paul may have had about baptism in addition to the one we have unearthed, he did see it, centrally, as also involving a cognitive element, as a matter of understanding and normative self-identification: as coming to see oneself as a Christ person. Baptism celebrates the change *from* identifying with one's individual, bodily being (**I**) and living for 'oneself' *to* identifying with Christ (**X**), thereby also coming to live for God—in short, I→X.

(iii) Let us use this result to address our third question concerning the extent to which Paul thought that baptized Christ-believers had attained a state of actual, realized sinlessness. Consider the so-called problem of the indicative and the imperative in the light of our results so far. With the understanding just given of what happens in baptism, it is entirely open for Paul to have had the following two thoughts concomitantly, one in the indicative mood, the other in the imperative mood: (*a*) in baptism the 'old man' *has been* crucified with Christ in order to make the body of sin inoperative so that the baptized person will no longer slave to sin (6:6); and (*b*) there still is a need to make this *come about completely and finally*. For it makes excellent sense to say that (*a*) in baptism a person has come to identify himself as one who lives for God through Christ Jesus, one who no longer sees his individual, bodily being as the locus of normativity, but (*b*) there is also a need to make this identification absolutely complete so that the body of sin will eventually be made entirely inoperative as such a locus. This reading takes something away from the finality of saying that in baptism the 'old man' *has* been crucified—but not much. It remains true to say this. It already *has* occurred. The point and logical role of baptism is to stamp 'death of the individual 'I' as the locus of normativity' on the self-identification of the believer. But since baptism is (whatever else it may be) also a matter of precisely such self-identification, of how one sees oneself and understands where one belongs, it may evidently be *deepened* until what was basically there to begin with has come to be *all* that there is, a *total* living for God through Christ Jesus. Within such an understanding of baptism there is ample room for both an indicative component, which speaks about what has already taken place, and an 'imperative' one, which addresses the need to bring this to its final consummation. In fact, it is noteworthy that Paul says that the 'old man' *has* been crucified in baptism *in order that* the body of sin *may* be made inoperative. He does not quite say that the latter thing already *has* happened.

Against this background we can make sense of what appears to be Paul's claim for actual, complete sinlessness in his addressees: that in baptism Christ-believers have altogether died to sin (6:2) and so apparently cannot but 'walk in a new life' (6:4). Let us put it like this. Paul's claim is that baptized Christ-believers *are* sinless—in principle, that is, in such a way that there may still be a need for parenesis in the form of *reminding* them of what they, in a manner of speaking, already are. There are two sides to this understanding. The first is that Paul does claim complete and realized sinlessness for Christ-believers. That, as we have come to see, is the very point of the Christ event. It was in order to generate, at long last, the kind of total directedness towards God that would also have this very precise consequence that God staged the Christ event in the first place. The kind of total directedness towards God that is the very content of Christ faith (cf. Romans 4) *implies* complete and realized sinlessness. Second, however, this state may not in fact always and everywhere be fully realized. Thus there *may* be a need for parenesis in the form of *reminding* Christ-believers of the earlier point. But there is no inconsistency. The second point does not cancel out the first. For both are matters *of the understanding* and here one may operate with degrees without doing damage to the logic.[12]

Is this good enough? Has it become possible to explain why the Christ event succeeded where, for instance, the law did not? What Paul would have to say is this: that the Christ event *may* generate complete and realized sinlessness (but does not *always* do this—hence the need for parenesis), whereas the law *cannot* do the same, as actual experience has also shown.[13] Can Paul make good this claim? Perhaps. At least, he appears to be attempting to do just this in Romans 4 when he develops the radical character of the Christ faith. The idea seems to be that it is the possibility of this *radical* form of relationship with God that also makes possible its radical *practice* (at the C-level): complete and realized sinlessness. *Could* the law not generate the same kind of relationship with God? Paul, at least, thought that it could not. That is what he spells out in 7:7 ff.

This discussion of our third question has been aimed to dissolve the so-called problem of the indicative and the imperative. It will be immediately clear that our (dis-)solution is exactly the same as the one given in our discussion of Galatians. Paul may speak in both the indicative and the imperative moods and there is no intrinsic problem in this. On the contrary, *just because everything takes place within the logical category of the understanding*, the use of the imperative, construed as stating a *reminder*, even *presupposes* the indicative. The discussion has also been aimed both at insisting that Paul takes complete and realized sinlessness to be a necessary consequence, and indeed part of the basic point, of the Christ event—and also at defusing the problem that may be felt with this, namely that it does not leave room for what is so manifestly there: parenesis. As against this, I have claimed that both points should be left standing and that they may in fact be so entirely unproblematically— *because* the basic logical category within which Paul is operating is that of understanding and self-identification.

(iv) Our fourth topic was two remarks in the chapter that throw further light on Paul's idea of what it is like to live in the Christ faith as opposed, e.g. to living under the law: the reference to obedience 'from the heart' (6:17, *ek kardias*) and to the 'weakness of your flesh' (6:19, *astheneia*).

Paul's reference to obedience 'from the heart' is of interest not only for the way it ties his perspective to the individual. It also immediately recalls his description of the 'real' Jew of 2:28–29, who was precisely circumcised on the heart. The connection is unsurprising since we took that Jew to be in fact the Christ-believer who had received the spirit (2:29). Still, the connection shows that the question of how the Christ-believer is structured internally is of major interest to Paul. It immediately comes up when he turns to consider the concrete life of his Christ-believing addressees. That too is unsurprising. For as we already know, it was universally held in the ancient ethical tradition as a whole that the internal structure settled how people would act. That topic moves into centre stage in 7:7 ff. There we shall see that in complete line with the ancient ethical tradition Paul took it that his eventual goal had only been reached once he could conceive of the Christ-believer as a person who had left behind even the smallest sign of internal disharmony and dissociation. Only the person who had overcome what in the ancient tradition was called 'weakness of the will' (*akrasia*) had arrived where the Christ faith was intended to bring him: to the state where he would do nothing but act correctly, the state of consistently correct C-level practice. The same motif is introduced in the reference to obedience 'from the heart', that is, complete and *undivided* obedience. Its presence here shows that this motif expresses a major concern of Paul's in 6:1–8:13 as a whole.

On the reading we are pursuing, that is not surprising either. For 6:1–
8:13 is precisely designed by Paul to show that Christ faith and righteousness *solve* the problem of failing to act correctly that he had diagnosed
in chapter 2 of the letter.

However, if that is the point of Paul's expression of his joy that they
have obeyed the new form of teaching from their heart, then why does
he refer in the next verse but one (6:19) to the 'weakness' of their flesh?
The concept of *astheneia* was central in the ancient moral psychology,
where it signified the internal weakness of the mind that accounts
precisely for cases of acting against one's better judgement, those Paul
will move on to discuss in chapter 7. (In Aristotle, *astheneia* is one of
two forms of *akrasia*, the other being *propeteia*, 'precipitation'. In
Stoicism, *astheneia* constitutes *the* basic form of *akrasia*.)[14] Apparently,
it is the risk of this form of uncontrolled action that prompts Paul's
parenesis in the present chapter too. But why refer to weakness, if Paul's
claim was, quite to the contrary, that his addressees had *already* 'obeyed
from the heart'? In fact, as we shall see, this reference strengthens rather
than weakens the claim that Paul's theme in chapter 6 as a whole is
consistently correct C-level practice.

However, Paul's reference here to *astheneia* has even wider implications.
They are of great importance since they lead us directly on to a central
Pauline idea. It is this: When a person has Christ faith, (*a*) not only will
he do everything that he *should* do (the previous point); (*b*) he will also
do it *freely* and as a direct consequence of his new self-understanding.
He will do it because he *wants* to, not merely because he must or because
it is a means to something else that he wishes to obtain. Clearly, to get
these two points out of Paul's reference to *astheneia* requires some work.
Let us look at the passage in more detail.

In 6:15 Paul has again asked a variant of the question with which he
began the chapter: should Christ-believers just go on sinning now that
they are under grace (6:1, 15)? Of course not (6:2, 15)! But whereas in
the first half of the chapter he had developed the reason for his denial by
showing, in effect, that being baptized they *cannot* (really) go on sinning,
in the second half he adopts another line. Here the idea is rather that
considering the weakness of their flesh, they should, as the frail humans
they are, see themselves as being *enslaved* to righteousness.

Paul presents this idea with some care. There is first a general principle:
by making oneself an 'obedient slave' (a *doulos eis hypakoēn*) of something, one *becomes* a slave to the thing one obeys; and here there are two
possibilities: either (to be a slave of) sin, which leads to death, or (of)
'obedience' (*hypakoē*), which leads to righteousness (6:16). In the light

of this principle Paul further notes with satisfaction that his addressees *were* slaves of sin,[15] but had 'obeyed from the heart' the new type of teaching to which they were introduced (6:17). It follows, by the principle of 6:16, that they have now become *slaves* to righteousness (6:18). Well and good. This change is one that Paul will then make use of in 6:19b: just as they then *presented* their limbs as slaves to sin, so now they should *present* them as slaves to righteousness. However, this is not all. For in 6:19a Paul interjects the remark that he is speaking 'in a human way only' (*anthrōpinon legō*) due to the weakness of their flesh.[16] This remark is intended as an apology. Paul apologizes for something and claims that he is forced by the weakness of his addressees' flesh to do what he apologizes for. But what does he apologize for? Only one answer seems possible. Since everything in the immediate context has to do with 'making oneself a slave' to something (cf. *doulon heauton paristanein*, 6:16, 19), Paul's apology must refer to that.[17] What Paul apologizes for is *using the language of slavery*: he only speaks in this 'human' way because of the weakness of his addressees' flesh. But why should he precisely *apologize* for using the language of slavery, particularly when Paul is otherwise so fond of describing himself as a 'slave' of Christ? Fortunately, the answer is not difficult to find. It trades on the specific manner in which Paul has described how his addressees had changed from being slaves to sin: they had 'obeyed from the heart' a new form of '*teaching*' (*didachē*, 6:17). In other words, they had *learned* something (the 'teaching') and *understood* it thoroughly, that is, made it their own ('from the heart')—and that *differs* from merely becoming a slave of something. So, when Paul after all does use the language of slavery (for which he apologizes), it is, so he suggests, because he is forced to speak in this 'all too human' way by his addressees' own weakness!

This train of thought shows that Paul operates with three different approaches in the chapter to the possibility of sin on the part of his addressees. (*a*) Being baptized, they should in principle have 'obeyed the new teaching from the heart' in such a way that there would be *no question at all* of continuing to sin. That was the point of the first half of the chapter. (*b*) If that situation did not in fact obtain, Paul would *remind* them that that was how things *should* be (6:11–13). (*c*) *Still*, in view of the weakness of their flesh Paul also felt that he needed to use *stronger* means. What he did was to introduce the idea of *enslaving* obedience, suggesting to his addressees that they should see themselves as *slaves* of righteousness and should apply this type of self-identification to their various limbs (6:15–19). Now it is enormously important to realize that the third approach was explicitly only applied by Paul as a 'human expedient' for which he apologizes. For that means that it is the two former approaches to the possibility of sin in Paul's addressees that represent the 'normal' situation, the one within which Paul generally saw himself as operating. In the 'normal' situation, Paul thought, his addressees would either have actually *stopped* sinning or else at least have done so in principle, in such a way that they only needed a little *reminding* to bring it off. What they would not 'normally' need to do is *submit* to some order, to become *slaves* to anybody or anything. Indeed, even if they did need to do that, they would still do it in the form of enslaving *themselves*, of *seeing themselves as* slaves. And therefore, when Paul does use the terminology of slavery and slave obedience, he precisely *apologizes* for it, explains to them why it is necessary to use it and indeed only uses it to enjoin them to make *their own* use of it, to apply it to themselves.

What all this shows is a point of great importance. Paul goes on to speak of the final end of it all (*telos*, cf. 6:22), which is eternal life given on the day of judgement. We should understand this as what we would call an 'objective' phenomenon, given by God and to be understood in the most vividly concrete and substantive form that anyone can imagine. Similarly, we should understand the righteousness to which Paul's addressees should consider themselves enslaved (6:19) as an objective status given by God. (Compare the fact that in 6:18 and 19 they are said to be enslaved to righteousness—but in 6:22 to God.) *Nevertheless*, these objective phenomena also *reflect* a state in human beings which is an *inner* one that makes them participate *actively and willingly* in these events as a result of an understanding on their part which they have made their own, namely, by coming to *identify* themselves, in the I→X movement, with God (through Christ). Moreover, this understanding is of such a kind that they will now want to do whatever God wants them to do *not* just as a means to some external end, say eternal life, or because somebody else (God) *orders* them to do it, *but for those things themselves*, because these things constitute the actual content of that (namely, God and God's will) *with* which these people have now (through Christ) come to identify themselves. Corresponding to the objective phenomena of eternal life and righteousness given by God, there is the 'subjective' side of human beings coming to see *for themselves* what needs to be done and wanting to do it *for what it itself is*, just because it reflects what, in the I→X-movement, they have now come to see as identifying *themselves*. Having experienced the Christ event and obtained Christ faith, these people are no longer just told to obey in the manner of slaves. Nor do they obey merely to avoid some greater evil or to make some extrinsic gain.

Is it convincing to get as much as this out of Paul's almost casual apology in 6:19? Here are two further arguments in addition to the basic one, that the reading gives a very precise sense to the passage.[18]

First, Paul's apology comes in a passage where he has just spoken of the meaning of baptism for the self-understanding of the baptized ones with regard to sinning, to Christ and to God. Against this background, it is striking to notice the way in which in Romans 8:14–15 Paul leads over from 6:1–8:13 to the concluding section (8:14–39) of chapters 1–8. Based on the central importance he has given in 8:1–13 to the spirit, he now describes the effect of spirit possession on those who 'let themselves be led by God's spirit':[19] they are 'sons of God' (8:14). But he then *explains* this (*gar*) by a reference, once more, to baptism: 'For you did not receive [namely, in baptism] a spirit of slavery leading to fear; instead you received a spirit of sonship by which we cry out [again in baptism]: Abba! Father!' (8:15). A spirit of slavery leading to fear: that is precisely the point. Baptism and reception of the spirit, which is part of baptism, do *not* mean *slavery*, presumably to God's will, or acting out of *fear*, presumably of the negative consequences of not doing what one should. They mean something else: the forward-looking identification with God as Father (which explains why one is now oneself a 'son of God'); and what this leads to is doing God's will because one *oneself wants* to, *not* out of fear in the manner of a slave. That new situation, however, makes it entirely possible that instead of being a 'chattel' slave to God one now sees oneself as a 'slave' of Jesus Christ, as one who *identifies* completely with Christ (and through him with God) and thus also takes oneself to *belong* to Christ.

Second, there is a far more general argument, which presupposes the idea of a comprehensive similarity between the logical categories and basic ideas in Paul and in the ancient ethical tradition generally and then points to the absolutely central place within the latter of precisely the idea that I claim is found in Paul too. It is the idea that the 'wise man', the fully virtuous person, will always and everywhere (*a*) do the right thing and (*b*) *for its own sake*—because it expresses what he takes himself to be and hence his 'happiness'. Both sides of this idea are present already in Aristotle. But let us concentrate here only on the second one. When Aristotle states that we choose, for instance, moral virtue both for its own sake and for the sake of 'happiness', what he means by the latter is that we choose it as one thing that directly goes into and is part of what we basically search for in our lives as a whole, 'happiness'.[20] Thus the two ideas support one another, leading to the conclusion that moral virtue is one thing that we choose in the most comprehensive sense for its own sake alone. The Stoics took over this bit of theory, even insisting that moral virtue is the *only* thing of which it holds. But they also developed the idea in a way that makes it closely comparable with Paul. This occurs in their theory of *oikeiōsis* when they spell out the idea of acting for the sake of the end (*telos*) or 'happiness' in terms of acting in a way that reflects what one takes oneself to be. In Stoicism the idea of choosing something for its own sake is directly connected with the idea of self-identification: one chooses something for its own sake because one sees it as expressing what one oneself is. Thus virtuous acts are chosen and done for their own sake by the Stoic wise man because he takes them to express that thing (X, namely, rationality) with which he has come to identify in the self-identificatory movement $I \rightarrow X$. Paul aims to say exactly the same: that through the Christ event Christ-believers have come to identify with God with the consequence that they may now (and *only* now) *want for themselves* to do what is (also) God's will.

Let me summarize on Romans 6 based on our four questions.

The chapter is important for a number of reasons. It shows conclusively that when Paul turns to develop the 'ethical' side of the Christ event conceived as the solution to the set of problems he has presented in 1:18–3:20, he operates centrally within the same logical categories as those that went into his presentation of those problems, the philosophical categories captured in the $I \rightarrow X \rightarrow S$-model. It also shows that he has the same conception of the thing that lay at the centre of the earlier problems but is now removed in baptism, the individual, bodily self understood as the locus of normativity. Perhaps we might also say that this has become even clearer here than it was before. It is precisely when Paul turns to explaining what is *positively* brought about by the Christ event that he makes entirely clear what he is talking about. In the same way, it was only when Paul turned to elucidate the new relationship with God generated by the Christ event that he clarified the radical character of the new situation. What was wrong with gentiles and Jews outside the Christ faith was that they did not identify *exclusively* with God, finding the *only* locus of normativity in him. Christ-believers by contrast do precisely this when they leave the individual, bodily self completely behind.

Romans 6 is also important for showing once and for all that the so-called 'problem' of the indicative and the imperative should never have been felt to be a problem at all. Baptized Christ-believers *have* come to identify exclusively with God. They *have* made their body of sin completely inoperative as a basis for action. Thus they *will* do what they know they should do. Still, this does not eliminate any possible need for parenesis in the form of reminding them of the self-identification which is already theirs. For the whole area in which Paul is operating is one of the understanding. And here one may quite unproblematically work with *degrees* ranging from an initial, basic grasp to a final, full one.

In the same connection, the chapter clarifies Paul's complex views on sinlessness. On the one hand, baptism and Christ faith do imply complete and realized sinlessness here and now. On the other, there is ample room for parenesis intended to bring this about finally and completely. And not only that. Paul may even use the idea of *voluntarily* enslaving oneself to righteousness as a means to that end, though only as a 'human' concession to the weakness of his addressees. In a description of the genuinely proper relationship to the proper practice, by contrast, a reference to slavery and slave obedience (as ordinarily understood) would be a mistake.

Finally, Romans 6 is important for showing just this: that the category of 'Thou shalt' has been exchanged for the one of 'I (or rather, we) will'. When baptized Christ-believers do what they should, they do it because they themselves want to. Behaving like that expresses directly what they take themselves to be when they identify with God. And so they want it. This is perhaps the place where Paul is most comprehensively and fundamentally in line with Stoicism as against any (theological) reading of Paul that stresses that Christ-believers will do what they must (to the extent that they do it) *because* they *must, because* God *orders* them to do it or the like. Such an idea goes directly against what Paul aims to say. Romans 6 shows this at exactly the place (6:16–19) where it has often been taken to say the very opposite.

The bodily self removed, II: 7:7–8:13

In chapter 6 Paul has shown that sinning was in principle excluded for Christ-believers. If it had not in fact gone away, then Paul's addressees should make it do so. Indeed, he went so far as to enjoin them to 'enslave' themselves to righteousness. In 7:7–8:13, he aims to show that Christ faith and spirit-reception constitute the *only* possible way of being brought away from the persistent risk of sinning. In particular, the law could not bring this about. Quite to the contrary, it precisely left people with a heightened awareness of the constant risk of sinning. Once more, however, the underlying thrust of the argument is parenetic. Since the Christ faith and spirit-reception constitute *the* way to get away from sin, Paul's addressees *must* now apply the spirit to practice if they have not already done so (8:12–13).

Our concern here should be neither with the exegetical details of the passage nor with Paul's more overt, literary purposes with it—those of separating the law from sin and maintaining the holy and good character of the law (cf. 7:12–13); of giving some response to the hints he has dropped about the role of the law within his overarching salvation-historical scheme (see 3:20–31, 4:15, 5:20); of suggesting an answer to the question about God's possible purpose with the law (7:13); and more. Instead, we shall concentrate on the main line of Paul's argument, which lies (*a*) in developing a phenomenology of life under the law which makes more precise the character of the human state 'under sin' to which the Christ faith constituted the solution (7:7–25) and (*b*) in insisting that the Christ event is in fact the solution to that problem (8:1–13).²¹ (*a*) In relation to 7:7–25, our discussion must focus on bringing out the set of concepts and the whole underlying theory through which Paul displays the negative character of life under the law. Here he relies crucially on the moral psychology which went into the analysis of weakness of will (*akrasia*) in the ancient ethical tradition. By his use of this material Paul becomes able to pinpoint the state of being 'under sin' as one of constantly *risking* to sin due to an incomplete internal transformation of the psyche. (*b*) Next we must consider whether the same philosophical theory may be seen to underlie his account in 8:1–13 of how being in Christ will overcome the predicament he has described in the previous section. On the surface Paul seems to be working in 8:1–13 with ideas that have very little to do with the vocabulary and categories in which he describes the problems about law-observance in 7:7–25. Since 7:7–25 lends itself immediately to the kind of philosophical analysis in terms of the I→X→S-model that we are pursuing, we must spend some time on the apparently more difficult 8:1–13 to see whether the two sections may in the end be held together in a satisfactory way that makes sense of the connection that Paul himself undoubtedly saw between them.

Its self-assertion: 7:7–25

The basic theme of 7:7–25 is straightforward, though also quite refined. It is the conscious acknowledgement and recognition of human sinfulness. Initially, this may not seem so clear. It is generally recognized that the account in 7:7–25 was meant by Paul to untangle the threads that connect the law and sin in what by 6:14 and 7:5–6 appeared to be a tightly wound knot. The task appears difficult, in view of the apparently quite different hints given earlier in the letter of the precise relationship between the law and sin: 3:20 (the law makes people *recognize* sin), 4:15

(the law generates wrath), 5:13 (there *was* sin in the world before the law, only it was not *registered*), 5:20 (the law came in sideways in order to *increase* transgression) and 6:14 (sin will not be lord over those who are not under the law). Will it in fact be possible to bring all this together under a single interpretation? Must we not rather conclude that Paul vacillates between a range of interpretations, e.g. a revelatory or cognitive one (that the law *teaches* man what is sin), a 'definitory' one (that the law *defines* sin as 'transgression') or a causative one (that the law *brings about* sinning)?[22] Let us try a patient reading of 7:7–13. The basic issue that we must decide is between a cognitive and a causative reading. We shall see, however, that a solution may lie in combining the two: by teaching man what is sin, the law may also, in a sense, generate sin.

Before there was a law, says Paul, nobody 'knew' sin (7:7). Did nobody sin at all? Is that the sense of 'not knowing' sin? That depends.[23] On the one hand, Paul states that sin was 'dead' or inoperative (*nekra*, 7:8) before the advent of the law. It only 'came alive' (*an-ezēsen*, 7:9) when the law issued its negative command 'Thou shalt not covet!' (7:7). The result of *this* was 'all forms of desire' (7:8). So, apparently the person did not previously sin. On the other hand, Paul has not said that sin only came into the world when the law came. It was already present, though admittedly without being 'operative', indeed it was this *pre*-existing sin which took the law as its starting point for generating all forms of desire (7:8). In what way would sin be present and in existence without being 'operative'? Here one is reminded of Paul's claim a couple of chapters earlier to the effect that sin was indeed present in the world before the coming of the law, quite precisely between Adam and Moses, only it was not registered in the account book (5:13–14)—for the very good reason that there was no such book. (For that, the law was needed.) This suggests that Paul is not operating with the idea of a period of primeval innocence before the law, a period when there was no behaviour or desire whatever of the kind which *when* the law had arrived *would* fall under sinful desire. Instead, what interests him is the fact of sin and desire *becoming known*, of their being understood and recognized *as* sin and (law-transgressing) desire. That only came through the law. Before the advent of the law, sin was dead and inoperative *as* sin—and so a person would not *sin* (as opposed to doing whatever would later *count* as sin). With the advent of the law, by contrast, sin came alive *as* sin.

This reading already combines the cognitive and the definitory interpretations. But it may also be said to cover the causative one. If the kind of sinning Paul has in mind is sinning experienced and recognized *as* sin, then it makes excellent sense to say that the law causes or generates *that* when it *reveals* sin's character *of* sin. And so one may of course also say that the law *increases* sin (cf. 5:20), not by making anybody sin *more*, but by making him now *sin* as opposed to doing what earlier did not *count* as sin. Let us focus this reading by coining some terms for it. What the law reveals, defines, generates and increases is sin-realized-as-sin. And the way it does it is by putting-a-name-on sin, by *saying* (cf. 7:7) 'Thou shalt not *covet*!'. Is law and sin then the same? Of course not. Sin was there already, and for that reason it is most appropriate to say that it is *sin* that is responsible for there being sin-realized-as-sin. Next, the law put a name on sin, presumably in order to keep it down or (possibly) remove it (cf. 'Thou shalt *not* covet!'). But sin, the power, then 'used' the law to generate the sinning that unfortunately *continued* to be there, but now *as* sin-realized-as-sin.

This reading makes intrinsic sense, as far as I can see, of everything that needs to be explained so far. The strongest point in its favour, however, is that it immediately explains the claim Paul goes on to make in 7:10 and through that the whole of 7:14 ff: that when sin came alive with the coming of the law, 'I' *died* and the law-command that was (intrinsically) meant to lead to life was 'found by me' to lead to *death*. This verse acts as a sort of headline for the section that begins in 7:14, in which Paul spells out precisely the experience of living under the law. That experience turns out to be nothing other than the *recognition* of human 'sinfulness', the *recognition* of an element of sin in oneself that is (apparently) *inescapable*. And that is felt as a 'death' (cf. 7:24). When the law made sin 'come alive', namely *as* sin, it *revealed* to the person living under it something intrinsically a part of him- or herself that now stood out as an element of sin. But that also meant that the law would be experienced as leading to death, namely, the death of (apparently) inescapable sinfulness that Paul describes so strikingly in 7:14–25.

7:13 should dispel any doubt that Paul is in fact speaking, not of obtaining right from the start those desires which under the law qualify as sinful desires, but of having them in the sense of recognizing them *under that description*. In addition to drawing his distinction between making the holy, just and good law responsible for the resulting misery (which one should not) and ascribing responsibility to sin (which one should), Paul also states that the purpose (presumably God's) of the development he has set out was that sin should 'become apparent (as) sin'.[24] That is quite explicit. Similarly, when he goes immediately on to state the purpose to be that 'sin should become very much a sinner', what he means is presumably that sin should *stand out as* sinful.[25]

The crucial insight is that in this account of life under the law, which is the most developed we have in Paul, what he focuses on as the essence of that life is a matter of the understanding: the recognition in a person living under the law of his own sinfulness (in the sense in which Paul goes on to develop it—that he constantly *risks* doing what he himself sees as sinful acts). This focus on the understanding is important. If living under the law issues in this kind of self-understanding, then it is a priori likely that the opposite of living under the law—living in Christ and the spirit—will contain a similar element of self-understanding. 8:1–13 must show whether that expectation is fulfilled.

We have left on one side the famous question of who the I is who is speaking throughout 7:7–25. We shall take it here without further discussion that it is a general I (possibly a prosopopoietic one) that stands for Jews living before and under the law. We shall also take it that Paul's account presupposes his own new Christ-believing perspective.[26] Thus no Jew (and certainly not the pre-Christ-believing Paul himself) need actually have had the experience he describes. This does not, however, in any way preclude that Paul is speaking of an experience, nor that he both means to say and is entitled to saying that it is one that people *should* have if they (now) live under the law. If Paul could show that the Christ faith *overcomes* human sinfulness of the form he says one experiences under the law, namely, the constant, uncontrollable risk of doing sinful acts, then he might also legitimately say that *viewed in the light of that (new) possibility*, life under the law *should* be experienced as being inescapably entangled in sinfulness in the way he explains in 7:7–25.

There is one point about Paul's use of 'I' in this section that needs to be emphasized. Paul very clearly chooses this form of speaking here because his whole theme is *the effect on the individual* (an I!) of the law, in the form of one's recognition of one's own sinfulness. This is so obvious that the point need hardly be made. But in the current climate of reaction to Rudolf Bultmann's very individualistic reading of Paul, it is necessary to insist that we recognize that Paul speaks of the individual whenever that is the plain meaning of the text. For all that, Paul need of course not have spoken of the individual in the specific way of Rudolf Bultmann. In fact he did not.

It should be obvious that Paul must be speaking quite distinctly of the individual in the present passage if his theme is the recognition of sinfulness. A recognition is something which has its logical locus in individuals, no matter how much they may also share it with others. In addition, when Paul spells out in 7:14–25 how the law was 'found by me' to lead to death (7:10) and how the holy law which was really 'my good' also 'became death for me' (7:13), what he does is of course to move into the individual and show how a person who lives under the law is torn in his interior between conflicting desires. And that is again something that necessarily takes place in an individual. Whether we like it or not, the whole theme of *akrasia* (weakness of will) necessarily focuses on the individual. In the ancient ethical tradition, it even focused distinctly on his or her psyche.

In the light of this, let us look a bit more closely at Paul's argument in 7:14 ff. His theme is the recognition of the kind of inner dissociation which occurs in *akrasia*.[27] The occurrence of this phenomenon shows, so Paul claims (7:14), that the 'I' is a fleshly being, sold under sin. Here the 'I' stands for the whole human being, which Paul then goes on to divide into different parts. This 'I-whole' of the person living under the law is the I with which Paul is basically concerned. And the problem he is analysing is a problem *of* the I-whole, one that has to do with a conflict *within* that I. This comes out whenever Paul speaks of the various psychic parts as parts *of* the I, e.g. 'sin living *in me*' (7:17), and also when he states that '*I* do what I hate' (7:15). It is of course also this I-whole he is talking about in his concluding exclamation (7:24): 'Wretched human that I am! Who will save me from this body of death?' As this verse makes clear, and as Paul had already said in 7:14, the I-whole is not distinct from the body of death. It *is* that body but of course as including the different parts that Paul identifies throughout his argument.[28]

Looking now at these parts, we see that there are two with a different relationship with the I-whole. One, the good one, is itself spoken of as an 'I'. This 'I-part' is the I that wills the good and does not will what the I-whole (from time to time) finds himself doing. The I-part agrees with the law that it is good (7:16) and declares that it is not this I which brings about what it hates (7:17). It finds joy in God's law and is identical with 'the inner man' (7:22) and the 'mind' (*nous*, 7:23, 25) as contrasted with the 'limbs' (*mele*, 7:23) and the 'flesh' (*sarx*, 7:25).

The point of speaking of both an I-whole and an I-part is evident. The part of the mind that we have called the I-part is precisely the one *with* which the I-whole *identifies*—hence precisely its name as an 'I'. And the whole problem that Paul is analysing lies in the two facts (*a*) that the other part, the non-I-part, is at the same time both *a real part of* the I-whole and also something with which the I-whole does *not identify* (but still recognizes as a part of itself)—and (*b*) that it is the non-I-part which from time to time '*acts*'. When that happens, the I-whole does not *identify* with 'his' acts. He merely *finds* that evil 'is present for me as something that lies alongside in me' (7:21). Or again, the I-whole merely *sees* or *observes* the presence of this other side of himself (7:23) without being able to *identify* with it. It is this *schizophrenic* aspect of weakness of will which makes it so unbearable (7:24).[29]

Paul's argument is clearly directed towards formulating this experience of dissociation, which is voiced several times in 7:21–23. For it is through having this experience that the I-whole recognizes his own sinfulness in the sense of the *presence in him* of something inherently sinful, something he does not in fact identify with, but which he cannot overcome however much he identifies and agrees with God's law. It is crucial to note, however, that even though Paul analyses the recognition of one's sinfulness as a recognition of something in oneself with which one does not identify, the sinfulness that is revealed with the coming of the law is a sinfulness of the individual person *as a whole*, the I-whole whose *inner* structure Paul has divided up into I-part and the 'other thing'.[30] It is the I-*whole*, with the individual body and limbs as one of its two parts, which is seen as sinful, no matter how disintegrated the two parts may be felt to be. Thus what Paul aims to identify in the passage as accounting for the continuing sinning of a person living under the law is something which, no matter how much the I-whole feels dissociated from it, is and remains an inherent part of that being. It is something '*in*' the individual human being, something tied to one's body, of which one cannot (apparently) entirely divest oneself as long as one remains an individual, bodily being.

So what is it? Exactly the same as we found already in connection with Romans 1: the individual *as* an individual, including the normative perspective that is part and parcel of being a bodily individual, the perspective of looking out *from* the bodily individual and evaluating things and events in the world in the light of whether they will further or counteract the interests of the individual. As we saw, these interests may be distinctly bodily ones, but they may also extend from the body to cover relations with others, those that remain directed towards the bodily individual him- or herself. Basically, what accounts for sinning on the part of a person living under the law is *a perspective*, the I-perspective.[31]

This reading situates Paul's account squarely within the picture of the I→X→S-model on its most distinctly Stoic interpretation. Think of the I-part and the non-I-part as belonging to an I-whole that is found at the I-pole of the model. Here the I-whole 'rejoices in God's law in the inner man': the inner man, that is, the I-part, is in itself directed 'upwards' towards God's law (X), and so is the I-whole too. Both the I-part and the I-whole in principle identify themselves with God's holy, just and good law (I→X). But nevertheless the non-I-part drags the I-whole down to the I-pole. Its uncontrolled and uncontrollable existence *as an* eliminable part of the I-whole means that the I→X movement can never be fulfilled.

In conclusion, Paul is suggesting, in a terminology that immediately translates into the I→X→S-model, that the law does not remove sin, indeed cannot remove it. Quite to the contrary, it makes sin stand out. Sin is tied to the individual body. It is a 'part' of the bodily self taken as a whole and no matter how much the I-whole may, in part, also identify with the law, there is a constant risk (if nothing more) that his inherent sinfulness, the individual self-directed perspective of the I-pole, may assert itself against all his law-abiding wishes. A risk? Yes, the risk of *akrasia*. For that is precisely the very essence of *akrasia* in the ancient ethical tradition: that one constantly *risks* 'acting' against one's better judgement.[32]

All of this makes intrinsic sense so far. By describing in terms of the phenomenon of *akrasia* the failure of the law to ensure that it is always followed by a person who lives under it, Paul has obtained a handle on accounting for life under the law which does not immediately call for any further elaboration. It is just a sufficiently common human experience that even when one subscribes to a law, one does not *necessarily* always follow it.

However, there are further questions that one could wish Paul had answered. For one thing, if a Jew had made the law his own not just as any old law, but as *God's own law* (cf. 7:22), perhaps even as part of a 'covenantal' relationship, would that not add something to mere 'law-keeping' which might take him further in the direction of always and everywhere observing the law? So, *why* was the law not sufficient? For another, if it is part of Paul's idea, as one may already surmise on the basis of chapter 6, that what was not possible through the law became possible through Christ, then how should that be explained? Exactly how may participation in the Christ event (I→X with *Christ* at X) bring about the complete removal of that factor in the individual psyche which the law could not keep entirely under control? That is, *why* is participation in the Christ event sufficient? Part of the answer to this second question has already been broached in our discussion of chapter 6. The secret must lie in the very emphatic sense that Paul must have given to the ideas of being 'dead to sin' and 'living for God through Christ Jesus' (6:11). When we now turn to 8:1–13, we must press this question again. We want to be shown exactly how the Christ event, as Paul describes its impact in 8:1–13, may be seen as a solution to the apparently unresolvable plight described in chapter 7. If we can see this, we may perhaps also become able to answer the first question and see why the law was understood by Paul not to be sufficient in all circumstances.

And its removal: 8:1–13

Paul's claim in 8:1–13 is, in complete accordance with what he had said in chapter 6, that as a result of the Christ event the body (*sōma*) of each of his addressees is 'dead' (*nekron*, 8:10). In other words, the 'other thing' described in chapter 7 has been put entirely out of action, made completely inoperative (cf. the use of *nekros* in 7:8).[33] There will no longer be anything 'bad lying next to the good in me' (cf. 7:21). The bodily self, which we interpreted as the individual self-directed perspective of the I-pole, has been entirely removed and the just demand of the law will now be fulfilled (8:4).[34] That is quite clearly what Paul wishes to tell his readers. But how does he get there? How will he *explain* that the Christ event may have had that effect, indeed has had it?

Initially, it appears somewhat difficult to answer this question in a satisfactory way on the basis of 8:1–13 alone. Paul's basic strategy here is to bring in *the spirit* in explanatory contrast with the law (cf. 8:2). Moreover, he appears to rely heavily on a number of strongly 'participationist' ideas. The most important are those of having the spirit 'in' one (8:9, 11), having Christ 'in' one (8:10), possessing the spirit of Christ and belonging to him (8:9), being 'in' Christ Jesus (8:2) and being 'in' the spirit (8:9) as opposed to 'in' the flesh (8:8–9). But the genuinely explanatory force of these locutions is not so easy to ascertain. Suppose we understand them both in a very substantive way and also in a manner that stresses the active role of God and Christ in bringing the new state about. Let us say that these people have been *invaded* by God's spirit. Within such a picture we might perhaps explain how sin in the individual being has been cancelled out. With a total invasion and takeover by God's spirit, there just is not room for it any longer. However, if there was nothing more to be said, we should be forced to conclude that Paul has relied on either a mere metaphor (with regard to the complete takeover brought about by God's invasion) or an unargued postulate (with regard to the radical difference between spirit-people and flesh-people). Once more, we come up against the fundamental problem of settling the question within what logical categories we should understand Paul. We need to read carefully, therefore, as we did with Paul's account of baptism, in order to discover ways of thinking that will give *genuinely explanatory force* to Paul's account of the new situation generated by the Christ event. We want to be *shown* how the Christ event may have had its striking effect of sinless practice and how, *for that reason*, it might be sufficient where the law was not. In other words, we want to be able to understand the change and the new situation in a terminology like that of the I→X→S-model—and to be convinced that Paul himself also understood them in that way.

Paul draws up a strong contrast between flesh and spirit (8:3–4, 5–11, 12–13). Where the person described in chapter 7 had in him two elements that pointed in different directions, what Paul has in mind now is an either-or for people as wholes. Some people 'are' 'in accordance with' flesh (8:5) or 'in' it (8:8). Others 'are' 'in' the spirit (8:9 ff). The first group in effect consists of those described in chapter 7. For according to 8:3, God sent Christ because of the law's 'weakness through the flesh'— clearly the weakness that Paul has just described in chapter 7.[35] Similarly, Paul lets his description of the first group issue in the claim that they *cannot* (*dynantai*) please God (8:8), since the flesh does not, indeed *cannot* (*dynatai*), be subjected to God's law (8:7)—again a clear reference to chapter 7. In itself it is a very strong claim that those described in chapter 7, who after all did rejoice in and identify with God's law in their inner being, should now be seen as people who 'are' in or in accordance with the flesh. Everything depends on whether Paul was able to develop with full explanatory force a contrast with these people which may not only convince us that those on the *other* side will in fact have overcome *completely* the earlier hindrance to law-fulfilment but also show us *how* that has come about.

Odds are not very favourable. I shall now go through some of the most important material in the passage in search for ideas we may use to account for the postulated difference between life under the law and in Christ. To avoid saddling Paul with mere reliance on metaphor or un-argued postulate, these ideas should be about how Christ-believers see things and how that will explain their supposed sinlessness. By contrast, we will not be satisfied with ideas that only speak in substantive and objective terms of what has been done from the outside to Christ-believers. The result of our search will be negative in the sense that we shall not be able to find anything in the way Paul describes Christ-believers here that will satisfy us. In other words, there is no clear trace of the whole way of thinking about these things that is encapsulated in the I→X→S-model— and was so clearly present in chapter 7. That should leave us in an impasse. I shall then argue, however, that there is a specific feature of the passage as a whole that will help us out.

Early in the section (8:3), Paul ties the eradication of sin directly to the Christ event. That event meant a realized judgement of sin in the flesh, a judgement that was, as it were, perpetrated on Christ. This recalls chapter 6 (6:7, 9), with which the present passage shares some important ideas. First, by dying in punishment for the sin that is tied to the flesh,

Christ has done justice to sin and has therefore escaped from it, leaving it completely behind. Sin no longer has any power over him. In his present, resurrected life he lives exclusively for God. Next, the Christ event also had precise implications for 'those in Christ Jesus'. For them too there no longer is any judgement (8:1). They too have escaped from sin. How? The answer given in 8:2 seems to point forward to the one we already know from 8:9–10: by having the spirit, by 'being in' Christ (8:2); that is, by having God's spirit, Christ's spirit, Christ 'in them', by being 'his' (8:9–10). Thus we seem to be staying within the categorial framework of the picture of a substantive event ('infusion'), a picture that might in fact also be involved in what Paul said about baptism in chapter 6. (But there, as we saw, that kind of language was far from the only kind.) To spell out Paul's meaning in 8:1–11, we might even introduce the customary point that Paul is relying on an ancient Jewish idea to the effect that what holds of the archetype of a chain (here Christ) holds of each individual item in the chain (here those 'in' Christ). However, that would not really be of much help. For what makes somebody belong in the chain? Should that itself be spelled out in substantive terms—or in some other way?

The situation does not look much better if we look at the verse (8:10) that states what we wish to be able to explain: that as a result of the Christ event, the body (of sin) in Paul's addressees is 'dead'. The body, says Paul, is dead 'because of sin'. We have taken this to mean 'because of the sin that goes with the body', 'because of its sinfulness'. But that hardly *explains* why it is dead. Then Paul refers to the spirit, meaning presumably the spirit (which is also Christ's spirit, cf. 8:9) that is 'in' each of his addressees. That spirit means 'life' 'because of righteousness'. Does that give us what we are looking for? Hardly. First on 'life'. If it could be taken here to refer specifically and pointedly to the right form of life here and now, we might perhaps have something to go on: 'life' now 'because of righteousness'—including because of faith? Will a veiled reference here to faith help us out? Does this give us what we were looking for: a reference to a way of seeing on the part of Christ-believers that will explain why *they*, of all people, may now fulfil the law? I doubt it. For in the light of the reference in 8:6 to the 'ultimate aim' (*phronēma*) of the spirit as being 'life and peace' (presumably in relation to God), it seems more natural to take 'life' in 8:10 to point (at least *also*) in the direction of eschatological life, certainly not exclusively to a law-fulfilling life here and now. That is supported by 8:11 too, which is explicitly eschatological. And the second half of 8:13, with its explicit reference to life in the future, virtually repeats the content of 8:10 (though now, of course, in directly parenetic form). Thus the 'life' vouched for by the spirit remains a very objective one, one that awaits Christ-believers in the eschatological future. Then on 'righteousness' in 8:10. It is presumably mentioned to counterbalance the reference to sinfulness of the body. The idea will be that the presence of the spirit in Paul's addressees means eschatological life for them due to the new status of righteousness they have received along with the spirit. It is of course true that such righteousness involves faith here and now on the part of those declared righteous. But we have already seen that that aspect does not seem to be within Paul's view. Instead, he appears to be staying wholly within the objective picture with its basically eschatological and future orientation.

We have thus reached an impasse. 8:1–13 raises a basic issue in relation to the kind of reading recommended in this book—and indeed to the immediately preceding section, 7:7–25. If this passage has described the problem of life under the law in the terminology of *akrasia*, which is also the terminology of the I→X→S-model, then how should we understand and handle Paul's apparent use of an altogether different kind of terminology in 8:1–13—when the latter passage also seems intended to bring in the solution to the problem developed in the earlier one? More generally, if we want an explanation of sinlessness in Christ that does not merely rely on 'participationist' ideas like 'infusion' and a substantive takeover, what shall we say of 8:1–13?

Let us put our question to 8:1–13 head-on: Do we find here some reference to a way of seeing on the part of Christ-believers? Do we even find such a reference that will genuinely explain how the Christ event as Paul describes it here might constitute the solution to the problem of *akrasia* under the law? Or are we left entirely with ideas about 'participation', 'infusion' and the like?

The correct answer, I suggest, is this: *Everything* Paul says in the passage refers to a way of seeing on the part of his addressees. The key feature lies in the overall character of the passage as a whole. Paul is not just describing what has *taken place*, objectively and from the outside, for 'those in Christ Jesus' (8:1). He is describing, from the inside, *what it is like to be* 'in Christ Jesus'—as it were for the consideration of his addressees. And he is, implicitly (8:1–11) and explicitly (8:12–13), *appealing* to them to *see* and *think of* themselves in this way—*as* people 'in Christ Jesus', *as* people who have God's spirit in them and so forth. If that is in fact the case, so the argument will be, then against our immediate impression, 8:1–13 too will be about a form of self-understanding, the correct one that Christ-believers will and should have and that will then also *explain* why *they*, that is, people with *that* self-understanding, have been removed from the constant risk of sin into a wholly new state of always acting properly.

To see this basic, *parenetic* direction of the passage, consider 8:4, where Paul states that God sent his son in order that the just demand of the law might be fulfilled 'among us who walk not in accordance with the flesh, but with the spirit'. What he means is not just: among us who do walk and so forth, but this: *when* we walk, *so long as* we walk, *if* we walk. Thus Paul is *describing* the Christian way of life *as part of* making an underlying *appeal* to his addressees. His aim is that they should come to *see themselves* in the light of his 'description'. Later (8:12–13), he will then make the implicit appeal of 8:4 explicit: they *owe* it, therefore, not to live in accordance with the flesh and so forth. Why? Because they *are* in the way he has just explained.

The suggestion is, then, that *all through* 8:1–11 Paul is basically making an appeal to the self-understanding of his addressees. His description is aimed to make them see who they themselves are. And that aim is *part of* his *parenetic* purpose. This is supported by the specific shape he gives to 8:5–11. When he opposes those who 'are' in accordance with the flesh (8:5–8) to those who 'are' in accordance with the spirit (8:9–11), he may initially appear to be merely describing two opposed groups that are implacably opposed to one another. Thus in 8:5–8 he certainly describes facts about what he takes it to be like to be one who 'is' in accordance with the flesh. Similarly, in 8:9 he begins by stating a fact: 'You (by contrast) are not in the flesh, but in the spirit'. However, that is not just pure description. Rather, Paul aims to make them recognize who and what they are. He also adds: '*if*, that is, God's spirit stays in you'. Of course Paul's *ei* and *eiper* may also mean 'inasmuch as' or 'since'. But that can hardly be the exclusive meaning here. For he goes immediately on with an *ei* that can only be genuinely conditional: 'If [*ei*] somebody should *not* possess Christ's spirit, then that person does not belong to Christ' (v. 9b). This sentence, with its genuinely conditional *ei*, presupposes that there was an *issue whether* some of Paul's addressees did or did not really 'possess Christ's spirit'. In that case, we should also take the two *ei*s with which Paul opens 8:10 and 8:11 to have a genuinely conditional force. Thus Paul is after all not just describing facts about his addressees, but stating what will (in fact!) hold of them *if* certain other things also hold. And *whether* these things do hold is—*up to the addressees themselves*.

On this reading, Paul is doing two things in 8:1–11 as a whole. (*a*) He is rehearsing the basic 'theological' content of the Christ faith: that God sent his own son and so forth (8:3); that there is henceforth no judgement for 'those in Christ Jesus' (8:1); that there is (eschatological) life and peace (with God) through reception of the spirit (8:6) and through God's intervention which creates righteousness (8:10)—and conversely, that the body of sin of 'those in whom Christ is' has (in whatever way) become dead and hence completely inoperative. (*b*) And then he is *exhorting his addressees to see themselves in this light*. That comes out in 8:12–13, which finally makes wholly explicit the parenetic force of 8:1–11 too.

Then comes the conclusion. If Paul does *both* things in 8:1–11, then one can see how the Christ event as described in this passage may in fact be taken to solve the problem of *akrasia* under the law. For what Paul is then saying in 8:1–11 is this. If his addressees *see themselves as* being 'in Christ Jesus' (8:1), if they *see themselves as* belonging to Christ (8:9b) through having Christ's spirit and *see themselves as* having Christ in them (8:10), in short, if they *see themselves as* having been taken over by God, Christ and the spirit, *then* their sinful body will in fact have been made inoperative, namely through that seeing. They will now identify completely and exclusively with Christ. Where 'they' *were*, there Christ now is. They have gone over completely to an altogether new kind of total directedness towards God. And that means that they have now also left behind altogether their own individual, bodily self. They no longer identify at all with that and will never allow it a role as the locus of normativity. In short, *then* the movement from **I** to **X** will have been *completed*.

There are two wholly different sides, therefore, to what Paul says and does in 8:1–13. There is first his objective account of the Christ event, the Christ *story*. This story, which tells of the Christ event, its purpose, character and result, issues in the factual claim that people who become part of this story cease altogether to sin. That, Paul claims, is the purpose itself, indeed the whole *raison d'être*, of the Christ event (8:4). It was to bring those gentiles and Jews *there*—those gentiles and Jews who were in dire need of it (1:18–3:20)—that God set the Christ event going to which gentiles and Jews might then respond with a faith like Abraham's (3:21–4:25). But then there is also Paul's *appeal* to his addressees, namely, that they *see themselves as* part of the objective story. If successful, this appeal will have definite consequences for the relationship with sin on the part of those to whom the appeal is addressed. *If* they *believe* Paul's story and thus become part of it *by* seeing and identifying themselves completely with the figure of Christ which constitutes the centre of the Christ story, then *these* people *will themselves in fact cease altogether* to sin. In *their* case, the risk of *akrasia* will finally have been completely overcome because they have given themselves over totally to Christ and God.

It is a quite different question, of course, *whether* a person should believe the story. Paul certainly believed it. Moreover, he presupposed that his addressees did the same. Against this background, what he then did was to insist that the Christ story made a totalizing claim *on* those who believed it. Therefore, if Christ-believers honoured this claim, as they were bound to do since that was what the story was all about, then they no longer *would* sin. They simply no longer *could* do so.

Have we also answered the other question, which asked why adherence to the law on the part of a devout Jew *could* not altogether exclude the risk of *akrasia*? Not quite. Paul himself does not address this question. He is satisfied with claiming that the law did not in fact achieve this. Would he have anything to say if we pressed him? The best answer seems to be that as Paul has rehearsed the Christ story in Romans 3:21 ff and indeed not least in 8:1–11 itself, it was *such* a striking story that *if* one believed it directly and literally and even as implying its imminent consummation, then it is more than likely that one would be taken over by it to such an extent that there would, as it were, be no room left for any other perspective on the world. But if it is *that* kind of event that was required to bring gentiles and Jews where God wanted them, then it does not seem unfair to say that the law was not the *kind* of thing that *could* bring them there. What the law could do was what Paul has described it in 7:7 ff as doing. More than that it could not. *Only* the Christ event could do more.[36]

Conclusion

7:7–8:13 as a whole, no less than chapter 6, is about the new possibility of actual, complete sinlessness that has been opened up by the Christ event. Both passages bring out how the kind of total directedness towards God that comes about through faith in the Christ event will make the 'body of sin' completely inoperative. It will remove the bodily self altogether, leaving behind only the person who belongs to and identifies him- or herself with God through Christ. Thus both passages serve to answer the basic question from which we started of how the type of faith described in 3:21–4:25 will help to solve the set of problems that Paul had identified in 1:18–3:20.

In bringing this out Paul keeps alive his basic strategy from 1:18–3:20 of showing that both gentiles and Jews are in need of the Christ faith in order to arrive where God wanted to bring them. He does this in a fascinating way. With regard to the Jews he drops a number of hints that the law is insufficient. And he then finally spells out in great detail how the law, which was itself both holy and just and as Paul no doubt thought the *best* available means to achieve the desired end, could not bring a person from the state that was closest to being the desired one over to the latter. The law could not remove the risk of *akrasia*. It could not, therefore, bring a person to the *unified* state of mind where he or she would *only* wish to do God's will because that had also become the person's own, exclusive will. But this account was also directly relevant to the gentiles. They too knew the phenomenon of *akrasia*. Indeed, that phenomenon had precisely been worked out in *gentile* thought in the ancient ethical tradition. So, whether they were themselves attracted to the Jewish law or not, they too would see that it was the Christ faith, and that alone, which would be able to bring them into the state where they would only wish to do God's will—and would therefore also actually do it. So by analysing the deficiency of what was otherwise the best available means, the *Jewish* law, in terms of a distinctly *Greek* idea (that of *akrasia*), Paul was able to show that both Jews and Greeks were in need of the Christ faith—and that once they *had* that, they would be able to *do* what the whole thing was about, God's will as rightly stated in the law. Thus 7:7–25 is very far from having the character of a digression, as has sometimes been claimed. It answers the question about the place of the law in Paul's system. But even more, it shows in relation to Paul's identification of the problem in 2:12–29 *precisely how* the Christ faith provides the ultimate solution to the problem as identified there. In the Christ faith even the risk of *akrasia* is overcome. God's will has now been completely internalized in such a way that the Christ-believer wills that for him- or herself alone.

All through the discussion, we have also been concerned to settle within what framework of logical categories Paul is here working. We have not excluded that he may have had strongly substantive ideas about what happened in baptism and in reception of the spirit. Also, he will definitely have thought that everything that happens is due to God's agency. But we have seen that all through he is also working within the set of logical categories that goes into the I→X→S-model centring on those of self-understanding and self-identification, the sense of where one oneself belongs—as in the Stoic theory of *oikeiōsis*. In chapter 6 and 7:7–25 this framework went directly into Paul's account of baptism and its consequences and life under the law. In 8:1–13 it was presupposed in a different way: the manner in which Paul expects his substantive and objective account of the Christ story, including its claims about what it is like to be 'in Christ Jesus', to appeal to his addressees so that they will themselves come to identify completely with God through Christ. We have also seen all through the discussion of 6:1–8:13 that this section is basically parenetic. It describes what the Christ faith means for actual practice. And it exhorts Paul's addressees, implicitly and explicitly, to realize this in both senses of the term: in understanding and in practice.

Against this background, we are entitled to sum up this reading by saying that Paul's basic theme all through 6:1–8:13 is, first, the possibility of actual sinless practice (at the C-level) that has been opened up when Christ-believers leave behind their individual bodily selves (I) as the normative locus of their self-identification and move up instead to X— and, second (the parenetic point), the need to actualize that possibility.

We may add that at the same time as Paul has claimed that complete law-fulfilment and in general sinless practice to the exclusion of any risk of *akrasia* is only possible in Christ, he has also raised the stakes for an adequate fulfilment of God's demands for righteousness. Law-fulfilment of a form that allowed for some transgression, which might then be amended, was not enough. Even complete and regular law-fulfilment that retained a bare risk of non-fulfilment was not enough. What was required was what had now also become possible: complete and unwavering law-fulfilment, completely sinless practice. That, Paul claimed, was only possible through Christ faith, which itself had the radical character that he had brought out in Romans 4.

10

Romans III
The Solution Developed

Summary of chapters on Romans 1–8, and two observations on Romans 9–11

Paul's argument in chapters 1–8 of Romans is complicated both in literary terms and also in the quite extravagant mixture of motifs that he brings in. But the specific line we have attempted to follow is not very complicated. At the risk of being repetitive, I shall summarize our findings so far in order to make the line stand out as clearly as possible.

Paul begins (1:18–3:20) by describing a pervasive state of being 'under sin', which he ascribes to both gentiles and Jews before Christ. Based on his description in 3:20 ff of the solution to this situation, we saw that the basic feature of the earlier state was a failure to stand in the proper relationship with God, the one of total human directedness towards God captured in the line I→X in the I→X→S-model. That line was broken and human beings had, to varying degrees, turned towards themselves: I→I. This was most clear in the case of gentiles (1:18–32); but Jews too (2:17–24) mistook their intrinsically correct relationship with God through the law as an occasion for adopting an attitude towards gentiles that reflected the same mistaken directedness towards themselves. The basic problem, then, was a lack of the proper, *total* directedness towards God.

However, Paul also developed this idea in an 'ethical' direction in two different ways. In the case of gentiles, he focused on the *substantive* 'ethical' implications of the failing 'religious' relationship: the immoral life that resulted from it. Here the line I→I, 'religiously' understood, turned into the same line, I→I, 'ethically' understood. Paul had a double target here, partly immoral acts related specifically to the body and partly acts that reflected a whole range of social vices. Both types were explained in terms of giving undue weight to the bodily individual and its intrinsically self-based and self-directed perspective. Instead of being whole-heartedly

directed towards God, gentiles were directed towards themselves even
when they engaged in relationships with others. Thus their state as described in 1:18–32 constituted a full and comprehensive negation of the
I→X→S-model.

In the case of the Jews, Paul focused on another, *formal* 'ethical' implication of their failing 'religious' relationship: a failure to *do* the law (as
opposed to merely having it), in particular a failure to avoid doing what
one knew to be forbidden by the law. Paul referred this failure back to a
lack of internalization, a failure to have the proper inner structure of the
psyche: to have the law written in one's heart and to be circumcised on
the heart (cf. 2:12–16, 25–29).

We were concerned to keep the two aspects of the 'ethical' failure
distinct. They are not about the same thing. What Paul said about gentiles
had to do with the substantive content of their 'ethical' failure. It pertained to the B-level (**Bb**). By contrast, what he said about the Jew had
to do with the more formal issue of doing or not doing what one knows
needs doing and avoiding or not avoiding what one knows must be
avoided. It thus pertained to the C-level. Both sides of the 'ethical' failure
fall under not being at the S-pole and both were to be explained by the
same feature: the restricted, self-directed perspective of the bodily individual that mirrors the basic, 'religious' failure (I→I).

Next, in his account of the new situation of Christ-believers, Paul
again took as his starting point the specifically 'religious' issue of their
relationship with God. That was the overall theme treated in 3:21–4:25
with a sharp focus on the idea of faith. Thus the theme was the restoration
of the proper line I→X. Paul also brought out very emphatically how
that restoration came about as a result of a movement in the opposite
direction, from X to I. It was God who made it possible through the
Christ event. The two themes of God's intervention (X→I) and the
restoration of the human relationship with God (I→X) were also central
in 5:1–11 and 8:14–39, which stayed within Paul's basic, 'religious' perspective. This raised the obvious question: How did Paul see the 'ethical'
implications of the 'religious' change he had described? Was the distinction between the B- and C-levels at the S-pole relevant for the new
situation too? Or had it been superseded by the new events?

The distinction was not superseded. What we saw in 6:1–8:13 was
precisely a preoccupation on Paul's part with its second side, the C-level
issue of the inner structure and doing. Both in chapter 6 and in 8:1–13
the basic idea was that by having become part of the Christ event Paul's
addressees had in fact died to sin. They had been taken over completely
by Christ in such a way that they no longer *could* sin. Instead, they

would automatically do what is right, including what the law requires. Even the risk of *akrasia* based on an internal division had been completely removed. For the inner structure of their psyche had been so completely changed that they would have no opposing desires whatever. Or at least: that is how they should understand what had happened to them in their faithful directedness towards God, so that they might finally bring it about, should any vestige remain of their 'old man'. We also saw that there was no inconsistency here in Paul's use of the indicative and imperative moods. For being in Christ was a matter of the understanding, in addition to whatever else it might be. And an understanding may be acquired, but may then also be in need of being deepened until it has completely cast out any remains of alternative perspectives.

However, if Paul had concentrated in 6:1–8:13 on the 'ethical' implications of the Christ faith with regard to the formal issue of practice (the C-level), then what about the other, substantive side, particularly the relationship with others (the B-level)? We saw how important that theme was, in its negative form, in 1:18–32. Has it dropped altogether out of view? Of course not. It becomes the overall theme of 12:1–15:13. Before we look at this, we should make two observations on chapters 9–11 to show how that section of the letter fits into the line we are drawing for the letter as a whole: the line of moving from I via X to S.

The first observation concerns 9:30–10:13, in which Paul produces one of his more striking formulations of the specific character of righteousness from faith (10:6–10). Paul makes the overall purpose of the first half of the three chapters (9:1–10:13) perfectly clear in 10:12–13: to show that there is no distinction (*diastolē*) between Jew and Greek in relation to the Lord. Thus he is recapitulating the account he gave in 2:12–3:31 of the place of Jews and gentiles in relation to God. Only where in that passage his point was that they were in the same position *negatively* ('for there is no *diastolē*', 3:22), his point now is that in relation to the Christ event too they are in the same position ('for there is no *diastolē*', 10:12), but now of course in positive terms. Just as earlier, Jews were under sin in no basic way differently from gentiles, so now, gentiles have been called by God, and again in no way differently from Jews.[1]

The reason why Paul spells this out in this particular way here is in most likelihood that he needs it as a foil for the step he goes on to take in chapter 11, where he castigates Christ-believing gentiles for thinking high-mindedly of themselves in relation to those Jews who have *not* (yet) turned to Christ. As we saw in an earlier chapter: (*a*) Paul's Christ-believing gentile addressees outside the law are on the same footing as Christ-believing Jews. For even though Jews have many advantages, after

Christ the law is not one of them. On the contrary, God has (also) called gentiles *outside* the law. (*b*) Still, by being called in this way, the gentiles have been grafted on to something *originally* Jewish. Therefore Paul's addressees must respect the Jews, even those who have not yet come round to the Christ faith.[2] We shall return to chapter 11 in a moment. What matters here is only that we get the implications right of Paul's talk in 9:30–10:13 of righteousness from faith and from the law. When he backs up his point in 10:12 that there is no distinction between Jew and Greek with the description of righteousness from faith given in 10:6–10, what he has in mind appears to be nothing other than the 'religious' point about the immediate and total directedness towards God that is brought about by the Christ event (I→X). In other words, in 9:30–10:13 he does not appear to be at all concerned with anything 'ethical'. What he seems to be saying is only that the relationship with God brought about by the Christ event is simple and straightforward, a matter of an unmediated directedness towards God which finds expression in two such unmediated and direct phenomena as confession with the mouth that Jesus is the Lord and faith in the heart that God has raised him from the dead (10:9). By contrast, Paul seems to imply, the law had come in as something that stood in the way of a similarly direct relationship with God.[3]

Thus the first half of chapters 9–11 does not contain material that gives further substance to Paul's use of the I→X→S-model in Romans. What it does, but certainly very emphatically, is only to provide a particularly strong expression of the basic idea of total directedness towards God (I→X). At the same time, what Paul does say fits in very well. Indeed, his talk of 'faith in the heart' (10:9) directly recalls his remarks in 6:17 and 2:29 about 'obedience from the heart' and 'circumcision of the heart'. And as we by now know, it is the idea of the total surrender to God (in, from and of the heart) that holds together the whole of Paul's theory, in its 'ethical' no less than its 'religious' aspects.

The second observation on chapters 9–11 brings us further. I am concerned here with Paul's criticism in 11:17–25 of Christ-believing gentiles for thinking in a high-minded manner about non-Christ-believing Jews. Here, at last, the issue of *other*-regarding 'ethical' behaviour is brought directly in: **Bb**. Taking up his point in 2:17 ff about the attitude of Jews outside Christ to gentiles, Paul now reverses it and applies it to the Christ-believing gentiles in relation to Jews outside Christ. The former must not 'boast against' or exult over (*katakauchasthai*) the latter (11:18), they must not have high thoughts (about themselves, 11:20) or take themselves to be wise (11:25). The most important reason for this is given in 11:20–

22. It basically amounts to the claim that Paul's addressees must take God seriously, both his severity and his clemency. For the latter will only remain operative towards them if they on their side 'cleave to' it (11:22). In short, only if they are themselves lenient and kind *towards the non-Christ-believing Jews*, will God remain lenient towards *themselves*. Here Paul makes direct and explicit use of his basic idea of seeing the ('religious') relationship with God and the ('ethical') relationship with other people as two sides of the same coin, the two sides that are formulated in the I→X→S-model when it has been completed by the addition of the S-pole. If Paul's addressees 'cleave to God's goodness', that is, if they retain their total directedness in faith (11:20, I→X) towards the God whose goodness showed itself in the Christ event, then and only then, will God continue in the same goodness towards them (X→I). But *if* they do that, then they too *will* be lenient and kind towards *others* (I→[X]→S). Then they just *cannot* think high-mindedly of themselves in relation to those others. We may ask, why? But we already know the answer: because total directedness towards God (I→X) *eliminates* what might otherwise have generated such high-minded thoughts, the self-directed, self-regarding attitude (I→I).

We should conclude that when Paul turns directly to the practical issues which, as I have claimed, underlie his writing the letter, he at long last draws out the *implications for 'ethical' behaviour in relation to others* (Bb) of the theme of total directedness towards God through Christ with which he has been preoccupied up to then. Thus the stage is set for addressing the new theme directly, as he does in 12:1 ff.

Total openness towards others, I: 12:1–13:14

Chapters 12–13 of Romans contain a large number of ideas which will enable us at long last to fill in the I→X→S-model in its entirety. The two chapters are exceedingly full and variegated and they warrant even closer study than they will receive here.[4] We shall look at them here with the general purpose of eliciting from them everything that throws light on what it is like to live within the group of Christ-believers as Paul understood this (in effect, as we shall see, at the S-pole of our model) and how the various elements in that state hang together. More specifically, we shall concentrate on the following four questions: (i) What do these chapters tell us about the I→X line as part of the full I→X→S-model? Is Paul's account here of the role of X in the move from I to S in line with what we have come to expect? (ii) Furthermore, how should we understand the full move from I *to* S via X? Exactly how does it come about? (iii) But also this: What is the form of the relationship between the individual and the others within the group of Christ-believers itself, that is, at the S-pole? Are they in some sense related *directly* to one another even though the relationship also goes via the relationship with God? Or is their relationship with one another only a derived one? Do Christ-believers love *each other* or do they merely love *God*? (iv) Finally, is there a difference between the attitude towards others on the part of people who belong at the S-pole—depending on whether those others are themselves members of the group or outsiders to it? And if there is, how should that be explained? Of these four questions the first mainly serves to make sure that we continue to be justified in reading the text in the light of the I→X→S-model. By contrast, our discussion of the other three will add importantly to our knowledge of how Paul conceived of life at the S-pole, the form of life that he aims to generate among his addressees. We need to pay careful attention to the way his argument proceeds in order to grasp its implications for these questions.

Four points in 12:1–2

12:1–2 make four points that are of interest to us. The first concerns the idea of turning one's body into a 'living, holy offering well-pleasing to God' (12:1). Seeing one's body as an offering to God is another very precise formulation of Paul's basic idea of the total directedness towards God (I→X). That idea thus stands as a headline for the 'ethical' discussion that follows. In other words, when Paul now discusses 'ethical' matters, which will in fact bring his readers to the S-pole of the I→X→S-model, he wishes these so-called 'ethical' matters to be understood as actually constituting the very content of the movement I→X. It is difficult to think of a more emphatic statement of the intrinsic connectedness of all sides of the I→X→S-model. In Paul there is no directedness towards God (I→X) that does not end at the S-pole, and that fact even serves to define the I→X directedness itself.[5]

A second point concerns the play between turning one's 'body' (*sōma*) into such an offering and doing it as one's 'mind's worship [of God]' (*logikē latreia*). Here the *logos* clearly stands for the mind or reason, the centre of understanding. And Paul goes immediately on to speak of the 'renewal of the *nous* (mind, intellect, rational understanding)' (12:2).[6] This is as clear proof as anyone could wish that he aims to develop the meaning and impact of the Christ event in the logical categories of the understanding, as I have contended all through this book. His theme is the mind's renewal, which will generate a total *metamorphosis* or change

(12:2) on the part of Christ-believers so that they will no longer 'model themselves after' (*syschēmatizesthai*) 'the present world' (*ho aiōn houtos*). What kind of change is this? The phrasing makes it difficult not to see it as being exactly what we would expect in terms of the I→X→S-model: a radical reversal in Christ-believers' *understanding* ('renewal of the *mind*') of where they *themselves* ('modelling themselves after') *belong* (*not* to 'the present world', *but* with 'God and his will'), that is, I→X. Once more Paul appears to be talking within the terms of the I→X→S-model in the highly distinct sense that we have given it of a change in normative self-identification, of how a person sees him- or herself.[7]

However, if the mind's worship and renewal is another, and more forceful, way of speaking of a total (intentional) directedness towards God, why does Paul start out from speaking of the body? Clearly, because he intends to say that he is not just talking of a 'mental' thing, some more or less superficial piece of understanding which does not really commit the person. Rather, it is an understanding which blots out completely any 'bodily' remains in the person. The person who has undergone this metamorphosis by the renewal of his mind has been *completely* turned into a holy offering to God, that is, down to the very last bit of his individual, bodily existence. In other words, the directedness towards X is in fact precisely the one that goes into I→X in the model, the one that leaves the normative role of the I-pole completely behind.[8]

Now this fits in closely with Paul's earlier talk of having one's 'old man' crucified with Christ, of having the 'body of sin' made inoperative and dead and so forth.[9] It is entirely appropriate, therefore, that Paul should end the two chapters with a small vice list (13:13) that concentrates on distinctly bodily vices (but precisely *also* includes such non-bodily, but nevertheless self-directed *social* vices as strife and envy)—and with an exhortation that his addressees (13:14) 'put on' (*endysasthai*, a distinctly bodily image) the Lord Jesus Christ and neglect completely the flesh (*sarx*) so as not to acquire any appetites (*epithymiai*). As we have seen so many times, the body as the centre and seat of the self-directed I that constitutes the I-pole of the model is thrust completely aside in the metamorphosis of the person as a whole that results from the mind's total directedness towards God. Once more, we are entitled to claim that Paul's various formulations here provide strong support for seeing him to be generally operating within the framework of the I→X→S-model as Stoically understood. When Paul speaks of *logos* (as implied in *logikos*, 12:1), of *nous* (12:2) and of *epithymiai* (13:14), he is employing concepts whose roots were solidly planted in the soil of the ancient ethical tradition, including the Stoic one. And when he describes a radical change that *leaves behind* the body as the seat of *epithymiai* and consists instead in a turning of the *nous* in the direction where one may speak of a *logos*-like worship, then he is equally certainly moving within a specifically Stoic form of thought.

A third point comes out of Paul's suggestion that the renewal of the mind will help his addressees to gauge what God's 'will' is (12:2). Again Paul is giving a headline for the ensuing discussion. This is of some importance since it supplies a bridge between I and S in the I→X→S-model. Our second question was how the full move from I to S via X should be understood to come about. An immediate answer would be this. The bodily self that has been removed in the total directedness towards God *not only* prevented a proper relation to God *but also* to others. That has now been changed and the road cleared for completely other-regarding behaviour. The point about God's will adds to this, however. It now looks as if it is God's *will that* human beings should precisely feel and act other-regardingly. We have already surmised as much when we spoke about God's purpose and plan with the Christ event. God wanted human beings to do what is morally right. And he acted so as finally to *enable* them to do *that*. There is a far closer connection, therefore, between I→X and I(→X)→S than the external, almost accidental one we noted at first.

Then, however, our third question immediately arises. If human directedness towards others follows more or less automatically from their directedness towards God or if it results from their awareness that other-regarding directedness is also what God wills, what kind of other-directedness do we end up with here? Is it only a derived, mediated and indirect one? Do Christ-believers actually love *each other* or do they merely love *God*? We shall have a great deal to say about this later.[10]

The fourth point of interest in 12:1–2 concerns Paul's general characterization of the content of God's will as 'the good, well-pleasing, perfect'. His use of the term 'perfect' (*teleion*) points in the direction of his idea of sinlessness. But then it is noteworthy that he is apparently also prepared to use the term 'good' (*agathon*) for what he has in mind. That is remarkable since *agathos* was such a general word—almost blandly so—for whatever qualified as morally and prudentially 'positive'. It will turn out that Paul has something far more specific in mind for 'the good' to be found within the group of Christ-believers. There it is *agapē*. In spite of this, however, he goes on in the two chapters to speak of the 'good' and the 'bad' (*ponēron* or *kakon*) both as general terms and also more specifically for the relationship of Christ-believers with those *outside* the group. In addition, he also relates his own bid for the most fundamental 'good', *agapē*, with another, traditional understanding of it: that expressed in the law (cf. 13:8–10). What all this points to is the following issue. If we compare Paul's own 'ethical' good, *agapē*, with perceptions of the 'ethical' good among people outside the group of Christ-believers—be it gentiles, who precisely speak of the *agathon* versus the *ponēron* or *kakon*, or Jews, who of course see it in terms of the law—we should conclude, as is generally done, that Paul's 'ethical' good is not in fact different in its basic content from those other conceptions. It may, however, be a more radical version of that shared content, precisely a conception of the 'good' *as* 'perfect'. This whole issue pertains to the fourth question we raised, of a potential difference in the relationship of Christ-believers with other people in and outside the group of believers.[11]

The line of thought in 12:3–21

In order to answer our questions, in particular the third and fourth one, we need to consider the exact way in which Paul's thought proceeds in the rest of chapter 12. It is best to take 12:3–9a together.[12] This section is exclusively concerned with interpersonal relations within the group of Christ-believers. It will throw light on our third question. It begins from another headline (12:3a), which urges Paul's addressees to have 'moderate thoughts' (*sōpronein*) as opposed to 'high thoughts' (*hyperphronein*), thoughts that may actually imply that one looks down on others from above (cf. *hyper*). Next (12:4–5), Paul introduces the famous image of being one body in Christ with the striking formulation that each Christ-believer is a limb on *the others* (12:5), not just on the body made up of them all, but directly on *them*.[13] Both points already suggest the idea of an immediate directedness towards one another among Christ-believers at the **Bb**-level, that is, a direct I→S line or even an S→S line, though certainly one that reflects and goes via a relationship with **X**.

Paul's use of the image of the body is a kind of indicative statement, which is followed in 12:6–9a by imperatival formulations.[14] He is now saying that no matter how his addressees may differ with respect to the 'measure of faith God has given them as their share' (12:3b), their other-regarding behaviour (to give in charity to someone, to act as leader to someone, to help someone in need) should be characterized by sincerity, eagerness and cheerfulness or gladness (*haplotēs*, *spoudē* and *hilarotēs* in 12:8). In short, their love (*agapē*) should be unfeigned (12:9a). It is important to see that Paul is making a very distinct point here. What concerns him is the *inner attitude* of those who, in the case he obviously has in mind, have the means to do good to others within the group and who actually do it. Not only should they do this. They should also have the proper inner attitude.

To what? One's immediate reaction is to say: to the acts themselves. When they give in charity to someone, they should be sincere in their wish to do just that—give in charity. That is, they must not do it for some ulterior purpose. However, will this also suffice to make sense of the point that they should act as leaders with 'eagerness'? Also, if I am right to take 12:9a on love as constituting a summary of what Paul has just been saying in 12:8b, the inner attitude he requires them to have cannot just be an attitude to those *acts*. For love is an attitude to *people*. That will also give a better sense to the point about eagerness. When they lead people, they should do it out of an eager concern for those being led! Perhaps, however, Paul did not distinguish very sharply here between seeing the attitude he is recommending to be directed at the acts themselves or towards those benefiting from the acts. Thus the best solution is probably to say that he is recommending that those, for instance, who give in charity should do it from a sincere wish to do just *that—and* do it to *them*. And similarly for the other attitudes.

What matters is that we here find Paul keenly and explicitly interested in the inner attitudes that lie behind a certain recommended behaviour. Moreover, his interest *includes* the aspect of those attitudes being directed towards the *people* who benefit from the acts. Thus he seems clearly to be talking of a direct I→S or S→S line—though still, of course, as *anchored* in (I→)X. This thought will then be summarized in the idea of unfeigned love, that is, a directedness towards others (within the group) that is genuinely directed towards *them*. That is apparently an important part of Paul's overall theme. Nor is it difficult to see, within the picture given by the I→X→S-model, why that should be so. For it is to be expected that life at the S-pole will turn out to reflect and mirror the I→X relationship in the form Paul saw that. And that relationship consisted in being directed towards a certain *person*, Christ.

The line of thought of 12:9b–21 may initially appear difficult to grasp. Is Paul not moving back and forth here between talking of relations within the group (12:9b–13, 15–17a) and towards outsiders (12:14, 17b–21)?[15] However, there is a solution to this quandary. The key lies in seeing that the participles of 12:9b–13, which are about relations within the group, all have the force I have suggested of leading up to a colon immediately after v. 13, a colon that then introduces Paul's version in v. 14 of the command to love one's enemies. With such a reading, the account of how Christ-believers should think, feel and act *within* the group (S→S) will be designed to *lay the ground for* Paul's remarks about how they should behave towards *outsiders*.[16]

Against this background, the precise way in which Paul develops his account of the internal relations in 12:9b–13 becomes important. In an extremely dense account he identifies the following elements: a general dedication to 'the good' and aversion from 'the bad' (v. 9b); a friendly attitude of friendly love (*philo-storgoi*) for one another (*allēlous*) among the brothers (cf. *phil-adelphia*) combined with an attitude of esteeming others more highly than oneself (v. 10); an inner eagerness that reflects a burning of their spirit (vv. 11a–b); four forms of a *'religious'* relatedness: being slaves to the Lord, rejoicing in hope, steadfast in tribulation, sticking to prayer (vv. 11c–12); and finally, two injunctions to specific and concrete behaviour of material support for the friends, the holy ones (v. 13). Note the quite striking care with which Paul differentiates between these various elements in the overall form of life he is depicting.[17] Starting from below, we may say that it includes (*c*) concrete material support for one another (v. 13). But such other-regarding *behaviour* should reflect (*b*) the proper *attitude*, and once more directly oriented towards *the others*: a burning eagerness in friendly love for one another that includes esteeming the others more highly than oneself (v. 10). And this genuinely other-regarding inner attitude will itself reflect (*a*) a basic total directedness towards Christ and God (vv. 11–12). In this way, the move from I to S via X will be complete. (*a*) The I-level will be left altogether behind to such a degree that the Christ-believers will in fact esteem the others *more* highly than themselves, as Paul says in a clear reformulation of his maxim as we know it from Philippians (2:4). (*b*) The result is a mutual directedness at the S-level (S→S) which will be completely internalized so as to have the character of genuine other-directed concern. It *derives* from the basic total directedness towards Christ and God (I→X) and itself involves a *shared* directedness upwards (S→X). But it also has the form of a person-to-person mutual directedness at the S-pole that has been internalized and solidified into an inner attitude that will then (*c*) be actualized in concrete other-regarding behaviour. This, the attitude (*b*) issuing in the practice (*c*), constitutes the ultimate target of the I→X→S-model as used by Paul in Romans—and indeed of the letter as a whole viewed, as I am arguing it should be, as a letter of parenesis.

In this way we have answered our third question concerning the relationship of Christ-believers to one another and to God through Christ. Christ-believers love each other. They do not merely love God and Christ. We have not quite answered *why* that is so. But the answer is not difficult to find as soon as one realizes to what extent this is all steeped in the way of thinking captured in the I→X→S-model Stoically understood. The movement I→X is a realization that 'I am a Christ person'. However, as soon as this realization is supplemented by another one, to the effect that 'These people too see themselves as Christ people', the road is clear for the final realization that 'I am one with *them*'. This may seem unpalatable to a modern sensibility. But it is certainly a Pauline thought. It is part of the metaphor Paul employs in 12:5 when he claims that 'we, the many, are one body in Christ', particularly when he adds that 'each individual among us is a limb of *the others*'. In addition, of course, it is a crucial, Stoic thought: that by coming to see themselves as rational beings (X), individuals become '*identical*' with all those who do the same (the wise, S→S) and let that self-identification govern their attitudes and acts towards those others.

From this picture of the relations within the group Paul moves directly on to the command to 'bless and not curse' their persecutors (12:14). I have suggested that his idea is this: that (c) internal mutual support (b) *derived from* mutual love (a) that is *based on* directedness towards Christ and God makes possible a sort of extension of the other-regarding attitude towards those outside the group, even its direct enemies. That reading immediately raises our fourth question, whether this attitude will also be one of love, that is, of a genuinely other-regarding openness towards the enemies as people. We shall return to the question in connection with 13:8–10. First, let us continue our reading of the text in order to elicit from it how Paul saw life at the S-pole and what the logical connections are between the various elements that go into this state.

How can we know that Paul saw a specific connection between the internal attitude and the one towards outsiders? Because he relies on it again in the verses that follow. 12:15–16 are clearly about relations within the group. Once more, Paul provides some quite striking formulations of those relations: 'rejoicing with those who are rejoicing' (12:15a), presumably (cf. 12:12) on the basis of an eschatological hope, and 'weeping with those who are weeping' (12:15b), presumably when faced with present tribulation (cf. 12:12).[18] In 12:16 he also repeats from 12:3 the basic idea of having 'moderate thoughts' (12:3), namely of 'thinking the same towards one another' (12:16). This is probably another formulation of the idea that was expressed in 12:9a in terms of *agapē*. Thus we remain within the group. Then follows 12:17, which moves smoothly from urging the addressees not to return evil (*kakon*) for evil to anybody (v. 17a) to stating that they should be concerned about the moral good (*ta kala*) with regard to *all* people (v. 17b). Since the verse follows immediately on 12:15–16, 17a should initially be taken to refer only to relations within the group. But v. 17b clearly refers also to those outside it. In short, Paul must have seen a specific *connection* between the internal attitude and the one towards outsiders. It is as if he is saying: rejoice and weep within the group in total internal unanimity (vv. 15–16); never return evil for evil to anybody (v. 17a—a rule that will *in fact* have relevance both in and outside the group); on the contrary, always be concerned about the moral good with regard to *all* (v. 17b—a rule that *explicitly* has relevance both in and outside the group). In other words, stand fast together within the special world-view and ethos that is yours; *then* you may also 'do the good' generally, even outside the group.[19] If this is the underlying idea, it is highly noteworthy that when Paul begins to speak of relations outside the group, he does not speak of love. Instead, he employs terms that had a very wide application: doing 'evil' (*kakon*) and being concerned about the 'moral good' (*kala*). Is the point that relations outside the group will not be characterized by love (*agapē*) in the specific form we saw Paul to be concerned with?

The final verses of the chapter (12:18–21) point in that direction. Here Paul is concerned that his addressees live 'at peace' with all (v. 18) and that they do not 'seek revenge' (v. 19). They must not let themselves be conquered by evil, but must themselves conquer evil by doing good (v. 21). We shall not go into the complexities of these verses (including the disastrously difficult reference in 12:20 to heaping coals of fire on the enemy's head). We may merely note here that the verses seem to employ a terminology that is distinctly free of anything that has to do with love. Living at peace with people and refraining from seeking revenge from them is certainly possible without loving them. And conquering evil by doing good (*to agathon*) both adds another term to the general moral terminology we noted and also allows for a sizeable portion of lack of *love* towards those whose evil behaviour one conquers by one's own good return.

Chapter 12 in context as revealing Paul's overall rhetorical strategy

Before leaving chapter 12, we should note two formulations in 12:16 which are so striking that they need special comment. Paul urges his addressees 'not to have high thoughts' (*mē ta hypsēla phronein*) and 'not to become wise in their own conceits' (*mē ginesthai phronimoi en heautois*). What makes this striking is not so much the content as the fact that these two phrases are repeated in virtually identical form from as unlikely a place as the final section of chapter 11, namely 11:20 and

11:25 respectively. Now in chapter 12 the two phrases fall immediately under the overall theme of that chapter, which is to bring out the intrinsic connection between the two sides of Paul's talk at the **B**-level: deriving 'ethical' parenesis concerning interpersonal relations (**B**b: S→S) from the new relationship with God (**B**a: I→X). But if Paul was *saying* the same in chapter 11, where he seemed to be engaged in a piece of highly specific parenesis of his addressees, did he also implicitly have *there* the idea that this piece of parenesis should be seen to follow directly from the new relationship with God? That possibility begins to suggest a point with very wide ramifications for understanding the letter as a whole.

The point is this. Chapters 1–8 of Romans are (in spite of 6:1–8:13) basically about the relationship with God (**B**a). The first half of chapters 9–11 is very much about the same thing, culminating as it does in the claim that the only thing that matters is confession with the mouth that Jesus is Lord and faith in the heart that God has raised him from the dead (10:9). With the second half, however, Paul moves into parenesis concerning interpersonal relations (**B**b). But in spite of his argument in 11:20–22, which we noted, he does not make the connection between the two themes wholly explicit. In 12:1 ff, however, he combines the two themes, and indeed quite explicitly. He engages in parenesis concerning interpersonal relations at the **S**-pole of our model (S→S) and he bases this directly on what he has said earlier in the letter about the movement I→X. This set of observations, I suggest, gives us the key to Paul's literary strategy in the writing of Romans. As Paul saw it, the relationship with God logically implied a certain interpersonal, 'ethical' relationship (the I→X→S-model as a whole)—*and vice versa*. Now the question of the proper interpersonal, 'ethical' relationship (**B**b) appears to have been *at issue* among Paul's Roman addressees. What better rhetorical strategy could one then think of than this: to set out the proper relationship with God that went into the Christ faith and then to *draw out* in explicit parenesis its implications for interpersonal, 'ethical' relations in general and for Paul's addressees in particular?[20] In chapter 11 Paul makes practical use of this strategy in a case of specific parenesis of his addressees. But it is not until chapter 12 that he makes the overall shape of his strategy clear. And just to state the obvious: on this picture, Paul's rhetorical strategy in Romans was neither more nor less than to *state* those ideas about the world (world-view *and* ethos) that *together* make up the I→X→S-model and then to *use* that model in explicit parenesis, aiming in this way to make his addressees put their state of being at the **S**-pole (**B**b) into practice (**C**).

This point draws on the shape of chapter 12 and its literal link back to chapter 11 in order to say something about chapters 1–11 as a whole. The point is of course greatly strengthened by the fact that a basic theme in Paul's parenesis, about the relationship between Jews and gentiles (see chapter 11 and again 14:1–15:13), also plays a central role in his earlier account of the relationship with God (1:18–4:25 and 9:1–10:13). But the link between chapters 11 and 12 also has forward-looking implications. It indicates that chapter 12 should not merely be understood as containing parenesis of a vague and general kind. Rather, in so far as it does stay at a general level, it will also be *laying the ground* for the *specific* parenesis that Paul turns to immediately after, in 13:1–7 and 14:1 ff. *Specific parenesis was Paul's ultimate aim.* He brought it in proleptically already in chapter 11. With chapter 12 he has then laid the *general* ground for the *specific* parenesis to which he now turns.

Two points in 13:1–7

There are only two points that need concern us in 13:1–7. This passage is, in the most general way, about doing 'the good' and avoiding 'the bad' (13:3–4), though of course as seen in relation to the political authorities. Thus Paul takes up 12:9b and, more importantly, 12:17 and 21. That raises our old question. Should Christ-believers *love* the authorities and do out of love what the latter demand? Or does Paul see doing the good and avoiding the bad as being, as it were, one step below that of loving? 13:1–7 does not itself answer this question. We shall return to it presently.

The other point concerns Paul's striking phrase in 13:5: 'not merely because of the wrath' (namely, that of the authorities—*and* of God), '*but also* because of the conscience' (namely, *their own*). Why this addition, which taken by itself is entirely superfluous for the argument?[21] There can only be one answer. Because Paul wanted to remind his addressees that the attitude towards the authorities that he was urging them to have was not just advantageous to them in purely prudential terms—so that they would not be punished (12:4), but rewarded for it (12:3). Instead, it was an attitude that should (also) spring from their own realization that 'the good' is *intrinsically* worth doing. They must *themselves wish* to do it. For they must themselves have come to see that it should be done. Where in Paul's framework will such a realization have a place? In the thought that those who perform the 'mind's worship of God' from which he began will not do what God wishes them to do *just because* that is God's will. They will have something more than the following kind of extrinsic relationship to their own acts: doing them in order to avoid punishment or wrath, or doing them for the only reason that God tells them to do so. Instead, they will *themselves* have come to wish to do them and to see that they should be done. They have *become* such people that they now wish for themselves to do those things. Here, then, there is not just a mindless 'slavery' to God, but willing for oneself what God (also) wills. And the way this is brought out is once more by a reference to the inner structure of Christ-believers, to their awareness of what they *themselves* want because it reflects what they have now come to take themselves to *be*. Once more, we see how the I→X→S-model in its specific, Stoic form helps to bring out Paul's meaning. It is because Paul has been talking of self-identification on the model of the Stoic talk of *oikeiōsis* that he can add here such a remark about their 'conscience', that is, their 'self-awareness' (*syn-eidēsis*).[22] Also, we see how Paul's turn to an inner attitude (here of who and what they are) again serves to make a quite central point about the state of being at the S-pole. Just as we saw that Christ-believers will love one another directly and not just as a reflex of the fact that that is the will of the God whom they also love, so we see here that they will also want to do 'the good' for themselves and not just because it reflects God's will.

The role of the law in 13:8–10

The connection of 13:1–7 with what precedes is intrinsic and close. But we shall leave it on one side.[23] The connection with what follows is equally close, but this time it is also directly germane to our inquiry. In 13:7 Paul has stated that the Christ-believers should render whatever they owe to the authorities. He takes this up in 13:8, stating that they must not owe anything to anybody—except loving one another. In other words, the one obligation that remains—one which they can never fulfil, as it were, once and for all—is that of mutual love. It is likely that this rather striking transition is meant to throw light back over 13:1–7. Is Paul not saying almost explicitly that subjection to the authorities is something good and to be done, indeed it reflects God's will and is even something one also wills for oneself—*but it is not a matter of love*? For it is something that one *can*, as it were, have done with. This is admittedly something of a guess.[24] If correct, it means, as we have already surmised, that Paul does distinguish between doing the good and loving. It presumably also means that Paul did not intend to tell his addressees quite generally to love those outside the group, including their enemies. To do good to them (and avoid doing bad) would be enough. Can such a distinction be maintained? 13:8b–10 points in this direction. Now we are finally ready to confront the issue directly.

At first blush this passage looks very odd. Why does Paul bring in the law here? Why should he have an interest in the law at this particular point in his argument? Why does he wish to argue that the law is fulfilled in love?[25] Let us first consider the argument Paul provides about the relationship between the law and love. It runs like this:

1. There is only one thing you always need to do: love (13:8a).
2. For: The one who loves his neighbour has fulfilled the law (13:8b). (Thus the law cannot add anything. Rather, it is in some way contained in love.)
   3a. For: The various (negative) commands of the law are summarized in the (positive) love command (13:9).
   3b. And in fact, love does not do anything bad (*kakon*) to one's neighbour (13:10a, viz. of the kind prohibited by the law).
4. Therefore, love is the fulfilment of the law (13:10b).
5. [Therefore, there is only one thing you always need to do: love (unexpressed).]

There are two ways of understanding the purpose of this argument. If we do take it that Paul had an independent, positive interest here in the law and its relationship with love, we may put either a negative or a positive interpretation on what he says about that relationship. If negative, we might take his point to be that the law has been *superseded* by (Christ-believing) love. If positive, we might take him to be saying that love '*consummates*' the law. We would therefore in fact be back with the issue of what gloss to put on Paul's claim that Christ is the *telos* of the law (10:4). As already noted, however, it is not entirely clear why Paul should at this point have been particularly interested in the law.

There is a better way of understanding Paul's purpose. It is to see him as aiming to show that there is *only one* continuous requirement, only one requirement that cannot, as it were, be fulfilled once and for all: that of loving one another. Now the emphasis will be on love and the ultimate purpose of the argument will be parenetic. In 13:7, as we saw, Paul has said to his addressees that they must 'discharge' their obligations towards the authorities. In 13:8 he begins by saying that similarly they must have no obligation whatever to anybody—*except* the one of loving one another. And it is in explanation of *this* that he then brings in the law. This makes sense if one presupposes that Paul generally saw the law as something one would think oneself *obliged* to do and indeed as the *most* important thing of that kind. In that case, what he is saying is that this (pen-)ultimate obligation no longer holds. *For* the person who loves his neighbour has *already fulfilled* the law in such a way that no law-governed obligations whatever remain alive as obligations. The latter point he then goes on to explain (13:9–10). On this reading, Paul brings in the law, not to make a negative or positive point about *that*, but to make a (positive) point about love: that loving one another is *the only* obligation that remains constantly and continuously alive.[26]

This reading has the advantage that it does justice to what Paul explicitly says in 13:8: that loving one another is *the only* obligation that remains alive (cf. *ei mē*, 'if only', 'except') and that this holds *because* the person who loves his neighbour (already) *has* fulfilled the law.[27] Before we consider some important implications of Paul's claim about love, on this reading, let us note exactly how he argues in 13:9–10 for the claim made in 13:8b and 10b: that love constitutes or contains a fulfilment of the law.

There are two points. First, a number of negative commands may, Paul claims, all be summarized in the one positive command to love one's neighbour (13:9). This point is wholly made, as it were, from within the horizon of the law. The idea is that if one fulfils the positive love command, then one will also honour the negative commands. Second, Paul claims that love does not do anything bad to the neighbour (13:10a). Now this will only add anything to the argument if by 'love' Paul means something other than what was immediately involved in 13:9. To put the point differently, the 'love' that Paul mentions in 13:10 cannot just mean 'loving as something commanded by the law'. For in that case 13:10a would constitute a mere repetition of 13:9. Instead, *hē agapē* in 13:10 must mean this: 'the love that I am talking about', 'love as *present* [though evidently also to be understood as the very thing that the law *commands*]'. Then the whole of 13:10a will mean this: 'love as present [the love I am talking about] does not *in fact* do any evil to the neighbour'. If that holds—and that is an issue that would in principle have to be settled *independently*—then it also follows that the kind of love that is Paul's theme fulfils the law. If *within* the horizon of the law the relationship between the many commands that prohibit bad acts towards others and the love command is as Paul has stated in 13:9, and if furthermore the love he is talking of is such a thing that when actualized it *actually* prevents people from doing to the neighbour the bad acts that are also prohibited by the law, then it truly follows that this love as present constitutes a fulfilment of the law in the sense from which Paul began: that the person who does love his neighbour has *already* fulfilled the law. For then he will by himself always *avoid* doing what the law (also) prohibits and he will by himself avoid doing *everything* that the law prohibits. And if that holds, then there remains only *one* constant *obligation*: to love one another. So do that!

On this reading, Paul should be seen to be operating with three different attitudes, only the first two of which fall within the horizon of the law. They are: (i) complying with the law's negative commands, as exemplified in 13:9a; (ii) complying with the law's positive love command (13:9b); (iii) and—love as present (13:10a). We saw that there had to be a difference between loving as commanded by the law (ii) and love as present (iii). Otherwise, 13:10a would be completely superfluous. But how would Paul be able to make good such a difference? The answer is far easier to find than one might perhaps expect. Love as present (13:10a), that is, actually loving one's neighbour (13:8b), is an inner attitude that is directed towards that other person, one's neighbour. Such an attitude is quite different from complying with the law's commands, be they negative or positive. As an inner attitude, it is there. It is in no need of being called into being. And as an attitude that is beforehand directed towards one's neighbour, it will, as Paul explicitly states (13:10a), be actualized in acts that will not do any evil to one's neighbour. The point is simple: with such a thing present—and as we know from chapter 12, that attitude precisely is present in Christ-believers—there is no longer any need for the law; all its requirements have *already* been fulfilled.

What we see in this passage, therefore, is what we have seen all through Romans: a preoccupation on Paul's part with inner attitudes. The point is of course not that he was uninterested in external and social behaviour. On the contrary, he was precisely interested in the proper prerequisite *for* external and social behaviour. And in the best ancient philosophical style that interest led him to think about inner attitudes.

To go back to our initial question, why did Paul bring in the law here? Did he intend to say something about the law, in particular? No. He wanted to say something about the kind of love that constitutes a main theme in chapters 12–13. When present that love has *beforehand* fulfilled that law which one would otherwise come to think of as the thing that would *most* constantly formulate obligations for human beings to fulfil. And so there is *only one* obligation that Paul's addressees need to fulfil: to love one another.

But is there not a problem here? Have I not argued that love as what Paul claims is present in his Christ-believing addressees is not something that falls under the mode of obligation? It is not something that is

required of them, not something they will have *because* God wills it or
even orders them to have it. For it is something actually present. It is
there. It is something they themselves already will. So is there not a
problem? No. For loving one another is an 'obligation' that they in actual
fact constantly fulfil. When Paul says to his addressees that they are only
'obliged' to do one thing, viz. love one another, he is doing exactly what
he did in 8:12–13 when he claimed that they (and he himself) were
'obliged' (again a form of *opheilein*) to live in accordance with the spirit.
And both manners of speech are closely similar to Paul's concluding
exhortation in Gal 5:24 that he and his addressees should walk in accordance with the spirit *since* they live by it—just after he has shown that
having the spirit means actually *having* those inner attitudes (the virtues)
which are headed by love. Thus Paul's point to his Roman addressees in
13:8 is just pure parenesis, as we have already claimed. It has no implications whatever to suggest that they are under an 'obligation' of a kind
that they either cannot or will not fulfil. On the contrary, since they *are*
Christ-believers, that is precisely what they both can and will.

Then we may at long last return to our fourth question: Did Paul
think that Christ-believers should *love* their enemies and the authorities
with the kind of love that he clearly thought should reign within the
group of Christ-believers? Everything speaks against this. First, he does
not actually speak of love in this connection, but of doing good and
avoiding the bad (12:17, 21, 13:3–4). Second, he tells his addressees not
to try to seek retribution, but to leave the punishment of their enemies in
God's hands (12:19)—not a very loving thought. Third, the relationship
to the authorities that he advocates seems rather far from being one
of love. Fourth, the move to love in 13:8 precisely sets this theme off
from what precedes. Fifth, the move in 13:11–14 to an eschatological
perspective clearly aims to set off the Christ-believers from those outside
the group. And finally there is this: As we have seen, Paul clearly aims in
chapters 12–13 as a whole to derive the 'ethical' form of life that he is
recommending from the new relationship with God that has been made
possible in the Christ event. Life at the S-level, with the special shape
that characterizes it (S→S), reflects the shared directedness of all involved
towards Christ (I→X in the form shared by all: S→X). And that is of
course only possible within the Christ group. It is true that Paul *could*
have said that Christ-believers should apply their own directedness
towards Christ also outwardly towards any human being irrespective of
his or her own relationship with Christ. But he does not. Rather, as we
saw, the life of shared love within the group works as the basis for
another kind of relationship towards outsiders, one which does good

and avoids the bad, but not as if the wall between inside and outside had been broken down—or even just perforated.

Summary of observations on chapters 12–13

Looking back over chapters 12 and 13, we see that Paul wanted to make a number of tightly connected points, all of which fit directly into the I→X→S-model in its Stoic form. There is first the point (12:1–2) about the total takeover of the individual, bodily self in his directedness towards God through Christ: I→X—and also the point (12:2) that this takeover has the form of a renewal of the mind, that is, a complete change in the understanding of where one oneself belongs, one's normative self-identification. Next there is the point (12:3 ff) that a person's directedness towards Christ generates a whole group of Christ-believers, in other words, that directedness towards Christ translates into a directedness towards others with the same relationship with Christ: I→X→S. Then there are a number of points about life at the S-pole. First, it is characterized by an inner attitude of genuine directedness towards the others themselves at the S-pole and also towards those acts (of goodwill, giving, caring and the like) that spring from such other-directedness (12:8–10, 11, 13, 15–16, 13:8, 10). Second, and correspondingly, life at the S-pole has of course left behind any special concern about the individual person's own body (13:13–14). Third, however, it is constantly informed by the shared sense of belonging to God through Christ: S→X. This motif is expressed in eschatological form: in the injunction that the addressees no longer conform to the pattern of the present world (12:2); in the play on their present trouble, on future-oriented prayer and on hope for the future (12:12, 15); in the references to God's future intervention (12:19–20); and in the concluding rehearsal of the basic, apocalyptic framework (13:11–14, forming an *inclusio* with the reference to the present world in 12:2).

We also saw that Paul aimed to be fairly precise about the form of life at the S-pole as seen in relation to those outside it. Here one did not find love, that is, the total openness towards others that is the basic point about life at the S-pole. Instead, it was a matter of doing good and avoiding evil, of not being conquered by evil, but conquering it by the good (12:17, 21, 13:3–4). To the extent that one may speak of directedness here, it is a directedness towards the morally good acts themselves, or towards such acts as expressing the proper values. Love, by contrast, contained a surplus: the inner attitude of directedness towards other *people* that *generated* those acts (13:8–10). Love may therefore be called the 'perfect' good (*to teleion*, 12:2), instead of being merely the 'good' (*to agathon*, 12:2, 21, 13:3) or the 'moral good' (cf. *kala*, 12:17).

Total openness towards others, II: 14:1–15:13

With 14:1 Paul turns to specific parenesis. The passage contains a number of motifs that fit immediately into the I→X→S-model as Paul has developed it in the rest of Romans. But it also adds considerably in complexity to the picture of life at the S-pole given in chapters 12–13. Here too the I→X→S-model may serve as the grid that will reveal the underlying logic.

Paul's general aim with the passage is to persuade his gentile addressees that they must show restraint with regard to the eating of certain forms of food when this creates problems for their weaker brothers, who, as we have previously seen, should be taken to be Jewish-oriented believers in Christ. As he says towards the end, he aims to bring it about that both groups may 'share the same thoughts with one another' (15:5). Only then will they be able to 'praise God with one accord and with one mouth' (15:6). Thus the final destination to which Paul aims to bring his addressees with his letter is a state that is just another formulation of his idea of life at the S-pole. It is noteworthy, however, that here, at the end of his argument, Paul develops more extensively than anywhere else in the letter the motif that life at the S-pole reflects the Christ event itself in a quite specific way: X→I or X→S. The idea is introduced in 15:1 when Paul states that 'we, the strong' must not 'please ourselves'. Instead, 'each of us' must 'please his neighbour' (15:2). *For* Christ too did not 'please himself' (15:3)—presumably in his death. On the contrary, as one may add (cf. 14:15), he acted for the sake of the others. Here Christ clearly functions as a model for life at the S-level: S→S *reflecting* the Christ event (X→I / S) and being *modelled* on Christ's own attitude and behaviour in that event. The same idea is taken up again in 15:5, where Paul prays that his addressees will 'share the same thoughts with one another' *in accordance with* (*kata*) Christ Jesus. This is all, in fact, quite close to the picture we drew out of the Christ 'hymn' in Philippians in relation to the immediately surrounding text.

Note then also that whereas Paul's immediate aim with the passage is indeed the 'ethical' one stated in 15:1–5, it may also be said to be the more directly 'religious' one of 15:6, which is about unanimously giving praise to God (*doxazein*), that is, S→X. This fits in closely with a major theme that was introduced already in chapters 1–3, when Paul argued that up to the Christ event all had fallen below God's glory (*doxa*, 3:23, cf. for Jews 2:23–24, and for gentiles 1:21–22). Thus even though the rhetorical line of Romans is, as I am arguing, to develop the idea of the proper relationship with God as a setting for specific, 'ethical' parenesis, Paul would certainly also insist that the aim of life in Christ (and indeed, of his own writing) might also be said to lie in complete directedness towards God. That is quite unproblematic, however—as long as it is remembered that this directedness is not just an individual one (I→X), but one that is precisely *shared*: S→X. For in this form it is, in the final analysis, inseparable from the 'ethical' directedness: S→S.

The same concern to connect the 'ethical' and the 'religious' dimensions of Paul's overall picture may be read off another feature of the concluding section of chapters 14–15: when Paul brings in hope as the basic framing category for his parenesis. Christ-believers should feel hope (*elpis*) based on the capacity for endurance (*hypomonē*) and on the energizing appeal (*paraklēsis*) to be found in scripture (15:4). Further, it is the God of endurance (*hypomonē*) and heartening appeal (*paraklēsis*) who will bring about their mutual unanimity (15:5). Also, it is the God of hope (*elpis*), so Paul prays, who will fill them with 'joy and peace' (*chara kai eirēnē*) in faith so that they may abound in hope (*elpis*) through the power of the holy spirit (15:13). Earlier, however, Paul had stated the 'kingdom of God' *here on earth* to be the very same thing: 'peace and joy in the holy spirit' (14:17). In short, Paul is placing a present life of peace, joy (14:17, 15:13) and sharing the same thoughts with one another (15:5), that is, S→S, within the framework of endurance and an energizing appeal that looks forward in hope to the prospect of finally being together with Christ and God in the kingdom of God: S→X. This repeats the basic idea underlying the structure of chapters 5–8 earlier in the letter, with 5:1–11 and 8:14–39 (on the forward-looking, eschatological hope) surrounding the parenetic section 6:1–8:13 (on how to live a Christ-believing life in the present). The kingdom of God is a life of peace and joy in the holy spirit here on earth that looks forward with hope to the eventual realization of the same thing in the future.

This, then, is the full form of the state to which Paul aims to bring his addressees. How does he attempt to achieve this in the earlier sections of the two chapters? One motif is the one we met in 15:1–3: that of using Christ (or even God) as a model. Thus Paul first urges his gentile addressees to 'receive in the group' (*proslambanesthai*) the (Jewish oriented) brother who is 'weak in faith' (14:1) and therefore not prepared to eat everything (14:2). Next, he urges the weak not to judge the other one; 'for God has received him in the group (*proslambanesthai*)' (14:3). Finally, he summarizes his whole message as follows: 'Therefore receive one another in

the group (again *proslambanesthai*), *just as Christ too* received you in
the group to the glory of God' (15:7). The motif of using Christ as a
model also makes an appearance in 14:15: the strong in faith must not
destroy the one for whose sake *Christ died*. This is as clear a statement as
anyone could wish of how events at the A-level were taken by Paul to
ground 'ethical' behaviour at the B- and C-levels.

More generally, Paul's strategy in the two chapters is a two-pronged
one. He first (14:4–12) argues that any form of judgement or scorn for
others with whom one disagrees over food is wrong. He clearly aims to
keep the balance between the 'Jew', whom he presents as judging (the
term is *krinein*, 14:3, 4, 10), and the 'gentile', whom he presents as being
scornful (the term is *exouthenein*, 14:3, 10), and the basic idea in 14:4–
12 is relevant for both parties (compare the use of *krinein* in 14:13a as
applied to *both*). It is that any kind of critical attitude towards others is
incompatible with the Christ faith. This holds, as it were, materially. If
one does have the Christ faith, one will do whatever one does (eat the
doubtful food *or not* eat it) *as* an expression of one's directedness towards
Christ and God, and that in itself vindicates the act (14:5–6, cf. v. 14).
Thus there is no material reason for criticizing the other. Indeed, the
Christ faith just *means* that: living and dying, not for oneself but for the
Lord (14:7–8a), *belonging* to the Lord (14:8b), in short I→X. And that
vindicates the act (no matter which) in this area of things *intrinsically*
indifferent. But it also holds, as it were, formally. For each individual
will have to give account of himself to God (14:10b–12) and therefore
has no business interfering with his brother over these issues (14:10a).

What Paul brings out very strongly here is the idea that even when
Christ-believers stand united at the S-level, the relationship with God
and Christ that regulates their shared form of life is an individual one
on the part of each member of the group on his or her own.[28] It is an
I→X relationship, though obviously *as part of* life at the S-pole. This
renders any form of interpersonal criticism illegitimate. For as we know,
the I→X relationship precisely does away with that I which lies behind
criticism of others. Such criticism, Paul thought, contained a basic element
of serving the self and this was excluded by the Christ faith.[29]

Another way of putting this point is to say that at the S-pole, where
every attitude and act is defined by the shared directedness towards Christ
(S→X), what each individual does in relation to the issue of eating or
not-eating certain types of food falls entirely under the category of 'indifferents', on the precise, Stoic construal of this notion. What matters here is
only the (shared) directedness towards Christ. Paraphrasing Gal 5:6 we
might summarize this first point (the one made in 14:4–12) by saying

that 'in Christ Jesus eating or non-eating makes no difference at all; what matters is only faith (S→X)'.[30]

In the second half of chapter 14 (14:13–23) Paul takes up the second prong of his argument, which brings in the remainder of that Galatian paraphrase: 'faith [S→X] that is active through love [S→S]'. Now his theme is that the strong, who have no trouble eating any kind of food, should actually desist from doing this out of a positive consideration for the weak ones. Here, where he is talking of a positive mutual relationship, Paul also brings in the term we have been waiting for: love (14:15). And he ties it in very closely with the Christ event itself and thus with the relationship between God and human beings. As Christ died for the weak brother (X→I resulting in I→X), so the strong person should act out of love for his weaker brother (S→S, 14:15)—and therefore desist from eating the troublesome food. Otherwise, he risks destroying his brother (14:15) or annulling God's work (14:20). For if, goaded on by his strong brother, the weak person were to eat the food, *he* would not do it as an act of faith and so would put himself out of reach of God's salvation. Instead, he would condemn himself (14:23). Being weak, he would not be able to eat it *as* something indifferent. And so, in his mind it would interfere with and weaken the only thing that matters, his faith relationship with Christ. By the same token, though Paul does not spell it out right here, his eating under those circumstances would precisely generate the kind of mutual distrust and interior fighting in the group that shows that there no longer is that state of total mutual openness which defines life at the S-pole.

In conclusion, 14:1–15:13 adds considerable complexity to the picture of life at the S-level that Paul had depicted in chapters 12–13. That is only fair since that life cannot alone consist in 'rejoicing with those who rejoice and weeping with those who weep'. It also has to tackle concrete differences of opinion which cannot just be denied.[31] But even here we see that the motifs Paul uses for tackling those specific issues remain the same as before. All through he is concerned to spell out different aspects of the I→X→S-model.

Conclusion: *the form of life of Christ-believers according to Romans*

Let us pull this reading of Romans together under four headings: (*a*) Paul's rhetorical strategy in the letter; (*b*) the relationship between world-view and ethos in the comprehensive picture he develops of the Christ-believing form of life; (*c*) the specific points of contact between Paul's application of the I→X→S-model and Stoicism; (*d*) and finally a number of special properties of the Christ-believing form of life that are high-lighted by the comparison with Stoicism.

(*a*) We have seen that the letter makes sufficient sense in relation to the implied letter situation if we take Paul to have had two connected purposes in writing: to prepare for a visit to Rome and to admonish his addressees and remind them of the meaning of the Christ gospel. We have also seen that the best way to make sense of the letter as a whole in relation to these two purposes is to see it as basically a letter of parenesis that relies for its underlying logical structure on the I→X→S-model. There are two connected points here. One is that the descriptive parts of the letter (1:18–5:21, 8:14–39, 9:1–11:12) should be understood as laying the ground for the more overtly prescriptive passages of parenesis (6:1–8:13, 11:13–36, 12:1–15:13). This fits closely with the view we have developed of the relationship between statements in the indicative and the imperative moods, in particular that the latter are to be understood not as forward-looking commands to bring something new into existence, but rather as backward-looking appeals in the form of reminders of something the addressees are taken to know, see and accept beforehand. For in that case there is plenty of room for the indicative type of statement, which aims to spell out *what* it is that they already know. Conversely, spelling out what *has* happened to them lays the ground for appealing to them to put these very things on display in actual practice. The logic here goes like this: this is where you, by common consent, *are*; *so show* it. In conformity with this logic, we may say that the descriptive sections of the letter are, as it were, tilted towards the prescriptive ones. The logical focus is on the parenesis, and indeed on the most topical one (11:13 ff, 14:1 ff, possibly 13:1–7), where Paul intervenes most directly in Roman affairs.

The other point is that the relationship between the descriptive and prescriptive parts as just sketched, in particular the point about the direction of that relationship, becomes far easier to grasp once one brings in the I→X→S-model and employs it as a lens through which to read the letter. The whole flow of the letter falls very clearly into place as soon as we look at it from within that perspective. Just to repeat the central points: (i) 1:18–2:10/11 and 2:11/12–29 set up the whole problem by describing a state where the I→X→S-model is precisely *not actualized*. Thus negatively, the two passages not only presuppose the model but even help to formulate it to Paul's readers—as it were by default. The details are quite precise here: concern about the individual self (I→I) prevents the 'religious' relationship with God (I→X) that *would* have generated the proper 'ethical' relationships (I→S); moreover Paul is careful to distinguish between two forms of the failing 'ethical' relationship: the substantive failure at the **Bb**-level and the formal failure at the C-level. (ii) Then follows a descriptive account of what has happened to Christ-believers by God's intervention. *3:21–4:25* describes how God intervened with the Christ event in order to *generate* the proper I→X relationship with himself and how that event in fact generated a response in human beings, namely Christ faith, with the radical character that was necessary to remove human beings from staying at the I-pole. *5:1–21* and *8:14–39* bring this descriptive account further by describing the shared, forward-looking state of Christ-believers once they have reached the S-pole (S→X). (iii) However, the sections referred to under (ii) have consistently stayed at the 'religious' level that we identified as **A** and **Ba**. Even as described in *5:1–21* and *8:14–39*, Christ-believers have in fact only reached the S-pole with respect to that 'religious' dimension (S→X). With *6:1–8:13*, then, Paul's focus moves directly on to the 'ethical' side, from (I→)X to life at the S-pole itself. And here, correspondingly, the mode of speech becomes basically prescriptive and parenetic. (iv) *6:1–8:13* is the first section that states the parenetic point to which the earlier, descriptive parts have been pointing. But we noted that Paul here focuses specifically on the formal issue of practice at the C-level. The substantive issue of the proper 'ethical' relationship at the **Bb**-level (S→S) he has reserved for *12:1–15:13*, which is the second section that states the parenetic point of the earlier, descriptive parts. (v) Finally, we noticed how in *chapters 9–11* Paul repeats his basic strategy in the letter as a whole. He starts out from a descriptive account of what has happened in and through God's call, which has resulted in both a false 'religious' relationship with God (on the part of non-Christ-believing Jews) and a proper one (on the part of Christ-believers including, in particular, non-Jewish ones). Based on that he then moves on to draw out certain 'ethical' implications (for the relationship of non-Jewish Christ-believers to non-Christ-believing Jews), which are presented in the prescriptive mode. The general point is that the I→X→S-model helps us hold together the onward-moving flow of the letter towards 'ethical' parenesis in a manner that renders it strikingly coherent.

In this connection we may ask, however, why Paul reverses what one might consider the natural order of the two 'ethical' levels. Why does he begin (*6:1–8:13*) with the C-level and only later (*12:1–15:13*) turn to the **Bb**-level? There are probably several reasons. One is the one we noted: that in response to the way Paul has set up in *1:18–3:20* the problem to which the Christ event constitutes the solution, he will have felt the need to show that *all* sides of the problem have been solved in Christ faith. That could be done precisely by focusing on the consequences of the Christ faith for 'ethical' *practice* (at the C-level) since practice of the good of course presupposes the proper knowledge of it (at the **Bb**-level). Another reason is that once the issue of the 'ethical' consequences had been comprehensively settled in the manner just mentioned, Paul would be free to develop and spell out at greater length the part of it that was particularly concerned with others. And that was the part that was *directly* relevant for what he aimed to achieve through his letter in relation to his addressees. This suggestion is supported by the fact that in the sections of Paul's most specific parenesis (11:13 ff and 14:1 ff) he responds to problems that were very specifically concerned with the relationship of his immediate addressees, who were gentiles, with certain others, namely Jews, whether Christ-believing (14:1 ff) or not (11:13 ff). It was these problems that constituted Paul's long-distance focus in writing the letter—a point that is strongly supported by the fact that he focuses so much from the very beginning of the letter on Jews and gentiles. And so he placed this treatment last.

Another point also connects the I→X→S-model with Paul's rhetorical strategy in the letter. Paul does not just proceed through the letter in a manner that an outside interpreter may then attempt to elucidate, *from* the outside, in terms of the model. Rather, he aims to make his addressees themselves see and understand all the various connections that together *make up* the model. In that way he virtually aims to make them *grasp the model itself*: *that* there are those many connections. At the risk of being a little too bold, one might put the point by saying that the letter is virtually *about* the I→X→S-model. The reason for Paul's procedure here is clear enough. For suppose he could make his addressees see and understand that the I→X→S-model described their own situation. Suppose they would come to see that they themselves belonged at the S-pole and that this would need to be shown in practice. In that case they would also come to do what Paul aimed to make them do: act on it. And then Romans as a letter of parenesis would have reached its aim.

This account of Paul's rhetorical strategy in the letter may appear one-sided. It certainly is. But that is not a vice. I am not suggesting that there are no other important elements in Paul's rhetorical strategy (indeed, we shall consider an extremely important one in a moment). Instead, I am claiming that this account manages to hold together a number of facts about the letter which would otherwise lie only very disparately alongside each other. The most important of these facts are the following: that Paul sets up in 1:18–2:29 the whole problem to which the Christ event constituted the solution in a manner that—seen from the perspective of the I→X→S-model—does constitute something like a theory about the explanation of human behaviour and does it in a terminology that from time to time draws explicitly on contemporary, philosophical theories; and that he does the same later in the prescriptive parts of the letter: 6:1–8:13, 12:1–13:14, 14:1–15:13. It remains possible, of course, to leave these various elements as isolated ideas that *could* (but need not) be connected by means of something like the I→X→S-model. Similarly, it remains possible to see Romans as a somewhat loosely organized letter, a sort of patchwork in which Paul has drawn on earlier ideas and added new ones as they occurred to him, but without having had anything that would qualify as a rhetorical strategy. There is a choice here for the modern interpreter to make. However, when so much falls into place with the more stringent approach, the choice should not be a difficult one.

(*b*) We asked about the relationship between world-view and ethos in the comprehensive picture that Paul develops of the Christ-believing form of life. This question is also relevant to the issue of rhetorical strategy. The account I have just given of that strategy could well be said to be mainly about ethos in the sense that the I→X→S-model itself pertains to the B- and C-levels that we have distinguished. Only at either end of the model, and actually outside the model itself, does it pertain to the A-level; and that level, as everybody will agree, contains a number of quite central features in the world-view that Paul is also very concerned to present in the letter. Thus 'before' the model, there is the idea of what God *has* done to human beings, whether gentiles or Jews, in particular of course what God has very recently done in the Christ event itself (X→I). And 'after' the model, there is the idea of what God *will* do in the future, something that Christ-believers look towards with fervent longing.

Now one might well say that setting out these various elements in a 'salvation historical' account constitutes Paul's clearest and most comprehensive rhetorical strategy in the letter. It is marked by such striking signposts as his claim about an ongoing 'revelation' of God's justice and his wrath (1:17–18), by the corresponding 'now' of the 'appearance' of God's justice (3:21), by Paul's evident wish to construct some kind of coherent story from Adam over Abraham to Moses and further on to Christ (chapters 4–5)[32] and finally by his earnest talk in the mode of a hope that looks ardently forward to the end of time (5:1–11, 8:14–39,

also 11:25–36 and 13:11–14). So is there not a problem? Can one have
a rhetorical strategy that focuses on ethos in the way I have set this
out—and also one that focuses on world-view in the way just given? Of
course one can. That is precisely the point of speaking in a Geertzian
manner of world-view and ethos. As we know, 'theology' and 'ethics'
cannot be separated. Rather, they work together to make a *single* point
about human life.

This claim could be supported in detail by a number of examples. Let
me just mention two. We saw how strongly Paul emphasizes in 5:1–11
the element of human response to God's act in the Christ event. By God's
'bowing down' to human beings in love (5:8), they on their side 'moved
upwards' in love (5:5) in a manner that virtually brought them out of the
present world. Should we then say that Paul's description of this new
state is an account of world-view or of ethos? Surely, the correct answer
is: both. Still, it remains true to say, as we did, that Paul's description in
5:1–11 is not *explicitly* an 'ethical' one (**Bb**- and **C**-levels). Correspondingly, and in fact quite closely related with the earlier point, we saw how
Paul made use in 14:1–15:13 of the motif of Christ's 'bowing down' to
human beings as a *model for* human beings doing the same in relation
to one another. Now that motif *was* used by Paul to make an 'ethical'
point (about the **Bb**-relationship). Also, it went into direct parenesis.
But logically, it describes exactly the same state as before of an 'outworldliness' on the part of Christ-believers where world-view and ethos
come completely together.

The upshot is that the two rhetorical strategies we have identified
must not be torn apart. Instead, they support one another. The world-
view *grounds* the ethos and the description of the ethos (as contained
in the I→X→S-model) spells out the significance for human beings of
what is *already* contained in the world-view's statements about God's
acts and will. But we have also seen that in Paul's actual presentation of
these connections there is a specific direction, towards parenesis. That
direction need not intrinsically have been there. It would be perfectly
possible to present the Christ-believing form of life in the abstract as an
amalgam of world-view and ethos without tilting one's account towards
any parenesis. Paul, however, does tilt it. That happens when in his
account of life at the S-pole, which in itself focuses specifically on ethos,
he even concentrates on the C-level and the issue of *practice* (6:1–8:13).
And more generally, it is clearly what the rhetorical strategy of the letter
is all about when Paul lets the flow of the letter move inexorably forward
not only towards specifically 'ethical' issues of life at the S-pole, but also
towards parenesis.

(*c*) From these remarks about Paul's rhetorical strategy in the letter, let us go back to the I→X→S-model itself and make a list of those elements in the model that are specifically Stoic, but are also to be found in Romans. Once we have reminded ourselves of these, we may move on to note some differences between the Christ-believing form of life as described by Paul and the Stoic one.

The following nine features are shared by Paul in Romans and the I→X→S-model in its Stoic form:

1 The relationship between I and X (**Ba**) is one of self-identification.
2 The I at the I-pole stands for the I-perspective of the individual bodily self.
3 That perspective is both a distinctly bodily one (in fact, a body-*centred* one: I→I) and a social one that formally relates with others. (In substantive terms, however, it is unfortunately egocentrical: again I→I.)
4 The relationship between I and S is one of (self-)identification with others. It generates social community and a moral life.
5 Being at S consists in having a certain inner attitude (a psychic *hexis*).
6 The attitude consists in directedness towards others who belong at the S-pole too, that is, wanting the good for them for *their* sake.
7 The attitude also consists in wanting to do certain acts for themselves.
8 It also issues in doing those acts (**C**).
9 Points 4–8, as reflecting the new self-identification in point 1, describe the only thing that matters after the change away from the state identified in points 2–3. Everything else is indifferent.

With these similarities settled, we may note two differences of very different kind and import. The first is the whole apocalyptic world-view that was Paul's, both his cosmological, spatial presuppositions about heaven and earth and his temporal ideas about what God *has* done and what he eventually *will* do. This is mainly relevant to Paul's account of what happens 'before' and 'after' the I→X→S-model. 'Before' the model, we have been operating with an X→I relationship signifying God's intervention in the Christ event. And 'after' the model we might add an S→X relationship (the resurrection and more) which will once more be triggered by an X→S relationship (the parousia). The expanded model would look like this: $X→/I→X→S/X→S→X$. The difference from Stoicism with respect to the added elements could hardly be greater. And there can be

no doubt that whether one has such a picture of the world or a different
one has enormous consequences both for what one might call one's general
'outlook' on life (compare, for instance, the very important category or
mode of thought in Paul that is *hope*) and also, one suspects, for practice.
These differences would be worth exploring. For instance, one would
expect them to have important consequences for whether the combined
amalgam of world-view and ethos is experienced as being more or less
real. Thus Paul will have experienced it as being overwhelmingly real, far
more strongly so than anything experienced by a Stoic (or, for that matter,
a non-apocalyptic Jew) concerning the reality of the main elements in *his*
world-view. However, from the very beginning I have decided not to
allow this whole dimension to prevent us from looking with a cool eye at
the logic of what the letters are most directly about: an exercise in community formation in which Paul *uses* his specific world-view in the ways
we should then analyse. In relation to our specific theme, therefore, Paul's
apocalyptic world-view constitutes what we may call an external difference
from Stoicism.

The second difference is an internal one and hence potentially more
interesting. It is also, in fact, much smaller. Still, at the risk of allowing it
to appear greater than it is, we should mention it. It revolves around
Paul's notion of love (*agapē*). In Stoicism one does of course find the
idea of a relationship with other human beings (namely, as rational)
which transcends the individual perspective. Also, Stoic reflections on
friendship among the wise involve the idea of a specific directedness
towards the others as people that we have also found in the Pauline
notion of love. But is it not directedness towards other people *as* rational
and wise? And so, is there not a vital difference here? However, the
Pauline idea of directedness towards other people is in fact also somewhat
restricted. For it is only a directedness towards others as *Christ* people.
As we saw, Paul does not operate with *love* for people outside the group
of Christ-believers. In addition, in Stoicism one even finds traces of the
idea of directedness towards other people even though they may *not* be
wise, but because being human they at least have the potential for being
so. One *might* claim, therefore, that in Stoicism there is a *wider* concern
for others as people than in Paul.[33]

Still, there is at least the following difference from Paul. In Stoicism
the logic goes from directedness towards reason to directedness towards
others as (at least in the abstract) rational beings. Similarly, in Paul
the directedness goes from directedness towards Christ to directedness towards others as Christ people. But since Christ is himself a person,
the step to directedness towards others as people is easier to take in

the Pauline case and more directly in line with what grounds it. We may even take this as another example of the difference between the more abstract character of Stoicism and the more immediate and real character of the Christ-believing form of life. Directedness towards Christ as a person so very easily translates into directedness towards others as persons as soon as they too are seen to be directed towards Christ. Still, the difference is not one that in any way diminishes the comprehensive area of overlap between Paul and the Stoics. To state that Pauline love is altogether different from anything one finds in the ancient ethical tradition would be totally false.

(*d*) Finally, let us note some elements in Paul's theory in Romans that are wholly in line with Stoicism and stand out *more* clearly when one reads the letter in the light of the I→X→S-model.

(*d*.1) A central element in Paul's account in 6:1–8:13 of how the proper 'ethical' practice would be achieved was his idea of obedience 'from the heart' and of overcoming the internal division of the psyche which was responsible for cases of *akrasia* in people living under the law. This idea of sinlessness *realized* in external acts and *based* on *a certain inner structure of the psyche* matched Paul's hints of the same in chapter 2, when he spoke of having the law written in one's heart and of being circumcised on the heart. It appears, then, that Paul wanted to make this particular dimension of his theory clear as early as possible. Paul was obviously very concerned about *doing* (the C-level), which is the comprehensive theme of 2:11/12–29 and again of 6:1–8:13. But that concern took the wholly specific form of asking about the inner structure of the psyche. Like his God (2:16), Paul himself looked into the interior of the mind.

The idea of a radical change in the inner structure of the psyche is one of the features of Paul's theory that connects it most closely with the ancient ethical tradition in general and with Stoicism in particular. In Stoicism, complete directedness towards the understanding of the world that was formulated by reason meant that all other, more particularistic perspectives were blotted out—their content was demoted to the status of 'indifferents' (*adiaphora*). Similarly, in Paul's case the idea is that total directedness towards God through Christ blots out any other element in the psyche. When people come to identify with God through Christ, all other sides of the person with which they have previously identified will be completely neglected. They will no longer be given any normative role. The psyche will therefore no longer be divided, but wholly directed towards one thing alone.

There is a striking thought here, both in Paul and Stoicism, to the effect that a form of directedness *outwards* that is total will result in an *inner* attitude that is undivided and whole. Of course, Pauline scholars regularly contrast the idea of an outward-directedness (to be found in Paul) with that of an inward-directedness (to be found in the Stoics). That is a misunderstanding. In Stoicism, identifying with (one's own) reason points distinctly outward. For 'one's own' reason is just a reflex of the larger reason that holds the world together and is indeed identical with (the Stoic conception of) God. Conversely, as a Stoic would immediately and rightly point out, the Pauline outward-directedness is itself an internal phenomenon, a psychic matter. In Paul too, God works through the understanding. The point stands, therefore, that in both cases a directedness outward towards something far larger than the individual, with which the individual has come to identify, may make the individual inwardly undivided and whole. He or she will no longer identify him- or herself with any other, more local and particularistic features of him- or herself and these features will no longer be given any normative role. Consequently, there will no longer be any particularistic desires based on any of these features. The psyche will be one and undivided.

We may ask from philosophical curiosity how a Christ-believer will live as an individual, bodily self before the return of Christ when all features of him- or herself that are specifically tied to their own bodily individuality have, as it were, been placed in parenthesis. Or again, how does a bodily individual live as disembodied and divested of his or her individuality? Paul nowhere tackles this question head-on, nor is it possible to put together a developed answer on the basis of what he does say. For a full answer, we should go elsewhere, e.g. to the Stoics, whose ethics revolve around this very issue.[34]

Be that as it may. We may at all events conclude that Paul was wholly in line with the ancient ethical tradition when he brought in the idea of the undivided psyche in 6:1–8:13 in explanation of his claim that the proper directedness towards God in Christ faith means actual, sinless practice. That tradition was very much concerned with the idea of actual ethical practice: that the ethical person is one who always and only does the good. And here too the explanation was given in terms of the inner structure of the psyche, of what this person has come to see and want for him- or herself. In Stoicism, furthermore, this was specifically brought out in terms of the connection we noted between self-identification and normativity. And the Stoics were alone among ancient ethicists in basing the idea of the undivided inner structure of the psyche on that of an outward-directedness towards one thing alone.

(*d*.2) There is a specific corollary of Paul's emphasis on the inner structure in 6:1–8:13, to which we have paid much attention since it should colour our whole understanding of his 'theology'. If Christ-believers now themselves *want*, and want alone, to do the good, then they will do it not only because it is God's will, but also because it is, as it were, 'their own will'. By coming to identify *themselves* with God (through *God's* act, of course) and placing the locus of normativity there, they have also come to will the good *for themselves*. Willing something for oneself is different from wanting to do it for extrinsic reasons: as a *means* to acquire or avoid something else or in the manner of a slave who is just *told* or *ordered* to do it. That is why Paul apologizes in 6:19 for exhorting his addressees to turn themselves into slaves of God's righteousness. And that is why he states in 8:15 that they have not received a spirit of slavery that was meant to bring them back to fear. Rather, being baptized and having the spirit in them, they will now want for themselves to do the good (and will therefore do it).

(*d*.3) In what Paul says about the **Bb**-level too (12:1–15:13), he was very much concerned with the inner, psychic structure of Christ-believers (*d*.1), their *willing* the good for others (*d*.2), but now also their willing the good for *them*, their directedness *towards* others in mutual love (*d*.3). We found a comprehensive pattern in what Paul says of the form of life at this level. It is grounded in the **A/Ba**-relationship, but focused on the interpersonal relationship within the group of Christ-believers. That is where willing the good for others, not just as the objective good but as *their* good, is primarily displayed. For that is where one may find the particular kind of relationship that accounts for this special form of willing: a total identification with Christ, a realization that there are others who in the same way totally identify with him, a translation of one's directedness towards Christ on to directedness towards those others with whom one is, through the shared identification with Christ, identical, and finally, an application of what 'Christ' stands for—namely, giving up one's individual self in love for the others—*to* those others with whom one sees oneself as identical. Only peripherally was this attitude then extended outwards to include an interpersonal relationship outside the group. In relation to outsiders too there was a 'willing the good', but no love, no wishing the good for others for *their* sake, because one is attached to *them*. That only comes within the group that is constituted by total directedness towards Christ.

(*d*.4) This emphasis on the inner structure and willing in the account of love between Christ-believers shows the extent to which the comparison with Stoicism helps to bring out something that is just as central to the letter to the Romans as to Paul's other letters: that they are all so many exercises in community formation. That is what is brought out with particular clarity by reading the letter in the light of the I→X→S-model in its Stoic form. It would be quite false to think that the emphasis on the inner structure and willing is opposed to a community-formative aim. On the contrary, Paul's idea is that the complete inner undivided-ness that results from total outward-directedness towards God through Christ leads to two results that are eminently community-formative in character: doing the proper acts—and these acts are themselves all other-regarding—and having the corresponding other-regarding attitudes, first among which is the genuinely other-directed one of love.

This intrinsic connection between inner structure and community formation is one that Paul shares with the ancient ethical tradition in general and with Stoicism in particular. It is appropriate, therefore, to end here by bringing in the Stoic conception of the kind of community with which they on their side were concerned. They spoke of it as being the whole world (*ouranos, mundus*). That might seem to remove it radically from the kind of *out*worldliness that Paul had in mind. It certainly is different, reflecting the fundamental difference in tangible world-view between the Stoics and Paul. But the Stoics defined their 'world' in a way that makes it closely similar to what we find in Paul: 'governed by the power of the gods', a 'city and state that is common to the gods and to human beings' and 'of which each individual human being is a member', which explains why 'each person will also place the common good of that city before his or her own good' (Cicero *Fin* III 64). Suppose we make this Stoic city outworldly in Paul's sense. Then it becomes identical with the city that is waiting for Paul's Christ-believers in heaven, the heavenly *politeuma* of Phil 3:20, the heavenly Jerusalem of Gal 4:26 and the target of their present hopes according to Rom 8:18–39. Suppose we try instead to situate it somewhere *within* the present world, while also giving it an essentially 'outworldly' character. Then there is one place to find it: in the concrete, historical communities that Paul aimed to bring into existence, in Rome no less than elsewhere, those constituting the *ekklēsia* or 'assembly' of God.

11

Conclusion

Paul

Paul was driven by a vision. Things *had* been done by God in the past. And things *would* be done in the future. But then there also was a meantime. Here Paul had a task and his addressees had one. Paul's task was partly the missionary one of spreading the word further—to the gentiles. That is clear from his own account in Gal 1–2, and Romans 15 spells out the urgency of his sense that he now had to move on, through Rome, to the second half of the Mediterranean area and preach the gospel there. Partly, however, Paul's task was directed to building up the congregations he had already founded. That is the purpose of his letters. His addressees too had a task. That was to bring to fruition what had happened to them when they were established as Christ-believers by Paul. Paul's upbuilding purpose with his letters was to help them fulfil that task.

For Paul's upbuilding task and for that of his addressees focus was on anthropology, on explicating the character of the *involvement* of the addressees (and indeed of Paul too) *in* the two framing events initiated by God. To elucidate this, Paul made use of a comprehensive, but also sharply focused model that had been developed in Stoicism, the I→X→S-model. In terms of this model he aimed to bring out the precise character of the *initial* involvement of his addressees, their 'conversion', their coming to Christ faith. That was captured in the movement I→X. But he also aimed to bring out the precise character of the final *goal* of their involvement. That was captured in the movement I→(X→)S and in his elaboration of the new form of life at the S-pole.

One crucially important result of our analysis was that although Paul was certainly able to keep these two themes apart logically and for purposes of presentation, they in fact hang inextricably together. Put differently, even though the movement I→X is very distinctly one under-taken by an individual as an individual, the eventual goal of the whole process is just as much a distinctly social one. We have seen how that could be so. The experience of Christ (X) as seen in the Christ event lifts the individual (I) out of his or her individuality, leaves it behind and carries him or her over to a state of communality (S) shared with all those who have undergone the same process. We have also seen that the model for this process is to be found in Stoicism.

The fact that Paul starts out, logically, from speaking of the individual and ends by speaking of the group—and the individual as nothing but a member of the group—cannot be overemphasized. It means that the heavy emphasis in scholarship after Bultmann on the social character of Pauline Christianity is both right and wrong. It is right for the reason just stated. But it is also wrong when it claims that Paul did not have a concept of the individual person as an individual. It is certainly true that Paul did not speak for a modern 'individualism' in a person's experience of God and Christ. To that extent the reaction to Bultmann's one-sided existentialist individualism is well taken. But it is equally certainly true that Paul did have the formal concept of the individual as an individual. That concept was both available in and indeed basic to the philosophical, ethical tradition on which he was drawing. It remains the case that the eventual goal was through and through social. And there too Paul was wholly in line with the philosophers, not least the Stoics whose Utopian thought ended in the idea of a shared form of life among the wise which is closely similar to what one may take to be the form of Paul's heavenly *politeuma* in Philippians 3.

Explicating the character of the involvement of Paul's addressees at the beginning and end was not something Paul did for its own sake. Instead, it is part of what the letters *are*, at the most fundamental level and from one end to the other: exercises in parenesis. We have seen that parenesis has two components. It consists in Paul's *reminding* his addressees of what *has* happened and his *appeal* to them to put it into *practice*. The various features of the I→X→S-model, including the two we just mentioned, come in as part of the first component of parenesis, the reminding. What Paul does is to set out a course of events that he himself and his addressees *have* undergone. They *have* been brought *from* some place (in fact, the I-pole) *to* somewhere else (the S-pole). This re-minding then issues in the direct appeal: *practise* it, since it *has* happened to us.

However, Paul's letters are not just through and through parenetic in this more abstract sense, but also quite literally so, that is, in *literary* terms. Thus we have seen how in Philippians Paul twice states what *has* happened to *himself* (Phil 1:12–26 and 3:4–14) as a background in the form of a reminder to his explicit paraklesis, the appeal that the Philippians now practise what in a similar way has also already happened to *them* (Phil 1:27–2:18 and 3:15–4:9). Indeed, Paul *begins* the letter with a thanksgiving section that precisely reminds them of this last thing (1:1–5) and moves on from there to paraklesis (1:9–11). Similarly, in Galatians he reminds his addressees of what has happened to *himself* (Gal 1:12–2:21) and indeed what happened to *them* (Gal 3:1–5 and 4:12–20) as a basis for his explicit parenesis (5:13–6:10) that they now *practise* this. Finally, Romans too describes what has already happened in the form of a comprehensive course of events (1:16–4:25), not now pertaining specifically to Paul himself or to the Romans in particular when *they* came to Christ faith, but to 'all': to Jews first and also, similarly, to gentiles. But in Romans too we saw that this all points towards two things: an account (5:1–21 and 8:14–39) of how Christ-believers now stand poised towards the *future* (the future framing event)—*and* parenesis proper (6:1–8:13, 11:13–25 and 12:1–15:13), that is, the explicit appeal that the addressees put into practice what has already happened to them.

It is crucial to see here that the content of Paul's reminder, that is, what he describes as having happened, is distinctly tilted towards what we may call its anthropological side: towards what the 'objective' Christ event set going by God has *meant* to Paul and his addressees, what happened *to them*. The 'objective' framework remains very solidly in place, of course. It is *God* who *has* done something in the Christ event and God and Christ who *will* do something in the future. But what Paul aims to spell out in his reminder is what effect this had on himself and his addressees. It is for this very precise purpose that he brings in, as part of his reminder, the various ideas that together constitute the I→X→S-model. What he does is try to *make the model itself clear to* his addressees—as a *basis* for his appeal to them to put it into practice. They must come to see what all that has happened to them *means*. Then they will *do* it. Then they will have fulfilled *their* task. And then Paul too will have fulfilled his own task in relation to them.

Just to state the obvious: on such a reading there will be no valid distinction between 'theology' and 'ethics' in Paul. All through Paul will be 'theologizing' in the sense of spelling out the meaning to human beings of what God has done (to them) through Christ. But all through he will also be concerned with what is the ultimate goal of his 'theologizing': practice. Nothing must be torn apart here. It all hangs intrinsically and inextricably together.

And his interpreters

Of course there is much more in Paul than parenesis in the comprehensive sense just stated. Here I take up two sets of issues that have particularly engaged his interpreters, one captured under the term 'participation' and the other under 'the law' and 'righteousness'.

We have seen all through that Paul's thought world was filled with what we have called substantive ideas of various sorts. There was no doubt in his mind about the 'real' character of the two framing events: Christ's descent into human form and his resurrection to a heavenly state, from which he will return to bring people up to that same state. Similarly, Paul had no doubt about God's intervention in history before Christ: his 'salvation-historical' sketch was just—history. Nor should we exclude the possibility that he reckoned with the 'reality' of a number of features in the involvement of Christ-believers in the Christ event. The 'old man' may have 'really' died and been buried with Christ in baptism. Christ-believers may have 'really' come to be *in* Christ. They certainly have Christ's spirit 'in them' and that presence may have had a 'real' character too.

Seeing this, commentators (from Wrede over Schweitzer to Sanders and onwards—e.g. to Dale Martin) have insisted on the 'real' character of this Pauline talk and coined the term 'participation' for it. They have also invariably claimed that this whole way of thinking fits well into the ancient thought world but is also one that we cannot take over. They are right on both counts. But it certainly does not follow that we should focus on this side of Paul's thought world alone to the exclusion of everything else. On the contrary, we should insist that Paul may speak both in the substantive terminology of participation language—and *also* in the quite different language of parenesis, which is through and through cognitive. How, then, should the two types of language be correlated? There is no explicit answer to this question in Paul himself and for a very good reason: that *he* did not see any problem here in the way we are likely to do—and precisely because *we* have access to the one kind of language *but not* to the other.

It is a different question whether Paul *should* have seen a problem in how to correlate cognitive language with substantive, reifying language of the kind he is obviously employing (at least in part). Is there an intrinsic incoherence in this, even if Paul did not see that? One version of the question would be to ask whether a belief in some form of external or pre-determination is intrinsically inconsistent with a belief in free human cognition and agency. This question has of course been discussed by philosophers and theologians since antiquity—and even in antiquity itself, e.g. by the Stoics, who famously insisted that there was *no* intrinsic inconsistency here. Unfortunately, it is far from clear—after all these centuries of discussion—what the answer should be. Personally I tend to think that there is no intrinsic inconsistency, and that the Stoics were right. But even if they were not, and even if one should therefore fault not only the Stoics (for their answer) but also Paul for not having seen the problem, that does not of course justify *neglecting* one side of Paul's thought (the cognitive one) and insisting that the other (the substantive one) expresses *all* there is to be said. The fact that this latter side is *in*accessible to us does not give it a *favoured* status.

The other set of issues that have engaged readers of Paul—on the law and righteousness—has been seen in sharply different ways by main interpreters of Paul throughout the 20th century. Wrede and Schweitzer saw it as being of subsidiary importance and as being closely tied to Paul's missionary enterprise: that of preaching the gospel to gentiles. Thus it pertained very specifically to the relationship between gentiles and Jews within that context. In Neo-Orthodoxy, by contrast, as represented by Bultmann and others, Paul's discussion of the law and righteousness regained its traditionally Protestant, strongly theological position as the 'centre of Paul'. Here what Paul said of law-abiding Judaism was seen as the quintessential expression of the state of fallen humanity that is rebelling against God, to which righteousness through faith constituted *the* answer. Sanders then broke decisively with this reading, partly by taking up Wrede's and Schweitzer's basic idea of situating Paul on the law and righteousness within his missionary enterprise as a question concerning the specific relationship between gentiles and Jews. But against Schweitzer in particular, Sanders did not see any intrinsic contrast or lack of connection between Paul's talk of righteousness (and the law) and his use of another favoured type of language, that of participation. Or at least that is how it appeared initially (in Sanders 1977). When it came to sorting out in more detail what Paul does say of the law (Sanders 1983), Paul turned out to be far less coherent, and Sanders frequently had to invoke Paul's alleged propensity for black and white thinking to explain apparently inconsistent Pauline claims. The same procedure may be noticed in Räisänen's careful and comprehensive discussion of Paul on the law, originally published in the same year as Sanders, 1983. For Räisänen too there was inconsistency and incoherence, indeed confusion, in what Paul says about the law.

My own approach has been to accept the rejection by Sanders and Räisänen of the Neo-Orthodox reading of Paul on the law and righteousness. It seems certain that the forceful restatement by these two scholars (and indeed by others) of ideas that were already present *in nuce* in Wrede has come to stay. Thus when Paul speaks of righteousness and the law, he is not enunciating any eternal truths about the relationship of 'fallen mankind' to God. Instead, his problem was the far more specific, *historical* one of how exactly to fit Jews into the new situation generated by the Christ event, and in particular how to sort out the relationship between gentiles and Jews now that gentiles had obtained access to Christ *without* the law—but when it was also the Jews who were the true ancestors of the new Christ faith. Against Sanders and Räisänen, however, I have been prepared to give Paul far more of the benefit of the doubt with respect to the *possibility* that there is a coherent, realistic and philosophically satisfying comprehensive account to be found in Paul of righteousness, the law, Christ faith, Jews and gentiles.

We may bring out what he does say by taking the three letters of Philippians, Galatians and Romans in turn.

Philippians: Righteousness was not through the law, not through any of the features that distinguished Paul himself as a Jew who *as* a Jew might justly point to his own excellent status. Instead, righteousness was through Christ faith, a state brought about by God (in the single act of the Christ event) and predicated on the faith (3:4–9). This is a sheer statement by Paul of his one, basic perspective: Christ and the Christ faith *alone*. There is no suggestion that there was anything specifically wrong with the law or with the distinctive characteristics of Paul's Jewishness, only a claim that these excellent features too belong on the side of everything that Paul has now left behind.

Galatians: Paul first states what is essentially the same message, but now in an extended discussion with and contrast to another view, according to which righteousness also required following the law (2:15–21). Paul denied this on behalf of his gentile Christ-believers. Christ was wholly sufficient for them, as he had become for Paul himself. Paul also attempted to find a different, intermediary role for the law (3:15–24, 4:1–3), and he suggested that seen in retrospect from the kind of life opened up by the Christ event, the law might be experienced as having a somewhat oppressive character (3:19–4:11). Still, there was nothing intrinsically wrong with it. On the contrary, even though it might not have been given directly by God (3:19–20) and even though that might possibly explain its oppressive character, it was given for a sensible purpose: of keeping down transgressions (3:19). Nor was it certainly *against* God's promises (3:21).

So far this is little more than the neutral statement of Philippians that righteousness was *not* through the law. But then Paul takes a huge step forward that has in fact been prepared by his various statements (in Phil 3:7–11 and Gal 2:19–20) of what did happen when a person (Paul himself) came to Christ faith. The step is taken (in Gal 5:13 ff) when Paul spells out the full, positive content of the kind of life implied by the Christ faith and when he then claims that this kind of life constitutes the essential content of—the law! We saw that this passage also brings us much further in understanding what Paul means by righteousness. Righteousness is (also) a state of mind, a certain form of character—namely the one that issues in actually acting in accordance with the law, in doing what the law says should be done and avoiding to do what the law prohibits. Thus Christ and the law are far more closely connected than appeared from Philippians and the first, neutral (and to some extent negative) part of Galatians. Now the message is that *Christ* was in fact able to *generate* what Paul's opponents falsely thought would be generated by *the law*. And now it also becomes clear that what Paul and his opponents were in fact discussing was the conditions for righteousness in the sense of actual, concrete sinlessness, of actually and concretely getting away from sinning. By bringing Christ and the law together in this way Paul also moves much closer to solving the question of how Judaism up to Christ fits into the new situation and correspondingly how the gentiles who have entered into Christ outside the law will then relate to the Jews.

Romans: Many of the issues left over in Galatians were then taken up and brought to some kind of conclusion in Romans. *Why* was it *only* the Christ event that might generate righteousness in the sense developed, as a state of mind responsible for sinlessness? Paul had given part of the answer in Gal 2:19–20 and 6:14–15 combined with 5:13–26 in particular. But Romans 1:18–4:25 spells out in far broader terms what it was that was wrong with both gentiles and Jews outside Christ (the I-directedness corresponding to an insufficient directedness towards God) and what was so special about the Christ faith that it might constitute the solution. Further, *why* was the law in particular *not* sufficient? Here Rom 7:7–25 provided the answer when taken together with the manner in which Paul had set up the problem in Rom 2:12–25. The law *could* not do any more than generate the next-best state, in which there was a constant *risk* of sinning (7:7–25). What was needed, however, was a state of circumcision of the heart (2:12–25), and that required the Christ event and faith.

As in Galatians, however, the outcome of *that* was the fulfilment—of the law (Rom 8:4). And so the issue was once more raised with extra force of how gentiles, who *through* the Christ faith and *without* the law had now gained full access to the new situation in Christ, would be related to the Jews, to whom belonged not only that *law* which would now actually be fulfilled (though only in Christ), but also the original promises and more. That question too Paul attempted to answer, in Romans 9–11 and 14:1–15:13. His answer was given in the image of the olive tree (standing for Judaism) onto which gentiles had been grafted and the idea of the original promises that had been given to the Jews— and had now been fulfilled in Christ. Gentiles did have *full* access *now* to the new situation on exactly the same footing as Jews. Still, they had to show special respect for Jews (whether Christ-believing or not) with whom they might—in itself reasonably enough—have some disagreement. For what they had gained access to was *originally*—in terms of its 'roots'—a distinctly Jewish possession.

Finally, there was righteousness itself. Galatians had shown that it stood for a state of mind of perfect sinlessness. But Galatians had also shown (5:5) that it remained something that belonged to the future, presumably in the form of God's future justifying verdict on the day of Christ. Both ideas are to be found in Romans too (the first certainly in 8:4, possibly in 8:10 and the repeated assertions in 3:21–5:11 that Christ-believers *have* been 'righteoused', that is, *made* righteous, through the Christ faith; the second in 5:9–10 and 8:31–39). But here a third idea of righteousness becomes very prominent too: the one introduced in Phil 3:9 of *God's* righteousness in his dealing with Jews and gentiles in accordance with his promises. Where the first type of righteousness is, one might say, presentic and anthropological, the second is future and forensic, and the third is past, present and future and (if one wishes) covenantal. But they all fit together and must not be separated. In his complete trustworthiness in spite of everything (3:3–5), God has—in the Christ event— made it possible for Jews and gentiles finally to *become* (by means of the faith) righteous, that is, sinless; and God may therefore also *declare* them righteous on the day of Christ.

Not all of Paul's solutions may seem equally persuasive. And history, with its parting of the ways between Judaism and Christianity, has shown up an intrinsic instability at the heart of his attempt to hold together Judaism and the Christ faith as interpreted by himself. Still, it seems fair to say that Paul's statements about the law and righteousness are part of a fairly rigorous attempt to think through how one might *spell out* the meaning of the Christ event *in addition* to speaking of it in 'participationist' categories—and that this attempt was relatively successful. There is more systematic thought on these issues in Paul than either Sanders or Räisänen would allow. In addition to everything else that Paul *also* was, he also *was* something of a thinker. That result may be interesting in itself. In this book, however, the two sets of issues I have highlighted in this section have been treated mainly in the form of corollaries to the analysis of Paul's parenesis broadly conceived. It is the fact that they fit into—and may be solved in terms of—the I→X→S-model as this underlies Paul's parenesis that is the genuinely interesting point. The thesis is that parenesis, and indeed Stoically informed parenesis, constitutes a key that will open the text up for a new and more fruitful discussion of the traditional questions posed under the two sets of issues.

Four theses

The proposal for an adequate reading of Paul that I have presented in this book may be summarized in four theses.

There is first a *historical* thesis: that there is a fundamental similarity in the basic model that structures both Stoic ethics and Paul's comprehensive parenesis in his letters as a whole. I have not been concerned to speculate about the possible roads of influence from Stoicism to Paul. The main reason is that such speculation would most likely remain just that—speculation. Nor have I been concerned to do what others have recently done with great success: analyse particular passages in the letters and show how these reflect a Paul who actively participated in the moral philosophical discourse of his day, though also (as everybody did) with his own special emphases. This has been done for topics ranging from specific concepts (like *syneidēsis*, *adiaphora*, *exousia*, *autarcheia*, *eleutheria* and more) to broader themes (like diatribe style, exhortation more generally and more). Instead, I have attempted to show that there is a single, basic thought structure that is formulated in both Stoic ethics and in Paul. And my claim has been that it is in terms of this structure that we should understand the other more restricted similarities.

There is no need to expatiate here on the consequences of this thesis if it is valid. Jerusalem and Athens, religion and philosophy, Christianity and humanism—all these supposed contrasts may have been validly drawn in later periods for the purposes for which they were coined. But if we want a truly historical understanding of earliest Christianity, at least as formulated by Paul, we must give them up. Instead, just as we have gradually learned to see Paul as a part of ancient Judaism, so we must gradually learn to see him as a part of the ancient ethical tradition. In this latter area there are no intrinsic contrasts at the centre of either

Paul's or Stoic thought that we may, as it were, settle *beforehand*—and then proceed to a comparison that may only point to certain relatively tangential similarities. Rather, the field of comparison is wide open with no demarcation lines settled in advance.

Second, there is an *exegetical* thesis: that a reading that draws on Stoic ideas helps to solve a number of problems that have traditionally engaged interpreters of Paul's letters. These problems include the following. (i) How do the letters hang together? Can we discover some kind of internal logic that will explain a sufficiently large part of what we actually find in them? (ii) In particular, what is the logical relationship between the descriptive and the prescriptive parts—the problem usually designated that of the 'indicative' and the 'imperative'? (iii) What is the relationship between the apparently non-contingent elements of Paul's thought and those that seem to make only a contingent appearance in each particular letter? (iv) How can we combine what appear to be different kinds of conceptuality in the letters, e.g. the substantive one we have spoken of and a cognitive one?

Questions like these have continued to tease Paul's interpreters— and will no doubt continue to do so. But some of them, I contend, have been answered through the approach adopted in this book. We have been much concerned about the literary structure of the three letters we have studied. And we have seen how they may be held together as documents of parenesis, when this concept is understood in the more comprehensive sense we have specified so as to *include* both descriptive ('indicative') and specifically prescriptive ('imperative') parts. Parenesis consists in reminding and appealing. And that is what happens *all through* Paul's letters. We have also observed how the 'non-contingent' elements in the letters are constantly being adjusted and put to use to help solving the contingent issues to which all the letters (Romans included) are basically addressed. Finally, we have seen that Paul operates through and through at a cognitive level—the one that is responsive to a philosophical reading of him. But we have also noted that this fact does not in the least go against finding other kinds of language in him, in particular what we have called substantive language. Paul did not himself see a contrast here. But then *we* need a certainty that we cannot probably obtain before *finding* a contrast between the two. And only then would we be justified in choosing to focus on one type of language to the *exclusion* of the other. As it is, we need to take both into account in a comprehensive reading of Paul.

Third, there is a *hermeneutical* thesis: that a kind of reading that draws on Stoicism to emphasize and develop those ideas of a cognitive type that are in fact there in Paul is positively *required* for an exegesis of his letters to have fulfilled its task. We have just seen that a responsible reading of Paul must allow for the existence of different types of language. But exegesis is a double-sided enterprise. On the one hand it must seek to elucidate the text as seen—so far as possible—from within its own thought world. That part of the enterprise will certainly never be able to step altogether out of the horizon of understanding within which the interpreter him- or herself is situated. Still, the interpreter's attempt is to be open to discovering new ways of putting together ideas to which the interpreter has at least access, ways, that is, which are specifically *different* from those that constitute the interpreter's own horizon of understanding. In historical research one element is therefore a kind of *backward movement* that places the interpreter's own, modern beliefs in brackets and makes the attempt (destined never to be entirely successful) of reconstructing a different horizon of understanding, one removed in time and place from one's own.

However, that is only the first half of the exegetical task. Just because of the difference between now and then, any kind of reading of a historical text will also be concerned, whether it knows it or not, to make a *forward movement*, that is, to see the understanding of the world that is being studied as constituting a 'real option' for the interpreter—not necessarily as something he or she will consider *the* correct understanding, but as an understanding that the interpreter *could* conceivably inhabit. With respect to this second half of the interpretation of Paul, I have insisted that we should recognize that one type of language that Paul uses, the substantive one, does not constitute a real option for us, whereas the other, cognitive one does. That has the consequence that we must do two things in reading Paul: both remain open to his use of substantive language (as part of the first half of the exegetical task), but also accept and insist that for the second half of the task it is the other, cognitive, type alone that may be used. That is the only type to which we have direct access and it is in terms of that type alone that we may *responsibly* do what *all* interpreters do: see what Paul says as presenting a real option to us. By contrast, if (as many scholars have in fact regrettably done) we begin to play with Paul's substantive language (in the way this was understood by him) as presenting something that constitutes a real option for us, then we are suffering from an illusion. What there is to be 'rescued' in Paul (in no more than this sense: that it constitutes a real option) is what is stated in cognitive language.

Finally, there is a *theological* thesis: that Paul must be read directly, philosophically, even naturalistically as a person who is speaking of *the world* as it is available to all partners in the dialogue, in exactly the same way as this was done by his fellow Jews (like Philo) and Greeks (like Plato or the Stoics). In particular, there is no radically different, privileged perspective (the perspective of revealed faith) that as it were settles any discussion in advance and on which Paul *just* wished to fall back if and when the dialogue broke down. Paul certainly *knew*. But he knew about *the world*. And he in principle expected that anybody else would become able to share his own knowledge of the world, to *see* it the way he did. That is the reason why it bothered him tremendously that his Jewish compatriots generally had *not* reached his own insight (Romans 9–11). The important thing is that it bothered him. For that shows that he was in principle working within a field of things to be seen and understood. The story (of the Christ event) might be a strange one, as Paul did not at all deny, but it was one to be accepted (or rejected) as any other account of the world. Paul's 'theologizing' stood in what we may call 'direct confrontation' with other accounts of the world, in the sense that they were logically operating at the same level. It was not secured logically beforehand in a way that would turn the dialogue into a sham.

We may think, indeed we should think, that Paul's belief in the story of the Christ event, in the direct form in which he understood it, was false. But we may let ourselves be stimulated by the *kind* of 'theologizing' that we find in Paul to think that we should ourselves adopt the same kind: one that attempts to tease out the meaning for human beings of the Christ event in a manner that makes immediate sense philosophically and in that way presents the special shape of the Christ-believing form of life as a real option to one's contemporaries.

Notes

Notes for Chapter 1

1. For references to the work of Malherbe, Meeks, Räisänen, Sanders and Stendahl, see later in this chapter. The works of Theissen I have mainly in mind are the well-known series of sociological studies of 1 Corinthians from the mid-70s published in Theissen 1983 (1979) and the psychological analysis of Pauline theology in Theissen 1983.

2. For a forceful questioning of the apologetic tendency underlying much traditional historical scholarship on early Christianity, see J. Z. Smith 1990.

3. Malherbe's major contributions are Malherbe 1983, 1986, 1987, 1989, 1994 and 1996. See also his exceedingly helpful overviews of the field in Malherbe 1990 and 1992.

4. In addition to the classic account of Paul's social world in Meeks 1983, Meeks' methodological profile is particularly clearly stated in Meeks 1986a, which lies behind the broader accounts in Meeks 1986b and 1993. Meeks does not, of course, in the least neglect 'ideas' (compare, e.g. the final chapter in Meeks 1983 on 'Patterns of belief and patterns of life' and the 'correlations' between the two). But he does not quite allow himself to see that distinctly philosophical developments of ideas may directly serve those social functions that he is rightly after.

5. The classic statements are Sanders 1977 and 1983 and Räisänen 1983. See also the relevant essays in Räisänen 1992.

6. See Engberg-Pedersen 1981 and 1983.

7. See Engberg-Pedersen 1986a and 1990.

8. I made an early attempt to read Paul and Greek ethics together in an essay on the first chapters of Romans, published only in Danish (Engberg-Pedersen 1986b). Ten years later (Engberg-Pedersen 1996), in a book that was also only published in Danish and does not discuss Paul, I attempted to identify the basic features of Greek ethics between Socrates and Marcus Aurelius. The argument was that in spite of the obvious differences, these features are sufficiently similar to turn this whole body of thought into a single, coherent ethical tradition.

9. Early representatives of this development are Wrede 1907 and Schweitzer 1930. Late representatives are Sanders 1977 and 1983 and Räisänen 1983.

10. This has happened in two fields, in particular: in the analysis of the epistles as letters (compare the summary account in Stowers 1986, drawing on milestones throughout the 20th century such as Deissmann 1908, Schubert 1939, Koskenniemi 1956, Thraede 1970) and as rhetorical texts (begun in Betz 1975 and 1979 and flourishing since then, compare, e.g. Porter and Olbricht [eds] 1993 and D. F. Watson 1995).

11. Bultmann 1984⁹ (1948–53), 192.

12. For a convincing discussion of the difference between 'formal and substantial individualism' see the British philosopher Bernard Williams 1995.

13. See, e.g. Malherbe 1994, 255.

14. For an example see Malherbe 1987, 32–3.

15. For a sophisticated analysis of 'comparison' in this whole area see J. Z. Smith 1990, ch. 2. Smith is right to emphasize that comparison takes place 'within the space of the scholar's mind' and 'for the scholar's own intellectual reasons' (51). That point underlies the claim about first looking for similarities between Paul and the moral philosophers.

16. One might have attempted to address this theme directly, e.g. in relation to the many motifs discussed in Malherbe 1992. In the present work, however, the point will only be made more indirectly, e.g. in the discussion of how the many different moral-philosophical motifs that make their appearance in the letter to the Philippians may be fitted together within a single pattern.

17. See Bultmann 1910 and the commentaries in the Handbuch zum Neuen Testament series by Lietzmann (Romans 1906 and Corinthians 1907) and Dibelius (Thessalonians and Philippians 1911, Colossians, Ephesians and Philemon 1912, the Pastorals 1913) plus the classic statement on parenesis in the latter's commentary on James 1921 in Meyer's Kritisch-exegetischer Kommentar series.

18. It is all a matter of degree here. Since Hengel 1969 there has been nothing new in claiming an intimate relationship between 'Judaism' and 'Hellenism'. There is a big step, however, from that towards the attitude of a total, merely 'curious' open-mindedness towards identifying 'original' Jewish and 'original' Greek ideas in the Hellenistic Jewish mix that is Paul—for the only valid purpose of analysing and understanding *Paul*. Examples of how that may be done are given in Engberg-Pedersen 1994a. Examples (by Dale B. Martin, Wayne A. Meeks and others) of how scholars need to be aware of the ideological components that are always present (in one way or the other) in the concepts of 'Judaism' and 'Hellenism' are given in Engberg-Pedersen forthcoming.

19. For bibliography on this see Malherbe 1992, 269–70 and Colish 1992, 367–8.

20. For a superb overview that also goes back to the beginnings in the 19th century (and before) see Malherbe 1992. Following on an introduction (I), Malherbe organizes his account around such themes as the 'Corpus Hellenisticum

Novi Testamenti' and the problem of parallels (II), epistolary paraenesis (III), the description of the wise man (IV), ancient psychagogy (V), the *Haustafeln* (VI), the diatribe (VII), the *topoi* (VIII) and such *varia* as the catalogues of virtues and vices, *peristasis* catalogues and individual concepts like humility and conscience (IX). That more or less covers the whole field, thereby also raising the question whether the intimate contact between the New Testament (or at least Paul) and the Hellenistic moralists over this wide range of apparently dissimilar topics may not reflect a deeper similarity that holds all the rest together. Malherbe does not restrict himself to the Stoics. For a historiographical overview that is restricted to Stoicism and the New Testament see Colish 1992. The main 20th-century contributions in that specific field are treated there on pp. 367–79. For Stoicism and Paul in particular, they include the famous discussion (focusing on Epictetus) between Bultmann (1912) and Adolf Bonhöffer (1911 and 1912) and works by Liechtenhan (1922b, focusing on Posidonius), Greeven 1935, Pohlenz 1949, Jagu 1958, Sevenster 1961 (Seneca), Braun 1962 (Epictetus), Hübner (1975) and again Jagu 1989 (Epictetus). The most recent major contributions are those of Jones 1987 (on the concept of freedom in Paul against its contemporary background), Vollenweider 1989 (on the same issue) and the series of works by Jaquette (1994–6, focusing on the Stoic 'indifferents' and their role in Paul). Colish's concluding observation is worth quoting in full: 'Over the centuries, the relations between Stoicism and early Christianity have been a vehicle for Christian apologists of all kinds, for intra-humanist rivalries, for humanists and anti-humanists, for Enlightenment rationalists and their opponents, for nationalists and internationalists, for ecumenists and the repudiators of antisemitism, as well as for the proponents of academic wrangles and educational reforms of various sorts ... our investigation has shown that the historical understanding of this whole subject has been anything but cumulative. Rather, the view of the relations between Stoicism and the New Testament have been notably fluid, and the approaches taken to it highly subjective, as each successive group of commentators has reinvented the topic and used it to mirror its own contemporary concerns' (379).

21. For major American contributions see Stowers 1981, Fiore 1986, Fitzgerald 1988 (all pupils of Malherbe) and Jaquette 1994, 1995a and 1996, and from the German side Jones 1987 and Vollenweider 1989.

22. This is one of the genuine insights of Segal 1990.

23. For a recent example of the kind of basically dichotomous thinking we should attempt to overcome, see deSilva 1995. This short paper carefully lists a long line of similarities between Paul and the Stoics (mainly Epictetus) with regard to Stoic terminology, phrases, conceptions, *topoi*, metaphors, figures, forms and ideas such as that of natural theology. But deSilva's conclusion is that Bruce Metzger was (after all) 'correct ... to qualify the relationship [between Paul and the Stoics] *strongly* by saying that 'the *theological presuppositions* and the *springs* of Paul's actions were very different from those of a Stoic

philosopher. It was the encounter with Christ, the experience of the Spirit ... that shaped Paul's message' (564, my italics). In other words, in the final account, when it comes to what is genuinely basic, the similarities with Stoicism turn out to be only relatively superficial.

24. Malina: 1986, 1993² (1981), 1996 and Malina and Neyrey 1996. Martin: especially 1995.

25. James Dunn quickly saw the 'newness' of this perspective, see Dunn 1983a (also in Dunn 1990), 1992a and the introduction (pp. 1–5) to Dunn 1996a. Thielman 1989, 2–27 provides a nice overview (clearly stimulated by Sanders' own sketch in Sanders 1977, 1–12) that situates Sanders, Räisänen and Dunn within a line of thinking that goes back to C. G. Montefiore and was then followed by G. F. Moore, W. D. Davies, H. J. Schoeps and others. But he also acknowledges the emphatic position of Sanders. For an excellent more recent assessment see Roetzel 1995. Roetzel at one point refers to the 'radical critique of Bultmann and the traditional Lutheran position' that came soon after the second world war 'from the shores of Britain and Scandinavia' (1995, 256). Within the latter group he singles out for mention Johannes Munck (1954) and Krister Stendahl. Munck's influence (as witnessed, e.g. in Sanders 1977 and in Segal 1990) is a chapter of its own. (Compare Roetzel 1995, 257: 'The genius of Munck's work was its insistence that Paul be viewed in light of his Judaism rather than juxtaposed against it.') Stendahl's hugely innovative contribution was his short paper on Paul and the 'introspective conscience of the West': Stendahl 1963.

26. For this reading see Frederiksen 1991.

27. Psychological explanation: Räisänen 1983, 14 and *passim*. Sanders 1983, 80 ('he thinks in black and white terms') and *passim*. Romans 2: Sanders 1983, 123–32. (This treatment of a fascinating chapter has always struck me as being particularly unpersuasive.)

28. Compare, e.g. Furnish 1990 and Keck 1993.

29. The latter term was very helpfully introduced by Jouette M. Bassler into the work of the Society of Biblical Literature Pauline Theology Group (1986–95). See Bassler 1993, 17 and Meyer 1997, 150.

30. Williams 1985, 160–1.

31. Williams 1985, 163–4 (Williams' emphasis).

32. See in particular Bultmann 1948 (1941), 1952a and 1965 (1958).

33. This de facto claim is made in Bultmann's concrete exegesis when he discovers his own *existential* reading in Paul's own text. A good example is the reading in Bultmann 1932 of the experience of death in Romans 7, repeated in the *Theologie* (1984⁹) on pp. 248–9.

34. See Käsemann 1961 and 1962. Also Bultmann's reaction in Bultmann 1964—and Käsemann's, e.g. in Käsemann 1972²b.

35. Of course, very much hangs here on who the 'we' are. I shall not address that question.

36. It is interesting to notice that at this point there is a certain overlap between the viewpoint of one or more of the modern approaches, which I have presented here as being only cognitively, as opposed to existentially, 'interested'—and the existentially interested viewpoint that I am elaborating.

Notes for Chapter 3

1. The tide is turning, however. Thus a book like Vollenweider 1989 on *eleutheria* in Paul 'and his *Umwelt*' does contain a substantial section (pp. 23–104) on the larger themes in Stoicism that underpin their notion of freedom. By contrast, the two (in themselves excellent) volumes by Klauck 1996 on 'the religious *Umwelt*' of early Christianity restrict themselves to comments on the individual philosophers considered most pertinent (Seneca and Epictetus), four very eclectic pages on 'the basic features of the system' and an only slightly more extensive treatment of three 'special themes': Stoic 'eschatology', the 'autonomy of conscience' and the freedom of the Stoic sage.

2. The impulse and basis here have been mainly Anglo-American. But gradually this new approach has spread to France, Germany, Scandinavia and elsewhere. Pioneers were Mates 1953 (on Stoic logic) and Sambursky 1959 (on Stoic physics). An early Scandinavian scholar to take up this challenge was Christensen (1962). For Stoic ethics in particular a pioneer who has continued to change the subject is A. A. Long (1967 onwards). An early German scholar to respond to this particular impulse was Forschner 1981. Since 1978 (see Schofield, Burnyeat, Barnes 1980) a series of international Symposia Hellenistica has cemented the new, philosophically more rigorous approach and its international appeal. For Stoic ethics in particular see the volume edited by Schofield and Striker 1986. Landmark studies within this field have been Inwood 1985 and Striker 1991. An excellent summary of the early results of this work was given in Long and Sedley 1987 (with key texts, incisive philosophical commentary, bibliography and more). But the search continues. See, e.g. Sihvola and Engberg-Pedersen 1998 on the analysis of passions in Stoic ethics.

3. For the influence of Stoicism in Latin literature and Christian Latin thought of late antiquity see in particular Colish 1985 (two volumes). For the post-Renaissance tradition see, e.g. Taylor 1989 or Schneewind 1998.

4. I use the Teubner edition (Leipzig: Teubner Verlag, 1915) by Th. Schiche (Cicero, *De finibus bonorum et malorum*). Translations are either by H. Rackham (Cicero XVII *De finibus bonorum et malorum*, LCL, Cambridge, Mass: Harvard University Press 1914 and later) with corrections or by myself.

5. Edition: H. S. Long, Oxford Classical Texts, 1964. The translation in the LCL (by R. D. Hicks, 1925) is very unsatisfactory.

6. 4 vols, Leipzig: Teubner Verlag, 1903–24.

7. I made this argument in Engberg-Pedersen 1990, 36–79, comparing the two basic accounts (in Diogenes Laertius and Cicero) of the Stoic theory of *oikeiōsis* (on which more below).

8. For a reliable textbook account of these various figures see Long 1974 (1986²).

9. For a more thorough discussion of Aristotle on *eudaimonia* see Engberg-Pedersen 1983, ch. 1. I have used the Oxford Classical Texts edition by I. Bywater (Oxford University Press, 1894). Translations are my own.

10. In addition to the difference with regard to this-worldliness, another one will immediately spring to mind in readers of Paul. Practical thought: is this not something 'done' by the deliberator 'him- or herself' in a manner that removes it radically from Paul, where everything is a gift from God? Is it not just another form of 'works righteousness'? Answer: Definitely not! It certainly is a 'gift of God' in Paul. But it equally certainly is something 'done' by Christ-believers 'themselves' (cf., most strikingly, Phil 2:12–13). The idea of an *opposition* here is a far later thought. Nor, on their side, did the philosophers conceive of practical thought as something engaged in by a person '*him- or herself*' in the later, radically heightened sense of something to be *contrasted* with what may come 'from the outside'. In fact, both the 'active *nous*' (in Aristotle, compare his *De Anima* 3.5) and *logos* (in Stoicism) were conceived as phenomena that distinctly transcend human individuals.

11. For this theme in relation to Aristotle see Engberg-Pedersen 1983, chs 2–4. See also Annas 1993 *passim* on the '*morality* of happiness'.

12. For more on this see Engberg-Pedersen 1983, ch. 8.

13. For the details of the Stoic takeover, cf. Engberg-Pedersen 1990, ch. 1.

14. For more detailed analysis see Engberg-Pedersen 1990, chs 3–4, from which I take over a few bits and pieces.

15. I employ 'loving' simply as a convenient stand-in for 'liking', 'feeling affection for', 'having a positive attitude towards', and so on.

16. It already crept into the title of an early paper on this theme: Kerferd 1972.

17. This is very clearly reflected in Aristotle's remark quoted above on the extension of 'self-sufficiency' to include parents, children, wife and so forth. This is another area where the Stoics radicalized the Aristotelian starting point so as to turn it into something quite new. For them an 'altruism' based in the ties of the individual person with others precisely belongs at the I-pole. It is therefore an attitude to be *overcome* and turned into an altogether different kind of altruism that has left the individual ties completely behind.

18. Note how carefully Cicero maintains the important logical distinction between the self and its 'constitution'.

19. The phrase *res agendae* may also be translated as 'acts to be done', but it is more likely that the gerundive has here the function of the non-perfect passive participle.

20. For a fascinating discussion of 'the view from above' in ancient philosophy, Goethe and others see Hadot 1995, 238–50. For an equally fascinating modern philosophical discussion see Nagel 1986.

21. Compare, e.g. Kerferd 1978.

22. See the passages collected in *SVF* III ch. V, par. 3.

23. For this idea see Seneca *Epistulae Morales* 42.1 and *SVF* 3.658 (Alexander of Aphrodisias).

24. Compare Aristotle's analysis in *Nicomachean Ethics* IV.iii.

25. I have analysed this in detail in Engberg-Pedersen 1990, ch. 8 (on 'Intention and Passion: Desire as Belief').

26. Note that this sentence explicitly parallels the two forms of *oikeiōsis*.

27. For what follows on *prokopē* and *kathēkonta* and *kathorthōmata*, I am relying on the full discussion in Engberg-Pedersen 1990, 126–40. For Chrysippus on *prokopē* compare *SVF* 3.510 and 539–43.

28. For texts on the two concepts see *SVF* 3.500–18. Also Long and Sedley 1987, 1.359–68.

29. Texts: *SVF* 3.377–490, Long and Sedley 1987, 1.410–23. Discussion: Engberg-Pedersen 1990, ch. 8. See also Sihvola and Engberg-Pedersen 1998, chs by Tad Brennan, John M. Cooper, Christopher Gill, Richard Sorabji, and Terence H. Irwin.

30. *SVF* 3.548, p. 147, l. 13.

31. *SVF* 3.112, p. 26, l. 41.

32. For the three 'good emotions', see *SVF* 3.431–42. These correspond, in the way to be explained, with the four basic types of passion: 'desire' (positive) and 'fear' (negative) with regard to the future and 'pleasure' (positive) and 'pain' (negative) with regard to the present. Compare, e.g. *SVF* 3.394.

33. For an account of Marcus Aurelius' handling of this theme, see Engberg-Pedersen 1998, 322–6.

34. The next few pages substantially repeat the relevant part of Engberg-Pedersen 1994b.

35. Compare, e.g. Bultmann 1910 on this *Umwertung der Werte* (Bultmann's expression): 27–30 for the Stoics and 80–5 for Paul.

36. Most recently by Erskine 1990, 18–27, and Schofield 1991, 3–56.

37. *On the Fortune of Alexander* 329B. For this tradition, compare Dawson 1992.

38. Christensen 1984, 45–54, esp. 51–2. Christensen speaks, rightly, of an anarcho-syndicalist *democracy* as the Stoic ideal model of society.

39. Compare Cicero *De Officiis* 1.128 and 148. E.g. 128 init.: 'But we should give no heed to the Cynics (or to some Stoics who are practically Cynics) who ...' (LCL translation by W. Miller, 1913). (There is no certainty that this comes from Panaetius but there is general agreement that the likelihood is great.)

40. Schofield 1991, ch. 2, argues for the recipe interpretation. He does so primarily by comparing Zeno with Plato, thus leaving out in effect the Cynic dimension in Zeno. This also explains why Schofield does not do justice to that element in Zeno's conception which made it possible to develop it in the way we find in Chrysippus (see below).

41. For Demetrius see Seneca *Epistulae Morales* 20.9 and 62.3. Epictetus: *Dissertations* 3.22. On these two texts see Billerbeck 1978 (Epictetus) and 1979 (Demetrius).

42. See in particular Goulet-Cazé 1990.

43. Text and translation: Lutz 1947.

44. On Epictetus see the excellent overview in Spanneut 1962.

Notes for Chapter 4

1. The overview over the various problems and the cautious suggestions as to their solution given in Kümmel 1980[20], 280–94 remain generally convincing. They pertain to the questions of (*a*) Paul's several aims in writing that together constitute the occasion for writing, (*b*) the time and location of writing, including the issue of (*c*) the various types of opponents that Paul refers to or warns against, and finally (*d*) the letter's integrity. What is particularly salutory is Kümmel's repeated claim that certain questions we would like to be able to answer cannot in fact be conclusively answered. By contrast, the in itself quite helpful overview over research on the letter between 1945 and 1985 in Schenk 1987 reveals a scholarly confidence in our ability to reach wholly specific answers to wholly specific questions that we should see as unwarranted.

2. These two immediate aims on Paul's part are rightly mentioned first by Kümmel (1980[20], 283). Nobody, it seems, seriously questions them. Ephesus: Kümmel (1980[20], 284–91) remains (in itself commendably) agnostic on the location of writing though claiming that of the three usual possibilities (Rome, Caesarea, Ephesus), Rome is the least probable. (O'Brien 1991, 25, by contrast, thinks that 'the balance of probability rather lies in favour of Rome'!) I have been convinced that Ephesus is the correct answer by the way this hypothesis has allowed Niels Hyldahl to hold together the three letters of Philippians, 1 and 2 Corinthians in terms of a single travel plan on Paul's part, which also involved Timothy, to Macedonia and Corinth. See Hyldahl 1986, 18–51.

3. Recent attempts to make the schism between Euodia and Syntyche come out as *the* occasion for writing seem overbold and one-sided. Compare, for instance,

the (rhetorically quite effectively buttressed) statement by Garland (1985, 172): 'It is my opinion that *all* of the preceding argument was intended to lead up to the pastoral confrontation of these two women' (my emphasis). Nils Dahl (1995, 14) claims that 'the disagreement between Euodia and Syntyche is the chief problem Paul faces and the main reason why his joy over the Philippians is less than complete', but rightly does not make this issue the very occasion for writing. Dahl argues persuasively that there is 'a remarkable correspondence between the initial, general exhortations in Phil 1:27–2:5 and the special appeal to Euodia and Syntyche in the context of 3:20–4:3' (1995, 9–10). But it is overdoing this point when he also quotes with approval a suggestion by G. B. Caird 'that when Paul wrote the more general exhortation, he already had this quarrel [between Euodia and Syntyche] in mind' (Dahl 1995, 9 quoting Caird 1976, 149–50). Black 1995 argues in a way that is very similar to, but arguably more cautious than, Dahl: 'the bulk of the letter is directed toward solving the issue of disunity arising from the exigence *reflected most clearly* in 4:2–3' (16, my emphasis). Black sees 'unity for the sake of the gospel' as 'a permeating, interlocking theme in Philippians' (1995, 44). This theme is reflected in the letter's 'comprehensive macrostructure', which has 'a specific communicative goal' that answers the letter's 'rhetorical exigence' (1995, 45). As will become clear, I wholly agree, but without feeling the need to press beyond the evidence for any absolutely specific letter situation. I remain sceptical, therefore, about the far more full-blown picture drawn by Peterlin 1995 on the basis of a reading that is closely similar to Black's both on the general theme of the letter and on the specific role of Euodia and Tyche. It is the very fact of its fullblown character, as witnessed, e.g. by Peterlin's 'reconstruction' of events before, up to and including the letter (219–27), that renders it too speculative. One wonders what the result would have been had Peterlin attempted to apply to his own reading the caution advocated, e.g. in J. M. G. Barclay 1987 on how to mirror-read a Pauline letter. He might have ended up with nothing more specific than the reading of Swift 1984 (from whom Peterlin both begins, 2, and ends, 228): that 'the theme' of Philippians is 'partnership in the gospel' (Swift 1984, 248). But that reading at least has the advantage of being on the right track.

4. Following on the well-known works by Schmithals 1957, Koester 1961–2, Gnilka 1965, Klijn 1964–5, Holladay 1969, Jewett 1970b and others, more recent discussions include Grayston 1985–6, Niebuhr 1992, Kähler 1994, Tellbe 1994 and Bateman 1998. O'Brien 1991, 26–35, gives a fine overview over the various suggestions that have been made. Seen from within the 'new perspective' on Paul, however, it is very difficult to decide whether, for instance, the opponents described in ch. 3 were Christ-believing Jews, non-Christ-believing Jews, or Christ-believing non-Jews with a Jewish orientation. That makes one wonder at the confidence with which scholars settle for one or the other possibility.

5. As argued, e.g. by Garland 1985, 166. This is another area where it is unwise to settle for any very definite answer. On the one hand, it does seem likely that

the Philippians had been faced with some people whom they would even themselves understand as opponents (1:28). On the other, it also seems likely that Paul mainly *uses* references to such opponents as a negative foil for his positive message (1:27–30, 3:2–21). The latter perspective is worked out most clearly in Stowers 1991, Schoon-Janssen 1991 (119–61) and (for 3:2–21) deSilva 1994.

6. See, for instance, Capper 1993, who builds on Sampley 1980. Compare, however, the cautious remarks on Capper in Berry 1996, 123–4, n. 70.

7. As suggested by Fitzgerald 1996b, 157–60.

8. For an exhaustive overview of the debate see Reed 1997, 124–52. Bormann 1995, 108–18 (himself a partitionist) provides a helpful overview over *Teilungs-hypothesen* in German scholarship since the second world war.

9. 3:1 has always been the stumbling-block for unitarians. For a careful analysis see now Reed 1996, which was apparently written later than the verbally almost identical (!) pp. 228–65 of Reed 1997. I shall build on Reed and make two further observations (regarding 'the same things' and 'security') that will strengthen his case for making 3:1 the hinge on which the whole letter turns.

10. Reed shows (1996, 65–72 and 73–6) that Paul's use of *oknēron* plays on an epistolary 'hesitation formula' that is well known from the papyri: 'I will not hesitate to …'. Reed helpfully distinguishes between a hesitation formula of *request* (my own example: 'Please, do not hesitate to …') and one of *notification* (Reed 1996, 66 and 70—my own example: 'I do not hesitate to …'). The latter 'reveal[s] the sender's desire to take some course of action on behalf of the recipient' (Reed 1996, 70), which is directly relevant to Paul. On *asphales*: Reed opts, rightly, for translating this term as 'trustworthy, unfailing' or 'not liable to fall, immovable, steadfast' (1996, 77–8). He rejects a suggestion originally made by V. P. Furnish (1963–4, 84–5) that the sense of 'certain, dependable' points in the direction of 'knowledge'. But Furnish may have been right. Thus the Stoics distinguished knowledge (*epistēmē*) from 'weak belief' by saying that *epistēmē* is a belief which, in addition to being both true and reflecting a so-called kataleptic *phantasia* (impression), is also 'steadfast (or sure, *asphalēs*), firm (or strong, *bebaia*) and unchangeable by reason'. See *SVF* 3.548 init. (= LS 41G) from Stobaeus *Eclogae* pp. 111, 18–112, 5W. Where Furnish goes wrong, I think, is in taking the 'same things' that Paul will repeat to refer to what Timothy and Epaphroditus will have transmitted *orally* (Furnish 1963–4, 86–7). This follows from his belief that 'there is no clear way in which the substance of chapter iii repeats anything in chapters i and ii' (Furnish 1963–4, 83). But there is, as we shall see.—Fridrichsen 1930, 300–1, quotes two passages from Dio Chrysostom (Or. 1.31.36 and Or. 2.17.2) that reveal the strongly *hortatory* connotations of *ouk oknēron* and *hymin asphales* respectively.

11. For further discussion of the various possibilities, including an external or 'cataphoric' (that is, forward-looking) reference, see Reed 1996, 79–80. He does not consider the possibility I shall suggest.

12. I suggested this possibility in a footnote in Engberg-Pedersen 1994b (258 n. 5). For other forward-looking proposals see nn. 13 and 18 below.

13. Compare Garland 1985, 157–9, specifically on the similarity of the Christ 'hymn' in 2:6–11 and 3:20–21. For other references on this, see Garland 1985, 158 n. 61. For wider repetitions, see Garland 1985, 159–62 and Rolland 1990. Kähler (1994, 55 n. 42) by contrast speaks of 'die durch 3,2ff. unerklärbare Bemerkung in 3,1 *ta auta graphein*', thus repeating a traditional point in German scholarship (still alive, for instance, in Schenk 1984, 243, and Müller 1993, 136). Fitzgerald 1996b, 154–5, shows that there is plenty to go on.

14. Porter and Reed 1998, 228–30, rightly caution against attaching too much significance to the repetition of single, common words—like *apōleia* here. But in the present instance there is repetition of a whole cluster of terms: the Philippians' living like citizens (1:27 *politeuesthai*, cf. 3:20 *politeuma*) in directedness towards Christ (1:27, 3:18) in such a way that they will themselves gain salvation (1:28 *sōtēria*, 3:20 Christ as *sōtēr*)—and their opponents will end with destruction (*apōleia*, 1:28, 3:19).

15. Black 1995, 41–2 gives a fine summary of the way in which 'the thrust of 3:1–4:9 is the same as that of 1:12–2:30'. Elsewhere he also speaks of 3:1 as 'a transitional element', namely 'to the warning against the Judaizers beginning in 3:2' (Black 1995, 40). But he does not combine his two observations: that 3:1 as a 'transitional element' introduces a *repetition* of the *whole* '*thrust*' of 1:12–2:30.

16. Commentators seem keen on exonerating Paul from voicing any criticism whatever of the Philippians. Compare, e.g. O'Brien 1991, 343–4: 'The apostle's words are tactful, courteous, and winning. He acknowledges ... a lack. ... Not a *hysterēma* occasioned by their doing less than they ought, but a lack *caused by their absence from him*' (my italics). This is more or less the standard interpretation. Until further proof has been given, I am convinced that Paul's reference here to 'your lack with respect to (your) contribution to me' should be read in the most straightforward way: that they had not yet paid what Paul had a right to expect from them. On the basis of Paul's usage elsewhere we may claim the following. (i) The lack (or want, *hysterēma*) may be construed in a number of ways. Thus, in 1 Cor 16:17 it probably refers to the lack of the *Corinthians' presence* together with Paul. In 2 Cor 8:14 it may refer to a *spiritual* lack or deficiency on the part of the Corinthians as compared with the Christ-believers in Jerusalem. In Col 1:24 the lack is one in 'Christ's afflictions'. (ii) In 2 Cor 9:12, however, and 11:9 the *context* makes it clear that Paul has a financial lack in mind, 9:12 by speaking among other things of a certain *leitourgia*. (iii) As Col 1:24 shows, Paul (or 'Paul') may define the particular area in which there is lack by adding the relevant substantives in the genitive. All of this points to the above reading of Phil 2:30. The suggestion of Dibelius 1937³, 85, that *anaplēroun to hysterēma tinos* means 'die Stelle eines Abwesenden vertreten' may be generally possible, but it will not fit the present text where Paul carefully defines

(*in tēs pros me leitourgias*) the respect in which the Philippians have been lacking.

17. Again, I remain convinced that *ēdē pote* ('at last') does indicate that Paul would have been justified in feeling some lack on the part of the Philippians. As Collange 1973, 130, saw (against 'most commentators'), that is precisely what causes him (i) to *take back* that slight element of criticism in *eph' hōi kai ephroneite, ēkaireisthe de* ('as you did think previously, but without having the proper opportunity'), and (ii) to hasten to add that he had *not* himself felt it as a material lack (*ouch hoti kath' hysterēsin legō*, 4:11). Here, as with 2:30, the challenge to scholars is to accept what, to me at least, appears as the initially quite straightforward meaning of the text and then to try to fit *that* into an overall interpretation of Paul's relationship with the Philippians. Contrast, e.g. O'Brien 1991, 517: 'At first sight Paul's language here seems to be chiding the Philippians gently for their delay in sending help to him ... But there is no intended reproach in these words'. (The suggestion in Baumert 1969 that parts of 4:10 should be differently translated is not relevant to this issue.)

18. One scholar has seen this with all clarity: Wick 1994, published in the same year as Engberg-Pedersen 1994b (cf. above n. 12), but seen much later by me. I am in complete agreement with Wick's basic analysis of the letter as consisting of two *parallel* sets of thematic blocks (Wick 1994, 40): 1:12–2:30 and 3:1 (or rather 3:2)–4:9 and also with some of his more detailed parallels, e.g. between his block 1 (= 1:12–26) and block 6 (= 3:1/2–16) and between block 5 (= 2:19–30) and block 10 (= 4:10–20). His further parallelisms—between block 2 (= 1:27–30) and block 7 (= 3:17–21), between block 3 (= 2:1–11) and block 8 (= 4:1–3) and between block 4 (= 2:12–18) and block 9 (= 4:4–9)—seem overspecific to me, as do his many lists of detailed supposed parallels. The problem is the usual one: an insight (in this case, a very important one) is driven to excess in the hope of being able to explain *everything*. Also, one should be cautious about putting too much emphasis on the notion of a 'parallelism' (or of seeing macrostructural 'chiasms' at work in the letter, cf. Porter and Reed 1998 in response to Luter and Lee 1995). Wick's grasp of the role of 3:1b in the letter is based on his realization of the 'comprehensive parallelism' of the letter body as a whole and on Paul's statement that he will write 'the same things' once more—in the plural (Wick 1994, 56–7). As Wick sees, the latter refers not only backward to the exhortation to rejoice or forward to the warning against the opponents, but to both things *and* everything that follows. It is true, Wick states, that not everything in what follows is a repetition of the first letter-half in a one-to-one sense, but also a supplementary addition and development. But in addition to much that is verbally repeated, the same basic themes are to be found everywhere (Wick 1994, 57). That is exactly right. This insight, as I go on to suggest, should strengthen decisively the recent trend towards unitarianism (for which see Jewett 1970a, Garland 1985, Alexander 1989, and of course Reed 1997). Wick agrees: Paul (himself) *shows* at a decisive place how he conceived the structure of this letter (Wick 1994, 57). For the view presented here of the basic structure of Philippians (two letter halves mirroring one another around the pivotal

3:1) see also the very brief (4 pages), but wholly convincing article by Rolland (1990).

19. Compare the previous note.

20. Thus 3:1 as a whole functions as a *Pauline bridge*. (For this concept compare Engberg-Pedersen 1995, 480.)

21. In particular, I would like to argue that Phil 1–2 shares two important features with 1 Thess 1–3. Both *recount* what has happened in the period after Paul left the two congregations and before he is now establishing contact with them again. And both are then followed by the term 'Well then' (*To loipon* in Phil 3:1, *Loipon* in 1 Thess 4:1). (For the meaning of that term see Cavallin 1941.)

22. Compare, for instance, Patte 1983 (for a general attempt and specifically pp. 164–89 for Philippians), Fowl 1990 (specifically for the Christ 'hymn' in Philippians, chs 3–4, pp. 49–101) and Hays 1983 (for the general idea and specifically for Gal 3:1–4:11).

23. It is generally recognized that Philippians is a 'letter of joy' (to quote Morrice 1984, 106), but I find no sustained attempt to integrate the notion of joy in a philosophical account of the form of life that Paul is depicting in the letter. See later in this chapter for some suggestions.

24. On the wholly concrete sense of this, see now Wansink 1996.

25. Compare for this Bloomquist 1993.

26. Nobody, it seems, has made much of this fact, probably because it only appears striking when one adopts a unitarian approach to the letter. Thus Walter 1977, who argues for the centrality of the theme of suffering, restricts this claim to hold for his 'main letter' B, namely 1:1–3:1—plus 4:[4]5–7.[8–9].[21–23]. By so doing he almost inadvertently confirms the fact.

27. Sampley 1980 first brought the motif of *koinōnia* into sharp relief. This has been taken up in different ways by others, e.g. Capper 1993, Witherington 1994 (who is sceptical of Sampley's emphasis on the pecuniary character of the partnership, see 119) and more extensively in Bormann 1995. I am in complete agreement with the potential fruitfulness of bringing out the framework of social conventions within which Paul's use of this motif should be seen. But it also has wider, 'ideological' connotations that I am intent on bringing out.

28. Paul has of course employed this term already in 1:12 to speak of the 'progress of the gospel'. This is a good example of his handling of terms that were originally and specifically Stoic: in a free way that is sometimes (as in 1:25), but not always (1:12), quite close to the original, technical sense in Stoicism. Here the connection between the two uses is at least close enough for it to be natural to see 1:12 and 1:25 as constituting an *inclusio*; compare Black 1995, 31 taken over from Garland 1985, 160.

29. For the meaning of *politeuma* see Lincoln 1981, 97–101, with discussion of older literature. Lincoln opts for 'state' or 'commonwealth' as translations with

'a dynamic constitutive force' that makes it stand for 'a realm which determines the quality of the lives of those who belong to it' (99). Unfortunately, he reads this very theologically to mean that the heavenly *politeuma* is 'determinative' of the Christian's existence in the sense of constituting the 'primary *binding* and *governing* relationship' (100, my emphases). (That reading is even more explicit in Böttger 1969, whose discussion remains valuable for its extensive quotation of the linguistic evidence.) But surely, the reason Paul has chosen *politeuma*—as *opposed*, e.g. to the term *basileia* with which Lincoln compares it (99)—is that he wanted to suggest that the Philippians were '*full* citizens' in the heavenly 'commonwealth'. On the whole, LSJ is better in spite of the fact that they placed our passage s.v. III: *citizen right*s, *citizenship* (a reading that Lincoln rightly rejects). From meaning II ('the concrete of *politeia*'—taken as 'civil polity, constitution of a state'—that is, the 'government' or 'form of government'), LSJ finally reaches home with meaning IV: [1] '*concrete, body of citizens ... sovereign body* ... 2. [a.] *corporate body of citizens*' (whether or not they are 'resident in a foreign city' like the Jews in Alexandria) and finally '*b*. generally, *corporate body, association*'.

30. The concept of a model has been fruitfully elaborated and applied to Philippians by Fowl 1990, 92–5 (Fowl speaks of an 'exemplar' following T. S. Kuhn) and Meeks 1991. The classical statement of its root in Hellenistic moral philosophy is Fiore 1986.

31. The motif of looking 'down' on the world and one's previous self 'from above' is probably Platonic in origin. It is employed to very good effect by Philo in his description of the contemplative life. As noted in ch. 3, Marcus Aurelius uses it repeatedly to express the relationship of the Stoic sage to the world and to non-wise others. See Marcus Aurelius 7.48, 9.30, 12.24.3 and discussion in Engberg-Pedersen 1998.

32. The concept of knowledge by acquaintance is derived from the philosophy of Bertrand Russell, where it is contrasted with knowledge 'by description'. To know something by acquaintance is for it to come before the mind without its being mediated by some description *that* the thing is thus and so. By contrast, knowledge by description is 'propositional'.

33. Compare, for instance, the Stoic account in Cicero *De Finibus* 3.34 of how a human being will arrive at the grasp of the 'absolute' character of perfect goodness and the perfect good: not by *comparison* with other things, but as something that is 'immediately', that is, from its own inherent properties, recognized and pronounced to be good.

34. Compare Russell's type of knowledge 'by description'.

35. This distinction will also account for 3:12–13 ('It is not that I have already grasped it or am already perfect'). For here too Paul is *directly* presenting himself as a model for the Philippians, that is, relating himself to *them*.

36. It is not, perhaps, so strange that nobody has apparently seen this since it requires that one has previously grasped the general parallelism of the two letter-

halves. But Black (1995), who almost grasps this (cf. above n. 15), to my mind misjudges the overall meaning of 3:1–4:9 when he states that this 'secondary development of the argument', namely for 'ecclesial unity', should be understood as consisting in a 'warning against pride in human achievement' (Black 1995, 43–4). That reeks of traditional theology, for which, as I see it, there is no justification in the text. (For instance, is 3:12–16 really a *warning against* perfection now', Black 1995, 44, my emphasis?) Wick (1994), who also grasps the general parallelism, thinks that Paul in 4:10–20 moves to a completely unqualified praise of the Philippians (Wick 1994, 129–34). That misses the way Paul *also* sets himself above the Philippians in that passage when he develops his own self-sufficiency; compare below.

37. See in particular Berry 1996, Fitzgerald 1996b and Malherbe 1996.

38. Again, Capper 1993, Witherington 1994 (118–21, who discusses the relationship between Paul and the Philippians under the rubric: 'Partners, Friends, or Family?') and the scholars mentioned in the previous note.

39. Peterman 1991 argues that Paul's famous 'thankless thanks' in 4:10–20 is in fact rather less thankless than it has normally been taken. On the contrary, it fits well into an ancient established pattern of communication among friends.

40. This translation is adapted from Malherbe (1996, 131). Compare also Gnilka 1968, 173.

41. Compare n. 17 above.

42. Compare the quotations from Bultmann 1962 in Malherbe 1996, 125–6.

43. See Malherbe 1996.

44. See *Nicomachean Ethics* I.vii.6–8, 1097b6–21.

45. Against Malherbe 1996, 138, who *contrasts* 'Stoic introspection' with a Paul who 'is essentially concerned with personal relationships rather than introspection'. What bothers me here is the 'rather than'. Of course, if one glosses the Pauline and Stoic talk of mental attitudes (and *autarkeia* is that kind of thing) as such a modern, or at least post-Augustinian, thing as 'introspection', Malherbe's contrast would be well taken. But that precisely does not fit—*either* the Stoics *or* Paul.

46. Malherbe 1996, 138. Compare also Berry 1996, 116. Malherbe and Berry are right to develop how in the ancient philosophical thought about friendship there was a tension between the claim to self-sufficiency on the part of the morally good man and his other-regardingness. This tension was overcome by postulating that the morally good man, who was self-sufficient in relation to external goods, would also ultimately transcend the particular being that he himself was—and would therefore in the final analysis be friends with *all* those who had done the same. *That* is the friendship of the wise that the Stoics, in particular, elaborated. In the present context, however, the point is that there is a tension here *to be overcome*. It is precisely this *tension* that Paul is playing on in the present text, not its eventual solution (compare *plēn*).

47. Depending on whether one accepts the argument of Peterman 1991 referred to above.

Notes for Chapter 5

1. This is common knowledge. Compare, e.g. O'Brien 1991, 203, with references. Dahl too speaks (1995, 11) of the verse as effecting a 'gradual transition' from the exhortation of 2:1–4 to the 'hymn'. As for the question of how to construe the syntax of the verse, sanity advises two positions: (1) one cannot *decide* a reading of the function of the 'hymn' as a whole ('soteriological' or 'kerygmatic'—with Käsemann 1950—or rather 'paradigmatic') on the basis of how one construes the syntax of 2:5; (2) there is no real issue concerning the latter, more special question. Considering the amount of ink that has been spent on 'solving' the syntax question, scholars will balk at the second point. But Dahl is right: 'The general meaning would have been sufficiently clear to the first readers, who hardly reflected on the syntax' (Dahl 1995, 11 n. 8). Black (1985, 304, 307), is particularly impressive on the connection between 2:1–4 and 2:6–11. Käsemann's attack on the traditional 'paradigmatic' or 'parenetic' reading was carefully discussed and rejected by Deichgräber 1967, 189–96, and Fowl 1990, 79–83.

2. Here are two different types of translation of this verse: (1) 'One should look out not only for one's own interests but for what is good for the others' (Dahl 1995, 10; similarly O'Brien 1991, 163). (2) '... not looking out for your own interests, but for the interests of others' (Black 1995, 36). The question of the exact rendering really matters here since the two translations obviously differ enormously in meaning. Should one—to some extent—look out for one's own interests or should one not? The question turns on the meaning of the *kai* after *alla*. Without wishing to argue the case fully here, I would claim that the *kai* means, not 'also', but 'precisely'. Thus the meaning will be 'not ... but precisely or rather', instead of 'not (only) ... but also'. Two observations point in this direction. First, that is an idiomatic meaning of the Greek *kai* in certain contexts. (Discussing the phrase *ou monon ... alla kai*, Denniston (1954², 3), quotes two passages—Sophocles, *Ajax* 1313 and Plato, *Phaedrus* 233B6-C1—where, as he thinks, '*kai* is retained and *monon* omitted'. He also suggests that in Lysias 6.13, where *monon* is also missing, '*kai*, if sound, perhaps means "actually"'. The truth is that in neither of these passages is the sense 'not *only* ..., but *also*', but rather 'not (so much) *this* ... , but rather precisely *this*'.) Second, it appears to suit 2:3 far better. (According to O'Brien 1991, 185 n. 148, Karl Barth apparently took the *kai* to emphasize what follows, wherefore he felt that it should be left untranslated. Barth's intuition was right. But the *kai* should in fact be translated as 'precisely'.)

3. The classic treatments of ancient and Senecan psychagogy are Rabbow 1954 and Hadot 1969, respectively. For Seneca see also Maurach 1996², 157–208.

4. Others who see Philippians as a hortatory letter (of friendship) are Stowers 1991, L. M. White 1990 (206: 'a friendly hortatory letter') and Fitzgerald 1996b, 147. Aune 1987 (210–11) called Philippians a 'letter of gratitude and paraenesis'. All are indebted to A. J. Malherbe's identification of 1 Thessalonians as a parenetic letter. See especially Malherbe 1983 and 1987. For the point that Pauline parenesis is not just to be identified with a specific parenetic section of his letters see also Stowers 1986, 23. And for specimens of parenetic letters (with discussion) see Stowers 1986, 94–106. In my discussion of Philippians I shall stick to the term 'paraklesis' as against 'parenesis'. The reason is twofold. First, Paul never himself uses a form of words derived from the Greek *parainein*, whereas he is of course quite fond of *parakaleisthai* with derivates. Second, Philippians itself employs the term *paraklēsis*, and in a very marked position (2:1).

5. For *parakalō* + *oun* see Rom 12:1 and 1 Cor 4:16 (also Eph 4:1). Nauck 1958 at least has the merit of having identified this *oun* as a 'parenetic *oun*' ('*oun*-paräneticum'). But his use of his observation (with regard to the question of where 'the third, parenetic main part' of Galatians begins—Nauck favours 5:1) is very superficial. Note in addition that the absolutely correct observation (by Malherbe and Stowers, see the previous note) that Paul's letters may be parenetic *all through* does not of course go against saying that there are certain sections in the letters in which the parenetic character is, as it were, intensified— like Rom 12:1ff.

6. The commentators (e.g. Lohmeyer 1930, 163–5, Gnilka 1968, 220) generally appreciate the very strong tone of this verse. Lohmeyer is also good at bringing out how the verse recalls 1:27–30, e.g. in the use of the central verb *stēkein*, 'stand fast'. In the light of our remarks about the structure of the letter (with 4:1 *repeating* 1:27–30 and 4:2–9 *repeating* 2:1 ff), that only serves to underscore the importance of 4:1. For 1:27 ff is precisely the place where Paul first turns directly to his basic, parenetic task. All in all, I find it difficult when reading Phil 4:1 not to be reminded of a similar verse in the letter to the Galatians that seems to summarize Paul's whole message in terms of steadfastness: Gal 5:1. (As we shall see in a moment, that does not go against claiming Phil 2:1 ff and 4:2 ff to have a similarly central role in the letter.)

7. Bjerkelund 1967 is generally referred to as a classic on the *parakalō* sentences in Paul. Bjerkelund's results need to be revised, however. Let me give two examples. First, as is well known, Bjerkelund's basic argument is that 'the first *parakalō* sentence in a letter contains the essential message (*Anliegen*) of the apostle' (189). Bjerkelund's own reading of Philippians does not, however, fit with this. He notices 'the only *parakalō* sentence' in the letter (4:2), but explains this in a *different* way: it occurs because Paul wishes to speak in a personal manner since his theme is enmities within the community (175–6). Thus Bjerkelund does not see that Phil 4:2 *supports* rather than deviates from his own general principle. As regards 2:1, Bjerkelund rejects seeing the use of *paraklēsis* as functionally equivalent with a *parakalō* sentence. (Instead he sticks to

translating *paraklōsis* as 'consolation' (*Trost*).) His reason: it does not fit 'our understanding of the *parakalō* sentences' (175). But it precisely does! Second, Bjerkelund does not wish to understand the *parakalō* sentences 'parenetically' ('*parakletisch*'), but rather as belonging to the genre of the *letter* ('*brieflich*', '*briefmässig*', as *opposed* to the 'genre' of parenesis, 189). And that holds too 'even when the *parakalō* sentences in fact introduce a parenetic section, like in Romans [12:1] and 1 Thessalonians [4:1]' (189). Bjerkelund's intention here is a good one—to situate the *parakalō* sentences squarely within the letter genre. But his *contrast* with a 'genre of parenesis' is, as we now know, false. It is far better to say that the (normal) letter function of the *parakalō* sentences that Bjerkelund has diagnosed *fits* with their parenetic role. For instance, the first *parakalō* sentence in 1 Corinthians (1:10) precisely identifies that letter as a whole as being a parenetic one (as, e.g. Mitchell 1991 has convincingly shown). Similarly, the overall parenetic character of Philippians comes out with all clarity by Paul's use of *paraklēsis* in 2:1 and *parakalō* in 4:2. (Black 1985, 305, is good on 2:1–4 as 'the primary hortatory passage and the high point of chap. 2'.)

8. Paul's reference to the *diapheronta* is a good example of his creative, half technical and half untechnical use of a Stoic idea. On the Stoic view some things are *a-diaphora*. That presumably implies that other things are those that matter and hence are *diapheronta*. The Stoics, however, did not use that term, even though they might very well have done so. Paul, by contrast, did.

9. Commentators regularly take *to auto phronēte* in the first half of 2:2 and *to hen phronountes* at the end of the verse to refer more or less to the same thing. Some therefore also speak of the two expressions as being 'seemingly redundant' (e.g. L. M. White 1990, 208). However, it seems to me that there may be a very good point in seeing Paul move *from* speaking of their 'having the same mind', namely, towards him and as he himself has towards them, *to* speaking of their 'having one mind', namely, among themselves. As I read the text, the shift occurs in *sympsychoi* ('of one soul', namely, among themselves—contrast the use of *isopsychos* in 2:20, which has precisely to do with Timothy's attitude to *Paul*).

10. The point has been repeatedly made, e.g. to very good effect by Meeks 1991.

11. 1 Cor 1–2 are of course relevant here.

12. The basic work for this is now Glad 1995.

13. I am somewhat reassured, however, by a similar boldness in L. M. White 1990. White both claims that the 'hymn' 'has been redacted by Paul into the parenetic function of the larger section 2:1–18' (208) and that it depicts Christ as a 'moral paradigm' of 'the supreme virtue of friendship' (213). Compare also Hawthorne 1987, 62: 'Does not context determine content? Could not the particular problems at Philippi addressed by this hymn have dictated its own special theme(s)?'

14. Rather: it *was* generally recognized after Ernst Lohmeyer's trend-setting analysis (1928). In his classic discussion, however, R. P. Martin, who ended up

accepting Lohmeyer's view, nevertheless stated that whereas German and French commentators had generally been persuaded by Lohmeyer, 'British scholars are inclined to dismiss the issue ... and then pass on as though the verses were authentically Paul's' (Martin 1967, 61). Recently, scholars (including German ones) have become even more sceptical, both regarding its pre-Pauline status and its character as a 'hymn'. See, for instance, Furness 1958–9, Hooker 1975 (e.g. 156: 'whatever its origins ...', 157: '[possibly] better described as a piece of rhythmic prose'), Caird 1976 (100–4), Kümmel 1980 (294), Black 1988 (a careful discussion), Fee 1992, Wick 1994 (178–9) and Brucker 1997 (310–15). The conclusion to O'Brien's discussion of the issue, 1991, 198–202, is revealing: 'It is possible that the hymn was composed independently of and prior to the writing of Philippians ... But Wright concludes his article [1986, 352] by stating that if someone were to argue that "the 'hymn' was originally written by Paul himself precisely in order to give christological and above all theological under-pinning to the rest of Philippians, ... I for one should find it hard to produce convincing counter-arguments".' For a methodologically sophisticated argu-ment for setting aside the question of the origin of the 'hymn' (in favour of analysing its function within the letter) see Fowl 1990, 31–45. My own claim, however, is the stronger one that the 'hymn' was in fact written by Paul himself for the purposes stated.

15. Compare the previous note. This is obviously not the place for an extended discussion. Let it just be noted that we are here once more confronted with the following basic methodological question. Should we feel sufficiently confident about a historical reconstruction of layers behind the text to let that recon-struction govern our interpretation of it? Or should our primary interpretive focus be the text as we have it? To me, at least, the fact that the kind of self-confidence that lies behind the Lohmeyer thesis has also led scholars to find 'hymns' behind 3:20–21 (see Becker 1971, with the discussion in Reumann 1984) and even 2:1–4 (see Black 1985) constitutes something of a *reductio ad absurdum* of that whole approach.

16. This theme is pervasive, in several forms, in recent analyses of early Christian christologies. Again, this is not the place to enter on a detailed discussion. It is highly noteworthy, however, that Paul himself explicitly compares the Christ event with the 'noble death': in Rom 5:7, where Christ's death comes out as an almost super-noble one (because it occurred, not on behalf of one who is just or good, but for the *un*godly).

17. See *Nicomachean Ethics* IX.viii.8, 1169a18–26.

18. Gnilka (1968, 198) notes that commentators have filled in the 'it' that Paul has not yet grasped in widely different ways: as the resurrection (Lütgert), knowledge of Christ (Michaelis), Christ himself (Dibelius), the heavenly prize (Bonnard, Beare, Delling). Gnilka's own solution consists in claiming that Paul may consciously have left out mentioning what he has in mind since that is not his immediate concern here. But surely the reason for all other solutions than

Lütgert's is the very difficulty of making sense of what would otherwise be the quite straightforward construction of the sentence. That just makes my point. O'Brien (1991, 421–2) takes the implied object to be 'Paul's overwhelming goal or ambition, expressed in a number of ways in vv. 8–11 as "gaining Christ", "being perfectly found in him", and "knowing him"'. Well and good, but when will that happen? At the resurrection!

19. The implied understanding of righteousness will make some scholars balk: that righteousness stands for a state of mind on the part of Christ-believers *and* for God's recognition of this on the day of Christ. Some of the unease may be dispelled by the immediately following remarks.

20. Compare, e.g. Bornkamm 1970[3] (1946), who starts out from 'our *ethical*' and 'our *religious* qualms concerning the idea of a reward' (69–70).

21. Thus the naive means–end picture should be rejected, not because it is ethically (or theologically) unattractive, but because it does not fit Paul's actual ways of speaking.

22. To be quite explicit, the reference to 'my own righteousness' has nothing to do with an idea of righteousness gained by one's own 'achievement'.

23. Compare the helpful overview of recent scholarship on this particular topic in Reumann 1996, 95–100.

24. Most of the essays in Fitzgerald (ed.) 1996a bear witness to the importance of friendship as constituting the best framework for addressing pupils in a way that will not put them off, but will rather make them wish for themselves to move in the direction sketched for them by their friendly teacher.

25. I have discussed the tension in Engberg-Pedersen 1994b. The issue obviously relates to the question whether some kind of power struggle was going on between Paul and the Philippians (or a group among them). It is difficult to get rid of this feeling (cf. also Ebner 1991, 358–64, and Peterlin 1995, *passim*), but I have already indicated my scepticism as to the possibility of ever reaching an absolutely clear answer to this question that will also generate some degree of consensus. Reumann (1996, 94) thinks that the possible fact of a power struggle would go against a friendship reading of the letter. White (1990, 214–15)—to my mind rightly—does not.

26. In their different ways, Wayne Meeks and Abraham Malherbe have made this notion the governing one for their analyses of the Pauline letters. It underlies Meeks 1983 and is brought to prominence in Meeks 1986b (especially chapter 5, 124–60) and Meeks 1993 (*passim*). In Malherbe's work the most explicit formulation is Malherbe 1987.

Notes for Chapter 6

1. One of the best general accounts is chs 2 ('The Galatians and the Demands of "the Agitators"') and 3 ('Paul's Response in the Main Body of the Letter') in

J. M. G. Barclay 1988, 36–105. See also J. M. G. Barclay 1987 for a careful methodological discussion of how to mirror-read a polemical letter like Galatians. Following E. P. Sanders, Barclay at a certain point distinguishes between views of Paul's opponents as 'certain or virtually certain', 'highly probable', 'probable', 'possible', 'conceivable' and 'incredible' (88–9). It is delightful—and wholly convincing—to see him include under the 'incredible' views of Paul's opponents this list: '1. They were Gnostics or gnosticizing to an appreciable degree. 2. They were libertines or played on the Galatians' "Hellenistic libertine aspirations". 3. They were syncretists with cosmic or mystical notions about circumcision, the law or keeping festivals. 4. They were directly commissioned by the Jerusalem apostles. 5. Paul was fighting against two distinct groups.' The most important discussion since Barclay is that of Martyn 1997a (Comment §6, 117–26, and Comment §46, 457–66) partly based on Martyn 1985, which was known to Barclay.

2. Following on Betz' innovative rhetorical approach as originally stated in Betz 1975 and spelled out in his commentary (1979), there have been a number of attempts to elucidate the structure of the letter along the same lines, e.g. Hester 1984 (for 1:11–2:14), Kennedy 1984, Hall 1987, Vouga 1988, Morland 1996. It is not clear, however, that just invoking the ancient rhetorical categories is able to *settle* any contested issue. For that, a more traditional, 'New Criticism' type of reading is in the last resort required. (Compare Porter 1993 for a broader questioning of the applicability of the three ancient types of speech to epistolary writings.) The same holds for other, more formal approaches that are in vogue at present, e.g. a reading informed by discourse analysis. Thus one should become sceptical when an (otherwise well-conducted) investigation like that in Holmstrand 1997 ends up (210–13) with the following structure of Galatians: 1:6–10, 1:11–2:21, 3:1–4:11 (no problem so far), 4:12–5:10, 5:11–6:13, 6:14–16 and 6:17. In spite of this, as regards the overall character and purpose of the letter, the discussion after Betz has at least made clear that if a choice need be made, Galatians belongs more to 'deliberative' than to 'forensic' rhetoric (thus Kennedy 1984, 144–52, Hall 1987, Vouga 1988). Paul is not so much defending himself as aiming to persuade the Galatians to refrain from a certain behaviour and to adopt a different one.

3. Martyn (1997a, 195–6 and 409–10) sees the close connection between 3:1–5 and 4:8–11 and 12–20. I am not persuaded, however, that there is an ABA¹B¹ relationship (A: 3:1–5, B: 3:6–4:7, A¹: 4:8–20, *B¹*: 4:21–5:1)—for this reason: it does not seem to make sufficient room for the extent to which 4:21–5:1 represents a new step in Paul's argument. ABA¹ is fine by letting 3:1–4:20 constitute a coherent, 'finished' section—that is one structural result of an *inclusio* like A–A¹. By contrast, Martyn's suggestion does not seem to allow for the forward-looking 'breath' that Paul takes at 4:21. Merk's carefully annotated discussion of where the 'parenetic section' of the letter begins (4:12? 4:21? 5:1? 5:2? 5:7? or 5:13?) is also relevant to the understanding of 4:21–5:1 (1969, esp. 92–8).

4. I shall take it as settled that the 'parenetic' section proper in Galatians—defined as a section that contains a high degree of 'parenetic' material of the type identified by Dibelius—begins at 5:13. Compare Merk 1969, J. M. G. Barclay 1988, 9–26, Dunn 1993a, 261, Martyn 1997a, 468 (against Betz 1979, who begins at 5:1 and is followed, e.g. by Harnisch 1987, 285 n. 20). A number of recent scholars divide 5:13–6:10 as follows: 5:13–24 + 5:25–6:10. See Schlier (1965⁴, 268–9), Betz (1979, 291–3), Barclay (1988, 155), Dunn (1993a, 286, 316) and Martyn (1997a, 541–2). My main reason for accepting the traditional division (5:13–26 + 6:1–10) will become clear in the next chapter when I analyse the tight argument contained in 5:16–25. Here we may note in addition that Paul's specific exhortation in 5:26 and 5:15 of the Galatians as a group to overcome internal strife constitutes a sort of *inclusio* of that argument (cf. the marked use of *allēlous* —'one another'—in both verses). Also, it is not clear that 5:25–6:10 consists merely of a string of more or less un-coordinated *sententiae* (Betz) or maxims (Barclay). If 5:25–26 belong with what precedes, it seems obvious that 6:1–5 go closely together, as do 6:7–10. Thus the only 'un-coordinated' verse will be 6:6. (Compare for this Lambrecht 1997–8.)

5. For an excellent survey of the various positions up until his own attempt to move forward, see J. M. G. Barclay 1988, 9–23. Barclay rightly distinguishes (9–16 and 16–23) between views that have seen 5:13–6:10 as a section 'wholly or largely unrelated' to the rest of the letter and views that have seen the passage as well 'integrated within the whole letter'. To the first group belong the classic views of Dibelius 1984⁶ (15–16: the genre of parenesis consists of 'sayings and groups of sayings very diverse in content, lacking any particular order, and containing no emphasis upon a special thought of pressing importance for a particular situation'), Lütgert 1919 (Paul is exhorting against a 'second front' of 'spirituals') and a string of later followers. To the latter belong those of Schmithals 1956 and 1983 (Paul is exhorting against libertinistic tendencies among the same group of opponents as in the rest of the letter, namely Jewish-Christian gnostics who preached circumcision but for the rest were living in a libertine rather than legalistic fashion), Jewett 1970–1 (the opponents are the same all through, namely, Hellenistic pneumatic libertinists) and Betz 1974 and 1979 (Paul was concerned to suggest a solution to the Galatians' moral confusion). As will be seen, there has been a clear movement in scholarship from 'disintegration' to 'integration'. For Barclay's and other more recent solutions see the next note.

6. Barclay's own argument is that '*the main body of the letter both points towards and renders necessary the ethical instruction at the end*' (J. M. G. Barclay 1988, 96, his italics). Throughout the letter Paul is concerned about 'Christian identity' and 'Christian behaviour': 'Paul's redefinition of Christian identity inevitably includes a concern for the practical aspects of Christian behaviour' (94 and *passim*). That is the point of the idea of 'obeying the truth' in Barclay's title: 'the "truth" that Paul expounds in the course of Gal 2–4 is ... meant to be "obeyed" and to determine the pattern of their "walk"' (94). However, the 'broad

descriptions of the Christian life as "living by faith" (2.19–20), continuing in the Spirit (3.1–5) and making faith work through love (5.1–6) ... do not yet meet the more practical requirements of the Galatians. ... Paul's argument would have been seriously deficient without some attempt to define how to continue in the Spirit or how to make faith work through love' (95). 'These verses [5:13 ff] are not an independent or dispassionate account of Christian ethics tacked on to the end of an argumentative letter, but a continuation and completion of the argument' (143). Elsewhere, Barclay speaks of Paul's concern to 'draw out the implications of justification by faith' (217, also 218) in an argument which 'complements and concludes' the earlier chapters (217).

As will gradually become clear, the solution I shall propose may sound very much like Barclay's. Like him I shall speak of identity (though in the sharpened form of self-identification) and of behaviour (though rather of practice in the sense of practising what one knows and wishes). And I completely agree that 'Paul's argument would have been seriously deficient without' 5:13–6:10. Still, there are important differences, points where I claim to be moving distinctly further, though in the same direction in which Barclay has already gone. Two are particularly important. First, in spite of the whole direction of his argument, Barclay continues to distinguish between 'identity' and 'behaviour' as two things that might, at least logically, be kept apart. One thing is a Christ-believing person's 'identity', another is his or her 'behaviour'. I completely reject this notional distinction. The whole point of Paul's argument, as we shall see with the help of the I→X→S-model, is that there is no new Christ-believing 'identity' (*as it were* I→X) which is not also a matter of 'behaviour' (or actual, social *practice*): the movement →S *spells out* the actual *content* of I→X. Thus I would never speak, with Barclay, of Gal 2–4 as 'the main body of the letter' and 5–6 as 'complementing and concluding' those earlier chapters. In point of fact, I consider that Barclay had not at the time freed himself completely from the traditional way of seeing the supposed 'main body' as being 'theological', with 5:13 ff fulfilling a more 'practical' and 'ethical' role. Second, I wholly reject the talk of 'obedience'. The movement →S does not constitute an 'obligation' for Christ-believers, something they *should* or *must* do. Rather, it expresses what they themselves both wish and do.

Others have moved further than Barclay. Thus Schoon-Janssen speaks, tantalizingly briefly (1989, 112), of Gal 5–6 as the *Hauptziel* of the letter. A more sustained, recent attempt along the same lines is Matera 1988. Matera attacks head-on the distinction between chs 1–4 as being 'theological' and chs 5–6 as being 'primarily ethical and exhortative' (79), claiming—rightly—that even though scholars like Barrett 1985 and Furnish 1968 have seen that it is 'difficult to separate paraenesis from doctrine' they have nevertheless gone on as if there were two separable themes here (89 n. 6). Against this Matera argues that chs 5–6 'are not only integral to Paul's argument, but are its culmination' (82). 'They are the climax of Paul's deliberative argument aimed at persuading the Galatians not to be circumcised' (80). How? Matera divides the two chapters as follows: '5.1–12 [gives] reasons for not accepting circumcision, 5.13–6.10 [contains] paraenetic material, 6.11–17 [again gives] reasons for not accepting circumcision' (83). And the point of the 'paraenetic material' is to *support* Paul's argument against circumcision by showing that 'those who accept it cannot be led by the Spirit' (80). As will become clear in a moment, we should basically agree with Matera's structural analysis. But 5:13 ff does not only provide 'support' for Paul's negative case against circumcision. As we shall see in the next chapter, it has a far more positive purpose of its own. (It is curious that Matera's later commentary—Matera 1992—makes far less of the insight he had formulated in 1988. Was he caught by the commentary genre?)

Finally, Suhl 1987 connects 5:13 ff, rightly as we shall see in the next chapter, with 2:15–21, arguing that the later passage brings the final proof that the lawfree gospel does not lead to sinning (3119–27). But Suhl too remains wedded to the old *contrast* between 'theological argumentation' and 'parenesis' when he urges that 5:13 ff is *not* parenesis *since* it has that other function in Paul's line of thought (e.g. 3119, 3122). That precisely does *not* follow.

7. Compare, e.g. R. N. Longenecker 1990, 199 who quotes Burton 1921, 251 for seeing the section as a 'supplementary argument' that occurred to Paul 'apparently as an afterthought' and refers to others (e.g. Oepke 1973[3], 147 and Mussner 1977[3]) for seeing it as 'a displaced portion of Paul's argument'. (In fact, Mussner thought that the new section 'occurred' to Paul because of the immediately preceding *aporoumai*, 'I am at a loss'—but also that it brings in the new idea of 'freedom' in Paul's line of thought, 316–17. The latter—correct—point was then taken up by Rohde 1989, 192.) Barrett (1976) rehearses some of the same perplexity among commentators. His solution was that Paul was forced to discuss the Hagar/Sarah story because his opponents had used it against him. Bouwman 1987 does not discuss the structural issue. Betz (1979, 238) saw the section as the 'sixth argument' in the *probatio* section (3:1–4:31), and in fact the most effective one (Betz 1979, 239–40). That has much to recommend it, particularly when one connects it with 5:1. This solution (or even Martyn's ABA[1]B[1] pattern, see above n. 3) seems far better than Longenecker's suggestion that the section is part of Paul's 'appeals and exhortations' (Longenecker 1990, 199) in what Longenecker sees as a major 'request section' in the letter: 4:12–6:10. We have two opposed views here: either to take 4:21–31 to go with the whole section that begins in 3:1 or to take it rather with what comes after the section (and as being introduced by 4:12–20). Solution? 4:21–31 is *a Pauline bridge*. It *continues* the line of thought from 3:1. But that line had been concluded by 4:20 (with 4:12–20 taking up 3:1–5). Thus 4:21–31 *also* points *forward*, as we shall see. (Structurally, the suggestion in Martyn 1990—which takes its departure from the analysis in Gaventa 1990 of Paul's reference in 4:19 to his birth-pangs— that 4:21 ff coheres intimately with 4:19–20 constitutes a genuinely new insight. For the new, overall reading of 4:21–31 that Martyn develops on that basis, see the next note.)

8. Compare J. M. G. Barclay (1988, 91), who speaks of 'a "tour de force", accompanied by strange and even arbitrary exegesis'. Walter (1986, 354), delightfully speaks of 'an extraordinarily discriminatory argumentation'. The counter-argument in Martyn 1990 is both important and persuasive: that Paul is contrasting, not Christianity and Judaism, but his own law-free mission with his prime target in the letter—that of a law-observant (and Christ-believing) mission to gentiles. Still, for the specific purposes of this particular letter Paul is out in 4:21–31 to malign *both* his Christ-believing law-observant opponents *and* non-Christ-believing (but law-observing) Judaism, whom he wishes to lump together. Thus Martyn's genuine insight has led him to distinguish too sharply between Paul's opponents and non-Christ-believing Jews more generally. Fortunately, the letter itself *also* shows that such maligning is very far from representing Paul's *full* view of the relationship between Christ faith and Judaism.

9. Let me just repeat my sense that seeing 4:21–31 as a Pauline bridge in this particular way at last allows us fully to understand the placing of that section. It does belong with 3:6–4:7 in terms of literary motif (the Abraham story) and specific idea (slavery and freedom) and also in terms of its argumentative character (if one likes, as part of Betz' *probatio* section). But it *also* belongs with what follows: 5:1 in particular—leading *up* to it (see in a moment)—but also 5:13 ff. It is, precisely, a Pauline bridge. (I shall continue to emphasize this notion until scholars begin to take it up.)

10. If asked for the verse that captures the whole essence of Paul's message to the Galatians, I would refer to 5:1. At the literary level, 5:1 constitutes a very pointed formulation of the whole brunt of Paul's argument so far, stated in that new and rhetorically highly effective vocabulary of freedom which Paul has created for himself in 4:21–31, and placed exactly before Paul begins on a formal summary of his previous argument (5:2–12, see below). But Dunn (1993a, 261) is right in saying that Paul apparently 'wanted the verse to stand on its own, not simply [to] serve as a conclusion' to the previous exposition. In terms of thought content, moreover, the verse also formulates the idea that Paul will then elaborate in 5:13 ff: what Christ-believing freedom concretely looks like. But this is quite different from saying that 'the parenetic section' *begins* with 5:1. Two of Martyn's arguments against this suggestion seem to me decisive: that 'the sharp expression "Look here! I, Paul, say to you" (5:2) signals a new turn in the argument' and that 'there are no imperative and hortatory verbs in 5:2–12' (Martyn 1997a, 468). Strangely, Martyn apparently does not see that 5:2 ff parallels 6:11 ff and so anticipates the formal conclusion of the letter. (More on this below.) S. K. Williams (1997, 132) got it just right on 5:1: 'Although 5:1 is connected thematically with what precedes and follows and indeed functions as a bridge passage between the allegory and the parenetic material of chapters 5 and 6, syntactically this verse stands in grand isolation. No particle or conjunction binds it to what precedes, and no conjunction or particle in 5:2 connects verse 1 to what follows.'

11. Compare the various suggestions mentioned above in n. 5.

12. See the next chapter for the exact way in which Paul argues this. Matera (1988) takes 5:13 ff to show that those who accept circumcision 'cannot be led by the Spirit' (80). He glosses this to mean that 'one *can* live an honorable [?] moral life apart from circumcision and the Law' (88, my emphasis). I take Paul to make the stronger claim that *only* by being led by the spirit can one live the kind of life that all were concerned about: one free of sin that actually fulfils the law by *doing* it. (More on this in the next chapter.)

13. In order to pinpoint the 'basis of obligation in Paul's Christology and ethics' Styler (1973) distinguished between 'four main points or stages ... in Paul's Christian assurance: (A) the act of God in Christ; (B) the initial response or conversion of the believer, marked by baptism; (C) the continuing Christian life, with its duties and the expectation of growth in holiness, love and knowledge; (D) the final judgement and salvation' (176). In the rest of this very short paper (twelve tautly written pages), Styler argued, among other things, for these claims: 'it is of the very essence of Paul's theology that the four stages adhere closely' (177); 'any attempt to make each of the four divisions self-supporting is doomed to failure' (177); 'beneath a liberty of language [in Paul] lies a firm substructure of belief' (177); (of Gal 2:19–20:) 'this is not the logical construction of a tidy scheme; it is something thrown up red-hot out of Paul's experience. And it is that experience which supplies the basis of Paul's thought, and therefore its logical substructure' (183); 'no place is now left in us for sin' (181); 'sin is unthinkable' (184).

My own experience with this paper is strange. I know that I read it more than ten years ago. In the meantime I have on and off had occasion to recall that it is one of a very few scholarly contributions that provides what I consider to be distinctly the best understanding of Gal 5:23b (the sense of *kata* here: not 'against', but 'dealing with', Styler 179 n. 11). I have had no inkling whatever of the close similarity between Styler's far more comprehensive ideas about the Pauline 'logical substructure' and so forth—and the way my own thought has been progressing in these matters. Either my original reading has been unconsciously at work or else the similarity is incidental—reflecting that that is where one *will* end if one asks with a sufficient degree of philosophical reflection about the relationship between 'theology and ethics' in Paul (which is where Styler too begins). In any case, while there are important points of difference between us (e.g. on 'obligation' and 'obedience', the reading of Romans 6 and other things), I see Styler's paper as a sort of blueprint for what I am trying to do in this book (albeit from an entirely different perspective—there is not a whisper about Stoicism in Styler).

14. The British philosopher J. L. Austin (1911–60) distinguished between three types of linguistic act (or speech-act): locutionary, illocutionary and perlocutionary acts. (See Austin 1975.) Illocutionary acts are acts done *in* saying something, e.g. such acts as *reminding* and *appealing*.

15. The pervasive presence of such illocutionary elements in 5:13–6:10 is what makes it natural to go on speaking of that section as specifically a piece or

section of parenesis. The section just exhibits a density of those particular elements that makes this a sensible scholarly policy. It does not follow, however, that all the rest is *not* (also) 'parenetic'. For in the rest, Paul *spells out* the normative knowledge that goes into the Christ faith (cf. point (*a*) in the text) and that (illocutionary) speech-act was also part of Pauline parenesis as defined. Thus one might well say that Paul's argument in Gal 3–4 is 'parenetic' too, only here the element of *appeal* is not made *explicit*. (This solves the apparent tension between saying, with Stowers 1986, 23, that Paul's letters are parenetic throughout and saying, with the scholarly community, that the parenesis is concentrated in specific sections.)

16. This analysis of Pauline parenesis should be compared with the comprehensive, classic account in Malherbe 1992 (written in 1972, compare the extensive use of it in Perdue 1981). Where Malherbe presented a wonderful collection of material and sorted it out in terms of its various concrete usages, I attempt to bring out the intrinsic logic of parenesis as engaged in specifically by Paul, where it is focused on the specific speech-act of reminding the addressees of something they are taken already to know. The ancient concept of *parenesis* is usefully discussed in Stowers 1986, 91–6, as part of an illuminating chapter (91–152) on ancient letters of exhortation and advice. The attempt to define an ancient literary 'genre' or 'form' of parenesis is notoriously difficult (compare Perdue and Gammie (eds) 1990 and the overview in Sensing 1996), indeed probably abortive. Instead, I use the concept as the term of art it has become in modern Pauline scholarship (though evidently as based on the corpus of ancient material collected by Malherbe and others).

17. I wholly agree with Martyn's identification of this particular sentence as 'one of the topic sentences for the whole of the letter' (Martyn 1997a, 90) and with his interpretation of it as strongly and distinctly apocalyptic. My quarrel with Martyn will be that this observation is very far from settling anything. On the contrary, that is where interpretation of the letter must *begin*.

18. For this, to my mind wholly correct, reading compare S. K. Williams 1997, 89–90: 'the curse, like the blessing, is *conditional*. . . . The Israelites [namely, according to Deuteronomy, which Paul quotes] are not cursed *because* they are a people whose charter is the Law of Moses. Rather, they are *subject* to the curse of God's punishment *if* they disobey that Law' (89, Williams' italics). Stanley 1990 (495, 498–500) in effect makes the same (important) point. Neither Lambrecht (1991b, 143 n. 25) nor Wright (1991b, 147 with 145 n. 26) accepted Stanley's point, which they knew. Neither did Cranford (1994, 251) or Hong (1994, esp. 177–8). Bonneau (1997, 73), by contrast, got it right. Garlington (1997) did not. He also shows how difficult it is for scholars to liberate themselves from the traditional understanding of Paul's relationship with Judaism. Thus he construes the curse of 3:10 with flying theological colours as the 'covenant', 'eschatological' curse that *has* been pronounced against the Jews and their followers, the Judaizers, as 'apostates'. As against this, Paul's point seems to be the far more restricted one that there is no need (indeed, it would be

entirely off-track) for gentile Christ-believers to place themselves under the conditional curse of the Jewish law—now that Christ has bought even Jews free from it.

19. For further discussion of this, Betz 1979, 150–1, seems to me the most helpful.

20. This, of course, is a post-Sanders point, which I wholly accept.

21. Martyn rightly singles this out for special treatment (Martyn 1997a, 370–3) though without at all stressing its experiential dimension.

22. I find it difficult not to connect these two things: Paul's talk in 3:1 of how the Galatians had had the crucified Christ Jesus depicted to their eyes (*kat' ophthalmous*)—presumably by Paul himself when he was with them for the first time—and his description in 4:13–15 of the (Christlike?) weakness that they had *seen* in him and to which they had reacted by receiving *him as* Christ Jesus and being prepared to give him their own most precious belonging—their eyes (again *ophthalmoi*). Is Paul not intimating that they had, as it were, seen Christ Jesus 'in' *him*?

23. The following remarks are very restricted in scope. On *hyper* in Paul see the classic treatment in Riesenfeld 1969. Also very helpful on ideas of atonement in relation to Paul is Breytenbach 1993 (on *hyper* esp. 67–9). An example of the difficulty of the whole area is that whereas Riesenfeld ends up deriving 'for the sake of our sins' from 'for our sake' (515), Breytenbach argues in effect the other way round (68–9). In general, Breytenbach very usefully questions the appropriateness of finding in Paul a fully developed notion of atonement (*Sühne*) and Christ's atoning death (*Sühnetod*).

24. This is supported partly by the fact that the manuscript tradition is here more or less evenly divided between *hyper* and *peri* and by the fact that the two prepositions are often interchangeable in Hellenistic Greek. (Compare, e.g. R. N. Longenecker 1990, 8, and Riesenfeld 1969, 515.) Riesenfeld (1969, 515) takes the meaning in 1:4 to be 'for the atonement [or removal, *Tilgung*—understood *theologically*] of sins'. That is strictly an overinterpretation, not least when Riesenfeld himself compares it with Rom 4:25 ('because of [*dia*] our trespasses').

25. Riesenfeld is generally right to begin (1969, 511) from a sense of *hyper* as 'for the sake of, for the benefit of, for' (*zugunsten von, zum Schutze von, für*).

26. We should agree with Martyn when he claims that Paul 'sees liberation rather than forgiveness as the fundamental remedy enacted by God' (Martyn 1997a, 90, compare also his excursus at 263–75). But we should also insist that this 'liberation' is not just an apocalyptic event of cosmic proportions. It also has concrete and tangible consequences in human beings—for instance, that they stop sinning. Furnish (1993, 113) agrees that 1:4 states 'not a conception of atonement for specific sins but the typically Pauline idea about release from sin's power'. But his understanding of this 'release' seems to be the traditional, wholly abstract one that through Christ faith believers *are* 'justified' irrespective

of how this may show in their practice. Finally, Breytenbach (1993, 68) too agrees that in 1:4 Paul describes Christ as having died 'in order to take "our sins" away'. But his gloss on this again seems unwarranted and influenced by later theology: 'Christ's death removes *the consequences* of sin, it breaks up the connection of deed and consequence [the German *Tat-Folge-Zusammenhang*] of sin and death' (my italics). Why does Christ's death 'take "our sins" away' in the sense that it removes our *death*? Why does it not remove our *sins*?

27. This is clear, among other things, from the fact that Paul here describes Christ as having 'felt *love* for me *and*' (*therefore*) 'given himself up for my sake'. Furnish (1993, 113–15) sees the importance of the reference to Christ's love. His gloss on the function of this Christological assertion is again traditional: 'to describe Jesus' death as an act of utterly selfless love is to suggest that justification is bestowed as a gift, quite apart from "works of the law"' (1993, 115). This misses completely both the fact that Paul is speaking specifically of *Jesus'* love (not just of God's act in the Christ event) and the concomitant, strongly experiential dimension on Paul's part of 2:19–20. (Berényi 1986, who argues well against seeing the latter half of 2:20 merely as a 'traditional phrase', also misses the extent to which Christ is here seen as *mediating* between Paul and God.) Riesenfeld (1969, 512–13) thinks that we should understand there to be a sort of logic that begins from vicariousness (*Stellvertretung*) and moves on to God's (or Christ's) salvific intention (*Heilsintention*). He quotes 2:20 in this same connection. However, the idea of vicariousness does not seem to be present here.

28 Christ *bought us free from* the curse, by (himself) *becoming* a curse—*hyper* us. Riesenfeld (1969, 512–13) and Breytenbach (1993, 68–9) agree in finding vicariousness here.

29. This is my version of the idea of 'interchange in Christ' that was introduced in 1971 by Morna Hooker and further developed in a series of papers on interchange and atonement, suffering and ethics. See Hooker 1971, 1978, 1981 and 1985, all conveniently collected in Hooker 1990, 13–69. The last paper in the series (Hooker 1985) is a powerful statement of a general reading of the relationship between 'theology' and 'ethics' in Paul that goes a long way in the direction that I am arguing for. With regard to the particular point of I→X *responding* to X→I, the first pages of that paper are illuminating. Here Hooker is explicitly after the 'logic' (Hooker 1985, 4) that holds Pauline 'theology' and 'ethics' together or the 'logical link' between them (Hooker 1985, 5). And she very suggestively shows how 'Paul's logic holds divine grace and human response firmly together' (Hooker 1985, 4). One reason for the success of this is that Hooker does *not* start out from the usual 'Reformation slogans' like 'justification by faith' (Hooker 1985, 11) or let herself be daunted by them. On one point, however, she has not liberated herself completely from that picture: notions like obedience, disobedience and the imperative still turn up from time to time.

30. Classical treatments from the last few decades are these: Howard 1967, 1973–4, 1979, Hultgren 1980, S. K. Williams 1980, 1987b, L. T. Johnson 1982, Hays 1983, Hooker 1989, Hays 1991, Dunn 1991b and B. W. Longenecker 1993. For a succinct rehearsal of the arguments see S. K. Williams 1997, 67–70. Martyn advocates that the genitive be 'classified somewhat loosely as an authorial genitive', meaning that 'Christ is the author of the faith spoken of' (Martyn 1997a, 251 n. 127, cf. 259 and 270). This appears as a theologically dictated attempt to avoid ascribing to Paul a straightforwardly subjective genitive. But if Christ had a *mind* (according to Paul, compare Phil 2:5–6 or 1 Cor 2:16), then why could he not also be faithful to God? Indeed, was he not precisely faithful to God *in* the Christ event—according to the Philippians 'hymn' (2:6–7)?

31. A hitherto unnoticed linguistic argument: S. K. Williams (1997, 75) has in effect noticed it (with his usual acumen). Quoting parts of 2:20 ('in faith I live— that [faith] of ...'), Williams says: 'The that-clause *defines* the faith in and by which Paul lives *as* the faith of God's son, that faith characteristic of the son and manifested in his love and self-giving' (first italics mine, second Williams'). Curiously, Hooker (1989, 336), who argues persuasively for the subjective reading of *pistis Christou*, quotes the phrase from 2:20 in the Greek as *en pistei ... tou hyiou theou*, thus omitting the crucial *tēi*!

32. Rom 3:25 too speaks (at least in some manuscripts) of *hē pistis*. L. T. Johnson (1982, 79–80) takes this to refer to the faithfulness of Christ. That may be correct, but his discussion shows that there is no certainty. (Similarly, *hē pistis* in Rom 3:30–31 and Gal 3:25 may refer to 'the faith *event*' taken more generally.) B. W. Longenecker (1993) attempts to buttress Johnson's argument, but the weaker reading continues to be possible. Consequently, there is no proof here—as there seems to be in Gal 2:20.

33. Sanders (1977, 440 ff, see esp. 453–72) revived this from Schweitzer (and partly Käsemann) and gave it prominence. He also insisted, with characteristic gusto, that this terminology is far better than merely to speak of 'a new understanding of one's self', as 'Bultmann and his pupils' (particularly Conzelmann and Bornkamm) famously did (453–4): 'The participatory union [that Paul has in mind for instance in 1 Cor 6:13–18] is not a figure of speech for something else; it is, as many scholars have insisted, real' (455); 'the general conception of participation permeated his thought' (456). However, in the end (Sanders' own final pages of the book: 522–3), Sanders raises what should really have been the obvious question from the very beginning: 'But what does this mean? How are we to understand it?' (522). And he answers: 'I must confess that I do not have a new category of perception to propose here' (522–3). This, however, does not make him wince: 'Although it is difficult today to formulate a perceptual category which is not magic [earlier: naive cosmological speculation and belief in magical transference on the one hand] and is not [a revised] self-understanding [on the other], we can at least assert that the realism of Paul's view indicates that he had one. To an appreciable degree, what Paul concretely thought cannot be directly appropriated by Christians today.' Still: 'What he really thought was just what

he said' (523). As I see the task of interpretation, our reaction should be this. Half of what Sanders says is entirely right. Paul did have those ideas. But that is only half the task of interpretation proper (as opposed to 'appropriation'). We need some kind of *translation too*, not in order to be able to *adopt* what Paul was saying, but in order to be able to *understand* it. Here *many* translation manuals will do, whether they be modern or of a more traditional kind. An apposite one is the one I am advancing in this book. That manual does trade on such a notion as 'self-understanding', not, however, in Bultmann's demythologizing existentialist sense (I am neither out to demythologize nor am I an existentialist) nor certainly because Bultmann employed a similar conception, but because it fits Paul's own text and fits it historically.

34. Martyn disagrees (1997a, 158) against Gaventa 1986 and Hays 1987 (281), arguing that (a) the rendering 'to me' is harmonious with v. 12, (b) the common Greek of Paul's day has many instances of a very weak *en* (in), and (c) this fits v. 24, where *en emoi* means 'because of (or for) me'. Neither argument is absolutely cogent, as Martyn recognizes. But what about this? Paul himself says in 2:20 what the result is of God's having revealed his son *en emoi*: that the son (Christ) *lives—en emoi*. In short, whether we explicitly take it with the same sense in 1:16 or, as it were, wait until 2:20, it seems clear what Paul wishes to say: that through God's revelation of Christ, he came to live *in* Paul. Our task, then, is to make *sense* of that. (Dunn too—1993a, 64—combines 1:16 with 2:20.)

35. Compare the emphatic position of *Christōi* in *Christōi synestaurōmai*. We should translate the two words: 'I have been crucified together with *Christ*'.

36. I take it that Paul's own *pistis*-relationship is a matter of faithfulness *towards God*, *trust* in God, namely, in the God who has set the Christ event going and will lead it to its glorious end. Even where *pistis Christou* does not refer to *Christ's* own faithfulness, but to the *pistis* of Christ-believers, it is not faith *in Christ*, but faith or trust in the God who was active in the Christ event.

37. Martyn reflects a traditional view when he states in a note to 4:6: 'For Paul there is no chronological order between adoption into God's family [namely as God's sons, cf. 3:26] and receipt of the Spirit' (1997a, 391 n. 11). Much as I would be prepared to accept that, I cannot see that it is borne out by Paul's own text. 3:14b and 4:6 seem to me to stand decisively against it. (As I read it, Betz' discussion with Schlier of the character and relationship of faith and baptism points in the same direction, see Betz 1979, 187–8.)

38. It is curious that the commentaries do not generally make any attempt to define the meaning of 'the flesh' in the letter. Why? Do we already know what it means? No. On the contrary, that question needs to be answered through *interpretation*, that is, by standing back and asking what Paul is at all talking about. For instance, it is insufficient (though in itself not false) to answer (with Käsemann, e.g. 1962 and 1972²b): 'a power'—or to discover (with Brandenburger 1968) the history-of-religions origin of the Pauline concept of 'the flesh' as a 'substantive force' and 'power of destruction'

(*Verderbensmacht*) in 'the dualistic wisdom thought of Hellenistic Judaism' (including Philo). That only invites even more interpretation: what were they talking about?

There are fine surveys of the meaning of *sarx* in the New Testament, and Paul in particular, in Schweizer 1964 (for the 'Hellenistic component' in the New Testament concept of *sarx* compare also Schweizer 1957) and Sand 1983 (the latter building on Sand 1967). Both reflect to varying degrees (Schweizer more than Sand) a traditional, mid-20th-century German understanding. Central features of Sand's analysis are the following. (i) The New Testament shares the Old Testament understanding of man as an indivisible whole (as against 'the dichotomous, trichotomous or dualistic perspective of Greek philosophy, Hellenism and Gnosticism' [Sand 1983, 549]). (ii) Still, in Paul there are three different fields of reference for the term: (*a*) to features connected with the human body, including the human being as a bodily one, and even humankind; in this usage *sarx* has an 'unspecific meaning' (Sand 1983, 550) and there is no 'special qualification' (551); examples from Galatians are 1:16, 2:16, 20, 4:13, 23, 29, 6:12, 13; (*b*) to features connected with an 'earthly-natural, merely worldly existence' (Sand 1983, 550) understood more broadly as reflecting a 'merely worldly (form of) acting and thinking' that is not (yet) specifically sinful (Sand refers, e.g. to Paul's talk in 1 Cor 1:26 of the few among the Christ-believing Corinthians who are wise 'in fleshly terms'); (*c*) finally, to the sphere of sin, an earthly-bodily sphere to which all human beings belong, but which also yields a truly sinful existence of enmity towards God due to the sheer power of sin (cf. Sand 1983, 552).

Moving on from a basis such as this one, J. M. G. Barclay (1988, 203–9) rightly attempts to formulate a 'general notion' (206) which could link together all the various uses of the term in Paul. He finds it in the idea of 'what is merely human' (206–9) to be understood within Paul's basic apocalyptic framework as what does not belong to the new eschatological age, the new creation established through the power of the spirit. (Here Barclay explicitly builds on Käsemann, 205.)

My reaction is this: If we aim only to codify and, to some degree, to sharpen what Paul says as seen from within his own perspective, the analyses by Schweizer, Sand and Barclay serve their purpose well. In fact, however, we need to do something more: to try to formulate what Paul is actually talking about in a language that is accessible to us. And here it is simply not enough to refer (with Käsemann) to Paul's apocalyptic framework, to his seeing sin as a power and so forth. For what does that actually mean? Can we in some way translate that into a language that is meaningful to us? That is what I shall attempt to do, building on the happy fact that Paul himself does talk, *partially* (cf. points (*a*) and (*b*) in Sand's analysis), of the flesh in wholly naturalistic terms.

39. This reading of the meaning of the flesh in Galatians may profitably be contrasted with the enormously influential one in Bultmann's *Theology* §§22–3 (Bultmann 1984⁹, 232–46). The basic difference lies in our respective perspec-

tives. Bultmann *begins* (logically) from above: whether one recognizes or denies God as creator. Starting from this, the flesh becomes 'fleshly being' (*Fleischlichkeit*) or 'creaturely being' (*Geschöpflichkeit*). By contrast, I begin (logically) from below, trying to give a naturalistic meaning to the idea of living 'in accordance with the flesh'. There is no disagreement, of course, that Paul was against that and that he aimed to make his addressees live 'in the spirit'. What is at issue is the meaning of this.

40. A classic account of Paul's complex use of 'boasting' is Bultmann 1938. It is pure Bultmann and it is fine. But it must now be regarded as obsolete, particularly due to its misrepresentation of Paul's idea of Jewish boasting. A more recent, careful and independent account is Zmijewski 1981. It too reflects a traditional Protestant German theology of Paul's understanding of righteousness (explicitly so, 686). This is not the place for the much-needed extensive discussion. Suffice it to say that I would, among other things, argue for this point: Paul *never* understands 'bad' boasting as pointing to one's own special qualities in an address that is directed to *God*. It never expresses 'self-confidence *before God*' (against, e.g. Barrett 1986, 366–8, who basically follows Bultmann). It is *always* harping on one's virtues in what one says *to other people* (though possibly, e.g. for Jews, with *reference* to one's own special relationship with God). This holds even of 1 Cor 1:29 where Paul denounces all human boasting 'in the face of God'. What he means is: all human boasting *over against other human beings*—when one is standing in the face of *God*.

41. Zmijewski (1981), who rightly looks for 'synonyms and contrasts' in the Pauline text in order to use them to settle the meaning of boasting itself, refers among other things to the term *pepoithenai* ('trust') in Phil 3:3 as a synonym. That is helpful. For this 'trust' is of course not 'the trust of man in himself as opposed to God' or something similar from the traditional German reading, but precisely the 'trust' that *goes into* normative self-identification. When one normatively identifies oneself in this or the other way, one *eo ipso* identifies what *has value*. That is what one (thereby) 'trusts'.

42. Betz (1979, 317–18) brings out well the paradoxical character of this kind of boasting. (I cannot, however, follow his gloss of 'the flesh' one may wrongly boast of as 'man's own achievements'. Paul was not against 'achievements'.)

43. Betz again (1979, 318): 'strictly speaking such "boasting in the Lord" is not boasting at all.'

44. Betz speaks of 'glorification' and thinks that ' "boasting in the Lord" would call for literary forms like "doxology" or "hymn" ' (1979, 318). The distinction may be a fine one, but I cannot hear the element of 'thanks' in *kauchasthai*. A better synonym would be *agalliasthai* ('exult'). Morrice (1984, 49–55) rightly includes a discussion of 'boasting', including 'justifiable boasting', in his *Joy in the New Testament*, translating it in some places (see 54–5) as 'joyful reliance', 'rejoicing' and the like.

Notes for Chapter 7

1. Major examples are Schweitzer 1930 and Sanders 1977 and 1983, though neither holds the position in exactly the way I have stated it. *Schweitzer* famously downplayed the centrality of the doctrine of righteousness by faith in favour of the mystical doctrine of being-in-Christ (201–21). And this latter was closely connected with possession of the spirit (163–70) and with ethics (286–7, 292–4), not with faith. By contrast, Paul never, Schweitzer claimed, attempted to bridge the gap between justification (including faith) and ethics: 'Never does he make the attempt to derive the ethics from righteousness by faith' (286). *Sanders* accepted sizeable parts of Schweitzer's position (see 1977, 438–41). But he also criticized Schweitzer for not having seen 'the *internal connection* between the righteousness by faith terminology and the terminology about life in the Spirit, being in Christ and the like ..., a connection which exists in Paul's own letters' (1977, 440, Sanders' italics). That is both fine and correct. However, in the 1983 book Sanders seems to have fallen implicitly back on a contrast between righteousness by faith and life in the spirit (e.g. 103–4, 208–9). The reason is probably that he here developed his own version of the old point from Schweitzer (1930, 216—and before him Wernle 1897, 83, and Wrede 1907, 72–9) that the language of righteousness by faith comes in when Paul opposes faith to the law as 'an *entrance* requirement', that is, when Paul explicitly addresses the relationship between Jews and gentiles in his missionary practice. Within such a framework, the spirit only makes its appearance in connection with Paul's talk of how people should then live *within* the new group. And so the contrast is fully present. On this particular issue, the page in the 1977 book from which I quoted is more helpful. Note, however, that even though we shall end up connecting *pistis* and the *pneuma* far more closely than either Schweitzer or Sanders (generally) allowed, it remains important to draw the *logical* distinction between the two instead of merely conflating them. Sanders was therefore quite right in chastising major representatives of Dialectical Theology like Bultmann (Sanders 1977, 439–40) and Furnish (1968—as he might then well be called, Sanders 440 n. 47) for relating ethics to justification by neglecting that Paul is actually not talking of righteousness in the passages to which they refer, but of living in the spirit, participating in Christ and the like.

2. S. K. Williams (1989) convincingly shows that Paul's *akoē pisteōs* means '"the hearing of faith", that "hearing" which Christians call *faith*' (90, Williams' italics). I had reached the same conclusion before reading Williams' article. Martyn (1997a, 286–9) argues for a quite different interpretation: the message enacted or uttered by God (through the apostle) that elicits faith! He refers to Rom 10:16–17 as making this reading 'almost certain' (288). But his reading here seems refuted by Rom 10:14: 'how will people *akouein* without there being somebody to proclaim the message (*kēryssein*)?' Does Paul mean 'how will people have the message proclaimed to them without there being somebody to proclaim it?'?!

3. I thus take the phrase *ek pisteōs* ('from faith') to qualify not the verb of the verse, but *pneumati* ('by the spirit', in the sense of 'by *having* the spirit', namely, from or as a result of faith). Commentators generally do not take it that way (e.g. neither Betz nor Martyn), but Paul's question in 3:2 seems to make this reading virtually certain: did you obtain the spirit from (*ex*) works of the law or *from* (*ek*) faith-hearing? S. K. Williams (1997, 138) is close to this reading. Burton (1921, 278) considered the possibility of the reading, which he found 'neither grammatically impossible ... nor un-Pauline in thought'. Yet he would have preferred the text *pneumati <tōi> ek pisteōs*. There is something to be said for this had Paul in general been writing 'correct', Xenophontic or Platonic Greek. But of course he is not. Furthermore, since, as we have seen, he is recapitulating crucial parts of his argument in ch. 3, it is far more likely that we should construe the grammar here on the basis of 3:14b, to which Burton rightly refers for the 'not un-Pauline' thought.

4. It is, of course, the latter part of this solution which distinguishes my understanding of the relationship between *pistis* and *pneuma* from those of Schweitzer and Sanders referred to in n. 1.

5. R. N. Longenecker (1990, 259–60) rightly warns against putting one or the other form of one-sided theology into Paul's use of the term 'fruit' (*karpos*) here (in contrast with the 'works of the flesh' of 5:19), e.g. a contrast between God's gift and human effort (as in Schlier 1965[4], 255–6). We shall eventually see, however, that Paul's use of that specific term does have a point. (For a general account of the use of the term in and outside the New Testament see Hauck 1938. The references in Betz 1979, 286 nn. 137–8, are valuable too.)

6. Note how 5:25 constitutes the conclusion of Paul's argument as begun in 5:16 and how 5:26 repeats the specific piece of exhortation concerning unity made in 5:15 just before Paul's argument began. (More on the whole argument below.) That argues fairly strongly against taking a new subsection (5:25–6:10) to begin with 5:25, one that consists of a scattered set of *sententiae* or 'maxims' (as in Betz 1979, 291–3, J. M. G. Barclay 1988, 155–66, Dunn 1993a, 316–17, Martyn 1997a, 541–5).

7. Betz (1979, 288) is right to see *pistis* not as specifically Christian faith, but as 'faithfulness', 'trustworthiness', namely for others.

8. It is interesting to compare Gal 5:13 and 5:14 in the light of our sharpened reading of Phil 2:4 as an exhortation, not just to care for others *too*, but *precisely* to care for others. Gal 5:14 might seem to support the *in*clusive reading of Phil 2:4, whereas Gal 5:13 supports an *ex*clusive reading. After all, a slave is not expected, *as* a slave, to care for himself too, but precisely for his master. Note then that 5:14 states the inherited, traditional rule, whereas 5:13 formulates Paul's own sharpened *understanding* of that.

9. This is so generally recognized that it needs no special discussion. Compare the classic treatment in Vögtle 1936, the first half of which contains an exhaustive and most helpful survey of the material in the New Testament, the Greco-Roman

world, the Old Testament and Hellenistic Judaism. By contrast, the second half (from p. 125) is a good example of how *not* to pursue the comparison between the 'secular Greek' and the 'New Testament' 'ideal of virtue'. Vögtle here draws a picture of 'similarity of content [!] and language'—but then also of a crucial difference between 'kernel and shell' on either side which turns the Christian ideal into a 'spiritual break-through'. Martyn too (1997a, 532–4) is keen on arguing that Paul so completely transforms the 'traditional lists' in the light of his 'apocalyptic vision', including the motif of 'cosmic warfare', that we should rather speak of 'transformed lists' and 'an apocalyptic transformation of the language of vices and virtues'. In this connection Martyn takes issue with Meeks 1993, whom he accuses of largely ignoring 'the degree to which apocalyptic frames of reference . . . led Paul to a radically new view of the cosmos itself'. This once more raises the fundamental issue of interpretation that underlies the present book. It is probably true that Paul would himself describe the relationship between 'his' catalogues of virtues and vices in the way suggested by Martyn. He does after all speak of a 'new creation' (6:15). Unfortunately, however, *we* cannot just repeat that, since Paul's own, quite straightforward understanding of the 'new creation' *cannot* be ours. It just is not Martyn's either, in the way it was understood by Paul himself. So whether we like it or not, we are *forced* to step back a little from Paul's own perspective. When we do that, we will also have to admit that against what Paul would probably himself have said, his catalogues of virtues and vices are not in fact much different from the traditional ones and that the way they function within Paul's overall thought is indeed closely similar to what we find in the popular (and also the not so popular) philosophers of his day. Since the language of the philosophers *is* more immediately accessible to us, we are virtually forced by a number of facts (that this language is so close to Paul's own, that Paul more or less explicitly uses it in places, and that other features in Paul may easily be fitted into what is basically a philosophical frame) to employ that framework in *our interpretation* of what Paul is talking about. It is not enough just to say: a new creation.

10. Two ideas in Stoicism point to this. First, one cannot fully or properly have a single virtue without having them all—the principle of the interconnectedness of the virtues. Second, the distinguishing mark of the wise man, who does have all the virtues, is that his acts are *katorthōmata*, *right* acts, as opposed to the *kathēkonta* of the person who has not yet quite learned (in Paul's language, Phil 1:10) to *dokimazein ta diapheronta* ('see the differences'). The wise man's acts are the *always* right acts.

11. Räisänen (1983, e.g. 42–83) is very good at bringing out what he perceives as an unacknowledged tension in Paul between an ideological position to the effect that Christ-believers *fulfil* the law (among other things, by actually doing what Jews living under the dominion of the Torah could not do) and a radical practice (with regard to circumcision and food laws) which in fact meant an *annulment* of the law. This tension is furthered, Räisänen thinks, by Paul's oscillating use of the term 'law' (*nomos*) in a 'looseness of speech' (28) which is

rhetorically effective, but covers up distinctions that should have been drawn (e.g. 16–28). The general problem with Räisänen's acute analyses, which delight in laying bare Paul's 'inconsistencies' and 'confusions', lies precisely here: that starting from the (entirely healthy) doubt that there was anything whatever to what Räsiänen perceives as Paul's criticism of Jews and the law, he does not give *Paul* enough of the benefit of the doubt; he does not allow that Paul *might* have a real *point* in his comparison of the effect of the law and Christ: that the Christ event and experience might actually deliver something that could not be brought about by the law. This is the (positive) possibility that we should explore. It has become easier to do so after we have realized (*through* the work of Räisänen himself, Sanders—and indeed, as Räisänen shows, 108 n. 79, already Paul Wernle) that Paul constructs his picture of the law and of the relationship between that and Christ as it were after the event. It has also become easier after we have realized that Paul is not in fact so critical of the law as Räisänen supposes. The basic point, however, is this: that due to the whole direction of his argument Räisänen was logically prevented from trying to find some point to Paul's wrestling with the law—instead of referring his supposed inconsistencies and confusions back to his psyche.

12. The NRSV translates v. 16 as follows: 'Live by the Spirit, I say, and do not gratify the desires of the flesh.' This is a complete misunderstanding of Paul's use of *ou mē* plus the subjunctive. (Many centuries ago, the Authorized Version was far better: 'This I say then, Walk in the Spirit, and ye shall not fulfil the lust of the flesh.') As e.g. Burton, Lietzmann, Mussner, Betz and Martyn recognize (but not, e.g. Bonnard 1953; Dunn too wavers, 1993a, 294 n. 1), this construction expresses 'the most definite form of negation regarding the future' (Betz 1979, 278 n. 59 quoting BDF/BDR, § 365). But Paul is hardly 'promising' anything (Betz). Rather he is affirming a fact: 'Walk by the Spirit, then [*kai*] you (most certainly) *will* not carry out the desire of the flesh.' The paraphrase in Lightfoot 1905[10], 209 is excellent: 'This is my command. Walk by the rule of the Spirit. If you do so, you will not, *you cannot*, gratify the lusts of the flesh.' (my emphasis). (S. K. Williams (1997, 148) too speaks of Paul as affirming 'a state of affairs', and explicitly against the NRSV, which otherwise constitutes Williams' primary translation of reference.) The point is very important since, as I have said, 5:17 ff constitutes an argument proper for the affirmative *statement of fact* made in the *second* half of 5:16. There also seems to be some confusion regarding the meaning of Paul's introductory *Legō de*. Betz (1979, 277 n. 51) refers to Gal 1:9, 3:17, 4:1 and 5:2. But of these the first and the last are not directly relevant. Paul's *introductory* use of *legō de* (4:1, 5:16—or *touto de legō*, 3:17) does not just mark the fact that Paul is about to make 'an important statement' (Betz 1979, 277). That fits the two other passages (1:9 and 5:2), where the use does not have the special, introductory character. Where the phrase does have this, it means 'what I mean is the following: . . .'. (Compare Schlier 1965[4], 247, who is wholly clear on this.)

13. For an excellent discussion see J. M. G. Barclay 1988, 111–15.

14. This argument works against, e.g. Betz' picture: 'Man is the battlefield of these forces within him, *preventing* him from carrying out his will. [Betz translates the *hina* : 'so that you do not do . . . .] The human "I" wills, but it is *prevented* from carrying out its will (*tauta poiēte*) because it is *paralyzed* through these dualistic forces within' (Betz 1979, 279–80, my emphases). Martyn too reads the *hina* in an 'ecbatic' way: 'the result being that you do not actually do the very things you wish to do' (1997a, 531). Curiously, Martyn, who otherwise has such an externalized view of the 'powers', also locates them within the souls of individuals. How, then, does he account for the connection between 5:17 and 5:16? By claiming that those who suffer what Paul describes in 5:17 are specifically those Galatians who are trying to 'direct their allegiance both to Christ and to the Sinaitic Law' (Martyn 1997a, 531, cf. 495 and 536–40). *They* will suffer the 'tragic failure' of 'attempting the impossible, that is to follow both Christ and the Sinaitic Law' (531). But my counterargument remains. If these people experience a sort of stalemate in such a way that they actually do not do what they (in accordance with their Christ and spirit side) do wish to do—then how will that *explain* (5:16) that if they do walk in the spirit, then they most certainly will not carry out the desire of the flesh?

15. This reading goes directly against two basic views of Martyn: 'Nothing is more foreign to Paul than the thought that the Flesh can be defeated by a course of human action'; 'for Paul the Spirit and the Flesh are not related to one another in such a way as to call upon the Galatians to decide for the one or the other' (Martyn 1997a, 529). The crucial point against Martyn is this. As is shown by both 5:16 and 5:18 ('If you *are being led*, that is, *let* yourselves be led, by the spirit, then . . .'), Paul's parenesis obviously does the only sensible thing of *presupposing* that those he is addressing may choose to *follow* his exhortation. In that light, 5:17 will mean that the two universal forces are at loggerheads with one another *aiming* to prevent the Galatians from doing what they, *if* they give access to the *other* side (no matter which), will *also* wish to do. Therefore, if *they* decide or choose *not* to pay exclusive heed to Paul's exhortation in 5:16, they will come within the purview of the flesh and its aim. And the result of *this* will be that they cannot in fact live wholly in accordance with the spirit. But it all hangs on what the Galatians will themselves decide. *If* they will let themselves be led by the spirit, *then* they will *not* be under the (law and) flesh. In discussing the motif of the spirit in relation to Paul's ethics, Haufe (1994, 188–91) emphasizes the 'normative' role of the spirit, which apparently means that the spirit sets up a certain substantive norm for the new life that Christ-believers will then apply in their own decisions (esp. 189). Haufe is right to emphasize the notion of decision, but it is unfortunate that he bases it directly on Bultmann and *opposes* it to the idea of seeing the spirit as an 'impersonal, mechanical power that directs human behaviour almost automatically' (189). There is no *contrast* here. And so Martyn may keep his emphasis on the spirit as 'power' without this allowing him to disparage a (non-Bultmannian) notion of decision or choice. Haufe's further point that the spirit stands for a 'faculty of cognition'

(*Erkenntnisvermögen*) that is responsible for the cognitive 'development' (*Entfaltung*) of the central Christ message that has been appropriated in faith (190–1, esp. 190) is very valuable. His gloss on 'walking in the spirit' is exactly right: 'to draw the practical consequences of the understanding [*Erkenntnis*] of the salvific event that has been mediated by the spirit, to let that understanding constitute the framework for one's own behaviour, to understand [*erkennen*] and practise [*praktizieren*] the behaviour on one's own part that matches the salvific behaviour of Christ' (191).

16. Commentators regularly ask why Paul so suddenly brings in the law in 5:18. I have not found anybody, however, who gives exactly the answer I suggest here: if the spirit, then not the flesh; but if not the flesh, then neither *that law which* (according to 3:19–24) *precisely served to control the flesh*. (Betz, however, is at least right—1979, 281 n. 90—in emphasizing that 5:18 should not be interpreted by drawing on the idea that the law *stimulates* sin—as, e.g. Schlier (1965⁴, 250), does.) It goes without saying that Paul is also out to connect the law and the flesh for the wider purposes of his argument (that if they do want to escape from sin, then Christ and the spirit—and not the law—is the answer). But the precise way he makes the connection is the one I have given. (*a*) It fits 3:19–24 completely (on which see later). (*b*) And it is simple and makes immediate sense. S. K. Williams (1997) thinks Paul's idea is that since the spirit is sufficient for the Christian life, the law is no longer needed 'as an indicator of unacceptable behaviors or as a moral guide. The works of the flesh ... are clear and evident even without the Law' (149–50). But if the spirit is sufficient (as it indeed is), then there is no need to focus on how the works of the flesh become *evident*. The sufficiency of the spirit means that there *are* no works of the flesh. There is nothing whatever, therefore, for the law to operate on.

17. There are two ways of understanding Paul's point about the law in relation to the attitudes he has listed. (Compare the discussion in J. M. G. Barclay 1988, 122–4, with references.) One may take it (with Martyn 1997a, 499–500; compare also R. A. Campbell 1996) as an assurance on Paul's part that if the Galatians will acquire these attitudes they will never risk doing anything that the law is against. So they need not fear any antinomian consequences of letting themselves be led by the spirit alone. In itself this might be good enough if we suppose (again with Martyn; see also Betz) that Paul is responding to a very specific situation where his opponents have warned the Galatians of the antinomian tendencies in Paul's preaching. Still, as has often been noted, it does sound very flat to have Paul say that the law is not *against* love and so forth, not least when he has just claimed that the whole law is actually *fulfilled* in the love command (5:14). Styler (1973, 179 n. 11) rightly argued that the usual translation 'is at best a massive understatement'. He therefore claimed that we should take Paul's *kata* ('against') to mean 'concerning' (equalling *peri*): "'there is no law dealing with such things as these'" (or 'the law does not deal'). That is the reading I argue for below. Betz (1979, 288 n. 164, with earlier predecessors like Robb 1944–5) refers to Aristotle's *Politics* (1284a 14–15) for what is verbally exactly

the same phrase. Here too, however, the *kata* does not directly mean 'against' (as Betz reads it), but rather 'concerning': the law does not *concern* such people or things, it is not *targeted* at them.

18. Note, for instance, the many plurals in the so-called vice list: *echthrai* ('hostile feelings and acts', Betz), *thymoi* ('outbursts of rage', Betz), *eritheiai* ('quarrels', Betz) and so forth. These are precisely not vices, considered as so many mental states, but the activities themselves, those that the law attempts to prevent. Similarly the list begins with *porneia*, which Betz rightly translates 'illicit sexual activities'. The next item is *akatharsia*, which (if we build on, e.g. Rom 1:24) similarly stands for a certain type of bodily *activity*. And so forth.

19. R. A. Campbell (1996) argues for translating 5:23b as follows: 'The Law does not condemn *people* like that'. He also connects this translation usefully with the problem treated in 2:15 ff: who are the sinners? It remains the case, however (as argued by J. M. G. Barclay 1988, 122–3), that the parallel between *tōn toioutōn* in 5:23b and *ta toiauta* in 5:21b ('such things') speaks for taking *tōn toioutōn* as neuter too. And more importantly, would Paul ever say that there is now no longer any condemnation *by the law* of people who are in Christ? (Certainly not in Rom 8:1, to which Campbell refers.) Rather, Paul aims to place the law together with the flesh and its acts on the side that has now been left behind—and the spirit together with its virtuous attitudes on the other. They fall altogether outside the realm of the law. To get to them one must do something new: crucify the flesh by coming to belong to Christ (5:24). Harnisch (1987, 291–2), who does not discuss 5:23b, has a clear grasp of the crucial contrast between the (plural) 'works' of the flesh and the (singular) 'fruit' of the spirit: 'Thus the parenetic section reaches its high point in a contrast which reflects the ontological difference [*Seinsdifferenz*] between old and new' (292). Unfortunately, however, Harnisch's contrast is basically a traditional, theological difference between a realm of the flesh where the human being is him- or herself 'active' and one of the spirit where 'any thought of human achievements' is excluded (292).

20. This verse, if not the whole argument of 5:16 ff, shows with unmistakable clarity that Martyn must be wrong when he states, as one of the basic results of his reading of the whole passage, that 'in Paul's view there is no thought that human beings may achieve perfection' (Martyn 1997, 529). 'Perfection', of course, is an enormously loaded term theologically. To me it is enough that Paul speaks of the *crucifixion* of the flesh with its passions and desires. Räisänen, who had no theological problem with finding an idea of perfection in Paul, acknowledges, as one of Paul's 'extravagant statements' (Räisänen 1983, 114 n. 103), that 'Christians really ... fulfil the law' (114). 'Galatians conveys an extremely "optimistic" picture of the spiritual life of the Christian community. It almost seems that the "Christians live on a new level of existence, and so their actions will automatically follow from this new kind of existence"' (115, quoting Drane 1975, 53).

21. I have earlier rejected the tendency among commentators to let Paul begin a section of more detailed, but scattered exhortation with 5:25. I noticed there that 5:26 recalls 5:15. Here we may particularly note how 5:25 repeats 5:16. After having written all this I noticed the following brief remark in S. K. Williams 1997, 153: 'Taken together, verses 24 and 25 (crucifying the flesh, following the Spirit's lead) mirror 5:16. Verse 26 then echoes verse 15.' That is exactly right. (Compare also R. A. Campbell 1996, 272, who speaks of verses 16 and 25 as 'framing' the intervening verses 'by a call to walk by the Spirit'.)

22. Martyn neglects the distinction by listing 'nine hortatory/imperative verbs' in 5:25–6:10 (1997a, 541–2). In a way Martyn is right. It does not matter much whether Paul uses a form of shared exhortation (1st person plural) or 2nd person plural imperatives. *But that is because the latter should be understood in the light of the former.* Paul's *imperatives too* have the logical character of appeals, not of orders.

23. It was *Wernle* (1897) who showed—one would have thought once and for all, and explicitly against the traditional Protestant reading (24–5, 54, 77–8, 93, 94, 106–9)—that Paul saw Christ-believers as straightforwardly sinless (15–16, 21, 30–1, 43, 45, 73, 89–90, 95). Since Paul's letters are also so full of exhortation to *become* sinless, Wernle also formulated with all clarity the resulting problem: that Paul will sometimes speak in the indicative about things that *have* happened to human beings and that *continue* to happen to them when the spirit grasps them and drives them forward without their contributing anything—*and* that he at other times also speaks in the imperative in a manner that is directed to the *will* of human beings, appealing to them to *make* those things happen that will happen anyway even if they contribute nothing (89). Paul, however, says Wernle, did not feel there to be any contradiction. 'Here an ethic of miracle and an ethic of the will intermingle with one another without any mediation' (89). Wernle's own solution was basically that Paul saw everything in the light of his (enthusiastic) belief that the 'ideal' situation that he had in mind had already become real. Any failure among his addressees to live up to that could be taken care of by exhortation (the imperative). And neither the failure nor the resulting use of exhortation posed any real problem.

Bultmann (1924) then formulated the alternative, quite different understanding of the relationship between the indicative and the imperative that is probably still the reigning one. For Bultmann the indicative of righteousness most decidedly did not connote sinlessness. There was still an urgent need, therefore, to try to move human beings further in that same direction (though they will never reach the goal). And that is the task performed by the imperative—which was not, however, Paul's so much as God's. In fact, it was a *part of* the indicative of righteousness. Or (if looked at from the perspective of Christ-believers) it had the character of obedience. Consequently, there was no 'antinomy' whatever—or rather, there was a 'paradoxical', '*genuine*' antinomy (123).

Two brief objections to this: (1) Wernle was right about sinlessness. Nothing Bultmann ever said could get around this fact. *Windisch* (1924), who very clearly shows the doctrinaire character of Bultmann's reading (the influence from Barth), was right to insist on this point: 'To my mind, the correctly understood Paul did have an ethic of sinlessness' (280). (2) (*a*) Paul's imperatives are his own, not God's. (*b*) And as we shall gradually see, they do not at all have the character of orders the proper reaction to which is one of obedience. In short, Bultmann's 'reading' of Paul is pure Protestant theology. It does provide a solution to a problem that neither Wernle nor Windisch had managed to solve (by their own admission). But it is a solution that has very little to do with the Paul of our texts.

24. One might, if one wanted to, make the point in terms of the distinction that is almost to be found in Haufe 1994 (190–1), between the initial *faith*-understanding of the Christ event and the final, *developed* understanding of it for which the *spirit* is responsible. In any case, 1 Cor 1–2 clearly shows that Paul did distinguish between degrees of understanding (in this case: the initial 'faith' and the hoped-for, final Christ-believing *sophia* or wisdom).

25. For discussion of the different types of strategy that went into the Stoic cure of passion, see Engberg-Pedersen 1990, 200–6.

26. Thus Paul belongs squarely with the Stoics in the sweep of 'discovery of the will' *between* Aristotle and Augustine. (See for this Kahn 1988.) It is only with the latter that what came to be understood as 'the' will was finally formulated. The Stoics had nothing of this kind. Nor did Paul.

27. The understanding of Paul's notion of 'new creation' that I favour is basically that expressed by Betz: 'Those who are now "in Christ" (cf. 3:26–28) have been given the "Spirit of Christ" (cf. 4:6) and have, in baptism, "put on" Christ (3:27); they "belong to Christ" (5:24), enjoy the "new life" (2:19 f; 5:25), and as such are "new creation"' (Betz 1979, 319). Betz is precisely right in saying that it is Christ-believers who *are* a 'new creation", cf. 2 Cor 5:17 which Betz correctly translates as follows: 'If someone is "in Christ," [he is a] new creation' (320 n. 82). This follows more or less directly from the similarity of 6:15 and 5:6. The 'new creation' as it were *consists* of 'faith that is active through love' and such faith is concretely *found* in a quite precise place: in Christ-believers. Compared with this I find Martyn's 'cosmic' talk of the 'new creation' far vaguer and less helpful (see e.g. his Comment #51 in Martyn 1997, 570–4). One may certainly make Paul's idea of the new creation as cosmic, apocalyptic, objective and all-encompassing as one will. That is entirely unproblematic. But one must also recognize that it has in addition a quite precise reference, which is indeed, in the jargon, 'anthropological'. It refers to those people who, individually, have Christ faith and who, together, constitute the group of Christ-believers. S. K. Williams (1997) expresses this with a rare degree of precision: 'What is "new" here? A [ii] new community of [i] new persons! 'New creation' names both [ii] new situation [in effect: S] and [i] new self [in effect: I→X], *for Paul can conceive of neither apart from the othe*r. [i] The believing "I" is *another self* [cf. I→X], a self configured around a *new center* [X!], empowered by the energy of the Spirit.

[ii] But this new self has another "home". The "world," this age and its *institutions and customs and values*, is its home no longer, not even if those institutions and customs and values are those of a religious tradition as noble as Judaism. Its home is *the family of others* [S] who look *and act* [!] like sisters and brothers because they have all "clothed (themselves) with Christ" (3:27)' (166, my italics and further disfigurations).

28. Sanders 1977 established this once and for all (442–7, 474–511). Neither Sanders nor Räisänen, however, who follows Sanders on this point, went on to address the urgent question that is raised by Sanders' insight. Granted that Paul constructed the human plight and the problem of the Jewish law on the basis of his grasp of the solution in Christ, could it not be that there was a valid *point* in Paul's *post eventum* construction of the plight and the problem? Could it not be that *as seen from the perspective of the solution* there *was* an *actual* 'plight' and an *actual* 'problem'—even though nobody would have seen it exactly like that before the solution was formulated?

29. For discussion with German representatives of that, like Hans Hübner (1978), see in particular Sanders 1983.

30. As will by now be clear, my main disagreement with Sanders and Räisänen on this issue is that in their wholly justified attempt to tear down traditional, systematizing and constructive readings of Paul's statements about the law, these two scholars have not themselves attempted to formulate some alternative reading with the same systematizing and constructive character. Instead, they both end up explaining Paul's many different statements about the law by referring them back, in a psychologizing way, to his habits of mind (e.g. his tendency to think in 'black and white' terms). One can easily understand this reductive strategy. Still, it does not follow that because one systematizing reading is false no other could be right. The task of interpretation therefore remains that of trying to formulate some alternative, systematizing account— without ever forgetting the many apparent inconsistencies that Sanders and Räisänen have diagnosed. In their various ways, scholars writing on Paul and the law after Sanders and Räisänen (like Westerholm 1988, Thielman 1989, B. L. Martin 1989, Weima 1990, Sloan 1991 and others) have all tried to salvage what they could from the wreck created by Sanders and Räisänen (the latter in particular). Seen from the perspective of the present book, however, they have all in fact remained too wedded to the traditional theological contrasts. Instead, we should try to see what may come out of analysing Paul's many statements about the law and Christ seen from a 'philosophical' perspective of the *kind* one finds, for instance, in Stoicism. That will effectively put a stop to any Christian triumphalism (one hopes) and thus hopefully lead to a reading that does not just harmonize Paul where Sanders and Räisänen have pointed up problems.

31. Sanders 1977 emphatically restated the importance of atonement in Jewish 'covenantal nomism' (e.g. 157–80, 422).

32. Paul's reference in 2:19 to his having died to the law *through* the law is and remains difficult. The reading for which I have decided, which connects the phrase with 3:13, is also adopted by J. M. G. Barclay (1988, 80–1 n. 14 with references to others, including Schlier) and now by Martyn (1997a, 257). (Betz, by contrast, refers to 3:19–25, 1979, 122.) For a more traditional sketch of how there is redemption and blessing 'in Christ' through a soteriological pattern of '(eschatological) salvation by representation and participation', see, e.g. Donaldson 1986, 105 with references (112 n. 80). (In fairness to Donaldson it should be said that this sketch is only somewhat incidental to his main theme, which concerns the role of the law within a salvation-historical scheme that stresses the redemption of Israel from the 'curse of the law' as being necessary for the inclusion of the gentiles.) Stanley (1990, 506) rightly states that 'the details of the conception behind v. [3:]13 remain obscure', indeed 'a mystery to the modern reader'.

33. That is one of the most important results of the rejection of the traditional Protestant reading of Paul that is part of the new perspective on him. In discussing why Paul held that righteousness cannot come by the law, Sanders (1983, 17–64) has shown once and for all that the answer is neither the 'quantitative' one (because it is *impossible* to do the entire law) nor the 'qualitative' one (because doing the law itself *estranges*). Either answer would make the law intrinsically wrong-headed, by placing human beings in a situation in which they *must* do something that they *cannot* do or must do something that they must *not*, after all, really try to do. Paul nowhere states that *that* was what was wrong with the law.

34. It is astonishing to me that commentators generally do not see that the sentence quoted from 3:21 constitutes a well-aimed *praise* of the law. It is obviously true that Paul goes directly against an ordinary Jewish understanding of the law, according to which it *was* given to generate life. That Paul certainly denies. But his *ontōs ... an ēn* ('then verily ... would have been ...') is intended to give the law *as much praise as possible* —once one has grasped that it was *not* meant the way Jews regularly understood it. That is the only reading that will (*a*) give the *ontōs ... an ēn* its usual meaning and (*b*) make the verse serve to *explain* (witness *gar*, 'for') Paul's strong denial that the law went against God's promises. Neither Betz nor Martyn sees this positive side to 3:21b. R. N. Longenecker (1990, 144) even concludes his exegesis of the verse as follows: 'Paul ... insists that no law can give life, and so righteousness in whatever its dimension, whether forensic or ethical, cannot be based on any law'. But that leaves the *ontōs ek nomou an ēn* entirely out of the summary! Similarly, Hartman (1993, 140–1) only retains from the verse the statement presupposed in its 'unreal condition': that the law was not life-giving and that righteousness does not come from the law. No attention is given to the *ontōs ... an ēn*. The same is true of the Greimasian analysis of the verse given by Hays (1983, 122–3). I suspect the reason for failing to see Paul's praise of the law in this verse is derived from a long tradition of translating the relevant sentence, a good example of which is Mussner's (1977³,

243): 'For (*only*) if [(*nur dann,*) *wenn*] a law had been given that could give life, would righteousness *in fact* [*wirklich*] had come from the law.' But *ontōs* does not have this *concessive* meaning. Rather, it has the positive, *affirmative* one to be found in 'verily', 'truly' and the like.

35. Everything is contested here. It is well known that Paul reaches a view in Romans according to which the law may in a sense be said to have had the purpose (God's, one supposes) to 'multiply' sin (5:20). That must be interpreted in its own context. It strikes me as almost inexplicable how commentators can settle for a similar interpretation for 3:19. That, however, is where both Betz and Martyn end (Betz 1979, 165: 'Rather than preventing transgressions, Paul's view [in Galatians and Romans, effectively taken together] is that the purpose of the Torah was to "produce" them.' Martyn 1997a, 355: 'the Law entered the picture, in its own time, in order to elicit transgressions (so also Rom 5:20)'). But how should Paul's Galatian addressees have had any chance of grasping his meaning if that was what he meant? Surely, a law, any kind of law—and 3:21b shows that Paul did see the Jewish Law as *a law* —has its whole *raison d'être* in *deterring* people from transgressing it. (Dunn 1993a, 189–90, is very close to seeing this.) Moreover, Betz himself shows that that was the traditional Jewish understanding too (as against Paul's own allegedly 'decidedly non-Jewish position'). Similarly, Räisänen (1983, 140), speaks of 'the good Jewish sense of '"preventing transgressions"'', but also declares that in the Pauline verse the phrase 'can hardly be taken' in that way. Why?

The issue obviously also pertains to the question of what picture of the function of the law Paul is giving in 3:22–5. The following comprehensive reading, partly proposed by Lull 1986, strikes me as simple and sane: the law was brought in (in the last resort probably by God himself) in order to keep sinning down *until* the arrival of Christ; in fulfilling this task, the law (that is, scripture) acted as a jailer (cf. 3:22), a guard (cf. 3:23) and a children's disciplinarian or pedagogue (cf. 3:24) who was relatively successful in preventing transgressions, but who for that very reason was also felt to be somewhat oppressive. Lull 1986 is excellent on 3:19: the law was given 'to curtail transgressions' (483), 'to *curb* or *prevent* transgressions until the ... arrival ... of Jesus Christ' (489)—and Romans is not of much use since 'even in Romans one can find various views of the Law that do not add up to a single, coherent view' (484–5). I cannot, however, agree with Lull that the law was meant to provide 'protective custody' (488), that the purpose of its '"enslaving character" ... is precisely one of "protection"' (496). Sanders (1983, 66–7), whom Lull quotes, is better: 'The law as pedagogue ... is more an enslaver than a protector.' Only this hardly implies—as Sanders seems to think— that the law was given to *produce* transgressions. The law said: you *must not* do—whatever sinful people would wish to do. And that was *felt to* have an enslaving character, namely, in relation to the sinful desire. Since the law could not *remove* the desire, it also makes sense to say that it enclosed the human being under sin.

It is important not to read into Paul's picture of the pedagogue the idea that he serves in the institution of 'education toward virtue' (for this general idea behind the notion of a pedagogue see Lull 1986, 491–3). Lull explicitly distinguishes his own position from the traditional one that gives to the law a preparatory role in relation to Christ (1986, 496–8). But the reason he needs to do this is precisely that he has ascribed to the law a quasi-positive role as a 'protector'. Leave that out and the function of the law will *only* be to curb transgressions as best it can. Belleville 1986 brings out well how the law as a pedagogue 'supervises', 'rebukes' and 'punishes' (59–60, esp. 60). Unaccountably, she also insists that existence 'under law' is neither positive nor negative (60), but 'neutral' (71). But Paul's repeated use of being *under* this or the other thing (3:10: a curse, 3:22: sin, 3:23/4:5: the law, 3:25: a pedagogue, 4:2: guardians and stewards, 4:3: the elements of the world) must, it seems, have a strong—and strongly negative—experiential component. S. K. Williams (1997) ends his careful analysis of 3:19–25 (97–103) by finding—rightly—in 3:19 a reference to 'the restraining role of that law—the Law of Moses—which instructed, rebuked, and punished' (103). Young (1987) brings out well the temporary role of the ancient pedagogue.

36. It is to the great credit of Suhl 1987 (3119, 3122) to have seen this specific connection of 5:13 ff with all that precedes. But Suhl does not at all draw the consequence for our understanding of Paul's idea of righteousness that I go directly on to formulate.

37. Much of this, though not all, can be found in Ziesler 1972 (e.g. 168–71). It is, as Ziesler says (1), 'at odds with the usual Protestant understanding' and—to make Ziesler's words my own—it 'was certainly not foreseen when the study was begun'.

38. The notoriously opaque details of this need not concern us.

39. For references compare, e.g. J. M. G. Barclay 1988, 63 n. 76.

Notes for Chapter 8

1. Donfried (ed.) 1991²a, lxiv–lxv, quotes the views of two such perceptive scholars as Achtemeier (1985) and Paul Meyer (1988) who question the search for a single meaning for the letter. While there is probably little to be gained from discussing this issue in the abstract, it is obviously very important that a reader of Romans be constantly aware of what kind of unity at what level of reading he or she is looking or arguing for.

2. That was the basic direction taken in the first edition of *The Romans Debate* (Donfried 1977, compare the introduction as repeated in Donfried (ed.) 1991²a, xli–xlvii), where some form of the older view was represented by Bornkamm 1991 (1963) and Manson 1991 (1948). By 1991 (the second edition, compare the introduction to that, Donfried (ed.) 1991²a, xlix–lxxii) the more topical interpretation had won the day. As Donfried says (1991²a, lxix): 'Without ques-

tion a consensus has been reached that Romans is addressed to the Christian community in Rome which finds itself in a particular historical situation.'

3. It seems to me, however, that the old issue raises its head again when scholars ask about Paul's *'theological'* intention, purpose or purposes in writing the letter (thus, e.g. Donfried (ed.) 1991²a, lxxi, reflecting a widespread approach among scholars), as if that particular kind of intention might differ from the more immediately situation-oriented one. However, one lesson that was learned from the intensive work done in the *Pauline Theology Group* under the Society of Biblical Literature was that 'theology' and 'topicality' must precisely not be separated. Beker's well-known distinction between 'coherence' and 'contingency' formulates this insight well, as long as it is understood that there is no theological coherence independently of the way in which 'the gospel' (*un*specified or stated only vaguely and generally) is in fact played out in Paul's handling of the topical contingencies of the particular situation with which he is dealing. (For Beker's distinction see, e.g. Beker 1980, 11–16.) Thus any analysis of Romans that attempts to find some unity of the letter at the general level of ('theological') ideas only in fact represents a step back to the traditional kind of reading the letter.

4. Klein 1991 (1969) helpfully distinguished between two general approaches to Romans, the first of which has regarded Paul as being more occupied with his own concerns than with those of the Roman community, whereas the second has seen Paul to address the Romans for their own sake (1991, 30).

5. Koester (1980, 575) speaks of Romans as a letter of 'self-recommendation'. As we shall see, the term itself is almost on target: *ein Empfehlungsschreiben des Paulus für sich selbst*. Paul did write primarily to prepare for a reasonably extended stay for himself in Rome. But his strategy for achieving this aim was quite different from just giving a calm exposé of the way he himself understood the gospel.

6. This is clear, e.g. from the way Koester (1980, 575–6) develops his understanding of the letter as one of self-recommendation.

7. Methodologically, I am in line here with the general approach advocated in J. M. G. Barclay 1987.—The literature on the *'Abfassungszweck'* or 'reasons for Romans' is extensive. There is a good overview of the issues in Fitzmyer 1993, 68–84. In addition to a number of independent weighty discussions (e.g. Wilckens 1974b, Kettunen 1979 and not least Wedderburn 1988), a good deal of the relevant shorter treatments are anthologized in Donfried (ed.) 1991²a. Fitzmyer is right in referring again to the suggestive discussion in Marxsen 1963, 85–97. Marxsen was one of the first to take the 'topical' approach to Romans sufficiently seriously to attempt a reading of the whole letter in that light. However, against Marxsen and other similar readings (like that of F. Watson 1986, part of which is anthologized in Donfried (ed.) 1991²a, 203–16), I shall insist on the greatest possible degree of minimalism. Thus I shall not be looking for a plural set of 'reasons for Romans' (like Wedderburn 1988) nor be happy

with the conclusion of Fitzmyer (1993, 80) that 'his [Paul's] purposes in writing Romans have been multiple'. Instead the task will be this: to find a single and simple reason for Romans that takes seriously the letter's character as a real letter (compare the epistolary framework, 1:1–15 + 15:14 ff) and is able to combine that with a 'topical' reading of the letter bulk as a whole.

8. Jerusalem: e.g. Jervell 1991 (1971). Spain: Jewett 1988, 1995.

9. The importance of 15:14–15 for determining Paul's aims with the letter is rightly emphasized by Sampley (1995b, 129).

10. Cranfield (1975–9, 753) takes it the latter way, arguing that Paul's *apo merous* ('partly') qualifies *egrapsa* ('I have written'), namely in 12:1–15:13. (Wilckens 1982, 117, concurs.) It is probably best to see *apo merous* as qualifying the *combined* phrase of *tolmēroteron ... egrapsa* ('I have written somewhat boldly in part'). But there is no necessity that this should refer specifically to 12:1ff. What, for instance, about 11:13–25 or 8:1–13? It will only seem 'natural' (Cranfield) to connect the phrase specifically with 12:1ff if one takes it that Paul here turns to something distinctly new, namely exhortation. But that, as I shall argue, is quite false.

11. This conclusion is shared, e.g. by Cranfield 1975–9, 86: '*euangelizesthai* is here used of preaching to those who are already believers'. (Compare also Dunn 1988, 33–4 and Fitzmyer 1993, 251.) Schlier (1977, 40) takes *euangelizesthai* in the sense of 15:20 and as different from making the Romans strong and achieving something among them, namely as referring to the addition of *new* members to the Roman congregations. But how will that fit Paul's declared readiness to 'preach the gospel' *to* 'you in Rome'? Wilckens (1978, 81–2) at least sees that Paul's *euangelizesthai* in 1:15 refers to what he goes immediately on to say (1:16 ff)—and hence to the rest of the letter. But since that is obviously directed to Christ-believers (compare 1:15 'you in Rome' with 1:6–7 'among whom you too are called of Jesus Christ, / to all in Rome (who are) God's beloved, holy called ones'), the meaning of *euangelizesthai* will be this: to do whatever Paul does in the letter to his Christ-believing addressees. And that he himself identifies at the end of the letter as a matter of 'admonishing' and 'recalling'. There is a strong German tradition for taking *euangelizesthai* in Paul to refer *only* to 'first time evangelization'. The motive for this is probably doctrinal. Wilckens in principle broke away from that. But the best comment is in Kümmel 1980[20], 272–3: 'Paul came to Rome to a congregation that had not been set up by himself, not in order to work there as a missionary; but being a *servant of Jesus Christ to the gentiles* (15:16) he was obviously *eager also to preach the gospel to you in Rome* (1:15) or, as he also formulates it, *to remind you* (of the gospel) *because of the grace I have received* (15:15); and the letter to the Romans is already the putting into practice [*Vollzug*] of such "reminding".'

12. In itself the scope of this claim is only fairly restricted: that *Paul* saw Romans as a letter in which he had 'preached the gospel' in the sense of 'admonished' his addressees and 'recalled' the basic elements in the Christ faith. Should we also

take Romans as a 'letter of parenesis' as modern scholars employ that term? It is not clear that the question of the 'literary genre' of parenesis (presumably to be taken in ancient terms) has received any genuinely satisfactory answer in the scholarly literature. The discussion of 'Letters of Exhortation and Advice' in Stowers 1986, 91–152 is particularly illuminating. Stowers sensibly draws a *modern* distinction between *protreptic* as standing for 'hortatory literature that calls the audience to a new and different way of life' and *parenesis* as standing for 'advice and exhortation to continue in a certain way of life' (92). Unaccountably (since Paul's assumed audience *had* been called), Stowers goes on to suggest that 'Paul's letter to the Romans is a protreptic letter' (114). He does qualify this later when discussing the 'letter of admonition': 'Romans is a protreptic letter that makes central use of indirect admonition . . . ; Paul acknowledges the admonitory character of the letter in 15:14–15'; this 'typical . . . assertion of the audience's lack of need for admonition . . . reflects the kinship between paraenesis and admonition. Admonition is correction for those whose moral health is fundamentally good. It is encouragement which reminds them to live up to what they are' (128). Surely what all this suggests is that, as Stowers has defined the terms, Romans just is a letter of *parenesis*, and not of *protreptic*. The same basic point—that Paul assumes that his Roman addressees already are converted and that there is therefore no need for *protreptic*—also holds against the suggestion by Aune (1991a, shorter version in Donfried (ed.) 1991²a, 278–96) that we should see Romans as a *logos protreptikos*.

13. In general I concur here with Stowers (1994, e.g. 21–3) who employs Dunn 1988 as a good example of how extraneous information about Jews and Christ-believers in Rome is brought into the interpretation of the letter. While Stowers' criticism is basically methodological (text versus history), I would also emphasize the speculative character of any comprehensive reconstruction like Dunn's. Scholars may not like such minimalist austerity. But I find it mandatory.

14. See in particular Stowers 1994, 29–33.

15. Stowers 1981 worked out the importance of taking into account Paul's use of diatribe style, e.g. for determining his encoded readership. This insight does not necessarily stand and fall with the further elaborations in Stowers 1994 of who the diatribal *sy* ('you') stands for in any particular passage. On the contrary, the basic point will stand even where some of the elaborations may fall.

16. This general understanding of Paul's addressees in 7:1–6 is now becoming standard, see, e.g. Dunn 1988, 359 and Fitzmyer 1993, 457.

17. Paul: 'Therefore, receive *one another* (*allēlous*), as Christ too received *you* (*hymas*, namely, gentiles!) into the glory of God'. That is, just as Christ received *you*, so *you* must receive 'one another', meaning the 'weak'. Note how the reading suggested here regarding who are being directly addressed in 14:1–15:13 fits in with Stowers' general point that the direct addressees are gentiles and that Jews are only addressed diatribally. Stowers himself, however (1994, 317), rejects

the reading of the passage that equates the 'weak' with Jewish-oriented Christ-believers and the 'strong' with gentile-oriented ones. On this see more below.

18. The aim of this section being what it is, I shall refrain from giving detailed references.

19. This is quite traditional, of course. Stowers argues (1994, chs 4–5) that 'reading 2:17–29 [and 3:1 ff] as a set of propositions about the sinfulness and depravity of Jews in general or all Jews constitutes an egregious misreading' (153). Instead, Paul is only addressing a special kind of Jewish 'teacher of gentiles'. Much as I would be prepared to consider such a 'rereading', I cannot let myself be persuaded that 3:9 means anything other than what it directly says: that Paul has 'already charged that both Jews and Greeks are all under sin'. (But see later on what that, more specifically, does mean.) The traditional content of much of what follows will be immediately clear to students of 'rereadings' like those in Gaston 1987, Stowers 1994 and Nanos 1996. While I applaud the strongly 'Jewish orientation' of these attempts—not least in acknowledgement of the wholly justified revolution in Pauline studies effected by the 'Jewish orientation' of scholars like Stendahl and Sanders—I cannot in the end make them fit the Pauline text. As everywhere in this book, my own claim to novelty has little to do with this particular kind of concrete historical reinterpretation. Instead, it operates on the somewhat more abstract level of Paul's system of ideas, trying to illuminate *that* by historically based reinterpretation. In this latter respect Stowers, in particular, is in line with the present approach, e.g. in his elaboration of the central importance for the argument of Romans of the concept of self-mastery.

20. For this point see the convincing discussion and rejection in Segal 1990, 129–32, of the view of Lloyd Gaston, in particular, that Paul allowed for 'two paths to salvation', Christ faith for gentiles without adoption of the law—but the law for Jews. Segal 1990, 334 n. 27: 'As a Jew, I would like very much to agree with ... Gaston that Paul never denies that salvation comes from the law, however I cannot do so on the basis of this passage [Gal 2:16].' As Segal sees, the same holds for Romans. For a thorough rejection of Gaston's basic idea, with particular respect to Romans 9–11, see also E. E. Johnson 1989, 176–205.

21. This is the excellent translation in Wright 1995, 35, which Wright bases on the interpretation in Cranfield 1975–9, 90–1.

22. (a) On the position of 8:12–13: Wilckens 1980, 120 has a good discussion of how to divide the text. He is right to reject separating 8:12–13 from 8:1–11 (as is done by Michel, Kuss, Käsemann, Cranfield, Schlier and Dunn). His argument to take 8:1–17 together is not convincing, however. He sees that 8:14–17 lays the substantive basis for the next section, but thinks that in formal terms it belongs with what precedes—because of the *gar*, which has an explanatory function. But this is problematic. 8:14 does not *explain* 8:13b in a backward-looking way. Rather, it develops or *explicates* it further in a manner that looks distinctly forward. Perhaps, on the basis of a passage like this one we should

speak of an 'explicatory *gar*' in Paul that is used to introduce a *new* thought. Others who divide at 8:14 include Schnackenburg (1975), von der Osten-Sacken (1975a), Byrne (1986), Elliott (1990) and Fitzmyer (1993).

(b) Few have recognized the basically parenetic character of 6:1–8:13. One can understand why. After all, Paul seems primarily intent on developing what *actually follows* with regard to sinning from participation in the Christ event. 'We' *are* dead and buried with Christ in baptism and so are also dead to sin (ch. 6). 'We' *are* dead to the law, so that we (now, actually) serve in the newness of the spirit (7:6). 'You' *are* in the spirit and not in the flesh (8:9)—consequently (*ara oun*), 'we' *are* obligated *not* to the flesh, to live according to the flesh … (8:12). However, 8:12–13 gives the game away: 'we' are—*obligated*; for if '*you*' live in accordance with flesh … ! In other words, Paul spells out what *has* happened to his Christ-believing addressees (with regard to sinning) as a *means* of *exhorting* them to *make* it happen. But that is precisely a central logical figure in Pauline parenesis. Who would claim that Paul is *only* describing in 6:1–8:13 what *has* happened to his addressees? If all therefore agree that he *also* intends to use such a description to exhort his addressees, *more* or *less* implicitly (no matter which), to *make* it happen—then the section *is* basically parenetic as Paul handles parenesis. To take but one example, Elliot (1990, 237) says this: 'The argumentation moves from the rhetorical question in 6.1 ("Shall we continue in sin that grace may abound?") toward the cumulative and definite answer (cf. *ara oun*) in 8.12–13 ("we are obligated, then, *not* to the flesh, to live according to flesh … ")'. This is exactly right on the coherence of 6:1 to 8:12–13. But in another way it is quite wrong. Paul does not merely aim to provide a 'definite *answer*' to the question of 6:1 as if it were a merely theoretical, indeed a 'theological' one. He aims, basically, to exhort. (Elsewhere, following Boers 1982, Elliott does recognize the *general* parenetic character of the letter, e.g. 1990, 290–1.)

One scholar saw both the 'parenetic direction' (*Tendenz*) of 7:6 (in relation to 7:5), 8:1ff (in relation to 7:14–25) and 8:12–13 in relation to 8:1–11—and also the connectedness of 8:12–13 to 8:1–11 as against 8:14: Schnackenburg 1975, 297–8 and 298 n. 29, which could not be better.

23. Dunn 1988, 844–5, brings this out well. Compare also Fitzmyer 1993, 705–6: 'The paragraph forms the conclusion to the hortatory section (12:1–15:13) and is the logical conclusion to the letter as a whole (1:16–15:13).'

24. There are various positions in this area. (a) Karris (1991 [1973]) originally declined to see any specific parenetic point to the general exhortation of 14:1–15:6 (77, 83). That view has few adherents. (b) Sampley (1995a, 48, and 1995b, 123–5), has recently argued against identifying the weak and strong as two distinct groups (as did Karris 1991, 77–81), but he certainly does take the passage to have direct, topical import (1995a, 42, 48–9)—and in fact to be about 'an ethnically grounded struggle' (48). His line is followed by Jaquette (1995a, 126–36) in a manner that makes it very close to position (d) below. (c) For the case against seeing the 'weak' to represent, basically, Jewish or Jewish-oriented Christ-

believers as against 'strong', non-Jewish-oriented Christ-believers, see—in addition to Karris (Sampley's reading is more complex): Stowers 1994, 317, 321 and W. S. Campbell 1995, 270–7. (But how does the latter's conclusion on p. 277 cohere with his sketch of a scenario on p. 275?) (d) For the opposite view see in particular the careful discussions in Cranfield 1975–9, 690–7, Wilckens 1982, 109–15, and J. M. G. Barclay 1996b, 288–93. Compare also Reasoner 1995, 288–90 (responding to Campbell 1995.) As will become clear, I am convinced by the arguments for the latter position, including the point that this reading alone will explain Paul's explicit talk of Jews and gentiles in 15:7–13. (J. M. G. Barclay declines to build on this, 1996b, 290 n. 10.) Still, Stowers is right on the general (moral philosophical) sense of 'weakness' (namely of conviction, compare also Rom 6:19). And Sampley is right on the very oblique character of Paul's argument in the two chapters.

25. See Sampley 1995a. Also, independently, J. M. G. Barclay 1996b, 289.

26. Wilckens (1982, 110) brought this out well.

27. References in Wilckens 1982, 114, and J. M. G. Barclay 1996b, 291 n. 15.

28. J. M. G. Barclay (1996b, 191) is right to emphasize this.

29. The syntax of 15:9 init. is notoriously difficult. Compare the careful analysis of Wilckens 1982, 106. I cannot agree with his final decision to let *doxasai* be governed by *legō*. Since *doxasai* is in the aorist, that would make the meaning come out as referring to the past: that the gentiles *have* glorified (or come to glorify) God. Cranfield (1975–9, 742–3) thinks that *doxasai* as governed by *legō* may have a present meaning ('I declare that ... but that the Gentiles are glorifying ...'). That seems to me altogether impossible Greek. We should rather conclude the other way round: if, as 15:6 and 7 together seem to imply, the reference to gentile glorification of God has a basically forward-looking meaning, then the tense of *doxasai* will *prove* that 15:9a continues 15:8b (*eis to bebaiōsai ktl.*) and is thus subordinate to the point that Christ has become a servant of the Jewish people. (That fits, as we shall see, the most plausible reading of chs 9–11.) Wright (1995, 62), Hays (1995, 84), and E. E. Johnson (1995, 220) read the two verses in the same way. For a full discussion see J. R. Wagner 1997, who proposes a new reading that runs as follows in translation: 'For I say that the Christ has become a servant of the circumcision on behalf of the truthfulness of God, in order to confirm the promises made to the patriarchs, and [a servant] with respect to the Gentiles on behalf of the mercy [of God] in order to glorify God.' However, (a) it seems impossible to move back to *Christon diakonon gegenēsthai* in front of *ta de ethnē* to obtain the desired grammatical subject for *doxasai* (namely, Christ)—and then to move back only to *eis to bebaiōsai* to obtain the required *eis* in front of *doxasai*. Also, (b) the reading of *ta de ethnē* as a sort of accusative of respect is very unpersuasive. Finally, (c) what Paul wishes to say, according to 15:7b, is that Christ *accepted 'you'*, that is, the gentiles, *into* glorification of God, which is precisely what he does say in the contested

sentence if it is read strictly consecutively: '(Christ became a servant to the *Jews*) in order to confirm … and (in order that) the *gentiles* might glorify God …' Meeks' comment on this is entirely apposite: 'Note the indirection of this claim: Christ accepted the *Gentile* Christians by being a *diakonos* of the *Jews*, in order to fulfil promises made in the Jewish scriptures to Jewish patriarchs about Gentiles' (Meeks 1987, 292, Meeks' italics).

30. Compare our remarks on this in ch. 7 n. 12.

31. Another way of putting this reading runs: For the gentiles to glorify God in the proper way is for them to be directed towards Christ (compare 15:11–12) together with the Jews (compare 15:10 *meta tou laou autou*, 'together with his people'). But the only way they can do this is by themselves repeating *Christ's* act of *receiving* themselves (as reflecting *God's* act of *mercy* to *them*)—when he became a servant *to the Jews*, that is, by themselves becoming servants to the Jews.

32. Furnish (1968, 101 and 106) has some excellent remarks that point in the direction I am suggesting we should go. I believe there remains a difference, however. Here is Furnish: 'The question is frequently raised whether the introductory *oun* ("therefore") of vs. 1 is only transitional and thus points to no important logical or inner connection between what precedes and what follows it, or whether it refers "to the result of the whole preceding argument"' (101, quoting Sanday and Headlam 1902⁵, 351). And more: 'The first verses of chap. 12 offer a fresh statement, now in the imperative mood, of what it means to receive by faith the revealing of God's righteousness (1:16–17). Romans 12–15 is not, therefore, just an appendix on Christian morals. These exhortations not only presuppose the "theological" assertions of chaps. 1–11, but supply a further and needed explication of that one gospel (God's power for salvation) which both "theology" and "ethics" seek to unfold' (106). 'Explication' is a good term. But 'point' would be even better. The very point of Paul's 'theologizing' lies in—action. And that is what Romans 12–15 brings out. Thus there are not just the two possible ways highlighted by Furnish of construing the relationship of the explicit parenesis in 12:1ff with what precedes. In addition, there is a third, which is even stronger than Furnish's second one: that 12:1ff spells out ('explicates') in directly *practicable* terms what all the rest (the comprehensive world-view) *points towards*, namely, *action*—which is something for which the addressees, on *their* side, are then responsible. If *they* understand and accept what *Paul* has said, then *they* will *act* accordingly. The 'theology', we might say, is *tilted towards* action.

33. See ch. 4 above.

34. I am pleased to note that that is where Sampley 1995a does end. A few quotations: 'All of Romans, from beginning to end, is an apostolic intervention, pastoral in style, in an intramural, ethnically grounded struggle over leadership and position in the Roman house-churches' (49). 'Rom 1:18–8:39 is not … the doctrinal base from which Paul will subsequently build ethical implications. In

chapters 1 through 8, indeed in 1 through 11, Paul's interest is not doctrine *per se* but the establishment of the broadest possible ground upon which all of the Roman believers, no matter what their ethnic background, can see that they stand in common' (50). Finally, Sampley speaks of 'the major sections of Romans as a sustained, cohesive, comprehensive address of the Roman factions, as a quest for unity' (50). For other similar statements about the relationship of chapters 1–11 to the rest, see, e.g. Marxsen 1963 (e.g. 94: 'In chapters 1–11, Paul prepares his solution to the Roman problem by more general statements of principle; but he only addresses the problem directly towards the end of the letter after these justifying considerations'), Bartsch 1967 (an article that has hardly made the impact it deserves), Boers 1982 (e.g. 194: 'Paul's letter to the Romans ... appears to be as much as any of his letters ... directed to what he believed to have been concrete pastoral issues of the church of Rome. The letter is as direct, and as hard-hitting, a moral confrontation as is Galatians, even though the tone and the reasoning is more relaxed'—curiously, in Boers 1994 there is nothing comparable to this strong emphasis on the basically parenetic character of Romans) and Meeks 1987 (e.g. 290: 'Paul's advice [in chs 12–15] about behavior in the Christian groups cannot be rightly understood until we see that the great themes of chapters 1–11 here receive their denouement. And we do not grasp the function and therefore the meaning of those theological themes in their epistolary context unless we see how Paul wants them to work out in the everyday life of the Roman house communities').

35. Note that the basic mistake of these people is that of negligence. There is no whisper of anything that has to do with the traditional idea of 'rebellion against God'. That belongs to later theology and matches the traditional misreading of Paul's understanding of Jewish *kauchēsis* as boasting *over against God*. With the point about negligence connect the fact that Paul is constantly speaking in 1:18–32 of a lack of understanding (an *'intellectual'* error), not one of 'will'. Paul's basic moral psychology is just different from (and more Stoic than) that of later theology, e.g. Augustine's.

36. Scholars who *reject* the traditional reading of these people as Jews (to counterbalance the gentiles of 1:18–32) include Bassler (1982, 135–6), Stowers (1981, 112, and 1994, 100–4) and Elliott (1990, 174–90).

37. That was Stowers' basic argument for adopting this reading.

38. Compare Bassler 1982, 136.

39. I presuppose here that the old question concerning the identity of the people referred to in this passage—gentile *Christians* or *non*-Christ-believing gentiles?—has been settled for the second alternative. For a convincing discussion see Bassler 1982, 141–5.

40. For a good discussion of this and other attempts to deny that Paul is speaking of gentiles 'really fulfilling the requirements of the law', see Räisänen 1987, 103–6. We should agree that 'Paul is really speaking of Gentiles who fulfil the

law outside the Christian community' (105). However, if that was *all* there is to be said, then Paul would be in real trouble. (Is he not out to argue that *only* the Christ faith 'solves' the 'problem' that he is aiming to identify?) That only suits Räisänen, who is intent on laying bare the apostle's incoherence. By contrast, if one is more inclined than Räisänen was to give Paul the benefit of the doubt, one will feel the need to press on where Räisänen (cheerfully) accepted defeat.

41. Räisänen (1987, 105 n. 64) too advances this argument while also noting that 'the train of thought would be clearer and the contrast more effective, if this verse, too, were intended as a reference to mere Gentiles'. However, that is only superficially so, as we shall see. In this final verse of comparison between gentiles and Jews, Paul apparently aims to suggest that the true *Jew* (2:28) and *also* the gentile who fulfils the law (2:26–27) is—the Christ-believer, who has been circumcised on the heart with God's spirit (2:29). This is both bold and compressed. And it would be worth nothing if we could not spell it out in a manner that makes empirical sense. But we can, as we shall see. Byrne (1996, 104) states well enough that 'it is a disservice to Paul's argument to "christianize" it "too early" and fail to appreciate the way in which it operates as an "inner-Jewish" indictment couched in biblical terms'. But that is precisely the point. It *is* an *inner*-Jewish indictment—that for Paul pointed towards the *Christ* belief. In a refreshingly bold article, Snodgrass (1986, 74–5) characterizes reading the true Jew as the Christ-believer as 'a rather strong case of Christian "provincialism"'. But again, it is precisely the kind of sectarian *Judaism* that was Paul's understanding of the Christ faith. That understanding did have its element of exclusivist 'provincialism'. Fridrichsen 1922 on the 'true' Jew is still worth reading, not least for the convincing manner in which he shows the Stoic context for the Pauline contrasts of 2:28–29. Fridrichsen (43–44) too rejected seeing the 'true' Jew of 2:29 as a Christ-believer. But that is partly because he failed to distinguish between on the one hand those described in 2:12–16 and 26–27 and on the other the 'true' Jew of 2:29, partly because he neglected the argument from the reference to the *pneuma*.

42. That is, neither by having the law nor, of course, through Christ; they 'simply' do it. For further discussion see Bassler 1982, 141–5, together with Pohlenz 1949, 75–82, Bornkamm 1970³ (1959) and Martens 1994. It is obvious that the whole of 2:12–16 is redolent with ideas that are *ultimately* derived from Greek philosophy and political thought. It also seems likely that Paul was aware of this. The important point, however, is that he was able to use this material *for his own purposes*, without feeling the need to be 'correct' and 'technical', *but also without any sense of moving into a different world of thought*. Here Paul was light years in advance of most of his modern commentators. Wilckens (1978, 135) is right on 2:14–15: 'The interpretation must stay closely with the intention (*Skopos*) of the text and must avoid misreadings on either side: neither claim that Rom 2:14–15 lays the foundation for a Christian theory of natural right nor reduce Paul's adoption of central ideas in the Hellenistic philosophical tradition to mere associations—or even deny it.'

43. I have been unable to find anybody who has asked about the specific point of Paul's reference in 2:15 to the internal battle and given the answer suggested here. The reason will be twofold: (*a*) that scholars do not regularly have the knowledge of the ancient ethical tradition which makes that reference stand out and (*b*) that scholars are not regularly open to finding anything like that *kind* of idea in the present text. However, the question calls for an answer. One can easily see why Paul brings in the *syneidēsis* ('conscience' or 'self-awareness') here. For that is what will bear witness on behalf of the gentile on the day when God will judge the interior of man. But why bring in the idea of an interior *battle*? To the person who knows the ancient ethical tradition (as Paul himself did) the answer will be immediately clear: because a *divided* interior is characteristic of either the weak-willed person (the *akratēs*), who though divided will regularly opt for the *wrong* decision—or of the strong-willed person whom Paul will have in mind here, the *enkratēs*, who will regularly do the right thing *even though* he is also divided. It is the idea of the gentiles of 2:12–16 as (no more than) *enkrateis* that will prove fruitful. For in the ancient ethical tradition the *enkratēs* points in the direction of another person: the truly good one whose character is such that there is no interior battle at all and who will therefore *always* do what is right. He is the one whom Paul will eventually introduce in 2:29.

44. Compare our analysis of the two kinds of 'boasting' (one wrong and one right) in ch. 6 above.

45. As Pauline scholarship has developed over the last 10 to 20 years, it is by now almost impossible to speak of 'the Jew' without this recalling the worst in Bultmann, Käsemann and others ('the Jew in us all', the *homo religiosus* and so forth). (*a*) But Paul does identify his dialogue partner in 2:17 ff in *general* terms as 'a *Ioudaios*' (2:17, 28, 29 and 3:1 ff) as opposed to *hē akrobystia* (2:26–27), that is, just gentiles. (*b*) This happens *after* he has three times (1:16, 2:9–10) spoken of 'the Jew first and also the Greek'. (*c*) And he ends by speaking about 'all Jews and Greeks' (3:9). It is impossible, therefore, not to take him to speak of 'the Jew' in the (totally innocent) sense of 'Jews'. Furthermore, as I have already suggested, in his dialogue with 'the Jew' Paul is not directing his remarks *to* Jews, but to his gentile addressees. He is putting 'a Jew' on stage in order to show *them* something, namely that outside Christ *they* are (or were) on the same footing as the Jews—that of being 'under sin'. This latter reading ultimately goes back to Stowers 1981. In his later book (1994), Stowers develops this reading away from seeing Paul as speaking of 'the Jew' in the sense of 'Jews as they are most'. Cf. n. 19 above.

46. Without wishing to argue anything here, let me just state my own understanding of 3:9: 'What then?' (asks Paul on behalf of his Jewish interlocutor). '*Are* we (Jews) (then, cf. 3:1 and the argument of 3:1–8) being held (by God) in a favoured position?' (namely, like courtiers by a Hellenistic king). 'Not' (Paul answers) 'in all respects' (*ou pantōs*—which is very different from *pantōs ou*: 'not at all') (—for instance not in this respect:) 'for we (I, Paul) have earlier (in

the letter, namely at 1:18–32 and 2:17–29) accused both Jews and Greeks of being all under sin'. That is, with regard to *sinning* (as opposed, e.g. to having had God's oracles entrusted to one, 3:2), 'we Jews' are *not* better off in relation to God. (Cranfield 1975–9, 189 n. 1, sadly considers the suggested reading of *proechometha* to be 'hardly ... more than a counsel of despair'. To me it seems quite straightforward. It is further supported by the fact that Paul employs the same political image later in the letter when he speaks of 'reconciliation' with God as a matter of gaining 'access' to him—as to a Hellenistic king, 5:2.)

47. The issue is discussed with great force in Räisänen 1987, 94–109. Räisänen aims to diagnose a strain and artificiality in Paul's 'theory that nobody can fulfil (or has fulfilled) the law' (107), which Räisänen rightly takes to be the brunt of Paul's argument in 1:18–32 and 3:9. Thus 2:12–16 shows that when Paul is not 'reflecting on the situation of the Gentiles [but 'only interested in proving the Jew guilty'], it is quite natural for him to think that they can fulfil the law' (106). Similarly, Paul elsewhere (Phil 3:6) shows that when he is not 'reflecting on the situation of the Jews from a certain theological angle he does not presuppose that it is impossible [for Jews] to fulfil the law' (106). Therefore, his account in Romans 2 of the failure of Jews is 'simply a piece of propagandist denigration' (101). Conclusion: 'Paul is *pushed to develop his argument into a preordained direction*' (108), 'Paul *does not succeed* in showing the sinfulness of the Jews in any empirically or logically convincing way' (108 n. 80, Räisänen's italics). As always, Räisänen focuses the issue very sharply: how can Rom 1:18–3:20 be understood as an 'empirically and logically convincing' argument that 'both Jews and Greeks are all under sin'? But once he has diagnosed the problem, he backs off from trying to solve it. Sanders (1983, 123–132) agrees with much in Räisänen's analysis: 'Let me put the matter clearly. Paul's case for universal sinfulness, as it is stated in Rom. 1:18–2:29, is not convincing: it is internally inconsistent and it rests on gross exaggeration' (125). In the end Sanders gives up finding any 'distinctively Pauline imprint in 1:18–2:29', taking it instead as a 'synagogue sermon' (129) that only belongs superficially in the letter. As against this, I shall eventually argue that chapter 2 in particular (which constitutes the true stumbling-block for Sanders) plays a crucial role since it goes a long way towards identifying what Paul saw as a *specific*, but wholly *pervasive* problem in human living outside the Christ faith (but of course *as seen from* the new perspective), a problem that will then be overcome *by* the Christ faith.

48. Wilckens (1978, 172) at least rightly paraphrases: 'All, Jews as well as Greeks, are under sin'. But it is not quite clear how he intends that to be understood. It is curious to see that commentators regularly do not discuss the issue. That follows from the fact that they more or less immediately begin to speak of 'the human condition'. But Paul speaks of 'Jews *and* Greeks'. It is a huge question *whether* the step should be taken from that to the human condition and *how* such a step should then be understood. Byrne (1996, 130, in a note on 3:23)

seems to have glimpsed the issue, but immediately lets it fall: 'As in 3:9 ... , "all" primarily envisages two groups—Jews and Gentiles—rather than all individuals, though the inclusion of all on an individual basis must [?] also be implied'—period!

49. Compare the relationship between 3:9b and 3:9a in the reading of the whole verse given above in n. 46. Right here in 3:9 Paul is after all engaged in a dialogue with a *Jewish* partner about the *Jewish* special relationship with God (3:1).

50. Thus it seems best to understand Paul's use here of *hystereisthai* with the genitive in the first place along the lines suggested by LSJ s.v. under III: (1) *lag behind, be inferior to* or (2) *fall below, fail to do justice to* a theme—and only secondarily as under IV.1, where our passage is actually mentioned: *fail to obtain, lack.* For the Jewish ideas that constitute the context for the latter understanding see, e.g. Byrne 1996, 130–1. As, e.g. 2 Cor 3:18 shows, that context is in fact highly relevant to Paul. But it does not seem to be at the forefront in the present passage, where it is the lack of human directedness *towards* God's glory that is mainly in view.

51. But once more, there is no suggestion of any 'rebellion' against God.

52. This is obviously not the place to discuss the issue of Paul and homosexuality. Two things should be more firmly acknowledged than is usually the case. First, Paul was clearly *against* homosexual practice. But secondly, he brings in the case of homosexual behaviour as an *example* of something *else*—that is his *real* target.

53. Please note that I am only exegeting what Paul was trying to say. Most of us would now say that in his remarks about same-sex relations he was just plain wrong. But the same among us would probably also agree that in his basic view of the intrinsic connection between the body and the self he was precisely, and profoundly, right. That probably constitutes the kernel of the challenge to us of Paul's construction of the (body- *and* self-*transcending*) Christ faith. What can— and will—we make of that?

54. This was very convincingly argued by Bassler (1982, 123–37). Strangely, this has not made any real impact on commentators like Dunn (1988) and Fitzmyer (1993). Even Stowers (1994) regularly speaks of 1:18–2:16. But Bassler's careful argument stands. Moreover 2:12–29 treats a quite distinct topic of its own: that of *doing* (an old theme)—*the law* (a new one).

55. Is it unacceptable to think that Paul thought that this is something that might actually happen, indeed that it sometimes did happen? Is it unacceptable to think that he was right in thinking so? As we are reading Paul here, he does not say that it *always* happens. Armed with the idea of an entirely new possibility in Christ (namely, that sinning *never* happens), he construes both gentiles and Jews as being 'under sin' in the sense of being *liable* to sin. Thus understood his critique of gentiles and Jews makes empirical sense. And the burden of argument

has now been changed to concern the claim that Christ-believers will be free even from the *risk* of sinning.

Notes for Chapter 9

1. This point, if not the specific construal of Paul's Jewish dialogue partner, is well brought out by Stowers (1994, 231 and *passim*).

2. Moxnes 1980 remains a valuable discussion of the argument of Romans 4 and the traditions behind it. Written in the main before the appearance of Sanders 1977 (Moxnes 1980, 104 n. 5), it to some extent reflects a traditional, contrastive understanding of Paul's relationship with Judaism. But its main conclusions stand and may easily be rephrased to take account of the new, post-Sanders perspective on Paul as one who saw himself as formulating what was now the true form of Judaism.

3. The understanding of 4:1–5 is strongly contested and a proper defence of the reading I shall briefly state here would involve a whole paper. But the issue does merit a rather longish note. 4:1: Against recent proposals I adopt a traditional understanding of this verse. 'What, then, shall we say that Abraham, our forefather in the flesh, has experienced?' (For this sense of *heuriskein* compare 7:21.) Following Hays 1985, Stowers translates: 'What then will we say? Have we found Abraham to be our forefather by his own human efforts [that is, according to the flesh]?' But (i) this construal of *kata sarka* seems to me syntactically impossible and (ii) *ton propatora hēmōn* cannot function as a predicate since it contains the article *ton*. (Wilckens 1978, 261, considers something like this reading and rightly rejects it. Hays does not consider the second objection, which I find decisive. By contrast, Zahn (1910, 215–16 n. 35), whose discussion Hays sensibly invokes, does consider the objection. His rejection of it does not, however, persuade. He reasonably compares with a sentence like *Iēsous estin ho Christos*, 'Jesus is the Christ', and then claims that an article was actually required in front of *propatora*, 'forefather': 'for Paul is not talking of any old forefather, but of the only one and the relationship of the Christians to him'. But how could Christ-believers conceivably have 'found' Abraham to be their *one and only* forefather according to the flesh?) 4:2–5: In reply to the question asked in 4:1, Paul states that Abraham has experienced being declared righteous from faith and not from any works: *For (gar)* if Abraham *had* been declared righteous on the basis of works, then—against what was said in the first half of 3:27—he *would* have a reason to boast (namely, of what he had achieved). In fact, however *(alla)*, he did *not* have such a reason in his relationship with God. *For* scripture says that Abraham was declared righteous because of his *trust* in God (that is, *not* of any works). Now if a person does works, this person will receive his reward not as an act of grace, but as something that is his due; but if (as was the case with Abraham) a person does not do works, but trusts the God who declares righteous even the person who is ungodly (that is, one who does

not do the proper works), then in the case of this person it is his trust that is reckoned as righteousness. (And that was what Abraham experienced.)

Three connected points on this: (*a*) 'Works' and 'do works' will still refer to works or acts that fall under the Jewish law. (*b*) Similarly, the 'ungodly' of 4:5 is the person who does not do works of the law. This follows from the flow of the sentence, which identifies *ho asebēs* ('the ungodly') with *ho mē ergazomenos* ('the one who does not do works of the law'). In 5:6 too 'we ungodly ones' similarly rephrases 'we *weak* ones', and that group will *include* Jews (like those described in 2:17–3:20). Thus, in the argument of 4:5 the 'ungodly' is not *necessarily* one who is *outside* the covenant. That is also made abundantly clear in 4:6–8 and even more so in 4:9, where Paul in effect says that David's praise as given in 4:6–8 touches not *only* Jews, but *also* non-Jews. It is true, as Paul goes on to say in 4:10 ff, that Abraham was *in fact* ungodly in the sense of being outside the covenant. For the covenant was just about to be instituted. But that does not touch the basic point, which is that God's grace is not seen here by Paul as something that had specifically to do with *non*-Jews. (*c*) If Abraham *had* been declared righteous from works of the law, he would be entirely justified in boasting of that (to others—or 'proud' of it in his relationship with God in the same way as Paul was himself proud of what he had achieved in his missionary work and ready to 'boast' of it on the day of Christ). Similarly, had he been reckoned righteous as a reward for doing works of the law, he would have been fully *entitled* to this reward, and there would have been nothing wrong with his obtaining it in that way. In fact, however, that was *not* what happened to Abraham.

The crucial point in all is that Paul does not in the least imply here that *had* Abraham been declared righteous from works of the law (*inside* the covenant once it had been instituted), there would have been anything wrong with this. Paul is not setting up a contrast between Abraham/Christ-belief on the one side and on the other a 'Judaism' that consists in doing the law. There is no criticism whatever of 'works righteousness' in these remarks that have so often been understood in that way. There is only a statement that works righteousness was *in fact* not what was involved.

4. Moxnes (1980, 104) briefly rejects an approach to Romans 4 that focuses on 'Paul's description of faith' in the chapter. He finds it 'psychological and individualistic' of the kind rightly criticized by Stendahl 1963 and 1976. But we are now learning that even though Stendahl was basically right in denying Paul's own pre-Christian psychological experiences to be the mainspring of his conversion and theologizing, and although Sanders was basically right in claiming that Paul's understanding of the 'solution' came before his theologizing development of the 'plight', this does not rule out an interest on Paul's part in 'psychology'. On the contrary, Paul was keenly interested in developing the 'psychological' shape of (Christ) faith, just as we have seen him to be keenly interested in developing the 'psychological' states that accounted for sin. Only, that interest is part of his (theologizing) development of *the solution*. It does not refer back

in any 'psychological and individualistic' manner to Paul's own, personal experiences.

5. It is worth pointing out that there is no indication that the idea of 'reconciliation' presupposes that of an earlier stage of 'rebellion' that was pointedly and explicitly directed *against* God—so that people did not do God's will *because* they *knew* it to be *God's* will. Rather, where they were previously directed towards *themselves* (I→I) in a manner that could well be *construed* from the *outside* (namely, from within the new perspective) as being 'inimical' and 'rebellious' in relation to God, they have now become totally directed towards God (I→X). That could then also be seen as implying a 'reconciliation' with God.

6. For this theme see in particular S. K. Williams 1980. (Also Kertelge 1967, 63–160, and Ziesler 1972, 186–209.)

7. For a forceful statement of this basic point see Byrne 1981, a paper that I (shamefully) did not know when writing Engberg-Pedersen 1995. In spite of the care with which Byrne addresses the issue, I am somewhat unhappy, though, with his claim that 6:1–8:13 should be seen against the presupposition of 'an intrinsic link between righteousness and the gaining of eternal life' (1981, 558). It would be better to say that Paul is spelling out to his addressees, for parenetic purposes, what the righteousness that they have been given concretely consists in. There is nothing for them to be *gained* here, only a 'living out the righteousness of God' (as Byrne's own title has it). Not surprisingly, I am not happy either with describing 6:1–8:13 as an 'ethical excursus' (even in scare quotes, Byrne 1981, 558 and 580). On the contrary, Paul is precisely spelling out what that righteousness, which through God's grace is now theirs, actually *consists* in. And that *is* something 'ethical'.

8. Schweitzer (1930, 214–16) even went to the opposite pole when he insisted that the doctrine of righteousness, of a 'cognitively (*gedanklich*) achieved salvation through faith', was 'only a fragment that had ripped itself off from the comprehensive, *mystical* doctrine of salvation' (215–16, my italics). That comes in reply to Schweitzer's own question, which is also mine: 'Do we find in Paul two conceptions of salvation side by side, one "substantive" [*naturhaft*] and one "cognitive" [*gedanklich*]?' (214). Where Schweitzer attacked the strategy of starting out from the doctrine of righteousness through faith (215) and moved on from there to his famous idea of seeing that doctrine rather as an unconnected *Nebenkrater*, I insist that we should *recognize* the two modes of thought but also see them as two different ways of expressing the *same* basic ideas. These *we* may bring out (through the I→X→S-model) in a manner that draws *directly* on one side of the supposed dichotomy but declines to see any contrast between what is said in either set of conceptual vocabulary.

Very much of what has now come to be seen as the special position of Schweitzer in fact goes back to Wrede 1907—who, strangely, made very little impact on Sanders 1977. (a) Wrede too begins from the doctrine of salvation (52 and 53–72) and relegates the doctrine of righteousness to a position of a far more subordinate *Kampfeslehre* as part of Paul's missionary enterprise (73–9). (*b*) In his account of the doctrine of salvation Wrede constantly emphasizes the 'substantive' character of entities like the flesh, sin, the law and death (e.g. 57). And he polemicizes against what he calls a 'onesidedly ethical interpretation of the Pauline doctrine', which is explained by the fact 'that people do not realize Paul's distance from modern ways of thought' (66). Instead Paul speaks of a *'substantive change of humankind* [Wrede's italics, namely, in Paul's quite 'realistically' (*eigentlich*) intended talk of 'dying with Christ' and the like, 62], *from* which the ethical change will then follow' (67, my italics). (*c*) Faith has no special role to play. It is nothing more than obedient acceptance of the message of salvation. 'Acceptance of that [message] immediately [*ohne weiteres*, 'without further ado'] produces that mystical [!] connection [*Verbindung*] with Christ through which his death and resurrection will now by itself [!] transfer itself to the believer, so that he too is dead and risen' (67). And so forth.

Wrede's account is no less fascinating in its forcefulness than Schweitzer's. But it is just as onesided. To give but one example, how could Wrede make his point about a 'substantive change of humankind from which the ethical change will then follow' (67)—when he has just (66) said this about the distinction between the 'merely substantive' (*das bloss Naturhafte*) and the 'ethical' (*das Sittliche*): *'Paul did not have this distinction'* (Wrede's own italics). Precisely! Why, then, insist onesidedly on the one aspect alone? Why not *recognize* the existence of both and try to work out their meaning by leaning on that side of the complex which is actually *accessible* to us (as the other one precisely is *not*)?

9. In addition to the major commentaries (e.g. Wilckens, Dunn, Fitzmyer, Byrne and Moo 1996), the bibliography of Fitzmyer (1993, 167–8, 439–43 and 452–3) gives access to the most helpful exegetical discussions.

10. E.g. Dunn (1988, 318): 'The societal and salvation-history dimension here should not be reduced to the pietistic experience of the individual'. What, however, if we did not understand the reference to the individual in the way suggested by Dunn's term 'pietistic'? And what if we did not seen any intrinsic opposition between Paul's talk of the individual and the 'societal and salvation-history' (or any other kind of collective) picture that he may also have had in mind?

11. Speaking of the Pauline expressions of having 'died with Christ' and been 'resurrected', Wrede (1907, 62) rejects an 'ethical' or 'metaphorical' interpretation of them: 'In truth, those expressions are through and through intended as *real* [*eigentlich*]. Paul is thinking of an actual [*wirklich*] death, of a dying of the same kind as Christ has himself experienced it, a participation [*Mitbeteiligung*] in his death' (Wrede's emphasis). Sanders (1977, 455) too has this thought: 'The participatory union is not a figure of speech for something else; it is, as many scholars have insisted [here Sanders refers to Schweitzer, Käsemann and J. A. T. Robinson], real.'

12. The point may also be put in terms of the phrase 'become (or be) what you are', which is sometimes (e.g. in Hooker 1985, 5) given as the proper gloss on the relationship between the indicative and the imperative—and sometimes precisely rejected as such (e.g. implicitly in Bultmann 1924, 127—and from then on in Dialectical Theology). As a better alternative one might suggest this: '*remain* what you are—and show it in practice'.

13. In a once quite often used terminology we can say the following. What is generated by the Christ event and Christ faith is this: *posse (non posse peccare)*— that it has now become *possible* that a person should arrive at a state in which he or she no longer *can* sin. Living under the law it was possible that somebody should not sin. But the possibility of sinning could not be *excluded*. The same in a way holds for living in Christ without further specification. But here the *possibility* is there of reaching a state in which even the risk of sinning is altogether excluded.

14. Aristotle: *Nicomachean Ethics* VII.vii.8, 1150b19–28. Stoics: *SVF* 3.471 p. 120 l. 31—p. 121 l. 3. Also 3.473 p. 123 ll. 1–3. In Stoicism *astheneia* is closely connected with the central idea of (psychic) *tonos* ('tension'), which is what accounts for the wise man's practice of right acts. For the precise understanding of the two terms in the Stoic explanation of passion (as basically a matter of weakness of will) see the detailed discussion in Engberg-Pedersen 1990, 182–200.

15. Note the emphatic position of *ēte* (you *were*), which has a correspondence in 7:6: *hote gar ēmen en tēi sarki* (when we *were* in the flesh).

16. For an extensive treatment of this phrase see Bjerkelund 1972. His comments on Rom 6:19 in particular are brief and not very helpful (93–4).

17. We should accept the interpretation of Cranfield here (1975–9, 325–6; also Fitzmyer 1993, 450–1, but rejected, e.g. by Moo 1996, 403–5, and Kaye 1979, 133). The basic argument is that this reading gives a very precise sense to the *gar* of the immediately following sentence: 'you became enslaved to righteousness (18). I speak in this human way only because of the weakness of your flesh. For just as you presented your limbs as slaves (*doula*) . . . , so you *must* now present your limbs as *slaves* (*doula*) to righteousness . . .' (19). Why does Paul change from speaking of making *oneself* a slave (6:16) to making one's *limbs* slaves (6:19)? Probably because in 6:19 he aims to focus very precisely on the concrete practice (the limbs) in which their status as 'slaves' *should* now express itself.

18. By contrast, it seems to me that such an otherwise sane and perspicuous commentator as Wilckens succumbs to the worst kind of theologizing in his exegesis of 6:19a (1980, 37–9)—to the effect that *finitum* is both *incapax* and *capax infiniti*.

19. For this expression compare what we got out of the identical expression in Gal 5:18.

20. See above, ch. 3.

21. In the light of this, the best reading of Paul's rhetorical strategy here is to see 7:7–25 as a systematically developed negative *foil* 'against which to highlight life in the Spirit (8:1–13)' (Byrne 1996, 216). This understanding, and the concomitant one that Paul is *not* speaking in 7:7–25 of the Christ-believer, is strengthened by noticing the careful way in which Paul has prepared for 7:7–8:13 in 7:5–6, with 7:5 giving the gist of 7:7–25 and 7:6 that of 8:1–13. For a closely similar reading see Schnackenburg 1975, 297–8. He saw the point about the negative foil (297), the 'appellative character' and 'parenetic tendency' of 7:6 and 8:1 (298)—and the fact that 8:12–13 go with 8:1–11 (298 n. 29).

22. These categories are taken from Räisänen 1987, 141. As always, Räisänen provides an excellent discussion of a given issue (here the 'negative purpose' of the law, 140–50) that sharpens one's understanding of the difficulties of interpretation. As always too, however, Räisänen stops short before trying to see whether it is not, after all, possible to find a reading that makes a coherent and consistent point. He never gives Paul the benefit of the doubt.

23. Commentators regularly take the phrase *hamartian gnōnai* in the sense of 'get to know' sin in the sense of *having* or 'experiencing' it. Dunn (1988, 378) sees that this does not quite fit the phrase *epithymian eidenai* in the last part of the verse, which 'tends to denote more rational knowledge'. Since this phrase is brought in to explain the other, that in itself points to a cognitive reading.

24. Nobody seems to question this understanding. But then this *hina* sentence ('in order that') should throw light on the next *hina* sentence in the verse, which appears to have a completely parallel function.

25. Fitzmyer (1993, 469) rightly exegetes: so that 'the true colors of sin might be shown *for what they are*' (my italics).

26. The classic treatment is Kümmel 1974 (1929). For an important qualification of reading the *egō* as a 'purely fictive I' see Theissen 1983, 194–204. Meyer (1990, 64–5) agrees with Kümmel that 'the passage is not autobiographical in any sense that allows it to yield details about Paul's personal life, either before his conversion or after. Paul is employing rather a rhetorical style in which the self functions in a representative way as a type or paradigm for others' (64). But he is also right to insist that 'it is impossible to dismiss all personal nuances from his use of "I"' (65). Paul is precisely *imagining* what—seen from his new vantage point—it *was* like, *as it were* for himself, to live under the law—now that a wholly new possibility has opened up.

27. I find it difficult to understand how such a perceptive and independent critic as Paul Meyer can deny that that is in fact Paul's theme (1990, 76), when he has even (cf. 83 n. 45) studied Theissen's careful collection (1983, 213–23) of the parallel material. There are probably two reasons for this, both of which go back to faulty German theologizing: (*a*) Paul views man as a whole, as against the ancient philosophical distinctions between various layers in the self. Compare Meyer (76): 'Paul is not talking about the conflict between the rational and the irrational in the human self, nor about two selves at different levels, as

though one were under the power of sin and the other not. Both "inmost self" (v. 22) and "members" (v. 23) are but two aspects of the same self that is "sold under sin". Does this not ultimately derive from the Protestant *simul iustus—et peccator*? (*b*) Meyer adopts (as a 'brilliant exegetical observation', 75) Bultmann's famous idea that the object of 'willing' throughout this passage is not the fulfilling of the law's commandments, but 'life', and conversely, that what in fact comes out of all our doing is 'death'. This seems sheer theologizing with next to no exegetical basis in the text itself. It is true that the object of *katergazesthai* ('to bring about, achieve') is 'death' in 7:13. But 7:18 *proves* that this same sense cannot be involved 'throughout vv. 15–20' (Meyer, 76), since the object is here explicitly said to be 'the morally good' (*to kalon*), that is (cf. 7:16), what the 'morally good' law says one should do. If so, that will be the sense in 7:15, 17 and 20 too. Finally, the contrast in 7:25b between 'my *nous* and 'my *sarx* (flesh)' again seems to prove that Paul's theme is, as it has always been taken, plain weakness of will.

28. Exegetically (and hence somewhat incidentally to our present concerns), I would like to suggest the following structure of Paul's argument from 7:14 onwards. 7:14 formulates two connected, but still distinguishable ideas: (*a*) that the law is 'spiritual' (and so holy, just and good, cf. 7:12) and (*b*) that 'I' am 'fleshly' and sold under sin. Point (*a*) is then argued for in 7:15–16: *in* acting the way I do, I *agree* that the law is good. By contrast, point (*b*) is argued for only in 7:17–20. It is first stated as something to be proved (17), then argued for and finally repeated as having now been proved (20b). Thus the *nuni de* and *ouketi* that introduce 7:17 means something like this: 'However, as things are it is in fact not I who bring it about.' Further, the *ei de* ('but if') of 7:16 and 7:20 both introduce the *Quod erat demonstrandum*. And both are immediately preceded (in 7:15b and 7:19) by the tag that Paul takes over from the customary *topos* of weakness of the will: 'what I will, I do not do'. With 7:21, then, Paul is ready to spell out how his 'discovery' of point (*b*) results in an internal, schizophrenic attitude to the law. Seen from within the perspective of his mind or reason (*nous*, 7:23, 25), the law (of Moses) is God's law (7:22, 25) in which the I delights in his inner being (7:22) and (willingly) serves (7:25). Seen from within the perspective of his 'limbs' (7:23) and flesh (7:25), the law (of Moses) *becomes* the 'law of sin' (7:23, 25), that is, the law of Moses *as* it functions to *keep down* sin. Thus there are two opposed ways in which the I is made to 'serve' (*douleuein*, cf. 7:25) the law (of Moses), one willingly and actively and the other unwillingly and ineffectually. The recognition of this split constitutes a 'death'.

29. It is this aspect too which explains why Paul may say that sin brought about death (for me) by means of the good law (7:13). It is certainly true that Paul will also have thought of 'death' and 'life' in eschatological terms (compare 6:21–22). But the reference to death in 7:13 has a much more precise and immediate meaning: the one *spelt out* in 7:14–23. 7:13 serves to introduce that account, which then reaches its concluding climax in the reference to death in 7:24b. In short, the term 'death'—referring to something generated by the law

(or rather by sin *through* the law)—is here used *metaphorically* of a certain state of mind.

30. Meyer (1990, 76) is therefore right *in a way* to say that 'both "inmost self" (v. 22) and "members" (v. 23) are but two aspects of the same self that is "sold under sin"'. But that is very far from implying that Paul is not speaking of plain and simple weakness of will. He is.

31. Note how Paul identifies it in 7:24: as something that belongs more or less intrinsically to *egō anthrōpos* ('I, wretched human being') and to the *sōma* ('body') of such a being. It is precisely a perspective that belongs with being a bodily individual. That perspective (of the 'body') is then also connected with death ('who will save me *from* the body *of that* death'): how? what death? Answer: the schizophrenia of weakness of will that Paul has spelt out in 7:14–23.

32. It is the element of risk in *akrasia* that explains why from Plato (in the *Protagoras*) onwards the Greek moral philosophers were so keenly engaged in finding an account of this philosophically (as opposed to experientially) strange phenomenon that would sufficiently *explain* it. *If* one *knew* what was right and *wanted* to do it, then *how come* that one did not actually do it, but did something else instead? Where was the *risk* of this to be *located*?

33. I am presupposing here the following translation of 8:10: 'But if Christ is in you, then while the body will be dead because of (the) sin (that goes with it), the spirit means life because of (the) righteousness (that you have received).' This describes the *present* state of Christ-believers, who have Christ 'in' them. In the next verse, Paul goes on to describe how in the *future* God will also make their 'mortal bodies' 'alive' through the spirit which *already* dwells in them. It is crucial to see the difference here between *nekron* ('dead', not 'mortal', as Byrne 1996, 245, has it) in 8:10 and *thnēton* ('mortal') in 8:11. In the present there can only be a '*moral*' liberation from a body that remains in existence, but precisely without exerting any influence whatever *on* the person who has Christ (and his spirit) in him. By contrast, in the future there will be an 'ontological' transformation *of* the body so that the body may now *itself* be carried over into the new existence. For discussion, compare Dunn 1988, 430–1, who wrongly rejects the readings by Käsemann, Osten-Sacken and Wilckens that are not far from the one given here. Dunn thinks that the weakness of that reading lies in 'the basic failure to appreciate the continuing two-sidedness of the believer's existence and experience for Paul'. But that supposed 'two-sidedness' cannot be in the picture here. 8:9–11 precisely states how 'you', Christ-believers, are *not* like those described in 8:5–8, who 'are in accordance with the flesh' (8:5). '*You*' are in the spirit (8:9), if God's spirit (8:9), that is, Christ's spirit (8:9), that is, Christ (8:10) is in 'you'. And *if* that holds, then the two things also hold that Paul goes on to describe, one for the present (that their sinful body is put out of action) and one for the future (that it will be transformed).

34. For a convincing discussion of what appears to be Paul's plain meaning here see Räisänen 1987, 65–7: 'The idea suggested [by 8:4] in the mind of readers is

that what was impossible to do under the dominion of the Torah is now done by the Christians who walk according to the Spirit'. It is one of the triumphs of Wilckens' work (within the German tradition) to have grasped this point so clearly, compare, e.g. in his Romans commentary (Wilckens 1980, 128–30). Compare also Reinmuth 1985, 66–73. Incidentally, it is curious to note how two excellent Catholic commentators, Byrne and Fitzmyer, feel the need to emphasize here that Paul's term 'fulfilled' is a 'theological passive' and hence excludes any notion of something 'achieved' or 'brought about' by Christians 'themselves', as a 'deed'. (See Fitzmyer 1993, 487–8.) That only shows the long shadow of traditional Protestantism. By contrast, Paul himself does not operate with any such contrast, as is shown, e.g. by Phil 2:12–13.

35. Note that 'weakness' (*astheneia*) is the very term used in the analysis of *akrasia* in the ancient ethical tradition. There, however, it is a 'weakness' of the person, here of the law. But the difference is negligible since Paul describes it further as the law's weakness *through the flesh*.

36. Please note that I am only attempting to give Paul an argument that might work, at least to some degree, on Paul's own premises. It is an entirely different question whether *we* should be convinced that there is a 'categorial' difference between having 'God's Christ' or 'God's law' as the focus of one's intentional directedness.

Notes for Chapter 10

1. Romans 9–11 is a storm centre in current Pauline scholarship. My brief remarks on the three chapters are not intended as an independent contribution to the debate, only to suggest a perspective on how to integrate them in a coherent reading of the letter as a whole. There are two basic points, one about the development of the argument and one about its eventual goal. The development: (a) Paul first (9:6–10:13) argues about God's call in a way that might be felt negatively by non-Christ-believing Jews and positively by gentiles—to the claim that there is no distinction (*diastolē*) between Jew and non-Jew in relation to the Lord; following on a transitional passage (10:14–21) which in effect describes the missionary activity of preachers of the gospel, (b) Paul next (11:1–36) affirms the special position of the Jews, beginning from himself and ending with those Jews who have not yet come round to the Christ faith. These are the two themes of God's (a) impartiality and (b) faithfulness rightly identified by E. E. Johnson (1995 *passim*, drawing on E. E. Johnson 1989) as the pair of concepts that holds the three chapters together. For the goal see the next note.

2. Thus I understand the goal of the three chapters as follows. Paul is not writing a theological essay trying to clarify God's trustworthiness or unpredictability as an issue of independent, theoretical interest. Instead, he is writing to his *gentile* addressees (compare Stowers 1994, 287–9) making use of his usual *diatribal* dialogue with a Jewish partner (9:14 ff) in order to make them realize

that (a) their own position within the Christ faith as compared with that of non-Christ-believing Jews (9:6–10:13) *requires* (b) that they themselves show respect for those same Jews, since the original promises are *theirs* and *they* too will eventually come round to the Christ faith goaded on by the gentiles (11:1–36). We should therefore speak of Paul's 'blatantly parenetic aims' not only with the direct address of 11:13–27 (E. E. Johnson 1995, 234), but also with the three chapters as a whole (as Johnson denies). And we should agree with Stowers (1994, 295), that 'the admonition [of 11:13–25 constitutes] a climactic moment in the letter's rhetoric'.

3. Let me just register my conviction that *telos* in 10:4 ('Christ is the *telos* of the law') means 'end' in the sense of 'cessation'. The discussion of Räisänen 1987, 53–6, is persuasive (to me) here. (Compare also Dunn 1988, 589–91.) But so is Räisänen's claim that 'Paul *could* have written that Christ is the goal of the law' (56). Conclusion? Perhaps, having studied the literature on the question, including the major commentaries and such specialized discussions as, e.g. P. W. Meyer 1980, Sanders 1983, 36–43, Räisänen 1987, 53–6, and last but not least Badenas 1985, scholars should try to avoid spending more energy on the question. At any rate, it seems fair to suggest that no stance on how to understand *telos* in 10:4 will be able to throw any *independent* light on Paul's understanding of the law in relation to Christ.

4. Monographs on these chapters include Ortkemper 1980 and Wilson 1991. They do not, however, regularly ask the questions we shall be pursuing.

5. Commentators have rightly fixed on a part of this theme when they have spoken of *Gottesdienst im Alltag der Welt* (Käsemann, 'worship of God in the worldly, everyday existence') or (Dunn 1988, 710) 'a whole-person commitment lived out in daily existence'. I am sharpening this in two respects: (a) There is no 'commitment' or 'worship of God' (I→X) of the kind Paul had in mind which is not, right from the beginning, a 'whole-person' one, since it precisely leaves the I-pole *behind*. (b) And the 'whole-person commitment' is *necessarily* both one that is *lived out* in daily existence and a *social* one (life at the S-pole). The move I→X already *contains* the move to the S-pole, which is constituted by a certain *actualized* and *social* form of life.

6. Betz (1988, 212) rightly insists that *logikos* means '*vernünftig*', that is 'rational', in the sense of something that may be 'advanced and interpreted with a rational backing' ('*mit Vernunftgründen vorgetragen und interpretiert*'). By contrast, translating *logikos* as 'spiritual' 'prevents a proper understanding of the text'.

7. This is not to deny that Paul may well also have had more 'substantive' ideas when he spoke of *syschēmatizesthai* and *metamorphousthai*.

8. Thus Dunn (1988, 710) was entirely right to speak of a 'whole-person commitment'. But he was not right to bring into his exegesis of these verses the hackneyed point about Paul's reference to the body (*sōma*) here as being in some kind of *contrast* with 'the more dualistic character of Greek anthropology'

(709). *Stoic* anthropology is *not* 'dualistic'. And the Stoics and Paul agree in giving what seems the most cogent interpretation we have from antiquity of the intrinsic connection of the 'I' and the body.

9. Many scholars have seen these close backwards connections of 12:1–2, e.g. Furnish 1968, 101–6: 'In 12:1–2 Paul is calling the brethren to a new life exactly opposite that which he has previously described' (103). Compare also Betz 1988, 214–15, and M. Thompson 1991, 78–83.

10. I have not come across any New Testament scholar who has raised this question directly. I suppose it derives from a more independent, philosophical interest. (Thus I have myself grappled with it in relation to the thought of Marcus Aurelius, see Engberg-Pedersen 1998.) But it does seem an important question for the careful explication of Paul's picture of the Christ-believing form of life.

11. Both Wilckens (1982, 7) and Dunn (1988, 715) take the three adjectives to refer to the same thing, which we may call the 'Christian good'. Surprisingly, they do not consider the different semantic range of the adjectives themselves. We should expect, however, that Paul's use of *three* adjectives to designate the *one* thing to which he is obviously referring may teach us something important about his understanding of the 'Christian good' in comparison with *other* conceptions of 'the good' that were around.

12. The syntax of 12:6–14 is difficult. We should probably be sceptical about the traditional idea that in Paul (and, for instance, 1 Peter) a present participle may function more or less directly as an imperative. (See, e.g. the discussion in Ortkemper 1980, 15–18, and Wilson 1991, 156–65.) Instead, we may prefer to see the participle at the beginning of 12:6, which governs everything down to 12:8a, as being broken off there with a sort of anacoluthic colon—after *en tēi paraklēsei*—that then introduces an imperatival thought. Thus *ho metadidous ktl.* means something like this: 'the one who gives in charity [*should do it*] in open-heartedness or sincerity [*haplotēs*], etc.' This line is then *summarized* in 12:9a: 'Your (*hē*) love [must be] unfeigned.' Following on that Paul embarks on a second round of participles that again leads forward to a colon (after *diōkontes*, 12:13), which is now followed by direct imperatives (in 12:14). It is not so easy to *prove* the correctness of such a reading. Here I shall leave it to the reader to judge for him- or herself.

13. Paul does not say, for instance: *to de kath' heis <tou henos sōmatos> melē*. Rather, each individual is a limb of *each other*. It seems to me that there is an important nuance here, which commentators generally miss.

14. See n. 12 above.

15. Compare, e.g. Dunn 1988, 738–9, and Byrne 1996, 377. Neither Dunn nor Byrne provides any solution to the problem. (Ortkemper 1980, 101–4 does not even discuss it.)

16. This is quite different from saying, with Wilckens 1982, 22, that 'the abruptness of this transition [from 12:13 to 12:14] shows that there is no basic

difference between the relationship with the brothers within the congregation and that with people outside it, neither with respect to its ethical importance nor to the manner of the relationship'. We should disagree. As we shall see, the 'manner of the relationship' is in fact quite different. In fact, we shall end agreeing with Stendahl (1962, 354) when he argued that 'neither Qumran, nor Paul speak about love for the enemies'. Stendahl at least paid careful attention to the question of when in chapters 12–13 Paul is speaking of insiders and when of outsiders: 'Beginning with Rom. 12:14 the attention is shifting from the insiders to the outsiders, to the persecutors and to the attitude toward the world at large, and in 13:1–7 we are told about the rôle of the authorities in this world. The admonitions in vv. 15–16, which repeat what has been said in v. 3, may well be understood as about the community under persecution. In any case vv. 19–20 speak about enemies. These must be the outsiders' (345). Later in the paper Stendahl in effect suggested the idea about 'laying the ground' in remarks about the insiders for their attitude to the outsiders. Referring to Phil 4:5 ('Let you gentleness [*to epieikes/hē epieikeia*] become known to *all* people. The Lord is near!') Stendahl suggests that this 'gentleness' is closely related to the attitude expressed in Rom 12:17–21; '*to epieikes* and *hē epieikeia* signify a graciousness out of strength, and the specific strength here lies in the words "the Lord is nigh"' (352). Graciousness out of strength: that is the point. Note then also that *if* this idea is valid, then the comment in Dunn 1988, 739 on 12:15–16 (which should then be considered as laying the ground for the rest) becomes particularly apposite: 'these verses were probably addressed to some of the tensions within the Roman congregations, particularly between Jewish and Gentile Christians'. That is exactly right: internal unity among the Christ-believers in Rome was *required* for them to have the proper relationship *externally*.

17. Dunn (1988, 737) reflects the general feeling among commentators when he says the following of 12:9–21: 'This is the most loosely constructed of all the paragraphs, consisting mainly of individual exhortations (stringing pearls) held together in part by particular words and thematic links (especially love: *agapē, philadelphia, philostorgos, philoxenia*—vv 9, 10, 13; bad: *ponēros, kakos*—vv 9, 17, 21; good: *agathos, kalos*—vv 9, 17, 21).' As against this I am trying to articulate the internal coherence of Paul's thought in the whole section in terms of the I→X→S-model.

18. Dunn (1988, 746) thinks, rightly, that 'the parallel with 1 Cor 12:26 and Phil 2:17–18 suggests that Paul had the internal relationships of the Christian congregations particularly in view', but adds: 'but there is no reason he should not have had wider associations in view as well' (referring, among others, to Furnish 1972, Cranfield 1975–9 and Wilckens 1982). No reason: if the idea of rejoicing does rely on the eschatological hope and that of crying on present tribulations, then of course there is every reason why Paul should have only the internal relationships in view. And what else *could* those two ideas refer to? Compare Stendahl 1962, 345, quoted above in n. 16.

19. Nobody, it seems, has paid attention to the precise manner in which 12:17 may thus be taken to provide a bridge between the talk about internal relationships in 12:15–16 and that about external relationships in 12:18.

20. For another, slightly looser, solution to the enigma of Paul's rhetorical strategy in Romans along similar lines compare Crafton 1990. Crafton rightly says that 'Paul theologizes the conflict situation in the Roman[s] house churches' (331). He is also right on target in claiming this: 'The imperatives of chapters 12–15 are firmly grounded in the indicatives of chapters 1–11; they are a *spelling out* of the practical commitment *inherent in* Paul's argumentation' (334, my italics). Finally, his basic idea is helpful that Paul attempts—for practical purposes—to draw his addressees into a 'rhetorical vision' of his own. Where I disagree is mainly with regard to Crafton's reconstruction of the letter situation, which I find too loose, and the somewhat general character of the 'vision' he ascribes to Paul.

21. Commentators do not regularly seem to be bothered by this. Bultmann (1947, 200) was. However, his suggestion that we should see 13:5 as a gloss that has crept in at the wrong place (it should be understood as a note on 13:6) has rightly not found followers. Wilckens (1982, 36–7) is right to end his discussion by coming down on the side of those who understand Paul's reference to conscience here to refer not to a special kind of conscience had by the Christian as opposed to the non-Christian, but rather to the conscience 'of each human being, and specifically in the sense of 2:15' (37). (So also Dunn 1988, 765: 'Paul does not conceive the operation of conscience as something distinctively Christian'.) Wilckens' further comment, however, that 'nevertheless, in 13:5 the scope is not that of the opposition between external fear of punishment and internal moral conviction' is unintelligible to me.

22. For general discussion of this concept, its use in Paul and the relationship between that use and Stoicism, see the bibliography in Fitzmyer 1993, 160, referring among others to Pierce 1955, Stelzenberger 1961 and Eckstein 1983. To this add the bibliographical references in Lüdemann 1983, 721, in particular to Jewett 1971 and Chadwick 1978. Two brief comments. (i) Fitzmyer (1993, 128) formulates as follows what is more or less the consensus at present on the possible derivation of the concept from Stoicism: 'It [the term 'conscience' in Paul] is certainly not borrowed by Paul from Stoic philosophy, for from at least the sixth century B.C. on it was a tenet of widespread Greek popular thinking.' That is correct—and also false. It is certainly true that the Stoics did not *invent* the notion of the conscience. But via the sharp focus in their philosophy on *akrasia* and the connection of this with their basic theory of *oikeiōsis*, they did develop a theoretical place for the notion of 'self-awareness' which gave it an added importance. (ii) As regards its place in Paul, Lüdemann (1983, 724) was right in saying (*a*) that the term is not central to Paul's anthropology or ethics, (*b*) that Paul never invoked the conscience as a 'moral principle' or as the seat of 'God's voice', (*c*) and that having taken it over 'presumably directly' from 'Hellenistic popular philosophy' (and 'less probably from the Corinthian

Christians'), Paul employs it in a number of different contexts without changing its basic meaning. In short, Paul did not (overtly) use the term in any very specific, technical philosophical sense. Right! However, if there is a technical *framework* of a distinctly philosophical kind that we may use with profit to illuminate Paul's thought more generally, then his apparently *non*-technical use of a term like *syneidēsis* may still, as it were, *come alive* within and as part of that framework.

23. I have in mind mainly points like these: (*a*) that the ultimate power is God's (13:1b with 12:19), including the explicit reuse of terminology (13:4 with 12:19), and (*b*) the pervasive concern (13:3–4 with 12:21) about doing the 'good' (*agathon*) and avoiding the 'bad' (*kakon*).

24. I presuppose here that there is a kind of wordplay on *opheilete* in 13:8: 'Be *in debt* to no one—except that you are *obliged* to love one another'. Much hangs on the relationship one posits between 'all' in 13:7 ('discharge your debts to all') and 'one another' in 13:8 as the object of love. Wilckens (1982, 67–8) thinks that Paul is talking in 13:8 quite generally of 'love of the neighbour' (*Nächstenliebe*) and that he begins to widen his perspective to include everybody already with the 'all' of 13:7. But the 'all' is defined by the reference that follows in the rest of the verse to those to whom tribute, tax, fear and respect are due. And Paul's use of *apodote* ('discharge') does suggest that these 'obligations' are debts that may be fulfilled once and for all. So the 'all' can hardly refer to a supposed *everybody* to whom love of neighbour *remains* a constant obligation. Dunn (1988, 775–6) also wishes to see Paul speak of indiscriminate love of neighbour, as against 'fellow believers', not least because Paul has had relationships with the wider community in view in the whole of the preceding section, at least in 12:17–13:7. That is certainly true. But it by no means follows that his theme has been love of all others. Moreover, the *difference* between 'all' and 'one another' (*allēlous* with its strong sense of mutuality) to my mind points distinctly in the direction of 'fellow believers' alone. It seems quite revealing that Dunn (1988, 776), ends his discussion as follows: 'Perhaps it would be best to say that Paul has fellow believers particularly in view [!] but not in any exclusive way [?]'. If one does take it in an exclusive way, the rendering given above becomes quite pointed with an emphasis on 'love' and 'one another'.

25. Compare Räisänen 1987, 64–6. Räisänen (64) rightly notes that the passage appears to prepare the discussion in 14:1–15:13, e.g. the idea of walking 'in accordance with love' (cf. 14:15), of the strong being 'obliged' to bear the burdens of the weak (cf. 15:1) and of the need to please one's 'neighbour' (cf. 15:2). As will become clear, we should agree with Räisänen's observation: 'It is love that is in focus in 13.8–10, rather than law' (64).

26. I have not seen any interpretation of 13:8–10 that points in this particular direction. I proceed to giving some arguments in its favour. In addition, it seems a fairly strong argument that the proposed reading makes the verses come out as having a specifically parenetic role (compare the inclusion of point 5 in my reconstruction). For Romans 12–13 is of course through and through parenetic.

By contrast, taking the purpose to be an elucidation of the relationship between the law and love presupposes a more independently 'theoretical' interest on Paul's part.

27. Note the perfect tense of *peplērōken* ('has fulfilled'). I consider Paul's use of this tense to give fairly strong support for the proposed reading, in the way I go on to explain.

28. For the notion of 'individuation' in Paul see the excellent discussion in Sampley 1990.

29. Compare for this general idea Gal 6:1–5. Also, it seems that Paul has implicitly prepared for this point in Romans as early as 2:1–3 in his strictures on 'judging' others.

30. This is wholly in line with the account of the passage given in Jaquette 1995a, 126–36.

31. This is well brought out in the final pages of J. M. G. Barclay 1996a.

32. I have said nothing in this book about the Adam–Christ section (5:12–21). Here Paul celebrates the 'new creation' (cf. Gal 6:15 and 2 Cor 5:17) that has been brought about by the Christ event to supersede the old Adamic creation —with the 'obedience' (Rom 5:19) of 'the one human being, Jesus Christ' (5:15) counterbalancing the 'disobedience of the one human being', Adam (5:19). However, Paul has a very specific rhetorical aim with this, which is to bring out as sharply as possible the ultimate contrast between death (as instituted by Adam) and life (as instituted by Christ). Thus throughout the section there is a distinctive move from death (brought about by Adam, 5:12–15), via God's grace and gift (5:15.16), his righteousness (5:16) and all three of them (5:17) to the life (5:17.18.21) that will finally and eternally (5:21) do away with death. Note then that this basic idea itself has the distinct, rhetorical purpose of setting up a 'choice' for Paul's addressees in the parenetic section that immediately follows (6:1–8:13)—the choice between death and life (*passim*, including 6:20–23, 7:24–8:2—and quite strikingly in the two last words of the whole section, end of 8:13). Here too, then, there is a clear line from world-view to ethos.

33. For one example of how this works in the Stoicism of Marcus Aurelius, see Engberg-Pedersen 1998, 330–4.

34. Compare, e.g. Engberg-Pedersen 1990 ch. 4 (on Stoic *apatheia*) and the whole of Engberg-Pedersen 1998 (for the issue in Marcus Aurelius).

Abbreviations

AB	Anchor Bible
AGP	*Archiv für Geschichte der Philosophie*
AnBib	Analecta Biblica
ANRW	*Aufstieg und Niedergang der römischen Welt*
AP	*Ancient Philosophy*
ATDan	Acta Theologica Danica
BBB	Bonner biblische Beiträge
BETL	Bibliotheca Ephemeridum Theologicarum Lovaniensium
BEvT	Beiträge zur evangelischen Theologie
BFCT	Beiträge zur Förderung christlicher Theologie
Bib	*Biblica*
BJRL	*Bulletin of the John Rylands University Library of Manchester*
BK	*Bibel und Kirche*
BSac	*Bibliotheca Sacra*
BulBR	*Bulletin for Biblical Research*
BulICS	*Bulletin of the Institute of Classical Studies*
BWANT	Beiträge zur Wissenschaft vom Alten und Neuen Testament
BZ	*Biblische Zeitschrift*
BZNW	Beihefte zur Zeitschrift für die neutestamentliche Wissenschaft
CBQ	*Catholic Biblical Quarterly*

CJ	*Classical Journal*
CNT	Commentaire du Nouveau Testament
ConBNT	Coniectanea Biblica, New Testament
ConJ	*Concordia Journal*
CTJ	*Calvin Theological Journal*
CTR	*Criswell Theological Review*
CurRBS	*Currents in Research: Biblical Studies*
EKKNT	Evangelisch-katholischer Kommentar zum Neuen Testament
EvQ	*Evangelical Quarterly*
EvT	*Evangelische Theologie*
ExpTim	*Expository Times*
FB	Forschung zur Bibel
FRLANT	Forschungen zur Religion und Literatur des Alten und Neuen Testaments
FS	Festschrift
GTA	Göttinger theologische Arbeiten
HNT	Handbuch zum Neuen Testament
HTKNT	Herders theologischer Kommentar zum Neuen Testament
HTKNTSup	Herders theologischer Kommentar zum Neuen Testament, Supplementband
HTR	*Harvard Theological Review*
HUCA	*Hebrew Union College Annual*
HUT	Hermeneutische Untersuchungen zur Theologie
ICC	International Critical Commentary
IBS	*Irish Biblical Studies*
Int	*Interpretation*
JAC	Jahrbuch für Antike und Christentum
JBL	*Journal of Biblical Literature*
JES	*Journal of Ecumenical Studies*
JETS	*Journal of the Evangelical Theological Society*
JR	*Journal of Religion*
JSNT	*Journal for the Study of the New Testament*

JSNTSup	Journal for the Study of the New Testament, Supplement Series
JSOT	*Journal for the Study of the Old Testament*
JTS	*Journal of Theological Studies*
KD	*Kerygma und Dogma*
LCL	Loeb Classical Library
LS	Long and Sedley, *The Hellenistic Philosophers*
LSJ	Liddell, Scott, Jones, *A Greek-English Lexicon*
MeyerK	H. A. W. Meyer, Kritisch-exegetischer Kommentar über das Neue Testament
MNTC	Moffatt, NT Commentary
Neot	*Neotestamentica*
NICNT	New International Commentary on the New Testament
NIGCT	The New International Greek Testament Commentary
NovT	*Novum Testamentum*
NovTSup	Novum Testamentum, Supplements
NTAbh	Neutestamentliche Abhandlungen
NTF	Neutestamentliche Forschungen
NTS	*New Testament Studies*
OSAP	*Oxford Studies in Ancient Philosophy*
PAS	*Proceedings of the Aristotelian Society*
PBACAP	*Proceedings of the Boston Area Colloquium of Ancient Philosophy*
Philol	*Philologus*
Phron	*Phronesis*
PQ	*Philosophical Quarterly*
QD	Quaestiones Disputatae
RAC	*Reallexikon für Antike und Christentum*
RB	*Revue biblique*
ResQ	*Restoration Quarterly*
RevExp	*Review and Expositor*
RevScRel	*Revue des sciences religieuses*
RHPR	*Revue d'histoire et de philosophie religieuses*

RMP	*Rheinisches Museum für Philologie*
RNT	Regensburger Neues Testament
SBLDS	Society of Biblical Literature Dissertation Series
SBLSP	Society of Biblical Literature Seminar Papers
SBT	Studies in Biblical Theology
SD	Studies and Documents
SEÅ	*Svensk Exegetisk Årsbok*
SNT	Studien zum Neuen Testament
SNTSMS	Society for New Testament Studies Monograph Series
ST	*Studia Theologica*
SUNT	Studien zur Umwelt des Neuen Testaments
SVF	*Stoicorum Veterum Fragmenta* (ed. Hans von Arnim)
TBei	*Theologische Beiträge*
TBü	Theologische Bücherei
Them	*Themelios*
THKNT	Theologischer Handkommentar zum Neuen Testament
TLZ	*Theologische Literaturzeitung*
TQ	*Theologische Quartalschrift*
TrinJ	*Trinity Journal*
TSK	*Theologische Studien und Kritiken*
TTZ	*Trierer theologische Zeitschrift*
TynBul	*Tyndale Bulletin*
TZ	*Theologische Zeitschrift*
VF	*Verkündigung und Forschung*
WBC	Word Biblical Commentary
WD	*Wort und Dienst*
WMANT	Wissenschaftliche Monographien zum Alten und Neuen Testament
WUNT	Wissenschaftliche Untersuchungen zum Neuen Testament
YCS	*Yale Classical Studies*
ZKG	*Zeitschrift für Kirchengeschichte*
ZNW	*Zeitschrift für die neutestamentliche Wissenschaft*
ZTK	*Zeitschrift für Theologie und Kirche*

Bibliography

The bibliography lists works that are quoted in the book. It also contains a number of unquoted works from which I have learnt or against which I have tested my own views. The fact that a given work is not actually quoted does not, of course, imply any adverse opinion on its quality or importance. For all abbreviations see the preceding list.

AAGESON, J. W. 1986. 'Scripture and Structure in the Development of the Argument in Romans 9–11'. *CBQ* 48, 265–89.

ACHTEMEIER, P. J. 1985. *Romans*. Interpretation: A Bible Commentary for Teaching and Preaching. Atlanta: Knox.

— 1996. 'The Continuing Quest for Coherence in St. Paul: An Experiment in Thought'. In Lovering, Jr. and Sumney (eds) 1996, 132–45.

ADAMS, E. 1997. 'Abraham's Faith and Gentile Disobedience: Textual Links between Romans 1 and 4'. *JSNT* 65, 47–66.

ALETTI, J.-N. 1987. 'L'Argumentation paulinienne en Rm 9'. *Bib* 68, 41–56.

— 1988. 'Rm 1,18–3,20. Incohérence ou cohérence de l'argumentation paulinienne?' *Bib* 69, 47–62.

— 1996. 'Romains 2. Sa cohérence et sa fonction'. *Bib* 77, 153–77.

— 1997. 'Romains 5,12–21. Logique, sens et function'. *Bib* 78, 3–32.

ALEXANDER, L. 1989. 'Hellenistic Letter-Forms and the Structure of Philippians'. *JSNT* 37, 87–101.

ALTHAUS, P. 1951. '". . . Dass ihr nicht tut, was ihr wollt" (Zur Auslegung von Gal. 5, 17)'. *TLZ* 76, 15–18.

AMADI-AZUOGO, C. A. 1996. *Paul and the Law in the Arguments of Galatians: A Rhetorical and Exegetical Analysis of Galatians 2,14–6,2*. BBB 104. Weinheim: Beltz Athenäum.

ANDRESEN, C. and G. KLEIN (eds) 1979. *Theologia Crucis—Signum Crucis*. FS E. Dinkler. Tübingen: Mohr (Siebeck).

384   Bibliography

ANNAS, J. 1993. *The Morality of Happiness*. New York: Oxford University Press.

AUNE, D. E. 1987. *The New Testament in Its Literary Environment*. Library of Early Christianity. Ed. Wayne A. Meeks. Philadelphia: Westminster.

— 1991a. 'Romans as a Logos Protreptikos in the Context of Ancient Religious and Philosophical Propaganda'. In Hengel and Heckel (eds) 1991, 91–121.

— 1991b. 'Romans as a *Logos Protreptikos*'. In Donfried (ed.) 1991²a, 278–96.

— 1996. 'Zwei Modelle der menschlichen Natur bei Paulus'. *TQ* 176, 28–39.

AUS, R. D. 1979. 'Paul's Travel Plans to Spain and the "Full Number of the Gentiles" of Rom. XI 25'. *NovT* 21, 232–62.

AUSTIN, J. L. 1975² (1961). *How to Do Things with Words*. Ed. J. O. Urmson and M. Sbisà. Cambridge, Mass.: Harvard University Press.

BACHMANN, M. 1993. 'Rechtfertigung und Gesetzeswerke bei Paulus'. *TZ* 49, 1–33.

BADENAS, R. 1985. *Christ the End of the Law: Romans 10.4 in Pauline Perspective*. JSNTSup 10. Sheffield: JSOT.

BADER, G. 1981. 'Römer 7 als Skopus einer theologischen Handlungstheorie'. *ZTK* 78, 31–56.

BALZ, H. and G. SCHNEIDER (eds) 1981. *Exegetisches Wörterbuch zum Neuen Testament* II. Stuttgart: Kohlhammer.

— (eds) 1983. *Exegetisches Wörterbuch zum Neuen Testament* III. Stuttgart: Kohlhammer.

BANDSTRA, A. J. 1990. 'Paul and the Law: Some Recent Developments and an Extraordinary Book'. *CTJ* 25, 249–61.

BANKS, R. 1980(/1994²). *Paul's Idea of Community: The Early House Churches in their Historical [²Cultural] Setting*. Grand Rapids: Eerdmans (Peabody, Mass: Hendrickson).

BARCLAY, J. M. G. 1986. 'Paul and the Law: Observations on Some Recent Debates'. *Them* 12, 5–15.

— 1987. 'Mirror-Reading a Polemical Letter: Galatians as a Test Case'. *JSNT* 31, 73–93.

— 1988. *Obeying the Truth: Paul's Ethics in Galatians*. Edinburgh: Clark.

— 1995. 'Paul Among Diaspora Jews: Anomaly or Apostate?' *JSNT* 60, 89–120.

— 1996a. *Jews in the Mediterranean Diaspora: From Alexander to Trajan (323 BCE–115 CE)*. Edinburgh: Clark.

— 1996b. '"Do we Undermine the Law?" A Study of Romans 14.1–15.6'. In Dunn (ed.) 1996a, 287–308.

BARCLAY, W. 1960–1. 'Hellenistic Thought in New Testament Times'. *ExpTim* 72, 28–31; 78–81; 101–4; 146–9; 164–6; 200–3; 227–30; 258–61; 291–4.

BARCLAY, W. 1962. *Flesh and Spirit: An Examination of Galatians 5.19–23.* London: SCM.

BARRETT, C. K. 1976. 'The Allegory of Abraham, Sarah and Hagar in the Argument of Galatians'. In Friedrich, Pöhlmann and Stuhlmacher (eds) 1976, 1–16.

— 1985. *Freedom and Obligation: A Study of the Epistle to the Galatians.* London: SPCK.

— 1986. 'Boasting (*kauchasthai, ktl.*) in the Pauline Epistles'. In Vanhoye (ed.) 1986, 363–8.

— 1991² (1957). *The Epistle to the Romans.* Black's New Testament Commentaries. London: Black.

— 1994. *Paul: An Introduction to His Thought.* Louisville: Westminster Knox.

BARTH, M. 1968. 'Jews and Gentiles: The Social Character of Justification in Paul'. *JES* 5, 241–67.

BARTSCH, H.-W. 1967. 'Die antisemitischen Gegner des Paulus im Römerbrief.' In W. P. Eckert, N. P. Levinson and M. Stöhr (eds), *Antijudaismus im Neuen Testament? Exegetische und systematische Beiträge.* Abhandlungen zum christlich-jüdischen Dialog, Bd. 2. 27–43. Munich: Kaiser.

BASSLER, J. M. 1982. *Divine Impartiality: Paul and a Theological Axiom.* SBLDS 59. Chico, Cal: Scholars.

— (ed.) 1991. *Pauline Theology I.* Minneapolis: Fortress.

— 1993. 'Paul's Theology: Whence and Whither?' In Hay (ed.) 1993, 3–17.

BATEMAN, H. W. 1998. 'Were the Opponents at Philippi Necessarily Jewish?' *BSac* 155, 39–61.

BAUMERT, N. 1969. 'Ist Philipper 4,10 richtig übersetzt?' *BZ* 13, 256–62.

BAUR, F. C. 1978 (1876). 'Seneca und Paulus, das Verhältniss des Stoicismus zum Christenthum nach den Schriften Senecas'. In Baur, *Drei Abhandlungen zur Geschichte der alten Philosophie und ihres Verhältnisses zum Christentum.* Ed. E. Zeller. 377–480. Aalen: Scientia.

BECHTLER, S. R. 1994. 'Christ, the *Télos* of the Law: The Goal of Romans 10:4'. *CBQ* 56, 288–308.

BECKER, J. 1971. 'Erwägungen zu Phil. 3,20–21'. *TZ* 27, 16–29.

— 1989. *Paulus: Der Apostel der Völker.* Tübingen: Mohr (Siebeck).

BEKER, J. C. 1980. *Paul the Apostle: The Triumph of God in Life and Thought.* Philadelphia: Fortress.

BELL, R. H. 1994. *Provoked to Jealousy: The Origin and Purpose of the Jealousy Motif in Romans 9–11.* WUNT 2/63. Tübingen: Mohr (Siebeck).

BELLEVILLE, L. L. 1986. '"Under Law": Structural Analysis and the Pauline Concept of Law in Galatians 3.21–4.11'. *JSNT* 26, 53–78.

BENOIT, P. 1946. 'Sénèque et Saint Paul'. *RB* 53, 7–35.

BERÉNYI, G. 1986. 'Gal 2,20: A Pre-Pauline or a Pauline Text?' In Vanhoye (ed.) 1986, 340–4.

BERGMEIER, R. 1996. 'Die Loyalitätsparänese Röm 13:1–7 im Rahmen von Römer 12 und 13'. *TBei* 27, 341–57.

BERRY, K. L. 1996. 'The Function of Friendship Language in Philippians 4:10–20'. In Fitzgerald (ed.) 1996a, 107–24.

BETZ, H. D. 1974. 'Spirit, Freedom, and Law: Paul's Message to the Galatian Churches'. *SEÅ* 39, 145–60.

— 1975. 'The Literary Composition and Function of Paul's Letter to the Galatians'. *NTS* 21, 353–79.

— 1979. *Galatians: A Commentary on Paul's Letter to the Churches in Galatia.* Hermeneia. Philadelphia: Fortress.

— 1986. 'The Problem of Rhetoric and Theology According to the Apostle Paul'. In Vanhoye (ed.) 1986, 16–48.

— 1988. 'Das Problem der Grundlagen der paulinischen Ethik'. *ZTK* 85, 199–218.

— 1991. 'Christianity as Religion: Paul's Attempt at Definition in Romans'. *JR* 71, 315–44.

BIDEZ, J. 1932. *La Cité du monde et la cité du soleil chez les stoïciens.* Collection d'études anciennes. Paris.

BILLERBECK, M. 1978. *Epiktet: Vom Kynismus.* Philosophia Antiqua 34. Leiden: Brill.

— 1979. *Der Kyniker Demetrius: Ein Beitrag zur Geschichte der frühkaiserzeitlichen Populärphilosophie.* Philosophia Antiqua 36. Leiden: Brill.

BJERKELUND, C. J. 1967. *Parakalô: Form, Funktion und Sinn der parakalô-Sätze in den paulinischen Briefen.* Oslo: Universitetsforlaget.

— 1972. '"Nach menschlicher Weise rede ich". Funktion und Sinn des paulinischen Ausdrucks'. *ST* 26, 63–100.

BLACK, D. A. 1985. 'Paul and Christian Unity: A Formal Analysis of Philippians 2:1–4'. *JETS* 28, 299–308.

— 1988. 'The Authorship of Philippians 2:6–11: Some Literary-Critical Observations'. *CTR* 2, 269–89.

— 1995. 'The Discourse Structure of Philippians: A Study in Textlinguistics'. *NovT* 37, 16–49.

BLOOMQUIST, L. G. 1993. *The Function of Suffering in Philippians.* JSNTSup 78. Sheffield: JSOT.

BOER, M. C. de 1989. 'Paul and Jewish Apocalyptic Eschatology'. In Marcus and Soards (eds) 1989, 169–90.

BOERS, H. 1982. 'The Problem of Jews and Gentiles in the Macro-Structure of Romans'. *SEÅ* 47, 184–96.

— 1994. *The Justification of the Gentiles: Paul's Letters to the Galatians and the Romans.* Peabody, Mass: Hendrickson.

BONHÖFFER, A. 1911. *Epiktet und das Neue Testament.* Religions-geschichtliche Versuche und Vorarbeiten 10. Giessen: Töpelmann.

— 1912. 'Epiktet und das Neue Testament'. *ZNW* 13, 281–92.

BONNARD, P. 1953. *L'Épître de Saint Paul aux Galates.* CNT 9. Neuchâtel: Delachaux and Niestlé.

BONNEAU, N. 1997. 'The Logic of Paul's Argument on the Curse of the Law in Galatians 3:10–14'. *NovT* 39, 60–80.

BORMANN, L. 1995. *Philippi: Stadt und Christengemeinde zur Zeit des Paulus.* NovTSup 78. Leiden: Brill.

— K. DEL TREDICI and A. STANDHARTINGER (eds) 1994. *Religious Propaganda and Missionary Competition in the New Testament World.* FS Dieter Georgi. NovTSup 74. Leiden: Brill.

BORNKAMM, G. 1966⁵ (1939). 'Taufe und neues Leben bei Paulus'. In *Das Ende des Gesetzes: Paulusstudien. Gesammelte Aufsätze I.* BEvT 16. 34–50. Munich: Kaiser.

— 1966⁵ (1952). 'Die christliche Freiheit (Gal 5 13–15)'. In *Das Ende des Gesetzes: Paulusstudien. Gesammelte Aufsätze I.* BEvT 16. 133–8. Munich: Kaiser.

— 1970³ (1946). 'Der Lohngedanke im Neuen Testament'. In *Studien zu Antike und Urchristentum. Gesammelte Aufsätze II.* BEvT 28. 69–92. Munich: Kaiser.

— 1970³ (1959). 'Gesetz und Natur: Röm 2 14–16'. In *Studien zu Antike und Urchristentum. Gesammelte Aufsätze II.* BEvT 28. 93–118. Munich: Kaiser.

— 1971 (1962). 'Der Philipperbrief als paulinische Briefsammlung'. In *Geschichte und Glaube II. Gesammelte Aufsätze IV.* BEvT 53. 195–205. Munich: Kaiser.

— 1991 (1963). 'The Letter to the Romans as Paul's Last Will and Testament'. In Donfried (ed.) 1991²a, 16–28.

BÖTTGER, P. C. 1969. 'Die eschatologische Existenz der Christen: Erwägungen zu Philipper 3 20'. *ZNW* 60, 244–63.

BOUWMAN, G. 1987. 'Die Hagar- und Sara-Perikope (Gal 4,21–31): Exemplarische Interpretation zum Schriftbeweis bei Paulus'. *ANRW* II.25.4, 3135–55.

BOYARIN, D. 1994. *A Radical Jew: Paul and the Politics of Identity*. Berkeley/Los Angeles: University of California Press.

BRANDENBURGER, E. 1968. *Fleisch und Geist: Paulus und die dualistische Weisheit*. WMANT 29. Neukirchen-Vluyn: Neukirchener.

BRAUN, H. 1962 (1967²). 'Die Indifferenz gegenüber der Welt bei Paulus und bei Epiktet'. In Braun, *Gesammelte Studien zum Neuen Testament und seiner Umwelt*, 159–67. Tübingen: Mohr (Siebeck).

BREYTENBACH, C. 1989. *Versöhnung: Eine Studie zur paulinischen Soteriologie*. WMANT 60. Neukirchen-Vluyn: Neukirchener.

— 1993. 'Versöhnung, Stellvertretung und Sühne: Semantische und traditionsgeschichtliche Bemerkungen am Beispiel der paulinischen Briefe'. *NTS* 39, 59–79.

BRIDOUX, A. 1966. *Le Stoicisme et son influence*. Paris: Vrin.

BROWN, R. E. 1983. 'Not Jewish Christianity and Gentile Christianity but Types of Jewish/Gentile Christianity'. *CBQ* 45, 74–9.

— 1990. 'Further Reflections on the Origins of the Church of Rome'. In Fortna and Gaventa (eds) 1990, 98–115.

BRUCKER, R. 1997. *'Christushymnen' oder 'epideiktische Passagen'? Studien zum Stilwechsel im Neuen Testament und seiner Umwelt*. FRLANT 176. Göttingen: Vandenhoeck & Ruprecht.

BUCHANAN, C. O. 1964. 'Epaphroditus' Sickness and the Letter to the Philippians'. *EvQ* 36, 157–66.

BUGG, C. B. 1991. 'Philippians 4:4–13'. *RevExp* 88, 253–7.

BULTMANN, R. 1910. *Der Stil der paulinischen Predigt und die kynisch-stoische Diatribe*. FRLANT 13. Göttingen: Vandenhoeck & Ruprecht.

— 1912. 'Das religiöse Moment in der ethischen Unterweisung des Epiktet und das Neue Testament'. *ZNW* 13, 97–110, 177–91.

— 1924. 'Das Problem der Ethik bei Paulus'. *ZNW* 23, 123–40.

— 1932. 'Römer 7 und die Anthropologie des Paulus'. In Bultmann 1967, 198–209.

— 1938. '*kauchaomai ktl.*' In Kittel (ed.) 1938, 646–54.

— 1947. 'Glossen im Römerbrief'. *TLZ* 72, 197–202. Also in Bultmann 1967, 278–84.

— 1948 (1941). 'Neues Testament und Mythologie. Das Problem der Entmythologisierung der neutestamentlichen Verkündigung'. In H. W. Bartsch (ed.), *Kerygma und Mythos* I, 15–48. Hamburg/Volksdorf: Reich Evangelischer.

— 1952a. 'Zum Problem der Entmythologisierung'. In H.W. Bartsch (ed.), *Kerygma und Mythos* II, 179–208. Hamburg/Volksdorf: Reich Evangelischer.

— 1952b. 'Zur Auslegung von Galater 2,15–18'. In Bultmann 1967, 394–9.

BULTMANN, R. 1962. *Das Urchristentum im Rahmen der antiken Religionen.* Munich: Rowohlt.

— 1964. 'Ist die Apokalyptik die Mutter der christlichen Theologie? Eine Auseinandersetzung mit Ernst Käsemann'. In Bultmann 1967, 476–82.

— 1965 (1958). 'Jesus Christus und die Mythologie'. In Bultmann, *Glauben und Verstehen. Gesammelte Aufsätze IV*, 141–89. Tübingen: Mohr (Siebeck).

— 1967. *Exegetica. Aufsätze zur Erforschung des Neuen Testaments.* Ed. Erich Dinkler. Tübingen: Mohr (Siebeck).

— 1984⁹ (1948–53). *Theologie des Neuen Testaments.* Tübingen: Mohr (Siebeck).

BURTON, E. DE W. 1921. *A Critical and Exegetical Commentary on the Epistle to the Galatians.* ICC. Edinburgh: Clark.

BYRNE, B., SJ 1981. 'Living out the Righteousness of God: The Contribution of Rom 6:1–8:13 to an Understanding of Paul's Ethical Presuppositions'. *CBQ* 43, 557–81.

— 1986. *Reckoning with Romans: A Contemporary Reading of Paul's Gospel.* Good News Studies 18. Wilmington, Del.: Glazier.

— 1996. *Romans.* Sacra Pagina 6. Collegeville: Liturgical.

CAIRD, G. B. 1976. *Paul's Letters from Prison.* Oxford University Press.

CALLAN, T. 1980. 'Pauline Midrash: The Exegetical Background of Gal 3:19b'. *JBL* 99, 549–67.

CAMPBELL, D. A. 1992. *The Rhetoric of Righteousness in Romans 3.21–26.* JSNTSup 65. Sheffield: JSOT.

— 1994. 'Romans 1:17—a *Crux Interpretum* for the *Pistis Christou* Debate'. *JBL* 113, 265–85.

— 1997. 'False Presuppositions in the *Pistis Christou* Debate: A Response to Brian Dodd'. *JBL* 116, 713–19.

CAMPBELL, R. A. 1996. '"Against such things there is no law"? Galatians 5:23b again'. *ExpTim* 107, 271–2.

CAMPBELL, W. S. 1981. 'Romans III as a Key to the Structure and Thought of the Letter'. *NovT* 23, 22–40.

— 1991. *Paul's Gospel in an Intercultural Context: Jew and Gentile in the Letter to the Romans.* Frankfurt: Lang.

— 1995. 'The Rule of Faith in Romans 12:1–15:13: The Obligation of Humble Obedience to Christ as the Only Adequate Response to the Mercies of God'. In Hay and Johnson (eds) 1995, 259–86.

CAPPER, B. J. 1993. 'Paul's Dispute with Philippi: Understanding Paul's Argument in Phil 1–2 from his Thanks in 4.10–20'. *TZ* 49, 193–214.

CARROLL, J. T., C. H. COSGROVE and E. E. JOHNSON (eds) 1990. *Faith and History.* FS Paul W. Meyer. Atlanta: Scholars.

CAVALLIN, A. 1941. '(to) *loipon*'. *Eranos* 39, 121–44.

CHADWICK, H. 1978. 'Gewissen'. In *RAC* 10, 1025–107. Stuttgart: Hiersemann.

CHRISTENSEN, J. 1962. *An Essay on the Unity of Stoic Philosophy*. Copenhagen: Munksgaard.

— 1984. 'Equality of Man and Stoic Social Thought'. *Commentationes Humanarum Litterarum Helsinki* 75, 45–54.

CLASSEN, C. J. 1991. 'Paulus und die antike Rhetorik'. *ZNW* 82, 1–33.

— 1993. 'St Paul's Epistles and Ancient Greek and Roman Rhetoric'. In Porter and Olbricht (eds) 1993, 265–91.

COLISH, M. L. 1985. *The Stoic Tradition from Antiquity to the Early Middle Ages*. 2 vols. Leiden: Brill.

— 1992. 'Stoicism and the New Testament: An Essay in Historiography'. *ANRW* II.26.1, 334–79. Berlin: de Gruyter.

COLLANGE, J.-F. 1973. *L'Épître de Saint Paul aux Philippiens*. CNT Xa. Neuchâtel: Delachaux and Niestlé.

COSGROVE, C. H. 1987. 'Justification in Paul: A Linguistic and Theological Reflection'. *JBL* 106, 653–70.

— 1992. 'The Justification of the Other: An Interpretation of Rom. 1:18–4:25'. In SBLSP 31, 613–34. Atlanta: Scholars.

COUSAR, C. B. 1995. 'Continuity and Discontinuity: Reflections on Romans 5–8 (In Conversation with Frank Thielman)'. In Hay and Johnson (eds) 1995, 196–210.

CRAFTON, J. A. 1990. 'Paul's Rhetorical Vision and the Purpose of Romans: Toward a New Understanding'. *NovT* 32, 317–39.

CRANFIELD, C. E. B. 1975–9. *A Critical and Exegetical Commentary on the Epistle to the Romans*. 2 vols. ICC. Edinburgh: Clark.

— 1990. 'Giving a Dog a Bad Name. A Note on H. Räisänen's *Paul and the Law*'. *JSNT* 38, 77–85.

— 1991. '"The Works of the Law" in the Epistle to the Romans'. *JSNT* 43, 89–101.

— 1994. 'Romans 6:1–14 Revisited'. *ExpTim* 106, 40–3.

CRANFORD, M. 1994. 'The Possibility of Perfect Obedience: Paul and an Implied Premise in Galatians 3:10 and 5:3'. *NovT* 36, 242–58.

CULPEPPER, R. A. 1980. 'Co-Workers in Suffering: Philippians 2:19–30'. *RevExp* 77, 349–58.

DAHL, N. A. 1969. 'The Atonement—an Adequate Reward for the Akedah? (Rom 8.32)'. In E. E. Ellis and M. Wilcox (eds), *Neotestamentica et Semitica*. FS Matthew Black. 15–29. Edinburgh: Clark. Also in Dahl 1991. *Jesus the Christ*. 137–51. Minneapolis: Fortress.

DAHL, N. A. 1977a. *Studies in Paul: Theology for the Early Christian Mission.* Minneapolis: Augsburg.

— 1977b. 'The Missionary Theology in the Epistle to the Romans'. In Dahl 1977a, 70–94.

— 1977c. 'The Doctrine of Justification: Its Social Function and Implications'. In Dahl 1977a, 95–120.

— 1995. 'Euodia and Syntyche and Paul's Letter to the Philippians'. In White and Yarbrough (eds) 1995, 3–15.

DAUBE, D. 1966. 'Paul a Hellenistic Schoolmaster?' In R. Loewe (ed.), *Studies in Rationalism, Judaism and Universalism.* 67–71. London: Routledge.

DAUTZENBERG, G. 1996. 'Die Freiheit bei Paulus und in der Stoa'. *TQ* 176, 65–76.

DAVIES, G. N. 1990. *Faith and Obedience in Romans: A Study in Romans 1–4.* JSNTSup 39. Sheffield: JSOT.

DAVIES, W. D. 1948. *Paul and Rabbinic Judaism: Some Rabbinic Elements in Pauline Theology.* London: SPCK.

— 1977–8. 'Paul and the People of Israel'. *NTS* 24, 4–39. Also in Davies 1984a, 123–52, 341–56.

— 1984a. *Jewish and Pauline Studies.* London: SPCK.

— 1984b (1978). 'Paul and the Gentiles: A Suggestion Concerning Romans 11:13–24'. In Davies 1984a, 153–63, 356–60.

DAWSON, D. 1992. *Cities of the Gods: Communist Utopias in Greek Thought.* New York: Oxford University Press.

DEICHGRÄBER, R. 1967. *Gotteshymnus und Christushymnus in der frühen Christenheit: Untersuchungen zu Form, Sprache und Stil der frühchristlichen Hymnen.* SUNT 5. Göttingen: Vandenhoeck & Ruprecht.

DEIDUN, T. J. 1981. *New Covenant Morality in Paul.* AnBib 89. Rome: Biblical Institute.

DEISSMANN, A. 1908. *Licht von Osten: Das Neue Testament und die neuentdeckten Texte der hellenistisch-römischen Welt.* Tübingen: Mohr (Siebeck).

DEISSNER, K. 1917. *Paulus und Seneca.* BFCT 21/2. Gütersloh: Bertelsmann.

DENNISON, W. D. 1979. 'Indicative and Imperative: The Basic Structure of Pauline Ethics'. *CTJ* 14, 55–78.

DENNISTON, J. D. 1954². *The Greek Particles.* Oxford University Press.

DESILVA, D. A. 1994. 'No Confidence in the Flesh: The Meaning and Function of Philippians 3:2–21'. *TrinJ* 15, 27–54.

— 1995. 'Paul and the Stoa: A Comparison'. *JETS* 38, 549–64.

DIBELIUS, M. 1912. *An die Kolosser Epheser. An Philemon.* HNT 12. Tübingen: Mohr (Siebeck).

DIBELIUS, M. 1913. *Die Pastoralbriefe.* HNT 13. Tübingen: Mohr (Siebeck).

— 1937³ (1911). *An die Thessalonicher I II. An die Philipper.* HNT 11. Tübingen: Mohr (Siebeck).

— 1984⁶ (1921). *Der Brief des Jakobus.* MeyerK 15. Göttingen: Vandenhoeck & Ruprecht.

DOBBELER, A. VON 1987. *Glaube als Teilhabe: Historische und semantische Grundlagen der paulinischen Theologie und Ekklesiologie des Glaubens.* WUNT 2/22. Tübingen: Mohr (Siebeck).

DODD, B. 1995. 'Romans 1:17—A *Crux Interpretum* for the *Pistis Christou* Debate?' *JBL* 114, 470–73.

DODD, B. J. 1996. 'Christ's Slave, People Pleasers and Galatians 1.10'. *NTS* 42, 90–104.

DODD, C. H. 1960 (1932). *The Epistle of Paul to the Romans.* MNTC. London: Hodder & Stoughton.

DONALDSON, T. L. 1986. 'The "Curse of the Law" and the Inclusion of the Gentiles: Galatians 3.13–14'. *NTS* 32, 94–112.

— 1989. 'Zealot and Convert: The Origin of Paul's Christ–Torah Antithesis'. *CBQ* 51, 655–82.

— 1993. '"Riches for the Gentiles" (Rom 11:12): Israel's Rejection and Paul's Gentile Mission'. *JBL* 112, 81–98.

— 1997. *Paul and the Gentiles: Remapping the Apostle's Convictional World.* Minneapolis: Fortress.

DONFRIED, K. P. (ed.) 1991²a (1977). *The Romans Debate: Revised and Expanded Edition.* Peabody, Mass: Hendrickson.

— 1991b (1974). 'False Presuppositions in the Study of Romans'. In Donfried (ed.) 1991²a, 102–25.

DOUGHTY, D. D. 1995. 'Citizens of Heaven. Philippians 3.2–21'. *NTS* 41, 102–22.

DOWNING, G. F. 1984. 'Cynics and Christians'. *NTS* 30, 584–93.

— 1996. 'A Cynic Preparation for Paul's Gospel for Jew and Greek, Slave and Free, Male and Female'. *NTS* 42, 454–62.

DRANE, J. W. 1975. *Paul: Libertine or Legalist? A Study in the Theology of the Major Pauline Epistles.* London: SPCK.

DUNN, J. D. G. 1983a. 'The New Perspective on Paul'. *BJRL* 65, 95–122. Also in Dunn 1990, 183–206 with Additional Note 206–14.

— 1983b. 'The Incident at Antioch (Gal. ii.11–18)'. *JSNT* 18, 3–57. Also in Dunn 1990, 129–74 with Additional Note 174–82.

— 1985. 'Works of the Law and the Curse of the Law (Galatians iii.10–14)'. *NTS* 31, 523–42. Also in Dunn 1990, 215–36 with Additional Note 237–41.

DUNN, J. D. G. 1987. 'Paul's Epistle to the Romans: An Analysis of Structure and Argument'. *ANRW* II.25.4, 2842–90. Berlin: de Gruyter.

— 1988. *Romans*. 2 vols. WBC 38. Dallas: Word.

— 1990. *Jesus, Paul and the Law: Studies in Mark and Galatians*. London: SPCK/ Louisville: Westminster.

— 1991a. 'The Theology of Galatians'. In Bassler (ed.) 1991, 125–46. Also in Dunn 1990, 242–64.

— 1991b. 'Once More, *Pistis Christou*'. SBLSP 30, 730–44. Atlanta: Scholars.

— 1991c. 'The Formal and Theological Coherence of Romans'. In Donfried (ed.) 1991²a, 245–50.

— 1992a. 'The Justice of God. A Renewed Perspective on Justification by Faith'. *JTS* 43, 1–22.

— 1992b. 'Yet Once More—"The Works of the Law": A Response'. *JSNT* 46, 99–117.

— 1993a. *The Epistle to the Galatians*. London: Black.

— 1993b. *The Theology of Paul's Letter to the Galatians*. Cambridge University Press.

— 1993c. 'Echoes of Intra-Jewish Polemic in Paul's Letter to the Galatians'. *JBL* 112, 459–77.

— (ed.) 1996a. *Paul and the Mosaic Law*. WUNT 89. Tübingen: Mohr (Siebeck).

— 1996b. '"The Law of Faith", "the Law of the Spirit" and "the Law of Christ"'. In Lovering, Jr. and Sumney (eds) 1996, 62–82.

— 1998. *The Theology of Paul the Apostle*. Grand Rapids: Eerdmans.

EBNER, M. 1991. *Leidenslisten und Apostelbrief: Untersuchungen zu Form, Motivik und Funktion der Peristasenkataloge bei Paulus*. FB 66. Würzburg: Echter.

ECKERT, J. 1996. '"Zieht den Herrn Jesus Christus an . . . !" (Röm 13,14): Zu einer enthusiastischen Metapher der neutestamentlichen Verkündigung'. *TTZ* 105, 39–60.

ECKSTEIN, H.-J. 1983. *Der Begriff Syneidesis bei Paulus: Eine neutestamentlich-exegetische Untersuchung zum 'Gewissensbegriff'*. WUNT 2/10. Tübingen: Mohr (Siebeck).

— 1996. *Verheissung und Gesetz: Eine exegetische Untersuchung zu Galater 2,15–4,7*. WUNT 86. Tübingen: Mohr (Siebeck).

— 1997. 'Auferstehung und gegenwärtiges Leben nach Röm 6,1–11. Präsentische Eschatologie bei Paulus?' *TBei* 28, 8–23.

ELLIOTT, N. 1990. *The Rhetoric of Romans: Argumentative Constraint and Strategy and Paul's Dialogue with Judaism*. JSNTSup 45. Sheffield: JSOT.

ELLIS, E. E. and E. GRÄSSER (eds) 1975. *Jesus und Paulus*. FS W. G. Kümmel. Göttingen: Vandenhoeck & Ruprecht.

ENGBERG-PEDERSEN, T. 1981. 'For Goodness' Sake: More on *Nicomachean Ethics* I vii 5'. *AGP* 63, 17–40 (repr. 1995 in T. Irwin [ed.], *Aristotle's Ethics*, New York: Garland, 127–50).

— 1983. *Aristotle's Theory of Moral Insight*. Oxford University Press.

— 1986a. 'Discovering the good: *oikeiosis* and *kathekonta* in Stoic ethics'. In M. Schofield and G. Striker (eds), *The Norms of Nature: Studies in Hellenistic Ethics*. 145–83. Cambridge University Press.

— 1986b. 'Paulus og græsk moralfilosofi' [Paul and Greek ethics]. *Fønix* 10, 13–32.

— 1990. *The Stoic Theory of Oikeiosis: Moral Development and Social Interaction in Early Stoic Philosophy*. Studies in Hellenistic Civilization 2. Aarhus University Press.

— 1994a (ed.). *Paul in His Hellenistic Context*. Edinburgh: Clark/Minneapolis: Fortress.

— 1994b. 'Stoicism in Philippians'. In Engberg-Pedersen 1994a (ed.), 256–90.

— 1995. 'Galatians in Romans 5–8 and Paul's Construction of the Identity of Christ Believers'. In Fornberg and Hellholm (eds) 1995, 477–505.

— 1996. *Antikkens etiske tradition: Fra Sokrates til Marcus Aurelius* [The Ancient Ethical Tradition. From Socrates to Marcus Aurelius]. Copenhagen: Gyldendal.

— 1998. 'Marcus Aurelius on Emotions'. In Sihvola and Engberg-Pedersen (eds) 1998, 305–37.

— forthcoming (ed.). *Paul Beyond the Judaism/Hellenism Divide*.

EPP, E. J. 1986. 'Jewish-Gentile Continuity in Paul: Torah and/or Faith? (Romans 9:1–5)'. *HTR* 79, 80–90.

ERSKINE, A. 1990. *The Hellenistic Stoa: Political Thought and Action*. London: Duckworth.

FEE, G. D. 1992. 'Philippians 2:5–11: Hymn or Exalted Pauline Prose?' *BulBR* 2, 29–46.

FEUILLET, A. 1980. 'Loi de Dieu, Loi du Christ et Loi de l'Esprit d'après les Épîtres pauliniennes'. *NovT* 22, 29–65.

FINSTERBUSCH, K. 1996. *Die Thora als Lebenweisung für Heidenchristen: Studien zur Bedeutung der Thora für die paulinische Ethik*. SUNT 20. Göttingen: Vandenhoeck & Ruprecht.

FIORE, B. 1986. *The Function of Personal Example in the Socratic and Pastoral Epistles*. Anbib 105. Rome: Biblical Institute.

FITZGERALD, J. T. 1988. *Cracks in an Earthen Vessel: An Examination of the Catalogues of Hardship in the Corinthian Correspondence.* SBLDS 99. Atlanta: Scholars.

— (ed.) 1996a. *Friendship, Flattery, and Frankness of Speech: Studies on Friendship in the New Testament World.* NovTSup 82. Leiden: Brill.

— 1996b. 'Philippians in the Light of Some Ancient Discussions of Friendship'. In Fitzgerald (ed.) 1996a, 141–60.

FITZMYER, J. A. 1993. *Romans: A New Translation with Introduction and Commentary.* AB 33. New York: Doubleday.

FORNBERG, T. and D. HELLHOLM (eds) 1995. *Texts and Contexts: Biblical Texts in their Textual and Situational Contexts.* FS Lars Hartman. Oslo: Scandinavian University Press.

FORSCHNER, M. 1981 (1995²). *Die stoische Ethik: Über den Zusammenhang von Natur-, Sprach- und Moralphilosophie im altstoischen System.* Stuttgart: Klett-Cotta (Darmstadt: Wissenschaftliche Buchgesellschaft).

FORTNA, R. T. and B. R. GAVENTA (eds) 1990. *The Conversation Continues: Studies in Paul and John.* FS J. Louis Martyn. Nashville: Abingdon.

FOWL, S. E. 1990. *The Story of Christ in the Ethics of Paul: An Analysis of the Function of the Hymnic Material in the Pauline Corpus.* JSNTSup 36. Sheffield: JSOT.

FREDERIKSEN, P. 1991. 'Judaism, the Circumcision of Gentiles, and Apocalyptic Hope: Another Look at Galatians 1 and 2'. *JTS* 42, 532–64.

FRIDRICHSEN, A. 1922. 'Der wahre Jude und sein Lob. Röm. 2 28 f.' *Symbolae Arctoae* 1, 39–49.

— 1930. 'Exegetisches zu den Paulusbriefen'. *TSK* 102, 291–301.

FRIEDRICH, G. (ed.) 1964. *Theologisches Wörterbuch zum Neuen Testament* VII. Stuttgart: Kohlhammer.

FRIEDRICH, J., W. PÖHLMANN and P. STUHLMACHER (eds) 1976. *Rechtfertigung.* FS Ernst Käsemann. Tübingen: Mohr (Siebeck)/Göttingen: Vandenhoeck & Ruprecht.

FURNESS, J. M. 1958–9. 'The Authorship of Philippians ii. 6–11'. *ExpTim* 70, 240–3.

FURNISH, V. P. 1963–4. 'The Place and Purpose of Philippians III'. *NTS* 10, 80–8.

— 1968. *Theology and Ethics in Paul.* Nashville: Abingdon.

— 1972. *The Love Command in the New Testament.* Nashville: Abingdon.

— 1990. 'Paul the Theologian'. In Fortna and Gaventa (eds) 1990, 19–34.

— 1993. '"He Gave Himself [Was Given] Up . . .": Paul's Use of a Christological Assertion'. In A. J. Malherbe and W. A. Meeks (eds), *The Future of Christology.* FS Leander E. Keck. 109–21. Minneapolis: Fortress.

GAMBLE, H., JR. 1977. *The Textual History of the Letter to the Romans: A Study in Textual and Literary Criticism.* SD 42. Grand Rapids: Eerdmans.

GARLAND, D. E. 1985. 'The Composition and Unity of Philippians: Some Neglected Literary Factors'. *NovT* 27, 141–73.

GARLINGTON, D. B. 1990. *'The Obedience of Faith': A Pauline Phrase in Historical Context.* WUNT 2/38. Tübingen: Mohr (Siebeck).

— 1994. *Faith, Obedience, and Perseverance: Aspects of Paul's Letter to the Romans.* WUNT 79. Tübingen: Mohr (Siebeck).

— 1997. 'Role Reversal and Paul's Use of Scripture in Galatians 3.10–13'. *JSNT* 65, 85–121.

GASTON, L. 1987. *Paul and the Torah.* Vancouver: University of British Columbia Press.

GAVENTA, B. R. 1986. 'Galatians 1 and 2: Autobiography as Paradigm'. *NovT* 28, 309–26.

— 1990. 'The Maternity of Paul: Exegetical Reflections on Galatians 4:19'. In Fortna and Gaventa (eds) 1990, 189–201.

GEERTZ, C. 1957. 'Ethos, World View, and the Analysis of Sacred Symbols'. *The Antioch Review* 17,4. Repr. in Geertz 1973. *The Interpretation of Cultures.* New York: Basic, 126–41.

GETTY, M. A. 1988. 'Paul and the Salvation of Israel: A Perspective on Romans 9–11'. *CBQ* 50, 456–69.

GLAD, C. E. 1995. *Paul and Philodemus: Adaptability in Epicurean and Early Christian Psychagogy.* NovTSup 81. Leiden: Brill.

GNILKA, J. 1965. 'Die antipaulinische Mission in Philippi'. *BZ* 9, 258–76.

— 1968. *Der Philipperbrief.* HTKNT 10.3. Freiburg: Herder.

— 1996. *Paulus von Tarsus: Apostel und Zeuge.* HTKNTSup 6. Freiburg: Herder.

GORDON, T. D. 1987. 'The Problem at Galatia'. *Int* 41, 32–43.

GOULET-CAZÉ, M.-O. 1990. 'Le Cynisme à l'époque impériale'. *ANRW* II.36.4. 2722–833. Berlin: de Gruyter.

GRANT, F. C. 1915. 'St Paul and Stoicism'. *The Biblical World* 45, 268–81.

GRÄSSER, E. and O. MERK (eds) 1985. *Glaube und Eschatologie.* FS Werner Georg Kümmel. Tübingen: Mohr (Siebeck).

GRAYSTON, K. 1985–6. 'The Opponents in Philippians 3'. *ExpTim* 97, 170–2.

GREEVEN, H. 1935. *Das Hauptproblem der Sozialethik in der neueren Stoa und im Urchristentum.* NTF 4. Gütersloh: Bertelsmann.

HAACKER, K. 1990. 'Der Römerbrief als Friedensmemorandum'. *NTS* 36, 25–41.

HAACKER, K. 1997a. 'Die Geschichtstheologie von Röm 9–11 im Lichte philoonischer Schriftauslegung.' *NTS* 43, 209–22.

— 1997b. *Paulus: Der Werdegang eines Apostels.* Stuttgarter Bibel-studien 171. Stuttgart: Katholisches Bibelwerk.

HADOT, I. 1969. *Seneca und die griechisch-römische Tradition der Seelenleitung.* Quellen und Studien zur Geschichte der Philosophie 13. Berlin: de Gruyter.

HADOT, P. 1995. *Philosophy as a Way of Life: Spiritual Exercises from Socrates to Foucault.* Oxford: Blackwell.

HAHN, F. 1976. 'Das Gesetzesverständnis im Römer- und Galaterbrief'. *ZNW* 67, 29–63.

— 1993. 'Gibt es eine Entwicklung in den Aussagen Über die Rechtfertigung bei Paulus?' *EvT* 53, 342–66.

HAINZ, J. 1994. 'Koinōnia bei Paulus'. In Bormann *et al.* 1994, 375–91.

HALL, R. G. 1987. 'The Rhetorical Outline for Galatians: A Reconsideration'. *JBL* 106, 277–87.

HARNISCH, W. 1987. 'Einübung des neuen Seins: Paulinische Paränese am Beispiel des Galaterbriefs'. *ZTK* 84, 279–96.

HARTMAN, L. 1993. 'Galatians 3:15–4:11 as Part of a Theological Argument on a Practical Issue'. In Lambrecht (ed.) 1993, 127–58.

HATCH, E. 1891². *The Influence of Greek Ideas and Usages upon the Christian Church.* London: Williams & Norgate.

HAUCK, F. 1938. 'karpos ktl.' In Kittel (ed.) 1938, 617–19.

HAUFE, G. 1994. 'Das Geistmotiv in der paulinischen Ethik'. *ZNW* 85, 183–91.

HAWTHORNE, G. F. 1987. *Philippians.* Word Biblical Themes. Waco, Texas: Word.

HAY, D. M. (ed.) 1993. *Pauline Theology II: 1 and 2 Corinthians.* Minneapolis: Fortress.

— and E. E. JOHNSON (eds) 1995. *Pauline Theology III: Romans.* Minneapolis: Fortress.

HAYS, R. B. 1980. 'Psalm 143 and the Logic of Romans 3'. *JBL* 99, 107–15.

— 1983. *The Faith of Jesus Christ: An Investigation of the Narrative Substructure of Galatians 3:1–4:11.* SBLDS 56. Chico, CA: Scholars.

— 1985. '"Have we found Abraham to be our Forefather according to the Flesh?" A Reconsideration of Rom 4:1'. *NovT* 27, 76–98.

— 1987. 'Christology and Ethics in Galatians: The Law of Christ'. *CBQ* 49, 268–90.

— 1989. '"The Righteous One" as Eschatological Deliverer: A Case Study in Paul's Apocalyptic Hermeneutics'. In Marcus and Soards (eds) 1989, 191–215.

HAYS, R. B. 1991. '*Pistis* and Pauline Christology: What is at Stake?' SBLSP 30, 714–29. Atlanta: Scholars.

— 1993. 'Christ Prays the Psalms: Paul's Use of an Early Christian Exegetical Convention'. In Malherbe and Meeks (eds) 1993, 122–36.

— 1995. 'Adam, Israel, Christ—The Question of Covenant in the Theology of Romans: A Response to Leander E. Keck and N. T. Wright'. In Hay and Johnson (eds) 1995, 68–86.

— 1996. 'The Role of Scripture in Paul's Ethics'. In Lovering, Jr. and Sumney (eds) 1996, 30–47.

HEILIGENTHAL, R. 1983. *Werke als Zeichen: Untersuchungen zur Bedeutung der menschlichen Taten im Frühjudentum, Neuen Testament und Frühchristentum*. WUNT 2/9. Tübingen: Mohr (Siebeck).

— 1984. 'Soziologische Implikationen der paulinischen Rechtfertigungslehre im Galaterbrief am Beispiel der "Werke des Gesetzes"'. *Kairos* 26, 38–53.

HEINEMANN, I. 1927. 'Die Lehre vom ungeschriebenen Gesetz im jüdischen Schrifttum'. *HUCA* 4, 149–71.

HELLHOLM, D. 1997. 'Die argumentative Funktion von Römer 7.1–6'. *NTS* 43, 385–411.

HENGEL, M. 1969. *Judentum und Hellenismus*. WUNT 10. Tübingen: Mohr (Siebeck).

— and U. HECKEL (eds) 1991. *Paulus und das antike Judentum*. WUNT 58. Tübingen: Mohr (Siebeck).

HESTER, J. D. 1984. 'The Rhetorical Structure of Galatians 1:11–2:14'. *JBL* 103, 223–33.

HOFIUS, O. 1976. *Der Christushymnus Philipper 2,6–11: Untersuchungen zu Gestalt und Aussage eines urchristlichen Psalmes*. WUNT 17. Tübingen: Mohr (Siebeck).

— 1983. 'Das Gesetz des Mose und das Gesetz Christi'. *ZTK* 80, 262–86.

— 1989a. *Paulusstudien*. WUNT 51. Tübingen: Mohr (Siebeck).

— 1989b (1983). 'Sühne und Versöhnung: Zum paulinischen Verständnis des Kreuzestodes Jesu'. In Hofius 1989a, 33–49.

— 1989c (1987). '"Rechtfertigung des Gottlosen" als Thema biblischer Theologie'. In Hofius 1989a, 121–47.

— 1989d (1986). 'Das Evangelium und Israel. Erwägungen zu Römer 9–11'. In Hofius 1989a, 175–202.

HOLLADAY, C. R. 1969. 'Paul's Opponents in Philippians 3'. *ResQ* 12, 77–90.

HOLMBERG, B. 1980. *Paul and Power: The Structure of Authority in the Primitive Church as Reflected in the Pauline Epistles*. Philadelphia: Fortress.

HOLMSTRAND, J. 1997. *Markers and Meaning in Paul: An Analysis of 1 Thessalonians, Philippians and Galatians*. ConBNT 28. Stockholm: Almqvist & Wiksell.

HONG, I.-G. 1993. *The Law in Galatians*. JSNTSup 81. Sheffield: JSOT.

— 1994. 'Does Paul Misrepresent the Jewish Law? Law and Covenant in Gal. 3:1–14'. *NovT* 36, 164–82.

HOOKER, M. D. 1971. 'Interchange in Christ'. *JTS* 22, 349–61. Also in Hooker 1990, 13–25.

— 1975. 'Philippians 2:6–11'. In Ellis and Grässer (eds) 1975, 151–64.

— 1978. 'Interchange and atonement'. *BJRL* 60, 462–81. Also in Hooker 1990, 26–41.

— 1981. 'Interchange and suffering'. In W. Horbury and B. McNeil (eds), *Suffering and Martyrdom in the New Testament*. FS G. M. Styler. Cambridge University Press. Also in Hooker 1990, 42–55.

— 1985. 'Interchange in Christ and Ethics'. *JSNT* 25, 3–17. Also in Hooker 1990, 56–69.

— 1989. 'Pistis Christou'. *NTS* 35, 321–42.

— 1990. *From Adam to Christ: Essays on Paul*. Cambridge University Press.

HORN, F. W. 1992. *Das Angeld des Geistes: Studien zur paulinischen Pneumatologie*. FRLANT 154. Göttingen: Vandenhoeck & Ruprecht.

HORST, P. W. VAN DER 1974. 'Musonius Rufus and the New Testament'. *NovT* 16, 306–15.

HOWARD, G. 1967. 'On the "Faith of Christ"'. *HTR* 60, 459–65.

— 1973–4. 'The "Faith of Christ"'. *ExpTim* 85, 212–15.

— 1979 (1990²). *Paul: Crisis in Galatia. A Study in Early Christian Theology*. SNTSMS 35. Cambridge University Press.

HÜBNER, H. 1975. 'Das ganze und das eine Gesetz: Zum Problemkreis Paulus und die Stoa'. *KD* 21, 239–56.

— 1978. 'Identitätsverlust und paulinische Theologie: Anmerkungen zum Galaterbrief'. *KD* 24, 181–93.

— 1978 (1980²). *Das Gesetz bei Paulus: Ein Beitrag zum Werden der paulinischen Theologie*. FRLANT 119. Göttingen: Vandenhoeck & Ruprecht.

— 1979–80. 'Pauli Theologiae Proprium'. *NTS* 26, 445–73.

— 1985. 'Was heisst bei Paulus "Werke des Gesetzes"?' In Grässer and Merk (eds) 1985, 123–33.

— 1993. *Biblische Theologie des Neuen Testaments. Band 2: Die Theologie des Paulus*. Göttingen: Vandenhoeck & Ruprecht.

HULTGREN, A. J. 1980. 'The *Pistis Christou* Formulation in Paul'. *NovT* 22, 248–63.

HVALVIK, R. 1990. 'A "Sonderweg" for Israel: A Critical Examination of a Current Interpretation of Romans 11.25–27'. *JSNT* 38, 87–107.

HYLDAHL, N. 1986. *Die paulinische Chronologie*. ATDan 19. Leiden: Brill.

INWOOD, B. 1985. *Ethics and Human Action in Early Stoicism*. Oxford University Press.

JAGU, A. 1958. 'Saint Paul et le stoïcisme'. *RevScRel* 32, 225–50.

— 1989. 'La Morale d'Epictète et le christianisme'. *ANRW* II.36.3, 2164–99.

JAQUETTE, J. L. 1994. 'Paul, Epictetus, and Others on Indifference to Status'. *CBQ* 56, 68–80.

— 1995a. *Discerning What Counts: The Function of the* Adiaphora *Topos in Paul's Letters*. SBLDS 146. Atlanta: Scholars.

— 1995b. 'Foundational convictions, ethical instruction and theologising in Paul'. *Neot* 29, 231–52.

— 1996. 'Life and Death, *Adiaphora*, and Paul's Rhetorical Strategies'. *NovT* 38, 30–54.

JERVELL, J. 1991 (1971). 'The Letter to Jerusalem'. In Donfried (ed.) 1991²a, 53–64.

JERVIS, L. A. 1991. *The Purpose of Romans: A Comparative Letter Structure Investigation*. JSNTSup 55. Sheffield: JSOT.

JEWETT, R. 1970a. 'The Epistolary Thanksgiving and the Integrity of Philippians'. *NovT* 12, 40–53.

— 1970b. 'Conflicting Movements in the Early Church as Reflected in Philippians'. *NovT* 12, 362–90.

— 1970-1. 'The Agitators and the Galatian Congregation'. *NTS* 17, 198–212.

— 1971. *Paul's Anthropological Terms: A Study of their Use in Conflict Settings*. Leiden: Brill.

— 1982. 'Romans as an Ambassadorial Letter'. *Int* 36, 5–20.

— 1985. 'The Law and the Coexistence of Jews and Gentiles in Romans'. *Int* 39, 341–56.

— 1988. 'Paul, Phoebe, and the Spanish Mission'. In Neusner, J. *et al.* (eds) 1988, 142–61.

— 1991 (1986). 'Following the Argument of Romans'. In Donfried (ed.) 1991²a, 265–77.

— 1995. 'Ecumenical Theology for the Sake of Mission: Romans 1:1–17+15:14–16:24'. In Hay and Johnson (eds) 1995, 89–108.

JOHNSON, E. E. 1989. *The Function of Apocalyptic and Wisdom Traditions in Romans 9–11*. SBLDS 109. Atlanta: Scholars.

— 1995. 'Romans 9–11: The Faithfulness and Impartiality of God'. In Hay and Johnson (eds) 1995, 211–39.

JOHNSON, E. E. and D. M. HAY (eds) 1997. *Pauline Theology IV: Looking Back, Pressing On*. Society of Biblical Literature Symposium Series 4. Atlanta: Scholars.

JOHNSON, L. T. 1982. 'Rom 3:21–26 and the Faith of Jesus'. *CBQ* 44, 77–90.

JOLY, R. 1968. *Le vocabulaire chrétien de l'amour est-il original? Philein et Agapan dans le grec antique*. Université libre de Bruxelles. Institut d'histoire du christianisme. Bruxelles: Presses Universitaires.

JONES, F. S. 1987. *'Freiheit' in den Briefen des Apostels Paulus: Eine historische, exegetische und religionsgeschichtliche Studie*. GTA 34. Göttingen: Vandenhoeck & Ruprecht.

JUDGE, E. A. 1972. 'St. Paul and Classical Society'. *JAC* 15, 19–36.

— 1979. '"Antike und Christentum": Towards a Definition of the Field. A Biographical Survey'. *ANRW* II.23.1, 3–58.

— 1984. 'Cultural Conformity and Innovation in Paul: Some Clues from Contemporary Documents'. *TynBul* 35, 3–24.

KÄHLER, C. 1994. 'Konflikt, Kompromiss und Bekenntnis: Paulus und seine Gegner im Philipperbrief'. *KD* 40, 47–64.

KAHN, C. H. 1988. 'Discovering the will: From Aristotle to Augustine'. In J. M. Dillon and A. A. Long (eds), *The Question of 'Eclecticism': Studies in Later Greek Philosophy*. Hellenistic Culture and Society 3. 234–59. Berkeley/Los Angeles: University of California Press.

KAMLAH, E. 1964. *Die Form der katalogischen Paränese im Neuen Testament*. WUNT 7. Tübingen: Mohr (Siebeck).

KARRIS, R. J. 1991 (1973). 'Romans 14:1–15:13 and the Occasion of Romans'. In Donfried (ed.) 1991²a, 65–84.

— 1991 (1974). 'The Occasion of Romans: A Response to Prof. Donfried'. In Donfried (ed.) 1991²a, 125–7.

KÄSEMANN, E. 1950. 'Kritische Analyse von Phil. 2, 5–11'. In Käsemann 1964a, 51–95.

— 1961. 'Gottesgerechtigkeit bei Paulus'. In Käsemann 1964b, 181–93.

— 1962. 'Zum Thema der urchristlichen Apokalyptik'. In Käsemann 1964b, 105–31.

— 1964a. *Exegetische Versuche und Besinnungen I*. Göttingen: Vandenhoeck & Ruprecht.

— 1964b. *Exegetische Versuche und Besinnungen II*. Göttingen: Vandenhoeck & Ruprecht.

— 1972²a (1969). *Paulinische Perspektiven*. Tübingen: Mohr (Siebeck).

— 1972²b (1969). 'Zur paulinischen Anthropologie'. In Käsemann 1972²a, 9–60.

KÄSEMANN, E. 1972²c (1969). 'Rechtfertigung und Heilsgeschichte im Römerbrief'. In Käsemann 1972²a, 108–39.

— 1973. *An die Römer.* HNT 8a. Tübingen: Mohr (Siebeck).

KAYE, B. N. 1979. *The Argument of Romans with Special Reference to Chapter 6.* Austin, Texas: Schola.

KAYLOR, R. D. 1988. *Paul's Covenant Community: Jew and Gentile in Romans.* Atlanta: Knox.

KECK, L. E. 1976. 'Justification of the Ungodly and Ethics'. In Friedrich, Pöhlmann and Stuhlmacher (eds) 1976, 199–209.

— 1977. 'The Function of Rom 3:10–18—Observations and Suggestions'. In J. Jervell and W. A. Meeks (eds), *God's Christ and His People.* FS Nils Alstrup Dahl. 141–57. Oslo: Universitetsforlaget.

— 1979. 'The Post-Pauline Interpretation of Jesus' Death in Rom 5,6–7'. In Andresen and Klein (eds) 1979, 237–48.

— 1984. 'Paul and Apocalyptic Theology'. *Int* 38, 229–41.

— 1990a. 'Christology, Soteriology, and the Praise of God (Romans 15:7–13)'. In Fortna and Gaventa (eds) 1990, 85–97.

— 1990b. 'Romans 15:43: An Interpolation?' In Carroll, Cosgrove and Johnson (eds) 1990, 125–36.

— 1993. 'Paul as Thinker'. *Int* 47, 27–38.

— 1995. 'What Makes Romans Tick?' In Hay and Johnson (eds) 1995, 3–29.

— 1996. 'The Accountable Self'. In Lovering, Jr. and Sumney (eds) 1996, 1–13.

— 1997. 'Searchable Judgments and Scrutable Ways'. In Johnson and Hay (eds) 1997, 22–32.

KEE, H. C. 1985. 'Pauline Eschatology: Relationships with Apocalyptic and Stoic Thought'. In Grässer and Merk (eds) 1985, 135–58.

KENNEDY, G. A. 1984. *New Testament Interpretation through Rhetorical Criticism.* Chapel Hill: University of North Carolina Press.

KERFERD, G. B. 1972. 'The Search for Personal Identity in Stoic Thought'. *BJRL* 55, 177–96.

— 1978. 'What Does the Wise Man Know?' In J. M. Rist (ed.) *The Stoics.* 125–36. Berkeley/Los Angeles: University of California Press.

KERTELGE, K. 1967. *'Rechtfertigung' bei Paulus: Studien zur Struktur und zum Bedeutungsgehalt des paulinischen RechtfertigungsBegriffs.* Münster: Aschendorff.

— 1968. 'Zur Deutung des Rechtfertigungsbegriffs im Galaterbrief'. *BZ* 12, 211–22. Also in Kertelge 1991, 111–22.

— 1971. 'Exegetische Überlegungen zum Verständnis der paulinischen Anthropologie nach Römer 7'. *ZNW* 62, 105–14. Also in Kertelge 1991, 174–83.

KERTELGE, K. 1984. 'Gesetz und Freiheit im Galaterbrief'. *NTS* 30, 382–94. Also in Kertelge 1991, 184–96.

— 1985. 'Die paulinische Rechtfertigungslehre nach Röm 3, 21–6'. In Kertelge 1991, 123–29.

— (ed.) 1986. *Das Gesetz im Neuen Testament*. QD 108. Freiburg: Herder.

— 1989a. 'Freiheitsbotschaft und Liebesgebot im Galaterbrief'. In H. Merklein (ed.), *Neues Testament und Ethik*. FS Rudolf Schnackenburg. 326–37. Freiburg: Herder. Also in Kertelge 1991, 197–208.

— 1989b. 'Rechtfertigung aus Glauben und Gericht nach den Werken bei Paulus'. In K. Lehmann (ed.), *Lehrverurteilungen—kirchentrennend? II. Materialien zu den Lehrverurteilungen und zur Theologie der Rechtfertigung*. 173–90. Freiburg/Göttingen. Also in Kertelge 1991, 130–47.

— 1991. *Grundthemen paulinischer Theologie*. Freiburg: Herder.

KETTUNEN, M. 1979. *Der Abfassungszweck des Römerbriefes*. Annales Academiae Scientiarum Fennicae, Dissertationes Humanarum Litterarum 18. Helsinki: Suomalainen Tiedeakatemia.

KITTEL, G. (ed.) 1938. *Theologisches Wörterbuch zum Neuen Testament III*. Stuttgart: Kohlhammer.

KLAUCK, H.-J. 1996. *Die religiöse Umwelt des Urchristentums II. Herrscher- und Kaiserkult, Philosophie, Gnosis*. Stuttgart: Kohlhammer.

KLEIN, G. 1976. 'Präliminarien zum Thema "Paulus und die Juden"'. In Friedrich, Pöhlmann and Stuhlmacher (eds) 1976, 229–43.

— 1988. 'Ein Sturmzentrum des Paulusforschung'. *VF* 33, 40–56.

— 1991 (1969). 'Paul's Purpose in Writing the Epistle to the Romans'. In Donfried (ed.) 1991²a, 29–43. Original version: 'Der Abfassungszweck des Römerbriefes'. In Klein 1969. *Rekonstruktion und Interpretation*, BEvT 50. 129–44. Munich: Kaiser.

KLIJN, A. F. J. 1964–5. 'Paul's Opponents in Phil iii', *NovT* 7, 278–84.

KLUMBIES, P.-G. 1987. 'Zwischen Pneuma und Nomos: Neuorientierung in den galatischen Gemeinden'. *WD* 19, 109–35.

— 1994. 'Der Eine Gott des Paulus: Röm 1,21–31 als Brennpunkt paulinischer Theo-logie'. *ZNW* 85, 192–206.

KOESTER, H. 1961–2. 'The Purpose of the Polemic of a Pauline Fragment (Philippians III)'. *NTS* 8, 317–32.

— 1980. *Einführung in das Neue Testament*. Berlin: de Gruyter.

KOSKENNIEMI, H. 1956. *Studien zur Idee und Phraseologie des griechischen Briefes bis 400 n.Chr*. Annales Academiae Scientiarum Fennicae Ser. B Tom. 102,2. Helsinki: Akateeminen Kirjakauppa.

KRANZ, W. 1951. 'Das Gesetz des Herzens'. *RMP* 94, 222–41.

KUCK, D. W. 1994. ' "Each Will Bear His Own Burden": Paul's Creative Use of an Apocalyptic Motif'. *NTS* 40, 289–97.

KÜMMEL, W. G. 1974 (1929). *Römer 7 und die Bekehrung des Paulus.* In *Römer 7 und das Bild des Menschen im Neuen Testament. Zwei Studien.* Munich: Kaiser.

— 1976. 'Albert Schweitzer als Paulusforscher'. In Friedrich, Pöhlmann and Stuhlmacher (eds) 1976, 269–289.

— 1977. 'Die Probleme von Römer 9–11 in der gegenwärtigen Forschungslage'. In Lorenzi (ed.) 1977, 13–33.

— 1980[20]. *Einleitung in das Neue Testament.* Heidelberg: Quelle & Meyer.

KUSS, O. 1957–78. *Der Römerbrief übersetzt und erklärt.* 3 vols. Regensburg: Pustet.

KUTSCH, E. 1987. 'Das *posse non peccare* und verwandte Formulierungen als Aussagen biblischer Theologie'. *ZTK* 84, 267–78.

LAGRANGE, M.-J. 1912. 'La philosophie religieuse d'Epictète et le christianisme'. *Revue biblique internationale* 9, 5–21, 192–212.

LAMBRECHT, J. 1977–8. 'The Line of Thought in Gal. 2.14*b*–21'. *NTS* 24, 484–95.

— 1986. 'Gesetzesverständnis bei Paulus'. In Kertelge (ed.) 1986, 88–127.

— 1991a. 'Transgressor by Nullifying God's Grace. A Study of Gal 2,18–21'. *Bib* 72, 217–36.

— 1991b. 'Curse and Blessing: A Study of Galatians 3,10–14'. *Collationes* 21, 133–57. Also in Lambrecht 1994, 271–98.

— (ed.) 1993. *The Truth of the Gospel: Galatians 1:1–4:11.* Monographic Series of 'Benedictina' 12. Rome: 'Benedictina', St Paul's Abbey.

— 1994. *Pauline Studies.* BETL 115. Leuven University Press.

— 1996. 'Paul's Reasoning in Galatians 2:11–21'. In Dunn (ed.) 1996a, 53–74.

— 1997. 'Paul's Coherent Admonition in Galatians 6,1–6: Mutual Help and Individual Attentiveness'. *Bib* 78, 33–56.

LAMPE, P. 1991. 'The Roman Christians of Romans 16.' In Donfried (ed.) 1991[2]a, 216–30.

LEIPOLDT, J. 1906. 'Christentum und Stoizismus'. *ZKG* 27, 129–65.

LIECHTENHAN, R. 1922a. 'Die Überwindung des Leides bei Paulus und in der zeitgenössischen Stoa'. *ZTK* 30, 368–99.

— 1922b. *Die göttliche Vorherbestimmung bei Paulus und in der posidonianischen Philosophie.* FRLANT 18. Göttingen: Vandenhoeck & Ruprecht.

LIETZMANN, H. 1907. *An die Korinther I II.* HNT 9. Tübingen: Mohr (Siebeck).

— 1971[4] (1932[3]). *An die Galater.* HNT 10. Tübingen: Mohr (Siebeck).

— 1971[5] (1906). *An die Römer.* HNT 8. Tübingen: Mohn (Siebeck).

LIGHTFOOT, J. B. 1903⁴. *Saint Paul's Epistle to the Philippians*. London: Macmillan & Co.

— 1905¹⁰. *Saint Paul's Epistle to the Galatians*. London: Macmillan & Co.

LINCOLN, A. T. 1981. *Paradise Now and Not Yet: Studies in the Role of the Heavenly Dimension in Paul's Thought with Special Reference to his Eschatology*. SNTSMS 43. Cambridge University Press.

LINDEMANN, A. 1986. 'Die biblischen Toragebote und die paulinische Ethik'. In W. Schrage (ed.), *Studien zum Text und zur Ethik des Neuen Testaments*. FS H. Greeven. BZNW 47. Berlin: de Gruyter.

LODGE, J. G. 1996. *Romans 9–11: A Reader-Response Analysis*. University of South Florida International Studies in Formative Christianity and Judaism 6. Atlanta: Scholars.

LOHMEYER, E. 1928. Kyrios Jesus: *Eine Untersuchung zu Phil. 2,5–11*. Sitzungsberichte der Heidelberger Akademie der Wissenschaften. Philosophisch-historische Klasse, Jahrgang 1927–8. 4. Abhandlung. Heidelberg: Winter.

— 1930 (1964¹³). *Die Briefe an die Philipper, an die Kolosser und an Philemon*. MeyerK 9. Göttingen: Vandenhoeck & Ruprecht.

LONG, A. A. 1967. 'Carneades and the Stoic *telos*'. *Phron* 12, 59–90.

— 1968a. 'The Stoic Concept of Evil'. *PQ* 18, 329–43.

— 1968b. 'Aristotle's Legacy to Stoic Ethics'. *BullCS* 15, 72–85.

— 1970–1. 'The Logical Basis of Stoic Ethics'. *PAS* 71, 85–104.

— (ed.) 1971a. *Problems in Stoicism*. London: Athlone.

— 1971b. 'Freedom and Determinism in the Stoic Theory of Human Action'. In Long (ed.) 1971a, 173–99.

— 1974 (1986²). *Hellenistic Philosophy: Stoics, Epicureans, Sceptics*. London: Duckworth.

— 1976. 'The Early Stoic Concept of Moral Choice'. In C. Laga (ed.), *Images of Man in Ancient and Medieval Thought*. FS Gerard Verbeke. Symbolae, Series A, Vol. 1. 77–92. Louvain: Presses universitaires.

— 1983. 'Greek Ethics After MacIntyre and the Stoic Community of Reason'. *AP* 3, 184–99.

— 1988. 'Stoic Eudaimonism'. *PBACAP* 4, 77–101.

— and D. N. SEDLEY 1987. *The Hellenistic Philosophers*. 2 vols. Cambridge University Press.

LONGENECKER, B. W. 1989. 'Different Answers to Different Issues: Israel, the Gentiles and Salvation History in Romans 9–11'. *JSNT* 36, 95–123.

— 1993. '*Pistis* in Romans 3:25: Neglected Evidence for the "Faithfulness of Christ"'. *NTS* 39, 478–80.

LONGENECKER, R. N. 1990. *Galatians*. WBC 41. Dallas: Word.

LORENZI, L. DE (ed.) 1977. *Die Israelfrage nach Röm 9–11*. Rome: Abtei von St Paul vor den Mauern.

— (ed.) 1979. *Dimensions de la vie chrétienne (Rm 12–13)*. Benedictina, Section biblico-oecuménique 4. Rome: Abbazia di San Paolo fuori le mura.

LOVERING, E. H., JR. and J. L. SUMNEY (eds) 1996. *Theology and Ethics in Paul and His Interpreters*. FS Victor Paul Furnish. Nashville: Abingdon.

LÜDEMANN, G. 1983. 'syneidēsis'. In Balz and Schneider (eds) 1983, 721–5.

LÜHRMANN, D. 1975. 'Wo man nicht mehr Sklave oder Freier ist: Überlegungen zur Struktur frühchristlicher Gemeinden'. *WD* 13, 53–83.

— 1978. *Der Brief an die Galater*. Zürcher Bibelkommentare zum Neuen Testament 7. Zürich: Theologischer.

LULL, D. J. 1980. *The Spirit in Galatia: Paul's Interpretation of* Pneuma *as Divine Power*. SBLDS 49. Chico, California: Scholars.

— 1986. '"The Law was our Pedagogue": A Study in Galatians 3:19–25'. *JBL* 105, 481–98.

LUSCHNAT, O. 1958. 'Das Problem des ethischen Fortschritts in der alten Stoa'. *Philol* 102, 178–214.

LUTER, A. B. and M. V. LEE 1995. 'Philippians as Chiasmus: Key to the Structure, Unity and Theme Questions'. *NTS* 41, 89–101.

LÜTGERT, W. 1919. *Gesetz und Geist: Eine Untersuchung zur Vorgeschichte des Galaterbriefes*. BFCT 22.6. Gütersloh: Bertelsmann.

LUTZ, C. E. 1947. 'Musonius Rufus'. *YCS* 10, 3–147.

LUZ, U. 1969. 'Zum Aufbau von Röm. 1–8.' *TZ* 25, 161–81.

LYONS, G. 1985. *Pauline Autobiography: Toward a New Understanding*. SBLDS 73. Atlanta: Scholars.

MALHERBE, A. J. 1983. 'Exhortation in First Thessalonians'. *NovT* 25, 238–56. Also in Malherbe 1989, 49–66.

— 1986. *Moral Exhortation: A Greco-Roman Sourcebook*. Library of Early Christianity 4. Ed. Wayne A. Meeks. Philadelphia: Westminster.

— 1987. *Paul and the Thessalonians: The Philosophic Tradition of Pastoral Care*. Philadelphia: Fortress.

— 1989. *Paul and the Popular Philosophers*. Minneapolis: Fortress.

— 1990. 'Hellenistic Moral Philosophy and the New Testament: A Retrospective Analysis'. Unpublished paper (35 pp.). SBL Annual Meeting New Orleans 1990.

— 1992. 'Hellenistic Moralists and the New Testament'. *ANRW* II.26.1, 268–333.

— 1994. 'Determinism and Free Will in Paul: The Argument of 1 Corinthians 8 and 9'. In Engberg-Pedersen (ed.) 1994a, 231–55.

MALHERBE, A. J. 1996. 'Paul's Self-Sufficiency (Philippians 4:11)'. In Fitzgerald (ed.) 1996a, 125–39.

— and W. A. MEEKS (eds) 1993. *The Future of Christology*. FS Leander E. Keck. Minneapolis: Fortress.

MALINA, B. J. 1986. *Christian Origins and Cultural Anthropology*. Atlanta: Knox.

— 1993² (1981). *The New Testament World: Insights from Cultural Anthropology*. Louisville: Westminster Knox.

— 1996. *The Social World of Jesus and the Gospels*. London: Routledge.

— and J. H. NEYREY 1996. *Portraits of Paul: An Archaeology of Ancient Personality*. Louisville: Westminster Knox.

MANSON, T. W. 1962a. *Studies in the Gospels and Epistles*. Ed. M. Black. Manchester University Press.

— 1962b (1939). 'The Date of the Epistle to the Philippians'. In Manson 1962a, 149–67.

— 1991 (1948). 'St Paul's Letter to the Romans—and Others'. In Donfried (ed.) 1991²a, 3–15. Also in Manson 1962a, 225–41.

MARCUS, J. 1986. 'The Evil Inclination in the Letters of Paul'. *IBS* 8, 8–21.

— 1988. '"Let God Arise and End the Reign of Sin!": A Contribution to the Study of Pauline Parenesis'. *Bib* 69, 386–95.

— 1989. 'The Circumcision and the Uncircumcision in Rome'. *NTS* 35, 67–81.

— and M. L. SOARDS (eds) 1989. *Apocalyptic and the New Testament*. FS J. L. Martyn. JSNTSup 24. Sheffield: JSOT.

MARSHALL, J. W. 1993. 'Paul's Ethical Appeal in Philippians'. In Porter and Olbricht (eds) 1993, 357–74.

MARTENS, J. W. 1994. 'Romans 2.14–16: A Stoic Reading'. *NTS* 40, 55–67.

MARTIN, B. L. 1989. *Christ and the Law in Paul*. NovTSup 62. Leiden: Brill.

MARTIN, D. B. 1990. *Slavery as Salvation: The Metaphor of Slavery in Pauline Christianity*. New Haven: Yale University Press.

— 1995. *The Corinthian Body*. New Haven: Yale University Press.

MARTIN, R. P. 1967 (1983²). *Carmen Christi: Philippians ii.5–11 in Recent Interpretation and in the Setting of Early Christian Worship*. SNTSMS 4. Cambridge University Press. (2nd ed.: Grand Rapids: Eerdmans.)

MARTIN, T. 1995. 'Apostasy to Paganism: The Rhetorical Stasis of the Galatian Controversy'. *JBL* 114, 437–61.

MARTYN, J. L. 1985. 'Apocalyptic Antinomies in Paul's Letter to the Galatians'. *NTS* 31, 410–24.

— 1990. 'The Covenants of Hagar And Sarah'. In Carroll, Cosgrove and Johnson (eds) 1990, 160–92.

MARTYN, J. L. 1996. 'The Crucial Event in the History of the Law (Gal 5:14)'. In Lovering, Jr. and Sumney (eds) 1996, 48–61.

— 1997a. *Galatians.* AB 33A. New York: Doubleday.

— 1997b. *Theological Issues in the Letters of Paul.* Edinburgh: Clark/Nashville: Abingdon.

MARXSEN, W. 1963. *Einleitung in das Neue Testament: Eine Einführung in ihre Probleme.* Gütersloh: Mohn.

MATERA, F. J. 1988. 'The Culmination of Paul's Argument to the Galatians: Gal. 5.1–6.17'. *JSNT* 32, 79–91.

— 1992. *Galatians.* Sacra Pagina 9. Collegeville, Minnesota: Glazier (Liturgical).

MATES, B. 1953. *Stoic Logic.* Berkeley/Los Angeles: University of California Press.

MAURACH, G. 1996² (1991). *Seneca: Leben und Werk.* Darmstadt: Wissenschaftliche Buchgesellschaft.

MAYER, B. 1987. 'Paulus als Vermittler zwischen Epaphroditus und der Gemeinde von Philippi: Bemerkungen zu Phil 2,25–30'. *BZ* 31, 176–88.

MEEKS, W. A. 1982. 'The Social Context of Pauline Theology'. *Int* 36, 266–77.

— 1983. *The First Urban Christians: The Social World of the Apostle Paul.* New Haven: Yale University Press.

— 1986a. 'Understanding Early Christian Ethics', *JBL* 105, 3–11.

— 1986b. *The Moral World of the First Christians.* Library of Early Christianity 6. Ed. Wayne A. Meeks. Philadelphia: Westminster.

— 1987. 'Judgment and the Brother: Romans 14:1–15:13'. In G. F. Hawthorne and O. Betz (eds), *Tradition and Interpretation in the New Testament.* FS E. Earle Ellis. 290–300. Grand Rapids: Eerdmans/Tübingen: Mohr (Siebeck).

— 1990. 'On Trusting an Unpredictable God: A Hermeneutical Meditation on Romans 9–11.' In Carroll, Cosgrove and Johnson (eds) 1990, 105–24.

— 1991. 'The Man from Heaven in Paul's Letter to the Philippians'. In Pearson (ed.) 1991, 329–36.

— 1993. *The Origins of Christian Morality: The First Two Centuries.* New Haven: Yale University Press.

MELL, U. 1989. *Neue Schöpfung: Eine traditionsgeschichtliche und exegetische Studie zu einem soteriologischen Grundsatz paulinischer Theologie.* BZNW 56. Berlin: Töpelmann.

MENGEL, B. 1982. *Studien zum Philipperbrief.* WUNT 2/8. Tübingen: Mohr (Siebeck).

MERK, O. 1968. *Handeln aus Glauben: Die Motivierungen der paulinischen Ethik.* Marburger theologische Studien 5. Marburg: Elwert.

— 1969. 'Der Beginn der Paränese im Galaterbrief'. *ZNW* 60, 83–104.

MEYER, P. W. 1979. 'The Holy Spirit in the Pauline Letters: A Contextual Exploration'. *Int* 33, 3–18.

MEYER, P. W. 1980. 'Romans 10:4 and the "End" of the Law'. In J. L. Crenshaw and S. Sandmel (eds), *The Divine Helmsman: Studies on God's Control of Human Events*. FS Lou H. Silberman. 59–78. New York: KTAV.

— 1988. 'Romans'. In *Harper's Bible Commentary*. Ed. J. L. Mays. 1130–67. San Francisco: Harper & Row.

— 1990. 'The Worm at the Core of the Apple: Exegetical Reflections on Romans 7'. In Fortna and Gaventa (eds) 1990, 62–84.

— 1997. 'Pauline Theology: A Proposal for a Pause in Its Pursuit'. In Johnson and Hay (eds) 1997, 140–60.

MICHEL, O. 1977¹⁴ (1955). *Der Brief an die Römer*. MeyerK 4. Göttingen: Vandenhoeck & Ruprecht.

MINEAR, P. S. 1971. *The Obedience of Faith: The Purpose of Paul in the Epistle to the Romans*. SBT 2/19. London: SCM.

— 1979. 'The Crucified World: The Enigma of Galatians 6,14'. In Andresen and Klein (eds) 1979, 395–407.

MITCHELL, M. M. 1991. *Paul and the Rhetoric of Reconciliation: An Exegetical Investigation of the Language and Composition of 1 Corinthians*. HUT 28. Tübingen: Mohr (Siebeck).

MOO, D. J. 1996. *The Epistle to the Romans*. NICNT. Grand Rapids: Eerdmans.

MORLAND, K. A. 1996. *The Rhetoric of Curse in Galatians: Paul Confronts Another Gospel*. Emory Studies in Early Christianity 5. Atlanta: Scholars.

MORRICE, W. G. 1984. *Joy in the New Testament*. Exeter: Paternoster.

MOULE, C. F. D. 1967. 'Fulfilment-Words in the New Testament: Use and Abuse'. *NTS* 14, 293–320.

MOXNES, H. 1980. *Theology in Conflict: Studies in Paul's Understanding of God in Romans*. NovTSup 53. Leiden: Brill.

MÜLLER, P. 1989. 'Grundlinien paulinischer Theologie (Röm 15,14–33)'. *KD* 35, 212–35.

MÜLLER, U. B. 1988. 'Der Christushymnus Phil 2 6–11'. *ZNW* 79, 17–44.

— 1993. *Der Brief des Paulus an die Philipper*. THKNT 11/I. Leipzig: Evangelische.

MUNCK, J. 1954. *Paulus und die Heilsgeschichte*. Acta Jutlandica. Theology Series 6. Copenhagen: Munksgaard.

— 1956. *Christus und Israel: Eine Auslegung von Röm 9–11*. Acta Jutlandica. Teologisk serie 7. Aarhus: Universitetsforlaget/Copenhagen: Munksgaard.

MUSSNER, F. 1977³ (1974). *Der Galaterbrief*. HTKNT 9. Freiburg: Herder.

NAGEL, T. 1986. *The View from Nowhere*. New York: Oxford University Press.

NANOS, M. D. 1996. *The Mystery of Romans: The Jewish Context of Paul's Letter*. Minneapolis: Fortress.

410   Bibliography

NAUCK, W. 1955. 'Freude im Leiden: Zum Problem einer urchristlichen Verfolgungstradition'. *ZNW* 46, 68–80.

— 1958. 'Das *oun*-paräneticum'. *ZNW* 49, 134–5.

NEUSNER, J., E. S. FRERICHS, P. BORGEN and R. HORSLEY (eds) 1988. *The Social World of Formative Christianity and Judaism*. FS Howard Clark Kee. Philadelphia: Fortress.

NIEBUHR, K.-W. 1992. *Heidenapostel aus Israel: Die jüdische Identität des Paulus nach ihrer Darstellung in seinen Briefen*. WUNT 62. Tübingen: Mohr (Siebeck).

NOACK, B. 1965. 'Current and Backwater in the Epistle to the Romans'. *ST* 19, 155–66.

O'BRIEN, P. T. 1991. *The Epistle to the Philippians: A Commentary on the Greek Text*. NIGCT. Grand Rapids: Eerdmans/Carlisle: Paternoster.

OEPKE, A. 1973³ (rev. J. Rohde) (1937). *Der Brief des Paulus an die Galater*. THKNT 9. Berlin: Evangelische.

ORTKEMPER, F.-J. 1980. *Leben aus dem Glauben: Christliche Grundhaltungen nach Römer 12–13*. NTAbh Neue Folge Band 14. Münster: Aschendorff.

OSTEN-SACKEN, P. VON DER 1975a. *Römer 8 als Beispiel paulinischer Soteriologie*. FRLANT 112. Göttingen: Vandenhoeck & Ruprecht.

— 1975b. 'Erwägungen zur Abfassungsgeschichte und zum literarisch-theologischen Charackter des Römerbriefes'. *Theologia Viatorum* 12, 109–20. Also in von der Osten-Sacken 1987a, 119–30.

— 1987a. *Evangelium und Tora: Aufsätze zu Paulus*. TBü 77. Munich: Kaiser.

— 1987b (1983). 'Heil für die Juden—auch ohne Christus?' In von der Osten-Sacken 1987a, 256–71.

— 1987c. 'Römer 9–11 als Schibbolet christlicher Theologie'. In von der Osten-Sacken 1987a, 294–314.

PATTE, D. 1983. *Paul's Faith and the Power of the Gospel*. Philadelphia: Fortress.

PEARSON, B. A. (ed.) 1991. *The Future of Early Christianity*. FS Helmut Koester. Minneapolis: Fortress.

PERDUE, L. G. 1981. 'Paraenesis and the Epistle of James'. *ZNW* 72, 241–56.

— and J. G. GAMMIE (eds) 1990. *Paraenesis: Act and Form*. Semeia 50. Atlanta: Scholars.

PERKINS, P. 1991. 'Philippians: Theology for the Heavenly *Politeuma*'. In Bassler (ed.) 1991, 89–104.

PETERLIN, D. 1995. *Paul's Letter to the Philippians in the Light of Disunity in the Church*. NovTSup 79. Leiden: Brill.

PETERMAN, G. W. 1991. '"Thankless Thanks": The Epistolary Social Convention in Philippians 4:10–20'. *TynBul* 42, 261–70.

PETERSEN, N. R. 1991. 'On the Ending(s) to Paul's Letter to Rome'. In Pearson (ed.) 1991, 337–47.

PIERCE, C. A. 1955. *Conscience in the New Testament*. SBT 15. London: SCM.

POHLENZ, M. 1949. 'Paulus und die Stoa'. *ZNW* 42, 69–104.

POIRIER, J. C. 1996. 'Romans 5:13–14 and the Universality of Law'. *NovT* 38, 344–58.

POLLARD, P. 1997. 'The "Faith of Christ" in Current Discussion'. *ConJ* 23, 213–28.

POPKES, W. 1982. 'Zum Aufbau und Charakter von Römer 1.18–32'. *NTS* 28, 490–501.

— 1995. 'James and Paraenesis, Reconsidered'. In Fornberg and Hellholm (eds), 1995, 535–61.

PORTER, S. E. 1993. 'The Theoretical Justification for Application of Rhetorical Categories to Pauline Epistolary Literature'. In Porter and Olbricht (eds) 1993, 100–22.

— 1996. 'Understanding Pauline Studies: An Assessment of Recent Research (Part One).' *Them* 22/1, 14–25.

— 1997. 'Understanding Pauline Studies: An Assessment of Recent Research (Part Two).' *Them* 22/2, 13–24.

— and T. H. OLBRICHT (eds) 1993. *Rhetoric and the New Testament: Essays from the 1992 Heidelberg Conference*. JSNTSup 90. Sheffield: JSOT.

— and J. T. REED 1998. 'Philippians as a Macro-Chiasm and its Exegetical Significance'. *NTS* 44, 213–31.

PRELLER, H. 1929. 'Paulus oder Seneca?' In A. Cartellieri, A. Leitzmann, Th. Meyer-Steineg (eds), *Festschrift Walther Judeich*. 68–80. Weimar: Böhlaus.

RABBOW, P. 1954. *Seelenführung: Methodik der Exerzitien in der Antike*. Munich: Kösel.

RÄISÄNEN, H. 1983 (1987²). *Paul and the Law*. WUNT 29. Tübingen: Mohr (Siebeck).

— 1985. 'Galatians 2. 16 and Paul's Break with Judaism'. *NTS* 31, 543–53.

— 1987. 'Römer 9–11: Analyse eines geistigen Ringens'. *ANRW* II.25.4, 2891–939.

— 1988. 'Paul, God, and Israel: Romans 9–11 in Recent Research'. In Neusner, J. *et al.* (eds) 1988, 178–206.

— 1992. *Jesus, Paul and Torah: Collected Essays*. Sheffield Academic Press.

REASONER, M. 1995. 'The Theology of Romans 12:1–15:13'. In Hay and Johnson (eds) 1995, 287–99.

REED, J. T. 1996. 'Philippians 3:1 and the Epistolary Hesitation Formulas: The Literary Integrity of Philippians, Again'. *JBL* 115, 63–90.

REED, J. T. 1997. *A Discourse Analysis of Philippians: Method and Rhetoric in the Debate over Literary Integrity*. JSNTSup 136. Sheffield Academic Press.

REINMUTH, E. 1985. *Geist und Gesetz: Studien zu Voraussetzungen und Inhalt der paulinischen Paränese*. Theologische Arbeiten 44. Berlin: Evangelische.

REUMANN, J. 1984. 'Philippians 3.20–21—a Hymnic Fragment?' *NTS* 30, 593–609.

— 1996. 'Philippians, Especially Chapter 4, as a "Letter of Friendship": Observations on a Checkered History of Scholarship'. In Fitzgerald (ed.) 1996a, 83–106.

RHYNE, C. T. 1985. '*Nomos Dikaiosynēs* and the Meaning of Romans 10:4'. *CBQ* 47, 486–99.

RIESENFELD, H. 1969. '*hyper*'. In G. Friedrich (ed.), *Theologisches Wörterbuch zum Neuen Testament* 8. 510–18. Stuttgart: Kohlhammer.

RIETH, O. 1933. *Grundbegriffe der stoischen Ethik: Eine traditions-geschichtliche Untersuchung*. Problemata 9. Berlin: Weidmannsche.

RISSI, M. 1987. 'Der Christushymnus in Phil 2,6–11'. In *ANRW* II.25.4, 3314–26. Berlin: de Gruyter.

ROBB, J. D. 1944–5. 'Galatians v. 23: An Explanation'. *ExpTim* 56, 279–80.

ROETZEL, C. J. 1995. 'Paul and the Law: Whence and Whither?' *CurRBS* 3, 249–75.

ROHDE, J. 1989. *Der Brief des Paulus an die Galater*. THKNT 9. Berlin: Evangelische.

RÖHSER, G. 1987. *Metaphorik und Personifikation der Sünde: Antike Sündenvorstellungen und paulinische Hamartia*. WUNT 2/25. Tübingen: Mohr (Siebeck).

ROLLAND, P. 1990. 'La structure littéraire et l'unité de L'Épître aux Philippiens'. *RevScRel* 64, 213–16.

RUSSELL, R. 1982. 'Pauline Letter Structure in Philippians'. *JETS* 25, 295–306.

RUSSELL III, W. B. 1997. *The Flesh/Spirit Conflict in Galatians*. Lanham, MD: University Press of America.

SAMBURSKY, S. 1959. *Physics of the Stoics*. London: Routledge and Kegan Paul.

SAMPLEY, J. P. 1980. *Pauline Partnership in Christ: Christian Community and Commitment in Light of Roman Law*. Philadelphia: Fortress.

— 1985. 'Romans and Galatians: Comparison and Contrast'. In J. T. Butler, E. W. Conrad, B. C. Ollenburger (eds), *Understanding the Word*. FS Bernhard W. Anderson. 315–39. JSNTSup 37. Sheffield: JSOT.

— 1990. 'Faith and Its Moral Life: A Study of Individuation in the Thought World of the Apostle Paul'. In Carroll, Cosgrove and Johnson (eds) 1990, 223–38.

SAMPLEY, J. P. 1991. *Walking Between the Times: Paul's Moral Reasoning.* Minneapolis: Fortress.

— 1995a. 'The Weak and Strong: Paul's Careful and Crafty Rhetorical Strategy in Romans 14:1–15:13'. In White and Yarbrough (eds) 1995, 40–52.

— 1995b. 'Romans in a Different Light: A Response to Robert Jewett'. In Hay and Johnson (eds) 1995, 109–29.

— 1996. 'Reasoning From the Horizons of Paul's Thought World: A Comparison of Galatians and Philippians'. In Lovering, Jr. and Sumney (eds) 1996, 114–31.

SAND, A. 1967. *Der Begriff 'Fleisch' in den paulinischen Hauptbriefen.* Biblische Untersuchungen 2. Regensburg: Pustet.

— 1983. '*sarx*'. In Balz and Schneider (eds) 1983, 549–57.

SANDAY, W. and A. C. HEADLAM 1902⁵ (1895). *A Critical and Exegetical Commentary on the Epistle to the Romans.* ICC. Edinburgh: Clark.

SANDERS, E. P. 1977. *Paul and Palestinian Judaism: A Comparison of Patterns of Religion.* London: SCM.

— 1983. *Paul, the Law, and the Jewish People.* Philadelphia: Fortress.

— 1990. 'Jewish Association with Gentiles and Galatians 2:11–14'. In Fortna and Gaventa (eds) 1990, 170–88.

SANDNES, K. O. 1991. *Paul—One of the Prophets? A Contribution to the Apostle's Self-Understanding.* WUNT 2/43. Tübingen: Mohr (Siebeck).

SCHENK, W. 1984. *Die Philipperbriefe des Paulus: Kommentar.* Stuttgart: Kohlhammer.

— 1987. 'Der Philipperbrief in der neuen Forschung (1945–1985)'. In *ANRW* II.25.4, 3280–313. Berlin: de Gruyter.

SCHLATTER, A. 1952² (1935). *Gottes Gerechtigkeit: Ein Kommentar zum Römerbrief.* Stuttgart: Calwer.

SCHLIER, H. 1965⁴ (1949). *Der Brief an die Galater.* MeyerK 7. Göttingen: Vandenhoeck & Ruprecht.

— 1977. *Der Römerbrief.* HTKNT 6. Freiburg: Herder.

SCHMELLER, T. 1995. *Hierarchie und Egalität: Eine sozialgeschichtliche Untersuchung paulinischer Gemeinden und griechisch-römischer Vereine.* Stuttgarter Bibelstudien 162. Stuttgart: Katholisches Bibelwerk.

SCHMITHALS, W. 1956. 'Die Häretiker in Galatien'. *ZNW* 47, 25–67.

— 1957. 'Die Irrlehrer des Philipperbriefes'. *ZTK* 54, 297–341.

— 1975. *Der Römerbrief als historisches Problem.* SNT 9. Gütersloh: Mohn.

— 1983. 'Judaisten in Galatien?' *ZNW* 74, 27–58.

SCHNACKENBURG, R. 1975. 'Römer 7 im Zusammenhang des Römerbriefes'. In Ellis and Grässer (eds) 1975, 283–300.

SCHNEEWIND, J. B. 1998. *The Invention of Autonomy: A History of Modern Moral Philosophy.* Cambridge University Press.

SCHOEPS, H. J. 1959. *Paulus: Die Theologie des Apostels im Lichte der jüdischen Religionsgeschichte.* Tübingen: Mohr (Siebeck).

SCHOFIELD, M. 1991. *The Stoic Idea of the City.* Cambridge University Press.

— and G. STRIKER (eds) 1986. *The Norms of Nature: Studies in Hellenistic Ethics.* Cambridge University Press.

—, M. BURNYEAT and J. BARNES (eds) 1980. *Doubt and Dogmatism: Studies in Hellenistic Epistemology.* Oxford University Press.

SCHOON-JANSSEN, J. 1991. *Umstrittene 'Apologien' in den Paulusbriefen: Studien zur rhetorischen Situation des 1. Thessalonicherbriefes, des Galaterbriefes, und des Philipperbriefes.* GTA 45. Göttingen: Vandenhoeck & Ruprecht.

SCHOTTROFF, L. 1979. 'Die Schreckensherrschaft der Sünde und die Befreiung durch Christus nach dem Römerbrief des Paulus'. *EvT* 39, 497–510.

SCHRAGE, W. 1961. *Die konkreten Einzelgebote in der paulinischen Paränese: Ein Beitrag zur neutestamentlichen Ethik.* Gütersloh: Mohn.

— 1964. 'Die Stellung zur Welt bei Paulus, Epiktet und in der Apokalyptik. Ein Beitrag zu 1Kor 7,29–31'. *ZTK* 61, 125–54.

SCHREINER, T. 1936. *Seneca im Gegensatz zu Paulus: Ein Vergleich ihrer Welt- und Lebensanschauung.* Tübingen: Göbel.

— 1993. *The Law and Its Fulfillment: A Pauline Theology of Law.* Grand Rapids: Baker.

SCHUBERT, P. 1939. *Form and Function of the Pauline Thanksgivings.* BZNW 20. Berlin: Töpelmann.

SCHULZ, A. 1969. 'Grundformen urchristlicher Paränese'. In J. Schreiner and G. Dautzenberg (eds), *Gestalt und Anspruch des Neuen Testaments.* 249–61. Würzburg: Echter.

SCHULZ, S. 1985. 'Der frühe und der späte Paulus: Überlegungen zur Entwicklung seiner Theologie und Ethik'. *TZ* 41, 228–36.

SCHWEITZER, A. 1930. *Die Mystik des Apostels Paulus.* Tübingen: Mohr (Siebeck).

SCHWEIZER, E. 1957. 'Die hellenistische Komponente im neutestamentlichen *sarx*-Begriff'. *ZNW* 48, 237–53.

— 1964. '*sarx ktl.*' In Friedrich (ed.) 1964, 98–104, 118–36.

— 1974. '"Der Jude im Verborgenen . . . , dessen Lob nicht von Menschen, sondern von Gott kommt". Zu Röm 2,28f und Mt 6,1–18'. In J. Gnilka (ed.), *Neues Testament und Kirche.* FS Rudolf Schnackenburg. 115–24. Freiburg: Herder.

SCOTT, J. M. 1993. '"For as Many as are of Works of the Law are under a Curse" (Galatians 3.10)'. In C. A. Evans and J. A. Sanders (eds), *Paul and the Scriptures of Israel.* JSNTSup 83. 187–221. Sheffield: JSOT.

SEGAL, A. F. 1990. *Paul the Convert: The Apostolate and Apostasy of Saul the Pharisee*. New Haven: Yale University Press.

SEIFRID, M. A. 1992. *Justification by Faith: The Origin and Development of a Central Pauline Theme*. NovTSup 68. Leiden: Brill.

— 1994. 'Blind Alleys in the Controversy over the Paul of History'. *TynBul* 45, 73–95.

SENSING, T. 1996. 'Towards a Definition of Paraenesis'. *ResQ* 38, 145–58.

SEVENSTER, J. N. 1961. *Paul and Seneca*. NovTSup 4. Leiden: Brill.

— 1966. 'Education or Conversion: Epictetus and the Gospels'. *NovT* 8, 247–62.

SHARP, D. S. 1914. *Epictetus and the New Testament*. London: Kelly.

SIHVOLA, J. and T. ENGBERG-PEDERSEN (eds) 1998. *The Emotions in Hellenistic Philosophy*. The New Synthese Historical Library 46. Dordrecht: Kluwer.

SILVA, M. 1988. *Philippians*. Wycliffe Exegetical Commentary. Chicago: Moody.

SLOAN, R. B. 1991. 'Paul and the Law: Why the Law Cannot Save'. *NovT* 33, 35–60.

SMITH, J. Z. 1990. *Drudgery Divine: On the Comparison of Early Christianities and the Religions of Late Antiquity*. Chicago University Press.

SNODGRASS, K. R. 1986. 'Justification by Grace—to the Doers: An Analysis of the Place of Romans 2 in the Theology of Paul'. *NTS* 32, 72–93.

— 1988. 'Spheres of Influence: A Possible Solution to the Problem of Paul and the Law'. *JSNT* 32, 93–113.

SOARDS, M. L. 1989. 'Seeking (*zētein*) and sinning (*hamartōlos* and *hamartia*) According to Galatians 2.17'. In Marcus and Soards (eds) 1989, 237–54.

SPANNEUT, M. 1962. 'Epiktet'. *RAC* 5, 599–681.

STANLEY, C. D. 1990. '"Under a Curse": A Fresh Reading of Galatians 3. 10–14'. *NTS* 36, 481–511.

STANTON, G. 1996. 'The Law of Moses and the Law of Christ: Galatians 3:1–6:2'. In Dunn (ed.) 1996a, 99–116.

STELZENBERGER, J. 1933. *Die Beziehungen der frühchristlichen Sittenlehre zur Ethik der Stoa: Eine moralgeschichtliche Studie*. Munich: Hueber.

— 1961. *Syneidesis im Neuen Testament*. Paderborn: Schöningh.

STENDAHL, K. 1962. 'Hate, Non-Retaliation, and Love. 1 QS x, 17–20 and Rom. 12:19–21'. *HTR* 55, 343–55.

— 1963. 'The Apostle Paul and the Introspective Conscience of the West'. *HTR* 56, 199–215. Also in Stendahl 1976.

— 1976. *Paul Among Jews and Gentiles*. Philadelphia: Fortress.

— 1995. *Final Account: Paul's Letter to the Romans*. Minneapolis: Fortress.

STOB, R. 1935. 'Stoicism and Christianity'. *CJ* 30, 217–24.

STOWERS, S. K. 1981. *The Diatribe and Paul's Letter to the Romans*. SBLDS 57. Chico: Scholars.

— 1984. 'Paul's Dialogue with a Fellow Jew in Romans 3:1–9'. *CBQ* 46, 707–22.

— 1986. *Letter Writing in Greco-Roman Antiquity*. Library of Early Christianity 5. Ed. Wayne A. Meeks. Philadelphia: Westminster.

— 1989. '*Ek pisteōs* and *dia tēs pisteēs* in Romans 3.30'. *JBL* 108, 665–74.

— 1991. 'Friends and Enemies in the Politics of Heaven: Reading Theology in Philippians'. In Bassler (ed.) 1991, 105–21.

— 1994. *A Rereading of Romans: Justice, Jews, and Gentiles*. New Haven: Yale University Press.

STRELAN, J. G. 1975. 'Burden-Bearing and the Law of Christ: A Re-examination of Galatians 6:2'. *JBL* 94, 266–76.

STRIKER, G. 1991. 'Following Nature: A Study in Stoic Ethics'. *OSAP* 9, 1–73.

STUHLMACHER, P. 1985. 'Paul's Understanding of the Law in the Letter to the Romans'. *SEÅ* 50, 87–104.

— 1991a (1986). 'The Purpose of Romans'. In Donfried (ed.) 1991²a, 231–42.

— 1991b (1988). 'The Theme of Romans'. In Donfried (ed.) 1991²a, 333–45.

STYLER, G. M. 1973. 'The Basis of Obligation in Paul's Christology and Ethics'. In B. Lindars and S. S. Smalley (eds), *Christ and Spirit in the New Testament*. FS C. F. D. Moule. 175–87. Cambridge University Press.

SUHL, A. 1987. 'Der Galaterbrief—Situation und Argumentation'. *ANRW* II.25.4, 3067–134. Berlin: de Gruyter.

SWIFT, R. C. 1984. 'The Theme and Structure of Philippians'. *BSac* 141, 234–54.

SYNOFZIK, E. 1977. *Die Gerichts- und Vergeltungsaussagen bei Paulus: Eine traditionsgeschichtliche Untersuchung*. GTA 8. Göttingen: Vandenhoeck & Ruprecht.

TAYLOR, C. 1989. *Sources of the Self: The Making of the Modern Identity*. Cambridge University Press.

TAYLOR, G. M. 1966. 'The Function of *Pistis Christou* in Galatians'. *JBL* 85, 58–76.

TELLBE, M. 1994. 'The Sociological Factors behind Philippians 3.1–11 and the Conflict at Philippi'. *JSNT* 55, 97–121.

THEISSEN, G. 1983²a (1979). *Studien zur Soziologie des Urchristentums*. WUNT 19. Tübingen: Mohr (Siebeck).

— 1983b. *Psychologische Aspekte paulinischer Theologie*. FRLANT 131. Göttingen: Vandenhoeck & Ruprecht.

THIELMAN, F. 1989. *From Plight to Solution: A Jewish Framework for Understanding Paul's View of the Law in Galatians and Romans.* NovTSup 61. Leiden: Brill.

—— 1995. 'The Story of Israel and the Theology of Romans 5–8'. In Hay and Johnson (eds) 1995, 169–95.

THOMPSON, M. 1991. *Clothed with Christ: The Example and Teaching of Jesus in Romans 12.1–15.13.* JSNTSup 59. Sheffield: JSOT.

THOMPSON, R. W. 1986a. 'How Is the Law Fulfilled in Us? An Interpretation of Rom 8:4'. *Louvain Studies* 11, 31–40.

—— 1986b. 'Paul's Double Critique of Jewish Boasting: A Study of Rom 3,27 in Its Context'. *Bib* 67, 520–31.

THRAEDE, K. 1970. *Grundzüge griechisch-römischer Brieftopik.* Zetemata 49. Munich: Beck.

TOBIN, T. H. 1993. 'Controversy and Continuity in Romans 1:18–3:20'. *CBQ* 55, 298–318.

DU TOIT, A. B. 1979. '*Dikaiosyne* in Röm 6: Beobachtungen zur ethischen Dimension der paulinischen Gerechtigkeitsauffassung'. *ZTK* 76, 261–91.

—— 1991. 'Faith and Obedience in Paul'. *Neot* 25, 65–74.

TYSON, J. B. 1968. 'Paul's Opponents in Galatia'. *NovT* 10, 241–54.

—— 1973. '"Works of the Law" in Galatians'. *JBL* 92, 423–31.

VANHOYE, A. (ed.) 1986. *L'Apôtre Paul: Personnalité, styles et conception du ministère.* BETL 73. Leuven University Press.

VÖGTLE, A. 1936. *Die Tugend- und Lasterkataloge im Neuen Testament, exegetisch, religions- und formgeschichtlich untersucht.* NTAbh 16. Münster: Aschendorff.

VOLLENWEIDER, S. 1989. *Freiheit als neue Schöpfung: Eine Untersuchung zur Eleutheria bei Paulus und in seiner Umwelt.* FRLANT 147. Göttingen: Vandenhoeck & Ruprecht.

—— 1996. 'Der Geist Gottes als Selbst der Glaubenden: Überlegungen zu einem ontologischen Problem in der paulinischen Anthropologie'. *ZTK* 93, 163–92.

VOS, J. S. 1994. 'Paul's Argumentation in Galatians 1–2'. *HTR* 87, 1–16.

VOUGA, F. 1988. 'Zur rhetorischen Gattung des Galaterbriefes'. *ZNW* 79, 291–2.

WAGNER, G. (ed.) 1996. *An Exegetical Bibliography of the New Testament. Vol. 4. Romans and Galatians.* Macon, Ga: Mercer University Press.

WAGNER, J. R. 1997. 'The Christ, Servant of Jew and Gentile: A Fresh Approach to Romans 15:8–9'. *JBL* 116, 473–85.

WALTER, N. 1977. 'Die Philipper und das Leiden: Aus den Anfängen einer heidenchristliche Gemeinde'. In R. Schnackenburg, J. Ernst, J. Wanke (eds), *Die Kirche des Anfangs.* FS Heinz Schürmann. 417–34. Leipzig: St Benno.

WALTER, N. 1986. 'Paulus und die Gegner des Christusevangeliums in Galatien'. In Vanhoye (ed.) 1986, 351–6.

WALTERS, J. C. 1994. *Ethnic Issues in Paul's Letter to the Romans: Changing Self-Definition in Earliest Roman Christianity.* Valley Forge, PA: Trinity Press International.

WANSINK, C. S. 1996. *Chained in Christ: The Experience and Rhetoric of Paul's Imprisonments.* JSNTSup 130. Sheffield Academic Press.

WATSON, D. F. 1995. 'Rhetorical Criticism of the Pauline Epistles since 1975'. *CurRBS* 3, 219–48.

WATSON, F. 1986. *Paul, Judaism and the Gentiles: A Sociological Approach.* SNTSMS 56. Cambridge University Press.

WATSON, N. M. 1983. 'Justified by Faith, Judged by Works—an Antinomy?' *NTS* 29, 209–21.

WEBSTER, J. B. 1986. 'The Imitation of Christ'. *TynBul* 37, 95–120.

WEDDERBURN, A. J. M. 1988. *The Reasons for Romans.* Studies of the New Testament and its World. Edinburgh: Clark.

WEIMA, J. A. D. 1990. 'The Function of the Law in Relation to Sin: An Evaluation of the View of H. Räisänen'. *NovT* 32, 219–35.

WEISS, H.-F. 1965. 'Zur Frage der historischen Voraussetzungen der Begegnung von Antike und Christentum'. *Klio* 43–5, 307–28.

WENGST, K. 1972. *Christologische Formeln und Lieder des Urchristentums.* Gütersloh: Mohn.

WERNLE, P. 1897. *Der Christ und die Sünde bei Paulus.* Freiburg/Leipzig: Mohr (Siebeck).

WESTERHOLM, S. 1984. 'Letter and Spirit: The Foundation of Pauline Ethics'. *NTS* 30, 229–48.

— 1988. *Israel's Law and the Church's Faith: Paul and His Recent Interpreters.* Grand Rapids: Eerdmans.

WHITE, L. M. 1990. 'Morality Between Two Worlds: A Paradigm of Friendship in Philippians'. In D. L. Balch, E. Ferguson, W. A. Meeks (eds), *Greeks, Romans, and Christians.* FS Abraham J. Malherbe. 201–15. Minneapolis: Fortress.

— and O. L. YARBROUGH (eds) 1995. *The Social World of the First Christians.* FS Wayne A. Meeks. Minneapolis: Fortress.

WIBBING, S. 1959. *Die Tugend- und Lasterkataloge im Neuen Testament und ihre Traditionsgeschichte unter besonderer Berücksichtigung der Qumran-Texte.* BZNW 25. Berlin: Töpelmann.

WICK, P. 1994. *Der Philipperbrief: Der formale Aufbau des Briefs als Schüssel zum Verständnis seines Inhalts.* BWANT 7/15. Stuttgart: Kohlhammer.

WILCKENS, U. 1974a. *Rechtfertigung als Freiheit: Paulusstudien*. Neukirchen-Vluyn: Neukirchener.

— 1974b. 'Über Abfassungszweck und Aufbau des Römerbriefs'. In Wilckens 1974a, 110–70.

— 1976. 'Christologie und Anthropologie im Zusammenhang der paulinischen Rechtfertigungslehre'. *ZNW* 67, 64–82.

— 1978–1980–1982. *Der Brief an die Römer*. 3 vols. EKKNT 6/1–3. Zürich: Benziger/Neukirchen-Vluyn: Neukirchener.

— 1982. 'Zur Entwicklung des paulinischen Gesetzesverständnisses'. *NTS* 28, 154–90.

WILLIAMS, B. 1985. *Ethics and the Limits of Philosophy*. London: Fontana/Collins.

— 1995. 'Formal and substantial individualism'. In Williams, *Making Sense of Humanity and Other Philosophical Papers 1982–1993*. 111–22. Cambridge University Press.

WILLIAMS, S. K. 1980. 'The "Righteousness of God" in Romans'. *JBL* 99, 241–90.

— 1987a. 'Justification and the Spirit in Galatians'. *JSNT* 29, 91–100.

— 1987b. 'Again *Pistis Christou*'. *CBQ* 49, 431–47.

— 1989. 'The Hearing of Faith: *Akoe Pisteos* in Galatians 3'. *NTS* 35, 82–93.

— 1997. *Galatians*. Abingdon New Testament Commentaries. Nashville: Abingdon.

WILLIS, W. L. 1996. 'Bibliography: Pauline Ethics, 1964–1994'. In Lovering, Jr. and Sumney (eds) 1996, 306–19.

WILSON, W. T. 1991. *Love without Pretense: Romans 12.9–21 and Hellenistic-Jewish Wisdom Literature*. WUNT 2/46. Tübingen: Mohr (Siebeck).

WINDISCH, H. 1924. 'Das Problem des paulinischen Imperativs'. *ZNW* 23, 265–81.

WINGER, M. 1992. *By What Law? The Meaning of Nómos in the Letters of Paul*. SBLDS 128. Atlanta: Scholars.

WITHERINGTON III, B. 1994. *Friendship and Finances in Philippi: The Letter of Paul to the Philippians*. The New Testament in Context. Valley Forge, Pa: Trinity Press International.

WOLTER, M. 1978. *Rechtfertigung und zukünftiges Heil: Untersuchungen zu Röm 5:1–11*. BZNW 43. Berlin: de Gruyter.

— 1997. 'Ethos und Identität in paulinischen Gemeinden'. *NTS* 43, 430–44.

WREDE, W. 1907. *Paulus*. Tübingen: Mohr (Siebeck).

WRIGHT, N. T. 1986. '*harpagmos* and the Meaning of Philippians 2.5–11'. *JTS* 37, 321–52. Also in Wright 1991a, 56–98.

WRIGHT, N. T. 1991a. *The Climax of the Covenant: Christ and the Law in Pauline Theology*. Edinburgh: Clark.

— 1991b. 'Curse and Covenant: Galatians 3.10–14'. In Wright 1991a, 137–56.

— 1995. 'Romans and the Theology of Paul'. In Hay and Johnson (eds) 1995, 30–67.

YOUNG, N. H. 1987. '*Paidagogos*: the Social Setting of a Pauline Metaphor'. *NovT* 29, 150–76.

ZAHN, T. 1910. *Der Brief des Paulus an die Römer*. Kommentar zum Neuen Testament 6. Leipzig: Deichert (Böhme).

ZELLER, D. 1973 (1976²). *Juden und Heiden in der Mission des Paulus: Studien zum Römerbrief*. FB 1 (8). Stuttgart: Katholisches Bibelwerk.

— 1985. *Der Brief an die Römer übersetzt und erklärt*. RNT. Regensburg: Pustet.

— 1993. 'Tyrann oder Wegweiser? Zum paulinischen Verständnis des Gesetzes'. *BK* 48, 134–40.

— 1996. 'Selbstbezogenheit und Selbstdarstellung in den Paulusbriefen'. *TQ* 176, 40–52.

ZIESLER, J. A. 1972. *The Meaning of Righteousness in Paul: A Linguistic and Theological Enquiry*. SNTSMS 20. Cambridge University Press.

— 1989. *Paul's Letter to the Romans*. Trinity Press International New Testament Commentaries. London: SCM/Philadelphia: Trinity Press International.

— 1990² (1983). *Pauline Christianity*. Oxford University Press.

ZMIJEWSKI, J. 1981. '*kauchaomai, kauchēma, kauchēsis*'. In Balz and Schneider (eds) 1981, 680–90.

Index of Modern Authors

Index of References

The index lists whole passages, and only individual verses or minor sections where these are given special treatment.

Index of Subjects

The subjects index is highly selective and should be used together with the two other indexes. It presupposes that the book has been read and lists only very specific discussions that the reader may wish to consult once more.